CONCISE EDITION

··

WORLDS TOGETHER,
WORLDS APART

Volume 1

CONCISE EDITION

WORLDS TOGETHER,
WORLDS APART

Volume 1: Beginnings through the 15th Century

Elizabeth Pollard | **Clifford Rosenberg** | **Robert Tignor**

with Jeremy Adelman, Stephen Aron, Peter Brown, Benjamin Elman,
Stephen Kotkin, Xinru Liu, Susanne Marchand, Holly Pittman,
Gyan Prakash, Brent Shaw, Michael Tsin

W. W. Norton & Company · New York · London

W. W. NORTON & COMPANY has been independent since its founding in 1923, when William Warder Norton and Mary D. Herter Norton first published lectures delivered at the People's Institute, the adult education division of New York City's Cooper Union. The firm soon expanded its program beyond the Institute, publishing books by celebrated academics from America and abroad. By midcentury, the two major pillars of Norton's publishing program—trade books and college texts—were firmly established. In the 1950s, the Norton family transferred control of the company to its employees, and today—with a staff of four hundred and a comparable number of trade, college, and professional titles published each year—W. W. Norton & Company stands as the largest and oldest publishing house owned wholly by its employees.

Editor: Jon Durbin
Associate Editor: Justin Cahill
Editorial Assistant: Penelope Lin
Developmental Editor: Ann Shin
Project Editor: Diane Cipollone
Marketing Manager, History: Sarah England
Manuscript Editor: Nancy Green
Managing Editor, College: Marian Johnson
Managing Editor, College Digital Media: Kim Yi
Production Manager: Andy Ensor
Media Editor: Lisa Moore
Media Project Editor: Penelope Lin
Media Editorial Assistant: Chris Hillyer
Design Director: Jillian Burr
Photo Editor: Nelson Colón
Permissions Manager: Megan Jackson
College Permissions Associate: Bethany Salminen
Composition: Cenveo® Publisher Services
Manufacturing: Courier, Kendallville

Permission to use copyrighted material is included on p. C-1.

The Library of Congress has cataloged the full edition as follows:

Tignor, Robert L.
    Worlds together, worlds apart : a history of the world from the beginnings of humankind to the present / by Robert Tignor, Jeremy Adelman, Stephen Aron, Peter Brown, Benjamin Elman, Stephen Kotkin, Xinru Liu, Suzanne Marchand, Holly Pittman, Gyan Prakash, Brent Shaw, and Michael Tsin. — Fourth edition.
        pages cm
    Includes bibliographical references and index.
    ISBN 978-0-393-92207-3 (hardcover : alk. paper) — ISBN 978-0-393-12376-0 (pbk. : alk. paper) 1. World history. I. Title.
    D21.T53 2013
    909—dc23
                        2013038525

ISBN: 978-0-393-91847-2 (pbk.)

W. W. Norton & Company, Inc., 500 Fifth Avenue, New York, N.Y. 10110
www.wwnorton.com

W. W. Norton & Company Ltd., Castle House, 75/76 Wells Street, London W1T 3QT

1 2 3 4 5 6 7 8 9 0

Contents in Brief

Contents

Chapter 1
BECOMING HUMAN   3

Chapter 2

RIVERS, CITIES, AND FIRST STATES, 3500–2000 BCE   **45**

Chapter 3

NOMADS, TERRITORIAL STATES, AND MICROSOCIETIES, 2000–1200 BCE   **83**

Chapter 4
FIRST EMPIRES AND COMMON CULTURES IN AFRO-EURASIA, 1250–325 BCE   **121**

Chapter 5
WORLDS TURNED INSIDE OUT, 1000–350 BCE   **159**

An "Axial Age"   162

Eastern Zhou China   162

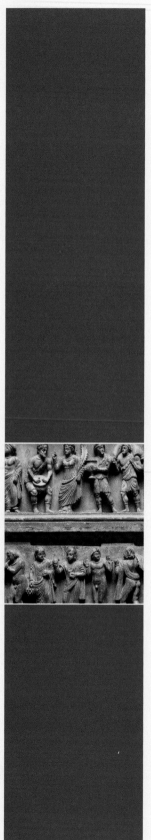

Chapter 6

SHRINKING THE AFRO-EURASIAN WORLD, 350–100 BCE **197**

Chapter 7

HAN DYNASTY CHINA AND IMPERIAL ROME, 300 BCE–300 CE   **233**

Chapter 8

THE RISE OF UNIVERSAL RELIGIONS, 300–600 CE   **267**

Chapter 9
NEW EMPIRES AND COMMON CULTURES, 600–1000 CE   **303**

Chapter 10
BECOMING "THE WORLD," 1000–1300 CE   341

Chapter 11

CRISES AND RECOVERY IN AFRO-EURASIA, 1300–1500   **383**

Current Trends in World History

Analyzing Global Developments

Global Themes and Sources

Maps

Preface

Worlds Together, Worlds Apart has set the standard for four editions for instructors who want to teach a globally integrated world history survey course. As the dynamic field of world history has evolved, so too has *Worlds Together, Worlds Apart*. Building on the successes of the full text, new co-authors Elizabeth Pollard (San Diego State University) and Clifford Rosenberg (City College of New York) and original author Robert Tignor (Princeton University) have created the new Concise Edition of *Worlds Together, Worlds Apart*. A full third shorter than its parent text and written with clear accessible prose and explanations, the Concise Edition continues to offer a coherent, cutting-edge survey of the field built around world history stories of significance. This concise globally integrated, chronological approach makes it possible for students to readily make connections and comparisons across time and place, and makes the teaching of the course more manageable for instructors. Some of the major stories dealt with in the chapters of the Concise edition are the spread of humans across the planet, the first global agricultural revolution, the creation of empires, the building of the Silk Roads, the spread of the Black Death across Afro-Eurasia, the impact of New World silver on global trade, alternative ways to organize societies during the rise of nineteenth-century capitalism, and the rise of the nation state.

HIGHLIGHTS OF THE CONCISE EDITION

The new Concise Edition is designed to be easy for students to read. It features a brand-new suite of pedagogical and media tools built around new Core Objectives, which are designed to guide students' reading and to aid them and their instructor in assessing their understanding of the material and concepts. Each of the book's 21 chapters begins with the innovative Before You Read This Chapter pedagogy, which highlights the Global Storylines and Core Objectives that students need to comprehend while reading the chapter. New Comparison Flags appear in the margins throughout the chapter to remind students of the Core Objectives while they read and to help them begin to make comparisons and connections on their own. The After You Read This Chapter pedagogy includes Tracing the Global Storylines, which shows the impact of the chapter's main storyline on each region of the world. The new Thinking About Global Connections questions highlight major themes that unify the book's global approach, and new Study Questions place the chapter's Key Terms into a historical context.

The new Concise Edition also provides students with new features that are designed to encourage critical thinking and to help them develop historical thinking skills. Chief among these is the new Global Themes and Sources feature, which gathers at the end of each chapter a new collection of primary source documents. This includes Competing Perspectives, which invites students to compare several documents on one of the themes discussed in the chapter; and a new Interpreting Visual Evidence activity that allows students to probe a world historical theme reaching across regions.

Within the narrative of each chapter appear two unique features that also encourage critical thinking and the development of historical thinking skills. The new Analyzing Global Developments feature engages students with real historical data, much of it the result of recent scholarship, and the new Current Trends in World History feature, which presents new research trends, demonstrates how historical research remains relevant to our world today.

The Concise Edition's compelling and unique focus on world history stories, themes, and Core Objectives is further reinforced in our new online and digital support materials for students and instructors. Lead author for media Alan Karras (University of California, Berkeley) has brought together a tremendous media team to create InQuizitive—Norton's new formative, adaptive learning program—and digital materials for the Norton Coursepack to support the text (see page xxxvii for information about student and instructor resources). This exciting new authorial team has worked together closely to ensure the tightest integration possible between the main text and the media materials to help students and instructors succeed in their world history course.

OUR MAJOR THEMES

The primary organizing framework of *Worlds Together, Worlds Apart*—one that runs through the chapters and connects the different parts of the volume—is the theme of **interconnection and divergence**. While describing movements that facilitated global connectedness, this book also shows how different regions developed their own ways of handling or resisting connections and change.

Themes that stand out in *Worlds Together, Worlds Apart* highlight the importance of trade and culture exchange through the recurring efforts of people at **crossing borders—religious, political, and cultural—that brought the world together**. Merchants and educated men and women traded goods and ideas. Whole communities, in addition to select groups, moved to safer or more promising environments. This transregional crossing of ideas, goods, and peoples produced **transformations and conflicts**—a second important theme. The movement of ideas, peoples, products, and germs over long distances upset the balance of power across the world and within individual societies. Such movements changed the relationship of different population groups with other peoples and areas of the world and led over time to dramatic shifts in the ascendancy of regions. **Changes in power arrangements** within and between regions explain which parts of the world and regional groups benefited from integration and which resisted it. Finally, we highlight **the important roles that gender and the environment play in shaping the evolution of societies**. These themes (trade and cultural exchange, transformation and conflict, gender and the environment, and alterations in the balance of power) weave themselves through every chapter of this work. While we highlight major themes throughout, we tell the stories of the people caught in these currents of exchange, conflict, and changing power relations, paying particular attention to the role that gender and the environment play in shaping the evolution of societies.

OVERVIEW OF VOLUME ONE

Volume One of *Worlds Together, Worlds Apart* deals with the period from the beginnings of human history through the Mongol invasions of the thirteenth century and the spread of the Black Death across Afro-Eurasia. It is divided into eleven chapters, each of which marks a distinct historical period. Hence, each chapter has an overarching theme or small set of themes that hold otherwise highly diverse material together.

Chapter 1, "Becoming Human," presents biological and cultural perspectives on the way that early hominids became truly human. We believe that this chapter is important in establishing the global context of world history. We believe too that our chapter is unique in its focus on a range of creation narratives that explain how humans became humans. We discuss how early humans became bipedal and how they developed complex cognitive processes such as language and artistic abilities. Recent research indicates that *Homo sapiens* originated in Africa, probably no more than 200,000 years ago. These early men and women walked out of the African landmass sometime between 120,000 and 50,000 years ago, gradually populating all regions of the world. What is significant in this story is that the different population groups around the world, the so-called races of humankind, have only recently broken off from one another. Also in this chapter, we describe the domestication of plants and animals and the founding of the first village settlements around the globe.

Chapter 2, "Rivers, Cities, and First States, 3500–2000 BCE," covers the period during which five of the great river basins experienced extraordinary breakthroughs in human activity. On the flood plains of the Tigris and Euphrates in Mesopotamia, the Nile in Egypt, the Indus valley in modern-day northern India and Pakistan, and the Yellow and Yangzi rivers in China, men and women mastered annual floods and became expert in seeding and cultivating foodstuffs. In these areas, populations became dense. River-basin cultures had much in common. They had highly developed hierarchical political, social, and cultural systems, priestly and bureaucratic classes, and organized religious and cultural systems. But they also differed greatly, and these differences were passed from generation to generation. The development of these major complex societies certainly is a turning point in world history.

Extensive climatic and technological changes serve as major turning points for **Chapter 3, "Nomads, Territorial States, and Microsocieties, 2000–1200 BCE."** Drought, environmental degradation, and political instability brought the first river-basin societies to a crashing end around 2000 BCE. When aridity forced tribal and nomadic peoples living on the fringes of the settled populations to move closer to settled areas, they brought with them an insurmountable military advantage. They had become adept at yoking horses to war chariots, and hence they were in a position to subjugate or intermarry with the peoples in the settled political organizations in the river basins. Around 2000 BCE these peoples established new territorial kingdoms in Mesopotamia, Egypt, the Indus valley, and China, which gave way a millennium later (1000 BCE) to even larger, militarily and politically more powerful states. In the Americas, the Mediterranean, sub-Saharan Africa, and the Pacific worlds, microsocieties arose as an alternative form of political organization in which peoples lived in much smaller-scale societies that showcased their own unique and compelling features.

Chapter 4, "First Empires and Common Cultures in Afro-Eurasia, 1250–325 BCE," describes the different ways in which larger-scale societies grew and became unified. In the case of the world's first empires, the neo-Assyrian and Persian, political power was the main unifying element. Both states established different models that future empires would emulate. The Assyrians used brutal force to intimidate and subjugate different groups within their societies and neighboring states. The Persians followed a pattern that relied less on coercion and more on tributary relationships, while permitting cultural diversity. The Zhou state in China offered yet a third way of political unity, basing its rule on the doctrine of the mandate of heaven, which legitimated its rulers' succession as long as they were able to maintain stability and order. Vedic society in South Asia offers a dramatically different model in which religion and culture were the main unifying forces.

The last millennium before the common era witnessed some of the most monumental developments in human history. In the six and half centuries discussed in **Chapter 5, "Worlds Turned Inside Out, 1000–350 BCE,"** teachers and thinkers, rather than kings, priests, and warriors, came to the fore. Confucius, the Buddha, Plato, and Aristotle, to name only the best known of this brilliant group, offered new insights into the natural world and provided new guidelines for how to govern justly and live ethically. In this era, small-scale societies, benefiting from more intimate relationships, took the place of the first great empires, now in decline. These highly individualistic cultures developed new strategies for political organization, even including experimenting with a democratic polity. In Africa, the Bantu peoples spread across sub-Saharan Africa, and the Sudanic peoples of Meroe created a society that blended Egyptian and sub-Saharan influences. These were all dynamic hybrid societies building on existing knowledge. Equally dramatic transformations occurred in the Americas, where the Olmec and Chavín peoples were creating hierarchical societies of the like never before seen in their part of the world.

Chapter 6, "Shrinking the Afro-Eurasian World, 350 BCE–100 CE," describes two major forces that simultaneously integrated large segments of the Afro-Eurasian landmass culturally and economically. First, Hellenism, whose leading figure, Alexander the Great, paved the way in North Africa and Southwest and central Asia for the first transregional cultural system in world history. Second, a trading network known as the Silk Roads, stretching from Palmyra in the west to central Asia in the east, came into being. Buddhism was the first religion to seize on the Silk Roads' more formal existence as its followers moved quickly with the support of the Mauryan Empire to spread their ideas into central Asia.

Chapter 7, "Han Dynasty China and Imperial Rome, 300 BCE–300 CE," compares Han China and the Roman Empire, the two political, economic, and cultural systems that dominated much of the Afro-Eurasian landmass from 200 BCE to 200 CE. Both the Han Dynasty and the Roman Empire ruled effectively in their own ways, providing an instructive comparative case study. Both left their imprint on Afro-Eurasia, and rulers for centuries afterward tried to revive these glorious empires and use them as models of greatness. This chapter also discusses the effect of state sponsorship on religion, as Christianity came into existence in the context of the late Roman Empire and Buddhism was introduced to China during the decline of the Han.

Out of the crumbling Roman Empire new political systems and a new religion emerged, the major topic of **Chapter 8, "The Rise of Universal Religions, 300–600 CE."** The Byzantine Empire, claiming to be the successor state to the Roman Empire, embraced Christianity as its state religion. The Tang rulers patronized Buddhism to such a degree that Confucian statesmen feared it had become the state religion. Both Buddhism and Christianity enjoyed spectacular success in the politically fragmented post-Han era in China and in the feudal world of western Europe. These dynamic religions represent a decisive transformation in world history. Christianity enjoyed its eventual successes through state sponsorship via the Roman and Byzantine empires and by providing spiritual comfort and hope during the chaotic years of Rome's decline. Buddhism grew through imperial sponsorship and significant changes to its fundamental beliefs, when adherents to the faith deified the Buddha and created notions of an afterlife. In Africa a wide range of significant developments and a myriad of cultural practices existed; yet large common cultures also arose. The Bantu peoples spread throughout the southern half of the landmass, spoke closely related languages, and developed similar political institutions based on the prestige of individuals of high achievement. In the Americas the Olmecs established their own form of the city-state, while the Mayans owed their success to a decentralized common culture built around a strong religious belief system and a series of spiritual centers.

In **Chapter 9, "New Empires and Common Cultures, 600–1000 CE,"** in a relatively remote corner of the Arabian Peninsula, another world religion, Islam, exploded with world-changing consequences. The rise of Islam provides a contrast to the way in which universalizing religions and political empires interacted. Islam and empire arose in a fashion quite different from Christianity and the Roman Empire. Christianity took over an already existing empire—the Roman—after suffering persecution at its hands for several centuries. In contrast, Islam created an empire almost at the moment of its emergence. By the time the Abbasid Empire came into being in the middle of the eighth century, Islamic armies, political leaders, and clerics exercised power over much of the Afro-Eurasian landmass from southern Spain, across North Africa, all the way to central Asia. The Tang Empire in China, however, served as a counterweight to Islam's power both politically and intellectually. Confucianism enjoyed a spectacular recovery in this period. With the Tang rulers, Confucianism slowed the spread of Buddhism and further reinforced China's development along different, more secular pathways. Japan and Korea also enter world history at this time, as tributary states to Tang China and as hybrid cultures that mixed Chinese customs and practices with their own. The Christian world split in this period between the western Latin church and the eastern Byzantine church. Both branches of Christianity played a role in unifying societies, especially in western Europe, which lacked strong political rule.

In the three centuries from 1000 to 1300 (**Chapter 10, "Becoming 'The World,' 1000–1300 CE"**) Afro-Eurasia experienced an unprecedented rise in prosperity and population that even spread into West and East Africa. Just as importantly, the world in this period divided into regional zones that are recognizable today. And trade grew rapidly. A view of the major trading cities of this time demonstrates how commerce transformed cultures. Sub-Saharan Africa also underwent intense regional integration via the spread of the Mande-speaking peoples and the Mali Empire. The Americas witnessed their

first empire in the form of the Chimu peoples in the Andes. This chapter ends with the Mongol conquests of the twelfth and thirteenth centuries, which brought massive destruction. The Mongol Empire, however, once in place, promoted long-distance commerce, scholarly exchange, and travel on an unprecedented scale. The Mongols brought Eurasia, North Africa, and many parts of sub-Saharan Africa into a new connectedness. The Mongol story also underscores the important role that nomads played throughout the history of the early world.

The Black Death brought Afro-Eurasia's prosperity and population growth to a catastrophic end as discussed in **Chapter 11, "Crises and Recovery in Afro-Eurasia, 1300–1500."** The dying and destruction of the fourteenth century saw traditional institutions give way and forced peoples to rebuild their cultures. The political systems that came into being at this time and the intense religious experimentation that took place effected a sharp break with the past. The bubonic plague wiped out as much as two-thirds of the population in many of the densely settled locations of Afro-Eurasia. Societies were brought to their knees by the Mongols' depredations as well as by biological pathogens. In the face of one of humanity's grimmest periods, peoples and societies demonstrated tremendous resilience as they looked for new ways to rebuild their communities, some turning inward and others seeking inspiration, conquests, and riches elsewhere. Volume One concludes on the eve of the "Columbian Exchange," the moment when "old" worlds discovered "new" ones and a vast series of global interconnections and divergences commenced.

OVERVIEW OF VOLUME TWO

The organizational structure for Volume Two reaffirms the commitment to write a decentered, global history of the world. Christopher Columbus is not the starting point, as he is in so many modern world histories. Rather, we begin in the eleventh and twelfth centuries with two major developments in world history: the Mongols and the Black Death. The first, set forth in **Chapter 10, "Becoming 'The World,' 1000–1300 CE,"** describes a world that was divided for the first time into regions that are recognizable today. This world experienced rapid population growth, as is shown by a simple look at the major trading cities from Asia in the east to the Mediterranean in the west. Yet nomadic peoples remain a force as revealed in the Mongol invasions of Afro-Eurasia.

Chapter 11, "Crises and Recovery in Afro-Eurasia, 1300–1500," describes how the Mongol warriors, through their conquests and the integration of the Afro-Eurasian world, spread the bubonic plague, which brought death and depopulation to much of Afro-Eurasia. Both these stories set the stage for the modern world and are clear-cut turning points in world history. The primary agents of world connection described in this chapter were dynasts, soldiers, clerics, merchants, and adventurers who rebuilt the societies that disease and political collapse had destroyed.

The Mongols joined the two hemispheres, as we describe in **Chapter 12, "Contact, Commerce, and Colonization, 1450–1600,"** bringing the peoples and products of the Western Hemisphere into contact and conflict with Eurasia and Africa. It is the collision between the Eastern and Western Hemispheres that sets in motion modern world history and marks a distinct divide or turning point between the premodern and the modern. Here, too, disease and increasing trade linkages were vital. Unprepared for the advanced military technology and the disease pool of European and African peoples, the Amerindian population experienced a population decline even more devastating than that caused by the Black Death.

Europeans sailed across the Atlantic Ocean to find a more direct, less encumbered route to Asia and came upon lands, peoples, and products that they had not expected. One item, however, that they had sought in every part of the world and that they found in abundance in the Americas was precious metal. **Chapter 13, "Worlds Entangled, 1600–1750,"** discusses how New World silver from Mexico and Peru became the major currency of global commerce, facilitating the long-distance trading networks that had been revived after the Black Death. The effect of New World silver on the world economy was so great that it, even more than the Iberian explorations of the New World, brought the hemispheres together and marked the true genesis of modern world history. Sugar also linked the economies and polities of western Europe, Africa, and the Americas and was a powerful force in a triangular trade centered on the Atlantic Ocean. This trade involved the shipment of vast numbers of African captives to the Americas, where they toiled on sugar, tobacco, cotton, and rice slave plantations.

Chapter 14, "Cultures of Splendor and Power, 1500–1780," investigates Ottoman scientists, Safavid and Mughal artists, and Chinese literati, as well as European thinkers, whose notable achievements were rooted in their own cultures but tempered by awareness of the intellectual activities of others. This chapter looks closely at how culture is created as a historical process and describe how the massive increase in wealth during this period, growing out of global trade, led to one of the great periods of cultural flourishing in world history. Around 1800, transformations reverberated outward from the Atlantic world and altered economic and political relationships in the rest of the world.

Chapter 15, "Reordering the World, 1750–1850," discusses political revolutions in the Americas and Europe, focusing on new ideas about how to trade and labor. It contends that a powerful rhetoric of freedom and universal rights underlay the beginning of "a great divide" between peoples of European descent and those who were not. These forces of laissez-faire capitalism, industrialization, the nation-state, and republicanism not only attracted diverse groups around the world; they also threatened groups that put forth alternative visions. New ideas of freedom, as manifested in trading relations, labor, and political activities, clashed with older notions of inherited rights and statuses and further challenged the way men and women had lived in earlier times. These political, intellectual, and economic reorderings changed the way people around the world saw themselves and thus represent something quite novel in world history.

These new ways of envisioning the world did not go unchallenged, as **Chapter 16, "Alternative Visions of the Nineteenth Century,"** makes clear. Here, intense resistance to evolving modernity reflected the diversity of peoples and their hopes for the future. Wahabbism in Islam, the strongman movement in Africa, Indian resistance in the United States and Mexico, socialism and communism in Europe, the Taiping Rebellion in China, and the Indian Mutiny in South Asia catapulted to historical prominence prophets and leaders whose visions often drew on earlier traditions and led these individuals to resist rapid change.

Chapter 17, "Nations and Empires, 1850–1914," deals with the political, economic, military, and ideological power that thrust Europe and North America to the fore of global events and led to an era of nationalism and modern imperialism, new forces in world history. Yet this period of seeming European supremacy was to prove short-lived.

As **Chapter 18, "An Unsettled World, 1890–1914,"** demonstrates, even before World War I shattered Europe's moral certitude, many groups at home (feminists, Marxists, and unfulfilled nationalists) and abroad (anticolonial nationalists) had raised a chorus of complaints about European and North American dominance. As in Chapter 14, this chapter looks at the processes by which specific cultural movements rose and reflected the concerns of individual societies. Yet here, too, syncretistic movements emerged in many cultures and reflected the sway of global imperialism, which by then had become a dominant force.

Chapter 19, "Of Masses and Visions of the Modern, 1910–1939," briefly covers World War I and then discusses how, from the end of World War I until World War II, different visions of being modern competed around the world. The development of modernism and its effects on multiple cultures integrate the diverse developments discussed in this chapter. In the decades between the world wars, proponents of liberal democracy struggled to defend their views and often to impose their will on authoritarian rulers and anticolonial nationalists.

Chapter 20, "The Three-World Order, 1940–1975," presents World War II as new adversaries arose after the war. A three-world order came into being—the First World, led by the United States and extolling capitalism, the nation-state, and democratic government; the Second World, led by the Soviet Union and favoring authoritarian polities and economies; and the Third World, made up of former colonies seeking an independent status and alternative routes to modernity for themselves in world affairs. The rise of this three-world order dominates the second half of the twentieth century and constitutes another major theme of world history.

Chapter 21, "Globalization, 1970–2000," explains that, at the end of the Cold War, the modern world, while clearly more unified than before, still had profound cultural differences and political divisions. At the beginning of the twenty-first century, capital, commodities, peoples, and ideas moved rapidly over long distances. But cultural tensions and political impasses continued to exist. The rise of this form of globalism represented a vital new element as humankind headed into a new century and millennium.

The **Epilogue, 2001–The Present,** tracks developments since the turn of the millennium. These last few years have brought profound changes to the world order, yet we hope readers of *Worlds Together, Worlds Apart* will see more clearly how this most recent history is, in fact, entwined with trends of much longer duration that are the chief focus of this book.

MEDIA ANCILLARIES

New lead author for media and pedagogy Alan Karras has helped us gather a team of innovative world history instructors, including Shane Carter, Wendy Eagan, Theresa Quindlen, and Sally West. Together, this team has ensured that the Concise Edition of *Worlds Together, Worlds Apart* is supported by an array of digital media with tools faculty need to meet course goals—in the classroom and online—and activities for students to develop core skills in reading comprehension, writing, and analysis, and to better understand the geography and contexts in world history surveys.

FOR STUDENTS

Quizzing to Learn

InQuizitive, Norton's new adaptive quizzing platform, uses interactive questions and guided feedback to motivate students to read and understand the text. Varied question types—featuring images, maps, and sources—prompt critical and analytical thinking on each of the chapter's Core Objectives. Robust grading functionality helps instructors track their students' progress on learning outcomes.

Student Site

This free site offers students access to additional primary source documents and images, Office Hour videos with the authors, and iMaps. It is ideal for instructors interested in granting students access to additional material without creating or administering online assignments.

Norton Ebooks

Norton Ebooks lets students access the entire book and much more: they can search, highlight, and take notes with ease, as well as collaborate and share their notes with instructors and classmates. Ebooks can be viewed on any device—laptop, tablet, phone, even a public computer—and will stay synced between devices.

FOR INSTRUCTORS

Norton Coursepacks

Free Norton Coursepacks (downloadable in Blackboard, WebCT, D2L, and Moodle; additional formats can be provided upon request), includes:

- **New Gradable Assignments** allow you to assign quizzes based on questions from the text including Assessing the Global Storylines, Competing Perspectives, and Interpreting Visual Evidence.
- **NEW Primary Source Exercises** include several primary sources from across cultures with a brief multiple choice exam and a short answer question.
- **Guided Reading Exercises,** keyed to each chapter's Core Objectives, instill the three-step Note-Summarize-Assess pedagogy. Each chapter has one exercise built around passages from the text.
- **Review Quizzes** include targeted feedback that highlights Core Objective, page reference, and difficulty. *Chrono-Quizzes* end each chapter quiz with a matching question.
- **Online Reader** provides over 100 primary-source documents and images.
- **Map Resources** include *iMaps*, where students can peel back each layer to highlight the information they want to see, *StoryMaps* where complex maps are broken into five annotated slides that focus on the *story* behind the *geography*. *World History Tours*, powered by Google Earth that are dynamic, interactive primary sources that trace global developments over time. *Map Worksheets* provide each map without labels for offline relabeling and quizzing.
- **Forum Prompts** for online and hybrid courses are a set of topics that can be used to launch discussions.
- **Key Term Flash Cards** allow students to self-study historical vocabulary.
- Links to **InQuizitive** for each chapter.

Classroom Presentation Tools

- **Lecture PowerPoints and Art PowerPoints** feature photographs and maps from the book, retouched for in-class presentation.
- *Story Maps* break complex maps into a sequence of five annotated screens that focus on the story behind the geography. Ten maps include such topics as The Silk Road, The Spread of the Black Death, and Population Growth and the Economy.

Instructor's Manual (Sharon Cohen)

The Instructor's Manual for *Worlds Together, Worlds Apart* Concise Edition has everything instructors need to prepare lectures and classroom activities: lecture outlines, lecture ideas, classroom activities. Our new Popular Fallacy section provides an exercise that helps to dispel common misconceptions students may have about each chapter.

Test Bank (Ryba Epstein)

The Test Bank features multiple-choice, true/false, and essay questions aligned with the chapter's Core Objectives and classified according to level of difficulty and Bloom's Taxonomy, offering multiple avenues for content and skill assessment. All Norton test banks are available with ExamView Test Generator software, allowing instructors to easily create, administer, and manage assessments.

ACKNOWLEDGMENTS

The quality and range of reviews on this project were truly exceptional. The final version of the manuscript was greatly influenced by the thoughts and ideas of numerous instructors.

Concise Edition Reviewers

Andreas Agocs, University of the Pacific
Anthony Barbieri-Low, University of California, Santa Barbara
Brett Berliner, Morgan State University
Carolyn Noelle Biltoft, Georgia State University
Gayle Brunelle, California State University, Fullerton
Grace Chee, West Los Angeles College
Stephen Colston, San Diego State University
Paula Devos, San Diego State University
Alan Karras, University of California, Berkeley
Elaine MacKinnon, University of West Georgia
Harold Marcuse, University of California, Santa Barbara
Eva Moe, Modesto Junior College
Alice Pate, Kennesaw State University
Chandrika Paul, Shippensburg University
Jared Poley, Georgia State University
Dana Rabin, University of Illinois
Masako Racel, Kennesaw State University
Charles Reed, Elizabeth City State University
Alice Roberti, Santa Rosa Junior College
Steven Rowe, Chicago State University
Lynn Sargeant, California State University, Fullerton
Robert Saunders, Farmingdale State College
Sharlene Sayegh-Canada, California State University–Long Beach
Jeffrey Shumway, Brigham Young University
Greg Smay, University of California, Berkeley
Lisa Tran, California State University, Fullerton
Michael Vann, California State University, Sacramento
Theodore Weeks, Southern Illinois University
Krzysztof Ziarek, University of Buffalo

For the Concise Edition we have some familiar and new friends at Norton to thank. Chief among them is Jon Durbin, who once again played a major role in bringing this edition to publication. Ann Shin, our developmental editor, did a remarkable job in helping to address reviewers' comments and streamline the whole book. Sarah England has put together a creative marketing plan for the book. Jillian Burr is responsible for the book's beautiful and effective new design. Justin Cahill and Penelope Lin have been invaluable with their work on the maps, illustrations, and new feature boxes. Lisa Moore, Tacy Quinn, and Chris Hillyer have done a masterful job strengthening the media support materials to meet the ever more complex classroom and assessment needs of instructors. Diane Cipollone, our project editor, and Andrew Ensor, our production manager, have done a great job getting the book published on time with a very tight schedule. Nancy Green did an assiduous job with the copyediting, turning the chapters around quickly to meet our schedule. A special shout out goes to Debra Morton-Hoyt and her team of cover designers. *Worlds Together, Worlds Apart* has always been incredibly creative and distinctive looking, and the Concise Edition covers are even more eye-catching and memorable than the first four editions. Last, but far from least, we thank the authors of the full edition for their participation in this Concise Edition work, while allowing the new authors considerable leeway to have their own input. Bravo!

Finally, and most importantly, we recognize that while this project often kept us apart from family members, their love and understanding holds our worlds together.

About the Authors

ELIZABETH POLLARD (*Ph.D. University of Pennsylvania*) is associate professor of history at San Diego State University. Her research expertise focuses on women accused of witchcraft in the Roman world and on the exchange of goods and ideas between the Mediterranean and the Indian Ocean. Her pedagogical interests include the effectiveness of web-based technology and world history in teaching, learning, and writing about ancient history.

CLIFFORD ROSENBERG (*Ph.D. Princeton University*) is associate professor of European history at City College and the Graduate Center, CUNY. He specializes in the history of modern France and its empire and is the author of *Policing Paris: The Origins of Modern Immigration Control Between the Wars*. He is working now on the spread of tuberculosis between France and Algeria since the mid-nineteenth century.

ROBERT TIGNOR (*Ph.D. Yale University*) is professor emeritus and the Rosengarten Professor of Modern and Contemporary History at Princeton University and the three-time chair of the history department. With Gyan Prakash, he introduced Princeton's first course in world history nearly twenty years ago. Professor Tignor has taught graduate and undergraduate courses in African history and world history and written extensively on the history of twentieth-century Egypt, Nigeria, and Kenya. Besides his many research trips to Africa, Professor Tignor has taught at the University of Ibadan in Nigeria and the University of Nairobi in Kenya.

ALAN KARRAS (*Ph.D. University of Pennsylvania*) is the Associate Director of International & Area Studies at the University of California, Berkeley, and has served as chair of the College Board's test development committee for world history and as co-chair of the College Board's commission on AP history course revisions. He studies the eighteenth-century Atlantic world and global interactions more broadly concerning illegal activities like smuggling.

JEREMY ADELMAN (*D.Phil. Oxford University*) is currently the Director of the Council for International Teaching and Research at Princeton University and the Walter S. Carpenter III Professor of Spanish Civilization and Culture. He has written and edited five books, including *Republic of Capital: Buenos Aires and the Legal Transformation of the Atlantic World*, which won the best book prize in Atlantic history from the American Historical Association, and most recently *Sovereignty and Revolution in the Iberian Atlantic*. Professor Adelman is the recent recipient of a Guggenheim Memorial Foundation Fellowship and the Frederick Burkhardt Award from the American Council of Learned Societies.

STEPHEN ARON (*Ph.D. University of California, Berkeley*) is professor of history at the University of California, Los Angeles, and executive director of the Institute for the Study of the American West, Autry National Center. A specialist in frontier and Western American history, Aron is the author of *How the West Was Lost: The Transformation of Kentucky from Daniel Boone to Henry Clay* and *American Confluence: The Missouri Frontier from Borderland to Border State*. He is currently editing the multivolume *Autry History of the American West* and writing a book with the tentative title *Can We All Just Get Along: An Alternative History of the American West*.

PETER BROWN (*Ph.D. Oxford University*) is the Rollins Professor of History at Princeton University. He previously taught at London University and the University of California, Berkeley. He has written on the rise of Christianity and the end of the Roman Empire. His works include *Augustine of Hippo, The World of Late Antiquity, The Cult of the Saints, Body and Society, The Rise of Western Christendom,* and *Poverty and Leadership in the Later Roman Empire*. He is presently working on issues of wealth and poverty in the late Roman and early medieval Christian worlds.

BENJAMIN ELMAN (*Ph.D. University of Pennsylvania*) is professor of East Asian studies and history at Princeton University. He is currently serving as the chair of the Princeton East Asian Studies Department. He taught at the University of California, Los Angeles, for over fifteen years. His teaching and research fields include Chinese intellectual and cultural history, 1000–1900; the history of science in China, 1600–1930; the history of education in late imperial China; and Sino-Japanese cultural history, 1600–1850. He is the author of five books: *From Philosophy to Philology: Intellectual and Social Aspects of Change in Late Imperial China; Classicism, Politics, and Kinship: the Ch'ang-chou School of New Text Confucianism in Late Imperial China; A Cultural History of Civil Examinations in Late Imperial China; On Their Own Terms: Science in China, 1550–1900;* and *A Cultural History of Modern Science in China.* He is the creator of Classical Historiography for Chinese History at www.princeton.edu/~classbib/, a bibliography and teaching website published since 1996.

STEPHEN KOTKIN (*Ph.D. University of California, Berkeley*) is professor of European and Asian history as well as international affairs at Princeton University. He formerly directed Princeton's program in Russian and Eurasian studies (1996–2009). He is the author of *Magnetic Mountain: Stalinism as a Civilization, Uncivil Society: 1989 and the Implosion of the Communist Establishment,* and *Armageddon Averted: The Soviet Collapse, 1970–2000.* He is a coeditor of *Mongolia in the Twentieth Century: Landlocked Cosmopolitan.* Professor Kotkin has twice been a visiting professor in Japan.

XINRU LIU (*Ph.D. University of Pennsylvania*) is associate professor of early Indian history and world history at the College of New Jersey. She is associated with the Institute of World History and the Chinese Academy of Social Sciences. She is the author of *Ancient India and Ancient China, Trade and Religious Exchanges, AD 1–600; Silk and Religion, an Exploration of Material Life and the Thought of People, AD 600–1200; Connections across Eurasia, Transportation, Communication, and Cultural Exchange on the Silk Roads,* coauthored with Lynda Norene Shaffer; and

A Social History of Ancient India (in Chinese). Professor Liu promotes South Asian studies and world history studies in both the United States and the People's Republic of China.

SUZANNE MARCHAND (*Ph.D. University of Chicago*) is professor of European and intellectual history at Louisiana State University, Baton Rouge. Professor Marchand also spent a number of years teaching at Princeton University. She is the author of *Down from Olympus: Archaeology and Philhellenism in Germany, 1750–1970* and *German Orientalism in the Age of Empire: Religion, Race and Scholarship.*

HOLLY PITTMAN (*Ph.D. Columbia University*) is professor of art history at the University of Pennsylvania, where she teaches art and archaeology of Mesopotamia and the Iranian Plateau. She also serves as curator in the Near East Section of the University of Pennsylvania Museum of Archaeology and Anthropology. Previously she served as a curator in the Ancient Near Eastern Art Department of the Metropolitan Museum of Art. She has written extensively on the art and culture of the Bronze Age in the Middle East and has participated in excavations in Cyprus, Turkey, Syria, Iraq, and Iran, where she currently works. Her research investigates works of art as media through which patterns of thought, cultural development, and historical interactions of ancient cultures of the Near East are reconstructed.

GYAN PRAKASH (*Ph.D. University of Pennsylvania*) is professor of modern Indian history at Princeton University and a member of the Subaltern Studies Editorial Collective. He is the author of *Bonded Histories: Genealogies of Labor Servitude in Colonial India, Another Reason: Science and the Imagination of Modern India,* and *Mumbai Fables.* Professor Prakash edited *After Colonialism: Imperial Histories and Postcolonial Displacements* and *Noir Urbanisms,* coedited *The Space of the Modern City* and *Utopia/Dystopia,* and has written a number of articles on colonialism and history writing. He is currently working on a history of the city of Bombay. With Robert Tignor, he introduced the modern world history course at Princeton University.

BRENT SHAW (*Ph.D. Cambridge University*) is the Andrew Fleming West Professor of Classics at Princeton University, where he is director of the Program in the Ancient World. He was previously at the University of Pennsylvania, where he chaired the Graduate Group in Ancient History. His principal areas of specialization as a Roman historian are Roman family history and demography, sectarian violence and conflict in Late Antiquity, and the regional history of Africa as part of the Roman Empire. He has published *Spartacus and the Slaves Wars*; edited the papers of Sir Moses Finley, *Economy and Society in Ancient Greece*; and published in a variety of books and journals, including the *Journal of Roman Studies*, the *American Historical Review*, the *Journal of Early Christian Studies*, and *Past & Present*.

MICHAEL TSIN (*Ph.D. Princeton*) is associate professor of history and international studies at the University of North Carolina at Chapel Hill. He previously taught at the University of Illinois at Chicago, Princeton University, Columbia University, and the University of Florida. Professor Tsin's primary interests include the histories of modern China and colonialism. He is the author of *Nation, Governance, and Modernity in China: Canton, 1900–1927*. He is currently writing a social history of the reconfiguration of Chinese identity in the twentieth century.

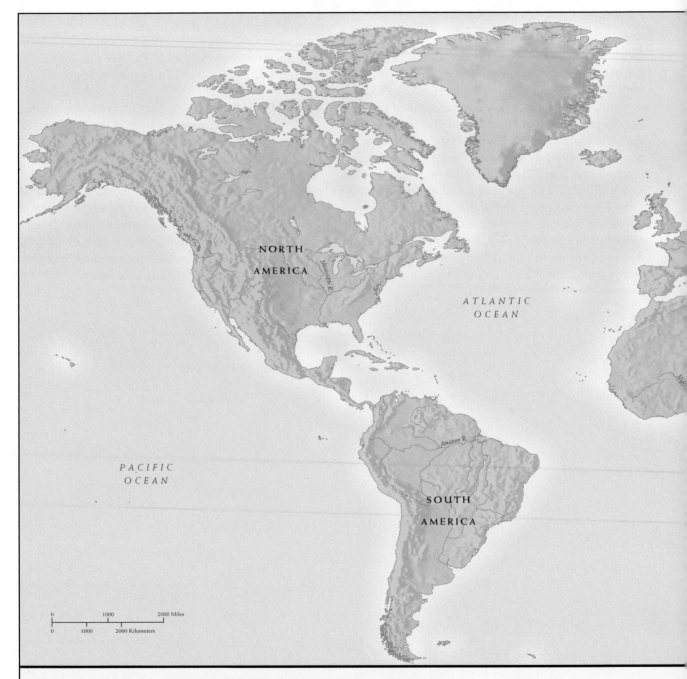

THE GEOGRAPHY OF THE ANCIENT AND MODERN WORLDS

Today, we believe the world to be divided into continents, and most of us think that it was always so. Geographers usually identify six inhabited continents: Africa, North America, South America, Europe, Asia, and Australia. Inside these continents they locate a vast number of subcontinental units, such as East Asia, South Asia, Southeast Asia, the Middle East, North Africa, and sub-Saharan Africa. Yet this geographical understanding would have been completely alien to premodern men and women, who did not think that they inhabited continents bounded by large bodies of water. Lacking a firm command of the seas, they saw themselves living on contiguous landmasses, and they

thought these territorial bodies were the main geographical units of their lives. Hence, in this volume we have chosen to use a set of geographical terms, the main one being Afro-Eurasia, that more accurately reflect the world that the premoderns believed that they inhabited.

The most interconnected and populous landmass of premodern times was Afro-Eurasia. The term Eurasia is widely used in general histories, but we think it is in its own ways inadequate. The preferred term from our perspective must be Afro-Eurasia, for the interconnected landmass of premodern and indeed much of modern times included large parts of Europe and Asia and significant regions in Africa. The major African territories that were regularly joined to Europe and Asia were Egypt, North Africa, and even parts of sub-Saharan Africa.

Only gradually and fitfully did the divisions of the world that we take for granted today take shape. The peoples inhabiting the northwestern part of the Afro-Eurasian landmass did not see themselves as European Christians, and hence as a distinctive cultural entity, until the Middle Ages drew to a close in the twelfth and thirteenth centuries. Islam did not arise and extend its influence throughout the middle zone of the Afro-Eurasian landmass until the eighth and ninth centuries. And, finally, the peoples living in what we today term the Indian subcontinent did not feel a strong sense of their own cultural and political unity until the Delhi Sultanate of the thirteenth and fourteenth centuries and the Mughal Empire, which emerged at the beginning of the sixteenth century, brought political unity to that vast region. As a result, we use the terms South Asia, Vedic society, and India in place of Indian subcontinent for the premodern part of our narrative, and we use Southwest Asia and North Africa to refer to what today is designated as the Middle East. In fact, it is only in the period from 1000 to 1300 that some of the major cultural areas that are familiar to us today truly crystallized.

WORLDS TOGETHER,
WORLDS APART

Volume 1

Before You Read This Chapter

GLOBAL STORYLINES

- Communities, from long ago to today, produce creation narratives in order to make sense of how humans came into being.

- Hominid development across millions of years results in modern humans (*Homo sapiens*) and the traits that make us "human."

- During the period from 200,000 to 12,000 years ago, humans live as hunter-gatherers and achieve major breakthroughs in language and art.

- Global revolution in domesticating crops and animals leads to settled agricultural-based communities, while other communities develop pastoral ways of life.

CORE OBJECTIVES

- **DESCRIBE** various creation narratives traced in this chapter, including the narrative of human evolution, and **EXPLAIN** why they differ.

- **TRACE** the major developments in hominid evolution that resulted in the traits that make *Homo sapiens* "human."

- **DESCRIBE** human ways of life and cultural developments from 200,000 to 12,000 years ago.

- **COMPARE** the ways communities around the world shifted to settled agriculture and **ANALYZE** the significance this shift had for social organization.

Becoming Human

In 2003, in a remote corner of the Ethiopian highlands of Africa, a team of evolutionary biologists came upon fossil remains lodged in volcanic rock. Identifying and reassembling these remains took six years, but the researchers eventually reconstructed one of the most revealing sets of human fossils ever found: a nearly complete skeleton of an adult male, and the partial remains of another adult and a juvenile. By establishing the age of the volcanic rock, the team determined that the bones were about 160,000 years old. Although the skeletal remains were not identical to those of modern men and women, they were close enough to form part of the family of modern humans. In short, the bones represented the oldest record of *Homo sapiens*. The fossil finds confirmed what earlier studies had suggested: *Homo sapiens*, or modern humans, originated in a small region of Africa about 200,000 years ago and migrated out of Africa between 100,000 and 50,000 years ago.

Most of the common traits of human beings—the abilities to make tools, engage in family life, use language, and refine cognitive abilities—evolved over many millennia and crystallized around the time *Homo sapiens* migrated out of Africa. Only with the beginning of settled agriculture did significant cultural differences develop between groups of humans, as artifacts such as tools, cooking devices, and storage containers reveal. The differences in humankind's cultures are less than 15,000 or 20,000 years old.

This chapter lays out the origins of humanity from its common source. It shows how many different hominids (represented today by humans, chimpanzees, gorillas, and orangutans) preceded modern humans, and that humans came from only one—very recent—stock of hominid migrants out of Africa. Fanning out across the world, our ancestors adapted to environmental constraints and opportunities. They created languages, families, and clan systems, often innovating to defend themselves against predators. One of the biggest breakthroughs was the domestication of plants and animals and the creation of settled agriculture. With this development, humans could stop following food and begin producing it where they desired.

Creation Narratives

For thousands of years, humans have constructed, out of their values and available evidence, narratives of how the world, and humans, came to be. These **creation narratives** have varied over time and across cultures, depending on a society's values and the evidence available. To understand the origins of modern humans, we must come to terms with scales of time: the billions, millions, and hundreds of thousands of years through which the universe, earth, and life on it, developed into what they are today. Though the hominids that eventually evolved into modern humans lived millions of years ago, our tools for telling the modern creation narrative are relatively new.

Only 350 years ago, English clerics claimed on the basis of biblical calculations and Christian tradition that the first day of creation was Sunday, October 23, 4004 BCE. Modern science, however, indicates that the origin of the universe dates back 13.8 billion years, and the hominid separation from African pongids (members of the ape family) began 6 or 7 million years ago. These new discoveries have proved as mind-boggling to Hindus and Muslims as to Christians and Jews—all of whom believed, in different ways, that the universe was not so old and that divine beings had a role in creating it and all life, including the first humans. (See Competing Perspectives: Creation Narratives.) For millennia, human communities across the globe have constructed narratives that extend back differing lengths of time and suggest various roles for humans and gods in the process of universal creation. For instance, the Judeo-Christian narrative portrays a single God creating a universe out of nothingness, populating it with plants, animals, and humans, in a span of six days. The centuries-old creation story of the Yoruba peoples of West Africa depicts a divine being descending from the heavens in human form and becoming the godlike king Oduduwa, who established the Yoruba kingdom and the rules by which his subjects were to live. The foundational texts of Hinduism, which date to the seventh or sixth century BCE, account that the world is millions, not billions, of years old. Chinese Han dynasty (206 BCE–220 CE) astronomers believed that at the world's beginning the planets were conjoined and that they would merge again at the end of time. The Buddhists' cosmos comprised millions of worlds, each consisting of a mountain encircled by four continents, its seas surrounded by a wall of iron.

Yet even the million-year time frames and multiple planetary systems that ancient Asian thinkers endorsed did not prepare their communities for the idea that humans are related to apes. In all traditional cosmologies, humans came into existence fully formed, at a single moment, as did the other beings that populated the world. Modern discoveries about humanity's origins have challenged these traditions, because no tradition conceived that creatures evolved into new kinds of life, that humans had descended from apes, and that all of humanity originated in a remote corner of Africa.

Hominids to Modern Humans

The modern scientific creation narrative of human evolution would have been unimaginable even just over a century ago, when Charles Darwin was formulating his ideas about human origins. As we will see in this section, scientific discoveries have shown that modern humans evolved from earlier hominids. Through adaptation to their environment, various species of hominids developed new physical characteristics and distinctive skills. Millions of years after the first hominids appeared, the first modern humans—*Homo sapiens*—emerged and spread out across the globe.

EVOLUTIONARY FINDINGS AND RESEARCH METHODS

New insights into the time frame of the universe and human existence have occurred over a long period of time. Geologists made early breakthroughs in the eighteenth century when their research into the layers of the earth's surface revealed a world much older than biblical time implied. Evolutionary biologists, most notably Charles Darwin (1809–1882), concluded that all life had evolved over long periods from simple forms of matter. In the twentieth century astronomers, evolutionary biologists, and archaeologists have developed sophisticated dating techniques to pinpoint the chronology of the universe's creation and the evolution of all forms of life on earth. Their discoveries have radically transformed humanity's understanding of its own history (see **Current Trends in World History: Determining the Age of Fossils and Sediments**). A mere century ago, who would have accepted the idea that the universe came into being 13.7 billion years ago, that the earth appeared about 4.5 billion years ago, and that the earliest life forms began to exist about 3.8 billion years ago?

Yet, modern science suggests that human beings are part of a long evolutionary chain stretching from microscopic bacteria to African apes that appeared about 23 million years ago, and that Africa's "Great Ape" population separated into three distinct groups of **hominids**: one becoming present-day gorillas; the second becoming chimpanzees; and the third group becoming modern humans only after following a long and complicated evolutionary process. Our focus will be on the third group of hominids, who became modern humans. A combination of traits, evolving over several million years, distinguished humans from other hominids, including: (1) lifting the torso and walking on two legs (bipedalism), thereby freeing hands and arms to carry objects and hurl weapons; (2) controlling and then making fire; (3) fashioning and using tools; (4) developing cognitive skills and an enlarged brain and therefore the capacity for language; and (5) acquiring a consciousness of "self." All these traits were in place at least 150,000 years ago. *Change*

Two terms central to understanding any discussion of hominid development are evolution and natural selection. **Evolution** is the process by which species of plants and animals change and develop over generations, as certain traits are favored in reproduction. The process of evolution is driven by a mechanism called *natural selection*, in which members of a species with certain randomly occurring traits that are useful for environmental or other reasons survive and reproduce with greater success than those without the traits. Thus, biological evolution (human or otherwise) does not imply progress to higher forms of life, only successful adaptation to environmental surroundings.

EARLY HOMINIDS, ADAPTATION, AND CLIMATE CHANGE

The term *modern humans* refers to members of the *Homo sapiens* subspecies that evolved about 200,000 years ago. Through evolution, *Homo sapiens* developed the traits that make us distinct from the many other species and subspecies of hominids (such as the australopithecines, *Homo habilis,* and *Homo erectus* discussed in this section). "Modern" (and "recent") when applied to humans is relative, especially when compared to the life of the universe (which dates to 13.8 billion years ago) and even to the earliest hominids

Determining the Age of Fossils and Sediments

Our knowledge of human origins has been the result of several remarkable scientific breakthroughs. Only recently have scholars been able to date fossil remains and to use biological research to understand the relationships among the world's early peoples.

The first major advance in the study of prehistory (the time before written historical records) occurred in the mid-twentieth century, and it involved the use of *radiocarbon dating*. All living things contain the radiocarbon isotope C^{14}, which plants acquire directly from the atmosphere and animals acquire indirectly when they consume plants or other animals. When these living things die, the C^{14} isotope begins to decay into a stable nonradioactive element, C^{12}. Because the rate of decay is regular and measurable, it is possible to determine the age of fossils that leave organic remains for up to 40,000 years.

A second major dating technique, the *potassium-argon method*, also involves analysis of the changing chemical structure of objects over time. Scientists can calculate the age of nonliving objects by measuring the ratio of potassium to argon in them, since potassium decays into argon. This method allows scientists to calculate the age of objects up to a million years old. It also enables them to date the sediments in which researchers find fossils—as a gauge of the age of the fossils themselves.

DNA (deoxyribonucleic acid) analysis is a third crucial tool for unraveling the beginnings of modern humans. DNA, which determines biological inheritances, exists in two places within the cells of all living organisms—including the human body. *Nuclear DNA* occurs in the nucleus of every cell, where it controls most aspects of physical appearance and makeup. *Mitochondrial DNA* occurs outside the nucleus of cells and is located in mitochondria, structures used in converting the energy from food into a form that cells can use. Nuclear and mitochondrial DNA exists in males and females, but only mitochondrial DNA from females passes to their offspring, as the females' egg cells carry their mitochondria with their DNA to the offspring; sperm cells from males do not donate any DNA to the egg cell at fertilization. By examining mitochondrial DNA, researchers can measure genetic relatedness and variation among living organisms—including human beings. Such analysis has enabled researchers to pinpoint human descent from an original African population to other, genetically related populations that lived approximately 100,000 years ago.

The genetic similarity of modern humans suggests that the population from which all *Homo sapiens* descended originated in Africa about 200,000 years ago. When these humans began to move out of Africa around 100,000 years ago, they spread eastward into Southwest Asia and then throughout the rest of Afro-Eurasia. One group migrated to Australia about 50,000 years ago. Another group moved into the area of Europe about 40,000 years ago. When the scientific journal *Nature* published these findings in 1987, it inspired a groundswell of public interest—and a contentious scientific debate that continues today.

As this chapter demonstrates, the environment, especially climate, played a major role in the appearance of hominids and the eventual dominance of *Homo sapiens*. But how do we know so much about the world's climate going so far back in time? This brings us to the fourth of the scientific breakthroughs, known as marine isotope stages. By exploring the marine

(7 million years ago). This section's discussion demonstrates that as modern humans evolved from earlier hominids, they passed through successive waves of adaptation, innovation, and migration.

Australopithecines In 1924, near Johannesburg, South Africa, a scientist named Raymond Dart discovered the pint-sized skull and bones of a creature that had both ape-like and humanoid features. Dart labeled his bipedal find *Australopithecus africanus*. **Australopithecines** existed not only in southern Africa but in the north as well. In 1974, an archaeological team working at a site in present-day Ethiopia unearthed a relatively intact skeleton of a young adult female australopithecine in the valley of the Awash River. While the technical name for the find became *Australopithecus afarensis*, the researchers who found the skeleton gave it the nickname Lucy, based on the popular Beatles song "Lucy in the Sky with Diamonds."

Neanderthal DNA Extraction This sample of fossilized bone from an early hominid will have its genetic material extracted and sequenced.

life, mainly pollen and plankton, deposited in deep seabeds and measuring the levels of oxygen-16 and oxygen-18 isotopes in these life forms, oceanographers and climatologists are able to determine the temperature of the world hundreds of thousands and even millions of years ago and thus to chart the cooling and warming cycles of the earth's climate.

QUESTIONS FOR ANALYSIS

- How has the study of prehistory changed since the mid-twentieth century? What are the consequences?
- How does the study of climate and environment relate to the origins of humans?

Explore Further

Lawrence Barham and Peter Mitchell, *The First Africans: African Archaeology from the Earliest Toolmakers to Most Recent Foragers* (2008).

Graeme Barker, *Agricultural Revolution in Prehistory: Why Did Foragers Become Farmers* (2006).

Lucy was remarkable. She stood a little over three feet tall, she walked upright, her skull contained a brain within the ape size range (i.e., one-third human size), and her jaw and teeth were human-like. Her arms were long, hanging halfway from her hips to her knees—suggesting that she might not have been bipedal at all times and sometimes resorted to arms for locomotion, in the fashion of a modern baboon. Above all, Lucy's skeleton was relatively complete and showed us that hominids were walking around as early as 3 million years ago. (See Table 1.1.) It is important to emphasize that australopithecines were not humans but that they carried the genetic and biological material out of which modern humans would later emerge. These precursors to modern humans had a key trait for evolutionary survival: they were remarkably good adapters. They could deal with dynamic environmental shifts, and they were intelligent.

Fossil Bones of Lucy Archaeologist Donald Johanson discovered the fossilized bones of this young female in the Afar region of Ethiopia. Lucy's bones are believed to date from approximately 3.2 million years ago and provide evidence of some of the first hominids to appear in Africa. This find was of great importance because the bones were so fully and completely preserved.

COMPARISON

TRACE the major developments in hominid evolution that resulted in the traits that make *Homo sapiens* "human."

TABLE 1.1 | Human Evolution

SPECIES	TIME
Orrorin tugenensis	6 MILLION YEARS AGO
Australopithecus anamensis	4.2 MILLION YEARS AGO
Australopithecus afarensis (INCLUDING LUCY)	3.4 MILLION YEARS AGO
Australopithecus africanus	3.0 MILLION YEARS AGO
Homo habilis (INCLUDING DEAR BOY)	2.5 MILLION YEARS AGO
Homo erectus and *Homo ergaster* (INCLUDING JAVA AND PEKING MAN)	1.8 MILLION YEARS AGO
Homo heidelbergensis (COMMON ANCESTOR OF *NEANDERTHALS* AND *HOMO SAPIENS*)	600,000 YEARS AGO
Neanderthals	200,000 YEARS AGO
Homo sapiens	200,000 YEARS AGO
Homo sapiens sapiens (MODERN HUMANS)	35,000 YEARS AGO

Adaptation For hominids, like the rest of the plant and animal world, survival required constant adaptation (the ability to alter behavior and to innovate, finding new ways of doing things). During the first millions of years of hominid existence, these slow changes involved primarily physical adaptations to the environment. The places where researchers have found early hominid remains in southern and eastern Africa had environments that changed from being heavily forested and well watered to being arid and desert-like, and then back again. (See Map 1.1.) Hominids had to keep pace with these changing physical environments or else risk extinction. In fact, many of the early hominid groups did die out.

In adapting, early hominids began to distinguish themselves from other mammals that were physically similar to themselves. It was not their hunting prowess that made the hominids stand out, because plenty of other species chased their prey with skill and dexterity. The single trait that gave early hominids a real advantage for survival was bipedalism: they became "two-footed" creatures that stood upright. At some point, the first hominids were able to remain upright and move about, leaving their arms and hands free for other useful tasks, like carrying food over long distances. Once they ventured into open savannas (grassy plains with a few scattered trees), about 1.7 million years ago, hominids had a tremendous advantage. They were the only primates (an order of mammals consisting of man, apes, and monkeys) to move consistently on two legs. Because

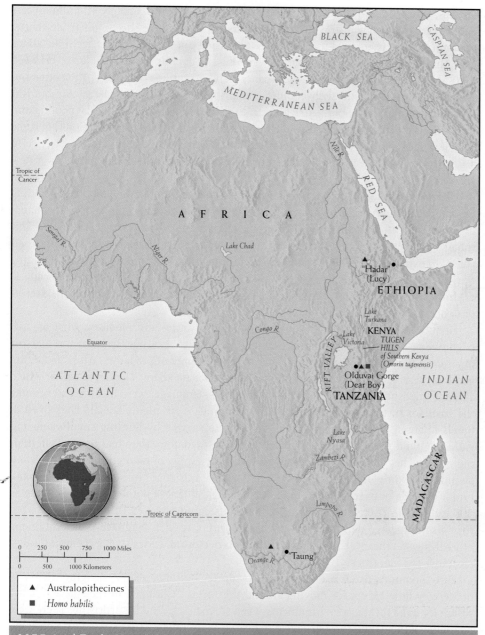

MAP 1.1 | Early Hominids

The earliest hominid species evolved in Africa millions of years ago.

- Judging from this map, what were the main geographic features of their environment?
- According to this chapter, how did the changing environment of eastern and southern Africa shape the evolution of these modern human ancestors?

they could move continuously and over great distances, they were able to migrate out of hostile environments and into more hospitable locations.

Environmental Changes The climate in eastern and southern Africa, where hominid development began, was conducive to the development of diverse plant and animal species. When the world entered its fourth great ice age approximately 40 million years ago, the earth's temperatures dropped and its continental ice sheets, polar ice sheets, and mountain glaciers increased. This ice age lasted until 12,000 years ago. Like all ice ages, this fourth ice age had alternating warming and cooling phases that lasted between 40,000 and 100,000 years each. Between 15 and 10 million years ago, the climate in Africa went through one such cooling and drying phase. To the east of Africa's Rift Valley, stretching from South Africa north to the Ethiopian highlands, the cooling and drying forced forests to contract and savannas to spread. It was in this region that some apes left the shelter of the trees, stood up, and learned to walk, to run, and to live in savanna lands—thus becoming the precursors to humans, and distinctive as a new species.

Using two feet for locomotion augmented the means for obtaining food and avoiding predators and improved the chances these creatures had to survive in constantly changing environments. In addition to being bipedal, hominids had opposable thumbs. This trait, shared with other primates, gave hominids great physical dexterity, enhancing their ability to explore and to alter materials found in nature. Manual dexterity and standing upright also enabled them to carry young family members if they needed to relocate, or to throw missiles (such as rocks and sticks) with deadly accuracy to protect themselves or to obtain food.

Hominids used their increased powers of observation and memory, what we call cognitive skills, to gather wild berries and grains and to scavenge the meat and marrow of animals that had died of natural causes or as the prey of predators. All primates are good at these activities, but hominids came to excel at them. Cognitive skills, which also included problem solving and—eventually—language, were destined to become the basis for further developments. Early hominids were highly social. They lived in bands of about twenty-five individuals, trying to survive by hunting small game and gathering wild plants. Not yet a match for large predators, they had to find safe hiding places. They thrived in places where a diverse supply of wild grains and fruits and abundant wildlife ensured a secure, comfortable existence. In such locations, small hunting bands of twenty-five could swell through alliances with others to as many as 500 individuals. Like other primates, hominids communicated through gestures, but they also may have developed a very basic form of spoken language that led (among other things) to the establishment of rudimentary cultural codes such as common rules, customs, and identities.

Early hominids lived in this manner for up to 3 million years, changing their way of life very little except for moving around the African landmass in their never-ending search for more favorable environments. Even so, their survival is surprising. There were not many of them, and they struggled in hostile environments surrounded by a diversity of large mammals, including predators such as lions.

As the environment changed over the millennia, these early hominids gradually changed as well. Over a period of 3 million years, their brains more than doubled in size; their foreheads became more elongated; their jaws became less massive; and they took on a much more human look. Adaptation to environmental changes also created new skills and aptitudes, which expanded the ability to store and analyze information. With larger brains, hominids could form mental maps of their worlds—they could learn, remember what they learned, and convey these lessons to their neighbors and offspring. In this fashion, larger groups of hominids created communities with shared understandings of their environments.

Diversity Recent discoveries in Ethiopia and Kenya suggest that hominids were both older and more diverse than early australopithecine finds had suggested. In southern

Kenya in 2000, researchers excavated bone remains, at least 6 million years old, of a chimpanzee-sized hominid (named *Orrorin tugenensis*) that walked upright on two feet. This discovery indicates that bipedalism must be millions of years older than scientists thought based on Lucy and the earlier *Australopithecus africanus* discovery. Moreover, these hominids' teeth indicate that they were closer to modern humans than to australopithecines. In their arms and hands, though, which show characteristics needed for tree climbing, the *Orrorin* hominids seemed more ape-like than the australopithecines. So *Orrorin* hominids were still somewhat tied to an environment in the trees. Other fossils, found at sites in the Afar depression in Ethiopia (just south of the area where Lucy was found) and in northern Kenya, have revealed additional distinct species of early hominids.

The fact that different kinds of early hominids were living in isolated societies and evolving separately, though in close proximity to one another, in eastern Africa between 4 and 3 million years ago indicates much greater diversity among their populations than scholars previously imagined. The environment in eastern Africa generated a fair number of different hominid populations, a few of which would provide our genetic base, but most of which would not survive in the long run.

TOOL-USE BY *HOMO HABILIS*

One million years after Lucy, the first beings whom we assign to the genus *Homo,* or "true human," appeared. Like early hominids, *Homo habilis* was bipedal, possessing a smooth walk based on upright posture. *Homo habilis* had an even more important

used arms to do things no[...]

advantage over other hominids: brains that were growing larger. Big brains are the site of innovation: learning and storing lessons so that humans could pass those lessons on to later generations, especially in the making of tools and the efficient use of resources (and, we suspect, in defending themselves). Mary and Louis Leakey, who made astonishing fossil discoveries in the 1950s at Olduvai Gorge in present-day north central Tanzania, identified these important traits. The Leakeys' finds included an intact skull that was 1.8 million years old. They nicknamed the creature whose skull they had unearthed Dear Boy.

Objects discovered with Dear Boy demonstrated that by this time early humans had begun to make tools for butchering animals and, possibly, for hunting and killing smaller animals. The tools were flaked stones with sharpened edges for cutting apart animal flesh and scooping out the marrow from bones. To mimic the slicing teeth of lions, leopards, and other carnivores, these early humans had devised these tools through careful chipping. Dear Boy and his companions had carried usable rocks to distant places where they made their implements with special hammer stones—tools to make tools. Unlike other tool-using animals (for example, chimpanzees), early humans were now intentionally fashioning implements, not simply finding them when needed. More

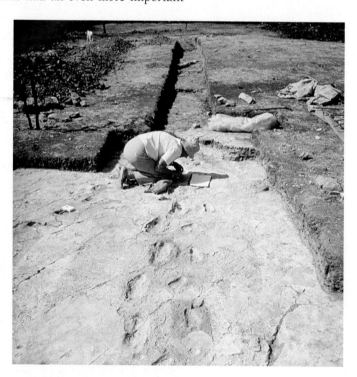

The Leakeys Louis Leakey and his wife, Mary, were dedicated archaeologists whose work in East Africa established the area as one of the starting points of human development. Mary Leakey was among the most successful archaeologists studying hominids in Africa. Her finds, including the one in this photograph from Laetoli, Tanzania, highlight the activities of early men and women in Africa. The footprints, believed to be those of an *Australopithecus afarensis*, date from 3.7 to 3 million years ago.

Olduvai Gorge, Tanzania Olduvai Gorge is arguably the most famous archaeological site containing hominid finds. Mary and Louis Leakey, convinced that early human beings originated in Africa, discovered the fossil remains of *Homo habilis* ("Skillful Man") in this area beginning in 1959. They argued that these findings represent a direct link to *Homo erectus*.

important, they were passing on knowledge of these tools to their offspring and, in the process, gradually improving the tools. The Leakeys, believing that making and using tools represented a new stage in the evolution of human beings, gave Dear Boy and his companions the name ***Homo habilis***, or "Skillful Man." While scholars today may debate whether tool making (rather than walking upright or having a large brain) is the key trait that distinguishes the first humans from earlier hominids, *Homo habilis*'s skills made them the forerunners, though very distant, of modern men and women.

MIGRATIONS OF *HOMO ERECTUS*

By 1 million years ago many of the hominid species that flourished together in Africa had died out. One surviving species, which emerged about 1.8 million years ago, had a large brain capacity and walked truly upright; it therefore gained the name ***Homo erectus***, or "Standing Man." Three important features distinguished *Homo erectus* from their competitors and made them more able to cope with environmental changes: their family dynamics, use of fire, and ability to travel long distances. Discoveries in Asia and Europe show that *Homo erectus* migrated out of Africa in some of the earliest waves of hominid migration around the globe.

Family Dynamics One of the traits that contributed to the survival of *Homo erectus* was the development of extended periods of caring for their young. Although their enlarged brain gave these hominids advantages over the rest of the animal world, it also brought one significant problem: their heads were too large to pass through the females' pelvises at birth. Their pelvises were only big enough to deliver an infant with a cranial capacity that was about a third an adult's size. As a result, offspring required a long period of protection by adults as they matured and their brain size tripled.

This difference from other species also affected family dynamics. For example, the long maturing process gave adult members of hunting and gathering bands time to train their children in those activities. In addition, maturation and brain growth required mothers to spend years breast-feeding and then preparing food for children after their weaning. In order to share the responsibilities of child-rearing, mothers relied on other women (their own mothers, sisters, and friends) and girls (often their own daughters) to help in the nurturing and protecting, a process known as _allomothering_ (literally, "other mothering").

Use of Fire _Homo erectus_ began to make rudimentary attempts to control their environment by means of fire. It is hard to tell from fossils when humans learned to use fire. The most reliable evidence comes from cave sites less than 250,000 years old, where early humans apparently cooked some of their food, but some have suggested that hominid mastery of fire occurred as early as 500,000 years ago. Fire provided heat, protection, a gathering point for small communities, and a way to cook food. It was also symbolically powerful: here was a source of energy that humans could extinguish and revive at will. The uses of fire had enormous long-term effects on human evolution. Because they were able to boil, steam, and fry wild plants, as well as otherwise undigestible foods (especially raw muscle fiber), early humans could expand their diets. Because cooked foods yield more energy than raw foods and because the brain, while only 2 percent of human body weight, uses between 20 and 25 percent of all the energy that humans take in, cooking was decisive in the evolution of brain size and functioning.

Early Migrations Being bipedal, _Homo erectus_ could move with a smooth and rapid gait, so they could cover large distances quickly. They were the world's first long-distance travelers, forming the first mobile human communities. Around 1 or 2 million years ago, _Homo erectus_ individuals migrated first into the lands of Southwest Asia. From there, they traveled along the Indian Ocean shoreline, moving into South Asia and Southeast Asia and later northward into what is now China. Their migration was a response in part to the environmental changes that were transforming the world. The Northern Hemisphere experienced thirty major cold phases during this period, marked by glaciers spreading over vast expanses of the northern parts of Eurasia and the Americas. The glaciers formed as a result of intense cold that froze much of the world's oceans, lowering them some

Skulls of Ancestors of _Homo sapiens_ Shown here are seven skulls of ancestors of modern-day men and women, arranged to highlight brain growth over time. The skulls represent (left to right): _Adapis,_ a lemur-like animal that lived 50 million years ago; _Proconsul,_ a primate that lived about 23 million years ago; _Australopithecus africanus; Homo habilis; Homo erectus; Homo sapiens_ from the Qafzeh site in Israel, about 90,000 years old; and Cro-Magnon _Homo sapiens sapiens_ from France, about 22,000 years old.

325 feet below present-day levels. These lower ocean levels made it possible for the migrants to travel across land bridges into Southeast Asia and from East Asia to Japan, as well as from New Guinea to Australia. The last parts of the Afro-Eurasian landmass to be occupied were in Europe.

Discoveries of the bone remains of "Java Man" and "Peking Man" (named according to the places where archaeologists first unearthed their remains) confirmed early settlements of *Homo erectus* in Southeast and East Asia. The remains of Java Man, found in 1891 on the island of Java, turned out to be those of an early *Homo erectus* that had dispersed into Asia nearly 2 million years ago. Peking Man, found near Beijing in the 1920s, was a cave dweller, toolmaker, and hunter and gatherer who settled in the warmer climate in northern China perhaps 400,000 years ago. Peking Man's brain was larger than that of his Javan cousins, and there is evidence that he controlled fire and cooked meat in addition to hunting large animals. He made tools of vein quartz, quartz crystals, flint, and sandstone. A major innovation was the double-faced axe, a stone instrument whittled down to sharp edges on both sides to serve as a hand axe, a cleaver, a pick, and probably a weapon to hurl against foes or animals. Even so, these early predecessors still lacked the intelligence, language skills, and ability to create culture that would distinguish the first modern humans from their hominid relatives.

HOMO SAPIENS: THE FIRST MODERN HUMANS

Homo sapiens—a bigger-brained, more dexterous, and more agile species of humans that appeared in the highlands of eastern Africa about 200,000 years ago—differed notably from their precursors, including *Homo habilis* and *Homo erectus*. Their distinctive traits, including greater cognitive skills, made *Homo sapiens* the first modern humans and enabled them to spread out from Africa and flourish in even more diverse regions across the globe than *Homo erectus* did.

Large-scale shifts in Africa's climate and environment about 200,000 years ago put huge pressures on all types of mammals, including hominids. In these extremely warm and dry environments, the smaller, quicker, and more adaptable mammals survived. What counted now was no longer large size and brute strength, but the ability to respond quickly, with agility, and with great speed. The eclipse of *Homo erectus* by *Homo sapiens* was not inevitable. After all, *Homo erectus* was already scattered around Africa and Eurasia by the time *Homo sapiens* emerged; in contrast, current thinking suggests that even as late as 100,000 years ago there were only about 10,000 *Homo sapiens* adults living in a small part of the African landmass. But when *Homo sapiens* moved out of Africa and the two species encountered each other in the same places across the globe, *Homo sapiens* individuals were better suited to survive—in part because of their greater cognitive and language skills.

The *Homo sapiens* newcomers followed the trails blazed by earlier migrants when they moved out of Africa sometime between 120,000 and 50,000 years

The Physical Evolution of Hominids These three figures show the femur bones of Lucy, *Orrorin tugenensis* (one of the earliest of the hominids, who may have existed as many as 6 million years ago), and *Homo sapiens*. *Homo sapiens* have a larger femur bone and were bigger than Lucy was—a representative of the hominid species *Australopithecus afarensis*—but have the same bone structure.

ago. (See Map 1.2.) In many places, they moved into the same areas as their genetic cousins, moving across Southwest Asia and from there into central Asia—but not into the area of Europe. They flourished and reproduced. By 30,000 years ago, the population of *Homo sapiens* had grown to about 300,000. Between 60,000 and 12,000 years ago, these modern humans were surging into areas tens of thousands of miles from the Rift Valley and the Ethiopian highlands of Africa (see **Analyzing Global Developments: The Age of the Universe and Human Evolution**).

In the area of present-day China, *Homo sapiens* were thriving and creating distinct regional cultures. Consider Shandingdong Man, a *Homo sapiens* who dates to about 18,000 years ago. His physical characteristics were closer to those of modern humans, and he had a similar brain size. His stone tools, which included choppers and scrapers for preparing food, were similar to those of the *Homo erectus* Peking Man. His bone needles, however, were the first stitching tools of their kind found in China, and they indicated the making of garments. Some of the needles measured a little over an inch in length and had small holes drilled in them. Shandingdong Man also buried his dead. In fact, a tomb of grave goods includes ornaments suggesting the development of aesthetic tastes and religious beliefs.

Homo sapiens were also migrating into the northeastern fringe of East Asia. In the frigid climate there, they learned to follow herds of large Siberian grazing animals. The bones and dung of mastodons made decent fuel and good building material. Pursuing their prey eastward as the large-tusked herds sought pastures in the steppes (treeless grasslands) and marshes, these groups migrated across the ice to Japan. Archaeologists have discovered a mammoth fossil in the colder north of Japan, for example, and an elephant fossil in the warmer south. Elephants in particular roamed the warmer parts of Inner Eurasia. The hunters and gatherers who moved into Japan gathered wild plants for sustenance, and they dried, smoked, or broiled meat by using fire.

About 16,000 years ago, *Homo sapiens* began edging into the weedy landmass that linked Siberia and North America (which hominids had not populated). This thousand-mile-long land bridge, later called Beringia, must have seemed like an extension of familiar steppe-land terrain. For thousands of years, modern humans poured eastward and southward into North America. The oldest known location of human settlement in the Americas is Broken Mammoth, a 14,000-year-old site in central Alaska. A final migration occurred about 8,000 years ago by boat, since by then the land bridge had disappeared under the sea. (See Table 1.2.)

Using their cognitive abilities to adapt to new environments and to innovate, these migrants, who were the first discoverers of America, began to fill up the landmasses. They found ample prey in the herds of woolly mammoths, caribou, three-ton giant sloths, and 200-pound beavers. But the explorers could also themselves be prey—for they encountered saber-toothed tigers, long-legged eagles, and giant bears that moved faster than horses. The melting of the glaciers about 8,000 years ago and the resulting disappearance of the land bridge eventually cut off the first Americans from their Afro-Eurasian origins. Thereafter, the Americas became a world apart from Afro-Eurasia.

Although modern humans evolved from earlier hominids, no straight-line descent tree exists from the first hominids to *Homo sapiens*. Increasingly, scientists view our origins as shaped by a series of progressions and regressions as hominid species adapted or failed to adapt and died out. The remains of now-extinct hominid species, such as *Homo ergaster*, *Homo heidelbergensis*, and *Homo neanderthalis* (see Table 1.1), offer intriguing glimpses of ultimately unsuccessful branches of the complex human evolutionary tree. Spreading into Europe and parts of Southwest Asia along with other hominids, Neanderthals, for example, had big brains, used tools, wore clothes, buried their dead, hunted, lived in rock

COMPARISON

COMPARE the narrative of human evolution to the creation narratives covered earlier.

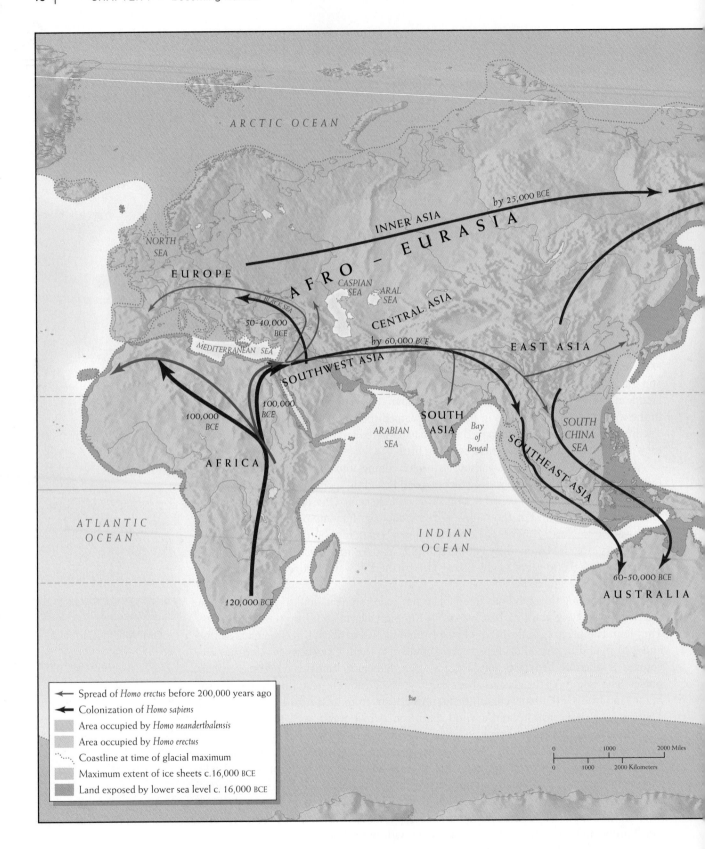

ARCTIC OCEAN

INNER ASIA

by 25,000 BCE

AFRO – EURASIA

NORTH
SEA

EUROPE

CASPIAN
SEA

ARAL
SEA

CENTRAL ASIA

EAST ASIA

BLACK SEA

50–40,000
BCE

by 60,000 BCE

MEDITERRANEAN SEA

SOUTHWEST ASIA

100,000
BCE

SOUTH
ASIA

SOUTH
CHINA
SEA

ARABIAN
SEA

Bay
of
Bengal

100,000
BCE

SOUTHEAST ASIA

AFRICA

ATLANTIC
OCEAN

INDIAN
OCEAN

120,000 BCE

60–50,000 BCE

AUSTRALIA

Spread of *Homo erectus* before 200,000 years ago

Colonization of *Homo sapiens*

Area occupied by *Homo neanderthalensis*

Area occupied by *Homo erectus*

Coastline at time of glacial maximum

Maximum extent of ice sheets c. 16,000 BCE

Land exposed by lower sea level c. 16,000 BCE

0		1000		2000 Miles

0	1000	2000 Kilometers

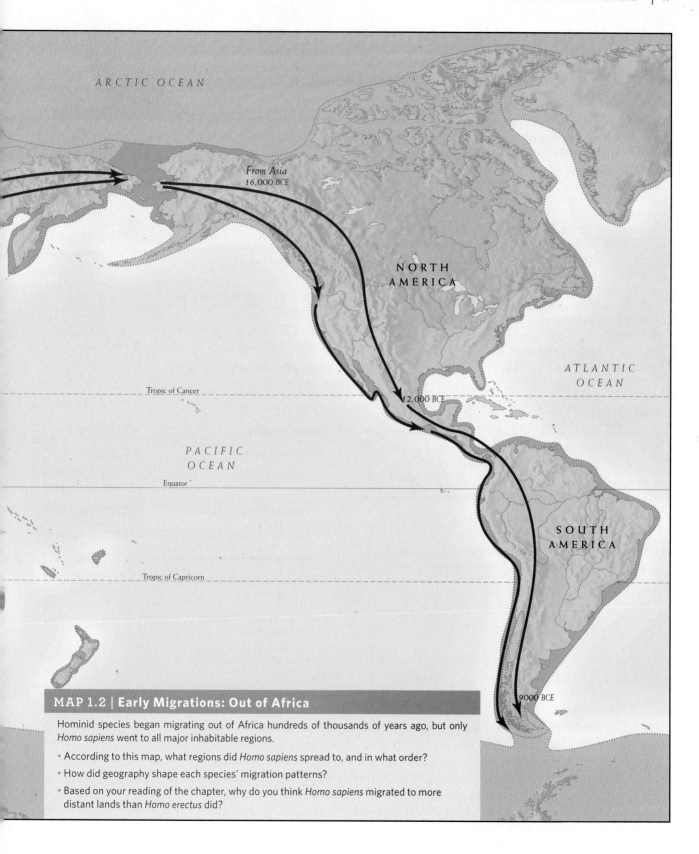

ARCTIC OCEAN

From Asia
16,000 BCE

NORTH AMERICA

ATLANTIC OCEAN

Tropic of Cancer

12,000 BCE

PACIFIC OCEAN

Equator

SOUTH AMERICA

Tropic of Capricorn

9000 BCE

MAP 1.2 | Early Migrations: Out of Africa

Hominid species began migrating out of Africa hundreds of thousands of years ago, but only *Homo sapiens* went to all major inhabitable regions.

- According to this map, what regions did *Homo sapiens* spread to, and in what order?
- How did geography shape each species' migration patterns?
- Based on your reading of the chapter, why do you think *Homo sapiens* migrated to more distant lands than *Homo erectus* did?

Analyzing Global Developments

The Age of the Universe and Human Evolution

Our universe is nearly 14 billion years old. Our sun, earth, and solar system appeared nearly 4.5 billion years ago, and the earliest life forms on earth appeared 3.8 billion years ago. Hominids, however, only appeared on the scene about 7 million years ago, which represents not even 1 percent of the total time that the earth has existed. They were for a long time confined to the African landmass, learning to walk on two legs there, devising simple tools at first and perfecting their use over time. Africa remained the homeland for many different hominid groups for nearly 5 million years before *Homo erectus* ventured out of the continent, moving into central Asia, East Asia, Southeast Asia, and Europe, though not into the Americas. There were probably other waves of hominid migrations out of Africa, but the most important of the migrations out of Africa occurred between 100,000 and 50,000 years ago when modern humans, *Homo sapiens*, left the continent and, with amazing rapidity, filled up all of the globe's landmasses. (See Map 1.2 to trace the migrations of *Homo erectus* and *Homo sapiens*.)

QUESTIONS FOR ANALYSIS

- Describe how we know the age of the universe. How do we know when and how hominids first appeared and their evolutionary patterns?
- Explain why hominids and *Homo sapiens* are so late in the evolutionary cycle. Why did they prevail over other hominids?
- In your opinion, which of the different families of hominids deserves the designation of the first humans and why?
- Why are scientists disinclined to see a straight-line evolution from the earliest hominids to modern humans?

The Big Bang Moment in the Creation of the Universe	13.8 BILLION YEARS AGO (BYA)
The Formation of the Sun, Earth, and Solar System	4.5 BYA
Earliest Life Forms appear	3.8 BYA
Multicellular Organisms appear	1.5 BYA
First Hominids appear	7 MILLION YEARS AGO (MYA)
Australopithecus afarensis appears (including Lucy)	3.4 MYA
Homo habilis appears (including Dear Boy)	2.5 MYA
Homo erectus appears (including Java and Peking Man)	1.8 MYA
Homo erectus leave Africa	1.5 MYA
Neanderthals appear	200,000 YEARS AGO
Homo sapiens appear	200,000 YEARS AGO
Homo sapiens leave Africa	100,000 to 50,000 YEARS AGO
Homo sapiens migrate into Asia	50,000 YEARS AGO
Homo sapiens migrate into Europe	40–50,000 YEARS AGO
Homo sapiens migrate into Australia	40,000 YEARS AGO
Homo sapiens migrate into the Americas	16,000 YEARS AGO
Homo sapiens sapiens appear (modern humans)	35,000 YEARS AGO

<1% of Earth's Existence

Sources: Chris Scarre (ed.), *The Human Past: World Prehistory and the Development of Human Societies* (2005); Ian Tattersall, *Masters of the Planet: The Search for Our Human Origins* (2012).

shelters, and even interacted with *Homo sapiens*. Yet when faced with environmental challenges, *Homo sapiens* survived, while Neanderthals died out 38,000 years ago.

Indeed, several species could exist simultaneously, but some were more suited to changing environmental conditions—and thus more likely to survive—than others. Although the examples emphasized in this chapter—*Homo habilis* and *Homo erectus*—were among some of the world's first human-like inhabitants, they probably were not direct ancestors of modern men and women. By 25,000 years ago, DNA analysis reveals, nearly all genetic cousins to *Homo sapiens* had become extinct. *Homo sapiens*, with their physical agility and superior cognitive skills, were ready to populate the world.

TABLE 1.2	Migrations of *Homo sapiens*	
SPECIES	**TIME**
Homo erectus leave Africa	c. 1.5 MILLION YEARS AGO
Homo sapiens leave Africa	c. 100,000 to 50,000 YEARS AGO
Homo sapiens migrate into Asia	c. 50,000 YEARS AGO
migrate into Europe	c. 50–40,000 YEARS AGO
migrate into Australia	c. 40,000 YEARS AGO
migrate into the Americas	c. 16–11,000 YEARS AGO

The Life of Early *Homo Sapiens*

In the period from 200,000 to around 12,000 years ago, early *Homo sapiens* were similar to other hominids in that they lived by hunting and gathering, but their use of language and new cultural forms represented an evolutionary breakthrough. Earlier hominids could not form large, lasting communities, as they had limited communication skills. While simple commands and hand signals developed over time, complex linguistic expression escaped them. This achievement was one of the last in the evolutionary process of becoming human; it did not occur until between 100,000 and 50,000 years ago. Many scholars view it as the critical ingredient in distinguishing human beings from other animals. It is this skill that made *Homo sapiens* "sapiens," which is to say "wise" or "intelligent"—humans who could create culture.

COMPARISON

DESCRIBE human ways of life and cultural developments from 200,000 to 12,000 years ago.

LANGUAGE

Few things set *Homo sapiens* off from the rest of the animal world more starkly than their use of language. Although the beginnings and development of language are controversial, scholars agree that the cognitive abilities involved in language development marked an evolutionary milestone. Some earlier hominids could express themselves by grunting, but natural language (the use of sounds to make words that convey meaning to others) is unique to modern humans. The development of language required a large brain and complex cognitive organization to create word groups that would convey symbolic meaning. Verbal communication required an ability to think abstractly and to communicate abstractions. Language was a huge breakthrough, because individuals could teach words and ideas to neighbors and offspring. Language thus enhanced the ability to accumulate knowledge that could be transmitted across both space and time.

Biological research has demonstrated that humans can make and process many more primary and distinctive sounds, called phonemes, than other animals can. Whereas a human being can utter fifty phonemes, an ape can form only twelve. Also, humans can process sounds more quickly than other primates can. With fifty phonemes it is possible to create more than 100,000 words; by arranging those words in different sequences and developing rules in language, individuals can express countless subtle and complex meanings. Recent research suggests that use of complex languages occurred about 100,000 years ago and that the nearest approximation to humanity's earliest language existing today belongs to two African peoples, the !Kung of southern Africa and the Hadza

MAP 1.3 | Original Language Family Groups

The use of complex language developed 100,000 years ago among *Homo sapiens* in Africa. As humans dispersed throughout the globe, nineteen language families evolved from which all modern languages originate.

- How many different landmasses did language evolve on? Which landmasses have a greater number of language families and why might that be?

- On the basis of this map, what geographic features kept emerging language families distinct from one another?

- Why do you think separate languages emerged over time?

of Tanzania. These peoples make a clicking sound by dropping the tongue down from the roof of the mouth and exhaling. As humans moved out of Africa and spread around the globe, they expanded their original language into nineteen language families, from which all of the world's languages then evolved. (See Map 1.3.) It was the development of language and the cultural forms discussed later in this section that allowed *Homo sapiens* to engage dynamically with their environments.

HUNTING AND GATHERING

Although these early humans were developing language skills that distinguished them from their hominid relatives, like their predecessors they remained hunters and gatherers until around 12,000 years ago (for almost 95 percent of our existence). As late as 1500 CE, as much as 15 percent of the world's population still lived by **hunting and gathering**. Early *Homo sapiens* hunted animals, fished, and foraged for wild berries, nuts, fruit, and grains, rather than planting crops, vines, or trees. Even today hunting and gathering societies endure, although only in the most marginal locations—often at the edge of deserts. Researchers consider the present-day San peoples of southern Africa as an isolated remnant continuing their traditional hunting-and-gathering modes of life. Modern scholars use the San to reveal how men and women must have lived hundreds of thousands of years ago.

The fact that hominid men and women (going back to *Homo erectus* and *habilis* and beyond) survived as hunters and gatherers for millions of years, that early *Homo sapiens* also lived this way, and that a few contemporary communities still forage for food suggests the powerful attractions of this way of life. Hunters and gatherers could find enough food in about three hours of foraging each day, thus affording time for other pursuits such as relaxation, interaction, and friendly competitions with other members of their bands. Scholars believe that these small bands were relatively egalitarian compared with the more male-dominated societies that arose later. They speculate that men specialized in hunting and women specialized in gathering and child-rearing. Scholars also believe that women made a larger contribution and had high status because the dietary staples of the community were cereals and fruits, whose harvesting and preparation were likely women's responsibility.

PAINTINGS, SCULPTURE, AND MUSIC

The ability to draw allowed *Homo sapiens* to understand their environment, to bond among their kin groups (groups related by blood ties), and to articulate important mythologies. Accomplished artwork from this era has been found across Afro-Eurasia. For instance, in a deep cave at Altamira in Spain more than two dozen life-size figures of bison, horses, and wild

The San Hunters and Gatherers of Southern Africa The San, who live in the Kalahari Desert in present-day Botswana, continue to follow a hunting and gathering existence that has died out in many parts of the world. Hunting and gathering was the way that most humans lived for millennia.

bulls, all painted in vivid red, black, yellow, and brown, are arranged across the ceiling of the huge chamber. More than 50,000 similarly stunning works of art have been found in caves across Europe and elsewhere. The images on cave walls accumulated over a period of 25,000 years, and they changed little in that time. The subjects are often large game—animals that early humans would have considered powerful symbols. The artists rendered these animals in such a way that the natural contours of the cave wall defined a bulging belly or an eye socket. The remarkably few human images show hunters, naked females, or dancing males. There are also many handprints made by blowing paint around a hand placed on the cave wall, or by dipping hands in paint and then pressing them to the wall. There are even abstract symbols such as circles, wavy lines, and checkerboards; often these appear at places of transition in the caves.

Scholars have rejected an initial theory that these paintings were decorative, for the deep caves were not homes and had no natural light to render the images visible. Perhaps the images helped the early humans to define themselves as separate from other parts of nature. Alternatively, they might have been the work of powerful shamans, individuals believed to hold special powers to understand and control the forces of the cosmos. The subjects and the style of the paintings are similar to images engraved or painted on rocks by some hunter-and-gatherer societies living today, especially the San and the !Kung peoples of southern Africa. In those societies, paintings mark important places of ritual: shamans make them during trances while mediating with the spirit world on behalf of their communities.

Paintings were not the only form of artistic expression for early humans. Archaeologists also have unearthed small sculptures of animals shaped out of bone and stone that are even older than the paintings. Most famous are figurines of rotund, and perhaps pregnant females. Statuettes like the so-called Venus of Willendorf, found in Austria, demonstrate that successful reproduction was a very important theme. Other sculptures represent animals in postures of movement or at rest. (See Interpreting Visual Evidence: Prehistoric Art.)

The caves of early men and women also resounded to the strains of music. In 2008 archaeologists working in southwestern Germany discovered a hollowed-out bone flute with five openings that they dated to approximately 35,000 years ago, roughly the same time that humans began to occupy this region. When researchers put the flute to musical tests, they also concluded that the instrument was capable of making harmonic sounds comparable to those of modern-day flutes.

Only *Homo sapiens* had the cognitive abilities to produce the abundant sculptures and drawings of this era, thus leaving a permanent mark on the symbolic landscape of human development. Such visual expressions marked the dawn of human culture and a consciousness of men's and women's place in the world. Symbolic activity of this sort enabled humans to make sense of themselves, nature, and the relationship between humanity and nature. That relationship with nature—which had remained static for hundreds of thousands of years of hunting and gathering—would change with the agricultural revolution.

Agricultural Revolution: Food Production and Social Change

About 12,000 years ago (around 10,000 BCE), a fundamental shift occurred in the way humans produced food for themselves—what some scholars have called an agricultural, or ecological, revolution. Around the same time, a significant warming trend that had begun around 11,000 BCE resulted in a profusion of plants and animals, large numbers of which began to exist closer to humans. In this era of major change, humans established greater control over nature. The transformation consisted of the **domestication** (the bringing under human control) of wild plants and animals. Population pressure was one factor that triggered the move to settled agriculture, as hunting and gathering alone could not sustain the growth in numbers of people. A revolution in agriculture, in turn, led to a vast population expansion because men and women could now produce more calories per unit of land. As various plants and animals were domesticated around the world, people settled in villages and social relationships changed.

THE BEGINNINGS OF SETTLED AGRICULTURE AND PASTORALISM

Learning to control environments through the domestication of plants and animals was a gradual process. Communities shifted from a hunting-and-gathering lifestyle (which requires moving around in search of food) to one based on agriculture (which requires staying in one place until the soil has been exhausted). **Settled agriculture** refers to the

Domestication This detail from a wall painting in the Tassili n'Ajjer mountain range in modern Algeria depicts early domestication of cattle and other animals.

application of human labor and tools to a fixed plot of land for more than one growing cycle. Alternatively, some people adopted a lifestyle based on **pastoralism** (the herding of domesticated animals), which complemented settled farming.

Early Domestication of Plants and Animals The formation of settled communities enabled humans to take advantage of favorable regions and to take risks, spurring agricultural innovation. In areas with abundant wild game and edible plants, people began to observe and experiment with the most adaptable plants. For ages, people gathered grains by collecting seeds that fell freely from their stalks. At some point, observant collectors perceived that they could obtain larger harvests if they pulled grain seeds directly from plants. The process of plant domestication probably began when people noticed that certain edible plants retained their nutritious grains longer than others, so they collected these seeds and scattered them across fertile soils. When ripe, these plants produced bigger and more concentrated crops. Plant domestication occurred when the plant retained its ripe, mature seeds, allowing an easy harvest. People used most seeds for food but saved some for planting in the next growing cycle, to ensure a food supply for the next year.

Dogs were the first animals to be domesticated (although in fact they may have adopted humans, rather than the other way around). Around 9000 BCE, in the area of present-day Iraq, dogs did more than comfort humans. They provided an example of how to achieve the domestication of other animals and, with their herding instincts, they helped humans to control other domesticated animals, such as sheep. In the central Zagros Mountains region, where wild sheep and wild goats were abundant, they became the next animal domesticates. Perhaps hunters returned home with young wild sheep, which then reproduced, and their offspring never returned to the wild. The animals accepted their dependence because the humans fed them. Since controlling animal reproduction was more reliable than hunting, domesticated herds became the primary source of protein in the early humans' diet.

When the number of animals under human control and living close to the settlement outstripped the supply of food needed to feed them, community members could move the animals to grassy steppes for grazing. These pastoralists herded domesticated animals, moving them to new pastures on a seasonal basis. Goats, the other main domesticated animal of Southwest Asia, are smarter than sheep but more difficult to control. The pastoralists may have introduced goats into herds of sheep to better control herd movement. Pigs and cattle also came under human control at this time.

Transhumant Herders and Nomadic Pastoralists Pastoralism appeared as a way of life around 5500 BCE, essentially at the same time that full-time farmers appeared (although the beginnings of plant and animal domestication had begun many millennia earlier). Over time, two different types of pastoralists with different relationships to settled populations developed: transhumant herders and nomadic pastoralists. Transhumant herders were closely affiliated with agricultural villages whose inhabitants grew grains, especially wheat and barley, which required large parcels of land. These herders produced both meat and dairy products, as well as wool for textiles, and exchanged these products with the agriculturalists for grain, pottery, and other staples. Extended families might farm and herd at the same time, growing crops on large estates and grazing their herds in the foothills and mountains nearby. They moved their livestock seasonally, pasturing their flocks in higher lands during summer and in valleys in winter. This movement over short distances is called *transhumance* and did not require herders to vacate their primary living locations, which were generally in the mountain valleys.

In contrast with transhumant pastoralism, *nomadic pastoralism* came to flourish especially in the steppe lands north of the agricultural zone of southern Eurasia. This way of

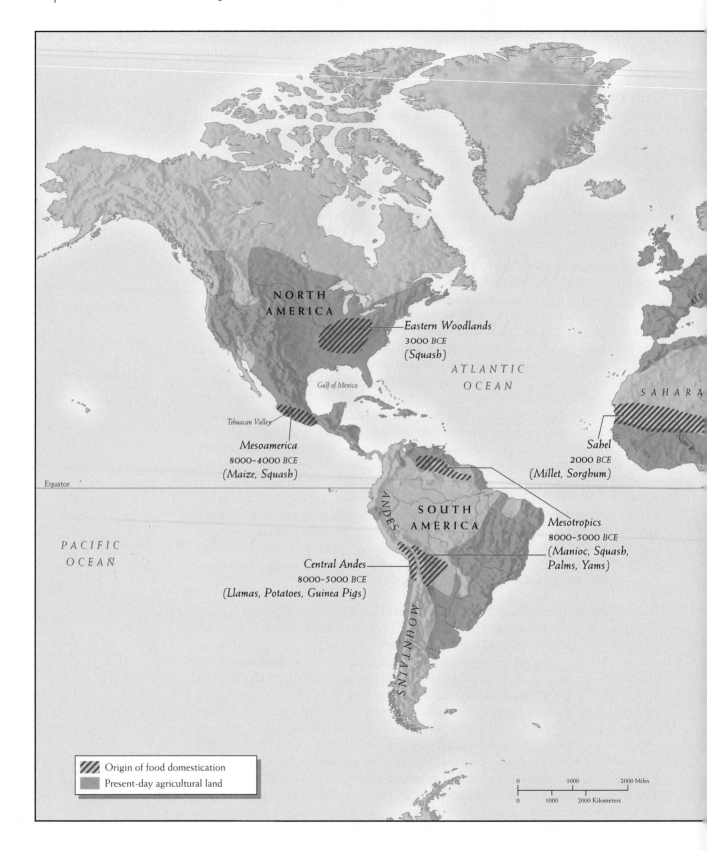

NORTH
AMERICA

Eastern Woodlands
3000 BCE
(Squash)

ATLANTIC
OCEAN

Gulf of Mexico

SAHARA

Tehuacan Valley

Mesoamerica
8000–4000 BCE
(Maize, Squash)

Sahel
2000 BCE
(Millet, Sorghum)

Niger R.

Equator

ANDES

SOUTH
AMERICA

Mesotropics
8000–5000 BCE
(Manioc, Squash,
Palms, Yams)

PACIFIC
OCEAN

Central Andes
8000–5000 BCE
(Llamas, Potatoes, Guinea Pigs)

MOUNTAINS

| | Origin of food domestication |
| | Present-day agricultural land |

0   1000   2000 Miles
0   1000   2000 Kilometers

MAP 1.4 | The Origins of Food Production

Agricultural production emerged in many regions at different times. The variety of patterns reflected local resources and conditions.

• How many different locations did agricultural production emerge in?

• Are there any common geographic features among these early food-producing areas?

• Based on your reading of the chapter, why do you think agriculture emerged in certain areas and not in others?

life was characterized by horse-riding herders of cattle and other livestock. Because horses provided decisive advantages in transportation and warfare, they gained more value than other domesticated animals. Thus, horses soon became the measure of household wealth and prestige. Unlike the transhumant herders, the nomadic pastoralists often had no fixed home, though they often returned to their traditional locations. They moved across large distances in response to the size and needs of their herds. The northern areas of the Eurasian landmass stretching from present-day Ukraine across Siberia and Mongolia to the Pacific Ocean became the preserve of these horse-riding pastoral peoples in a region unable to support the extensive agriculture necessary for large settled populations. Historians know much less about these horse-riding pastoral nomads than about the agriculturalists and the transhumant herders, as their numbers were small and they left fewer archaeological traces or historical records. Their role in world history, however, is as important as that of the settled societies. In Afro-Eurasia, they domesticated horses and developed weapons and techniques that at certain points in history enabled them to conquer sedentary societies. As we will see in the next section (and later chapters), they also transmitted ideas, products, and people across long distances, maintaining the linkages that connected east and west.

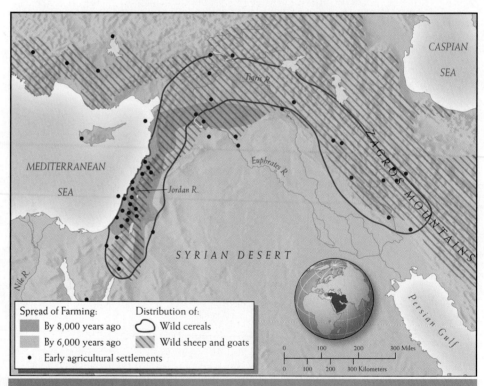

MAP 1.5 | The Birth of Farming in the Fertile Crescent

Agricultural production occurred in the Fertile Crescent starting roughly at 9000 BCE. Though the process was slow, farmers and herders domesticated a variety of plants and animals, which led to the rise of large-scale, permanent settlements.

▪ What does the map reveal about the environment and natural resources in and around the Fertile Crescent?

▪ Where do farming and agricultural settlements appear to develop or not? Based on the map, what factors appear to influence the location of agricultural settlements and farming?

▪ What relationship existed between cereal cultivators and herders of goats and sheep?

AGRICULTURAL INNOVATION: AFRO-EURASIA AND THE AMERICAS

The agricultural revolutions that occurred worldwide between 9000 and 2000 BCE had much in common: climatic change; increased knowledge about plants and animals; and the need for more efficient ways to feed, house, and promote the growth of a larger population. These concerns led peoples in Eurasia, the Americas, and Africa to see the advantages of cultivating plants and domesticating wildlife.

Some communities were independent innovators, developing agricultural techniques based on their specific environments. In Southwest Asia, East Asia, Africa, and the Americas, the distinctive crops and animals that humans first domesticated reflect independent innovation. As we will see in the following section, other communities (such as those in Europe) were borrowers of ideas, which spread through migration and contact with other regions. In all of these populations, the shift to settled agriculture was revolutionary.

Southwest Asia: Cereals and Mammals The first agricultural revolution occurred in Southwest Asia in an area bounded by the Mediterranean Sea and the Zagros Mountains, a region known today as the Fertile Crescent because of its rich soils and regular rainfall. Around 9000 BCE, in the southern corridor of the Jordan River valley, humans began to domesticate the wild ancestors of barley and wheat, which were the easiest to adapt to settled agriculture and the easiest to transport. Although the changeover from gathering wild cereals to regular cultivation took several centuries and saw failures as well as successes, by 8000 BCE cultivators were selecting and storing seeds and then sowing them in prepared seedbeds. Moreover, in the valleys of the Zagros Mountains on the eastern side of the Fertile Crescent, similar experimentation was occurring with animals around the same time. Of the six large mammals—goats, sheep, pigs, cattle, camels, and horses—that have been vital for meat, milk, skins, and transportation, humans in Southwest Asia domesticated all except horses. With the presence of so many valuable plants and animals, Southwest Asia led the agricultural revolution and gave rise to many of the world's first major city-states (see Chapter 2).

COMPARISON

COMPARE the ways communities around the world shifted to settled agriculture.

Large Two-handled Yangshao Pot This pot comes from the village of Yangshao in Henan Province, along the Yellow River in northwest China, where remains were first found in 1921 of a people who lived more than 6,000 years ago. The Yangshao lived in small, rammed-earth fortresses and, without the use of pottery wheels, created fine white, red, and black painted pottery with human faces and animal and geometric designs. This jar dates to the third or second millennium BCE.

East Asia: Water And Rice A revolution in food production also occurred among the coastal dwellers in East Asia although under different circumstances. (See Map 1.6.) As the rising sea level created the Japanese islands, hunters in that area tracked a diminishing supply of large animals, such as giant deer. When big game became extinct, men and women sought other ways to support themselves, and before long they settled down and became cultivators of the soil. In this postglacial period, divergent human cultures flourished in northern and southern Japan. Hunters in the south created primitive pebble and flake tools, whereas those in the north used sharper blades about a third of an inch wide. Production of earthenware pottery—a breakthrough that enabled people to store food more easily—also may have begun in this period in the south. Throughout the

MAP 1.6 | The Spread of Farming in East Asia

Agricultural settlements appeared in East Asia later than they did in the Fertile Crescent.

• According to this map, where did early agricultural settlements appear in East Asia?

• What types of crops and animals were domesticated in East Asia?

• How did the physical features of these regions lend themselves to agricultural production?

rest of East Asia, the spread of lakes, marshes, and rivers created habitats for population concentrations and agricultural cultivation. Two newly formed river basins, along the Yellow River in northern China and the Yangzi River in central China, became densely populated areas that were focal points for intensive agricultural development.

What barley and wheat were for Southwest Asia, rice along the Yangzi and millet along the Yellow River were for East Asia—staples adapted to local environments that humans could domesticate to support a large, sedentary population. Archaeologists have found evidence of rice cultivation in the Yangzi River valley in 6500 BCE, and of millet cultivation in the Yellow River valley in 5500 BCE. Innovations in grain production, including the introduction of a faster-ripening rice from Southeast Asia, spread through internal migration and wider contacts. Ox plows and water buffalo plowshares were prerequisites for large-scale millet planting in the drier north and the rice-cultivated areas of the wetter south. By domesticating plants and animals, the East Asians, like the Southwest Asians, laid the foundations for more populous societies.

Africa: The Race with the Sahara

The evidence of settled agriculture in the various regions of Africa is less clear. Most scholars think that the Sahel area (spanning the African landmass just south of the Sahara Desert) was most likely where hunters and gatherers became settled farmers and herders without borrowing from other regions. In this area, an apparent move to settled agriculture, including the domestication of large herd animals, occurred two millennia before it did along the Mediterranean coast in North Africa. From this innovative heartland, Africans carried their agricultural breakthroughs across the landmass.

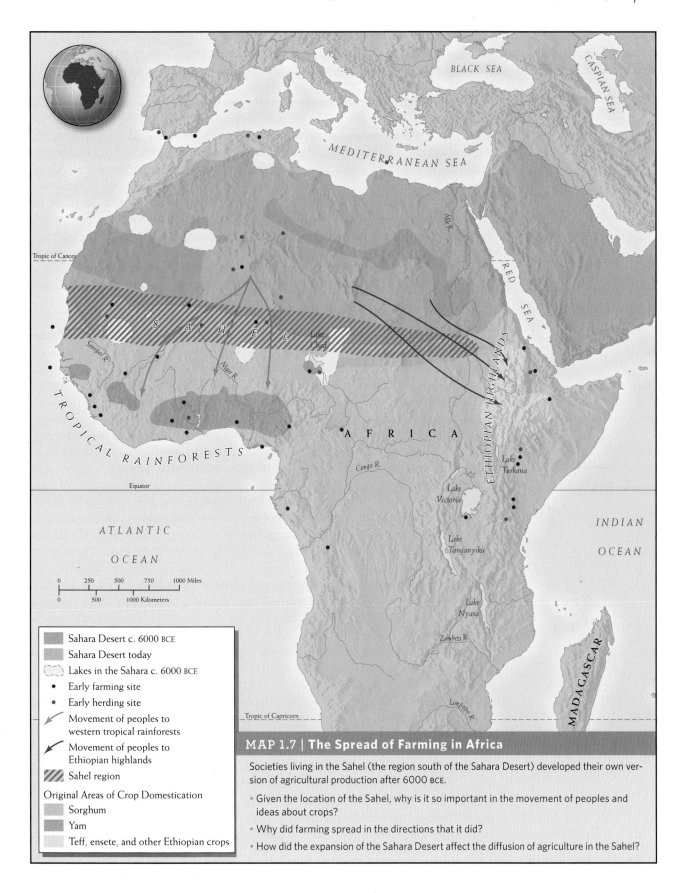

MAP 1.7 | **The Spread of Farming in Africa**

Societies living in the Sahel (the region south of the Sahara Desert) developed their own version of agricultural production after 6000 BCE.

• Given the location of the Sahel, why is it so important in the movement of peoples and ideas about crops?

• Why did farming spread in the directions that it did?

• How did the expansion of the Sahara Desert affect the diffusion of agriculture in the Sahel?

Legend:

Sahara Desert c. 6000 BCE
Sahara Desert today
Lakes in the Sahara c. 6000 BCE
• Early farming site
• Early herding site
↓ Movement of peoples to western tropical rainforests
↘ Movement of peoples to Ethiopian highlands
Sahel region

Original Areas of Crop Domestication
Sorghum
Yam
Teff, ensete, and other Ethiopian crops

In the wetter and more temperate locations of the vast Sahel, particularly in mountainous areas and their foothills, villages and towns developed. These regions were lush with grassland vegetation and teeming with animals. Before long, the inhabitants had made sorghum, a cereal grass, their principal food crop. Residents constructed stone dwellings, underground wells, and grain storage areas. In one such population center, fourteen circular houses faced each other to form a main thoroughfare, or a street.

The Sahel was colder and moister in 8000 BCE than it is today. As the world became warmer and the Sahara Desert expanded, around 2000 BCE, this region's inhabitants had to disperse and take their agricultural and herding skills into other parts of Africa. Some went south to the tropical rainforests of West Africa, while others trekked eastward into the Ethiopian highlands. In their new environments, farmers searched for new crops to domesticate. The rainforests of West Africa yielded root crops, particularly the yam and cocoyam, both of which became the principal life-sustaining foodstuffs. The enset plant, similar to the banana, played the same role in the Ethiopian highlands. Thus, the beginnings of agriculture in Africa involved both innovation and diffusion, as Africans applied the techniques that first emerged in the Sahel to new plants and animals.

The Americas: A Slower Transition The shift to settled agriculture occurred more slowly in the Americas. When people crossed Beringia into the Americas, the plants and animals were different enough that early settlers devised ways of living that distinguished them from their ancestors in Afro-Eurasia. When the glaciers melted and water covered the land bridge between East Asia and America, the Americas and their peoples truly became a whole world apart. Early humans in America, called "Clovis people" after an archaeological site near Clovis, New Mexico, used chipped blades and pointed spears to pursue their prey. Although scientists once thought that Clovis communities had wiped out the large Ice Age mammals in the Americas, recent research suggests that climatic change destroyed indigenous plants and trees—the feeding grounds of large prehistoric mammals. This left undernourished mastodons, woolly mammoths, bison, and other mammals vulnerable to human and animal predators. As in Afro-Eurasia, the arrival of a long warming cycle compelled those living in the Americas to adapt to different environments and to create new ways to support themselves. Thus, in the woodland area of the present-day northeastern United States, hunters learned to trap smaller wild animals for food and furs. To supplement the protein from meat and fish, these people also dug for roots and gathered berries. Even as most communities adapted to the settled agricultural economy, they did not abandon basic survival strategies of hunting and gathering.

Food-producing changes in the Americas were different from those in Afro-Eurasia because this area did not undergo the sudden cluster of innovations that revolutionized agriculture in Southwest Asia and elsewhere. Independent innovation occurred more slowly here. Tools ground from stone, rather than chipped implements, appeared in the Tehuacán Valley by 6700 BCE, and evidence of plant domestication there dates back to 5000 BCE. But villages, pottery making, and sustained population growth came later. For many early American inhabitants, the life of hunting, trapping, and fishing went on as it had for millennia. Indeed, researchers have found the remains of ancient shellfishing throughout the coastal Americas from Alaska to Chile on the Pacific Ocean side. On the coast of what is now Peru, people found food by fishing and gathering shellfish from the Pacific. Archaeological remains include the remnants of fishnets, bags, baskets, and textile implements; gourds for carrying water; and stone knives, choppers, scrapers, bone awls, and thorn needles. Some made breakthroughs in the management of fire that enabled them to manufacture pottery; others devised irrigation and water sluices in floodplains. And some even began to send their fish catches inland in return for agricultural produce.

The earliest evidence of plant experimentation in Mesoamerica dates from around 8000 BCE, and the peoples living there continued to domesticate new plants for a long time. Maize, squash, and beans (first found in what is now central Mexico) became dietary staples. The early settlers foraged small seeds of maize, peeled them from ears only a few inches long, and planted them. Maize offered real advantages because it was easy to store over long periods of time, nutritious, and easy to cultivate alongside other plants. Nonetheless, it took 5,000 years for farmers to complete its domestication. Over the years, farmers had to mix and breed different strains of maize for it to evolve from thin spikes of seeds to cobs rich with kernels, with a single plant yielding big, thick ears to feed a growing permanent population. Thus, the agricultural changes afoot in Mesoamerica were slow and late in maturing. The pace was even more gradual in South America, where early settlers clung to their hunting and gathering traditions.

Across the Americas, the settled, agrarian communities found that legumes (beans), grains (maize), and tubers (potatoes) complemented one another in keeping the soil fertile and offering a balanced diet. Unlike the Afro-Eurasians, however, the settlers did not use domesticated animals as an alternative source of protein. In only a few pockets of the Andean highlands is there evidence of the domestication of tiny guinea

Head of Mayan Corn God Corn, or maize, was a revered crop in Mesoamerica, where people ritually prayed to their deities for good harvests. Notice the crown made not of precious metals and stones but of corn husks as an example of the cultural emphasis on maize.

pigs. Nor did people in the Americas tame animals that could protect villages (as dogs did in Afro-Eurasia) or carry heavy loads over long distances (as cattle and horses did in Afro-Eurasia). Although llamas could haul heavy loads, they were uncooperative and only partially domesticated, and thus mainly useful only for their fur, which was used for clothing.

Nonetheless, the domestication of plants and animals in the Americas, as well as the presence of villages and clans, suggests significant diversification and refinement of agricultural techniques. At the same time, the centers of such activity were numerous, scattered, and more isolated than those in Afro-Eurasia—and thus more narrowly adapted to local geographical climatic conditions, with little exchange among them. This fragmentation was a distinguishing force in the gradual pace of change in the Americas, and it contributed to their taking a path of development separate from Afro-Eurasia's.

BORROWING AGRICULTURAL IDEAS: EUROPE

In some places, agricultural revolution occurred through the borrowing of ideas from neighboring regions, rather than through innovation. Peoples living at the western fringe of Afro-Eurasia, in Europe, learned the techniques of settled agriculture through contact with other regions. By 6000–5000 BCE, people in parts of Europe close to the

MAP 1.8 | The Spread of Agriculture in Europe

The spread of agricultural production into Europe after 7000 BCE represents geographic diffusion. Europeans borrowed agricultural techniques and technology from other groups, adapting those innovations to their own situations.

- Where did the ideas and techniques originate?

- Through what two pathways did agriculture spread across Europe?

- Did Europe's settled agricultural communities have different features from those that appeared in Southwest Asia, East Asia, and Africa?

societies of Southwest Asia, such as Greece and the Balkans, were abandoning their hunting-and-gathering way of life for an agricultural one. The Franchthi Cave in Greece, for instance, reveals that around 6000 BCE the inhabitants learned how to domesticate animals and plant wheat and barley, having borrowed that innovation from their neighbors in Southwest Asia.

The emergence of agriculture and village life occurred in Europe along two separate paths of borrowing. The first and most rapid trajectory followed the northern rim of the Mediterranean Sea: from what is now Turkey through the islands of the Aegean Sea to mainland Greece, and from there to southern and central Italy and Sicily. Whether the process involved the actual migration of individuals or, rather, the spread of ideas, connections by sea quickened the pace of the transition. Within a relatively short period of time, hunting and gathering gave way to domesticated agriculture and herding.

The second trajectory of borrowing took an overland route: from Anatolia, across northern Greece into the Balkans, then northwestward along the Danube River into the Hungarian plain, and from there farther north and west into the Rhine River valley in modern-day Germany. This route of agricultural development was slower than the Mediterranean route for two reasons. First, domesticated crops, or individuals who knew about them, had to travel by land, as there were few large rivers like the Danube. Second, it was necessary to find new groups of domesticated plants and animals that could flourish in the colder and more forested lands of central Europe, which meant planting crops in the spring and harvesting them in the autumn, rather than the other way around. Cattle rather than sheep became the dominant herd animals.

In Europe, the main cereal crops were wheat and barley (additional plants such as olives came later), and the main herd animals were sheep, goats, and cattle—all of which had been domesticated in Southwest Asia. Hunting, gathering, and fishing still supplemented the new settled agriculture and the herding of domesticated animals.

Thus, across Afro-Eurasia and the Americas, humans changed and were changed by their environments. While herding and gathering remained firmly entrenched as a way of life, certain areas with favorable climates and plants and animals that could be domesticated began to establish settled agricultural communities, which were able to support larger populations than hunting and gathering could sustain.

REVOLUTIONS IN SOCIAL ORGANIZATION

In addition to creating agricultural villages, the domestication of plants and animals brought changes in social organization, notably changes in gender relationships.

COMPARISON

ANALYZE the significance the shift to settled agriculture had for social organization across global regions.

Life in Villages Agricultural villages were established near fields for accessible sowing and cultivating, and near pastures for herding livestock. Villagers collaborated to clear fields, plant crops, and celebrate rituals in which they sang, danced, and sacrificed to nature and the spirit world for fertility, rain, and successful harvests. They also produced stone tools to work the fields, and clay and stone pots or woven baskets to collect and store the crops. The earliest dwelling places of the first settled communities were simple structures: circular pits with stones piled on top to form walls, with a cover stretched above that rested on poles. Social structures were equally simple, being clan-like and based on kinship networks. With time, however, population growth enabled clans to expand. As the use of natural resources intensified, specialized tasks evolved and divisions of labor arose. Some community members procured and prepared food; others built terraces and defended the settlement. Later, residents built walls with stones or mud bricks and clamped them together with wooden fittings. Some villagers became craftworkers, devoting their time to producing pottery, baskets, textiles, or tools, which they could trade to farmers and pastoralists for food. Craft specialization and the buildup of surpluses contributed to social stratification (the emergence of distinct and hierarchically arranged social classes), as some people accumulated more land and wealth while others led the rituals and sacrifices.

"Long House" The people who opened up the whole of central Europe to agriculture typically lived in communities of six to twelve "long houses." Although large in size (varying between 60 and 120 feet in length), long houses were built on simple principles: a framework of wooden beams and posts with walls made of mud and woven branches beneath a thatched roof. These dwellings probably sheltered large extended family or kinship units that cooperated to provide the hard work needed to carve out pioneer farming settlements along river valleys. This cutaway reconstruction of a long house shows the placement of wall timbers and internal support posts.

Archaeological sites in Southwest Asia have provided evidence of what life was like in some of the earliest villages. At Wadi en-Natuf, for example, located about ten miles from present-day Jerusalem, a group of people known historically as Natufians began to dig sunken pit shelters and to chip stone tools around 12,500 BCE. In the highlands of eastern Anatolia, large settlements clustered around monumental public buildings with impressive stone carvings that reflect a complex social organization. In central Anatolia around 7500 BCE, at the site of Çatal Höyük, a dense honeycomb settlement featured rooms with artwork of a high quality. The walls were covered with paintings, and sculptures of wild bulls, hunters, and pregnant women enlivened many rooms.

After 5500 BCE, people moved into the river valley in Mesopotamia (in present-day Iraq) along the Tigris and Euphrates rivers, and small villages began to appear. They collaborated to build simple irrigation systems to water their fields. Perhaps because of the increased demands for community work to maintain the irrigation systems, the communities in southern Mesopotamia became stratified, with some people having more power than others. We can see from the burial sites and myriad public buildings uncovered by archaeologists that, for the first time, some people had higher status derived from birth rather than through the merits of their work. A class of people who had access to more luxury goods, and who lived in bigger and better houses, now became part of the social organization.

Men, Women, and Evolving Gender Relations Gender roles became more pronounced during the gradual transition to agriculturally based ways of life. For millions of years, biological differences—the fact that females give birth to offspring and lactate to nourish them and that males do not—determined female and male behaviors and attitudes toward each other. One can speak of the emergence of "gender" relations and roles (as opposed to biological differences) only with the appearance of modern humans (*Homo sapiens*). Only when humans began to think in complex symbolic ways and give voice to these perceptions in a spoken language did true gender categories as *man* and *woman* crystallize. At that point, around 150,000 years ago, culture joined biology in governing human interactions.

As human communities became larger, more hierarchical, and more powerful, the rough gender egalitarianism of hunting and gathering societies eroded. Although as the primary gatherers women's knowledge of wild plants had contributed to early settled agriculture, they did not necessarily benefit from that transition. Advances in agrarian tools introduced a harsh working life that undermined women's earlier

Hunting This wall painting from Çatal Höyük (in present-day Turkey) depicts humans hunting a bull.

status as farmers. Men, no longer so involved in hunting and gathering, now took on the heavy work of yoking animals to plows. Women took on the backbreaking and repetitive tasks of planting, weeding, harvesting, and grinding the grain into flour. Thus, although agricultural innovations increased productivity, they also increased the drudgery of work, especially for women. Fossil evidence from Abu Hureyra, Syria, reveals damage to the vertebrae, osteoarthritis in the toes, and curved and arched femurs, all suggesting that the work of bending over and kneeling in the fields took its toll on female agriculturalists. The increasing differentiation of the roles of men and women also affected power relations within households and communities. The senior male figure became dominant in these households, and males became dominant over females in leadership positions.

The agricultural revolution marked a greater division among men, and particularly between men and women. Where the agricultural transformation was most widespread, and where population densities began to grow, the social and political differences created inequalities. As these inequalities affected gender relations, patriarchy (the rule of senior males within households) began to spread around the globe.

Conclusion

Over thousands of generations, African hominids evolved from other primates into bipedal, toolmaking, fire-using *Homo erectus*, who migrated far from their native habitats to fill other landmasses. They did so in waves, often in response to worldwide cycles of climatic change. *Homo sapiens*, with bigger brains and consequently greater cognition, emerged in Africa about 200,000 years ago and migrated out of Africa between 100,000 and 50,000 years ago. With greater adaptive skills, they were better prepared to face the elements when a cooling cycle returned, and eventually they became the only surviving branch of the tree of human ancestors. *Homo sapiens* used language and art to engage in abstract, representational thought, and to convey the lessons of experience to their neighbors and descendants. As modern humans stored and shared knowledge, their adaptive abilities increased.

Although modern men and women shared an African heritage, these individuals adapted over many millennia to the environments they encountered as they began to fill the earth's corners and practice hunter-gatherer ways of life. Some settled near lakes and took to fishing, while others roamed the northern steppes hunting large mammals. No matter where they went, their dependence on nature yielded broadly similar social and cultural structures. It took another warming cycle for people ranging from Africa to the Americas to begin putting down their hunting weapons and start domesticating animals and plants.

The changeover to settled agriculture was not uniform worldwide. As communities became more settled, the world's regions began to vary as humans learned to modify nature to fit their needs. The varieties of animals that they could domesticate and the differing climatic conditions and topography that they encountered shaped the ways in which people drifted apart in spite of their common origins. What these settled communities shared, however, was increasing social hierarchy, including an unequal status between men and women.

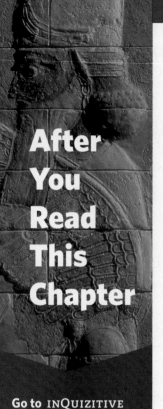

After You Read This Chapter

Go to INQUIZITIVE to see what you've learned—and learn what you've missed—with personalized feedback along the way.

FOCUS ON: *What Makes Us Human*

- *Bipedalism:* Hominids come down from the trees in Africa, become upright, and walk on two legs.

- *Big brains:* Ancestors to modern humans make tools and fire and acquire larger brains.

- *Cognitive skills: Homo sapiens* develop the capacity for language and learn to communicate with one another, develop a sense of self, and produce art.

- *Village life:* People domesticate plants and animals, and begin to live in more socially complex communities.

CHRONOLOGY

AFRO-EURASIA	◆ *Australopithecus africanus* hominid species appears 3 mya
	◆ *Homo habilis* appears 2.5 mya
	Homo erectus appears and migrates 2.5-1 mya
	Beginnings of Ice Age Across the Northern Hemisphere 2.5-1 mya
AFRICA	
EUROPE AND THE MEDITERRANEAN	
SOUTHWEST AND INNER ASIA	
EAST ASIA	*millions of years ago
THE AMERICAS	**years ago

5 MYA*   1 MYA

- ***Thinking about Exchange Networks and Human Evolution*** Across several million years, the hominid ancestors of humans, especially *Homo erectus*, and then *Homo sapiens,* migrated out of Africa. What role did evolution play in making it possible for our hominid ancestors and then *Homo sapiens* to migrate across the globe?

- ***Thinking about the Environment and Human Evolution*** Climate change and environmental conditions have played a recurring role in the narrative recounted in this chapter. In what specific ways did climate change and the environment help shape the evolution of humans and influence the shift from hunting and gathering to settled agriculture?

- ***Thinking about Changing Gender Relationships and the Agricultural Revolution*** Some scholars have argued that the hunting-and-gathering ways of life for both *Homo erectus* and *Homo sapiens* allowed women—biologically, through their lactation and child-rearing, and calorically, through their dominant role as gatherers—to make a larger and more significant contribution to their communities than their male counterparts. In what ways might the development of settled agriculture usher in a shift, or not, in these gender roles?

1. Why do human communities produce **creation narratives** and what do creation narratives have in common?

2. How do natural selection and adaptation play a role in **evolution**?

3. What are some of the distinctive features of **hominids**, especially **australopithecines**, *Homo habilis*, and *Homo erectus*?

4. In what ways are humans, *Homo sapiens*, different from our hominid ancestors?

5. How did *Homo sapiens* come into being? In what ways did **hunting and gathering** shape the dynamics of early human communities?

6. What do cave art and the so-called Venus figurines suggest about the values of human communities prior to the agricultural revolution?

7. Where, when, and how did the agricultural revolution take place, and what were the results? Describe the process of plant and animal domestication and how that led to **settled agriculture** (via both innovation and borrowing).

8. What is **pastoralism**, and how did varying types of pastoralists (both transhumant herders and nomadic pastoralists) interact with settled agricultural communities?

Human migration from Afro-Eurasia begins 18,000 ya ◆
Ice Age ends 16,000–10,000 BCE
Homo sapiens emerges in Africa 200,000 ya
Homo sapiens migrates out of Africa 100,000 to 50,000 ya
Cave Art develops in Europe 30,000 ya ◆
Beginnings of agricultural revolution in Southwest Asia 9000 BCE ◆
Agricultural settlements emerge in Southwest Asia 6000–5000 BCE
Pastoralism begins in Inner Asia 3000 BCE ◆
Millet cultivation in Yellow River valley develops 6500 BCE ◆
Rice cultivation in Yangzi River valley develops 5500 BCE ◆
Maize cultivation emerges in central Mexico 2000 BCE ◆

| 200,000 YA** | 150,000 YA | 100,000 YA | 50,000 YA | 10,000 YA | 1 CE |

Competing Perspectives

Creation Narratives

Humans at many times and in many places have attempted to explain where they came from by constructing creation narratives. Creation narratives draw on a particular society's knowledge and beliefs to offer an account of human, and even universal, origins. The documents here represent a range of varied creation narratives.

The first excerpt, from the *Rig Veda*, provides a Hindu creation narrative centered on the sacrifice of a primordial being named Purusha. It dates to around 1500 BCE when Vedic peoples migrated into South Asia. As we see in the second document, Judeo-Christian scripture opens with an account of a singular God bringing order from chaos over the course of six days. Another understanding of creation is recorded in the *Huainanzi*, from second-century BCE Han China. This Confucian text takes the form of dialogues between a prince and court scholars; it also reflects Daoist ideas, such as the role of the complementary forces of *yin* and *yang*. The Mayans of Mesoamerica believed that humans were created by an assembly of divine beings, a story preserved in the excerpt from the *Popul Vuh*. In the final document, a Yoruba creation narrative from West Africa depicts the god Obatala creating and populating the land with palm trees and humans. These creation narratives offer wide-ranging ideas about where the story of humanity begins and reveal a great deal about the values and beliefs of the communities that produce and preserve them.

PRIMARY SOURCE 1.1

"The Sacrifice of Purusha" from Rig Veda *(1500 BCE)*

Thousand-headed Purusha, thousand eyed, thousand-footed—he, having pervaded the earth on all sides, extends ten fingers beyond it.

Purusha alone is all this—whatever has been and whatever is going to be. Further, he is the lord of immortality and also of what grows on account of food.

Such is his greatness; greater, indeed than this is Purusha. All creatures constitute but one-quarter of him, his three-quarters are the immortal in the heaven. With his three-quarters did Purusha rise up; one-quarter of him again remains here. With it did he variously spread out on all sides over what eats and what eats not. . . . When the gods performed the sacrifice with Purusha as the oblation, then the spring was its clarified butter, the summer the sacrificial fuel, and the autumn the oblation.

The sacrificial victim, namely, Purusha born at the very beginning, they sprinkled with sacred water upon the sacrificial grass. With him as oblation, the gods performed the sacrifice, and also the Sādhyas [a class of semidivine beings] and the rishis [ancient seers].

From that wholly offered sacrificial oblation were born the verses and the sacred chants; from it were born the meters [*chandas*]; the sacrificial formula was born from it.

From it horses were born and also those animals who have double rows [i.e., upper and lower] of teeth; cows were born from it, from it were born goats and sheep.

When they divided Purusha, in how many different portions did they arrange him? What became of his mouth, what of his two arms? What were his two thighs and his two feet called?

His mouth became the brāhman; his two arms were made into the rājanya; his two thighs the vaishyas; from his two feet the shūdra was born.

The moon was born from the mind, from the eye the sun was born; from the mouth Indra and Agni, from the breath [*prāna*] the wind [*vāyu*] was born.

From the navel was the atmosphere created, from the head the heaven issued forth; from two feet was born the earth and the quarters (the cardinal directions) from the ear. Thus did they fashion the worlds.

Source: *Sources of Indian Tradition*, vol. 1, *From the Beginning to 1800*, edited and revised by Ainslie T. Embree, 2nd ed. (1988), pp. 18–19.

PRIMARY SOURCE 1.2

Genesis 1:1–31 from The Bible

[1]In the beginning God created the heavens and the earth. [2]The earth was without form and void, and darkness was upon the face of the deep; and the Spirit of God was moving over the face of the waters. [3]And God said, "Let there be light"; and there was light. [4]And God saw that the light was good; and God separated the light from the darkness. [5]God called the light Day, and the darkness he called Night. And there was evening and there was morning, one day. [6]And God said, "Let there be a firmament in the midst of the waters, and let it separate the waters from the waters." [7]And God made the

firmament and separated the waters which were under the firmament from the waters which were above the firmament. And it was so. [8]And God called the firmament Heaven. And there was evening and there was morning, a second day.

[9]And God said, "Let the waters under the heavens be gathered together into one place, and let the dry land appear." And it was so. [10]God called the dry land Earth, and the waters that were gathered together he called Seas. And God saw that it was good. [11]And God said, "Let the earth put forth vegetation, plants yielding seed, and fruit trees bearing fruit in which is their seed, each according to its kind, upon the earth." And it was so . . . . [13]And there was evening and there was morning, a third day. [14]And God said, "Let there be lights in the firmament of the heavens to separate the day from the night; and let them be for signs and for seasons and for days and years, [15] and let them be lights in the firmament of the heavens to give light upon the earth." And it was so. . . . [19]And there was evening and there was morning, a fourth day.

[20]And God said, "Let the waters bring forth swarms of living creatures, and let birds fly above the earth across the firmament of the heavens." . . . [23]And there was evening and there was morning, a fifth day.

[24]And God said, "Let the earth bring forth living creatures according to their kinds: cattle and creeping things and beasts of the earth according to their kinds." And it was so. . . .

[26]Then God said, "Let us make man in our image, after our likeness; and let them have dominion over the fish of the sea, and over the birds of the air, and over the cattle, and over all the earth, and over every creeping thing that creeps upon the earth." [27]So God created man in his own image, in the image of God he created him; male and female he created them. [28]And God blessed them, and God said to them, "Be fruitful and multiply, and fill the earth and subdue it; and have dominion over the fish of the sea and over the birds of the air and over every living thing that moves upon the earth." . . . . [31]And God saw everything that he had made, and behold, it was very good. And there was evening and there was morning, a sixth day.

Source: *The New Oxford Annotated Bible: New Revised Standard Version with The Apocrypha,* Fully Revised Fourth Edition. (New York: Oxford University Press, 2010), 11–13.

PRIMARY SOURCE 1.3

"The Creation of the Universe" from the Huainanzi (*ca. 1100 BCE*)

Before Heaven and Earth had taken form all was vague and amorphous. Therefore it was called the Great Beginning. The Great Beginning produced emptiness, and emptiness produced the universe. The universe produced material-force, which had limits. That which was clear and light drifted up to become Heaven, while that which was heavy and turbid solidified to become Earth. It was very easy for the pure, fine material to come together but extremely difficult for the

heavy, turbid material to solidify. Therefore Heaven was completed first and Earth assumed shape after. The combined essences of Heaven and Earth became the yin and yang; the concentrated essences of the yin and yang became the four seasons; and the scattered essences of the four seasons became the myriad creatures of the world. After a long time the hot Force of the accumulated yang produced fire, and the essence of the fire force became the sun; the cold force of the accumulated yin became water, and the essence of the water force became the moon. The essence of the excess force of the sun and moon became the stars, while Earth received water and soil. [3:1a]

When Heaven and Earth were joined in emptiness and all was unwrought simplicity, then, without having been created, things came into being. This was the Great Oneness. All things issued from this Oneness, but all became different, being divided into various species of fish, birds, and beasts. . . . Therefore while a thing moves it is called living, and when it dies it is said to be exhausted. All are creatures. They are not the uncreated creator of things, for the creator of things is not among things. If we examine the Great Beginning of antiquity we find that man was born out of nothing to assume form as something. Having form, he is governed by things. But he who can return to that from which he was born and become as though formless is called a "true man." The true man is one who has never become separated from the Great Oneness. [14:1a]

Source: *Sources of Chinese Tradition, Volume 1: From the Earliest Times to 1600,* 2nd edition, compiled by Wm. Theodore de Bary and Irene Bloom (New York: Columbia University Press, 1999), 346–347.

PRIMARY SOURCE 1.4

Popul Vuh (*date of origin unknown*)

Here, then, is the beginning of when it was decided to make man, and when what must enter into the flesh of man was sought.

And the Forefathers, the Creators and Makers, who were called Tepeu and Gucumatz said: "The time of dawn has come, let the work be finished, and let those who are to nourish and sustain us appear, the noble sons, the civilized vassals: let man appear, humanity, on the face of the earth." Thus they spoke.

They assembled, came together and held council in the darkness and in the night; then they sought and discussed, and here they reflected and thought. In this way their decisions came clearly to light and they found and discovered what must enter into the flesh of man.

It was just before the sun, the moon, and the stars appeared over the Creators and Makers.

From Paxil, from Cayalá, as they were called, came the yellow ears of corn and the white ears of corn. These are the names of the animals which brought the food: *yac* [the mountain cat], *utiú* [the coyote], *quel* [a small parrot], and *hob* [the crow]. These four animals gave tidings of the yellow ears of corn and the white ears of corn, they told them that they should go to Paxil and they showed them the road to Paxil.

And thus they found the food, and this was what went into the flesh of created man, the made man; this was his blood; of this the blood of man was made. So the corn entered [into the formation of man] by the work of the Forefathers.

• • •

The animals showed them the road. And then grinding the yellow corn and the white corn, Xmucané made nine drinks, and from this food came the strength and the flesh, and with it they created the muscles and the strength of man. This the Forefathers did, Tepeu and Gucumatz, as they were called.

After that they began to talk about the creation and the making of our first mother and father; of yellow corn and of white corn they made their flesh; of corn meal dough they made the arms and the legs of man. Only dough of corn meal went into the flesh of our first fathers, the four men, who were created.

• • •

It is said that they only were made and formed, they had no mother, they had no father. They were only called men. They were not born of woman, nor were they begotten by the Creator nor by the Maker, nor by the Forefathers. Only by a miracle, by means of incantation were they created and made by the Creator, the Maker, the Forefathers, Tepeu and Gucumatz. And as they had the appearance of men, they were men; they talked, conversed, saw and heard, walked, grasped things; they were good and handsome men, and their figure was the figure of a man.

They were endowed with intelligence; they saw and instantly they could see far, they succeeded in seeing, they succeeded in knowing all that there is in the world. When they looked, instantly they saw all around them, and they contemplated in turn the arch of heaven and the round face of the earth.

The things hidden [in the distance] they saw all, without first having to move; at once they saw the world, and so, too, from where they were, they saw it.

Great was their wisdom; their sight reached to the forests, the rocks, the lakes, the seas, the mountains, and the valleys. In truth, they were admirable men, Balam-Quitzé, Balam-Acab, Mahucutah, and Iqui-Balam.

Then the Creator and the Maker asked them: "What do you think of your condition? Do you not see? Do you not hear? Are not your speech and manner of walking good? Look, then! Contemplate the world, look [and see] if the mountains and the valleys appear! Try, then, to see!" they said to [the four first men].

And immediately they [the four first men] began to see all that was in the world. Then they gave thanks to the Creator and the Maker: "We really give you thanks, two and three times!"

Source: Adrian Recinos, from *Popol Vuh: The Sacred Book of the Ancient Quiché Maya*, trans. Delia Goetz and Sylvanus G. Morley, pp. 165–68. Copyright © 1950 by the University of Oklahoma Press. Reprinted with permission of University of Oklahoma Press.

PRIMARY SOURCE 1.5

Yoruba Creation Narrative (date of origin unknown)

In the beginning was only the sky above, water and marshland below.

The chief god Olorun ruled the sky, and the goddess Olokun ruled what was below.

Obatala, another god, reflected upon this situation, then went to Olorun for permission to create dry land for all kinds of living creatures to inhabit. He was given permission, so he sought advice from Orunmila, oldest son of Olorun and the god of prophecy.

He was told he would need a gold chain long enough to reach below, a snail's shell filled with sand, a white hen, a black cat, and a palm nut, all of which he was to carry in a bag. All the gods contributed what gold they had, and Orunmila supplied the articles for the bag. When all was ready, Obatala hung the chain from a corner of the sky, placed the bag over his shoulder, and started the downward climb. When he reached the end of the chain he saw he still had some distance to go.

From above he heard Orunmila instruct him to pour the sand from the snail's shell, and to immediately release the white hen.

He did as he was told, whereupon the hen landing on the sand began scratching and scattering it about.

Wherever the sand landed it formed dry land, the bigger piles becoming hills and the smaller piles valleys. Obatala jumped to a hill and named the place Ife. The dry land now extended as far as he could see.

He dug a hole, planted the palm nut, and saw it grow to maturity in a flash. The mature palm tree dropped more palm nuts on the ground, each of which grew immediately to maturity and repeated the process. Obatala settled down with the cat for company.

Many months passed, and he grew bored with his routine.

He decided to create beings like himself to keep him company. He dug into the sand and soon found clay with which to mold figures like himself and started on his task, but he soon grew tired and decided to take a break.

He made wine from a nearby palm tree, and drank bowl after bowl. Not realizing he was drunk, Obatala returned to his task of fashioning the new beings; because of his condition he fashioned many imperfect figures.

Without realizing this, he called out to Olorun to breathe life into his creatures.

The next day he realized what he had done and swore never to drink again, and to take care of those who were deformed, thus becoming Protector of the Deformed.

The new people built huts as Obatala had done and soon Ife prospered and became a city.

When Obatala returned to his home in the sky for a visit, Olokun summoned the great waves of her vast oceans and sent them surging across the land. Wave after wave she unleashed, until much of the land was underwater and many of the people were drowned. Those that had fled to the high-est land beseeched the god Eshu who had been visiting, to re-turn to the sky and report what was happening to them. Eshu demanded sacrifice be made to Obatala and himself before he would deliver the message.

The people sacrificed some goats, and Eshu returned to the sky.

When Orunmila heard the news he climbed down the golden chain to the earth, and cast many spells which caused the flood waters to retreat and the dry land reappear.

So ended the great flood

Source: "Yoruba Creation Narrative," trans. P. J. Criss, *P. J. Criss's Internet homepage* <http://www.cyhercomm.net/~grandpa/creation.html>. Reprinted in "'Ak Tengiz': The Dis-appeared Ice Age Sea-Size Lake of Siberia" by Polat Kaya, *Turk Dunyasi Arastirmalari* no. 121 (August 1999), 38–39.

QUESTIONS FOR ANALYSIS

1. What is created, and in what order, in each of these narratives? Who is doing the creating? Out of what? How long does it take? What seem to be the creator's (or creators') motives—if any—for creation?

2. What do you think accounts for the differences and similarities in these creation narratives?

3. Compare these historical creation narratives with the narrative of human origins outlined in this chapter. What does the modern creation narrative of evolution have in common with these creation narratives? How is it different?

Interpreting Visual Evidence

Prehistoric Art

Prehistoric art provides some of the best direct evidence for the thoughts and experiences of humans who lived prior to the invention of writing (which as we'll see in Chapter 2 has only been around for 5,000 years). Paintings showing the outlines of hands, images of animals, and even hunting scenes adorn the walls of caves across Afro-Eurasia, put there by humans over tens of thousands of years.

The artwork in Chauvet Cave in southwestern France may be the oldest in Europe, dating to about 35,000 years ago. In the first two images below, horses and bison from Chauvet Cave convey both perspective and movement. The overlapping of horses suggests a powerfully galloping herd and the bison image uses a doubling effect—drawing additional hindquarters and legs—to give the bison the appearance of motion and speed. In central India, cave paintings at Bhimbekta date to as long as 30,000 years ago; the painting reproduced here includes several herds of different types of animals. Other images from this site painted over thousands of years include humans dancing and even having sex. Cave paintings from other areas like Lascaux in southeastern France (20,000 years old), Altamira in Spain (17,000 years old), and Tassil-n-Ajjer in North Africa (8,000 years old) provide similar insights into the artists' lives.

In addition to making paintings, early humans carved figurines. Small female figurines, often with emphasized breasts and genitalia, have been found at Willendorf in Austria, Dolni Vestonice in the Czech Republic, Cernavoda in Romania, and Malta in Siberian Russia. These figurines, carved from limestone, mammoth tusk, and reindeer horn, also range from about 35,000 to 8,000 years old. The figurine known as the Venus of Hohle Fels, found in Germany, dates to more than 35,000 years ago. This 2.4-inch carving may have been worn as an amulet. The 6-inch Venus of Willendorf from more than 25,000 years ago wears only a headdress (or braided hairstyle) and rests her arms across her breasts. The apparent continuity in both the cave art and figurines across thousands of years is striking.

Horses from Chauvet Cave.

Bison from Chauvet Cave.

Cave painting at Bhimbetka.

Willendorf Venus.

Venus of Hohle Fels.

QUESTIONS FOR ANALYSIS

1. Based on these cave paintings and figurines, what types of subjects did humans in the prehistoric period depict in their art? Why do you think they chose those subjects?

2. Compare these paintings and figurines. Given that there was not likely any interaction between the communities that produced them, what do you think might account for the similarities and differences?

3. Imagine an artist in a dark cave, painting with plant-made pigments by the light of a flickering torch; or a man or woman spending a hundred hours to carve a figurine from limestone. What might spur the creation of such artworks? How does this art change your understanding of the hunter-gatherer lifestyle?

Before You Read This Chapter

Rivers, Cities, and First States,

3500–2000 BCE

One of the first urban centers in the world was the ancient city of Uruk. Located in southern Mesopotamia on a branch of the Euphrates River, it was home to more than 10,000 people by the late fourth millennium BCE and boasted many large public structures and temples. One temple had stood there since before 3000 BCE; with plastered mud-brick walls that formed stepped indentations, it perched high above the plain. In another area, administrative buildings and temples adorned with elaborate facades stood in courtyards defined by tall columns. Colored stone cones arranged in elaborate geometric patterns covered parts of these buildings. An epic poem devoted to its later king, Gilgamesh, described Uruk as the "shining city."

Over the years Uruk became an immense commercial and administrative center. A huge wall with seven massive gates surrounded the metropolis, and down the middle ran a canal carrying water from the Euphrates. On one side of the city were gardens, kilns, and textile workshops. On the other was the temple quarter where priests lived, scribes kept records, and lu-gal ("the big man") conferred with the elders. As Uruk grew, many small industries—including potters, metalsmiths, stone bowl makers, and brickmakers—became centralized in response to the increasing sophistication of construction and manufacturing.

Uruk was the first city of its kind in world history. Earlier humans had settled in small communities scattered over the landscape. As some communities gradually became focal points for trade, a few of these hubs grew into cities with large populations and institutions of economic, religious, and political power. Most inhabitants no longer produced their own food, working instead in specialized professions.

Between 3500 and 2000 BCE, a handful of remarkable societies clustered in a few river basins on the Afro-Eurasian landmass. These regions—in Mesopotamia (between the Tigris and Euphrates rivers), in northwest India (on the Indus River), in Egypt (along the Nile), and in China (near the Yangzi and Yellow rivers)—became the heartlands for densely populated settlements with complex cultures. Here the world saw the birth of the first large cities and territorial states. One of these settings (Mesopotamia) brought forth humankind's first writing system, and all laid the foundations for kingdoms radiating out of opulent cities. This chapter describes how each society evolved, and it explores their similarities and differences. It is important to note how exceptional these large cities and territorial states were, and we will see that many smaller societies prevailed elsewhere. The Aegean, Anatolia, western Europe, the Americas, and sub-Saharan Africa offer reminders that most of the world's people dwelt in small communities, far removed culturally from the monumental architecture and accomplishments of the big new states.

Settlement and Pastoralism

COMPARISON

IDENTIFY the earliest river-basin societies and **ANALYZE** their shared characteristics.

Around 3500 BCE, cultural changes, population growth, and technological innovations gave rise to complex societies. Clustered in cities, these larger communities developed new institutions, and individuals took on a wide range of social roles, resulting in new hierarchies based on wealth and gender. At the same time, the number of small villages and pastoral nomadic communities grew.

Water was the key to settlement, since predictable flows of water determined where humans settled. Reliable water supplies allowed communities to sow crops adequate to feed large populations. Abundant rainfall allowed the world's first villages to emerge, but the breakthroughs into big cities occurred in drier zones where large rivers formed beds of rich soils deposited by flooding rivers. With irrigation innovations, soils became arable. Equally important, a worldwide warming cycle expanded growing seasons. The **river basins**—with their fertile soil, irrigation, and available domesticated plants and animals—made possible the agricultural surpluses needed to support city dwellers.

Early Mesopotamian Waterworks From the sixth millennium BCE, irrigation was necessary for successful farming in southern Mesopotamia. By the first millennium BCE, sophisticated feats of engineering allowed the Assyrians to redirect water through constructed aqueducts, like the one illustrated here on a relief from the palace of the Assyrian king Sennacherib at Nineveh.

EARLY CITIES ALONG RIVER BASINS

The material and social advances of the early cities occurred in a remarkably short period—from 3500 to 2000 BCE—in three locations: the basin of the Tigris and Euphrates rivers in central Southwest Asia; the northern parts of the Nile River flowing toward the Mediterranean Sea; and the Indus River basin in northwestern South Asia. About a millennium later a similar process began along the Yellow River and the

Yangzi River in China. (See Map 2.1.) In these regions humans farmed and fed themselves by relying on intensive irrigation agriculture. Gathering in cities inhabited by rulers, administrators, priests, and craftworkers, they changed their methods of organizing communities by worshipping new gods in new ways and by obeying divinely inspired monarchs and elaborate bureaucracies. New technologies appeared, ranging from the wheel for pottery production to metal- and stoneworking for the creation of both luxury objects and utilitarian tools. The technology of writing used the storage of words and meanings to extend human communication and memory.

With cities and new technologies came greater divisions of labor. Dense urban settlement enabled people to specialize in making goods for the consumption of others: weavers made textiles, potters made ceramics, and jewelers made precious ornaments. Soon these goods found additional uses in trade with outlying areas. And as trade expanded over longer distances, raw materials such as wool, metal, timber, and precious stones arrived in the cities. (See Map 2.2.) One of the most coveted metals was copper: easily smelted and shaped (not to mention shiny and alluring), it became the metal of choice for charms, sculptures, and valued commodities. When combined with arsenic or tin, copper hardens and becomes **bronze**, which is useful for tools and weapons. Consequently, this period is often called a Bronze Age, though the term simplifies the breadth of the breakthroughs.

The emergence of cities as population centers created one of history's most durable worldwide distinctions: the **urban-rural divide**. Where cities appeared alongside rivers, people adopted lifestyles based on specialized labor and the mass production of goods. In contrast, most people continued to live in the countryside, where they remained on their lands, cultivating the land or tending livestock, though they exchanged their grains and animal products for goods from the urban centers. The two ways of life were interdependent and both worlds remained linked through family ties, trade, politics, and religion.

PASTORAL NOMADIC COMMUNITIES

Around 3500 BCE, Afro-Eurasia also witnessed the growth and spread of pastoral nomadic communities. The transhumant herder communities that had appeared in Southwest Asia around 5500 BCE (see Chapter 1) continued to be small and their settlements impermanent. They lacked substantial public buildings or infrastructure, but their seasonal moves followed a consistent pattern. Across the vast expanse of Afro-Eurasia's great mountains and its desert barriers, and from its steppe lands ranging across inner and central Eurasia to the Pacific Ocean, these transhumant herders lived alongside settled agrarian people, especially when occupying their lowland pastures. They traded meat and animal products for grains, pottery, and tools produced in the agrarian communities.

In the arid environments of Inner Mongolia and central Asia, transhumant herding and agrarian communities initially followed the same combination of herding animals and cultivating crops that had proved so successful in Southwest Asia. However, because the steppe environment could not support large-scale farming, these communities came to focus on animal breeding and herding. As secondary pursuits they continued to fish, hunt, and farm small plots in their winter pastures. Their economy centered on domesticated cattle, sheep, and horses. As their herds increased, these horse-riding nomads had to move often to new pastures, driving their herds across vast expanses of land. By the second millennium BCE, they had become full-scale nomadic pastoral communities, and they dominated the steppes. In these pastoral nomadic economies of the arid zones of central Eurasia, horses became crucial to survival. These nomadic and transhumant groups played a vital role in connecting cities and spreading ideas throughout Afro-Eurasia.

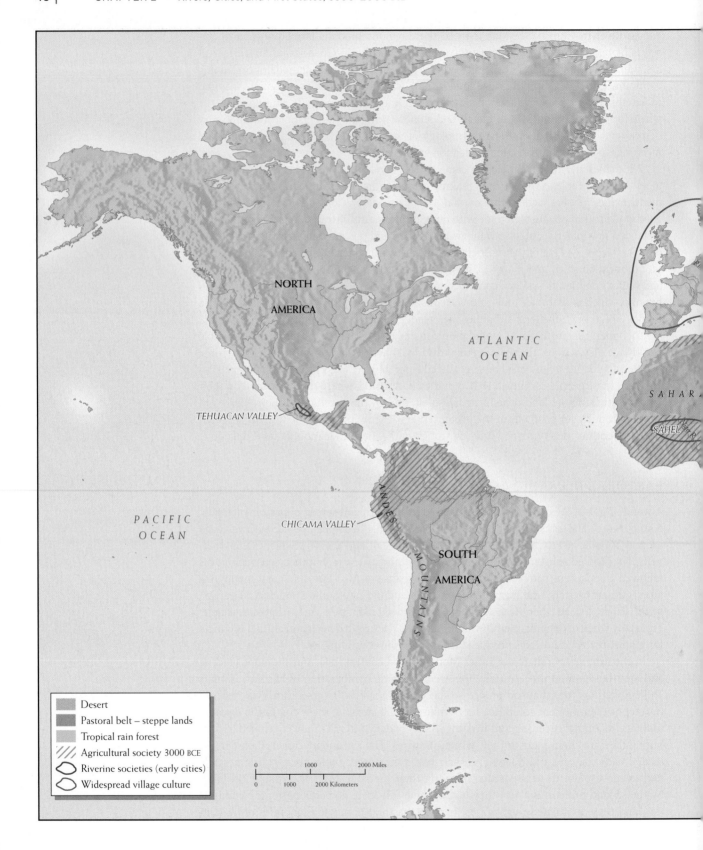

NORTH
AMERICA

ATLANTIC
OCEAN

SAHARA

SAHEL

TEHUACAN VALLEY

PACIFIC
OCEAN

CHICAMA VALLEY

ANDES MOUNTAINS

SOUTH
AMERICA

Desert
Pastoral belt – steppe lands
Tropical rain forest
Agricultural society 3000 BCE
Riverine societies (early cities)
Widespread village culture

0   1000   2000 Miles
0   1000   2000 Kilometers

MAP 2.1 | The World in the Third Millennium BCE

Human societies became increasingly diversified as agricultural, urban, and pastoral nomadic communities expanded.

• In what different regions did pastoralism and river basin societies emerge?

• Considering the geographic features highlighted on this map, why do you think cities appeared in the regions that they did?

• How did geographic and environmental factors promote interaction between nomadic pastoral and sedentary agricultural societies?

MAP 2.2 | Trade and Exchange in Southwest Asia and the Eastern Mediterranean—Third Millennium BCE

Extensive commercial networks linked the urban cores of Southwest Asia.

- Of the traded raw materials shown on the map, which ones were used for building materials, and which ones for luxury items?
- Why were there more extensive trade connections between Mesopotamians and people to their northwest and east than with Egypt to the west?
- According to the map, in what ways did Mesopotamia become the crossroads of Afro-Eurasia?

Between the Tigris and Euphrates Rivers: Mesopotamia

COMPARISON

EXPLAIN the religious, social, and political developments that accompany early urbanization in the river basin societies from 3500 to 2000 BCE.

The world's first complex society arose in Mesopotamia. Here the river and the first cities changed how people lived. Mesopotamia, whose name is a Greek word meaning "[region] between two rivers," is a landmass including all of modern-day Iraq and parts of Syria and southeastern Turkey. From their headwaters in the mountains to the north and east to their destination in the Persian Gulf, the Tigris and Euphrates rivers are wild and unpredictable. Unpredictable floodwaters could wipe out years of hard work, but when managed properly they could transform the landscape into verdant and productive fields.

Both rivers provided water for irrigation and, although hardly navigable, were important routes for transportation and communication by pack animal and by foot. Mesopotamia's natural advantages—its rich agricultural land and water, combined with easy access to neighboring regions—favored the growth of cities and later territorial states. These cities and states became the sites of important cultural, political, and social innovations.

TAPPING THE WATERS

The first rudimentary advances in irrigation occurred in the foothills of the Zagros Mountains along the banks of the smaller rivers that feed the Tigris. Converting the floodplain of the Euphrates River into a breadbasket, however, required mastering the unpredictable waters. (A floodplain is an area where the river overflows and deposits fertile soil.) Both the Euphrates and the Tigris, unless controlled by waterworks, were unfavorable to cultivators because the annual floods occurred at the height of the growing season, when crops were most vulnerable. Low water levels occurred when crops required abundant irrigation. To prevent the river from overflowing during its flood stage, farmers built levees along the banks and dug ditches and canals to drain away the floodwaters. Engineers devised an irrigation system whereby the Euphrates, the riverbed of which is higher than the Tigris, essentially served as the supply and the Tigris as the drain. Storing and channeling water year after year required constant maintenance and innovation by a corps of engineers.

The Mesopotamians' technological breakthrough was in irrigation, not in agrarian methods. Because the soils were fine, rich, and constantly replenished by the floodwaters' silt, soil tillage was light work. Farmers sowed a combination of wheat, millet, sesame, and barley (the basis for beer, a staple of their diet).

CROSSROADS OF SOUTHWEST ASIA

Though its soil was rich and water was abundant, southern Mesopotamia had few other natural resources apart from the mud, marsh reeds, spindly trees, and low-quality limestone that served as basic building materials. To obtain high-quality, dense wood, stone, metal, and other materials for constructing and embellishing their cities with their temples and palaces, Mesopotamians had to interact with the inhabitants of surrounding regions. In return for textiles, oils, and other commodities, they imported cedar wood from Lebanon, copper and stones from Oman, more copper from Turkey and Iran, and the precious blue gemstone called lapis lazuli, as well as the ever-useful tin, from faraway Afghanistan. Maintaining trading contacts was easy, given Mesopotamia's open boundaries on all sides. The area became a crossroads for the peoples of Southwest Asia, including Sumerians, who concentrated in the south; Hurrians, who lived in the north; and Akkadians, who populated western and central Mesopotamia. Trade and migration contributed to the growth of cities throughout the river basin, beginning with the Sumerian cities of southern Mesopotamia.

THE WORLD'S FIRST CITIES

During the first half of the fourth millennium BCE, a demographic transformation occurred in the Tigris-Euphrates river basin, especially in the southern area called Sumer. The population expanded as a result of the region's agricultural bounty, and many Mesopotamians migrated from country villages to centers that eventually became cities. (A **city** is a large, well-defined urban area with a dense population.) The earliest Sumerian cities—Eridu, Nippur, and Uruk—developed over about 1,000 years, dominating the southern part of the floodplain by 3500 BCE. Buildings of mud brick show successive layers of urban development, as at Eridu, where more than twenty reconstructed temples were piled atop one

Layout of Eridu Over several millennia, temples of increasing size and complexity were built atop each other at Eridu in southern Iraq. The culmination came with the elaborate structure of level VII.

another across four millennia, resulting in a final temple that rose from a platform like a mountain, visible for miles in all directions.

As the temple grew skyward, the village expanded outward and became a city. From their homes in temples located at the center of cities, the cities' gods broadcast their powers. In return, urbanites provided luxuries, fine clothes, and enhanced lodgings for the gods and their priests. In Sumerian cosmology, created by ruling elites, man existed solely to serve the gods, so the urban landscape reflected this fact: a temple at the core, with goods and services flowing to the center and with divine protection and justice flowing outward.

Some thirty-five cities with religious sanctuaries dotted the southern plain of Mesopotamia. Sumerian ideology glorified a way of life and a territory based on politically equal city-states, each with a guardian deity and sanctuary supported by its inhabitants. (A **city-state** is a political organization based on the authority of a single, large city that controls outlying territories.) Because early Mesopotamian cities served as meeting places for peoples and their deities, they gained status as religious and economic centers. Whether enormous (like Uruk and Nippur) or modest (like Ur and Abu Salabikh), all cities were spiritual, economic, and cultural homes for Mesopotamian subjects.

Simply making a city was therefore not enough: urban design reflected the city's role as a wondrous place to pay homage to the gods and their human intermediary, the king. Within their walls, early cities contained large houses separated by date-palm plantations and extensive sheepfolds. As populations grew, the Mesopotamian cities became denser, houses smaller, and new suburbs spilled out beyond the old walls. The typical layout of Mesopotamian cities reflected a common pattern: a central canal surrounded by neighborhoods of specialized occupational groups. The temple marked the city center, with the palace and other official buildings on the periphery. In separate quarters for craft production, families passed down their trades across generations. In this sense, the landscape of the city mirrored the growing **social hierarchies** (distinctions between the privileged and the less privileged).

GODS AND TEMPLES

The worldview of the Sumerians and, later, the Akkadians included a belief in a group of gods that shaped their political institutions and controlled everything—including the weather, fertility, harvests, and the underworld. As depicted in the *Epic of Gilgamesh* (a second-millennium BCE composition based on oral tales about Gilgamesh, a historical but mythologized king of Uruk), the gods could give but could also take away—with droughts, floods, and death. Gods, and the natural forces they controlled, had to be revered and feared. Faithful subjects imagined their gods as immortal beings whose habits were capricious, contentious, and gloriously work-free.

Each major god of the Sumerian pantheon (an officially recognized group of gods) dwelled in a lavish temple in a particular city that he or she had created, giving rise to each city's character, institutions, and relationships with its urban neighbors. Inside these temples were altars displaying the god's image. Benches lined the walls, with statues of humans standing in perpetual worship of the deity's images. By the end of the third millennium BCE, the temple's platform base had changed to a stepped platform called a *ziggurat*, with the main temple on top. Surrounding the ziggurat were buildings that housed priests, officials, laborers, and servants.

Temples functioned as the god's estate, engaging in all sorts of productive and commercial activities. Temple dependents cultivated cereals, fruits, and vegetables by using extensive irrigation and cared for flocks of livestock. Other temples operated workshops for manufacturing textiles and leather goods, employing craftworkers, metalworkers, masons, and stoneworkers. Enormous labor forces were involved in maintaining this high level of production.

ROYAL POWER, FAMILIES, AND SOCIAL HIERARCHY

Like the temples, royal palaces reflected the power of the ruling elites. Royal palaces appeared around 2500 BCE and served as the official residence of a ruler, his family, and his entourage. As access to palaces and temples over time became limited, gods and kings became inaccessible to all but the most elite. Although located at the edge of cities, palaces were the symbols of permanent secular, military, and administrative authority distinct from the temples' spiritual and economic power.

The Royal Cemetery at Ur shows how Mesopotamian rulers used elaborate burial arrangements to reinforce their religious and socioeconomic hierarchies. Housed in a mud-brick structure, the royal burials held not only the primary remains but also the bodies of more than eighty men and women who had been sacrificed. Huge vats for cooked food, bones of animals, drinking vessels, and musical instruments suggest the lifestyle of those who joined their masters in the graves. Honoring the royal dead by including their followers and possessions in their tombs underscored the social hierarchies—including the vertical ties between humans and gods—that were the cornerstone of these early city-states.

Social hierarchies were an important part of the fabric of Sumerian city-states. Ruling groups secured their privileged access to economic and political resources by erecting systems of bureaucracies, priesthoods, and laws. Priests and bureaucrats served their rulers well, championing rules and norms that legitimized the political leadership. Occupations within the cities were highly specialized, and a list of professions circulated across the land so that everyone could know his or her place in the social order. The king and priest in Sumer were at the top of the list, followed by bureaucrats (scribes and household accountants), supervisors, and craftworkers, such as cooks, jewelers, gardeners, potters, metalsmiths, and traders. The biggest group, which was at the bottom of the hierarchy, comprised workers who were not slaves but who were dependent on their

The Royal Tombs of Ur The Royal Tombs of Ur, excavated in the 1930s, contained thousands of objects in gold, silver, lapis lazuli, and shell that were buried along with elites of the First Dynasty of Ur. Pu-Abi, identified as a queen by the cylinder near her body, was buried in a separate chamber. She was interred in full regalia, including the elaborate headdress shown here.

employers' households. Movement among economic classes was not impossible but, as in many traditional societies, it was rare.

The family and the household provided the bedrock for Sumerian society, and its patriarchal organization, dominated by the senior male, reflected the balance between women and men, children and parents. The family consisted of the husband and wife bound by a contract: she would provide children, preferably male, while he provided support and protection. Monogamy was the norm unless there was no son, in which case a second wife or a slave girl would bear male children to serve as the married couple's offspring. Adoption was another way to gain a male heir. Sons would inherit the family's property in equal shares, while daughters would receive dowries necessary for successful marriage into other families. Some women joined the temple staff as priestesses and gained economic autonomy that included ownership of estates and productive enterprises, although their fathers and brothers remained responsible for their well-being.

FIRST WRITING AND EARLY TEXTS

Mesopotamia was the birthplace of the world's first writing system, inscribed to promote the economic power of the temples and kings. Those who wielded new writing tools were **scribes**; from the very beginning they were near the top of the social ladder, under the big man and the priests. As the writing of texts became more important to the social fabric of cities, and facilitated information sharing across wider spans of distance and time, scribes consolidated their elite status.

Mesopotamians were the world's first record keepers and readers. The precursors to writing appeared in Mesopotamian societies when farming peoples and officials who had been using clay tokens and images carved on stones to seal off storage areas began to use them to convey messages. These images, when combined with numbers drawn on clay tablets, could record the distribution of goods and services.

Around 3200 BCE, someone, probably in Uruk, understood that the marks (most were pictures of objects) could also represent words or sounds. Before long, scribes connected visual symbols with sounds, and sounds with meanings, and they discovered they could record messages by using abstract symbols or signs to denote concepts. Such signs later came to represent syllables, the building blocks of words. By impressing signs into wet clay with the cut end of a reed, scribes pioneered a form of wedge-shaped writing that we call *cuneiform;* it filled tablets with information that was intelligible to anyone who could decipher it, even in faraway locations or in future generations. Developing over 800 years, this Sumerian innovation enhanced the urban elites' ability to trade goods, to control property, and to transmit ideas through literature, historical records, and sacred texts. The result was a profound change in human experience, because representing symbols of spoken language facilitated an extension of communication and memory.

Much of what we know about Mesopotamia rests on our ability to decipher cuneiform script. By around 2400 BCE, texts began to describe the political makeup of southern Mesopotamia, giving details of its history and economy. Adaptable to different languages, cuneiform was borrowed by cities in northern Mesopotamia to write their Semitic language.

City life and literacy gave rise also to written narratives, the stories of a "people" and their origins. "The Temple Hymns," written around 2100 BCE, describe thirty-five divine sanctuaries. The Sumerian King List, known from texts written around 2000 BCE, recounts the reigns of kings by city and dynasty and narrates the long reigns of legendary kings before the so-called Great Flood. A crucial event in Sumerian identity, the Great Flood, found also in Biblical narrative, explained Uruk's demise as the gods' doing. Flooding was the most powerful natural force in the lives of those who lived by rivers, and it helped shape the foundations of Mesopotamian societies.

SPREADING CITIES AND FIRST TERRITORIAL STATES

No single state dominated Mesopotamia in the fourth and third millennia BCE, but the most powerful and influential were the Sumerian city-states (2850–2334 BCE) and their successor, the Akkadian territorial state (2334–2193 BCE). In the north, Hurrians urbanized their rich agricultural zone around 2600 BCE. (See Map 2.3.)

Sumerian city-states, with their expanding populations, soon found themselves competing for agrarian lands, scarce water, and lucrative trade routes. And as pastoralists far and wide learned of the region's bounty, they journeyed in greater numbers to the cities, fueling urbanization and competition. The world's first great conqueror—Sargon the Great (r. 2334–2279 BCE), king of Akkad—emerged from one of these cities. By the end of his reign he had united (by force) the independent Mesopotamian cities south of modern-day Baghdad and brought the era of competitive independent city-states to an end. Sargon's unification of the

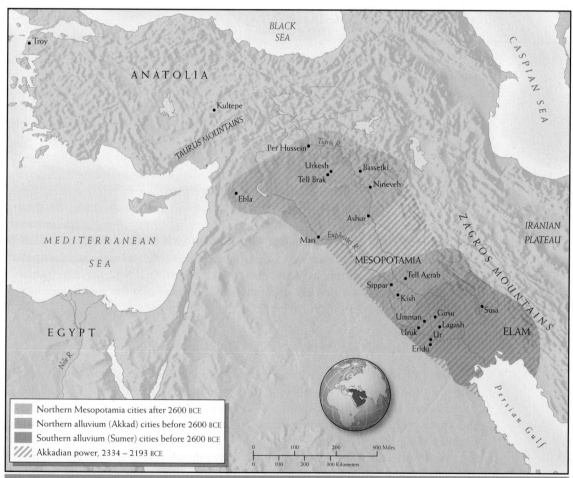

MAP 2.3 | The Spread of Cities in Mesopotamia and the Akkadian State, 2600–2200 BCE

Urbanization began in the southern river basin of Mesopotamia and spread northward. Eventually, the region achieved unification under Akkadian power.

• According to this map, what were the natural boundaries of the Mesopotamian cities?

• How did proximity to the Zagros Mountains affect the new urban centers?

• How did the expansion northward reflect the continued influence of geographic and environmental factors on urbanization?

southern cities by alliance, though relatively short-lived, created a **territorial state**. (A territorial state is a form of political organization that holds authority over a large population and landmass; its power extends over multiple cities.) Sargon's dynasty sponsored monumental architecture, artworks, and literary works, which in turn inspired generations of builders, architects, artists, and scribes. And by encouraging contact with distant neighbors, many of whom adopted aspects of Mesopotamian culture, the Akkadian kings increased the geographic reach of Mesopotamian influence. Just under a century after Sargon's death, foreign tribesmen from the Zagros Mountains conquered the capital city of Akkad around 2190 BCE, setting the beginning of a pattern that would fuel epic history writing, namely the struggles between city-state dwellers and those on the margins who lived a simpler way of life. The impressive state created by Sargon was made possible by Mesopotamia's early innovations in irrigation, urban development, and writing. While Mesopotamia led the way in creating city-states, Egypt went a step further, unifying a 600-mile-long landmass under a single ruler.

"The Gift of the Nile": Egypt

In Egypt, complex societies grew on the banks of the Nile River, and by the third millennium BCE their peoples created a distinctive culture and a powerful, prosperous state. The earliest inhabitants along the banks of the Nile were a mixed people. Some had migrated from the eastern and western deserts in Sinai and Libya as these areas grew barren from climate change. Others came from the Mediterranean. Equally important were peoples who trekked northward from Nubia and central Africa. Ancient Egypt was a melting pot where immigrants blended cultural practices and technologies.

Like Mesopotamia, Egypt had densely populated areas whose inhabitants depended on irrigation, built monumental architecture, gave their rulers immense authority, and created a complex social order based in commercial and devotional centers. Yet the ancient Egyptian culture was profoundly shaped by its geography. The environment and the natural boundaries of deserts, river rapids, and sea dominated the country and its inhabitants. Only about 3 percent of Egypt's land area was cultivable, and almost all of that cultivable land was in the Nile Delta—the rich alluvial land lying between the river's two main branches as it flows north of modern-day Cairo into the Mediterranean Sea. This environment shaped Egyptian society's unique culture.

THE NILE RIVER AND ITS FLOODWATERS

Knowing Egypt requires appreciating the pulses of the Nile. The world's longest river, it stretches 1,238 miles from its sources in the highlands of central Africa to its destination in the Mediterranean Sea. Egypt was deeply attached to sub-Saharan Africa; not only did its waters and rich silt deposits come from the African highlands, but much of its original population had migrated into the Nile valley from the west and the south many millennia earlier.

The Upper Nile is a sluggish river that cuts through the Sahara Desert. Rising out of central Africa and Ethiopia, its two main branches—the White and Blue Niles—meet at present-day Khartoum and then scour out a single riverbed 1,500 miles long to the Mediterranean. The annual floods gave the basin regular moisture and enriched the soil. Although the Nile's floodwaters did not fertilize or irrigate fields as broad as those in Mesopotamia, they created green belts flanking the broad waterway. These gave rise to a society whose culture stretched along the navigable river and its carefully preserved banks. Away from the riverbanks, on both sides, lay a desert rich in raw materials but largely uninhabited. (See Map 2.4.) Egypt had no fertile hinterland like the sprawling plains of Mesopotamia. In this way, Egypt was arguably the most river-focused of river-basin cultures.

MAP 2.4 | Old Kingdom Egypt, 2686–2181 BCE

Old Kingdom Egyptian society reflected a strong influence from its unique geographical location.

- What geographical features contributed to Egypt's isolation from the outside world and the people's sense of their unity?

- What natural resource enabled the Egyptians to build the Great Pyramids?

- Based on the map, why do you think it was important to the people and their rulers for Upper and Lower Egypt to be united?

The Nile's predictability as the source of life and abundance shaped the character of the people and their culture. In contrast to the wild and uncertain Euphrates and Tigris rivers, the Nile was gentle, bountiful, and reliable. During the summer, as the Nile swelled, local villagers built earthen walls that divided the floodplain into basins. By trapping the floodwaters, these basins captured the rich silt washing down from the Ethiopian highlands. Annual flooding meant that the land received a new layer of topsoil every year. The light, fertile soils made planting simple. Peasants cast seeds into the alluvial soil and then had their livestock trample them to the proper depth. The never-failing sun, which the Egyptians worshipped, ensured an abundant harvest. In the early spring, when the Nile's waters were at their lowest and no crops were under cultivation, the sun dried out the soil.

The peculiarities of the Nile region distinguished it from Mesopotamia. The Greek historian and geographer Herodotus 2,500 years ago noted that Egypt was the gift of the Nile and that the entire length of its basin was one of the world's most self-contained geographical entities. Bounded on the north by the Mediterranean Sea, on the east and west by deserts, and on the south by waterfalls, Egypt was destined to achieve a common culture. Due to these geographical features, the region was far less open to outsiders than was Mesopotamia, which was situated at a crossroads. Egypt created a common culture by balancing a struggle of opposing forces: the north or Lower Egypt versus the south or Upper Egypt; the red sand versus the black, rich soil; life versus death; heaven versus earth; order versus disorder. For Egypt's rulers the primary task was to bring stability or order, known as *ma'at*, out of these opposites. The Egyptians believed that keeping chaos, personified by the desert and its marauders, at bay through attention to *ma'at* would allow all that was good and right to occur.

THE EGYPTIAN STATE AND DYNASTIES

Once the early Egyptians harnessed the Nile to agriculture, the area changed quickly from being scarcely inhabited to socially complex. A king, called pharaoh and considered semidivine, ensured that the forces of nature, in particular the regular flooding of the Nile, continued without interruption. This task had more to do with appeasing the gods than with running a complex hydraulic system. The king protected his people from chaos-threatening invaders from the eastern desert, as well as from Nubians on the southern borders. In wall carvings, artists portrayed early kings carrying the shepherd's crook and the flail, indicating their responsibility for the welfare of their flocks (the people) and of the land. Under the king an elaborate bureaucracy organized labor and produced public works, sustaining both his vast holdings and general order throughout the realm.

The narrative of ancient Egyptian history follows its thirty-one dynasties, spanning nearly three millennia from 3100 BCE down to its conquest by Alexander the Great in 332 BCE. Since the nineteenth century, scholars have recast the story around three periods of dynastic achievement: the Old Kingdom, the Middle Kingdom, and the New Kingdom. At the end of each era, cultural flourishing suffered a breakdown in central authority, known respectively as the First, Second, and Third Intermediate Periods.

PHARAOHS, PYRAMIDS, AND COSMIC ORDER

The Third Dynasty (2686–2613 BCE) launched the foundational period known as the Old Kingdom, the golden age of ancient Egypt. By the time it began, the basic institutions of the Egyptian state were in place, as were the ideology and ritual life that legitimized the dynastic rulers.

The pharaoh—king as god—presented himself to the population by means of impressive architectural spaces, and the priestly class performed rituals reinforcing his supreme status within the universe's natural order. One of the most important rituals was the Sed festival, which renewed the king's vitality after he had ruled for thirty years and sought to ensure the perpetual presence of water. King Djoser, of the Third Dynasty, celebrated the Sed festival at his tomb complex at Saqqara. This magnificent complex is the world's oldest stone structure, dating to around 2650 BCE. Djoser's architect, Imhotep, designed a step pyramid that ultimately rose some 200 feet above the plain. The whole complex became a stage for state rituals that emphasized the divinity of kingship and the unity of Egypt.

Pharaohs used their royal tombs, and the ritual of death leading to everlasting life, to embody the state's ideology and the principles of the Egyptian cosmos. The pharaoh also employed symbols, throne names, and descriptive titles for himself and his advisers to represent his own power and that of his administrators, the priests, and the landed elite. The Egyptian cosmic order was one of inequality and stark hierarchy, not dissimilar to the hierarchies of Mesopotamia. Established at the time of creation, the universe was the king's responsibility to maintain for eternity.

TABLE 2.1	Dynasties of Ancient Egypt
SPECIES	**TIME**
Pre-dynastic Period dynasties I and II	3100–2686 BCE
Old Kingdom dynasties III–VI	2686–2181 BCE
First Intermediate Period dynasties VII–X	2181–2055 BCE
Middle Kingdom dynasties XI–XIII	2055–1650 BCE
Second Intermediate Period dynasties XIV–XVII	1650–1550 BCE
New Kingdom dynasties XVIII–XX	1550–1069 BCE
Third Intermediate Period dynasties XXI–XXV	1069–747 BCE
Late Period dynasties XXVI–XXXI	747–332 BCE

Source: Compiled from Ian Shaw and Paul Nicholson, eds., The Dictionary of Ancient Egypt *(1995), pp. 310–11.*

The step pyramid at Djoser's tomb complex was a precursor to the grand pyramids of the Fourth Dynasty (2613–2494 BCE). These kings erected their monumental structures at Giza, just outside modern-day Cairo and not far from the early royal cemetery site of Saqqara. The pyramid of Khufu, rising 481 feet above ground, is the largest stone structure in the world, and its corners are almost perfectly aligned to due north, west, south, and east. Surrounding these royal tombs at Giza were those of high officials, almost all members of the royal family. The enormous amount of labor involved in building these monuments came from peasant-workers, slaves brought from Nubia, and captured Mediterranean peoples. Through their majesty and complex construction, the Giza pyramids reflect the degree of centralization and the surpluses in Egyptian society at this time.

GODS, PRIESTHOOD, AND MAGICAL POWER

Egyptians understood their world as inhabited by three groups: gods, kings, and the rest of humanity. Official records only showed representations of gods and kings. Yet the people did not confuse their kings with gods—at least during the kings' lifetimes. Mortality was the bar between rulers and deities; after death, kings joined the gods whom they had represented while alive.

As in Mesopotamia, every region in Egypt had its resident god. Some gods, such as Amun (believed to be physically present in Thebes, the political center of Upper Egypt), transcended regional status because of the importance of their hometown. Over the centuries the Egyptian gods evolved, combining often-contradictory aspects into single deities, including: Horus, the hawk god; Osiris, the god of regeneration and the underworld; Isis, who represented the ideals of sisterhood and motherhood; Hathor, the goddess of childbirth and love; Ra, the sun god; and Amun, a creator considered to be the hidden god.

Official religious practices took place in the main temples. The king and his agents offered respect, adoration, and thanks to the gods in their temples. In return, the gods maintained order and nurtured the king and —through him— all humanity. In this contractual relationship, the gods were passive while the kings were active, a difference that reflected their unequal relationship.

The tasks of regulating religious rituals and mediating among gods, kings, and society fell to one specialist class: the priesthood. Creating this class required elaborate rules for selecting and training the priests. Only priests could enter the temples' inner sanctuaries, and the gods' statues only left the temples for great festivals. Thus, priests monopolized communication between spiritual powers and their subjects.

Unofficial religion was also important. Ordinary Egyptians matched their elite rulers in faithfulness to the gods, but their distance from temple life caused them to find different ways to fulfill their religious needs and duties. They visited local shrines, where they prayed, made requests, and left offerings to the gods. Magic had a special importance for commoners, who believed that amulets held extraordinary powers, such as preventing

Egyptian Gods Osiris (*left*) is the dying god who rules over the netherworld. Most frequently he is depicted as a mummy wearing a white crown with plumes and holding the scepter across his chest. The god Horus (*right*), who was also rendered as Ra-Horakhty, is the falcon-headed Egyptian sky god. Horus is the earliest state god of Egypt and is always closely associated with the king. Horus is a member of the nine deities of Heliopolis and is the son of Osiris and Isis.

illness and guaranteeing safe childbirth. To deal with profound questions, commoners looked to omens and divination. Spiritual expression was central to Egyptian culture at all levels, and religion helped shape other cultural achievements, including the development of a written language.

WRITING AND SCRIBES

Egypt, like Mesopotamia, was a scribal culture. By the middle of the third millennium BCE, literacy was well established among small circles of scribes in Egypt and Mesopotamia. The fact that few individuals were literate heightened the scribes' social status. Most high-ranking Egyptians were also trained as scribes working in the king's court, the army, or the priesthood. Some kings and members of the royal family learned to write as well. Although in both cultures writing emerged in response to economic needs, people soon grasped its utility for commemorative and religious purposes. As soon as literacy took hold, Mesopotamians and Egyptians were drafting historical records and literary compositions.

Ancient Egyptians used two forms of writing. Elaborate *hieroglyphs* (from the Greek "sacred carving") served in formal temple, royal, or divine contexts. More common, however, was *hieratic* writing, a cursive script written with ink on papyrus or pottery. (*Demotic* writing, from the Greek *demotika*, meaning "popular" or "in common use," developed much later and became the vital transitional key on the Rosetta Stone that ultimately allowed the nineteenth-century decipherment of hieroglyphics. (See **Analyzing Global Developments: The Development of Writing**.) Used for record keeping, hieratic writing also found uses in letters and works of literature—including narrative fiction, manuals of instruction and philosophy, cult and religious hymns, love poems, medical and mathematical texts, collections of rituals, and mortuary books.

Egyptian Hieroglyphs and "Cursive Script" The Egyptians wrote in two distinctive types of script. The more formal is hieroglyphs, which is based on pictorial images that carry values of either ideas (logograms) or sounds (phonemes). All royal and funerary inscriptions, such as this funerary relief from the Old Kingdom, are rendered in hieroglyphic script. Daily documents, accountings, literary texts, and the like were most often written in a cursive script called hieratic, which was written with ink on papyrus. The form of the cursive signs is based on the hieroglyphs but is more abstract and can be formed more quickly.

Analyzing Global Developments

The Development of Writing

Agricultural surplus, and the urbanization and labor specialization that accompanied it, prompted the earliest development of writing and the profession of the scribes whose job it was to write. Early forms of writing were employed for a variety of purposes such as keeping economic and administration records, recording the reigns of rulers, and preserving religious events and practices (calendars, rituals, and divinatory purposes). By the third millennium BCE, some early societies (Mesopotamia and Egypt, in particular) used writing to produce literature, religious texts, and historical documents. Different types of writing developed in early societies, in part because each society developed writing for different purposes (see table below):

- Ideographic/Logographic/Pictographic Systems: symbols represent words (complex and cumbersome).
- Logophonetic and Logosyllabic Systems: symbols represent sounds, usually syllables (alphabetic, fewer symbols).
- Syllabic Systems: symbols represent syllables.

- Non-alphabetic Systems: symbols are letters that are assembled to create words.

Scholars know more about early cultures whose writing has since been deciphered. Undeciphered scripts, such as the Indus Valley script and Rongorongo, offer intrigue and promise to those who would attempt their decipherment.

QUESTIONS FOR ANALYSIS

- What is the relationship between writing and the development of earliest river basin societies? (See also Map 2.1.)
- To what extent does the type of society (river basin, seafaring, etc.) seem to impact the development of writing in that region (date, type, purpose, etc.)?
- How has the decipherment, or lack thereof, of these scripts impacted scholars' understandings of the societies that produced them?

NAME/TYPE OF SOCIETY	WRITING FORM AND DATE OF EMERGENCE	TYPE OF WRITING AND PURPOSE	DATE AND MEANS OF DECIPHERMENT
Mesopotamia (Sumer)/Riverine (Tigris-Euphrates)	Cuneiform, 3200 BCE	Transitions from c. 1,000 pictographs to about 400 syllables (record keeping)	Deciphered in 19th century via Behistun/Beisitun inscription
Egypt (Old Kingdom)/ Riverine (Nile)	Hieroglyphs, 3100 BCE	Mixture of thousands of logograms and phonograms (religious)	Deciphered in early 19th century via trilingual Rosetta Stone (written in hieroglyphs, demotic script, and Greek)
Harappa/Riverine (Indus)	Indus Valley script, 2500 BCE	375–400 logographic signs (nomenclature and literature)	Undeciphered
Minoan/Mycenaean Greece/Seafaring micro-society	Phaistos Disk and Linear A (Minoan Crete); Linear B (Mycenaean, Crete and Greece) 1900–1300 BCE	Phaistos Disk (45 pictographic symbols in a spiral); Linear A (90 logographic-syllabic symbols); Linear B (roughly 75 syllabic symbols with some logographs) (record keeping)	Phaistos (undeciphered); Linear A (undeciphered); Linear B (deciphered in mid-20th century)
Shang Dynasty/ Riverine (Yellow River)	Oracle bone script, 14th–11th century BCE	Thousands of characters (divinatory purposes)	Deciphered in early 20th century
Maya/Central American rainforest	Mayan glyphs, 250 BCE	Mixture of logograms (numeric glyphs) and phonograms (around 85 phonetic glyphs), and hundreds of "emblem glyphs" (record of rulers and calendrical purposes)	Decipherment begun in 20th century
Vikings/Seafaring (Scandinavia)	Futhark (runic alphabet), 200 CE	24 alphabetic runes (ritual use; or to identify owner or craftsperson)	Deciphered in 19th century
Inca/Andean highlands	Quipu, 3000? BCE	Knotted cords, essentially a tally system (record keeping)	Deciphered
Easter Island/Seafaring micro-society	Rongorongo, 1500 CE	120 glyphs (calendrical or genealogical)	Undeciphered

Sources: Chris Scarre (ed.), *The Human Past: World Prehistory and the Development of Human Societies* (2005); Luigi Luca Cavalli-Sforza, *Genes, Peoples, and Languages,* translated by Mark Selestad from the original 1996 French publication (2000).

Literacy spread first among upper-class families. Most students started training when they were young. After mastering the copying of standard texts in hieratic cursive or hieroglyphs, students moved on to literary works. The upper classes prized literacy as proof of high intellectual achievement. When they died, they had their student textbooks placed alongside their corpses as evidence of their talents. The literati produced texts mainly in temples, where these works were also preserved. Writing in hieroglyphs and the composition of texts in hieratic, and later demotic, script continued without break in ancient Egypt for almost 3,000 years.

PROSPERITY AND THE DEMISE OF OLD KINGDOM EGYPT

Cultural achievements, agrarian surpluses, and urbanization ultimately led to higher standards of living and rising populations. Under pharaonic rule, Egypt enjoyed spectacular prosperity. Its population swelled from 350,000 in 4000 BCE to 1 million in 2500 BCE and nearly 5 million by 1500 BCE. However, expansion and decentralization eventually exposed the weaknesses of the Old and Middle Kingdom dynasties.

The state's success depended on administering resources skillfully, especially agricultural production and labor. Everyone, from the most powerful elite to the workers in the field, was part of the system. In principle, no one possessed private property; in practice, Egyptians treated land and tools as their own—but submitted to the intrusions of the state. The state's control over taxation, prices, and the distribution of goods required a large bureaucracy that maintained records, taxed the population, appeased the gods, organized a strong military, and aided local officials in regulating the Nile's floodwaters.

Royal power, and the Old Kingdom, collapsed with the death of Pepy II in 2184 BCE. Local magnates assumed hereditary control of the government in the provinces and treated lands previously controlled by the royal family as their personal property. An extended drought strained Egypt's extensive irrigation system, which could no longer water the lands that fed the region's million inhabitants. (See **Current Trends in World History: Climate Change at the End of the Third Millennium BCE in Egypt, Mesopotamia, and the Indus Valley**.) In this so-called First Intermediate Period (2181 to 2055 BCE), local leaders plunged into bloody regional struggles to keep the irrigation works functioning for their own communities until the century-long drought ended. Although the Old Kingdom declined, it established institutions and beliefs that endured and were revived several centuries later.

The Indus River Valley: A Parallel Culture

Cities emerged in the Indus River valley in South Asia in the third millennium BCE. The urban culture of the Indus area is called "Harappan" after the urban site of Harappa that arose on the banks of the Ravi River, a tributary of the Indus. Developments in the Indus basin reflected local tradition combined with strong influences from Iranian plateau peoples, as well as indirect influences from distant Mesopotamian cities. Villages appeared around 5000 BCE on the Iranian plateau along the Baluchistan Mountain foothills, to the west of the Indus. By the early third millennium BCE, frontier villages had spread eastward to the fertile banks of the Indus River and its tributaries. (See Map 2.5.) The river-basin settlements soon yielded agrarian surpluses that supported greater wealth, more trade with neighbors, and public works. Urbanites of the Indus region and the Harappan peoples began to fortify their cities and to undertake public works similar in scale to those in Mesopotamia, but strikingly different in function.

The Indus Valley ecology boasted many advantages—especially compared to the area near the Ganges River, the other great waterway of the South Asian landmass. The melting

Climate Change at the End of the Third Millennium BCE in Egypt, Mesopotamia, and the Indus Valley

During the long third millennium BCE, the first urban centers in Egypt, Mesopotamia, Iran, central Asia, and South Asia flourished and grew in complexity and wealth in a wet and cool climate. This smooth development was sharply if not universally interrupted beginning around 2200 BCE. Both archaeological and written records agree that across Afro-Eurasia, most of the urban, rural, and pastoral societies underwent radical change. Those watered by major rivers were selectively destabilized, while the settled communities on the highland plateaus virtually disappeared. After a brief hiatus, some recovered, completely reorganized and used new technologies to manage agriculture and water. The causes of this radical change have been the focus of much interest.

After four decades of research by climate specialists working together with archaeologists, a consensus has emerged that climate change toward a warmer and drier environment contributed to this disruption. Whether this was caused solely by human activity, in particular agriculture on a large scale, or was also related to cosmic causes such as the rotation of the earth's axis away from the sun, is still a hotly debated topic. It was likely a combination of factors.

The urban centers dependent on the three major river systems in Egypt, Mesopotamia, and the Indus Valley, all experienced disruption. In Egypt, the hieroglyphic inscriptions tell us that the Nile no longer flooded over its banks to replenish the fields with fresh soil and with water for crops. Social and political chaos followed for more than a century. In southern Mesopotamia, the deeply down-cut rivers changed course, disrupting settlement patterns and taking fields out of cultivation. Other fields were poisoned by salts brought on through overcultivation and irrigation without fallow periods. Fierce competition for water and land put pressure on the central authority. To the east and west, transhumant pastoralists, faced with shrinking pasture for their flocks, pressed in on the river valleys, disrupting the already challenged social and political structure of the densely urban centers.

In northern Mesopotamia, the responses to the challenges of aridity were more varied. Some centers were able to weather the crisis by changing strategies of food production and distribution. Some fell victim to intraregional warfare, while others, on the rainfall margin, were abandoned. When the region was settled again, society was differently organized. Population did not drastically decrease, but rather it distributed across the landscape more evenly in smaller settlements that required less water and food. It appears that a similar solution was found by communities to the east on the Iranian plateau, where the inhabitants of the huge urban center of Shahr i Sokhta abruptly left the city and settled in small communities across the oasis landscape.

The solutions found by people living in the cities of the Indus Valley also varied. Some cities, like Harappa, saw their population decrease rapidly. It seems that the bed of the river shifted, threatening the settlement and its hinterland. Mohenjo Daro, on the other hand, continued to be occupied for another several centuries, although the large civic structures fell out of use, replaced by more modest structures. And to the south, on the Gujarat Peninsula,

snows in the Himalayas watered the semitropical Indus Valley, ensuring flourishing vegetation, plus the region did not suffer the yearly monsoon downpours that flooded the Ganges plain. The expansion of agriculture in the Indus basin, as in Mesopotamia, Egypt, and China, depended on the river's annual floods to replenish the soil and avert droughts. From June to September, the rivers inundated the plain. Once the waters receded, farmers planted wheat and barley, harvesting the crops the next spring. Villagers also improved their tools of cultivation. Researchers have found evidence of furrows, probably made by plowing, that date to around 2600 BCE. These developments suggest that, as in Mesopotamia and Egypt, farmers were cultivating harvests that yielded a surplus that allowed many inhabitants to specialize in other activities.

In time, rural wealth produced urban splendor. More abundant harvests, now stored in large granaries, brought migrants into the area and supported expanding populations. By 2500 BCE cities began to replace villages throughout the Indus River valley, and within a few generations towering granaries marked the urban skyline. Harappa and Mohenjo Daro, the two largest cities, each covered a little less than half a square mile and may have housed 35,000 residents.

population and the number of settlements increased. They abandoned wheat as a crop, instead cultivating a kind of drought-enduring millet that originated in West Africa. Apparently conditions there became even more hospitable, allowing farming and fishing communities to flourish well into the second millennium BCE.

The evidence for this widespread phenomenon of climate change at the end of the third millennium BCE is complex and contradictory. This is not surprising, because every culture and each community naturally had an individual response to environmental and other challenges. Those with perennial sources of freshwater were less threatened than those in marginal zones where only a slight decrease in rainfall can mean failed crops and herds. As important, certain types of social and political institutions were resilient and introduced innovations that allowed them to adapt, while others were too rigid or short-sighted to find local solutions. A feature of human culture is its remarkable ability to adapt rapidly. When faced with challenges, resilience, creativity, and ingenuity lead to cultural innovation and change. This is what we can see, even in our own times, during the period of environmental stress.

Millet This hardy grain, cultivated for its resistance to drought, persists in the desert environment of present-day western Pakistan.

QUESTIONS FOR ANALYSIS

- What technological innovations resulted from the drought in the Indus Valley? Why?

- Imagine that the climate during the third millennium BCE had not changed. How do you think this might have affected the development of ancient Egypt?

- How has our understanding of global climate change affected the way we study prehistory?

Explore Further

Wolfgang Behringer, *A Cultural History of Climate* (2010).

Barbara Bell, "The Dark Ages in Ancient History. 1. The First Dark Age in Egypt," *American Journal of Archaeology*, vol. 75, no. 1 (January 1971), pp. 1–26.

Max Weiss et al., "The Genesis and Collapse of Third Millennium North Mesopotamian Civilization," *Science*, New Series, vol. 261, no. 5124 (August 20, 1993), pp. 995–1004.

Harappan cities sprawled across a vast floodplain covering 500,000 square miles—two or three times the Mesopotamian cultural zone. At the height of their development, the Harappan peoples reached the edge of the Indus ecological system and encountered the cultures of northern Afghanistan, the inhabitants of the desert frontier, the nomadic hunter-gatherers to the east, and the traders to the west. Although scholars know less about Harappan society than about Mesopotamia or Ancient Egypt, what we know about their urban culture and trade routes is impressive.

HARAPPAN CITY LIFE AND WRITING

The well-planned layout of Harappan cities and towns included a fortified citadel housing public facilities alongside a large residential area. The main street running through the city had covered drainage on both sides, with house gates and doors opening onto back alleys. Citadels were likely centers of political and ritual activities. At the center of the citadel of Mohenjo Daro was the famous great bath. The location, size, and quality of

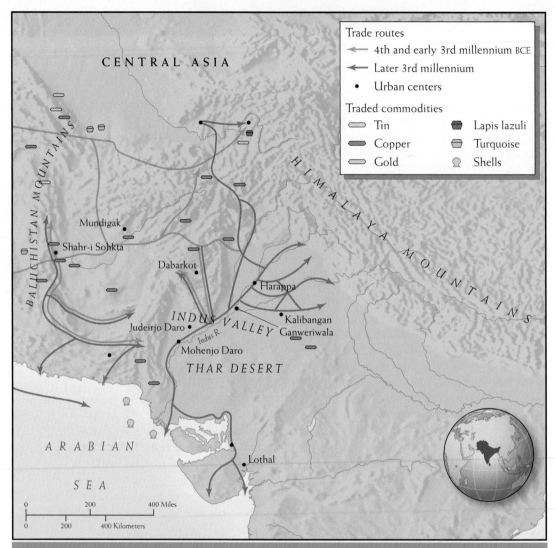

CENTRAL ASIA

BALUCHISTAN MOUNTAINS

HIMALAYA MOUNTAINS

Mundigak

Shahr-i Sohkta

Dabarkot

Harappa

Kalibangan

Ganweriwala

Judeirjo Daro

INDUS VALLEY

Indus R.

Mohenjo Daro

THAR DESERT

ARABIAN

SEA

Lothal

Trade routes

⟵ 4th and early 3rd millennium BCE

⟵ Later 3rd millennium

• Urban centers

Traded commodities

▭ Tin ⬡ Lapis lazuli

▭ Copper ⬡ Turquoise

▭ Gold ⚱ Shells

0   200   400 Miles

0   200   400 Kilometers

MAP 2.5 | The Indus River Valley in the Third Millennium BCE

Historians know less about the urban society of the Indus Valley in the third millennium BCE than they do about its contemporaries in Mesopotamia and Egypt. Recent scholarship has even suggested the importance of a second river, the Chagar-Hakra (Saraswati) to the east of the Indus, in this region. Archaeological evidence gives insight into this urban context.

• Where were cities concentrated in the Indus Valley?

• How did the region's environment shape urban development?

• What functions do you think outposts such as Lothal played in Harappan society?

the bath's steps, mortar and bitumen sealing, and drainage channel all suggest that the structure was used for public bathing rituals.

The Harappans used brick extensively—in houses for notables, city walls, and underground water drainage systems. Workers used large ovens to manufacture the durable construction materials, which the Harappans laid so skillfully that basic structures remain intact to this day. A well-built house had private bathrooms, showers, and toilets that drained into municipal sewers, also made of bricks. Houses in small towns and villages were made of less durable and less costly sun-baked bricks.

Many of the remains of Harappan culture lie buried under deep silt deposits accumulated over thousands of years of heavy flooding. Consequently, we know less about it than about

Mohenjo Daro Mohenjo Daro, the "mound of dead," is a large urban site of the Harappan culture. The view of the city demonstrates a neat layout of houses and civic facilities such as sewer draining.

other contemporary cultures of Afro-Eurasia. Additionally, scholars are still working to identify the Indus peoples' language and decipher the script of about 400 symbols. Although a ten-glyph-long public inscription has been found at the Harappan site of Dholavira, most of what remains of the Indus Valley script appears on a thousand or more stamp seals and small plaques excavated from the region, which may represent the names and titles of individuals rather than complete sentences. Moreover, because the Harappans did not produce King Lists (as the Mesopotamians and Egyptians did)—and may not even have had kings—scholars cannot chart a Harappan political history by tracing the rise and fall of dynasties and kingdoms. Relying only on fragmentary archaeological evidence, scholars have been unable to draw the rich portraits of Harappan life that they have supplied for the Mesopotamians and the Egyptians.

TRADE

The Harappans engaged in trade along the Indus River, through the mountain passes to the Iranian plateau, and along the coast of the Arabian Sea as far as the Persian Gulf and Mesopotamia. They traded copper, flint, shells, and ivory, as well as pottery, flint blades, and jewelry created by their craftworkers, in exchange for gold, silver, gemstones, and textiles. Carnelian, a precious red stone, was a local resource, but lapis lazuli had to come from what is now northern Afghanistan. Some of the Harappan trading towns nestled in remote but strategically important places. Consider Lothal, a well-fortified port at the head of the Gulf of Khambhat (Cambay). Although distant from the center of Harappan society, it provided vital access to the sea and to valuable raw materials. Its many workshops processed precious stones, both local and foreign. Because the demand for gemstones and metals was high on the Iranian plateau and in Mesopotamia, control of their extraction and trade was essential to maintaining the Harappans' economic power. So the Harappans built fortifications and settlements near sources of carnelian and copper mines.

Through a complex and vibrant trading system, the Harappans maintained access to mineral and agrarian resources. To facilitate trade, rulers relied not just on Harappan script but also on a system of weights and measures that they devised and standardized. Archaeologists have found Harappan seals, used to stamp commodities with the names of their owners or the nature of the goods, at sites as far away as the Persian Gulf, Mesopotamia, and the Iranian plateau.

COMPARISON

TRACE and **ANALYZE** the trade connections stretching from Mesopotamia to the Indus River Valley societies.

Dholavira inscription This is an artist's rendering of the 10 glyph-long inscription from Dholavira, an exceptional specimen of Indus Valley script both for its size, length, and inscription in stone. While Indus Valley script is still undeciphered, the excavator of this inscription has suggested it might record the name of a ruler or of the town, or even an incantation of some sort. Most examples of Indus Valley script are much briefer and appear on small seal stones along with images of animals and human figures.

The general uniformity in Harappan sites suggests a centralized and structured state. Unlike the Mesopotamians and the Egyptians, however, the Harappans apparently built neither palaces nor grand royal tombs. What the Indus River people show us is how much the urbanized parts of the world were diverging from one another, even as they borrowed from and imitated their neighbors.

The Yellow and Yangzi River Basins: East Asia

Like the Mesopotamians, Egyptians, and Harappans, East Asian peoples clustered in river basins. Their settlements along the Yellow River in the north and the Yangzi River to the south became the foundation of the future Chinese state. By 5000 BCE, both millet in the north and rice in the south were under widespread cultivation.

Yet in the following three millennia (when Mesopotamia, Egypt, and the Indus Valley were creating complex, city-based cultures), the Chinese moved slowly toward urbanization. (See Map 2.6.) Like the other regions' waterways, the Yellow and Yangzi rivers had annual floods and extensive floodplains suitable for producing high agricultural yields and supporting dense populations. In China, however, the evolution of hydraulic works, big cities, priestly and bureaucratic classes, and a new writing system took longer. A lack of easily domesticated animals and plants contributed to the different developmental path in China, as did geographic barriers. The Himalayan Mountains and the Taklamakan and Gobi deserts prevented large-scale migrations between East Asia and central Asia and hindered the diffusion of cultural breakthroughs occurring elsewhere in Afro-Eurasia.

FROM YANGSHAO TO LONGSHAN CULTURE

China's classical histories have claimed that China's cultural traditions originated in the Central Plains of the Yellow River basin and spread outward to less developed regions inside and even beyond mainland China. These histories place the beginnings of Chinese culture at the Xia dynasty, dating from 2200 BCE. Archaeological studies of river-basin environments in East Asia tell a different story, however. Whether or not the Xia existed as a historical dynasty, archaeological evidence suggests our study of the Yellow River basin and Yangzi delta should begin earlier—in the two millennia from 4000 to 2000 BCE.

China in 4000 BCE was very different geographically and culturally from what it is today. A warmer and moister climate divided its vast landmass into distinctive regions. Recent archaeological research records that at least eight distinct regional cultures appeared between 4000 and 2000 BCE, and only as these communities interacted did their institutions and ways of life come together to create a unified Chinese culture.

Although it was geographically divided, China was never devoid of outside influences. Some travelers did arrive via the ocean, but more came via the Mongolian steppe, through which nomads introduced important technologies such as metalworks. Nomads were drawn to the agricultural settlements (as they were in Mesopotamia), and they brought innovations, such as bronze and other goods, from the west. Through trade and migration, nomadic cultures and technologies filtered from the steppes to settled communities on the rivers.

MAP 2.6 | River Basin Peoples in East Asia, 5000–2000 BCE

Complex agricultural societies emerged in East Asia during the third millennium BCE.

- What were the regional cultures that flourished here during this time?
- What are the major geographic differences between the northern and southern regions of China in this period?
- Based on geographic differences among the areas, how were these cultures different, and how were they similar?

The major divide in China was between the northern Yellow and more centrally located Yangzi river basins. Not only did these two regions rely on different crops—millet in the north and rice to the south—but they built their houses differently, buried their dead in different ways, and produced distinctive pottery styles. The best known of the early cultures developed along the Yellow River and in the Central Plains area and is known as the Yangshao culture.

Yangshao villages typically covered ten to fourteen acres and were composed of houses erected around a central square. Villagers had to move frequently because they practiced slash-and-burn agriculture. Once having exhausted the soil, residents picked up their

Yangshao Bowl with Dancing Figures, c. 5000–1700 BCE The Yangshao, also referred to as the "painted pottery" culture, produced gray or red pottery painted with black geometric designs and occasionally with pictures of fish or human faces and figures. Because the potter's wheel was unknown at the time, the vessels were probably fashioned with strips of clay.

belongings, moved to new lands, and constructed new villages. Their lives were hard. Excavated cemeteries reveal that nearly 20 percent of the burials were of children fifteen years and younger; only a little more than half of those buried lived past the age of forty.

Around 3000 BCE the Yangshao culture gave way to the Longshan culture, which had an even larger geographical scope and would provide some of the cultural foundations for the first strong states that emerged in the Central Plains. Longshan flourished from 3000 BCE to 2000 BCE, and had its center in Shandong Province. Although the Longshan way of life first took form in coastal and southern China, outside the Central Plains, it moved quickly into this hub of economic and political activity. Proof of its widespread cultural influence can be seen from the appearance of a unique style of black pottery, stretching all the way from Manchuria in the north through the Central Plains to the coast and beyond to the island of Taiwan.

The Longshan people likely migrated in waves from the peripheries of East Asia to the eastern China seashore. Their achievements, compared to those of the Yangshao, suggest marked development between 5000 and 2000 BCE. Several independent regional cultures in northern and southern China began to produce similar pottery and tools and to plant the same crops, probably reflecting contact. They did not yet produce city-states, but agriculture and small settlements flourished in the increasingly populated Yellow River valley.

Some of the hallmarks of early urban life are evident in the archaeological remains. Longshan communities built defensive walls for protection and dug wells to supply water. They buried their dead in cemeteries outside their villages. Of several thousand graves uncovered in southern Shanxi province, the largest ones contain ritual pottery vessels, wooden musical instruments, copper bells, and painted murals. Shamans performed rituals using jade axes. Jade quarrying in particular indicated technical sophistication, as skilled craftworkers incised jade tablets with powerful expressions of ritual and military authority. The threat of organized violence among Longshan villages was real. Discoveries at one Longshan site revealed a household whose members were scalped. At this same site, attackers filled the water wells with five layers of human skeletons, some decapitated. Clearly, the villages' defensive walls were essential.

As communities became more centralized, contact between regions increased. Links between northern and southern China arose when Longshan peoples began to migrate along the East Asian coast to Taiwan and the Pearl River delta in the far south. Similarities in artifacts found along the coast and at Longshan sites in northern China, such as the form and decoration of pottery and jade items, also point to a shared sphere of culture and trade.

Archaeologists also have found evidence of short-lived political organizations. Although they were nothing like the dynastic systems in Egypt, Mesopotamia, and the Indus Valley, they were wealthy—if localized—polities. They constituted what scholars call the era of Ten Thousand States (*Wan'guo*). One of them, the Liangzhu, has drawn particular interest for its remarkable jade objects and its sophisticated farming techniques. The Liangzhu grew rice and fruits and domesticated water buffalo, pigs, dogs, and sheep. Archaeologists have discovered the remains of net sinkers, wooden floats, and wooden paddles, which demonstrate a familiarity with water-craft and fishing. Artisans produced a black pottery from soft paste thrown on a wheel, and like the Long-shan they created ritual objects from several variet-ies of jade. Animal masks and bird designs adorned many pieces, revealing a shared cosmology that in-formed the rituals of the Liangzhu elite.

In the late third millennium BCE, a long drought hit China (as it did Egypt, Mesopotamia, and India). Although the climate change limited progress and forced migrations to more dependable habitats, the Chinese recovered early in the second millennium BCE. Now they created elaborate agrarian systems along the Yellow and Yangzi rivers that were similar to earlier irrigation systems along the Euphrates, Indus, and Nile. Extensive trading networks and a stratified social hierarchy emerged; like the other river-basin complexes of Asia and North Africa, China became a centralized polity. Here, too, a powerful monarchy eventually united the independent communities. But what developed in China was a social and political system that emphasized an idealized past and a tradi-tion represented by sage-kings, which later ages emu-lated. In this and other ways, China diverged from the rest of Afro-Eurasia.

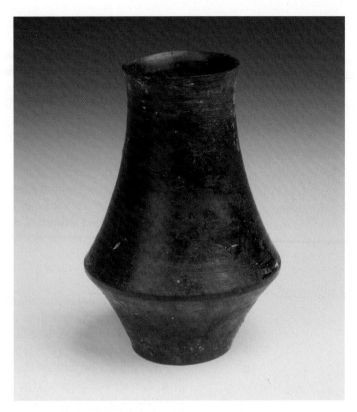

Longshan Beaker, c. 2500 BCE Longshan has been called the "black pottery" culture, and its exquisite black pottery was not painted but rather decorated with rings, either raised or grooved. Longshan culture was more advanced than the Yangshao culture, and its distinctive pottery was likely formed on a potter's wheel.

Life Outside the River Basins

In 3500 BCE, the vast majority of humans lived outside of the complex cities that emerged in parts of Afro-Eurasia. At the other end of the spectrum, many peoples continued to live as hunters and gatherers, or in small agricultural villages or nomadic groups. In between were worlds such as those in the Aegean, Anatolia, Europe, and parts of China, where towns emerged and agriculture advanced, but not with the leaps and bounds of the great river-basin civilizations.

Some cultures outside the river basins—in the Aegean, Anatolia, and in Europe—had a distinctive warrior-based ethos, such that the top tiers of the social ladder held chiefs and military men instead of priests and scribes. In Europe and Anatolia especially, weaponry rather than writing, forts rather than palaces, and conquest rather than commerce dominated everyday life. Settlements in the Americas and sub-Saharan Africa were smaller and remained based around agriculture. Here, too, the inhabitants moved beyond stone implements and hunting and gathering, but they remained more egalitarian than river basin peoples.

AEGEAN WORLDS

Contact with Egypt and Mesopotamia affected the worlds of the Aegean Sea (the part of the Mediterranean Sea between the Greek Peloponnese and Anatolia), but it did not transform them. Geography stood in the way of significant urban development on the mountain-ous islands of the Aegean, on the Anatolian plateau, and in Europe. Even though people from Anatolia, Greece, and the Levant had populated the Aegean islands in the sixth

COMPARISON

COMPARE early urbaniza-tion with the ways of life in small villages and among pastoral nomads.

millennium BCE, their small villages, of 100 inhabitants or fewer, endured for 2,000 years before becoming more complex. On mainland Greece and on the Cycladic islands in the Aegean, fortified settlements housed local rulers who controlled a small area of agriculturally productive countryside. Metallurgy developed in both the island of Crete and the Cyclades. There is evidence of more formal administration and organizations in some communities by 2500 BCE, but the norm was scattered settlements separated by natural obstacles. By the early third millennium BCE, Crete had made occasional contact with Egypt and the coastal towns of the Levant, encountering new ideas, technologies, and materials as foreigners arrived on its shores. People coming by ship from the coasts of Anatolia and the Levant, as well as from Egypt, traded stone vessels and other luxury objects for the island's abundant copper. Graves of Aegean elites, such as those at Knossos on Crete, with their gold jewelry and other exotic objects, show that the elites did not reject the niceties of cultured life, but they knew that their power rested as much on their rugged landscape's resources as on self-defense and trade with others.

ANATOLIA

The highland plateau of Anatolia (in the region of modern-day Turkey) shows clear evidence of regional cultures focused on the control of trade routes and mining outposts. True cities did not develop here until the third millennium BCE, and even then they were not the sprawling population centers typical of the Mesopotamian plain. Instead, small communities emerged around fortified citadels housing local rulers who competed with one another. Two impressively fortified centers were Horoz Tepe and Alaça Hüyük, which have yielded more than a dozen graves—apparently royal—full of gold jewelry, ceremonial standards, and elaborate weapons. Similarly, the settlement at Troy was characterized by monumental stone gateways, stone-paved ramps, and high-status graves filled with gold and silver objects, vessels, jewelry, and other artifacts. Parallel grave finds on Crete, the Greek mainland, and as far away as Ur indicate that Troy participated in the trading system linking the Aegean and Southwest Asian worlds. At the same time, Troy faced predatory neighbors and pirates who attacked from the sea—an observation that explains its impressive fortifications.

EUROPE: THE WESTERN FRONTIER

At the western reaches of the Eurasian landmass was a region featuring cooler climates with smaller population densities. Its peoples—forerunners of present-day Europeans—began to make objects out of metal, formed permanent settlements, and started to create complex societies. Here, hierarchies began to undermine egalitarian ways. Yet, as in the Aegean worlds, population density and social complexity had limits.

More than in the Mediterranean or Anatolia, warfare dominated social development in Europe. Two contributing factors were the persistent fragmentation of the region's peoples and the type of agrarian development they pursued. The introduction of the plow and the clearing of woodlands expanded agriculture. Flint mining at an industrial level slashed the cost and increased the availability of raw materials needed to make tools for clearing forested lands and tilling them into arable fields. Compared to the river-basin societies, Europe was a wild frontier where violent conflicts over resources were common.

By 3500 BCE the more developed agrarian peoples had combined into large communities, constructing impressive monuments that remain visible today. In western Europe, large ceremonial centers shared the same model: enormous shaped stones, some weighing several tons each, set in common patterns—in alleyways, troughs, or circles—known as *megalithic* ("great stone") constructions. These daunting projects required cooperative planning and work. In the British Isles, where such developments occurred later, the

MAP 2.7 | Settlements on the Margins: The Eastern Mediterranean and Europe, 5000–2000 BCE

Urban societies in Southwest Asia had profound influences on peripheral societies.

- What three peripheral worlds did the urban societies of Southwest Asia influence?
- In what ways did the spread of flint and copper tools and weapons transform Aegean and European societies?
- How did agriculture spread from Southwest Asia to these worlds?

famous megalithic complexes at Avebury and Stonehenge probably reached their highest stages of development just before 2000 BCE.

By 2000 BCE, the whole of the northern European plain came to share a common material culture based on agriculture, the herding of cattle for meat and milk, the use of the plough, and the use of wheeled vehicles and metal tools and weapons, mainly of copper. Increasing communication, exchange, and mobility among the European communities led to increasing wealth but also sparked organized warfare over frontier lands and valuable resources. In an ironic twist, the integration of local communities led to greater friction and produced regional social stratification. The violent men who now protected their communities received ceremonial burials complete with their own drinking cups and weapons. Archaeologists have found these warrior burials in a swath of European lands extending from present-day France and Switzerland to present-day central Russia.

Stonehenge This spectacular site, located in the Salisbury Plain in Wiltshire in southwestern England, is one of several such megalithic structures found in the region. Constructed by many generations of builders, the arrangement of the large stone uprights enabled people to determine precise times in the year through the position of the sun. Events such as the spring and autumn equinoxes were connected with agricultural and religious activities.

Because the agricultural communities now were producing surpluses that they could store, residents had to defend their land and resources from encroaching neighbors.

An aggressive culture was taking shape based on violent confrontations between adult males organized in "tribal" groups. War cultures arose in all western European societies. Armed groups carried bell-shaped drinking cups across Europe, using them to swig beer and mead distilled from grains, honey, herbs, and nuts.

Warfare had the effect of accentuating the borrowing among the region's competing peoples. The violent struggles and emerging kinship groups fueled a massive demand for weapons, alcohol, and horses. Warrior elites borrowed from Anatolia the technique of combining copper with tin to produce harder-edged weapons made of the alloy bronze. Soon smiths were producing them in bulk—as evidenced by hoards of copper and bronze tools and weapons from the period found in central Europe. Traders used the rivers of central and northern Europe to exchange their prized metal products, creating one of the first commercial networks that covered the landmass.

THE AMERICAS

In the Americas, techniques of food production and storage, transportation, and communication restricted the surpluses for feeding those who did not work the land. Thus these communities did not grow in size and complexity. For example, in the Chicama Valley of Peru, which opens onto the Pacific Ocean, people still nestled in small coastal villages to fish, gather shellfish, hunt, and grow beans, chili peppers, and cotton (to make twined textiles, which they dyed with wild indigo). By around 3500 BCE, these fishermen abandoned their cane and adobe homes for sturdier houses, half underground, on streets lined with cobblestones.

Hundreds if not thousands of such villages dotted the seashores and riverbanks of the Americas. Some made the technological breakthroughs required to produce pottery; others devised irrigation systems and water sluices in areas where floods occurred. Some even began to send their fish catches inland in return for agricultural produce. Ceremonial structures highlighted communal devotion and homage to deities, and rituals to celebrate birth, death, and the memory of ancestors.

In the Americas, the largest population center was in the valley of Tehuacán (near modern-day Mexico City). Here the domestication of corn created a food source that enabled people to migrate from caves to a cluster of pit-house villages that supported a growing population. By 3500 BCE the valley held nothing resembling a large city. People lived in clusters of interdependent villages, especially on the lakeshores: here was a case of high population density, but not urbanization.

SUB-SAHARAN AFRICA

The same pattern occurred in sub-Saharan Africa, where the population grew but did not concentrate in urban communities. About 12,000 years ago, when rainfall and temperatures increased, small encampments of hunting, gathering, and fishing communities congregated around the large lakes and rivers flowing through the region that would later become the Sahara Desert. Large game animals roamed, posing a threat but also providing a source of food. Over the millennia, in the wetter and more temperate locations of this vast region—particularly the upland mountains and their foothills—permanent villages emerged.

As the Sahara region became drier, people moved to the desert's edges, to areas along the Niger River and the Sudan. Here they grew yams, oil palms, and plantains. In the savannah lands that stretched all the way from the Atlantic Ocean in West Africa to the Nile River basin in present-day Sudan, settlers grew grains such as millet and sorghum, which spread from their places of origin to areas along the lands surrounding the Niger River basin. Residents constructed stone dwellings and dug underground wells and food storage areas. As an increasing population strained resources, groups migrated south toward the Congo River and east toward Lake Nyanza, where they established new farms and villages. Although population centers were often hundreds or thousands of miles apart and were smaller than the urban centers in Egypt and Mesopotamia, the widespread use of the same pottery style, with rounded bottoms and wavy decoration, suggests that they maintained trading and cultural contacts. In these respects sub-Saharan Africa matched the ways of life in Europe and the Americas.

Conclusion

Over the fourth and third millennia BCE, the world's social landscape changed in significant ways. In a few key locations, where giant rivers irrigated fertile lands, complex human cultures began to emerge. These areas experienced all the advantages and difficulties of expanding populations: occupational specialization; social hierarchy; rising standards of living; sophisticated systems of art and science; and centralized production and distribution of food, clothing, and other goods. Ceremonial sites and trading crossroads became cities that developed centralized religious and political systems. As scribes, priests, and rulers labored to keep complex societies together, social distinctions within the city (including the roles of men and women) and the differences between country folk and city dwellers sharpened.

Although river-basin cultures shared basic features, each one's evolution followed a distinctive path. Where there was a single river—the Nile or the Indus—the agrarian hinterlands that fed cities lay along the banks of the waterway. In these areas cities were small; thus the Egyptian and Harappan worlds enjoyed more political stability and less rivalry. In contrast, cities in the immense floodplain of the Tigris and Euphrates needed large hinterlands to sustain their populations. Because of their growing power and need for resources, Mesopotamian cities vied for preeminence, and their competition often became violent.

In most areas of the world, however, people still lived in simple, egalitarian societies based on hunting, gathering, and basic agriculture—as in the Americas and sub-Saharan Africa. In Anatolia, Europe, and parts of China, regional cultures emerged as agriculture advanced and populations grew. Some of them, as in the Aegean and Europe, forged warrior societies. Beyond these frontiers, farmers and nomads survived as they had for many centuries. Thriving trading networks connected many, but not all, of these regions to one another.

Changes in climate affected everyone and could slow or even reverse development. How—and whether—cultures adapted depended on local circumstances. As the next chapter will show, the human agents of change often came from the fringes of larger settlements and urban areas.

After You Read This Chapter

Go to INQUIZITIVE to see what you've learned—and learn what you've missed—with personalized feedback along the way.

FOCUS ON: *Societies in the Great River Basins*

MESOPOTAMIA

- Peoples living along the Tigris River and Euphrates River control floodwaters and refine irrigation techniques.

- Mesopotamians establish the world's first large cities, featuring powerful rulers, social hierarchies, and monumental architecture.

- Mesopotamia is the birthplace of writing.

EGYPT

- Peoples of Egypt use Nile River waters to irrigate their lands and create a bountiful agriculture.

- Egyptian rulers known as pharaohs unify their territory, establish a powerful state, and develop a vibrant economy.

- Egyptians build magnificent burial chambers (pyramids) and worship a pantheon of gods.

INDUS VALLEY

- South Asian peoples harness the Indus River and create cities like Harappa and Mohenjo Daro.

EAST ASIA

- Peoples dwelling in the basins of the Yellow River and the Yangzi River control the waters' flow and expand agriculture.

- These people develop elaborate cultures, which scholars later label Yangshao and Longshan, respectively.

CHRONOLOGY

SOUTHWEST ASIA AND EGYPT	Earliest Sumerian cities appear in Mesopotamia ◆ 3500 BCE	
	First Dynasty emerges in Egypt 3100 BCE ◆	
SOUTH ASIA		
EAST ASIA	Yangshao culture thrives along Yellow River 4000–3000 BCE	
EUROPE AND THE MEDITERRANEAN		
THE AMERICAS	Chicama Valley culture thrives on Pacific coast of South America ◆ 3500 BCE	
	Tehuacán Valley in Mexico thrives ◆ 3500 BCE	
INNER AND CENTRAL ASIA	Dense village life along many lakes and rivers ◆ 3500 BCE	
	Spread of nomadic pastoralism begins ◆ 3500 BCE	

4000 BCE   **3000 BCE**

- **Thinking about River-Basin Civilizations and the Environment** Human interaction with the environment—including climate, geography, the characteristics of the rivers, and the continued cultivation of crops and herds—played a significant role in shaping each early river-basin civilization. Describe ways that these environmental factors influenced the unique characteristics of each river basin civilization.

- **Thinking about Exchange Networks Among Early River-Basin Civilizations** Carnelian from the Indus region buried in elite tombs of Egypt; lapis lazuli from the region of modern-day Afghanistan on necklaces adorning Harappan necks; shell from the Indus floodplain inlaid on Mesopotamian grave goods—these examples provide evidence of how trade in raw materials bound river-basin civilizations together in the third millennium BCE. What routes might such goods have traveled? What does this exchange of commodities suggest about other types of exchange that may have been taking place between these river basin societies?

- **Thinking about Changing Power Relationships in River-Basin Civilizations** From 3500–2000 BCE, as civilizations developed in the river basins of Mesopotamia, Egypt, South Asia, and East Asia, more intensive cultivation brought agricultural surpluses that ushered in a wide range of impacts. Explain, with examples from each of the river-basin civilizations, how food surpluses led to job specialization, wealth accumulation, and the resulting social hierarchies.

1. Where and how did **river basins** contribute directly to the emergence of cities, from 3500–2000 BCE? What were some similarities and differences in irrigation techniques among these early civilizations?

2. In what ways did cities in Mesopotamia, Egypt, and the Indus Valley differ from pastoral nomadic communities? How did the development of these cities introduce a hitherto unknown **urban-rural divide**?

3. What are some similarities and differences among the **cities** and **city-states** that developed in Mesopotamia, Egypt, and the Indus Valley? Compare, for example, developments in **social hierarchies**, religion, and the production of monumental architecture (including temples and palaces).

4. Compare technological developments, including writing (**scribes**) and other technologies (such as the use of **bronze** and jade), in the various river-basin societies. What might account for the regional variations in technologies?

5. How did long-distance trade influence the political, economic, and technological development of urban societies in Egypt, Mesopotamia, and the Indus Valley?

6. Contrast the agricultural developments in East Asia with those taking place in Mesopotamia, Egypt, and the Indus Valley at about the same time (3500–2000 BCE).

7. Identify shared characteristics of settlements in Europe, Anatolia, the Aegean, the Americas, and Africa between 5000 and 2000 BCE.

Old Kingdom Egypt 2649–2152 BCE

Sargon's Akkadian territorial state in Mesopotamia 2334–2103 BCE

Cities appear in Indus Valley 2500 BCE

Longshan Culture flourishes in Yellow River Valley 4000–2000 BCE

Fortified villages in the Aegean 2500 BCE

Stonehenge constructed 2000 BCE

2000 BCE

1000 BCE

Competing Perspectives

Early Writing

As agricultural production increased and labor became more specialized in river-basin societies, scribes developed and mastered elaborate writing systems that recorded everything from economic transactions to religious ideas. The excerpts provided here demonstrate several unique types of early writing, as well as the variety of ways it was used.

From Mesopotamia, where the world's first writing system developed (ca. 3200 BCE), one Sumerian myth attributes the invention of cuneiform writing to Enmerkar, the Lord of Kulaba, who did not trust his messenger's memory to deliver a complicated message to the leader of the far-off land of Aratta. Although writing appeared in Egypt just 100 years after it did in Mesopotamia, the hieroglyphs preserved in the pyramid of Pharaoh Unas (2375–2345 BCE) represent the earliest religious writing from Egypt. These pyramid texts, such as the example included here, contain a range of rituals to facilitate the pharoah's passage into the afterlife.

Writing systems gradually emerged in other areas as well. As early as 2500 BCE, Indus Valley scribes made notations — usually pictorial emblems and five to six signs—on steatite seal stamps, pots, and even jewelry. The seal stamps shown here offer an example of this still undeciphered script. In China, marks on pots produced by Yangshao peoples (ca. 5000 BCE) may have been used for record-keeping, but the earliest full writing system did not appear until the Shang Dynasty (1600-1045 BCE). Shang kings used oracle bone predictions—etched on animal bones (like the one pictured here), which were heated until they cracked—to divine the answers to questions about the will of their ancestors and the weather. The earliest deciphered Greek writing, known as Linear B, did not appear until around 1450 BCE among the Mycenaeans, although other forms of Greek writing developed several hundred years earlier on Crete among the Minoans. The example here comes from the Mycenaean palace at Pylos, on mainland Greece.

PRIMARY SOURCE 2.1

Sumerian Origins of Writing

His speech was substantial, and its contents extensive. The messenger, whose mouth was heavy, was not able to repeat it. Because the messenger, whose mouth was tired, was not able to repeat it, the lord of Kulaba patted some clay and wrote the message as if on a tablet. Formerly, the writing of messages on clay was not established. Now, under that sun and on that day, it was indeed so. The lord of Kulaba inscribed the message like a tablet. It was just like that. The messenger was like a bird, flapping its wings; he raged forth like a wolf following a kid. He traversed five mountains, six mountains, seven mountains. He lifted his eyes as he approached Aratta. He stepped joyfully into the courtyard of Aratta, he made known the authority of his king. Openly he spoke out the words in his heart. The messenger transmitted the message to the lord of Aratta:

> *"Your father, my master, has sent me to you; the lord of Unug, the lord of Kulaba, has sent me to you." "What is it to me what your master has spoken? What is it to me what he has said?"*
>
> *"This is what my master has spoken, this is what he has said. My king is like a huge mes̃ tree, . . . son of Enlil; this tree has grown high, uniting heaven and earth; its crown reaches heaven, its trunk is set upon the earth. He who is made to shine forth in lordship and kingship, Enmerkar, the son of Utu,*

has given me a clay tablet. O lord of Aratta, after you have examined the clay tablet, after you have learned the content of the message, say whatever you will say to me, and I shall announce that message in the shrine E-ana as glad tidings to the scion of him with the glistening beard . . . .

After he had spoken thus to him, the lord of Aratta received his kiln-fired tablet from the messenger. The lord of Aratta looked at the tablet. The transmitted message was just nails, and his brow expressed anger. The lord of Aratta looked at his kiln-fired tablet. At that moment, the lord worthy of the crown of lordship, the son of Enlil, the god Iškur, thundering in heaven and earth, caused a raging storm, a great lion, in . . . He was making the mountains quake . . . , he was convulsing the mountain range . . . ; the awesome radiance . . . of his breast; he caused the mountain range to raise its voice in joy. (lines 500–551)

Source: J. A. Black, G. Cunningham, E. Fluckiger-Hawker, E. Robson, and G. Zólyomi, *The Electronic Text Corpus of Sumerian Literature* (Oxford, 1998–2006), www.etcsl.orinst .ox.ac.uk/.

PRIMARY SOURCE 2.2

Egyptian Mouth-Opening Ritual

Cleansing the Mouth with Salt Water

These your cool waters, Osiris—these your cool waters, oh
   Unis—have come from your son, have come from
   Horus.

I have come having gotten Horus' eye, that your heart
may become cool with it; I have gotten it under
your feet.

Accept the outflow that comes from you: your heart will not
become weary with it.

Recitation 4 Times: Come, you have been invoked.

Cool Water; 2 pellets of natron.

Condensed milk, condensed milk, that parts your
mouth, ho, Unis! may you taste its taste in front of
those of the gods' booths: the spittle of Horus,
condensed milk; the spittle of Seth, condensed
milk; the reconciliation of the two gods' hearts,
condensed milk.

Recitation 4 Times: Your natron-salt is among Horus's
Followers.

5 pellets of Nile-Valley natron of Nekheb.

Your natron is Horus's natron;
   your natron is Seth's natron;
   your natron is Thoth's natron;
   your natron is the god's natron:
   your own natron is amongst them.

Your mouth is the mouth of a milk-calf on the day he
is born.

5 Pellets of Delta natron of Shetpet.

Your natron is Horus's natron, your natron is Seth's natron,
your natron is Thoth's natron, your natron is the god's
natron; your natron is your ka's natron, your natron is
your natron's natron: this your own natron is amongst
your brothers, the gods.

Your natron is on your mouth: you should clean all your
bones and end what is (bad) against you.

Osiris, I have given you Horus's eye: provide your face with
it disseminated.

1 Pellet of natron.

The Mouth-Opening Ritual

Ho, Unis! I have fixed your jaws spread for you.

The flint spreader.

Osiris Unis, Let me part your mouth for you.

*An ingot of Nile-Valley god's-metal; an ingot of Delta
god's-metal.*

Unis, accept Horus's eye, which went away: I have gotten it
for you that I might put it in your mouth.

Nile-Valley Zrw-salt; Delta Zrw-salt.

Ho, Unis! Accept Osiris's šjkw-mineral.

Šjkw-mineral.

Here is the tip of the breast of Horus's own body: accept (it)
to your mouth.

A jug of milk.

Here is the breast of your lactating sister Isis, which you
should take to your mouth.

An empty jar.

Giving cool water; taking around.

Here are Horus's two eyes, black and white: take them to
your countenance, that they may brighten your face.

A white jar, a black jar; lifting up.

Source: James P. Allen, *Writings of the Ancient World: The Ancient Pyramid Texts* (Atlanta,
Georgia: Society of Biblical Literature, 2005), pp. 19–20.

Pyramid of Unas.

PRIMARY SOURCE 2.3

Harappan Seal Stones

Harappan Seal Stamps.

Shang Dynasty Oracle Bone

A partial translation of the left-hand side of this oracle bone reads:

[PREFACE:] Crack making on gui-si day, Que divined:

[CHARGE:] In the next ten days there will be no disaster.

[PROGNOSTICATION:] The king, reading the cracks, said, "There will be no harm; there will perhaps be the coming of alarming news."

[VERIFICATION:] When it came to the fifth day, ding-you, there really was the coming of alarming news from the west. Zhi Guo, reporting, said, "The Du Fang [a border people] are besieging in our eastern borders and have harmed two settlements." The Gong-fang also raided the fields of our western borders.

Source: This translation follows, with slight modifications by Bryan W. Van Norden, David N. Keightley, *Sources of Shang History* (Berkeley: University of California Press, 1978), p. 44.

Oracle Bone.

Early Greek Writing (Linear B)

The plot of Qelequhontas: this much seed: 276 l. of wheat

R. slave of the god, holds a lease: so much seed: 12 l. of wheat

W. the priest holds a lease: so much seed: 12 l. of wheat

Thuriatis, female slave of the god, dependant of P. the old man: so much seed: 108 l. of wheat

The plot of Admaos, so much seed: 216 l. of wheat. . . .

T. slave of the god, holds a lease: so much seed: 32 l. of wheat

The plot of A . . . eus, so much seed: 144 l. of wheat. . . .

The plot of T. slave of the god, holds a lease: 18 l. of wheat

The plot of R., so much seed: 138 l. of wheat. . . .

The plot of Aktaios, so much seed: 384 l. of wheat. . . .

Source: M. Ventris and J. Chadwick, *Documents in Mycenaean Greek*, 2nd ed. (Cambridge: Cambridge University Press, 1973), doc. 116.

Linear B from Pylos.
From the excavated Mycenean palace at Pylos, this is a typical Linear B document inscribed on clay with linear marks representing syllables and signs.

QUESTIONS FOR ANALYSIS

1. What sorts of topics does each example of early writing address? What do the topics discussed in these texts suggest about the function of writing in their respective societies?

2. Looking at the examples, what differences or similarities do you notice in letter/symbol forms and the context for the writing, in particular the objects on which the writing was etched?

3. What do these similarities and differences suggest about whether the writing spread through borrowing versus independent development?

Interpreting Visual Evidence
Burials and Long-Distance Trade

One of the most intriguing types of evidence from the river basin societies discussed in this chapter is the elaborate burials of the elite. These burials often contained tremendous wealth in the form of finely crafted items. A number of these items show not only highly specialized artisanship but also evidence of long-distance trade in raw materials among these third-millennium BCE civilizations.

Consider the types of objects pictured here and the materials used to make them. Queen Hetepheres I of the 4th Dynasty of Egypt (ca. 2550 BCE) was buried at Giza (near Memphis and Saqqara) with silver bracelets decorated with butterflies made of turquois, lapis lazuli, and carnelian. In southern Mesopotamia, "Queen" Pu-abi was interred in the magnificent Royal Tombs of Ur (ca. 2600-2400 BCE), which contained artifacts such as the Royal Standard of Ur pictured on the first page of this chapter. Among the many items found in Pu-abi's tomb was a lyre made with lapis lazuli and shell set in bitumen, shown in the second image below. Excavation reports describe this lyre as being found in the arms of a female lyrist who may have been a sacrificial victim at the death of Pu-abi. Harappan artisans in the Indus River valley used a bow drill to perforate tiny beads in order to craft the necklace shown here from lapis lazuli, carnelian, and other semi-precious stones. Much earlier, around 4000 BCE at Varna on the coast of the Black Sea (see Map 2.7), a "big man" of a farming village was buried with 990 gold objects (mostly decorative pieces sewn onto his clothing), as well as the flint daggers, axes, and spearheads in the final image.

Bracelets of Queen Hetepheres I.

Harp, or "Queen's Lyre," from the Royal Tombs of Ur.

Harappan gemstone necklace with lapis lazuli and carnelian.

Male warrior burial at Varna.

QUESTIONS FOR ANALYSIS

1. Looking at Map 2.2, where did the raw materials used to make each of the items here come from? Along what trade routes would these raw materials have travelled? What does that suggest about trade between river basin societies in the third millennium BCE?

2. What does the presence of these highly-crafted items in the graves of elite individuals suggest about river basin societies, especially in terms of wealth accumulation, labor specialization, and the beginnings of social stratification?

3. What does the ability and willingness to bury so much wealth in the dirt suggest about these third-millennium BCE societies, especially as compared with earlier, more subsistence-based hunter-gatherer communities?

Before You Read This Chapter

Nomads, Territorial States, and Microsocieties

2000–1200 BCE

Around 2200 BCE, the Old Kingdom of Egypt collapsed. The collapse did not occur because of incompetent rulers, of which there were many, or a decline in the arts and sciences, which is evident in unfinished building projects; the Old Kingdom fell because of radical changes in climate—namely, a powerful warming and drying trend that blanketed Afro-Eurasia between 2200 and 2150 BCE. The Mesopotamians and Harappans were as hard hit as the Egyptians.

In Egypt the environmental disaster yielded a series of low floods of the Nile because the usual monsoon rains did not arrive to feed the river's upper regions. With less water to irrigate crops, farmers could not grow enough food for the river basin's million inhabitants. Documents from this period reveal widespread suffering and despair. Consider the following tomb inscription: "All of Egypt was dying of hunger to such a degree that everyone had come to eating his children." Or another: "The tribes of the desert have become Egyptians everywhere. . . . The plunderer is everywhere, and the servant takes what he finds." Herders and pastoral nomads also felt the pinch. As these outsiders pressed upon permanent settlements in search of food, the governing structures in Egypt—and elsewhere, in Mesopotamia and the Indus Valley—broke down. The pioneering city-states may have created unprecedented differences between elites and commoners, between urban-ites and rural folk, but everyone felt the effects of this disaster.

This chapter focuses on two related developments. The first focus is the impact of climate change on the peoples of Afro-Eurasia: famines occurred, followed by political and economic turmoil. The old order gave way as river-basin states in Egypt, Mesopotamia, and the Indus Valley collapsed. Herders and pastoral nomads, driven from grazing areas that were drying up, forced their way into the heartlands of these great states in pursuit of better-watered lands. Once there, they challenged the traditional ruling elites. The nomads also brought with them a new military weapon—the horse-drawn chariot. Nomads and their chariots form the second focus of this chapter, for chariots introduced a type of warfare that would dominate the plains of Afro-Eurasia for a half a millennium. The nomads' advantage proved only temporary, however. Soon the Egyptians, Mesopotamians, Chinese, and many others learned from their chariot-driving conquerors: they assimilated some of their foes into their own societies and drove others away, adopting the invaders' most useful techniques. This chapter also examines worlds apart from the expanding centers of population and politics, where climate change and chariot-driving nomads were shaping world history. The islanders of the Pacific and the Aegean did not interact with one another with such intensity—and therefore their political systems evolved differently. In these locales, microsocieties (small-scale, loosely interconnected communities) were the norm.

Nomadic Movement and the Emergence of Territorial States

COMPARISON

EXPLAIN the relationship between climate change and human settlement patterns in the second millennium BCE.

As nomads and herders brought new pressures and new technologies to settled communities, innovations in governance spurred the rise of larger, expansionist territorial states. At the end of the third millennium BCE, drought and food shortages led to the overthrow of ruling elites throughout central and western Afro-Eurasia. Walled cities could not defend their hinterlands. Trade routes lay open to predators, and pillaging became a lucrative enterprise. Clans of horse-riding **pastoral nomads**—from the relatively sparsely populated and isolated Inner Eurasian steppes—swept across vast distances, eventually threatening settled people in cities. **Transhumant herders**—who lived closer to agricultural settlements and migrated seasonally to pasture their livestock—also advanced on populated areas in search of food and resources. These migrations of pastoral nomads and transhumant herders occurred across Eurasia, in the Arabian Desert and Iranian plateau in the west, and in the Indus River valley and the Yellow River valley in the east. (See Map 3.1.) Many transhumant herders and nomadic pastoralists settled in the agrarian heartlands of Mesopotamia, the Indus River valley, the highlands of Anatolia, Iran, China, and Europe. After the first wave of newcomers, more migrants arrived by foot or in wagons pulled by draft animals. Some sought temporary work; others settled permanently. They brought horses and new technologies that were useful in warfare; religious practices and languages; and new pressures to feed, house, and clothe an ever-growing population. This millennia-long process is sometimes referred to as Indo-European migrations.

Perhaps the most vital breakthroughs that nomadic pastoralists transmitted to settled societies were the harnessing of horses and the invention of the **chariot**, a two-wheeled horse-drawn vehicle used in warfare and later in processions and races. On the vast steppe lands north of the Caucasus Mountains, during the late fourth millennium BCE,

War Chariots *Upper left:* A large vase typical of Mycenaean art on the mainland areas of Greece. The regular banding and presentation of scenes reflect a society that is more formally ordered and rigidly hierarchical than that on Minoan Crete. Note the presence of the horse-drawn chariot. Possessing this more elaborate means of transport and warfare characterized the warrior elites of Mycenaean society and linked them to developments over wide expanses of Afro-Eurasia at the time. *Upper right:* This wooden chest covered with stucco and painted on all sides with images of the Egyptian pharaoh in his war chariot was found in the fabulously wealthy tomb of Tutankhamun in the Valley of the Kings in Egypt. The war chariot was introduced into Egypt by the Hyksos. By the reign of Tutankhamun in the New Kingdom, depictions of the pharaoh single-handedly smiting the enemy from a war chariot drawn by two powerful horses were common. *Bottom right:* The Shang fought with neighboring pastoral nomads from the central Asian steppes. To do this, they imported horses from central Asia and copied the chariots of nomads they had encountered. This gave Shang warriors devastating range and speed for further conquest.

settled people had domesticated horses in their native habitat. Elsewhere, as on the northern steppes of what is now Russia, horses were a food source. Only during the late third millennium BCE did people harness horses with cheek pieces and mouth bits in order to facilitate the control of horses and their use for transportation. Parts of horse harnesses made from wood, bone, bronze, and iron, found in tombs scattered across the steppe, reveal the evolution of headgear from simple mouth bits to full bridles with headpiece, mouthpiece, and reins.

Sometime around 2000 BCE, pastoral nomads in the mountains of the Caucasus joined the bit-harnessed horse to the two-wheeled chariot. Various chariot innovations began to unfold: pastoralists lightened chariots so their warhorses could pull them faster; spoked wheels made of special wood bent into circular shapes replaced solid-wood wheels that were heavier and prone to shatter; wheel covers, axles, and bearings (all produced by settled people) were added to the chariots; and durable metal went into the chariot's moving parts. Hooped bronze and, later, iron rims reinforced the spoked wheels. Initially iron was a decorative and experimental metal, and all tools and weapons were bronze.

BALTIC SEA

EUROPE

E U R A

URAL MOUNTAINS

HUNGARIAN
PLAIN

Dnieper R.

Dniester R.

Danube R.

Volga R.

BLACK SEA

CASPIAN
SEA

ARAL
SEA

Oxus R.

C E N T R A L   A S I A

Lake
Balkas

PAMIR MTS.

HINDU KUSH MTS.

A F R O

ANATOLIAN
PLATEAU

Tigris R.

Euphrates R.

MEDITERRANEAN SEA

IRANIAN
PLATEAU

ZAGROS MTS.

S O U T H W E S T   A S I A

HIM

Indus R.

A F

Nile R.

RED SEA

Persian Gulf

ARABIAN
DESERT

SOUTH

ARABIAN SEA

Legend	
←	Transhumant migrations
←	Spread of wheeled vehicles
←	Spread of war chariots
←	Dispersal of nomads
▨	Pastoral nomads c. 2000 – 1500 BCE

Southwest Asian Society
Zone of urban civilization

0   500   1000 Miles

0   500   1000 Kilometers

Lake Baikal

ALTAI MOUNTAINS

TIEN SHAN MTS.

TAKLAMAKAN DESERT

GOBI DESERT

Yellow R.

EAST ASIA

SEA OF JAPAN

JAPAN

MOUNTAINS

Ganges R.

ASIA

Yangzi R.

SOUTHEAST ASIA

Bay of Bengal

SOUTH CHINA SEA

PACIFIC

OCEAN

MAP 3.1 | Nomadic Migrations in Afro-Eurasia, 2000–1000 BCE

Nomads were on the move in this period, moving into many of the settled regions.

- According to this map, what parts of the world did pastoral peoples migrate from?
- What areas did they move into? What regions did they bring into closer connection?
- How did nomadic pastoral migrations affect settled, agriculture-based societies?

Iron's hardness and flexibility, however, eventually made it more desirable for reinforcing moving parts and protecting wheels, like those on the chariot. Thus the horse chariots combined innovations by both nomads and settled agriculturalists.

These innovations—combining new engineering skills, metalworking, and animal domestication—revolutionized the way humans made war. The horse chariot slashed travel time between capitals. Slow-moving infantry now ceded to battalions of chariots. Each vehicle carried a driver and an archer and charged into battle with lethal precision and ravaging speed. The mobility, accuracy, and shooting power of warriors in horse-drawn chariots tilted the political balance. After the nomads perfected this type of warfare (by 1600 BCE), they challenged the political systems of Mesopotamia and Egypt, and chariots soon became central to the armies of Egypt, Assyria, Persia, the Vedic kings of South Asia, and the Zhou rulers in China, and to local nobles as far west as Italy, Gaul, and Spain. Only with the development of cheaper armor made of iron (after 1000 BCE) did foot soldiers recover their military importance. And only after states developed cavalry units of horse-mounted warriors did chariots lose their decisive military advantage. For much of the second millennium BCE, then, charioteer elites prevailed in Afro-Eurasia.

For city dwellers in the river basins, the first sight of horse-drawn chariots must have been terrifying, but they quickly understood that war making had changed, and they scrambled to adapt. The pharaohs in Egypt probably copied chariots from nomads or neighbors, and they came to value them highly. For example, the young pharaoh Tutankhamun (r. c. 1336–1327 BCE) was a chariot archer who made sure his war vehicle and other gear accompanied him in his tomb. A century later the Shang kings of the Yellow River valley, in the heartland of agricultural China, likewise were entombed with their horse chariots.

While nomads and transhumant herders toppled the riverine cities in Mesopotamia, Egypt, and China through innovations in warfare such as the chariot, the turmoil that ensued sowed seeds for a new type of regime: the territorial state. While Sargon and the Akkadians set up a short-lived territorial state in earlier Mesopotamia (2334–2193 BCE) (see Chapter 2), the martial innovations and political and environmental crises of the early second millennium helped to spur their more enduring development elsewhere. The **territorial state** was a centralized kingdom organized around a charismatic ruler. The new rulers of these territorial states exerted power not only over localized city-states, but also over distant hinterlands. They enhanced their stability through rituals for passing the torch of command from one generation to the next. People no longer identified themselves as residents of cities; instead, they felt allegiance to large territories, rulers, and broad linguistic and ethnic communities. These territories for the first time had identifiable borders, and their residents felt a shared identity. Territorial states differed from the city-states that preceded them in that the new territorial states in Egypt, Mesopotamia, and China based their authority on monarchs, widespread bureaucracies, elaborate legal codes, large territorial expanses, definable borders, and ambitions for continuous expansion.

The Territorial State in Egypt

The first of the great territorial states of this period arose from the ashes of chaos in Egypt. The long era of prosperity associated with Old Kingdom Egypt ended when drought brought catastrophe to the area. For several decades the Nile did not overflow its banks, and Egyptian harvests withered. (See **Analyzing Global Developments: Climate Change and the Collapse of River-Basin Societies.**) As the pharaohs lost legitimacy and fell prey to feuding among rivals for the throne, regional elites replaced the

Analyzing Global Developments

Climate Change and the Collapse of River-Basin Societies

The three great river-basin societies discussed in Chapter 2—Egypt, Mesopotamia, and the Indus Valley—collapsed at around the same time. The collapse in Egypt and Mesopotamia was almost simultaneous (roughly between 2200 BCE and 2100 BCE). In contrast, while the collapse was delayed in the Indus Valley for approximately 200 years, when it came, it virtually wiped out the Harappan state and culture. At first, historians focused on political, economic, and social causes, stressing bad rulers, nomadic incursions, political infighting, population migrations, and the decline of long-distance trade. In more recent times, however, a group of scientists that included paleobiologists, climatologists, sedimentationists, and archaeologists have studied these societies and found convincing evidence that a truly radical change in the climate—a 200-year-long drought spreading across the Afro-Eurasian land mass—was a powerful factor in the collapse of these cultures. But how can these researchers know so much about the climate 4,000 years ago? The following table assembles the evidence for their assertions, drawing on their scholarly studies on Egypt, Mesopotamia, and the Indus Valley.

QUESTIONS FOR ANALYSIS

- Why did more standard historical explanations for the collapse of the large river-basin societies precede the more recent emphases on climate change?

- Few scholars are willing to regard climate change as the overwhelming factor in the collapse of these river-basin societies. Why do you think that this is the case?

- On the basis of your reading, do you think that the evidence for climate change is convincing for all three societies? Which ones are the more persuasive, which the less convincing?

RIVER-BASIN SOCIETY	DATE OF COLLAPSE	CLIMATOLOGICAL EVIDENCE	ARCHAEOLOGICAL EVIDENCE	LITERARY EVIDENCE
Egypt	The Old Kingdom collapsed and ushered in a period of notable political instability, the First Intermediate Period (2184–2055 BCE).	Sedimentation studies reveal markedly lower Nile floods and an invasion of sand dunes into cultivated areas.	Much of the sacred sites of the Old Kingdom and their artwork is believed to have been destroyed in this period due to the political chaos.	An abundant literary record is full of tales of woe. Poetry and stelae call attention to famine, starvation, low Nile floods, even cannibalism.
Mesopotamia	The last effective ruler of the Kingdom of Akkad (2334–2193 BCE) was Naram Sin (r. 2254–2218 BCE).	Around 2100 BCE, inhabitants abruptly abandoned the Haabur drainage basin, whose soil samples reveal marked aridity as determined by the existence of fewer earthworm holes and wind-blown pellets.	Teil Leilan and other sites indicate that the large cities of this region began to shrink around 2200 BCE and were soon abandoned, and remained unoccupied for 300 years.	Later UR III scribes described the influx of northern "barbarians" and noted the construction of a wall, known as the Repeller of the Amorites, to keep these northerners out.
Indus Valley and the Harappan Society	Many of the Harappan peoples migrated eastward, beginning around 1900 BCE, leaving this region largely empty of people.	Hydroclimatic reconstructions show that precipitation began to decrease around 3000 BCE, reaching a low in 2000 BCE, at which point the Himalayan rivers stopped incising. Around 1700 BCE, the Ghaggar-Hakra rivers dried up.	Major Harappan urban sites began to shrink in size and lose their urban character between 1900 and 1700 BCE.	No literary source material because the Harappan script has still to be deciphered.

Sources: Barbara Bell, "The Dark Ages in Ancient History," *American Journal of Archaeology,* vol. 75, no. 1 (January, 1971), pp. 1–26; Max Weiss et al., "The Genesis and Collapse of Third Millennium North Mesopotamian Civilization," *Science, New Series,* vol. 261, no. 5124 (August 20, 1993), pp. 995–1004; H. M. Cullen et al., "Climate Change and the Collapse of the Akkadian Empire," *Geology,* vol. 28, no. 4, April 2000, pp. 379–82; Liviu Giosan et al., "Fluvial Landscapes of the Harappan Civilization," *Proceedings of the National Academy of Science, published online,* May 29, 2012; and Karl W. Butzer, "Collapse, Environment, and Society," *Proceedings of the National Academy of Science,* published online, March 6, 2012, vol. 109, no. 10, pp. 3632–39. For a general overview of climate change and historical studies, consult Wolfgang Behringer, *A Cultural History of Climate* (2010).

authority of the centralized state. Egypt, which had been one of the most stable corners of Afro-Eurasia, endured more than a century of tumult before a new order emerged. The pharaohs of the Middle Kingdom and, later, the New Kingdom reunified the river valley and expanded south and north.

RELIGION AND TRADE IN MIDDLE KINGDOM EGYPT (2055–1650 BCE)

Around 2050 BCE, after a century of drought, the Nile's floodwaters returned to normal and crops grew again. In the centuries that followed, pharaohs at Thebes consolidated power in Upper Egypt and began new state-building activity, ushering in a new phase of stability that historians call the Middle Kingdom. The rulers of this era developed Egypt's religious and political institutions in ways that increased state power, creating the conditions for greater prosperity and trade.

Religion and Rule Spiritual and worldly powers once again reinforced each other in Egypt. Gods and rulers together replaced the chaos that people believed had brought drought and despair. Amenemhet I (1985–1955 BCE), first pharaoh of the long-lasting Twelfth Dynasty (1985–1795 BCE), elevated a formerly less significant god, Amun, to prominence. The king capitalized on the god's name, which means "hidden," to convey a sense of his own invisible omnipresence throughout the realm. Because Amun's attributes of air and breath were largely intangible, believers in other gods were able to embrace his cult. Amun's cosmic power appealed to people in areas that had recently been impoverished.

The pharaoh's elevation of the cult of Amun unified the kingdom and brought even more power to Amun and the pharaoh. Consequently, Amun eclipsed all the other gods of Thebes. Merging with the formerly omnipotent sun god Re, the deity now was called Amun-Re: the king of the gods. Because the power of the gods and kings was intertwined, the pharaoh as Amun's earthly champion enjoyed enhanced legitimacy as the supreme ruler.

The massive temple complex dedicated to Amun-Re offers evidence of their joint power. Middle Kingdom rulers tapped into their kingdom's renewed bounty, their subjects' loyalty, and the work of untold slaves and commoners to build Amun-Re's temple complex at Thebes (present-day Luxor). For 2,000 years, Egyptians and slaves toiled to erect monumental gates, enormous courtyards, and other structures in what was arguably the largest, longest-lasting public works project ever undertaken. Middle Kingdom rulers also nurtured a cult of the pharaoh as the good shepherd whose prime responsibility was to care for his human flock. By instituting charities, offering homage to gods at the palace to ensure regular floodwaters, and performing ceremonies to honor their own generosity, the pharaohs portrayed themselves as these shepherds. As a result, the cult of Amun-Re was both a tool of political power and a source of spiritual meaning for Egyptians.

Amun This sculpture of the head of the god Amun was carved from quartzite during the Eighteenth Dynasty, around 1335 BCE. At Thebes in Upper Egypt, a huge temple complex was dedicated to the combined god Amun-Re. The powerful kings of the Middle and New Kingdoms each added a courtyard or a pylon, making this one of the largest religious structures in the ancient world.

Expanding Trade Networks Prosperity gave rise to an urban class of merchants and professionals who used their wealth and skills to carve out new opportunities for themselves. They indulged in leisure activities such as formal banquets with professional dancers and singers, and they honed their skills in hunting, fowling, and fishing. In a sign of their upward mobility and autonomy, some members of the middle class constructed tombs filled with representations of the material goods they would use in the afterlife as well as the occupations that would engage them for eternity. This new merchant class did not rely on the king's generosity and took burial privileges formerly reserved for the royal family and a few powerful nobles.

As they centralized power and consolidated their territorial state, Egyptians also expanded their trade networks (see Map 3.2). Because the floodplains had long since been deforested, the Egyptians needed to import massive quantities of wood by ship. Most prized were the cedars from Byblos (a city in the land soon known as Phoenicia, roughly present-day Lebanon), crafted into furniture and coffins. Commercial networks extended south through the Red Sea to present-day Ethiopia; importing precious metals, ivory, livestock, slaves, and exotic animals such as panthers and monkeys. Expeditions to the Sinai Peninsula searched for copper and turquoise. Expansion southward into Nubia for gold and other resources continued in the early New Kingdom. As part of Egyptian colonization southward, a series of forts extended as far south as the second cataract of the Nile River (just south of the modern-day border between Egypt and Sudan).

MIGRATIONS AND EXPANDING FRONTIERS IN NEW KINGDOM EGYPT (1550–1069 BCE)

The success of the new commercial networks lured pastoral nomads who were searching for work. Later, chariot-driving Hyksos invaders from Southwest Asia attacked Egypt, setting in motion the events marking the break between what historians call the Middle and New Kingdoms of Egypt. Although the invaders challenged the Middle Kingdom, they also inspired innovations that enabled the New Kingdom to thrive and expand.

Hyksos Invaders Sometime around 1640 BCE, a western Semitic-speaking people, whom the Egyptians called the **Hyksos** ("Rulers of Foreign Lands"), overthrew the unstable Thirteenth Dynasty (toward the end of Egypt's Middle Kingdom period). The Hyksos had mastered the art of horse chariots. Thundering into battle with their war chariots and their superior bronze axes and composite bows (made of wood, horn, and sinew), they easily defeated the pharaoh's foot soldiers. The victorious Hyksos did not destroy the conquered land, but adopted and reinforced Egyptian ways. Ruling as the Fifteenth Dynasty, the Hyksos asserted control over the northern part of the country and transformed the Egyptian military.

After a century of political conflict, an Egyptian who ruled the southern part of the country, Ahmosis (r. 1550–1525 BCE), successfully used the Hyksos weaponry—horse chariots—against the invaders themselves, and became pharaoh. This conquest marked the beginning of what historians call New Kingdom Egypt. Hyksos invasions had taught Egyptian rulers that they must vigilantly monitor their frontiers, for they could no longer rely on deserts as buffers. Ahmosis assembled large, mobile armies and drove the Hyksos "foreigners" back. Diplomats followed in the army's path, as the pharaoh initiated a strategy of interference in the affairs of Southwest Asian states. Such policies laid the groundwork for statecraft and an international diplomatic system that future Egyptian kings used to dominate the eastern Mediterranean world.

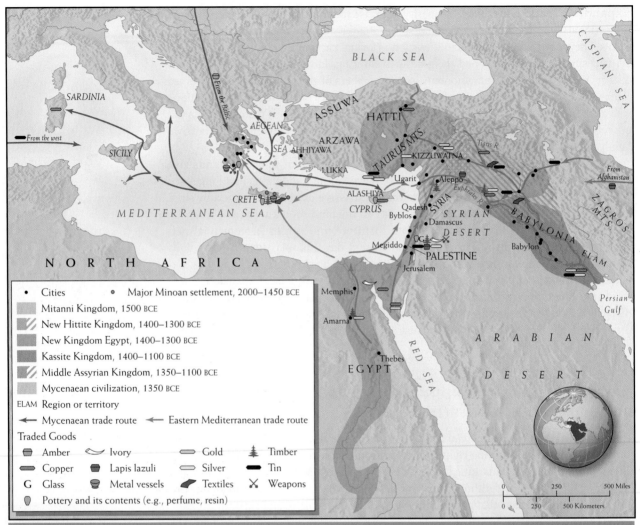

MAP 3.2 | Territorial States and Trade Routes in Southwest Asia, North Africa, and the Eastern Mediterranean, 1500–1350 BCE

Trade in many commodities brought the societies of the Mediterranean Sea and Southwest Asia into increasingly closer contact.

- What were the major trade routes and the major trading states in Southwest Asia, North Africa, and the eastern Mediterranean during this time?

- What were the major trade goods?

- Did trade enhance peaceful interactions among the territorial states?

Migrations and invasions introduced new techniques that the Egyptians adopted to consolidate their power. These included bronze working (which the Egyptians had not perfected), an improved potter's wheel, and a vertical loom. South Asian animals such as humped zebu cattle, as well as vegetable and fruit crops, now appeared on the banks of the Nile for the first time. Other significant innovations pertained to war: the horse and chariot, the composite bow, the scimitar (a sword with a curved blade), and other weapons from western Eurasia. These weapons transformed the Egyptian army from a standing infantry to a high-speed, mobile, and deadly fighting force. Egyptian troops extended the military frontier as far south as the fourth cataract of the Nile River (in northern modern-day Sudan), and the kingdom now stretched from the Mediterranean shores to Ethiopia.

Expanding Frontiers By the beginning of the New Kingdom, the territorial state of Egypt was projecting its interests outward: it defined itself as a superior, cosmopolitan society with an efficient bureaucracy run by competent and socially mobile individuals. As mentioned above, Egypt expanded its control southward into Nubia, as a source of gold, exotic raw materials, and manpower.

Historians identify this expansion most strongly with the reign of Egypt's most powerful woman ruler, Hatshepsut. She served as regent for her young son, Thutmosis III, who came to the throne in 1479 BCE. When he was seven years old, Hatshepsut proclaimed herself "king," ruling as coregent until she died two decades later. During her reign there was little military activity, but trade contacts into the Levant and Mediterranean and southward into Nubia flourished. When he ultimately came to power, Thutmosis III (r. 1479–1425 BCE) launched another expansionist phase, northeastward into the Levant, which lasted for 200 years. At the Battle of Megiddo (1469 BCE), the first recorded chariot battle in history, Thutmosis III, whose army employed nearly 1,000 war chariots, defeated his adversaries and established an Egyptian presence in Palestine. Having evolved into a strong, expansionist territorial state, Egypt was now poised to engage in commercial, political, and cultural exchanges with the rest of the region.

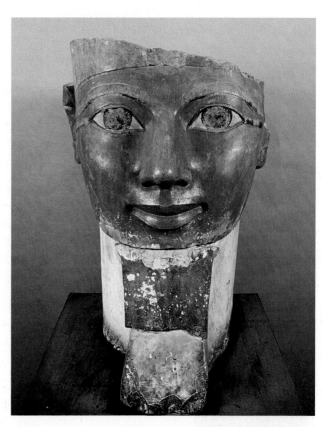

Hatshepsut The only powerful queen of Egyptian pharaonic history was Hatshepsut, seen here in a portrait head created during her reign. Because a woman on the throne of Egypt would offend the basic principles of order (*ma'at*), Hatshepsut usually portrayed herself as a man, especially late in her reign. This was reinforced by the use of male determinatives in the hieroglyphic renditions of her name.

Territorial States in Southwest Asia

Climatic change and invasions by migrants also transformed the societies of Southwest Asia, and new territorial kingdoms arose in Mesopotamia and Anatolia. Here, as in Egypt, the drought at the end of the third millennium BCE was devastating. Harvests shrank, the price of basic goods rose, and the social order broke down. In southern Mesopotamia cities were invaded by transhumant herders (not chariot-driving nomads) who sought grazing lands to replace those swallowed up by expanding deserts. A millennium of intense cultivation, combined with severe drought, brought disastrous consequences: rich soil in the river basin was depleted of nutrients; saltwater from the Persian Gulf seeped into the marshy deltas, contaminating the water table; and the main branch of the Euphrates River shifted to the west. Many cities lost access to their fertile agrarian hinterlands and withered away. Mesopotamia's center of political and economic gravity shifted northward, away from the silted, marshy deltas of the southern heartland.

As scarcities mounted, transhumant peoples began to press in upon settled communities more closely. Mesopotamian city dwellers were scornful of the rustic migrants, whom they called **Amorites** ("westerners"), invading their cities. While these

COMPARISON

COMPARE the varied processes by which territorial states formed and interacted with each other in Egypt and Southeast Asia.

Hammurapi's Code The inscription on the shaft of Hammurapi's Code is carved in a beautiful rendition of the cuneiform script. Because none of the laws on the code were recorded in the thousands of judicial texts of the period, it is uncertain if Hammurapi's Code presented actual laws or only norms for the proper behavior of Babylonian citizens.

transhumant herders may have been western "foreigners" to those living in the urban centers of Mesopotamia, they were not strangers. These rural folk had wintered in villages close to the rivers to water their animals, which grazed on fallow fields. In the scorching summer, they retreated to the cooler highlands. Their flocks provided wools, leather, bones, and tendons to the artisan-based industries of the urban centers of Mesopotamia. In return, the herders purchased crafted products and agricultural goods. They also paid taxes, served as warriors, and labored on public works projects, but had few political rights within city-states.

Around 2000 BCE, Amorites from the western desert joined allies from the Iranian plateau to bring down the Third Dynasty of Ur, which had controlled all of Mesopotamia and southwestern Iran for more than a century. These Amorites and their allies founded the Old Babylonian kingdom, centered on the southern Mesopotamian city of Babylon, near modern-day Baghdad. Other territorial states arose in Mesopotamia in the millennium that followed, sometimes with one dominating the entire floodplain and sometimes with multiple powerful kingdoms vying for territory. As in Egypt, a century of political instability followed the demise of the old city-state models. Here, too, pastoralists played a role in the restoration of order, increasing the wealth of the regions they conquered and helping the cultural realm to flourish. The Old Babylonian kingdom expanded trade and founded territorial states with dynastic ruling families and well-defined frontiers. As we will see, pastoralists also played a key role in the development of territorial kingdoms in Anatolia.

MESOPOTAMIAN KINGSHIP

The new rulers of Mesopotamia changed the organization of the state and promoted a distinctive culture, as well as expanding trade. Herders-turned-urbanite-rulers mixed their own nomadic social organization with that of the once dominant city-states to create the structures necessary to support much larger territorial states. The basic social organization of the Amorites, out of which the territorial states in Mesopotamia evolved, was tribal (dominated by a ruling chief) and clan-based (claiming descent from a common ancestor). Over time, chieftains drew on personal charisma and battlefield prowess to become kings; kings allied with the merchant class and nobility for bureaucratic and financial support; and kingship became hereditary.

Over the centuries, powerful Mesopotamian kings expanded their territories and subdued weaker neighbors, inducing them to pay tribute in luxury goods, raw materials, and manpower as part of a broad confederation of city-states under the kings' protection. Control over military resources (metals for weaponry and, later, herds of horses for pulling chariots) was necessary for dominance. The ruler's charisma also mattered. Unlike the more institutionalized Egyptian leadership, Mesopotamian kingdoms could vacillate from strong to weak, depending on the leader's personality.

The most famous Mesopotamian ruler of this period was Hammurapi (or Hammurabi) (r. 1792–1750). Continuously struggling with powerful neighbors, he sought to centralize state authority and to create a new legal order. Using diplomatic and military skills to become the strongest king in Mesopotamia, he made Babylon his capital. He implemented a new system to consolidate power, appointing regional governors to manage outlying provinces and to deal with local elites. Like the Egyptian pharaohs of the Middle Kingdom, Hammurapi was shepherd and patriarch of his people, responsible for proper preparation of the fields and irrigation canals and for his followers' well-being. Balancing elite privileges with the needs of the lower classes, the king secured his power. **Hammurapi's Code**, with its "eye-for-an-eye" reciprocity of crime and punishment, is an example of this balancing act.

Its compilation of more than 300 edicts outlines crimes and their punishments. The Code places an emphasis on the king's control, as divine agent, over public matters; the vital role of the family in orderly relations; and the rights and responsibilities of each social class (free, dependent, and slave). Such an overarching legal code underscored the authority of the king as well as the hierarchies of power within the territorial state.

Power and Culture Mesopotamian rulers commissioned public art and works projects and promoted institutions of learning. The court supported workshops for skilled artisans and schools for scribes, the transmitters of an expanding literary culture. To dispel their image as rustic foreigners and to demonstrate their familiarity with the region's core values, new Mesopotamian rulers valued the oral tales and written records of the earlier Sumerians and Akkadians. Scribes copied the ancient texts and preserved their tradition. Royal hymns portrayed the king as a legendary hero of quasi-divine status.

Heroic narratives about legendary founders, based on traditional stories about the rulers of ancient Uruk, legitimized the new rulers. The most famous tale was the *Epic of Gilgamesh*, one of the earliest surviving works of literature. Originally composed more than a millennium earlier, in the Sumerian language, this epic narrated the heroism of the legendary king of early Uruk, Gilgamesh. Preserved by scribes in royal courts through centuries, the epic offers an example of how the Mesopotamian kings invested in cultural production to explain important political relations, unify their people, and distinguish their subjects from those of other kingdoms.

Trade and the Rise of a Private Economy Another feature of the territorial state in Mesopotamia was its shift away from economic activity dominated by the city-state and toward independent private ventures. Mesopotamian rulers designated private entrepreneurs rather than state bureaucrats to collect taxes. People paid taxes in the form of commodities such as grain, vegetables, and wool, which the entrepreneurs exchanged for silver. They, in turn, passed on the silver to the state after pocketing a percentage for their profit. This process generated more private economic activity and wealth, and more revenues for the state.

Gilgamesh This terra-cotta plaque is one of the few depictions of Gilgamesh (on the left wielding the knife) and his sidekick, Enkidu. It illustrates one of the episodes in their shared adventures, the killing of Humwawa, the monster of the Cedar Forest. The style of the plaque indicates that it was made during the Old Babylonian period, between 2000 and 1600 BCE.

Mesopotamia was a crossroads for caravans leading east and west. Peace and good governance allowed trade to flourish. The ability to move exotic foodstuffs, valuable minerals, textiles, and luxury goods across Southwest Asia won Mesopotamian merchants and entrepreneurs a privileged position as middlemen. Merchants also used sea routes for trade with the Indus Valley. Before 2000 BCE, mariners had charted the waters of the Red Sea, the Gulf of Aden, the Persian Gulf, and much of the Arabian Sea. And during the second millennium BCE, shipbuilders figured out how to construct larger vessels and to rig them with towering masts and woven sails—creating seaworthy craft that could carry bulkier loads. Shipbuilding required wood (particularly cedar from Phoenicia) as well as wool and other fibers (from the pastoral hinterlands) for sails. Such reliance on imported materials reflected a growing regional economic specialization and an expanding sphere of interaction across western Afro-Eurasia. The benefits and risks of trade in Mesopotamia are evident from royal edicts of debt annulment (to help merchants who had overstretched) and formalized commercial rules governing taxes and duties. In trade and other exchanges, Mesopotamia became a crucial link between Egypt, Anatolia, and southwestern Iran. Centralized control of the region facilitated a thriving trade in such precious commodities as horses, chariots, and lapis lazuli, which was exchanged for gold, wood, and ivory.

THE OLD AND NEW HITTITE KINGDOMS (1800–1200 BCE)

Chariot warriors known as the Hittites established territorial kingdoms in Anatolia, to the northwest of Mesopotamia. Anatolia (modern-day Turkey) was an overland crossroads that linked the Black and Mediterranean seas. Like other plateaus of Afro-Eurasia, it had high tablelands, was easy to traverse, and was hospitable to large herding communities. During the third millennium BCE Anatolia had become home to numerous communities run by native elites. These societies combined pastoral ways of life, agriculture, and urban commercial centers. Before 2000 BCE, peoples speaking Indo-European languages began to enter the plateau, probably coming from the steppe lands north and west of the Black Sea. The newcomers lived in fortified settlements and often engaged in regional warfare, and their numbers grew. Splintered into competing clans, they fought for regional supremacy. They also borrowed extensively from the cultural developments of the Southwest Asian urban cultures, especially those of Mesopotamia.

In the early second millennium BCE, the chariot warrior groups of Anatolia grew powerful on the commercial activity that passed through their region. Chief among them were the **Hittites**. Hittite lancers and archers rode chariots across vast expanses to plunder their neighbors and demand taxes and tribute. In the seventeenth century BCE, the Hittite leader Hattusilis I unified these chariot aristocracies, secured his base in Anatolia, defeated the kingdom that controlled northern Syria, and then campaigned along the Euphrates River, even sacking Babylon in 1595 BCE.

Two centuries later, the Hittites enjoyed another period of political and military success. In 1274 BCE, they fought the Egyptians at the Battle of Qadesh (in modern Syria), the largest and best-documented chariot battle of antiquity. Hittite control—spanning from Anatolia across the region between the Nile and Mesopotamia—was central to balancing power among the territorial states that grew up in the river valleys.

A COMMUNITY OF MAJOR POWERS (1400–1200 BCE)

Between 1400 and 1200 BCE, the major territorial states of Southwest Asia and Egypt perfected instruments of international diplomacy. A cache of 300 letters discovered at the present-day Egyptian village of Amarna offers intimate views of the interactions among the powers of Egypt and Southwest Asia. The letters include communications between Egyptian pharaohs and various leaders of Southwest Asia, including Babylonian and Hittite kings. The leaders of these powers settled their differences through treaties and diplomatic negotiations rather than on the battlefield. Each state knew its place in the political pecking order. It was an order that depended on constant diplomacy, based on communication, treaties, marriages, and the exchange of gifts. As nomadic peoples combined with settled urban polities to create new territorial states in Egypt, Mesopotamia, and Anatolia, and as those territorial states came into contact with one another through trade, this diplomacy was vital to maintaining the interactions among this community of major powers in Southwest Asia.

COMPARISON

DESCRIBE the impact of transhumant herders and pastoral nomads on settled communities in Egypt, Southwest Asia, and the Indus River Valley.

Nomads and the Indus River Valley

Compared with those in Egypt and Mesopotamia, territorial states emerged more slowly in the Indus River valley. Late in the third millennium BCE, drought ravaged the Indus River valley as it did other regions. By 1700 BCE, the population of the old Harappan heartland had plummeted. Here, too, around 1500 BCE, yet another group of nomadic peoples, calling themselves Aryans ("respected ones"), emerged from their homelands in the steppes of Inner Eurasia. In contrast to Egypt, Anatolia, and Mesopotamia, these pastoral nomads did not immediately establish large territorial states. Crossing the northern highlands of central Asia through the Hindu Kush, they descended into the fertile Indus River basin (see Map 3.3) with large flocks of cattle and horses. They sang chants called Rig Veda as they sacrificed some of their livestock to their gods. Known collectively as the Veda ("knowledge"), these hymns served as the most sacred texts for the newcomers, who have been known ever since as the *Vedic peoples*. Sanskrit, the spoken language of the Vedic peoples, is one of the earliest known Indo-European languages and a source for virtually all of the European languages, including Greek, Latin, English, French, and German. (See **Current Trends in World History: How Languages Spread**.)

Like other nomads from the northern steppe, they brought domesticated animals—especially horses, which pulled their chariots and established their military superiority. Not only were Vedic peoples superb horse charioteers, but they were also masters of copper and bronze metallurgy and wheel making. Their expertise in these areas allowed them to produce the very chariots that transported them into their new lands.

The Vedic peoples were deeply religious. They worshipped a host of deities, the most powerful of which were the sky god and the gods that represented horses. They were confident that their chief god, Indra (the deity of war), was on their side. The Vedic peoples also brought elaborate rituals of worship, which set them apart from the indigenous populations.

Indra with Buddha The Vedic peoples worshipped their gods by sacrificing and burning cows and horses and by singing hymns and songs, but they never built temples or sculptured idols. Therefore we do not know how they envisioned Indra and their other gods. However, when Buddhists started to make images of Buddha in the early centuries CE, they also sculpted Indra and Brahma as attendants of the Buddha. Indra in Buddhist iconography evolved into Vajrapani, the Diamond Lord. In this plate, the one on the left holding a stick with diamond-shaped heads is Indra/Vajrapani.

MAP 3.3 | Indo-European Migrations, Second Millennium BCE

One of the most important developments of the second millennium was the movement of Indo-European peoples.

• Where did the Indo-European migration originate?

• Where did Indo-European migrations spread to during this time?

• How did widespread drought push or draw the migrants into more settled agricultural regions, such as the Indus Valley?

As with many Afro-Eurasian migrations, the outsiders' arrival led to fusion as well as to conflict. While the native-born peoples eventually adopted the newcomers' language, the newcomers themselves took up the techniques and rhythms of agrarian life. The Vedic peoples used the Indus Valley as a staging area for migrations throughout the northern plain of South Asia. As they mixed agrarian and pastoral ways and borrowed technologies (such as iron working) from farther west, their population expanded and they began to look for new resources. With horses, chariots, and iron tools and weapons, they marched south and east. By 1000 BCE, they reached the southern foothills of the Himalayas and began to settle in the Ganges River valley. Five hundred years later, they had settlements as far south as the Deccan plateau.

Each wave of occupation involved violence, but the invaders did not simply dominate the indigenous peoples. Instead, the confrontations led them to embrace many of the ways of the vanquished. In particular, the Vedic newcomers were impressed with inhabitants' farming skills and knowledge of seasonal weather. These they adapted even as they continued to expand their territory. They moved into huts constructed from mud, bamboo, and reeds. They refined the already sophisticated production of beautiful carnelian stone beads, and they further aided commerce by devising standardized weights. In addition to raising domesticated animals, they sowed wheat and rye on the Indus plain, and they learned to plant rice in the marshy lands of the Ganges River valley. Later they mastered the use of plows with iron blades, an innovation that transformed the agrarian base of South Asia. This turn to settled agriculture was a major shift for the nomadic pastoral Vedic peoples. After all, their staple foods had always been dairy products and meat, and they were used to measuring their wealth in livestock (horses were most valuable, and cows were more valuable than sheep). Moreover, because they could not breed their prized horses in South Asia's semitropical climate, they initiated a brisk import trade from central and Southwest Asia.

As the Vedic peoples filled the relative void left by the collapse of the Harappans and adapted to their new environment, their initial political organization took a somewhat different course from those of Southwest Asia. Whereas competitive kingdoms dominated the landscape in Southwest Asia, competitive and balanced regimes were slower to emerge in South Asia. The result was a slower process of political integration.

The Shang Territorial State in East Asia (1600–1045 BCE)

China's first major territorial state combined features of earlier Longshan culture with new technologies and religious practices. Climatic change affected East Asia much as it had central and Southwest Asia. Stories supposedly written on bamboo strips and later collected into what historians call the "Bamboo Annals" tell of a time at the end of the legendary Xia dynasty when the sun dimmed, frost and ice appeared in summer, and a long drought followed heavy rainfall and flooding. According to Chinese mythology, the first ruler of the Shang dynasty defeated a despotic Xia king and then offered to sacrifice himself so that the drought would end. This leader, Tang, survived to found the territorial state called Shang, around 1600 BCE in northeastern China.

The Shang state was built on four elements that the Longshan peoples had already introduced: a metal industry based on copper; pottery making; walled towns; and divination using animal bones. To these Longshan foundations the Shang dynasty added hereditary rulers whose power derived from their relation to ancestors and gods; written records; large-scale metallurgy; tribute; and various rituals.

COMPARISON

COMPARE state formation in Shang China to Mesopotamia and Egypt.

STATE FORMATION

A combination of these preexisting Longshan strengths and Shang innovations produced a strong Shang territorial state and a wealthy and powerful elite, noted for its intellectual achievements and aesthetic sensibilities.

How Languages Spread: The Case of Nomadic Indo-European Languages

Linguistics, or the study of language, is an important tool in world history. Language arose independently in a number of places around the world. All languages change with time, and their divergence from a mother tongue serves as a tool in determining at what point different languages, like German or French, broke apart. Scholars call related tongues with a common origin "language families." Even though members of the same language family diverged over time, they all share grammatical features and root vocabularies.

While technically there are more than a hundred language families, a much smaller number have influenced vast geographic areas. For example, the *Altaic* languages spread from Europe to central Asia. The *Sino-Tibetan* language family includes Mandarin, the most widely spoken language in the world. The *Uralic* family, which includes Hungarian and Finnish, occurs mainly in Europe. The *Afro-Asiatic* language family contains several hundred languages spoken in North Africa, sub-Saharan Africa, and Southeast Asia, Hebrew and Arabic among them.

One language family that linguists have studied extensively, and the one with the largest number of speakers today, is *Indo-European*. It was identified by scholars who recognized similarities in grammar and vocabulary among classical Sanskrit, Persian, Greek, and Latin. Living languages in this family include English, Irish, German, Norwegian, Portuguese, French,

Russian, Persian, Hindi, and Bengali. For the past 200 years, comparative linguists have sought to reconstruct Proto-Indo-European, the parent of all the languages in the family. They have drawn conclusions about its grammar, hypothesizing a highly inflected language with different endings on nouns and verbs according to their use. They have also made suggestions about its vocabulary.

For example, after analyzing patterns of linguistic change, scholars have proposed that the basic Indo-European root that means "horse"—in Sanskrit, *a'sva;* Persian, *aspa;* Latin, *equus;* and Greek, *hippos* (ίππος)—is *ekwo-. Table 3-1 demonstrates the similarity of words in some of the major Indo-European languages. We have emphasized numbers, which are especially stable in language systems because people do not like to change the way they count. We have also provided the equivalents in two Semitic languages (Arabic and Hebrew) to show how different these basic words are in another language family (the Afro-Asiatic).

Attempts to locate the homeland of the original speakers of Proto-Indo-European involve mapping the reconstructed vocabulary onto a matching geography. For example, some of the vocabulary contains words for "snow," "mountain," and "swift river," as well as for animals that are not native to Europe, such as "lion," "monkey," and "elephant." Other words describe agricultural practices and farming tools that date back as far as 5000 BCE.

Many linguists believe that nomadic and pastoral peoples of the Eurasian steppes took this language—along with their precious horses and chariots—as far as the borderlands of what is now Afghanistan and eastern Iran.

We know that the early speakers of Indo-European languages used chariots and had words for "wheel," "yoke," and "axle." In fact, the earliest pictures of horse-drawn chariots, used in battle, came from the steppe region east of the Ural Mountains. Indo-European-speaking nomads inhabited this area and subsequently migrated to South Asia and the Iranian plateau. Thus, the chariot was literally the vehicle for cultural mingling and, ultimately, the spread of the people's language.

Migration is only one of the possible reasons that languages move and change over vast areas and periods of time. Other influential factors are invasions, climatic conditions, natural resources, and ways of life. Even within one language, words can change through generations of use. And words from a common root can sometimes take on very different meanings while remaining similar phonetically. (To use an Indo-European root as an example, the Sanskrit *a'sura* means "demonic creature" whereas the Persian *ahura* means "Supreme God.")

Linguistic analysis sheds light on the geographic and demographic details of language penetration into different regions. Part of its allure is the fact

Shang kings used a personalized style of rule, making regular trips around the country to meet, hunt, and conduct military campaigns. With no rival territorial states on its immediate periphery, the Shang state did not create a strongly defended, permanent capital, but rather moved its capital as the frontier expanded and contracted. Bureaucrats used written records to oversee the large and expanding population of the Shang state.

Advanced Shang metalworking—the beginnings of which appeared in northwestern China at pre-Shang sites dating as early as 1800 BCE—was vital to the Shang territorial state. Shang bronze work included weapons, fittings for chariots, and ritual vessels.

that some issues defy resolution (for example, in some cases whether a given language was the dialect of the conquerors or the conquered). Nonetheless, the study of language families and their history underscores the key role of language in the intermingling of cultures throughout time.

QUESTIONS FOR ANALYSIS

• What relationships does Table 3.1 suggest among the Semitic languages and the Indo-European languages?

• How does the study of linguistics enhance our understanding of human geography?

Explore Further

David W. Anthony, *The Horse, the Wheel, and Language: How Bronze-Age Riders from the Eurasian Steppes Shaped the Modern World* (2007).

Joseph T. Shipley, *The Origins of English Words: A Discursive Dictionary of Indo-European Roots* (2001).

TABLE 3.1 | Similarity of Words in Some Major Indo-European Languages

	WORDS OF COMMON ORIGIN IN INDO-EUROPEAN LANGUAGES						SEMITIC LANGUAGES	
	SANSKRIT	HINDI	GREEK	LATIN	FRENCH	GERMAN	ARABIC	HEBREW
Numbers								
one	eka	ek	hen	unus	un	ein	wahid	ehad
two	dva	do	duo	duo	deux	zwei	ithnin	shnayim
three	tri	teen	treis	tres	trois	drei	thalatha	shlasha
four	catur	chār	tessara	quattuor	quatre	vier	arba'a	arba'a
five	pañca	pānch	penta	quinque	cinq	fünf	khamsa	hamisha
ten	daśa	das	deka	decem	dix	zehn	ashra	asara
hundred	śata	sau	hekaton	centum	cent	hundert	mi'a	me'a
Other common words								
father	pitṛ	pitā	pater	pater	père	vater	abu	aba
mother	mātṛ	mātā	mêter	mater	mère	mutter	umm	em
son	sūnu	betā	huios	filius	fils	sohn	ibn	ben
heart	hṛdaya	dil	kardia	cor	coeur	herz	qalb	lev
foot	pada	pair	pous	pes	pied	fuss	qadam	regel
god	deva	dev	theos	deus	dieu	gott	Allah	yahweh

Because copper and tin were available from the North China plain, only short-distance trade was necessary to obtain the resources that a bronze culture needed. (See Map 3.4.) Shang bronze-working technique involved the use of hollow clay molds to hold the molten metal alloy, which, when removed after the liquid had cooled and solidified, produced firm bronze objects. The casting of modular components that artisans could assemble later promoted increased production and permitted the elite to make extravagant use of bronze vessels for burials. The bronze industry of this period shows the high level not only of material culture (in the practical function of the physical objects) but also of cultural development (in the

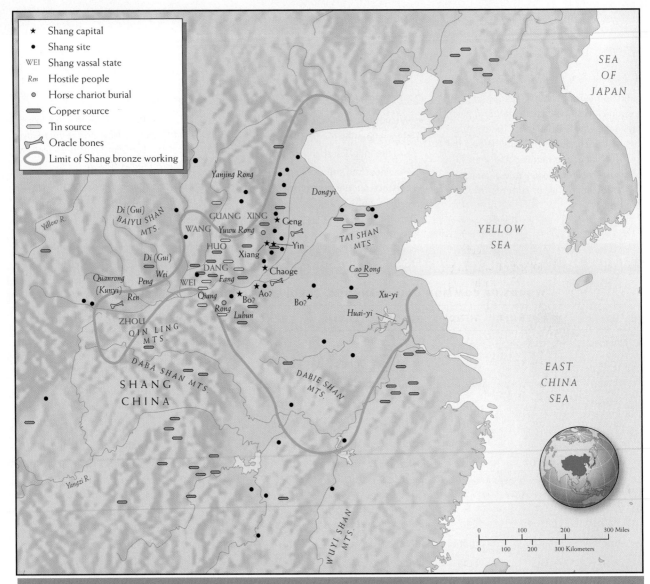

MAP 3.4 | Shang Dynasty in East Asia

The Shang state was one of the most important and powerful of early Chinese dynasties.

• Based on your analysis of this map, what raw materials were the most important to the Shang state?

• Why were there so many Shang capitals?

• Why were there no clear territorial boundaries for the Shang state?

aesthetic sense of beauty and taste conveyed by the choice of form). Since Shang metalworking required extensive mining, it necessitated a large labor force, efficient casting, and a reproducible artistic style. Although the Shang state highly valued its artisans, it treated its copper miners as lowly tribute laborers. By controlling access to tin and copper and to the production of bronze, Shang kings prevented their rivals from forging bronze weapons and thus increased their own power and legitimacy. With their superior weapons, Shang armies by 1300 BCE could easily destroy armies wielding wooden clubs and stone-tipped spears.

Chariots entered the Central Plains of China with no-mads of the north around 1200 BCE, much later than their appearance in Egypt and Southwest Asia. They were quickly adopted by the upper classes. Chinese chariots were larger (fitting three men standing in a box mounted on eighteen- or twenty-six-spoke wheels) and much better built than those of their neighbors. As symbols of power and wealth, they were often buried with their owners. Yet, unlike elsewhere in Afro-Eurasia, they were at first little used in warfare during the Shang era, perhaps because of the effectiveness and shock value of large Shang infantry forces, composed mainly of foot soldiers, armed with axes, spears, arrow-heads, shields, and helmets, all made of bronze. The chariot's primary purposes in Shang China were hunting and as a marker of high status. Shang metalworking and their incor-poration of the chariot gave the Shang state a huge advantage and unprecedented power over its neighbors.

AGRICULTURE AND TRIBUTE

The Shang dynastic rulers also understood the impor-tance of agriculture for winning and maintaining power, so they did much to promote its development. The activ-ities of local governors and the masses revolved around agriculture. Rulers controlled their own farms, which supplied food to the royal family, craftworkers, and the army. Farmers drained low-lying fields and cleared for-ested areas to expand the cultivation of millet, wheat, barley, and possibly rice. Their tools included stone plows, spades, and sickles. Farmers also cultivated silk-worms and raised pigs, dogs, sheep, and oxen. Thanks to the twelve-month, 360-day lunar calendar developed by Shang astrologers, farmers were better able to track the growing season. By including leap months, this calendar maintained the proper re-lationship between months and seasons, and it relieved fears about solar and lunar eclipses by making them predictable.

The ruler's wealth and power depended on tribute from elites and allies. Elites supplied warriors and laborers, horses and cattle. Allies sent foodstuffs, soldiers, and workers and "assisted in the king's affairs"—perhaps by hunting, burning brush, or clearing land—in return for his help in defending against invaders and making predictions about the harvest. Commoners sent their tribute to the elites, who held the land as grants from the king. Farm-ers transferred their surplus crops to the elite landholders (or to the ruler if they worked on his personal landholdings) on a regular schedule. Tribute could also take the form of turtle shells and cattle scapulas (shoulder blades), which the Shang used for divination (see below). Divining the future was a powerful way to legitimate royal power—and then to justify the right to collect more tribute. By placing themselves symbolically and literally at the center of all exchanges, the Shang kings reinforced their power over others.

SOCIETY AND RITUAL PRACTICE

The advances in metalworking and agriculture gave the state the resources to sustain a complex society, in which religion and rituals reinforced the social hierarchy. The core

Bronze At the height of the Shang state, circa 1200 BCE, its rulers erected massive palaces at the capital of Yin, which required bronze foundries for its wine and food vessels. In these foundries, skilled workers produced bronze weapons and ritual objects and elaborate ceremonial drinking and eating vessels, like the one pictured.

organizing principle of Shang society was familial descent traced back many generations to a common male ancestor. Grandparents, parents, sons, and daughters lived and worked together and held property in common, but male family elders took precedence. Women from other male family lines married into the family and won honor when they became mothers, particularly of sons.

The death ritual, which involved sacrificing humans to accompany the deceased in the next life, reflected the importance of family, male dominance, and social hierarchy. Members of the royal elite were often buried with full entourage, including wives, consorts, servants, chariots, horses, and drivers. The inclusion of personal slaves and servants indicates a belief that the familiar social hierarchy would continue in the afterlife.

The Shang state was a full-fledged theocracy: it claimed that the ruler at the top of the hierarchy derived his authority through guidance from ancestors and gods. Shang rulers practiced ancestral worship, which was the major form of religious belief in China during this period. Ancestor worship involved performing rituals in which the rulers offered drink and food to their recently dead ancestors with the hope that they would intervene with their more powerful long-dead ancestors on behalf of the living. Divination was the process by which Shang rulers communicated with ancestors and foretold the future. The technique involved diviners' applying intense heat to the shoulder bones of cattle or to turtle shells and interpreting the cracks that appeared on these objects as auspicious or inauspicious signs from the ancestors regarding royal plans and actions. On these so-called **oracle bones**, scribes subsequently inscribed the queries asked of the ancestors to confirm the diviners' interpretations. Thus, Shang writing began as a dramatic ritual performance in which the living responded to their ancestors' oracular signs.

The oracle bones and tortoise shells offer a window into the concerns and beliefs of the elite groups of these very distant cultures. The questions put to diviners most frequently as they inspected bones and shells were about the weather, hardly surprising in communities so dependent on growing seasons and good harvests, about family health and well-being, and especially about the prospects of having male children, who would extend the family line.

In Shang theocracy, because the ruler was the head of a unified clergy and embodied both religious and political power, no independent priesthood emerged. Diviners and scribes were subordinate to the ruler and the royal pantheon of ancestors he represented. Ancestor worship sanctified Shang control and legitimized the rulers' lineage, ensuring that the ruling family kept all political and religious power. Because the Shang gods were ancestral deities, the rulers were deified when they died and ranked in descending chronological order. Becoming gods at death, Shang rulers united the world of the living with the world of the dead.

SHANG WRITING

In the process of scribes' and priests' using their script on oracle bones for the Shang king, the formal character-based writing of East Asia developed over time. So although Shang scholars did not invent writing in East Asia, they perfected it. Evidence for writing in this era comes entirely from oracle bones, which were central to political and religious authority under the Shang. Other written records may have been on materials that did not survive. This accident of preservation may explain the major differences between the ancient texts in China (primarily divinations on bones) and in the Southwest Asian societies that impressed cuneiform on clay tablets (primarily for economic transactions, literary and religious documents, and historical records). In comparison with Mesopotamia and Egypt, the transition of Shang record keeping (for example, questions to ancestors, lineages of rulers, or economic transactions) to literature (for example, myths about the founding of states) was slower. Shang rulers initially monopolized writing through their scribes, who positioned the royal families at the top of the social and political hierarchy. And priests wrote on the oracle bones to address the otherworld and gain information about the future so that the ruling family would remain at the center of the political system.

As Shang China cultivated developments in agriculture, ornate bronze metalworking and divinatory writing on oracle bones, the state did not face the repeated waves of pastoral nomadic invaders seen in other parts of Afro-Eurasia. It was nonetheless influenced by the chariot culture that eventually filtered into East Asia. Given that so many of the developments in Shang China bolstered the authority of the dynastic rulers and elite, it is perhaps not surprising that the chariot in China was initially more a marker of elite status than an effective tool for warfare.

Microsocieties in the South Pacific and in the Aegean

As environmental circumstances drove pastoral nomads and transhumant herders toward settled agriculturalists, leading ultimately to the development of powerful and somewhat intertwined territorial states in Egypt, Southwest Asia, the Indus River Valley, and Shang China, other pressures drove migrations across the South Pacific and Aegean. These maritime migrations led to the development after 2000 BCE, in such places as Austronesia and the Aegean, of **microsocieties**: small-scale, fragmented, and dispersed communities that had limited interaction with others.

COMPARISON

EXAMINE the development of microsocieties in the South Pacific and the Aegean and **EXPLAIN** the role geography played in their development.

THE SOUTH PACIFIC (2500 BCE–400 CE)

Austronesian-speaking peoples with origins in coastal South China migrated into the South Pacific during this period and formed microsocieties there. Using their double-outrigger canoes, which were 60 to 100 feet long and bore huge triangular sails, the early Austronesians crossed the Taiwan Straits and colonized key islands in the Pacific. Their vessels were much more advanced than the simple dugout canoes used in inland waterways. In good weather, double-outrigger canoes could cover more than 120 miles in a day. The invention of a stabilization device for deep-sea sailing sometime after 2500 BCE triggered further Austronesian expansion into the Pacific. By 400 CE, these nomads of the sea had reached most of the islands of the South Pacific. Their seafaring skills enabled the Austronesians to monopolize trade wherever they went.

By comparing the vocabularies and grammatical similarities of languages spoken today by the remaining tribal peoples in Taiwan, the Philippines, and Indonesia, scholars have traced the ancient Austronesian-speaking peoples back to coastal South China in the fourth millennium BCE. Pottery, stone tools, and domesticated crops and pigs also provide markers for tracking Austronesian settlements throughout the coastal islands and in the South Pacific. According to archaeologists, the same cultural features had spread from Taiwan to the Philippines (by 2500 BCE), to Java and Sumatra (by 2000 BCE), and parts of Australia and New Guinea (by 1600 BCE). The Austronesians then ventured farther eastward into the South Pacific, apparently arriving in Samoa and Fiji in 1200 BCE

Austronesian Canoe Early Austronesians crossed the Taiwan Straits and colonized key islands in the Pacific using double-outrigger canoes from 60 to 100 feet long equipped with triangular sails. In good weather, such canoes could cover more than 120 miles in a day.

and on mainland Southeast Asia in 1000 BCE. (See Map 3.5.) The Austronesians reached the Marquesas Islands, strategically located for northern and southern exploration, in the central Pacific around 200 CE. Over the next few centuries, some moved on to Easter Island to the south and Hawaii to the north. The immense thirty-ton stone structures on Easter Island represent the monumental Polynesian architecture produced after their arrival.

Equatorial lands in the South Pacific have a tropical or subtropical climate and, in many places, fertile soils containing nutrient-rich volcanic ash. In this environment the Austronesians cultivated dry-land crops (yams and sweet potatoes), irrigated crops (more yams, which grew better in paddy fields or in rainy areas), and tree crops (breadfruit, bananas, and coconuts). In addition, colonized areas beyond the landmass, such as the islands of Indonesia, had labyrinthine coastlines rich in maritime resources, including coral reefs and mangrove swamps teeming with wildlife. Island hopping led the adventurers to encounter new food sources, but the shallow waters and reefs offered sufficient fish and shellfish for their needs.

In the South Pacific, the Polynesian descendants of the early Austronesians shared a common culture, language, technology, and stores of domesticated plants and animals. These later seafarers came from many different island communities (hence the name *Polynesian*, "belonging to many islands"), and after they settled down, their numbers grew. Their crop surpluses allowed more densely populated communities to support craft specialists and soldiers. Most settlements boasted ceremonial buildings to promote local solidarity and forts to provide defense. On larger islands, communities often cooperated and organized workforces to enclose ponds for fish production and to build and maintain large irrigation works for agriculture. In terms of political structure, Polynesian communities ranged from tribal or village units to multi-island alliances that sometimes invaded other areas.

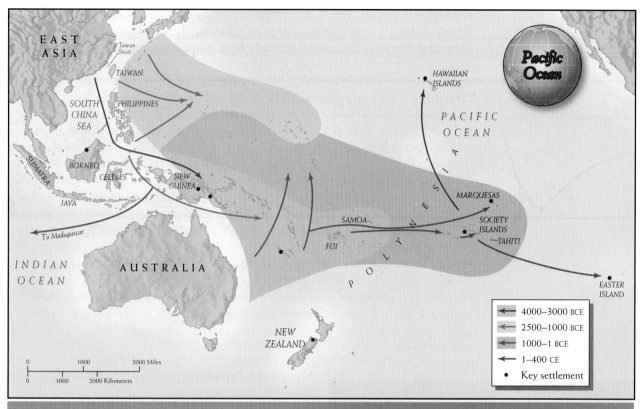

MAP 3.5 | Austronesian Migrations

The Pacific Ocean saw many migrations from East Asia.

- Where did the Austronesian migrants come from?
- What were the boundaries of their migration?
- Why, unlike other migratory people during the second millennium, did Austronesian settlers in Polynesia become a world apart?

The expansion of East Asian peoples throughout the South Pacific and their trade back and forth, however, did not integrate the islands into the mainland culture. Expansion could not overcome the tendency of these Austronesian microsocieties, dispersed across a huge ocean, toward fragmentation and isolation.

THE AEGEAN WORLD (2000–1200 BCE)

In the region around the Aegean Sea (the islands and the mainland of present-day Greece), no single power emerged before the second millennium BCE, but island microsocieties (the Minoans and the Mycenaeans) developed an expanding trade network and distinctive cultures. Settled agrarian communities were linked only by trade and culture. Fragmentation was the norm—in part because the landscape had no great riverine systems or large common plain. In its fragmentation, the island world of the eastern Mediterranean initially resembled that of the South Pacific.

As an unintended benefit of the lack of centralization, there was no single regime to collapse when the droughts arrived. Thus, in the second millennium BCE, peoples of the eastern Mediterranean did not struggle to recover lost grandeur. Rather, they enjoyed a remarkable though gradual development, making advances based on influences they absorbed from Southwest Asia, Egypt, and Europe. Residents of Aegean islands like Crete and Thera enjoyed extensive trade with the Greek mainland, Egypt, Anatolia, Syria, and Palestine. It was also a time of population movements from the Danube region and central Europe into the Mediterranean. Groups of these migrants settled in mainland Greece in the centuries after 1900 BCE; modern archaeologists have named them Mycenaeans after their famous palace at Mycenae. Soon after settling in their new environment, the Mycenaeans turned to the sea to look for resources and interaction with their neighbors.

At the outset, the main influence on the Aegean world came from the east by sea. As the institutions and ideas that had developed in Southwest Asia moved westward, they found a ready reception along the coasts and on the islands of the Mediterranean. Trade was the main source of eastern influences, with vessels carrying cargoes from island to island and up and down the commercial centers along the coast. (See Map 3.6.) Mediterranean trade centered on tin from the east and readily available copper, both essential for making bronze (the primary metal in tools and weapons). Islands such as Cyprus and Crete, located in the midst of the active sea-lanes, flourished. Cyprus had large reserves of copper ore, which started to generate intense activity around 2300 BCE. By 2000 BCE, harbors on the southern and eastern sides of the island were shipping and transshipping goods, along with copper ingots, as far west as Crete, east to the Euphrates River, and south to Egypt.

Seaborne Trade The size of the seaborne trade is revealed most spectacularly in the shipwrecks recovered by underwater archaeologists. One of these ships, sunk off the southern coast of Anatolia around 1325 BCE, was transporting ten tons of copper in 354 oxhide-shaped ingots, as well as more than a hundred amphorae (large, two-handled jars) containing all kinds of high-value commodities.

Minoan Culture Crete, too, was an active trading node in the Mediterranean, and its culture reflected outside influences as well as local traditions. Around 2000 BCE, a large number of independent palace centers began to emerge on Crete, at Knossos (ultimately the most impressive of them) and elsewhere. Scholars have named the people who built these elaborate centers the Minoans, after the legendary King Minos who may have ruled Crete at this time. The Minoans sailed back and forth across the Mediterranean, and by 1600 BCE they were colonizing other Aegean islands as trading and mining centers. The Minoans' wealth soon became a magnet for the Mycenaeans, their mainland competitors, who took over Crete around 1400 BCE.

As the island communities traded with the peoples of Southwest Asia, they borrowed some ideas but also kept their own cultural traditions. In terms of borrowing, the monumental architecture of Southwest Asia found small-scale echoes in the Aegean world—notably in the palace complexes built on Crete between 1900 and 1600 BCE.

In terms of a distinctive cultural element, worship on the islands focused on a female deity, the "Lady," but there are no traces of large temple complexes similar to those in Mesopotamia, Anatolia, and Egypt. Nor, apparently, was there any priestly class of the type that managed the temple complexes of Southwest Asian societies. Moreover, it is unclear whether these societies had full-time scribes.

Perhaps not surprisingly for a fragmented microsociety, there was significant regional diversity within this small

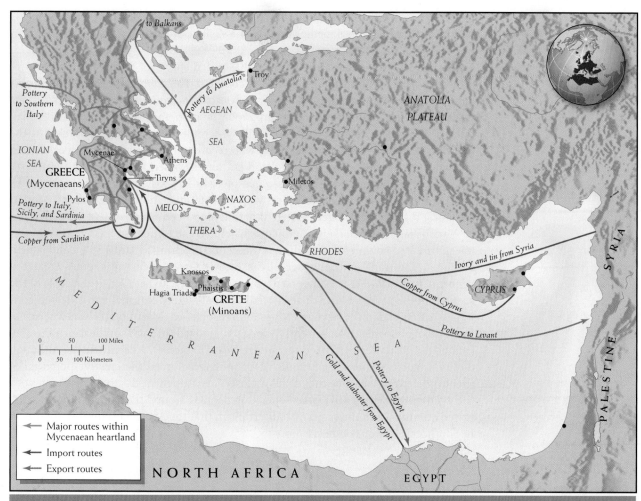

MAP 3.6 | Trade in the Eastern Mediterranean World

Greece, Egypt, and Cyprus were trade hubs in the eastern Mediterranean.

- What were the major commodities that were traded in the eastern Mediterranean?
- Why did trade originally move from east to west?
- What role did geographic location play in terms of the Mycenaeans eventually conquering the Minoans?

Aegean world. On Crete, the large, palace-centered communities controlled centrally organized societies with a high order of refinement. Confident in their wealth and power, the sprawling, airy palaces had no fortifications and no natural defenses. On Thera, a small island to the north of Crete, a trading city centered not on a major palace complex, but rather featured private houses, with bathrooms including toilets and running water and other rooms decorated with exotic wall paintings.

Mycenaean Culture The Mycenaean culture was more war-oriented than that of the peaceful, seafaring Minoans. When the Mycenaeans migrated to Greece from central Europe, they brought their Indo-European language, their horse chariots, and their metalworking skills. Their move was gradual, lasting from about 1850 to 1600 BCE, but ultimately they dominated the indigenous population. They maintained their dominance with their powerful weapon, the chariot, until 1200 BCE. The battle chariots and festivities of chariot racing described in the centuries-later epic poetry of Homer express memories of glorious chariot feats that echo Vedic legends from South Asia.

The Mycenaean material culture emphasized displays of weaponry, portraits of armed soldiers, and illustrations of violent conflicts. The main palace centers at Tiryns and Mycenae were the hulking fortresses of warlords surrounded by rough-hewn stone walls and strategically located atop large rock outcroppings. In these fortified urban hubs, a preeminent ruler (*wanax*) stood atop a complex bureaucratic hierarchy. At the heart of the palace society were scribes, who recorded the goods and services allotted to local farmers, shepherds, and metalworkers, among others. Tombs of the Mycenaean elite contain many gold vessels and ostentatious gold masks. Amber beads in the tombs indicate that the warriors had contacts with inhabitants of northern European coniferous forest regions, whose trees secreted that highly valued resin.

Mycenaean expansion eventually overwhelmed the Minoans on Crete. The Mycenaeans created colonies and trading settlements, reaching as far as Sicily and southern Italy. The trade and language of these early Greek-speaking peoples created a veneer of unity linking the dispersed worlds of the Aegean Sea. Yet, at the close of the second millennium BCE, the eastern Mediterranean faced internal and external convulsions that ended the heyday of these microsocieties. Most notable was a series of migrations of peoples from central Europe who moved through southeastern Europe, Anatolia, and the eastern Mediterranean (see Chapter 4). The invasions, although often destructive, did not extinguish but rather reinforced the creative potential of this frontier area. Because theirs was a closed maritime world—in comparison with the wide-open Pacific—the Greek-speaking peoples around the Aegean quickly reasserted dominance in the eastern Mediterranean that the Austronesians did not match in Southeast Asia or Polynesia.

Aegean Fresco This is one of the more striking wall paintings, or frescoes, discovered by archaeologists in the 1970s and 1980s at Akrotiri on the island of Thera (Santorini) in the Aegean Sea. Its brilliant colors, especially the blue of the sea, evoke the lively essence of Minoan life on the island. Note the houses of the wealthy along the port and the flotilla of ships that reflects the seaborne commerce that was beginning to flourish in the Mediterranean in this period.

Conclusion

The second millennium BCE was an era of migrations, warfare, and territorial state building in Afro-Eurasia. Whereas river-basin societies had flourished in the fourth and third millennia BCE in Mesopotamia, Egypt, the Indus Valley, and East Asia, now droughts shook the agrarian foundations of their economies. Old states crumbled; from the steppes and plateaus pastoral nomads and transhumant herders descended in search of food, grazing lands, and other opportunities. As transhumant herders pressed into the river-basin societies, the social and political fabric of these communities changed. Likewise, horse-riding nomads from steppe communities in Inner Eurasia conquered and settled in the agrarian states, bringing key innovations. Foremost were the horse chariots, which became a military catalyst sparking the evolution from smaller states to larger territorial states encompassing crowded cities, vast hinterlands, and broadened trade networks. The nomads and herders also adopted many of the settled peoples' beliefs and customs. On land and sea, migrating peoples created zones of long-distance trade that linked agrarian societies.

Through a range of trade, migrations, and conquest throughout the second millennium BCE, the Nile Delta, the basin of the Tigris and Euphrates rivers, the Indus Valley, and the Yellow River basin were brought into even closer contact than before. In Southwest Asia and the Nile River basin, the interaction led to an elaborate system of diplomatic relations. The first territorial states appeared in this millennium, composed of multiple communities living under common laws and customs. An alliance of farmers and warriors united agrarian production with political power to create and defend territorial boundaries. The new arrangements overshadowed the nomads' historic role as predators and enabled them to become military elites within these new states. Through taxes and drafted labor, villagers repaid their rulers for local security and state-run diplomacy. The rhythms of state formation differed where regimes were not closely packed together. In East Asia, for example, the absence of strong rivals allowed the emerging Shang dynasty to develop more gradually. Where landscapes had sharper divisions—as in the island archipelagos of the South Pacific and in the Mediterranean—small-scale, decentralized, and fragmented microsocieties emerged. But fragmentation is not the same as isolation. Even peoples in the worlds apart from the developments across Afro-Eurasia were not entirely secluded from the increasing flows of technologies, languages, goods, and migrants.

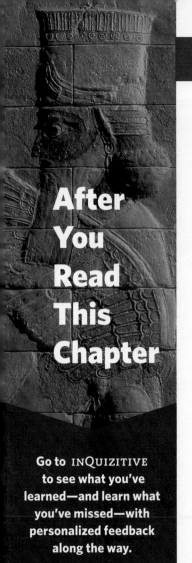

After You Read This Chapter

Go to INQUIZITIVE to see what you've learned—and learn what you've missed—with personalized feedback along the way.

FOCUS ON: *The Emergence of Territorial States*

EGYPT AND SOUTHWEST ASIA

- Invasions by nomads and transhumant herders lead to the creation of larger territorial states: New Kingdom Egypt, Hittites, Mesopotamian states.

- A centuries-long peaceful era, a community of major powers, emerges among the major states as the result of shrewd statecraft and diplomacy.

INDUS RIVER VALLEY

- Migratory Vedic peoples from the steppes of Inner Eurasia use chariots and rely on domesticated animals to spread out and begin integrating the northern half of South Asia.

SHANG STATE (CHINA)

- Shang dynastic rulers promote improvements in metalworking, agriculture, and the development of writing, leading to the growth of China's first major state.

MICROSOCIETIES

- Substantial increases in population, migrations, and trade lead to the emergence of microsocieties among peoples in the South Pacific (Austronesians) and the Aegean world (Minoans and Mycenaeans).

CHRONOLOGY

EGYPT AND SOUTHWEST ASIA		Middle Kingdom in Egypt 2055-1650 BCE
SOUTH ASIA		
EAST ASIA		
THE MEDITERRANEAN		
SOUTH PACIFIC		Austronesian migrations 2500 BCE-400 CE
	2500 BCE	**2000 BCE**

- *Thinking about Environmental Impacts and Territorial States* Around 2000 BCE, a series of environmental disasters helped to destroy the civilizations that had thrived in parts of Afro-Eurasia in the third millennium BCE. What were the short-term and long-term impacts of these environmental troubles? How did they influence the movement of peoples and the formation of territorial states in the second millennium BCE?

- *Thinking about Transformation & Conflict and Territorial States* The second millennium BCE witnessed large-scale migrations of nomadic peoples who brought with them their domesticated horses and their chariot technology. These people are referred to by scholars as Indo-Europeans, largely on the basis of their languages (see Current Trends in World History: How Languages Spread). Contrast the impact of migrations into Southwest Asia (Anatolia and Mesopotamia), Egypt, South Asia, and East Asia. To what extent did conflict play a role in the impact of Indo-European-language speakers on the formation of territorial states?

- *Thinking about Interconnection & Divergence and Territorial States* While territorial states formed in Egypt, Mesopotamia, South Asia, and East Asia, microsocieties formed in the South Pacific and in the Aegean Sea. What factors influenced whether a region might host a territorial state as opposed to a microsociety? What areas of the planet were still worlds apart? What ways of life continued to predominate in those worlds apart from the territorial states and microsocieties discussed in this chapter?

1. Explain the differences between **pastoral nomads** and **transhumant herders**. How did each shape Afro-Eurasian history during the second millennium BCE?

2. Analyze the impact on Afro-Eurasia of the domestication of horses and the invention of the **chariot**. How did these developments affect both nomadic and settled peoples?

3. Define the term **territorial state**. In what areas of Afro-Eurasia did this new form of political organization emerge and thrive?

4. How do Amun-Re, Ahmosis, and Hatshepsut contribute to an understanding of Egypt as a territorial state? Explain the role of the **Amorites** and **Hammurapi's Code** in the formation of territorial state in Mesopotamia. What do these developments suggest about the religious, political, and legal dimensions of territorial states?

5. In what ways did the **Hyksos** and **Hittites** influence territorial state formation in Egypt and Mesopotamia? How does the Battle of Qadesh offer an example of that interaction?

6. Contrast the formation of territorial states in Egypt and Mesopotamia with the impact of Vedic peoples in South Asia.

7. Contrast the formation of the Shang state in East Asia with developments happening at the same time in Egypt, Mesopotamia, and South Asia. Explain the role of metallurgy and **oracle bones** in supporting Shang authority.

8. Define the term **microsociety**. Compare and contrast Polynesian microsocieties of the South Pacific with the Minoans and Mycenaeans of the Aegean.

New Kingdom in Egypt 1550-1070 BCE

Hammurapi's Babylonia 1792-1750 BCE

Community of major powers 1400-1200 BCE

Vedic migration into Indus River valley begins 1500 BCE

Vedic migration into Ganges River valley begins 1000 BCE

Shang state 1600-1046 BCE

Minoan culture in Aegean 2000-1600 BCE

Mycenaean culture in Greece and Aegean 1850-1200 BCE

Competing Perspectives

Law Codes of Territorial States and Pastoral Nomads

In addition to charismatic monarchs and complex bureaucracies, one of the ways territorial states brought order to the large regions under their control was through clear codes of law. These could range from elaborate legal codes, such as that of Hammurapi, to more general instructions to leaders on how to administer justice. Pastoral nomadic groups, like the Hebrews and Vedic peoples, also developed law codes, especially as they began to settle down. Some law codes operated on an "if/then" formula (*if* a certain crime is committed, *then* a certain punishment is to be meted out), others laid out clear and forceful rules for proper behavior, while yet others deliberated on procedure and punishment. Some law codes mention gods specifically, while others appear to focus primarily on human interactions and appeal to earthly authority. Many of the law codes of territorial states reveal distinctions based on class, occupation, and gender.

Presented here is a series of early law codes. From a Babylonian territorial state in Mesopotamia, Hammurapi's Code with its 282 laws covering everything from property ownership to marriage is one of the earliest recorded law codes, dating to the 18th century BCE. No comprehensive law codes survive from Middle or New Kingdom Egypt, but a set of instructions to Rekhmire, a pharaoh's vizier (chief minister), from around 1450 BCE, gives a keen sense of how judgments were made at the Egyptian court. Hundreds of laws are contained in the priestly Levitical codes of Hebrew scripture; but the Ten Commandments are perhaps the clearest, most direct statement of the laws binding this nomadic people with their god and one another. The fourth document, the Code of Manu, is thought to represent some of the earliest laws of the nomadic Vedic peoples of South Asia. The code's nearly 2,700 verses were written down in Sanskrit sometime after 200 BCE, but the laws about social interactions in the excerpt here may well date to a much earlier time. The Chinese text included here is from the sixth century BCE and suggests that Shang kings did not publicize a penal code, but did create a clear system of punishments.

PRIMARY SOURCE 3.1

The Code of Hammurapi (ca. 18th century BCE)

1. If a man bring an accusation against a man, and charge him with a (capital) crime, but cannot prove it, he, the accuser, shall be put to death.

2. If a man charge a man with sorcery, and cannot prove it, he who is charged with sorcery shall go to the river, into the river he shall throw himself and if the river overcome him, his accuser shall take to himself his house (estate). If the river show that man to be innocent and he come forth unharmed, he who charged him with sorcery shall be put to death. He who threw himself into the river shall take to himself the house of his accuser.

3. If a man, in a case (pending judgment), bear false (threatening) witness, or do not establish the testimony that he has given, if that case be a case involving life, that man shall be put to death.

• • •

6. If a man steal the property of a god (temple) or palace, that man shall be put to death; and he who receives from his hand the stolen (property) shall also be put to death.

7. If a man purchase silver or gold, manservant or maid servant, ox, sheep or ass, or anything else from a man's son, or from a man's servant without witnesses or contracts, or if he receive (the same) in trust, that man shall be put to death as a thief.

8. If a man steal ox or sheep, ass or pig, or boat—if it be from a god (temple) or a palace, he shall restore thirty-fold; if it be from a freeman, he shall render tenfold. If the thief have nothing wherewith to pay he shall be put to death.

• • •

45. If a man rent his field to a tenant for crop-rent and receive the crop-rent of his field and later Adad (*i.e.*, the Storm God) inundate the field and carry away the produce, the loss (falls on) the tenant.

46. If he have not received the rent of his field and he have rented the field for either one-half or one-third (of the crop), the tenant and the owner of the field shall divide the grain which is in the field according to agreement.

• • •

128. If a man take a wife and do not arrange with her the (proper) contracts, that woman is not a (legal) wife.

129. If the wife of a man be taken in lying with another man, they shall bind them and throw them into the water. If the

husband of the woman would save his wife, or if the king would save his male servant (he may).

130. If a man force the (betrothed) wife of another who has not known a male and is living in her father's house, and he lie in her bosom and they take him, that man shall be put to death and that woman shall go free.

• • •

138. If a man would put away his wife who has not borne him children, he shall give her money to the amount of her marriage settlement and he shall make good to her the dowry which she brought from her father's house and then he may put her away.

139. If there were no marriage settlement, he shall give to her one mana of silver for a divorce.

140. If he be a freeman, he shall give her one-third mana of silver.

141. If the wife of a man who is living in his house, set her face to go out and play the part of a fool, neglect her house, belittle her husband, they shall call her to account; if her husband say: "I have put her away," he shall let her go. On her departure nothing shall be given to her for her divorce. If her husband say: "I have not put her away," her husband may take another woman. The first woman shall dwell in the house of her husband as a maid servant.

142. If a woman hate her husband, and say: "Thou shalt not have me," they shall inquire into her antecedents for her defects; and if she have been a careful mistress and be without reproach and her husband have been going about and greatly belittling her, that woman has no blame. She shall receive her dowry and go to her father's house.

Source: *The Code of Hammurabi, King of Babylon, About 2250 B.C*, 2nd edition, trans. Robert Francis Harper (Union, New Jersey: The University of Chicago Lawbook Exchange, Ltd., 1999): 11, 13, 27, 45, 49, 51.

Instruction to Vizier Rekhmire (ca. 15th century BCE)

[L]et one be afraid of thee, (for) a prince is a prince of whom one is afraid. . . . Be not known to the people; and they shall not say: "He is (only) a man." . . . As for every act of this official, the vizier while hearing in the hall of the vizier, he shall sit upon a chair, with a rug upon the floor, and a dais upon it, a cushion under his back, a cushion under his feet, . . . and a baton at his hand. . . . Then the magnates of the South (shall stand) in the two aisles before him, while the master of the privy chamber is on his right, the [receiver of income] on his left, the scribes of the vizier at his (either) hand; one [corresponding] to another, with each man at his proper place. One shall be heard after another, without allowing one who is behind to be heard

before one who is in front. . . . Let not any official be empowered to judge [against a superior] in his hall. . . . It is the vizier who shall punish him, in order to expiate his fault. Let not any official have power to punish in his hall. . . . It is he who dispatches the official staff, to attend to the water-supply in the whole land. It is he who dispatches the mayors and village sheiks to plow for harvest time. It is he who [appoints] the overseers of hundreds in the hall of the king's-house. It is he who [arranges] the hearing of the mayors and village sheiks who go forth in his name, of South and North. Every matter is reported to him; there are reported to him the affairs of the southern fortress . . . . It is he who takes every deposition; it is he who hears [it]. It is he who dispatches the [district] soldiers and scribes to carry out the [administration] of the king. The records of the nome are in his hall. . . . It is he who makes the boundary of every nome . . . all divine offerings and every contract. . . . It is he who appoints every appointee to the hall of judgment, when any litigant comes to him from the king's-house. It is he who hears every edict.

Source: *Ancient Records of Egypt: Historical Documents from the Earliest Times to the Persian Conquest*, Volume 2, trans. James Henry Breasted (Chicago, Ill.: The University of Chicago Press, 1906): 269–70, 273, 275, 279.

The Ten Commandments, Exodus 20:1-17 from The Bible

Exodus 20: [1]Then God spoke all these words, saying, [2]"I am the LORD your God, who brought you out of the land of Egypt, out of the house of slavery. [3]you shall have no other gods before me. [4]You shall not make for yourself an idol whether in the form of anything that is in heaven above, or that is on the earth beneath, or that is in the water under the earth; [5]you shall not bow down to them or worship them; for I the LORD your God am a jealous God . . . [6]but showing steadfast love to thousands of those who love me and keep my commandments. [7]You shall not take the name of the LORD your God in vain; for the LORD will not acquit anyone who takes his name in vain. [8]Remember the sabbath day, to keep it holy. [9]Six days you shall labor and do all your work. [10]But the seventh day is a sabbath to the LORD your God; you shall not do any work—you, or your son, or your daughter, your male or female slave, your cattle, or the alien within your towns; [11]for in six days the LORD made heaven and earth, the sea, and all that is in them, and rested the seventh day; . . . [12]Honor your father and your mother so that your days may be long in the land which the LORD your God gives you. [13]You shall not kill. [14]You shall not commit adultery. [15]You shall not steal. [16]You shall not bear false witness against your neighbor. [17]You shall not covet your neighbor's house; you shall not covet your neighbor's wife, or male or female slave, or ox, or donkey, or anything that belongs to your neighbor."

Source: *The New Oxford Annotated Bible: New Revised Standard Version with The Apocrypha, Fully Revised Fourth Edition.* (New York: Oxford University Press, 2010), 110–1.

PRIMARY SOURCE 3.4

The Code of Manu (ca. 200 BCE)

CHAPTER I. 1. The great sages approached Manu, who was seated with a collected mind, and, having duly worshipped him, spoke as follows: 2. 'Deign, divine one, to declare to us precisely and in due order the sacred laws of each of the (four chief) castes (varna) and of the intermediate ones. 3. 'For thou, O Lord, alone knowest the purport, (i.e.) the rites, and the knowledge of the soul, (taught) in this whole ordinance . . . which is unknowable and unfathomable.' 4. He [Manu], whose power is measureless, being thus asked by the high-minded great sages, duly honoured them, and answered, 'Listen!'. . .

CHAPTER IX. 1. I [Manu] will now propound the eternal laws for a husband and his wife who keep to the path of duty, whether they be united or separated. 2. Day and night women must be kept in dependence by the males (of) their (families). . . 3. Her father protects (her) in childhood, her husband protects (her) in youth, and her sons protect (her) in old age; a woman is never fit for independence. 4. Reprehensible is the father who gives not (his daughter in marriage) at the proper time; reprehensible is the husband who approaches not (his wife in due season), and reprehensible is the son who does not protect his mother after her husband has died. 5. Women must particularly be guarded against evil inclinations, however trifling (they may appear); for, if they are not guarded, they will bring sorrow on two families. 6. Considering that the highest duty of all castes, even weak husbands (must) strive to guard their wives. 7. He who carefully guards his wife, preserves (the purity of) his offspring, virtuous conduct, his family, himself, and his (means of acquiring) merit. . . . 10. No man can completely guard women by force; but they can be guarded by the employment of the (following) expedients: 11. Let the (husband) employ his (wife) in the collection and expenditure of his wealth, in keeping (everything) clean, in (the fulfilment of) religious duties, in the preparation of his food, and in looking after the household utensils. 12. Women, confined in the house under trustworthy and obedient servants, are not (well) guarded; but those who of their own accord keep guard over themselves, are well guarded. 13. Drinking (spirituous liquor), associating with wicked people, separation from the husband, rambling abroad, sleeping (at unseasonable hours), and dwelling in other men's houses, are the six causes of the ruin of women.

Source: *The Laws of Manu, Translated with Extracts from Seven Commentaries,* trans. Georg Bühler (Oxford at the Clarendon Press, 1886): 1, 2, 327–9.

PRIMARY SOURCE 3.5

Advisor Zichan of Zheng's Compilation of Laws (ca. 6th century BCE)

In the third month, the people of Zheng cast a penal text. Shu Xiang dispatched to Zichan a text. It stated, "Formerly, I had hope for you, but have now given it up. In the past, former kings consulted on affairs to decide them but did not make penal compilations, for they feared that the people would grow litigious. Still unable to control them, they restrained them with rightness, bound them with [good] governance, and raised them with humanness. They institutionalized emoluments and ranks to encourage their obedience and determined strict punishments so as to overawe their perversity. Fearing that that was not enough, they taught them of loyalty, rewarded good conduct, instructed them in their duties, deployed them with harmony, supervised them respectfully, supervised them with might, and adjudged them with firmness. Still they sought sagacious and erudite superiors, intelligent and astute officials, loyal and trustworthy elders, and kind and beneficent masters. It was only under such conditions that the people could be employed without disaster or disorder resulting. When the people are aware of a legal compilation, they will have no wariness of their superiors. All become contentious, appealing to the texts, and achieve their goals through lucky conniving. They cannot be governed. When the Xia had a disorderly government, they composed the *Punishments of Yu.* When the Shang had disorderly administration, they composed the *Punishments of Tang.* When the Zhou had disorderly administration, they composed the *Nine Punishments.* All three of these penal compilations arose in terminal ages. Now as advisor to the kingdom of Zheng you have rectified fields and ditches, established a reviled administration, instituted the tripartite compilation, and cast the penal text [in bronze], in order to calm the populace. Is this not difficult?"

Source: *Zuozhuan,* trans. Earnest Caldwell in "Social Change and Written Law in Early Chinese Legal Thought," *Law and History Review* 32. 1 (February 2014): 15.

QUESTIONS FOR ANALYSIS

1. What issues do territorial states, such as those of Babylon, New Kingdom Egypt, and Shang China, attempt to legislate? What sorts of issues appear to matter to the nomadic Hebrews and Vedic peoples?

2. What can you generalize about the concerns in a settled territorial state as compared with those of a more nomadic group?

3. What sorts of social distinctions (class, gender, occupation) are evident in the codes?

4. What seems to be the source of authority for each law code? What is the range of punishments? Who is responsible for enforcement? What do these variations suggest about the source of power at the heart of these societies?

Interpreting Visual Evidence

Bronze-Working

An important development in many of the territorial states of the second millennium BCE was bronze-working, which involved the smelting of copper and tin to make durable objects. Bronze was used for weapons, chariot parts (wheel-rims and lynchpins), tools, decorative objects, and ritual vessels.

The methods for casting bronze varied in different parts of Afro-Eurasia. In the east, in Shang China, artisans used an approach called the piece-mold method. In this method, artists would make a model of the item to be cast, cover it in clay to make a mold, cut the clay-mold away in pieces (even etching the clay mold to add further detail), cast the bronze into the cut pieces of the clay mold, and then reassemble the bronze pieces to make the finished product. This process allowed the artists to achieve a much greater level of detail than the lost-wax method used in the Mediterranean, in which a model is made in wax, clay formed around it, the clay form heated to melt and remove the wax, and then bronze poured into the cavity where the wax had been.

While bronze-working thrived across Afro-Eurasia in the second millennium BCE, scholars agree that Shang bronze metallurgy was far and away the most advanced. Stunning examples of intricate Shang bronze-working have been unearthed in tombs in the Yellow River valley. Shang Chinese developed a range of vessel types, one of which was the jia-type vessel (an example from ca. 15th–14th century BCE is pictured here), used for heating wine libations for ceremonies venerating ancestors. To the far west, bronze casters in Middle and New Kingdom Egypt crafted a range of items that have been found in burials. One example, dating to the 16th–13th centuries BCE is this razor handle depicting an African man playing an instrument. From Mycenae in Greece, a gold-inlay dagger from the 16th century BCE shows a Nile-scene, with papyrus flowers and cats chasing birds.

Shang "jia" vessel.

Egyptian razor handle.

Mycenaean bronze dagger.

QUESTIONS FOR ANALYSIS

1. Compare the bronze work from China, Egypt, and Greece. What does the varied craftsmanship suggest about the spread of this vital skill among territorial states in the second millennium BCE?
2. Compare what each of these items was used for and where they were found. What can you surmise about territorial states—about their hierarchies, their similarity to river basin societies—based on the find-spots for these items (elite graves) and their purpose (ritual, decorative, etc.)?
3. What does the decorative imagery on these bronze items suggest about trade and exchange among territorial states?

Before You Read This Chapter

GLOBAL STORYLINES

- Climate change, migrations, technological advances, and administrative innovations contribute to the development of the world's first great empires.
- The Neo-Assyrians and then the Persians employ two different approaches to consolidate and maintain empires in Southwest Asia.
- South Asia becomes more culturally integrated despite the absence of a strong, centralized political authority.
- The Zhou dynasty establishes loose political integration in East Asia.

CORE OBJECTIVES

- **DESCRIBE** the factors that contributed to the rise of early empires in 1250–325 BCE and the characteristics of these empires.
- **COMPARE** empire formation, or the lack thereof, in Southwest Asia, South Asia, and East Asia in this period.
- **EVALUATE** the connection between empires and war, religion, and trade.
- **ANALYZE** the relationships between empires and the peoples on their peripheries.

First Empires and Common Cultures in Afro-Eurasia

1250–325 BCE

Sennacherib—ruler of the Neo-Assyrian Empire early in the seventh century BCE—writes that at the end of one successful campaign he took "200,150 people, great and small, male and female, horses, mules, asses, camels, and sheep without number, I brought away from them and counted them my spoil." The booty about which Sennacherib boasts was unheard of in earlier ages. The immensity of such conquest highlights the arrival of a new era that involved empires with even larger geographical, political, economic, and cultural ambitions and achievements than the territorial states that preceded them (see Chapter 3). Given the nature and process of their formation, these early empires arguably replaced, rather than descended from, the earlier territorial states.

One key factor shaping these developments was warfare spurred by military innovation. Additionally, radical climate change drove many of the warrior/political leaders from the fringes of formerly powerful territorial states to the centers of power. There they established hybrid societies uniting cities and their hinterlands, among the Neo-Assyrians and Persians of Southwest Asia, Vedic parts of South Asia, and Zhou China. Imperial ideologies and religious beliefs supported the new empires. Farming yields increased and populations grew. On the fringes of empires, microsocieties arose and made significant contributions to human development: the seafaring Phoenicians developed a simplified alphabet, the Israelites espoused a strict monotheism, and Greek city-states came to the fore and even began to challenge the power of the Persian Empire.

Forces of Upheaval and the Rise of Early Empires

COMPARISON

DESCRIBE the factors that contributed to the rise of early empires in 1250–325 BCE and the characteristics of these empires.

Four related forces shaped the development of early empires in the first millennium BCE: climate change, migrations, new technologies, and administrative innovations. Migrants driven by climate change mingled with settled peoples. Ambitious leaders used innovations in technology and administration to create new states that went on to conquer other kingdoms. Gradually, a new political organization came into being: the **empire**. An empire is a group of states or different ethnic groups brought together under a single sovereign power. With varying degrees and types of centralization (as we will see in Southwest Asia, South Asia, and East Asia), empires connected distant regions through common languages, unifying political systems, trade, and shared religious beliefs. While most regions of Afro-Eurasia did not experience the rise of empire, those which did, and their neighbors, were profoundly impacted by the development.

CLIMATE CHANGE

Beginning around 1200 BCE, another prolonged period of drought gripped Afro-Eurasia, causing social upheavals and migrations and utterly destroying settled societies and long-established governments. Many regions that had enjoyed rapid population growth in the second millennium BCE now found themselves unable to support such large numbers, forcing peoples to leave their homes in search of food and fertile land. (See Map 4.1.)

From the Mediterranean to East Asia, this wave of drought led to dramatic political shifts. In Egypt, low Nile floods forced pharaohs to spend their time securing food supplies and repelling Libyans from the desert and "Sea People" marauders from the coast. In Anatolia, Hittite kings dispatched envoys to the rulers of all of the major agricultural areas, pleading for grain shipments to save their starving people. Even taking the drastic step of moving their capital to northern Syria, where food was more plentiful, did not prevent Hittite collapse. In mainland Greece, Mycenaean culture disintegrated when diminished rains made it impossible for farmers there to export wine, olives, and timber. Likewise in East Asia, radical climate change was a major factor in political developments. Arid conditions on the plains of central Asia resulted in powerful hot and dry winds carrying immense quantities of dust onto the North China plain. The dust storms reduced the soil's ability to retain moisture and led to a sharp decline in soil fertility. Some groups, like the Zhou peoples, went on the move in search of arable land.

MIGRATIONS

The violent movement of peoples, driven in part by climate change, disrupted urban societies and destroyed the administrative centers of kings, priests, and dynasties. Invaders, moving out of loosely organized peripheral societies, assaulted the urban centers and

Camels Dromedary camels (*left*) are good draft animals for travel and domestic work in the deserts of Arabia, Afghanistan, and India. Two-hump camels (*right*) are much bigger than dromedary camels. They are more suited to the extreme dry and cold weather in Iran and central Asia.

territorial kingdoms of mainland Greece, Crete, Anatolia, Mesopotamia, Egypt, and East Asia, causing the collapse of many of these once powerful states. Marauders from the Mediterranean basin and the Syrian desert upset the diplomatic relations and the elaborate system of international trade that had linked Southwest Asia and North Africa. In East Asia, the Zhou peoples, who by the twelfth century BCE were settled in the valley of the Yellow River's most important tributary, the Wei River in northwestern China, tangled with the Shang authorities and eventually overwhelmed the regime. In the Indus Valley, waves of nomads pressed down from the northwest, lured by fertile lands to the south. The upheavals caused by these migrations opened the way for new empires to develop, but only after centuries of turmoil and decline.

NEW TECHNOLOGIES

Technological innovations were crucial in reconstructing communities that had been devastated by drought and violent population movements. Advances in the use of pack camels, seaworthy vessels, iron tools for cultivation, and iron weapons for warfare facilitated the rise of empires.

The camel—first the one-humped Saharan dromedary and later the hardier two-humped Bactrian camel—helped to open up trade routes across Afro-Eurasia. The fat stored in camels' humps allows them to survive long journeys and harsh desert conditions, and thick pads under their hoofs enable them to walk smoothly over the difficult terrain that had previously hindered such long-distance exchange. Similarly, new shipbuilding technologies made a significant impact. Whereas boats had once been designed for limited transport on rivers and lakes and along shorelines, new ships boasted larger and better-reinforced hulls. Stronger masts and improved rigging allowed billowing sails to harness wind power more effectively. These innovations, along with improvements in ballast and steering, propelled bold mariners to venture out across large bodies of open water like the Mediterranean Sea.

Innovations in metalworking, in which bronze was supplanted by the harder iron, also facilitated the rise of empires. Iron became the most important and widely used metal from this time onward (hence the term Iron Age, sometimes used to describe this period). Although far

NORTH
SEA

BALTIC SEA

EUROPE

URAL MOUNTAINS

E U

Dnieper R.

Dniester R.

C E N T

ARAL
SEA

Volga R.

Danube R.

BLACK SEA

CASPIAN
SEA

MYCENAEANS   Troy
AEGEAN
SEA
Tiryns
CRETE

O

ANATOLIA

HITTITES   Nineveh
MITANNI   Ashur

IRANIAN PLATEAU

CYPRUS

SYRIAN
DESERT

ELAMITES   ZAGROS MTS.

M E D I T E R R A N E A N   S E A

F   R

LEVANT

Tyre

Jericho
Jerusalem

Babylon

SOUTHWEST ASIA

Persian Gulf

NORTH AFRICA

F

Amarna

EGYPT
Thebes

ARABIAN
PENINSULA

S A H A R A

A

Sub-Saharan periphery:
Increased population
and gradual adoption
of agriculture

Niger R.

NUBIA

RED SEA

S U B -

S A H A R A N   A F R I C A

ATLANTIC
OCEAN

Tropical woodlands:
Yams and palm nuts
cultivated

Congo R.

Lake
Victoria

	Urban cores
	Vedic settlement by 900 BCE
→	Nomadic incursions (sea peoples)
→	Nomadic incursions (pastoralists)
■	Destroyed site
•	City

A S I A

INNER ASIA

Lake Baikal

ALTAI MOUNTAINS

GOBI DESERT

L ASIA

TIEN SHAN

Lake Balkas

Oxus R. PAMIR MTS.

HINDU KUSH MTS.

TAKLAMAKAN DESERT

EAST ASIA

Yellow R.

SHANG CHINA

HIMALAYA MOUNTAINS

Indus R.

THAR DESERT

• Mithila

Ganges R.

SOUTH ASIA

Yangzi R.

DECCAN PLATEAU

Dantapura •

Ganges Valley:
Rice-farming villages

Mainland Southeast Asia:
Rice-farming villages, bronze tools and ornaments

ARABIAN SEA

Bay of Bengal

SOUTHEAST ASIA

SOUTH CHINA SEA

Maritime Southeast Asia:
Slow transition from hunting and gathering to agriculture

MAP 4.1 | Afro-Eurasia, 1200 BCE—Urban Cores and Nomadic Invaders

Nomadic incursions shattered the social and political status quo in Afro-Eurasia at this time. While destroying old polities, these migrations fostered a new social and political order in a variety of regions.

• Where did nomadic groups originate, and to where did they migrate?

• What is a major difference between the invasions of the Sea Peoples in this period versus pastoral invasions?

• Why do you think that so many of the nomadic movements were toward populated areas?

Big Forces in Early Empires

Conflict has always been a part of the human condition. But organized warfare and the use of "big force," that is large, well-disciplined armies, appears only with the formation of complex societies. The military units created in these complex societies became crucial vehicles for expanding the lands and peoples under the control of single states and broadcasting the influence of these states well beyond the territories that they controlled militarily.

Evidence for intermittent conflict among the city-states of Sumer in the fourth millennium BCE and in Old Kingdom Egypt (2649–2152 BCE) shows that local populations were drafted into a common army when needed. Permanent forces, first recorded in the Old Akkadian period in the third millennium BCE, were used to forge unity, dominate trade routes, and repel threatening "barbarians." Over the next two millennia, across the full extent of Afro-Eurasia, the technologies and structure of war machines developed along similar paths, leading to large standing armies equipped with new and improved weapons, marked by continual innovation and addition of new capabilities.

The earliest armies of Sumer were soldiers on foot arranged in a box-like (*phalanx*) formation. The men were protected by the same types of leather capes and helmets and carried the same large shields to deflect spears and arrows. This mass-formation fighting of infantry that was enabled by uniform training, uniform armaments, and state provisioning became the norm for land forces in Egypt, Assyria and, later, the Greek city-states. By the early second millennium, horse-drawn chariots were added to the force, adding mobility and the potential of surprise to an ever-larger infantry force (see Chapter 3). Mounted cavalry was introduced late in the middle of the first millennium BCE in Assyria when fighting in mountainous terrain rendered the chariot impractical. Camels, long used as pack animals, were also used in warfare, primarily by Arab tribesmen conscripted into the Assyrian army. And elephants were one of the four components of the South Asian Vedic armies, combined with cavalry, infantry, and chariots into a highly effective fighting force.

Even before the rise of complex societies and large military forces, the weapons of warfare had been those of the hunter: bows and arrows, spears, and slings. Like these weapons, knives, daggers, axes and maces were also incorporated into armies and were wielded by infantries in hand-to-hand combat. The compound bow, first used in warfare by the Sumerians, was refined by the Assyrians into a powerful projectile that could achieve an arc of more than 200 yards, raining destruction down on the opposing infantry. Although bronze was the most important metal for weapons, the introduction of iron toward the end of the second millennium BCE expanded the availability of metal for these state war machines. Since war was often conducted to acquire land, cities had to be conquered by force. Battering rams, first documented in Egypt, were added to mobile siege machines; towers supporting archers are pictured on the Assyrian stone sculptures. Levers and breaking-bars as well as tunneling were used to undermine the integrity of the walls. And scaling ladders were thrown against the fortification for the final assault.

In China, the same elements of infantry, chariots, and archers were at the core of the army from as early as the Shang dynasty.

more abundant than the tin and copper used to make bronze, iron is more difficult to extract from ore and to fabricate into useful shapes. When the technology to smelt and harden iron advanced, iron tools and weapons replaced those made of bronze. This revolution in metallurgy brought shifts in agrarian techniques, such as forged-iron-edged plows that allowed farmers to cultivate crops far beyond the traditional floodplains of riverbanks. Farmers could now till more difficult terrain to remove weeds, break up sod, and unearth fertile subsoil. These technological innovations supported larger, more integrated societies.

ADMINISTRATIVE INNOVATIONS

The expansion of the first empires depended on military might, and control of expanded territories required new administrative techniques. Beginning in the ninth

While their original goal was to capture prisoners needed for sacrifice to the ancestors, soon defensive forces were needed to protect them against their neighbors. The Zhou gradually defeated the Shang through their superior forces and more ingenious and agile tactics. A fundamental advance was made with the invention around 475 BCE of the crossbow, a far more powerful personal killing machine, and the torsion catapult, which threw both heavy projectiles and fiery masses onto the enemy. From the beginning, the techniques and technologies of war were rapidly shared across cultural boundaries as a natural result of adapting and improving on the achievements of the enemy. What mattered most for success was the ability to integrate and coordinate the increasing number of elements that went into a fighting force. The Persians learned at the hands of the Greeks that numbers and sheer firepower could not overcome agility, communication, and integration.

Towards the end of the second millennium BCE, new forms of force were appearing not just on land but also on the sea. The construction of purpose-built ships for the conduct of war on water—the world's first "battleships"—occurred over the course of the eighth century BCE in

Lachisch relief Advancing forces from reliefs in Sennacherib's palace at Nineveh commemorating the brutal Neo-Assyrian assault of Lachish in 701 BCE.

the eastern Mediterranean. These special ships were built mainly by the Phoenician and the Greek city-states whose livelihood depended on commerce on the high seas. They were not designed like the slow-sailing bulky ships used for the transport of large cargoes but were sleek and slim—about 120 feet long and only 15 wide—with little room for anything other than the men rowing them. With up to 170 rowers, they were designed and constructed for speed and power. They had no purpose other than the deliberate sinking of other

ships. At first, the rowers in ships were arranged with two banks (called "biremes" by the Greeks) and later with three (called "triremes"). The ships were armed with bronze "beaks" or rams that were used to cave in the sides of enemy ships. These ships were costly to construct, to man, to provision, and to command. As with the maintenance, training, and arming of large land forces, only relatively wealthy states and governments could afford to mount this kind of power on the high seas.

QUESTIONS FOR ANALYSIS

- What are some of the military innovations that are characteristic of "Big Forces"?
- From your reading of this chapter, what other ways could you compare empires in addition to "Big Forces"?
- Why is the comparison of empires useful for historians?

Explore Further

Pierre Briant, *From Cyrus to Alexander: A History of the Persian Empire* (2002).

Harold M. Tanner, *China: A History: From Neolithic Cultures through the Great Qing Empire (10,000 BCE – 1799 CE)*, (2009).

century BCE, fierce Neo-Assyrian soldiers, equipped with iron weaponry and armor, established their king's rule over the countryside. The Neo-Assyrians used mass deportations to break resisters' unity, to provide slave labor in parts of the empire that needed manpower, and to integrate the realm. Over 300 years, they constructed an infrastructure of roads, garrisons, and relay stations throughout the entire territory, making it easier to communicate and to move troops. Moreover, they forced subject peoples to send tribute in the form of grains, animals, raw materials, and people, in addition to precious goods such as gold and lapis lazuli, which they used to build imperial cities and to enrich the royal coffers. In later centuries, such innovations—well-equipped armies, deportation, road systems for transit and communication, and tribute—became common among empires. (See **Current Trends in World History: Big Forces in Early Empires**.)

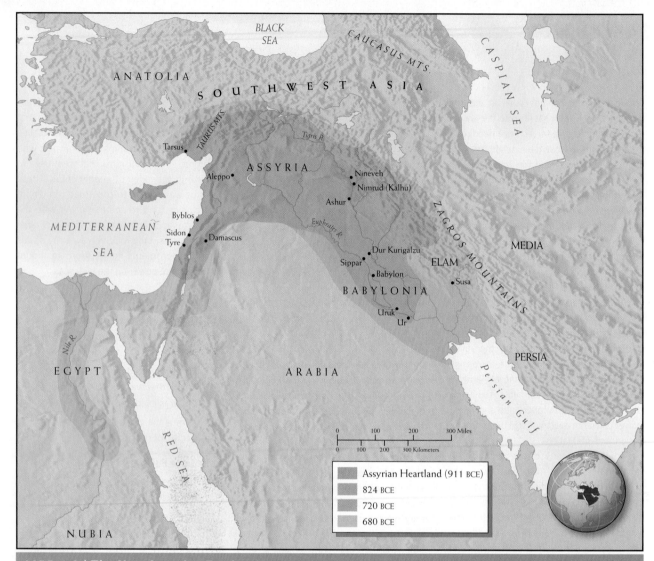

MAP 4.2 | The Neo-Assyrian Empire

The Neo-Assyrians built the first strong regional empire in Afro-Eurasia. In the process, they faced the challenge of promoting order and stability throughout their diverse realm.

- Where did the Neo-Assyrian Empire expand?
- Which parts of the empire were "the Land of Ashur," and which were "the Land under the Yoke of Ashur"?
- Why do you think expansion after 720 BCE led to the empire's destruction?

Empire in Southwest Asia: The Neo-Assyrian and Persian Empires

COMPARISON

COMPARE empire formation, or the lack thereof, in Southwest Asia, South Asia, and East Asia between 1250–325 BCE.

In Southwest Asia, the Neo-Assyrians and then the Persians offered some of the world's first experiments with true imperial control. The Neo-Assyrians (911–612 BCE) perfected early techniques of imperial rule, many of which became standard in later empires. The Neo-Assyrians also revealed the raw military side of imperial rule: constant, harsh warfare and the brutal exploitation of subjects. On the other hand, the Persians (ca. 560–331 BCE), who took control of Southwest Asia after the Neo-Assyrians, balanced their vast multicultural empire through a gentler combination of centralized administration and imperial ideology.

THE NEO-ASSYRIAN EMPIRE (911-612 BCE)

Defining features of the Neo-Assyrian empire included deportations, forced labor, and a rigid social hierarchy. Neo-Assyrian rulers divided their empire into two parts and ruled them in different ways. The core of empire, which the Assyrians called the "Land of Ashur," included such ancient cities as Ashur and Nineveh on the upper reaches of the Tigris River, and the lands between the Zagros Mountains and the Euphrates River. (See Map 4.2.) The king's appointees governed these interior lands, whose inhabitants had to supply food for the temple of the national god Ashur, manpower for the god's residence in the city of Ashur, and officials to carry out the state's business. Outside of Assyria proper lay "the Land under the Yoke of Ashur," whose inhabitants were not considered Assyrians. In these peripheral territories, local rulers held power as subjects of Assyria. These subordinated states were expected to deliver massive amounts of tribute in the form of gold and silver, as opposed to the manpower or agricultural goods supplied by those in the "Land of Ashur." Tribute went directly to the king, who used it to pay for his extravagant court and ever-increasing military costs.

Forced labor—including serving in the military—and deportations helped integrate the empire and undermine local resistance. The Neo-Assyrian armies were hardened and disciplined professional troops led by officers promoted on the basis of merit, not birth. Their military combined infantry, cavalry, iron weapons, horse-drawn chariots armored with iron plates and carrying expert archers, and siege warfare (complete with massive wheeled siege towers and iron-capped battering rams). The Neo-Assyrian army evolved over time from an all-Assyrian army that conducted annual summer campaigns to a several-hundred-thousand-strong, year-round force composed of Assyrians and conquered peoples. By the seventh century BCE, different ethnic groups in the Neo-Assyrian army performed specialized military functions: Phoenicians provided ships and sailors; Medes served as the king's bodyguards; and Israelites supplied charioteers. In addition to a military force, the Neo-Assyrian state needed huge labor forces for agricultural work and for enormous building projects. The Neo-Assyrians recruited most agricultural and construction workers from conquered peoples. Over three centuries the Neo-Assyrian Empire relocated more than 4 million people—a practice that not only supported its stupendous work projects but also undermined local resistance efforts.

Tiglath Pileser III The walls of the Neo-Assyrian palaces were lined with stone slabs carved with images of the victories of the king. This fragmentary slab from the palace of Tiglath Pileser III (r. 745–728 BCE) originally decorated the wall of his palace at Nimrud. It shows the inhabitants and their herds being forced to leave after the defeat of their town by the Assyrians. Below is Tiglath Pileser III, shaded by his royal umbrella, in his war chariot.

Neo-Assyrian Ideology and Propaganda Neo-Assyrian imperial ideology supported and justified its system of expansion, exploitation, and inequality. Even in the early stages of expansion, Assyrian inscriptions and art expressed a divinely determined destiny that drove the regime to expand westward toward the Mediterranean Sea. The national god Ashur had commanded all Assyrians to support the forcible growth of the empire, whose goal was

The Annals of Ashurbanipal
This ten-sided baked clay cylinder carries a portion of the annals of the Neo-Assyrian king, Ashurbanipal (r. 668–627 BCE). It was found at Nineveh along with thousands of other tablets preserved in his famous library. The annals of Ashurbanipal were detailed, almost novelistic accounts of his military and civic achievements. Unlike earlier annals, there is first-person discourse, indirect discourse, flashbacks, and lively description of events and places.

to establish and maintain order and keep an ever-threatening cosmic chaos at bay. Only the god Ashur and his agent, the king, could bring universal order. The king conducted holy war to transform the known world into the well-regulated Land of Ashur, intensifying his campaign of terror and expansion with elaborate propaganda. A three-pronged propaganda program—including elaborate architectural complexes and ceremonies, texts such as inscriptions and year-by-year accounts (annals) of kings' achievements, and vivid images of the army's brutal campaigns—proclaimed that Neo-Assyria's triumph was inevitable.

Neo-Assyrian Social Structure The Neo-Assyrians also exploited a rigid social hierarchy. At the top was the king, who as the sole agent of the god Ashur conducted war to expand the Land of Ashur. Below the king were military elites, rewarded through gifts of land, silver, and exemptions from royal taxes. Over time, these military elites became the noble class and controlled vast estates that included both the land and the local people who worked it. The king and the elites owned the most populous part of the society, the peasantry, in which various categories of workers had differing privileges. Many workers were enslaved because they could not pay their debts, but they were allowed to marry nonslave partners, conduct financial transactions, and even own property with other slaves attached to it. Foreigners enslaved through conquest, however, had no rights and were forced to do hard manual labor on the state's monumental building projects. Those peoples forcibly relocated were not slaves but became attached to the lands that they had to work. Families were small and lived on modest plots of land, where they raised vegetables and planted vineyards.

Women in Neo-Assyria were far more restricted than their counterparts in the earlier periods of Sumerian and Old Babylonian Mesopotamia. Under the Neo-Assyrians' patriarchal social system, women had almost no control over their lives. Because all inheritance passed through the male line, it was crucial that a man be certain of the paternity of the children borne by his wives. As a result, all interactions between men and women outside of the family were highly restricted. The so-called "Middle Assyrians" of the thirteenth century BCE had introduced the practice of veiling, requiring it of all respectable women. Prostitutes who serviced the men of the army and worked in the taverns were forbidden to wear the veil, so that their revealed faces and hair would signal their disreputable status. Any prostitute found wearing the veil would be dragged to the top of the city wall, stripped of her clothing, flogged, and sometimes even killed.

The queens of Neo-Assyria obeyed the same social norms, but their lives were more comfortable and varied than the commoners'. They lived in a separate part of the palace with servants who were either women slaves or eunuchs (castrated males). Though Neo-Assyrian queens rarely wielded genuine power, they enjoyed respect and recognition, especially in the role of mother of the king. In fact, a queen could serve as regent for her son if the king died while his heir was still a child.

The Instability of the Neo-Assyrian Empire At their peak, the Neo-Assyrians controlled most of the lands stretching from Persia to Egypt. Yet their empire was unstable, as it required occupying armies to be spread across vast territories and a relentless propaganda machine. Discontent among nobles ultimately led to civil war, which made the Neo-Assyrian Empire vulnerable to external threats as well. The conquest of Nineveh by a combined force of Medes, Neo-Babylonians, and other groups contributed to the collapse of the Neo-Assyrian Empire in 612 BCE.

THE PERSIAN EMPIRE (CA. 560–331 BCE)

After a brief interlude of Neo-Babylonian rule, the Persians asserted power and created a gentler form of imperial rule in Southwest Asia, based more on persuasion and mutual

MAP 4.3 | The Persian Empire, 550–479 BCE

Starting in the sixth century BCE, the Persians succeeded the Assyrians as rulers of the large regional empire of Southwest Asia and North Africa. Compare the Persian Empire's territorial domains to those of the Neo-Assyrian Empire in Map 4.2.

• Geographically, how did the Persian Empire differ from the Neo-Assyrian state?

• Analyzing the map, how many Persian satrapies existed, and what role do you think they played in the success of the Persian Empire?

• How does geography help explain why the Greeks were able to defeat the Persians twice?

benefit than on raw power. A nomadic group speaking an Indo-Iranian language, the Persians had arrived on the Iranian plateau from central Asia during the second millennium and gradually spread to the plateau's southwestern part. These expert horsemen shot arrows from horseback with deadly accuracy in the midst of battle. After Cyrus the Great (r. 559–529 BCE) united the Persian tribes, his armies defeated the Lydians in southwestern Anatolia and took over their gold mines, land, and trading routes. He next overpowered the Greek city-states on the Aegean coast of Anatolia. In building their immense empire, the Persians, whose ancestors were pastoralists and had no urban traditions to build on, adapted the ideologies and institutions of the Babylonians, the Neo-Assyrians, and indigenous peoples, modifying them to fit their own customs and political aims.

The Integration of a Multicultural Persian Empire From their base on the Iranian plateau, the Persian rulers developed a centralized, yet multicultural empire that reached from the Indus Valley to northern Greece and from central Asia to the south of Egypt. (See Map 4.3.) Cyrus, the founder of the Persian Empire, presented himself as a benevolent ruler who claimed to have liberated his subjects from the oppression of their own kings. He pointed to his victory in Babylon as a sign that the city's gods had turned against its king as a heretic. Cyrus released the Jews from their captivity in Babylon, to which they had been exiled by the Neo-Babylonian king Nebuchadnezzar II around 587 BCE; whereupon they returned to Jerusalem to begin rebuilding their temple in 538 BCE. Even the Greeks, who later defeated the Persians, saw Cyrus as a model ruler.

In the aftermath of Cyrus's death on the battlefield, Darius I (r. 521–486 BCE) overcame his main rival for power and put the new empire on a solid footing. First he suppressed revolts across the lands, recording this feat on the Behistun Inscription, a monumental rock relief overhanging the road to his capital, Persepolis. Then he conquered territories held by dozens of different ethnic groups, stretching from the Indus River in the east to the Aegean and Mediterranean seas in the west, and from the Black, Caspian, and Aral seas in the north to the Nile River in the south. To manage this huge domain, Darius introduced dynamic administrative systems that enabled the empire to flourish for another two centuries. Its new bureaucracy combined central and local administration and made effective use of the strengths of local tradition, economy, and rule—rather than forcing Persian customs on subject people via rigid central control.

This empire was both centralized and multicultural. The Persians believed that all subject peoples were equal; the only requirements were to be loyal to the king and to pay tribute—which was considered an honor, not a burden. Although local Persian administrators used local languages, Aramaic (a dialect of a Semitic language long spoken in Southwest Asia) became the empire's official language because many of its literate scribes came from Mesopotamia. Darius brought the wealth of the periphery to the imperial center by establishing a system of provinces, or **satrapies**, each ruled by a governor (called a satrap) who was a relative or a close associate of the king. The local bureaucrats and officials who administered the government worked under close monitoring by military officers, central tax collectors, and spies (the so-called eyes of the king) who enforced the satraps' loyalty. Darius established a system of fixed taxation and formal tribute allocations. Moreover, he promoted trade throughout the empire by building roads, establishing a standardized currency including coinage, and introducing standard weights and measures. These strategies helped integrate and centralize the empire's vast territories.

Zoroastrianism, Ideology, and Social Structure The Persians built their ideology of kingship and their social structure on religious foundations. They drew their religious ideas from their pastoral and tribal roots, and thus their ideology reflected traditions of warrior and priestly classes similar to those preserved in the Vedic texts of the Indus Valley. Zoroaster (also known as Zarathustra), who most likely lived sometime after 1000 BCE in eastern Iran, crystallized the region's traditional beliefs into a formal religious system. The main source for the teachings of Zoroaster is the *Avesta*, a collection of holy works initially transmitted orally by priests and then, according to legend, written down in the third century BCE. **Zoroastrianism** ultimately became the religion of the empire.

Zoroaster promoted belief in the god Ahura Mazda, who had created the world and all that was good. In dualistic contrast, Ahura Mazda's adversary, Ahriman was deceitful and wicked. The Persians saw these two forces as engaged in a cosmic struggle for control of the universe. Zoroastrianism treated humans as capable of choosing between good and evil. Human choices had consequences: rewards or punishments in the afterlife.

Persians believed that their kings were appointed by Ahura Mazda as ruler over all peoples and all lands of the earth and charged by him with maintaining perfect order from which all creation would benefit. As such, kings enjoyed absolute authority. In return, they were expected to follow moral and political guidelines that reflected Zoroastrian notions

Persepolis. In the highland valley of Fars, the homeland of the Persians, Darius and his successors built a capital city and ceremonial center at the site of Persepolis. On top of a huge platform, there were audience halls, a massive treasury, the harem, and residential spaces. The building was constructed of mud brick. The roof was supported by enormous columns projecting the images of bulls.

of ethical behavior. Kings also had to show physical superiority that matched their moral standing. They had to be expert horsemen and peerless in wielding bows and spears. These were qualities valued by all Persian nobles, who revered the virtues of their nomadic ancestors. According to the ancient Greek historian Herodotus, Persian boys were taught three things only: "to ride, to shoot with the bow, and to tell the truth."

The Persian social order included four diverse groups with well-defined roles. A ruling class consisted of priests maintaining the ritual fire in temples, nobles administering the state, and warriors protecting and expanding the empire. An administrative and commercial class included scribes and bureaucrats who kept imperial records and merchants who secured goods from distant lands. The other two groups were made up of artisans and, finally, peasants who grew the crops and tended the flocks that fed the imperial machine.

The powerful Persian hereditary nobility surrounded and supported the king. These nobles had vast landholdings and often served the king as satraps or advisers. Also close to the king were wealthy merchants who directed trade across the vast empire. Royal gifts solidified the relations between king and nobles, reinforcing the king's place at the top of the political and social pyramid. In public ceremonies the king presented gold vessels, elaborate textiles, and jewelry to reward each recipient's loyalty and demonstrate dependence on the crown. Any kind of failure would result in the withdrawal of royal favor. Should such failures be serious or treasonous, the offenders faced torture and death. In Persian society, class and royal favor counted for everything.

Public Works and Imperial Identity The Persians undertook significant building projects that helped unify their empire and consolidate imperial identity. For one, the Persians engaged in large-scale road building and constructed a system of rapid and dependable communication. The key element in the system was the Royal Road, which followed age-old trade routes some 1,600 miles from western Anatolia to the heart of the empire in southwestern Iran, continuing eastward across the northern Iranian plateau and into central Asia. Traders used the Royal Road, as did the Persian army; subjects took tribute to the king, and royal couriers carried messages to the satraps and imperial armies over this road.

In addition to the Royal Road, the Persians devised other ways to connect the far reaches of the empire with its center. Darius oversaw the construction of a canal more

Persian Water-Moving Technique. The Persians perfected the channeling of water over long distances through underground channels called *qanats*. This technique, an efficient way to move water without evaporation, is still used today in hot, arid regions. In this example near Yazd, in central Iran, the domed structure leading to the underground tunnel is flanked by two brick towers called "badgir," an ancient form of air-conditioning that cools the water using wind (*bad* in Persian).

than 50 miles long linking the Red Sea to the Nile River. Additionally, Persians developed a system of *qanats,* underground tunnels through which water flowed over long distances without evaporating or being contaminated. Laborers from local populations toiled on these feats of engineering as part of their obligations as subjects of the empire.

Until Cyrus's time, the Persians had been pastoral nomads who lacked traditions of monumental architecture, visual arts, or written literature or history. Multiple capitals—at Persepolis, Pasargadae, and Susa—expressed a Persian imperial identity. Skilled craftsmen from all over the empire blended their distinct cultural influences into a new Persian architectural style. The Persians used monumental architecture with grand columned halls and huge open spaces to provide reception rooms for thousands of representatives bringing tribute from all over the empire and as a way to help integrate subject peoples by connecting them to one central, imperial authority. In the royal palace, three of the columned halls stood on raised platforms accessed via processional stairways that were lined with elaborate images of subjects bringing gifts and tribute to the king. This highly refined program of visual propaganda showed the Persian Empire as a society of diverse but obedient peoples. The carvings on the great stairway of Persepolis demonstrate the range of peoples each bringing distinctive tribute: the Armenians presenting precious metal vessels, the Lydians carrying gold armlets and bowls, the Egyptians offering exotic animals, and the Sogdians leading proud horses.

While the stream of tribute ebbed and flowed over time, the multicultural Persian Empire was able to hold power in Southwest Asia for more than 200 years, weakened by challenges posed by Greek city-states to their west in the fifth century and falling only to the invading army of Alexander the Great in 331 BCE. First the Neo-Assyrians, and then later the Persians, had fashioned their own brands of empire that used a combination of military force, rigid political and social organization, and religious ideology to maintain successive control over Southwest Asia. (See **Analyzing Global Developments: City-States to Empires**.)

Analyzing Global Developments

City-States to Empires

Dramatic developments in urban growth, agricultural production, military innovations, and governance in Southwest Asia in this period led to the emergence of the largest states known to that time, which we have called the first empires. Larger than either city-states or territorial states, empire represented a quantum leap in scale and size. In four distinct periods between 2900 and 350 BCE, this region was transformed from being governed by city-states, each covering less than 4 square miles with 30,000 people, to large-scale empires covering 3,000,000 square miles and governing 35,000,000 people. The Persian Empire (560–331 BCE) rivaled the Roman and Han empires in terms of its size and scale.

QUESTIONS FOR ANALYSIS

- By what scales of magnitude did each stage of empires increase? How much larger were the empires than the world's first states?
- When did the biggest leaps in development between stages occur?
- By what sort of mechanisms did these very large states come about?

STATE/EMPIRE	EST. AREA (SQ. MILES)	EST. POPULATION	NOTES
STAGE ONE: City States (2900–2100 BCE)			
Ur, Uruk, and Nipur	1–4 sq. miles	20–30,000 people	Uruk was the largest city-state for 2,000 years.
STAGE TWO: First Small Empire (c. 1800–1600 BCE)			
The Babylonian Empire	65,000 sq. miles	200,000 people	The city of Babylon was possibly the largest in the world, with 150,000 people.
STAGE THREE: First Large-Scale Empires (c. 910–540 BCE)			
The Neo-Assyrian Empire (c. 910–625 BCE)	540,000 sq. miles	15,000,000 people	Major cities included Kalhu, Nineveh, and Assur.
The Neo-Babylonian Empire (c. 625–540 BCE)	200,000 sq. miles	15,000,000 people	Babylon remained the largest city in the world, surrounded by 8–9 miles of walls.
STAGE FOUR: The Largest Empire in the Ancient World (c. 560–331 BCE)			
The Persian Empire (c. 560–331 BCE)	3,000,000 sq. miles	35,000,000 people	Largest empire ever (measured as a percentage of the global population).

Sources: T. Boiy, *Late Achaemenid and Hellenistic Babylon*; Pierre Briant, *Histoire de l'empire perse*, Paris, Fayard, 1996; Amélie Kuhrt, *The Ancient Near East, 3000–330 BCE*, 2 vols., London, RKP, 1995; J. N. Postgate, *Early Mesopotamia: Society and Economy at the Dawn of History*, London-New York, Routledge, 1992; M. Roaf, *Cultural Atlas of Mesopotamia and the Ancient Near East*, New York, Facts on File, 1990; W. Scheidel, "The Dynamics of Ancient Empires" New York, Oxford University Press, 2010; Marc van de Mieroop, *A History of the Ancient Near East, ca. 3000–323*, 2nd ed., Oxford, Blackwell, 2007; Marc van de Mieroop, *The Ancient Mesopotamian City*, Oxford, Clarendon Press, 1997.

Imperial Fringes in Western Afro-Eurasia

A very different world emerged on Afro-Eurasia's western edges. Although their powerful neighbors affected them, western peoples—such as the Sea Peoples, the Greeks, the Phoenicians, and the Israelites—retained their own languages, beliefs, and systems of rule. While their communities were smaller than those in Southwest Asia, each asserted power and had long-lasting influence disproportionate to their size.

COMPARISON

ANALYZE the relationships between empires and the peoples on their peripheries in Southwest Asia, South Asia, and East Asia.

SEA PEOPLES

New migrations brought violent change to long-established kingdoms and states in the Mediterranean and Southwest Asia. Beginning around 1200 BCE as the full effects of drought struck, new waves of Indo-European-speaking peoples left the Danube River basin in Central Europe. A rapid rise in population and the development of local natural resources, particularly iron, spurred this group, who came to be known as the **Sea Peoples** to move down the Danube toward the Black Sea. The invaders, armed with iron weaponry, brought turmoil to the peoples living in southeastern Europe, the Aegean, and the eastern Mediterranean.

The Hittites of Anatolia were the first to fall to their invasion. Once the invaders reached the Mediterranean, they mainly used boats for transportation, hence the label Sea Peoples (not a name they called themselves but rather one from the perspective of those whom they attacked). The Egyptians knew them as the Peleset, and only with great difficulty did the pharaohs repel them. The Sea Peoples ultimately settled along the southern coast of Southwest Asia, where they became known as the Philistines.

In the Mediterranean, the Sea Peoples' intrusion shook the social order of the Minoans on the island of Crete (see Chapter 3). Agricultural production in the region declined and, as the palace-centered bureaucracies and priesthoods of the second millennium BCE vanished, more violent societies emerged that relied on the newcomers' iron weapons. This was the culture of warrior-heroes described in the *Iliad,* an epic poem about the Trojan War, based on oral tales passed down for centuries before their compilation by Homer in the eighth century BCE. The Greek descendants of these warrior-heroes developed dynamic communities and, as we will see in the next section, offered one of the most significant challenges to the Persians.

THE GREEKS

Among the small-scale societies that emerged in Persia's shadow, the Greeks were particularly influential. Greek-speaking people in different cities sometimes cooperated with the Persians, even borrowing their ideas, but sometimes strongly resisted them. In 499 BCE, some Greek city-states and others in the eastern Mediterranean revolted against the Persians, who claimed control over the Greek islands and mainland. During the six-year struggle, some Greek communities sided with the Persians and suffered condemnation by other Greeks for doing so. On the mainland, most Greek cities resisted the Persian king's authority. In 490 BCE, Darius and his vast army invaded mainland Greece but suffered a humiliating defeat at the hands of the much smaller force of Athenians at Marathon, near Athens. The Persians retreated and waited another decade before challenging their western foe again. Meanwhile, however, Athens was becoming a major sea power.

Under the leadership of Themistocles in the 480s BCE, Athens became a naval power whose strength was its fleet of triremes (battleships). When Greek and Persian forces clashed again in 480 BCE, Persian land forces led by Darius's successor Xerxes fought through Leonidas's 300 Spartans (and other Greeks) at Thermopylae only to have their navy lose the pivotal sea battle at Salamis. A year later, the

Mycenaean Arms and Armor This Mycenaean vase illustrates the central role of arms and war to the societies on mainland Greece in the period down to 1200 BCE. The men bear common suits of armor and weapons—helmets, corsets, spears, and shields—most likely supplied to them by the palace-centered organizations to which they belonged. Despite these advantages, they were not able to mount a successful defense against the land incursions that destroyed the Mycenaean palaces toward the end of the thirteenth century BCE.

MAP 4.4 | The Mediterranean World, 1000–400 BCE

Peoples on the fringes of the great regional empires of Southwest Asia and North Africa had strong influences beyond their borders, despite their political marginalization. Though politically dwarfed by the Neo-Assyrian and Persian empires, various groups in the Mediterranean basin displayed strong cultural and economic power.

- What were the borderland communities and what did they trade?
- How far did their trading networks and settlement patterns extend?
- According to your reading, why were such small communities able to flourish in terms of trade and settlement?

Persians suffered a decisive defeat on land and eventually lost the war. Persian military defeats changed the balance of power. For the next 150 years Persia lost ground to the Greeks, who gradually regained territory in southeastern Europe and western Anatolia. That expanded territory, and its governance, would become in the fifth century BCE the root of Greek civil discord (see Chapter 5).

THE PHOENICIANS

Another important group on the fringes extended their influence across the Mediterranean through their seafaring and trade: these were the Chanani (called "Canaanites" in the Bible) living in the region of modern-day Lebanon. We know these entrepreneurial people by the name that the Greeks gave them—**Phoenicians** ("Purple People")—because of an expensive purple dye that they manufactured and traded. A mixture of the local population and the more recently arrived Sea Peoples, these traders preferred opening up new markets and new ports to subduing frontiers. The Phoenicians maintained their autonomy from Neo-Assyrian kings by supplying them with exotic luxuries. Phoenician coastal cities were ideally situated to develop trade throughout the entire Mediterranean basin. Inland stood an extraordinary forest of massive cedars—perfect timber for making large, seaworthy craft, and a highly desirable export to the treeless heartlands of Egypt and Mesopotamia (see Map 4.4).

Innovations in shipbuilding and seafaring enabled Phoenicians to sail as far west as present-day Morocco and Spain, carrying huge cargoes of such goods as timber, dyed cloth, glassware, wines, textiles, copper ingots, and carved ivory. Their trading colonies all around the southern and western rims of the Mediterranean (including Carthage in modern-day Tunisia) became major ports that shipped goods from interior regions throughout the Mediterranean. There they competed with Greek colonies that were similarly settling in the western Mediterranean to pursue commerce and relieve population pressures. While the Phoenicians are noteworthy for their seafaring and trade, they are perhaps best known for their revolutionizing of commerce and communication through their development of the **alphabet** in the mid second millennium BCE. This new method of writing arrived in the west in 800 BCE, probably through Greek traders working in Phoenician centers. The alphabet allowed educated people to communicate directly with one another, dramatically reducing the need for professional scribes. Phoenician trade and their alphabet allowed this "fringe" group to exert influence far beyond the confines of their political borders.

THE ISRAELITES

To the south of the mountains of Lebanon, the homeland of the Phoenicians, another minor region extended to the borderlands of Egypt. In this narrow strip of land between the Mediterranean Sea to the west and the desert to the east, an important microsociety emerged, that of the Israelites. The Israelites' own later stories emphasized their origins in Mesopotamia to the east, with the patriarch Abraham from Ur on the Euphrates. Later stories stressed connections with Egypt of the pharaohs to the west and the mass movement of a captive Israelite population out of Egypt under Moses in the late second millennium BCE. Archaeological evidence suggests that a local culture emerged in the area of present-day Israel between 1200 and 1000 BCE. These developments culminated in a kingdom centered at Jerusalem under King David (ca. 1000–960 BCE). The kingdom that David and his successor Solomon (ca. 960–930 BCE) established around Jerusalem, centered on the great temple that Solomon built in the city, did not last long. It fragmented immediately after Solomon's reign, forming the small kingdom of Israel in the north and the smaller Judah in the south.

Within the small kingdom founded by David and Solomon, profound religious and cultural changes took place. Solomon's great temple in Jerusalem outranked all other shrines in the land. The educated upper classes especially, who were linked to the temple, focused on one god, YHWH, over other regional deities in a form of reverence modern scholars call *henotheism* (the recognition of the power of one god over other spirits and deities that still exist). Gradually, however, there was a move to **monotheism** (the acceptance of only one god to the exclusion of all others).

PHENICIAN	ANCIENT GREEK	LATER GREEK	ROMAN
		A	A
		B	B
		Γ	C
		Δ	D
		E	E
			F
		Z	Z
			H
		Θ	Th
		I	I
		K	K
		Λ	L
		M	M
		N	N
		Ξ	X
		O	O
		Π	P
			Q
		P	R
		Σ C	S
		T	T

The Phoenician Alphabet *Left*: The first alphabet was written on clay tablets using the cuneiform script. It was developed by Phoenician traders who needed a script that was easy to learn so that they could record transactions without specially trained scribes. This tablet was found at the port town of Ugarit (Ras Shamra) in Syria and is dated to the fourteenth century BCE. *Right*: The forms of the letters in the Phoenician alphabet of the first millennium BCE are based on signs used to represent the Aramaic language. These Phoenician letters were then borrowed by the ancient Greeks. Our alphabet is based on that used by the Romans, who borrowed their letterforms from the later Greek inscriptions.

The long transition to monotheism, completed by the seventh century BCE, did not take place without resistance. Challenging the power of kings and priests, prophets like Isaiah (ca. 720s BCE), Ezra (ca. 600s BCE), and Jeremiah (ca. 590s BCE) helped articulate the Israelites' monotheistic religion. Prophets threatened divine annihilation for groups that opposed the new idea of one temple, one god, and one moral system to the exclusion of all others. The Neo-Assyrians to the east figured large in many of the prophets' warnings. Ultimately, the Torah—a series of books that encapsulated the laws governing all aspects of life, including family and marriage, food, clothing, sex, and worship—became an exclusive "contract" between all these people and their one and only god. As Jewish people scattered over time across Afro-Eurasia, their monotheism would come to have a far-reaching impact.

Foundations of Vedic Culture in South Asia (1500–600 BCE)

In South Asia, language and belief systems—rather than a unified political system enforced and enlarged by military conquests—brought people together. Indo-European-speaking peoples, also known as Vedic peoples for the religious traditions they brought with them, entered South Asia through the passes in the Hindu Kush Mountains in the middle of the second millennium BCE and eventually occupied the whole of what are today Pakistan, Bangladesh, and northern India (see Chapter 3). Here the migrant population, together with the indigenous inhabitants, fostered a flourishing culture. Unlike societies in Southwest Asia, the new rulers in this region did not have previous states on which to found their power. Floods and earthquakes had weakened the earlier Harappan urban centers in the Indus River valley (see Chapter 2), and its urban culture had died out several centuries earlier. Vedic newcomers integrated this territory through a shared culture. Even though the Vedic migrants changed the social and cultural landscape of the region, they did not give it greater political coherence by creating a single, unified regional kingdom.

VEDIC CULTURE SETTLES DOWN

The men and women who migrated into the northern lands of South Asia were illiterate, chariot-riding, and cattle-keeping pastoral peoples, who lacked experience of cities and urban life. They brought with them much beloved and elaborate rituals, mainly articulated in hymns, called **Vedas** (Sanskrit for wisdom or knowledge), which they retained as they entered a radically different environment and which they relied on to provide a foundation for assimilating new ways. Transmitted orally, but eventually written down in Sanskrit, Vedic hymns reflected their earlier lives on the plains of central Asia and were infused with images of animals and gods. For example, in some of these Vedic poems storms "gallop" across the heavens, and thunder sounds like the "neigh of horses."

These Indo-European-speaking migrants, equipped with their Vedic traditions, encountered indigenous people who either lived in agricultural settlements or were herders like themselves. They allied themselves with some peoples and made enemies of others. In their interactions with local peoples, the Vedic migrants kept their own language and religious rituals but also absorbed local words and deities. Allies and defeated enemies who became part of their society had to accept Vedic culture. By the middle of the first millennium BCE, the Vedic peoples covered all of what is now northern India, and their language and rituals had become dominant in their new land (see Map 4.5).

Vedic elites, with their pastoral nomadic roots, never lost their passion for fine horses and they created trading routes to the northwest, beyond the Hindu Kush, to maintain a supply of these horses. But as the Vedic people entered the fertile river basins, they gradually settled down and turned to agriculture and herding. Indigenous farmers taught the Vedic newcomers farming techniques. For example, the iron plow was crucial for tilling the Ganges plain and transforming the Deccan plateau into croplands. In the drier north, the Vedic people grew wheat, barley, millet, and cotton; in the wet lowlands, they cultivated rice paddies. Farmers also produced tropical crops such as sugarcane and spices like pepper, ginger, and cinnamon. With farming success came increased populations and urban settlements across the region, fueled by agricultural surplus and trade in goods, both raw (grain) and manufactured (sugarcane into sugar).

SOCIAL DISTINCTIONS: CLANS AND *VARNA*

Over time, Vedic societies became more complex and less egalitarian than those of their pastoral ancestors. In the process of fanning out across the five tributaries of the Indus River and settling in the plain between the Ganges and Yamuna Rivers, the Vedic peoples created small regional governments and chieftainships. Jockeying for land and resources, they fought fiercely with the indigenous peoples and even more fiercely among themselves.

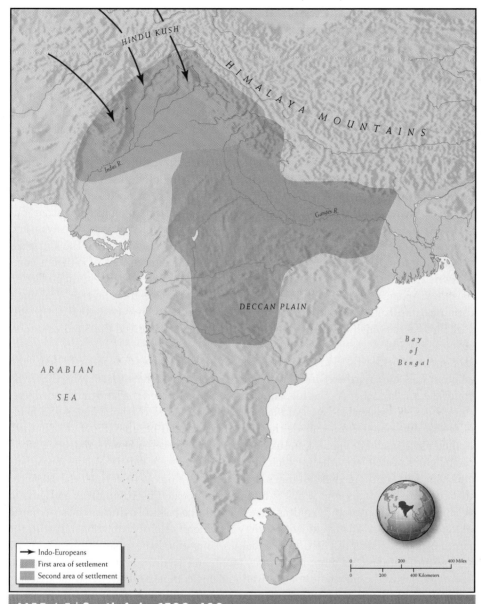

MAP 4.5 | South Asia, 1500–400 BCE

Indo-European peoples crossed over mountainous areas and entered northern South Asia, bringing with them their nomadic ways. They were, however, quick to learn settled agriculture from the local inhabitants.

- Where did the Indo-Europeans originally come from?
- Where did they settle? What geographical features may have influenced the stages of expansion southward?
- Based on your reading, why did Vedic culture prosper and provide a basis of unity for such large populations?

Vedic chieftainships eventually became small kingdoms with inhabitants bound to each other through lines of descent from a common ancestor. They traced their lineage—identified as either solar or lunar—through blood ties, marriage alliances, and invented family relations. The two lineages, solar and lunar, included many *clans* (groups of households claiming descent from a common ancestor) in which seniority determined one's power and importance. The Vedic peoples absorbed many local clans into their own lineages. Clans that adopted the Vedic culture became part of the lineage (through marriage or made-up ties) and were considered insiders. In contrast, clans that had other languages and rituals were considered to be uncivilized outsiders. These two lineages became less important over time, but were memorialized in the later *Mahabharata*, one of the two major Sanskrit epics of ancient India, which recalls the last phase of the lunar lineage, and the *Ramayana*, the second Sanskrit epic, which celebrates a hero of the solar lineage.

As Vedic peoples settled into agrarian communities after 1000 BCE, their social structure became even more complex and hierarchical. Among other distinctions, divisions developed between those who controlled the land and those who worked it. Vedic peoples used the term **varna** to refer to their rigid status distinction and recognized four ranked social groups into which one was born—Brahmans, Kshatriyas, Vaishyas, and Shudras. Since the Sankrit word *varna* means color, its use suggests that the four-class system originated in the encounter between clans and communities of different complexions and cultures. Vedic hymns described the origins of the *varnas* in their creation narrative. When the gods sacrificed Primeval Man to create the universe, Brahmans (priests) came from his mouth, his arms produced the Kshatriyas (warriors), the thighs gave birth to the Vaishyas (commoners), and from the feet emerged the Shudras (laborers and servants).

Clan members who had been politically the most powerful and had led their communities into northern India claimed the status of Kshatriyas. It was they who controlled the land. Less powerful clan members, who worked the land and tended livestock, became Vaishyas. Slaves and laborers who served in the households and fields of the Vaishyas came from outside the Vedic lineages and became known as Shudras. Brahmans claimed the highest status, for they performed the rituals and understood the religious principles without which life was believed to be unsustainable. Brahmans and Kshatriyas reinforced each other's high status. Brahmans performed the sacrifices that converted warriors into kings and kings reciprocated by paying fees and gifts to the Brahmans. Vaishyas and Shudras were left with the tasks of assuring the sustenance of the elite. The Brahmans guided a society in which the proper relationship with the forces of nature as represented by the deities constituted the basis of prosperity. As agriculture became ever more important, Brahmans acted as agents of Agni, the god of fire, to purify the new land for cultivation. This complex hierarchy so inextricably connected with Vedic religion provided the primary unifying structure for society in South Asia.

UNITY THROUGH THE VEDAS AND UPANISHADS

A Vedic culture, transmitted from generation to generation by the Brahmans, unified what political rivalries had divided. A common language (Sanskrit); belief in Agni, Indra, and other gods; and shared cultural symbols linked the dispersed communities and gave Vedic peoples a collective identity. Though Sanskrit was a language imported from central Asia, the people used it to transmit the Vedas orally. By expressing sacred knowledge in the rhythms and rhymes of Sanskrit, the Vedas effectively passed on their culture from one generation to the next.

The Vedas promoted cultural unity and pride through common ritual practices and support for hereditary leaders. As the priests of Vedic society, the Brahmans were responsible for memorizing the Vedic works. These included commentaries on sacred works from early nomadic times as well as new rules and rituals explaining the settled, farming way of life. The main body of Vedic literature includes the four Vedas: Rig-Veda, Sama-Veda, Yajur-Veda, and Atharva-Veda. The Rig-Veda, the earliest text, is a collection of hymns praising the gods, including Indra (god of war), Agni (god of fire), and Varuna (god of water). The Sama-Veda is a textbook of songs for priests to perform when making ritual sacrifices; most of their stanzas also appear in the Rig-Veda. The Yajur-Veda is a prayer book for the priest who conducted rituals for chariot races, horse sacrifices, or the king's coronation. The Atharva-Veda includes charms and remedies; many address problems re-

Gold coin of Kumaragupta I Kumaragupta I's coin, dating from the fifth century CE, intentionally drew on much older Vedic concepts (including the *ashvamedha*, or horse sacrifice from the Yajur-Veda) and imagery (here, a Hindu goddess).

lated to agriculture, a central aspect of life. Although the Vedic period left no impressive buildings and artifacts, the Vedas laid the socio-religious foundations for South Asia.

During the middle of the first millennium BCE, some thinkers (mostly Brahman ascetics dwelling in forests) felt that the Vedic rituals no longer provided satisfactory answers to the many questions of a rapidly changing society. The result was a collection of works known as the **Upanishads**, or the supreme knowledge, which expanded the Vedic cultural system. Taking the form of dialogues between disciples and a sage, the Upanishads offered insights into the ideal social order. The Upanishads teach that people are not separate from each other but belong to a cosmic universe called Brahma. While the physical world is always changing and is filled with chaos and illusion, *atman*, the eternal being, exists in all people and all creatures. Atman's presence in each living being makes all creatures part of a universal soul. Although all living beings must die, atman guarantees eternal life, ensuring that souls are reborn and transmigrate into new lives. This cycle continues with humans as they are reborn either as humans or as other living creatures, like cows, insects, or plants.

These unique views of life and the universe, as outlined in the Vedas and Upanishads, were passed along as principles of faith, bringing spiritual unity to the northern half of South Asia because local gods could easily be absorbed into the system. Unlike Southwest Asia, here in the kingdoms of the Indus Valley and the Ganges plain the common Vedic culture—rather than larger political units—was the unifying bond.

The Early Zhou Empire in East Asia (1045–771 BCE)

In China, the Zhou succeeded the Shang state, and Zhou rulers built a powerful tributary empire, claiming the "mandate of heaven." The Zhou had been only a minor state during the Shang's political preeminence, living side by side, trading and often allying with one another to fend off raiders from the northwest. The appearance of a dynamic leader among the Zhou peoples, King Wu, and the need to find more resources after drought-related dust storms swept across the North China plain emboldened the Zhou to challenge the Shang. At a battle in 1045 BCE, the Zhou prevailed. King Wu of the Zhou owed his success to his army of 45,000 troops and their superior weaponry, which included

COMPARISON

EVALUATE the connection between empires and war, religion, and trade in Southwest Asia and East Asia.

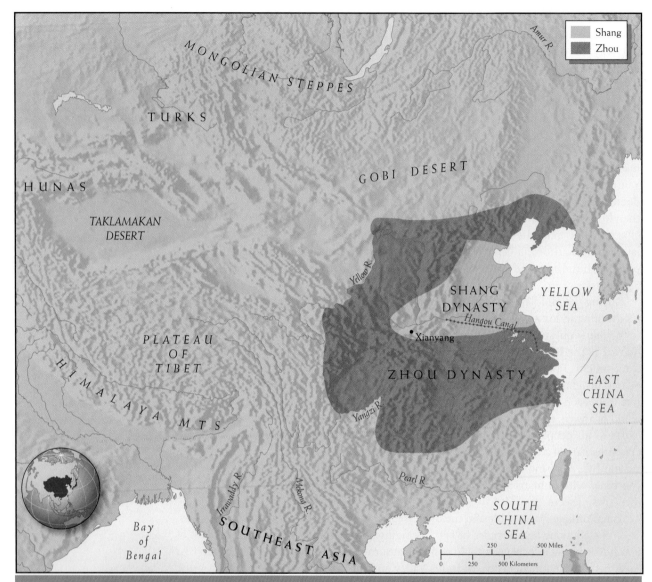

MAP 4.6 | The Shang and Zhou Dynasties, 2200–256 BCE

Toward the end of the second millennium BCE, the Zhou state supplanted the Shang dynasty as the most powerful political force in East Asia. Using the map above, compare and contrast the territorial reach of the Zhou state with that of the Shang.

• In what direction did the Zhou state expand the most dramatically?

• As you view the map, why do you think that the Zhou did not expand further northward and westward?

• Based on your reading, how did the Zhou integrate their geographically large and diverse state?

dagger axes, bronze armor, and 300 war chariots (small numbers by Southwest Asian standards, but overwhelming in East Asia). (See Map 4.6.) In the centuries that followed, innovations in politics, agriculture, and social structures helped the Zhou integrate their empire.

DYNASTIC INSTITUTIONS AND CONTROL OF THE LAND

When the Zhou took over from the Shang, their new state consisted of a patchwork of more than seventy small states, whose rulers, however, accepted the overarching authority of the Zhou kings. To solidify their power, the Zhou copied the Shang's patrimonial state structure, centered on ancestor worship in which the rulers' power passed down through a lineage of male ancestors reaching back to the gods. Thirty-nine Zhou kings followed one after the other, mostly in an orderly father-to-son succession, over a span of eight centuries.

Even though the Zhou drew heavily on Shang precedents, their own innovations produced some of the most significant contributions to China's distinctive cultural and political development. Regarding all those whom they governed as a single people, the Zhou employed the term *Huaxia,* or Chinese, when referring to their subjects. Contrary to political reality, Zhou leaders claimed that their territories were at heart unified, naming their lands *Zhongguo,* which at the time meant "the central states," but later came to mean "the middle kingdom" (and is a term still used for the modern state of China). Moreover, the Zhou kings of this middle kingdom, in addition to being required to rule justly, believed that they had a duty to extend their culture to "less civilized" peoples living in outlying regions.

Having defeated the Shang, and established Zhou control in northwestern China, King Wu (r. 1049–1043) and his successors expanded north toward what is now Beijing and south toward the Yangzi River valley. Seeking to retain the allegiance of the lords of older states and to gain the support of new lords, whom they appointed in annexed areas, Zhou kings rewarded their political supporters with

Zhou Chariots This 17th-century painting (on silk) shows a pivotal Zhou king, emperor Mu Wang (of the 10th century BCE), riding in a chariot driven by a legendary charioteer. The Zhou adapted the use of chariots and archers from their predecessors to defeat the Shang around 1045 BCE. Regional lords who owed allegiance to the Zhou king distinguished themselves in the aristocratic hierarchy by using chariots for battle and travel.

lands that they could pass on to their descendants. As the Zhou expanded their territory, its new colonies often consisted of garrison towns where the Zhou colonizers lived, surrounded by fields (inhabited by local farmers). As under the Shang, Zhou regional lords supplied military forces as needed, paid tribute, and appeared at the imperial court to pledge their continuing allegiance.

Not only through dynastic institutions, but also through agricultural advances (including the iron plow, irrigation, and canals) did the Zhou leaders promote the integration of China. Wooden and, much later, iron plows enabled farmers to break the hard sod of lands beyond the river basins, and over time cultivators learned the practice of field rotation to prevent soil nutrients from being exhausted. In the middle of the first millennium BCE, regional states organized local efforts to regulate the flow of the main rivers. They built long canals to promote communication and trade, and they dug impressive irrigation networks to convert arid lands into fertile belts. This slow agrarian revolution enabled the Chinese population to soar, reaching perhaps 20 million by the late Zhou era.

Under the Zhou, landowners and rulers organized the construction of dikes and irrigation systems to control the floodplain of the Yellow River and Wei River valley surrounding the capital at Xianyang (present-day Xi'an). For centuries, peasants labored over this floodplain and its tributaries—building dikes, digging canals, and raising levees as the waters flowed to the sea. When their work was done, the bottom of the floodplain was a latticework of rich, well-watered fields, with carefully manicured terraces rising in gradual steps to higher ground. Eventually, irrigation works grew to such a scale that they required management by the Zhou rulers, centered in the Wei River valley, and their skilled engineers. The engineers also designed canals that connected rivers and supported commerce and other internal exchanges. Tens of thousands of workers spent countless days digging these canals, paying tribute in the form of labor.

The canals linked China's two breadbaskets: wheat and millet fields in the north and rice fields in the south. And as with the Yellow River in the north, engineers controlled the Yangzi River in the south. Nomads in mountainous areas or on the Zhou frontiers, who often fought with the Zhou ruler and his regional lords, began to depend on trade with the fertile heartlands. In these ways, the Zhou promoted greater unity within their territory and among the peoples living in and around it.

"MANDATE OF HEAVEN"

In addition to promoting a Chinese ethnic and political identity and cultivating advances in agriculture, Zhou rulers also introduced the long-enduring concept of the **mandate of heaven**, which provided a justification for their rule. Attributed by later Chinese intellectuals to King Wu's younger brother Zhou Gong (often referred to as the Duke of Zhou), the mandate asserted that Zhou moral superiority justified taking over Shang wealth and territories and that heaven had imposed a moral mandate on them to replace the Shang, whom they characterized as evil men whose policies brought pain to the people through waste and corruption, and return good governance to the people.

At first Zhou leaders presented the mandate of heaven as a religious compact between the Zhou people and their supreme "sky god" in heaven, but over time Zhou kings and the court detached the concept from the sky god and made the mandate into a free-standing Chinese political doctrine. The Zhou argued that since worldly affairs were supposed to align with those of the heavens, heavenly powers conferred legitimate rights to rule only on their chosen representative. In return, the ruler was duty-bound to uphold heaven's principles of harmony and honor. Any ruler who failed in this duty, who let instability creep into earthly affairs, or who let his people suffer, would lose the mandate. Under this system, spiritual authority withdrew support from any wayward dynasts and found other, more worthy, agents. The Zhou rulers had to acknowledge that any group of rulers, even they themselves, could be ousted if they lost the mandate of heaven because of improper practices.

As part of maintaining their mandate and their legitimacy as rulers, Zhou kings created royal calendars, official documents that defined times for undertaking agricultural activities and celebrating rituals. Unexpected events such as solar eclipses or natural calamities could throw into question the ruling house's mandate. Since rulers claimed that their authority came from heaven, the Zhou perfected the astronomical system on which they based their calendar. Zhou astronomers precisely calculated the length of a lunar month (29.53 days) and the solar year. To resolve the discrepancy between a solar year (365.25 days) and a lunar year (354.36 days), the Zhou occasionally inserted a leap month. Scribes dated the reigns of kings by days and years within a repeating sixty-year cycle.

Zhou legitimacy was also grounded in their use of bronze ritual vessels, statues, ornaments, and weapons, the large-scale production of which they borrowed from their Shang predecessors. Like the Shang, the Zhou developed an extensive system of bronze metalworking that required a large force of tribute labor. Many of its members were Shang, who were sometimes forcibly transported to new Zhou towns to produce the bronze ritual objects. These objects, sold and distributed across the lands and used in ceremonial rituals, symbolized Zhou legitimacy.

SOCIAL AND ECONOMIC CONTROLS

As the Chinese social order became more integrated, it also became more class-based. Directly under the Zhou ruler and his royal ministers were the hereditary nobles, divided into ranks. These regional lords had landholdings of different sizes. They all owed allegiance to the Zhou king, and they supplied warriors to fight in the king's army and laborers to clear land, drain fields, and do other work. The regional lords periodically appeared at court and took part in complex rituals to reaffirm their allegiance to the king. Below the regional lords were high officers at the Zhou court, as well as ministers and administrators who supervised the people's work. Aristocratic warriors stood at the bottom of the noble hierarchy.

Among commoners, an elaborate occupation-based hierarchy developed over time. Early on, most of the population worked as farmers on fields owned by great landholding families, while some commoners were artisans, such as bronze-workers or silk-weavers. The later occupation-based system, however, divided people more precisely by function—landholders who produced grain, growers of plants and fruit trees, woodsmen, breeders of cattle and chickens, artisans, merchants, weavers, servants, and those with no fixed occupation—and the central government exerted considerable control over how each group did its job. While reports of this control may be overstated, it does show a unique attempt by the Zhou government to assert power over the empire's diverse peoples.

Zhou Wine Vessel Under the Zhou, bronze metallurgy depended on a large labor force. Many workers initially came from Shang labor groups, who were superior to the Zhou in technology. The use of bronze, such as for this wine vessel, exemplified dynastic continuity between the Shang and Zhou.

The Zhou also made political and legal use of family structures. In their patrilineal society, the Zhou established strict hierarchies for both men and women. Both art and literature celebrated the son who honored his parents. Men and women had different roles in family and ceremonial life. On landholdings, men farmed and hunted, while women produced silk and other textiles and fashioned them into clothing. Wealth increasingly trumped other distinctions, however. In particular, rich women high in the Zhou aristocracy enjoyed a greater range of actions than other women. And wealthy merchants in emerging cities challenged the authority of local lords.

LIMITS AND DECLINE OF ZHOU POWER

The Zhou state relied on culture (its bronzes) and statecraft (the mandate of heaven) to maintain its leadership among competing powers and lesser principalities in its territories. Rather than having absolute control of an empire (like the Assyrians or Persians) or a primarily socio-religious unity (as among the Vedic peoples of South Asia), the Zhou state was first among many regional economic and political allies.

The Zhou dynasty was not highly centralized; instead, it expected regional lords to control the provinces. Military campaigns continued to press into new lands or to defend Zhou holdings from enemies. Rulers interacted with neighbors and allies by giving them power, protecting them from aggression, and intermarrying between dynastic family members and local nobles. Consequently, Zhou subordinates had more than autonomy; they had genuine resources that they could turn against the dynasts at opportune moments.

The power of the Zhou royal house over its regional lords declined in the ninth and eighth centuries BCE. In response, the Zhou court at Xianyang introduced ritual reforms with grandiose ceremonies featuring larger, standardized bronze vessels. Even this move could not reverse the regime's growing political weakness in dealing with its steppe neighbors and internal regional lords. In 771 BCE, northern steppe invaders forced the Zhou to flee their western capital, ushering in the beginning of what would come to be known as the Spring and Autumn Period of the Eastern Zhou dynasty centered at Luoyi (modern Luoyang).

The Zhou dynastic period, like the Shang, was later idealized by Chinese historians as a golden age of wise kings and officials. In fact, the Zhou model of government, culture, and society became the standard for later generations. Though the Neo-Assyrian and Persian superpowers were capable of greater expansion during this period, China was sowing the seeds of a more durable state.

Conclusion

Around 1000 BCE, dramatic changes in political and social structures took place across Afro-Eurasia. Consolidations of power, with varying degrees and types of centralization, formed in Southwest Asia (Neo-Assyrians and Persians), Vedic South Asia, and East Asia (among the Zhou). Driving these socio-political developments were changes in climate, invasions by nomadic peoples, technological innovations, and new administrative strategies.

A spectrum of power consolidation—from the highly centralized to the more culturally unified—occurred across Afro-Eurasia. The tightly consolidated Neo-Assyrian and Persian empires differed in fundamental ways from the earlier city-states and territorial states of this area. They created ideologies, political institutions, and economic ties that extended their power across vast regions. Their strong imperial institutions enabled them to exploit human and material resources at great distances from the imperial centers. At the other end of Afro-Eurasia, the Zhou in China established loose integration of diverse peoples and territories through a powerful dynastic arrangement buttressed by a mandate from heaven; but they could not overcome the power of local nobles or fully protect the western frontier from nomadic attacks. In the Vedic world of the Indus Valley and Ganges plain, shared values and revered texts did not lead to a single major state. An unparalleled degree of cultural, as opposed to political or economic, integration bound together northern South Asia. Many centuries would pass before a regime would layer a state over this shared cultural world.

Empire building did not occur everywhere. The majority of the world's people still lived in smaller political groupings. Even within Afro-Eurasia, some areas were completely untouched. And even where the Neo-Assyrian and Persian rulers, soldiers, and traders came into contact with certain groups, they did not necessarily crush them. For example, the nomadic peoples of the northern steppes and the southern desert locations throughout

Eurasia continued to be autonomous. But fewer and fewer were untouched by the technological, cultural, and political pulses of empires.

The peoples living in Southwest Asia (under the Neo-Assyrians and then Persians), in the Vedic society of South Asia, and in the Zhou kingdom of China made lasting contributions to the cultural and religious history of humanity. Late Vedic South Asia spun out the concept of cyclic universal time in the form of reincarnation. And in late Zhou China, an ideal of statecraft and social order took shape. On the fringes of these empires, other groups made lasting contributions. The Phoenicians traversed the whole of the Mediterranean basin and spread their simplified alphabet. From the land of Israel, a budding monotheism sprouted. All evolved into powerful cultural forms that in time spread their influences far beyond their sites of origin.

After You Read This Chapter

FOCUS ON: *First Empires and Smaller States*

ANCIENT NEAR EAST

- Neo-Assyrians use raw military power and massive population relocations to build and maintain the world's first empire.

- Persians rely on persuasion and tolerance to build a cosmopolitan empire.

MEDITERRANEAN WORLD

- Greeks, Phoenicians, and Israelites show the advantages of small-scale states with innovations in writing, trading, and religious thought.

SOUTH ASIA

- Vedic peoples build a unified common culture through religious and economic ties.

CHINA

- Zhou dynasty constructs a powerful tributary state and legitimates its rule via the mandate of heaven doctrine (good governance together with upright behavior equates to legitimate rule).

CHRONOLOGY

SOUTHWEST ASIA AND NORTHERN AFRICA		
THE MEDITERRANEAN		
SOUTH ASIA		
EAST ASIA		
	1500 BCE	**1200** BCE

- *Thinking about Power Relationships and the Formation of Empires* From 1200 to 350 BCE, several regional empires with centralized rule developed: in Southwest Asia, the Neo-Assyrians and then Persians established tightly controlled empires; in East Asia, the Zhou achieved loose political unification; and a culturally integrated people thrived in South Asia. Compare the use of military force and its relationship to political centralization in each of these cases. How does religion help to bring unification?

- *Thinking about the Environment and the Formation of Empires* Just as climate change around 2000 BCE contributed to the demise of earlier civilizations, prolonged drought around 1200 BCE again brought dramatic changes to many areas. Compare the environmental crises in Egypt, Southwest Asia, and East Asia in the late second millennium BCE and their results, especially with respect to empire formation.

- *Thinking about Exchange Networks and the Formation of Empires* While this chapter focuses on the formation of empires, the majority of the world's people lived outside or on the fringes of these empires. The Sea Peoples, after disrupting the Hittites, Greeks, and Egyptians, settled down on the coast of Southwest Asia and became the Philistines; the Phoenicians expanded their trade across the Mediterranean; the Greeks effectively resisted Persian authority; and Jewish Israelites founded a kingdom centered on monotheism. Which had the most significant impact on human history: the centralized empires or the peoples on the fringes and beyond? Why?

1. Describe how climate change, migrations, technological developments, and administrative innovations contributed to the formation of empires in the later second millennium BCE.

2. What are the common features of **empires** across Eurasia from 1200–350 BCE? What are the similarities and differences in how empires formed, or did not form, in Southwest Asia, South Asia, and East Asia?

3. How did the Assyrian and Persian empires consolidate their imperial control over vast territories? What role did religious and political innovations such as **Zoroastrianism** and **satrapies** play in that consolidation?

4. How did peoples on the margins of Assyria and Persia—including the **Sea Peoples**, the **Phoenicians** (with their **alphabet**), the Israelites (and their **monotheism**), and the Greeks—interact with these imperial powers?

5. How did the Zhou Dynasty establish control in East Asia and what role did the **mandate of heaven** play in their maintenance of power?

6. How did socio-religious developments such as *varna*, the **Vedas**, and the **Upanishads** enable South Asia to become integrated without a centralized imperial state?

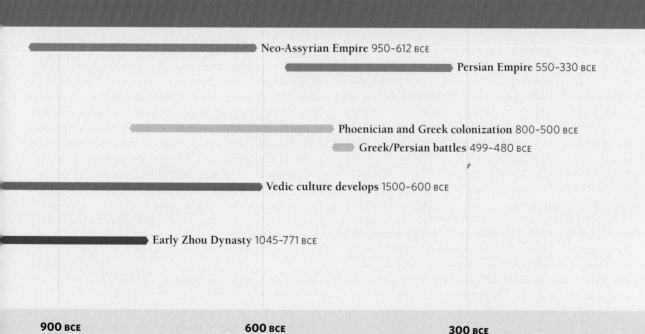

Neo-Assyrian Empire 950-612 BCE

Persian Empire 550–330 BCE

Phoenician and Greek colonization 800–500 BCE

Greek/Persian battles 499–480 BCE

Vedic culture develops 1500–600 BCE

Early Zhou Dynasty 1045–771 BCE

900 BCE　　　　　　　　　**600 BCE**　　　　　　　　　**300 BCE**

Competing Perspectives

Consolidating Early Empires

The early empires described in this chapter used a combination of military might, political organization, and religious ideology to control the peoples who lived within their territory. The Neo-Assyrians, for instance, combined brute force and tight political administration to consolidate a highly centralized empire. The Persians used some of the same strategies, but allowed greater multicultural variation and self-rule within their domain. Zhou leaders justified their rule via the mandate from heaven; but this justification required ongoing demonstration of a mandate in a world of unpredictable events such as sickness and crop devastation. In South Asia, Indo-European Vedic immigrants brought a degree of social, but not political, unification through their religious ideas, most notably the hierarchically arranged *varna*.

The texts presented here illustrate the varied methods of imperial control utilized in each of these regions. Inscribed on a stone pillar next to his throne room, the banquet stele of Neo-Assyrian ruler Assurnasirpal II (r. 883–859 BCE) describes the extravagant ten-day celebration he hosted on the occasion of the palace's completion and demonstrates his power over subject lands. To commemorate his consolidation of power over the Persian state, Darius I (r. 522–486 BCE) commissioned the trilingual Behistun inscription excerpted here; it was posted on a major road connecting Mesopotamia with western Iran. The *Shangshu* (Book of History) preserves an account of the transition of power (c. 1043 BCE) from King Wu to the Duke of Zhou, in which ancestors were consulted via oracle bones and the mandate from heaven was in doubt. The final excerpt, from the *Upanishads,* tells a story dating to the seventh century BCE or earlier of a young man struggling to determine his place in Vedic society. Each text gives a glimpse of the practical and ideological forces that bound peoples and empires together in the first millennium BCE.

PRIMARY SOURCE 4.1

The Banquet Stele of Assurnasirpal II (c. 865 BCE)

(102) When Ashur-nasir-apli, king of Assyria, consecrated the joyful palace, the palace full of wisdom, in Kalach [and] invited inside Ashur, the great lord, and the gods of the entire land; 1,000 fat oxen, 1,000 calves [and] sheep of the stable, 14,000 . . . sheep which belonged to the goddess Ishtar my mistress, 200 oxen which belonged to the goddess Ishtar my mistress, 1,000 . . . -sheep, 1,000 spring lambs, 500 *ayalu*-deer, 500 deer, 1,000 ducks [*issūrū- rabûtu*], 500 ducks [*usū*], 500 geese, 1,000 wild geese, 1,000 *qaribu*-birds, 10,000 pigeons, 10,000 wild pigeons, 10,000 small birds, 10,000 fish, 10,000 jerboa, 10,000 eggs, 10,000 loaves of bread, 10,000 jugs of beer, 10,000 skins of wine, 10,000 containers of grain [and] sesame, 10,000 pots of hot . . . , 1,000 boxes of greens, 300 [containers of] oil, 300 [containers of] malt, 300 [containers of] mixed *raqqatu*-plants, 100 [containers of] *kudimmus*, 100 [containers of] . . . , 100 [containers of] parched barley, 100 [containers of] *ubuhšennu*-grain, 100 [containers of] fine *billatu*, 100 [containers of] pomegranates, 100 [containers of] grapes, 100 [containers of] mixed *zamrus*, 100 [containers of] pistachios, 100 [containers of] . . . , 100 [containers of] onions, 100 [containers of] garlic, 100 [containers of] *kunipbūs*, 100 bunches of turnips, 100 [containers of] *biñbiñu*-seeds, 100 [containers of] *giddū*, 100

[containers of] honey, 100 [containers of] ghee, 100 [containers of] roasted *abšu*-seeds, 100 [containers of] roasted *šu'u*-seeds, 100 [containers of] *karkartu*-plants, 100 [containers of] *tiatu*-plants, 100 [containers of] mustard, 100 [containers of] milk, 100 [containers of] cheese, 100 bowls of *mīzu*-drink, 100 stuffed oxen, 10 homers of shelled *dukdu* nuts, 10 homers of shelled pistachios, 10 homers of . . . , 10 homers of *hăbbaququ*, 10 homers of dates, 10 homers of *titip*, 10 homers of cumin, 10 homers of *sahūnu*, 10 homers of . . . , 10 homers of *andahšu*, 10 homers of *šišanibu*, 10 homers of *simberu*-fruit, 10 homers of *hāšú*, 10 homers of fine oil, 10 homers of fine aromatics, 10 homers of . . . , 10 homers of *nassabu*-gourds, 10 homers of *zinzimmu*-onions, 10 homers of olives; when I consecrated the palace of Kalach, 47,074 men [and] women who were invited from every part of my land, 5,000 dignitaries [and] envoys of the people of the lands Suhu, Hindanu, Patinu, Hatti, Tyre, Sidon, Gurgumu, Malidu, Hubushkia, Gilzanu, Kumu, [and] Musasiru, 16,000 people of Kalach, [and] 1,500 *zarīqū* of my palace, all of them—altogether 69,574 [including] those summoned from all lands and the people of Kalach—for ten days I gave them food, I gave them drink, I had them bathed, I had them anointed. [Thus] did I honour them [and] send them back to their lands in peace and joy.

Source: Assyrian Royal Inscriptions, Part 2: From Tiglath-pileser I to Ashur-nasir-apli II, compiled and translated by Albert Kirk Grayson, vol. 2 of *Records of the Ancient Near East,* edited by Hans Goedicke (Wiesbaden: Otto Harrassowitz, 1976), pp. 175–76.

The Behistun Inscription (520 BCE), Darius I

4.31–2. Saith Darius the King: These IX kings I took prisoner within these battles.

4.33–6. Saith Darius the King: These are the provinces which became rebellious. The Lie made them rebellious, so that these [men] deceived the people. Afterwards Ahuramazda put them into my hand; as was my desire, so I did unto them.

4.36–40. Saith Darius the King: Thou who shalt be king hereafter, protect thyself vigorously from the Lie; the man who shall be a Lie-follower, him do thou punish well, if thus thou shalt think, "May my country be secure!"

4.40–3. Saith Darius the King: This is what I did; by the favor of Ahuramazda, in one and the same year I did [it]. Thou who shalt hereafter read this inscription, let that which has been done by me convince thee; do not thou think it a lie.

4.43–5. Saith Darius the King: I turn myself quickly to Ahuramazda, that this [is] true, not false, [which] I did in one and the same year. . . .

4.52–6. Saith Darius the King: Now let that which has been done by me convince thee; thus to the people impart, do not conceal it: if this record thou shalt not conceal, [but] tell it to the people, may Ahuramazda be a friend unto thee, and may family be unto thee in abundance, and may thou live long!

4.57–9. Saith Darius the King: If this record thou shalt conceal, [and] not tell it to the people, may Ahuramazda be a smiter unto thee, and may family not be to thee!

4.59–61. Saith Darius the King: This which I did, in one and the same year by the favor of Ahuramazda I did; Ahuramazda bore me aid, and the other gods who are.

4.61–7. Saith Darius the King: For this reason Ahuramazda bore aid, and the other gods who are, because I was not hostile, I was not a Lie-follower, I was not a doer of wrong—neither I nor my family. According to righteousness I conducted myself. Neither to the weak nor to the powerful did I do wrong. The man who cooperated with my house, him I rewarded well; whoso did injury, him I punished well.

4.67–9. Saith Darius the King: Thou who shalt be king hereafter, the man who shall be a Lie-follower or who shall be a doer of wrong—unto them do thou not be a friend, [but] punish them well.

4.69–72. Saith Darius the King: Thou who shalt hereafter behold this inscription which I have inscribed, or these sculptures, do thou not destroy them, [but] thence onward protect them; as long as thou shalt be in good strength!

Source: Roland G. Kent, *Old Persian: Grammar, Texts, Lexicon*, 2nd rev. ed. (New Haven: American Oriental Society, 1953), pp. 131–32.

Zhou Succession Crisis (c. 1043 BCE), King Wu

After he had completed the conquest of the Shang people, in the second year, King Wu fell ill and was despondent. The two lords, the duke of Shao and Tai-kung Wang, said, "For the king's sake let us solemnly consult the tortoise oracle." But the duke of Chou [King Wu's younger brother, named Tan] said, "We must not distress the ancestors, the former kings."

The duke of Chou then offered himself to the ancestors, constructing three altars within a single compound. . . . Then he made this announcement to the Great King, to King Chi, and to King Wen, his great grandfather, grandfather, and father, and the scribe copied down the words of his prayer on tablets:

"Your chief descendant So-and-so [King Wu's personal name is tabooed] has met with a fearful disease and is violently ill. If you three kings are obliged to render to Heaven the life of an illustrious son, then substitute me, Tan, for So-and-so's person. I am good and compliant, clever and capable. I have much talent and much skill and can serve the spirits. . . ."

Then he divined with three tortoises, and all were auspicious. He opened the bamboo receptacles and consulted the documents, and they too indicated an auspicious answer. The duke of Chou said to the king, "According to the indications of the oracle, you will suffer no harm."

[The king said,] "I, the little child, have obtained a new life from the three kings. I shall plan for a distant end. I hope that they will think of me, the solitary man."

After the duke of Chou returned, he placed the tablets containing the prayer in a metal-bound casket. The next day the king began to recover.

[Later, King Wu died and was succeeded by his infant son, King Ch'eng. The duke of Chou acted as regent and was slandered by King Wu's younger brothers, whom he was eventually forced to punish.]

In the autumn, when a plentiful crop had ripened but had not yet been harvested, Heaven sent great thunder and lightning accompanied by wind. The grain was completely flattened and even large trees were uprooted. The people of the land were in great fear. The king and his high ministers donned their ceremonial caps and opened the documents of the metal-bound casket and thus discovered the record of how the duke of Chou had offered himself as a substitute for King Wu. . . . .

The king grasped the document and wept. "There is no need for us to make solemn divination about what has happened," he said. "In former times the duke of Chou toiled diligently for the royal house, but I, the youthful one, had no way of knowing it. Now Heaven has displayed its terror in order to make clear the virtue of the duke of Chou. I, the little child, will go in person to greet him, for the rites of our royal house approve such action."

When the king came out to the suburbs to meet the duke of Chou, Heaven sent down rain and reversed the wind, so that the grain all stood up once more. The two lords ordered the people of the land to right all the large trees that had been blown over and to earth them up. Then the year was plentiful. (*Chin t'eng.*)

Source: Translated in Burton Watson, *Early Chinese Literature* (New York: Columbia University Press, 1962), pp. 35–36.

PRIMARY SOURCE 4.4

Indian Brahman Priesthood (before 7th cent. BCE), from The Upanishads

1. Satyakâma, the son of Gabâlâ, addressed his mother and said: 'I wish to become a Brahmakârin [religious student], mother. Of what family am I?'

2. She said to him: 'I do not know, my child, of what family thou art. In my youth when I had to move about much as a servant [waiting on the guests in my father's house] I conceived thee. I do not know of what family thou art. I am Gabâlâ by name, thou art Satyakâma [Philalethes]. Say that thou art Satyakâma Gâbâla.'

3. He going to Gautama Hâridrumata said to him, 'I wish to become a Brahmakârin with you, Sir. May I come to you, Sir?'

4. He said to him: 'Of what family are you, my friend?' He replied: 'I do not know, Sir, of what family I am. I asked my mother, and she answered: "In my youth when I had to move about much as a servant, I conceived thee. I do not know of what family thou art. I am Gabâlâ by name, thou art Satyakâma," I am therefore Satyakâma Gâbâla, Sir.'

5. He said to him: 'No one but a true Brâhmana would thus speak out. Go and fetch fuel, friend, I shall initiate you. You have not swerved from the truth.' Having initiated him, he chose four hundred lean and weak cows, and said: 'Tend these friend.'

He drove them out and said to himself. 'I shall not return unless I bring back a thousand.' He dwelt a number of years [in the forest], until the cows became a thousand.'

Source: *The Upanishads*, translated by F. Max Muller, vol. 1 of *Sacred Books of the East*, edited by F. Max Muller (1900; reprint, New Delhi: Motilal Banarsidass, 1981), pp. 60–61.

QUESTIONS FOR ANALYSIS

1. What is the focus of each text? Based on this central concern and the details surrounding it, explain how each text is a reflection of what you know (from this chapter) of the degree of imperial centralization in each region.

2. What is the role of religion in each text? What does that suggest about religion as a unifying force within each region?

3. From what perspective, elite or nonelite, is the text written and what does that suggest about the nature of empire, or lack of empire, in that region?

Interpreting Visual Evidence

Tribute

One method early empires of the first millennium BCE used to consolidate their power was the collection of tribute from the areas under their control. The examples gathered here depict the payment of various forms of tribute in different empires.

In his palace complex at Nimrud, the Neo-Assyrian king Shalmaneser III (r. 858–824 BCE) erected a black limestone obelisk decorated on four sides with reliefs and inscriptions commemorating his conquests and the peoples who paid tribute to him. This obelisk includes a famous scene thought to show the tribute offered by King Jehu of Israel. Another series of images on the obelisk, shown below, record the exotic gifts from Muṣri (literally, "Borderlands") including two-humped Bactrian camels, an elephant, and three monkeys. At the Persian capital of Persepolis, grand staircases leading to the main audience hall of the palace were decorated with scenes of the king and his courtiers as well as the delegations bringing tribute to the center of the empire. The second image depicts tribute-bearers bringing animals and other items (in bowls) as gifts to the Persian king. Those delivering their tribute would have walked past these scenes on their way to pay obeisance to the Persian king. In Zhou China, tribute was often rendered in human labor, to build the irrigation system of canals and dikes. But another form of tribute to Zhou dynasts may have been textiles, such as the woven silk with a geometric and dragon motif shown in the final image. The silk was dyed red with cinnabar, a rare and expensive ingredient whose use would have been limited to luxury textiles of the elite. The differing types of tribute and their display indicate the varying levels of centralized control these first-millennium empires exerted over their subject peoples.

Black obelisk of Shalmaneser III.

Tribute scene from palace at Persepolis.

Woven textile from Eastern Zhou.

QUESTIONS FOR ANALYSIS

1. Compare the grand display of tribute in the Neo-Assyrian and Persian empires with the tribute suggested by the Zhou textile. What do these varied tributes (their type and display) suggest about the nature of early empire in each of these regions?

2. Compare the symbolic political value versus the actual economic impact of the specific tributes visible here.

3. Imagine yourself as a tribute bearer ascending the steps to the reception hall of the Persian king or visiting the Neo-Assyrian capital of Shalmaneser III. Now imagine yourself as a member of the Persian or Neo-Assyrian elite. How would your experience of viewing these scenes differ depending on your identity?

Before You Read This Chapter

Worlds Turned Inside Out

1000–350 BCE

In the midst of violent struggles for power and territory in China in the sixth century BCE, Master Kong Fuzi instructed his disciples on how to govern, saying: "Guide them by edicts, keep them in line with punishments, and the people will stay out of trouble but will have no sense of shame. Guide them by virtue, keep them in line with the rites, and they will, besides having a sense of shame, reform themselves" (Confucius, *The Analects*, II, 3).

Master Kong, also known as Confucius, represented a new breed of influential leaders who were teachers and thinkers, not kings, priests, or warriors. Nonetheless, it was the convulsions around them—incessant warfare, population growth, migrations, and the emergence of new cities—that motivated their search for insights. By viewing the world in innovative ways, these teachers instructed rulers on how to govern justly and showed ordinary individuals how to live ethically.

The teachers and founders of new ways of thinking from the first millennium BCE, who figure prominently in this chapter, were some of the most influential in history. In China, Confucius elaborated a set of principles for ethical living that has guided the Chinese population up to modern times. In South Asia, Siddhartha Gautama (the Buddha) laid out social and spiritual tenets that challenged

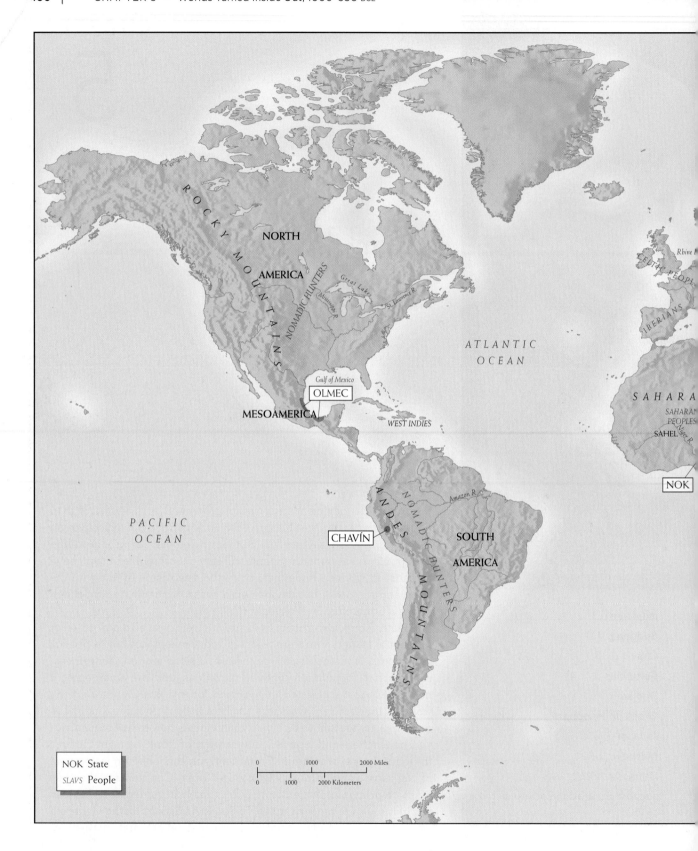

NOK State
SLAVS People

0   1000   2000 Miles
0   1000   2000 Kilometers

MAP 5.1 | The World in an Axial Age, c. 500 BCE

By the middle of the first millennium BCE, complex agriculture-based societies beyond the regional empires of Southwest Asia and North Africa contributed to the flowering of new cultural pathways and ideas.

- According to your reading, where did these second-generation societies appear?

- Which societies had greater opportunities for cultural mixing, and which ones were more isolated?

- How did proximity to others or relative isolation shape these societies' development?

the traditional social hierarchy based on birth and with it, the power of the ruling priests and warriors. In Greece, Socrates, Plato, and Aristotle described a world that conformed to natural laws.

The philosophers, theologians, poets, political leaders, and merchants of this era founded literary traditions, articulated new belief systems, and established new political and economic institutions that spread well beyond the places that inspired them. While wars and havoc occurred within their societies and long-distance trade and travel linked societies, these centuries were dominated by a search for order and an appetite for new thinking.

An "Axial Age"

Some modern thinkers call the mid-first millennium BCE the **axial age**, to emphasize its pivotal and transitional role between the declining empires of ancient Egypt, Southwest Asia, northern India, and Zhou China, and the later empires of Alexander the Great, Rome, and the Han Chinese (see Chapters 6 and 7). This dynamic period gave rise to the ethical, philosophical, and religious underpinnings of cultures in India, China, and Europe.

In this axial age of the first millennium BCE, societies on the edges of regional empires or within declining empires of Afro-Eurasia started to follow innovative paths. (See Map 5.1.) These new communities were not just extensions of old ways of life. In each, dramatic innovations in cultural and religious beliefs were expanding people's social, political, and cultural options. Although each of the resulting cultures—in East Asia, South Asia, and the Mediterranean—was distinct from the others, we might call them all **second-generation societies**, given that they built on their predecessors yet represented a departure from ancient legacies.

While Afro-Eurasia experienced an axial age and the emergence of second-generation societies, other parts of the world saw complex, urban-based societies emerge for the first time.. The first of these in the Americas was established by the Olmecs in Mesoamerica, with artistic and religious reverberations well beyond their homelands. In Africa, distinct regional identities spread in the Upper Nile (in Nubia) and West Africa. One of the most striking features of the first millennium BCE is the long-lasting impact of both the axial age second-generation societies that stretched across Afro-Eurasia and the first complex societies isolated from them by oceans and desert.

Eastern Zhou China

COMPARISON

DESCRIBE the challenges that Afro-Eurasian empires and states faced in the first millennium BCE.

Destruction of the old political order paved the way for radical thinkers and cultural flourishing in Eastern Zhou China. Centered at Luoyang, the turbulent Eastern Zhou dynasty was divided by ancient Chinese chroniclers into the Spring and Autumn period (722–481 BCE) and the Warring States period (403–221 BCE). One writer from the Spring and Autumn period described over 500 battles among states and more than 100 civil wars within states, all taking place within 260 years. Fueling this warfare was the spread of cheaper and more lethal weaponry, made possible by new iron-smelting techniques, which in turn shifted influence from the central government to local authorities and allowed warfare to continue unabated into the Warring States period. Regional states became so powerful that they undertook large-scale projects, including dikes and irrigation systems, which had to this point been feasible only for empires. At the beginning of the Warring States period, seven large territorial states dominated the Zhou world. (See Map 5.2.) Their wars and shifting political alliances involved the mobilization of armies and resources on an unprecedented scale. Qin, the most powerful state, which ultimately replaced the Eastern Zhou dynasty in 221 BCE, fielded armies that combined huge infantries in the tens of thousands with lethal cavalries and skilled archers using state-of-the-art crossbows.

The conception of central power changed dramatically during this era, as royal appointees replaced hereditary officeholders. By the middle of the fourth century BCE, power was so concentrated in the major states' rulers that each began to call himself "king" (*wang*). Despite the constant warfare, scholars, soldiers, merchants, peasants, and artisans thrived in the midst of an expanding agrarian economy and interregional trade.

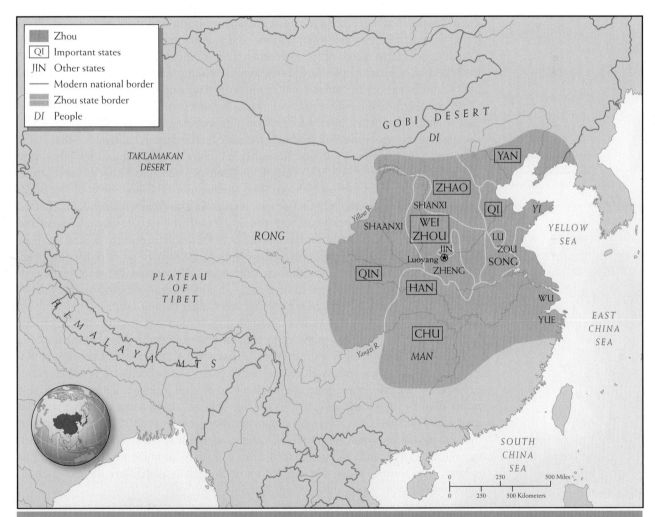

MAP 5.2 | Zhou China in the Warring States Period

The Warring States period witnessed a fracturing of the Zhou dynasty into a myriad of states.

• Find the Zhou capital of Luoyang on the map. Where was it located relative to the other key states?

• What about this map tells us why diplomacy was so important during this period?

• How do you think so many smaller states could survive when they were surrounded first by seven and then by three even larger and more powerful states (Qin, Qi, and Chu)?

COMPARISON

IDENTIFY axial age thinkers and **ANALYZE** their distinctive ideas.

INNOVATIONS IN THOUGHT

Out of this turmoil came new visions that would shape Chinese thinking about the individual's place in society and provided the philosophical underpinnings for the world's most enduring imperial system (lasting from the establishment of the Qin dynasty in 221 BCE until the abdication of China's last monarch in 1912). Often it was the losers among the political elites, seeking to replace their former advantages with new status gained through service, who sparked this intellectual creativity. Many important teachers emerged in China's axial age, each with disciples. The philosophies of these "hundred masters," a term mostly used at the time by itinerant scholars, constituted what came to be known as the Hundred Schools of Thought. Among the most influential were Confucianism and Daoism.

Confucius (551–479 BCE) was very much the product of the violent Spring and Autumn period. Serving in minor governmental positions, he believed the founders of the Zhou dynasty had established ideals of good government and principled action. Frustrated, however, by the realities of division and war among rival states all around him, Confucius set out in search of an enlightened ruler. Confucius's teachings stemmed from his belief that human beings behaved ethically not to achieve salvation or heavenly reward but because it was in their human makeup to do so. Humanity's natural tendencies, if left alone, produced harmonious existence. Confucius saw family and filial submission (the duty of children to parents) as the foundation of proper ethical action, including loyalty to the state and rulers. His idea of modeling the state on the patriarchal family—that is, the ruler respecting heaven as if it were his father and protecting his subjects as if they were his children—became a bedrock principle of Confucian thought. Although he regarded himself as a transmitter of ancient wisdom, Confucius established many of the major guidelines for Chinese thought and action: respect for the pronouncements of scholars, commitment to a broad education, and training for all who were highly intelligent and willing to work, whether noble or humble in birth. This equal access to training for those willing and able offered a dramatic departure from past centuries, when only nobles were believed capable of ruling. Nonetheless, Confucius's distinctions between gentlemen-rulers and commoners continued to support a social hierarchy—although an individual's position in that hierarchy now rested on education rather than on birth.

Confucius's ethical teachings were preserved by his followers in *The Analects*. In his effort to persuade his contemporaries to reclaim what he regarded as the lost ideals of the early Zhou, Confucius proposed a moral framework stressing correct performance of ritual (*li*), humaneness (*ren*), loyalty to the family (*xiao*), and perfection of moral character to become a "superior man" (*junzi*)—that is, a man defined by benevolence and goodness rather than by the pursuit of profit. Confucius believed that a society of such superior men would not need coercive laws and punishment to achieve order. Confucius left court, discouraged by the continuing state of warfare, in 484 BCE. His transformational ideology remained, however; and has shaped Chinese society for millennia, both through its followers and through those who adopted traditions that developed as a distinct counterpoint to Confucian engagement.

Another key philosophy was **Daoism**, which diverged sharply from Confucian thought by scorning rigid rituals and social hierarchies. Its ideas originated with a Master Lao (Laozi, "Old Master"), who—if he actually existed—may have been a contemporary of Confucius. His sayings were collected in *The Daodejing,* or *The Book of the Way and Its Power* (c. third century BCE). Master Lao's book was then elaborated by Master Zhuang (Zhuangzi, c. 369–286 BCE). Daoism stressed that the best path (*dao*) for living was to follow the natural order of things. Its main principle was *wuwei*, "doing nothing." Spontaneity, noninterference, and acceptance of the world as it is, rather than attempting to change it through politics and government, were what mattered. In Laozi's vision, the ruler who interfered least in the natural processes of change was the most successful. Zhuangzi focused on the enlightened individual living spontaneously and in harmony with nature, free of society's ethical rules and laws and viewing life and death simply as different stages of existence.

Apart from the philosophical discourse of the "hundred masters," with its far-reaching impact across Chinese society, elites and commoners alike tried to maintain stability in their lives through religion, medicine, and statecraft. The elites' rites of divination to predict the future and medical recipes to heal the body found parallels in the commoners' use of ghost stories and astrological almanacs to understand the meaning of their lives and the significance of their deaths. Elites recorded their political discourses on wood and bamboo slips, tied together to form scrolls. They likewise prepared military treatises, ritual texts, geographic works, and poetry. The growing importance of statecraft and philosophical discourse promoted the use of writing, with 9,000 to 10,000 graphs or signs required to convey these elaborate ideas.

What emerged from all this activity was a foundational alliance of scholars and the state. Scholars became state functionaries dependent on rulers' patronage. In return, rulers recognized scholars' expertise in matters of punishment, ritual, astronomy, medicine, and divination. Philosophical deliberations focused on the need to maintain order and stability by preserving the state. These bonds that rulers forged with their scholarly elites were a distinguishing feature of governments in Warring States China, as compared with other Afro-Eurasian societies at this time.

INNOVATIONS IN STATE ADMINISTRATION

Regional rulers of the Spring and Autumn period enhanced their ability to obtain natural resources, to recruit men for their armies, and to oversee conquered areas. This trend continued in the Warring States period, as the elites in the major states created administrative districts with stewards, sheriffs, and judges and a system of registering peasant households to facilitate tax collection and army conscription. These officials, who had been knights under the Western Zhou, were now bureaucrats in direct service to the ruler. These administrators were the "superior men" (*junzi*) of Confucian thought. They were paid in grain, titles, and gifts of gold and silver from the ruler. The most successful of these ministers was the Qin statesman Shang Yang (fourth century BCE). Lord Shang's reforms—including a head tax, administrative districts for closer bureaucratic control of hinterlands, land distribution for individual households to farm, and reward or punishment for military achievement—positioned the Qin to become the dominant state of its time.

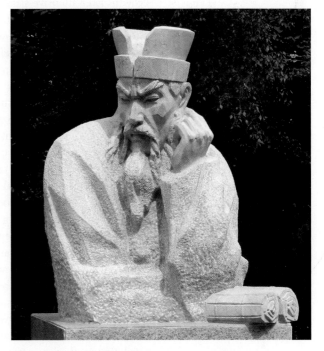

Shang Yang of Qin An important statesman of Qin during the Warring States period, Shang Yang introduced administrative reforms that enhanced the power of the central government.

INNOVATIONS IN WARFARE

With administrative reforms came reforms in military recruitment and warfare. In earlier periods, nobles had let fly their arrows from chariots while conscripted peasants fought beside them on the blood-stained ground. The Warring States, however, relied on massed infantries of peasants, whose conscription was made easier by the registration of peasant households. Bearing iron lances and unconstrained by their relationships with nobles, these peasants fought fiercely. In addition to this conscripted peasant infantry, armies boasted elite professional troops equipped with iron armor and weapons, and wielding the recently invented crossbow. The crossbow's tremendous power, range, and accuracy enabled archers to kill lightly armored cavalrymen or charioteers at a distance. With improved siege technology, enemy armies assaulted the new defensive walls of towns and frontiers, either digging under them or using counterweighted siege ladders to scale them. Campaigns were no longer limited to an agricultural season, but now might stretch over a year or longer. The huge state armies contained as many as 1,000,000 commoners in the infantry, supported by 1,000 chariots and 10,000 bow-wielding cavalrymen. During the Spring and Autumn period, one state's entire army would face another state's; but by the Warring States period, armies could divide into separate forces and wage several battles simultaneously.

ECONOMIC, SOCIAL, AND CULTURAL CHANGES

While a growing population presented new challenges, the continuous warfare in these periods spurred economic growth in China. An agricultural revolution on the North China plain along the Yellow River led to rapid population growth, and the inhabitants of the Eastern Zhou reached approximately 20 million. Several factors contributed to increased agricultural productivity beginning in the Spring and Autumn period. Some rulers gave peasants the right to own their land in exchange for taxes and military service, which in turn increased productivity because the farmers were working to benefit themselves. Agricultural productivity was also enhanced by innovations such as crop rotation (millet and wheat in the north, rice and millet in the south) and oxen-pulled iron plowshares to prepare fields.

With this increased agricultural yield came the pressures of accompanying population growth. Ever-attentive peasant farmers tilling the fields of North and South China produced more rice and wheat than anyone else on earth, but that agricultural success was often outpaced by their growing families. As more people required more fuel, deforestation led to erosion of the fields. Many animals were hunted to extinction. Many inhabitants migrated south to domesticate the marshes, lakes, and rivers of the Yangzi River delta; here they created new arable frontiers out of former wetlands. When the expansion into arable land invariably hit its limits, Chinese families faced terrible food shortages and famines. The long-term economic result was a declining standard of living for massive numbers of Chinese peasants.

Despite these long-term cycles of population pressures and famine, larger harvests and advances in bronze and iron casting enabled the beginning of a market economy: trade in surplus grain, pottery, and ritual objects. Peasants continued to barter, but elites and rulers used minted coins. Grain and goods traveled along roads, rivers, and canals. Rulers and officials applied their military and organizational skills for public projects enhancing water works.

Economic growth had repercussions at all levels of society. Rulers attained a high level of cultural sophistication, as reflected in their magnificent palaces and burial sites. Archaeological evidence also suggests that commoners could purchase bronze metalwork, whereas previously only Zhou rulers and aristocrats could afford to do so. Social relations became more fluid as commoners gained power and aristocrats lost it. In Qin, for example, peasants who served in the ruler's army could be rewarded with land, houses, slaves, and even status change for killing enemy soldiers. While class relations had a revolutionary fluidity, gender relations became more rigid for elites and nonelites alike as male-centered kinship groups grew. The resulting separation of the sexes and male domination within the family affected women's position. An emphasis on monogamy, or at least the primacy of the first wife over additional wives and concubines, emerged. Relations between the sexes became increasingly ritualized and constrained by moral and legal sanctions against any behavior that appeared to threaten the purity of authoritarian male lineages.

Even with the endless cycles of warfare and chaos—or perhaps because of them—many foundational beliefs, values, and philosophies for later dynasties sprang forth during the Spring and Autumn and Warring States periods. By the middle of the first millennium BCE, China's political activities and institutional and intellectual innovations affected larger numbers of people, over a much broader area, than comparable developments in South Asia and the Mediterranean.

Knife Coin Zhou dynasty coins, like the later Han coin shown here, were made of bronze and produced in a variety of shapes, some resembling spades and knives, depending on the region. Each of the Warring States had its own currency.

The New Worlds of South Asia

While Chinese scholar-officials were theorizing about how to govern and organize their society, the Vedic peoples who settled in the Ganges valley were assimilating earlier residents and forging their own new political institutions, economic activities, and belief systems. The heartland of South Asian developments in this period was the mid-Ganges plain, a roughly 70,000-square-mile area in the northeast of present-day India and the southern tip of Nepal. (See Map 5.3.) Waves of Vedic peoples migrated into this region around 600 BCE, clearing land, establishing new cities and trade routes, expanding rice cultivation, and experimenting with new political forms. Abundant monsoon rains made the land suitable for rice farming, as opposed to the wheat and barley farming of the Indus Valley. Vedic migrants cleared land by setting fire to the forests and using iron tools—fashioned from ore mined locally—to remove what was left of the jungle. Two major kinds of states appeared in the mid- and lower Ganges plain: those ruled by hereditary monarchs and those ruled by a small elite (oligarchy). South Asian oligarchies were led by the Kshatriya class of warriors and officials. Kshatriya oligarchs controlled the land and other resources, overseeing the work of slaves and foreign workers.

In the kingdoms and oligarchic cities of northern India, a new system of hierarchy emerged alongside the old four-fold *varnas* (Brahman priests, Kshatriya warriors, Vaishya commoners, and Shudra laborers). *Varnas* remained the overarching theoretical basis for ranking the social order; but, since booming agriculture allowed for greater variation in professions, occupation and birth received new emphasis. Each occupational group established its own sublevels, called *jatis* (the Sanskrit word for birth). *Jatis* were organized not only by kinship and profession, but even by product. In the emerging urban centers, for instance, traders were regarded as "purer" than artisans, while those making gold utensils had higher status than those making copper or iron products. Yet members of each group colluded to restrict internal competition, and they closed ranks to preserve their status. Sub-*jatis* banned intermarriage to prevent other groups from accessing their knowledge. Religion buttressed this hierarchical system. Brahmanical texts, some from an earlier period and some from the present, invoked the principle of purity and pollution to rank *varnas* and *jatis* and to hinder movement between them. Occupations were made hereditary, and taboos were placed on intermarriage and interdining. These injunctions ensured that individuals did not move out of their inherited occupation. Thus, the basis of what would later become the caste system, which still plays an important role in Indian society, was laid at this time.

Map labels (clockwise/as positioned):

KAMBOJA

GANDHARA
• Taxila

H I M A L A Y A M T S.

Indus R.
THAR DESERT

KURU

PANCHALA

Mathura •
SURA-
SENA

MATSYA

• Mathura

KOSHALA
• Sāvatthī

Sākata •

MALLA

VRIJJI
CONFEDERACY
• Kusīnāra

Ganges R.

ANGA

VATSA
• Kausāmbi

KASHI

CHEDI

AVANTI
•
VINDHYA
RAUSE

MAGADHA
• Rajagrīha

ARABIAN
SEA

ASMAKA

WESTERN GHATS

EASTERN GHATS

Bay
of
Bengal

VATSA	Important states
ANGA	Other states
•	Cities

```
0        200        400 Miles
0    200    400 Kilometers
```

MAP 5.3 | Sixteen States in the First Millennium in South Asia

South Asia underwent profound transformations in the first millennium BCE that reflected growing urbanization, increased commerce, and the emergence of two types of states: monarchies and oligarchies.

• Where did the new states and cities appear?

• What geographic and environmental features encouraged social and cultural integration?

• According to this map, what other regions had influence on South Asia, and where might South Asian culture spread?

NEW CITIES AND A CHANGING ECONOMY

Supported by rice agriculture, cities began to emerge on the Ganges plain around 500 BCE and became centers of commercial and intellectual exchange. Some, such as Shravasti and Rajagriha, thrived as artisanal centers; while others, like Taxila, prospered through trade. These cities of the Ganges plain were dominated by men and women whose occupations—bankers, merchants, and teachers—did not fit easily into the old *varnas*. Precisely laid out streets were crowded with vendors, and wealthy residents employed elephants and horse-drawn chariots to move them about. Alleys leading from the main streets zigzagged between houses built with pebbles and clay. Although city expansion was often haphazard, civic authorities showed great interest in sanitation. The many squares dotting each city had garbage bins, and dirty water drained away in deep sink wells underground. Streets were graded so that rainfall would wash them clean.

The new cities offered exciting opportunities and innovations. Rural householders who moved into them prospered by importing rice and sugarcane from villages to sell in the markets; they then transported manufactured goods such as sugar, salt, and utensils back to their villages. The less affluent turned to craftwork, fashioning textiles, needles, fine pottery, copper plates, ivory decorations, and gold and silver utensils. Other professions included physicians, launderers, barbers, cooks, tailors, and entertainers. The elaborate division of labor suggests high degrees of specialization and commercialization. Those with money became bankers who financed trade and industry. As in Greece and China, coins came into use in these cities at about this time. Traders and bankers established municipal bodies that issued the coins and vouched for their worth. Made of silver, the coins had irregular shapes but specific weights, which determined their value; they also were punch-marked, or stamped with symbols of authority on one side.

Yet, the opportunities and innovations of the new cities did not ensure success for everyone. Many came to cities in search of work, and some fared better than others. As a whole, city dwellers had more material wealth, but their lives were far more uncertain. In addition, urban life created a new social class: those who did the dirtiest jobs, such as removing garbage and sewage, and were therefore viewed as physically and ritually impure "untouchables." Even though their work kept the cities clean, they were forced to live in

Taxila (*Left*) Taxila became the capital of Gandhara, a kingdom located in what is today northern Pakistan and eastern Afghanistan at the time that it was occupied by the Persian Empire in the fifth century BCE. Dharmarajika was one of the most important monasteries. The walkway around the stupa, a mound-like structure containing Buddhist relics, was covered with glass tiles, and the stupa itself was decorated with jewels. (*Right*) This corner of a stupa exhibits a variety of the architectural styles that prevailed in Gandharan art at its height. Both square and round columns are covered by Corinthian capitals. The right arch gate shows the style of Sanchi, the famous stupa in central India.

shantytowns outside the city limits. These outcasts became receptive audiences for those who would challenge Vedic rituals and Brahman priests.

BRAHMANS, THEIR CHALLENGERS, AND NEW BELIEFS

COMPARISON

COMPARE the range of solutions the axial age thinkers devised.

To the Brahmans, nothing about the cities seemed good, and their efforts to retain their superior status prompted new challenges to traditional beliefs. The Brahmans thought that *varnas* and *jatis* mixing indiscriminately polluted society. Moreover, lowborn persons grasping at higher status by acquiring wealth or skill skewed established hierarchies. When an alphabetic script appeared around 600 BCE, sacred knowledge became more accessible, and thus the Brahmans' ability to control the definition of right and wrong was undermined. Formerly, all of Vedic literature had been memorized, and only the brightest Brahmans could master the tradition. (See Chapter 4.)

Frightened by these urban threats, Brahmans sought to strengthen their relationships with the kings by establishing the idea of a monarch endowed with divine power. Kingship had been unnecessary in a long-ago golden age, according to Brahmanic scripts; a moral code and priests to uphold it had been enough to keep things in order. Over time, though, the world deteriorated due to rivalry for wealth. According to Brahmanic writings, the gods then decided that people on earth needed a king to maintain order. The gods enticed a reluctant Manu ("Man") with a range of promises, including one-tenth of the grain harvest, one-fiftieth of the cattle, merits for subjects' good behavior, and the most beautiful woman in his domain. In this Brahmanic account, royal power had a divine origin: the gods chose the king and protected him. Priests and Vedic rituals were essential to royal power, since kingly authority was validated through religious ceremonies carried out by Brahman priests. This emphasis on divine kingship solved some problems but created new ones. The Brahmans' claim to moral authority caused resentment among the Kshatriyas—especially those in the oligarchic republics, whose leaders did not assert divine power. Merchants and artisans also chafed at the Brahmans' claims to superiority. Such resentments provoked challenges to the Brahmans' domination. Some thinkers in South Asia believed that they were in an age of acute crisis because their culture's ancient harmony had been lost. And like many scholars and philosophers elsewhere in this axial era, a new group of South Asian scholars and religious leaders developed their own answers to questions about human existence.

Dissident South Asian thinkers challenged the Brahmans' worldview by refusing to recognize the gods that populated the Vedic world. Some of these rebels sprang from inside the Vedic tradition; though Brahmans, they rejected the idea that sacrificial rituals pleased the gods. To them, God was a universal concept, not a superhuman creature. Also, they felt that the many cows that priests slaughtered for ritual sacrifices could serve more practical uses, such as plowing the land and producing milk. Their discussions and teachings about the universe and life were later collected in the *Upanishads*. Other dissidents, such as Mahavira and the Buddha, came from outside the Vedic tradition.

Mahavira and Jainism Vardhamana Mahavira (c. 540–468 BCE) popularized the doctrines of **Jainism**, which had emerged in the seventh century BCE. Born a Kshatriya in an oligarchic republic, Mahavira left home at age thirty to seek the truth about life; he spent twelve years as an ascetic (one who rejects material possessions and physical pleasures) wandering throughout the Ganges valley before reaching enlightenment. He taught that the universe obeys its own everlasting rules and cannot be affected by any god or other supernatural being. He also believed that the purpose of life is to purify one's soul through asceticism and to attain a state of permanent bliss. The Jains' religious doctrines emphasized the idea that asceticism, rather than knowledge, would enable one to avoid harming other creatures and thereby purify the soul. Since the doctrine of *ahimsa* ("no hurt") held that every living creature has a soul—killing even an ant would result in an unfavorable rebirth—believers had to watch every step to avoid inadvertently becoming murderers. The extreme nonviolence of Jainism was impossible for peasants, who could not work the land without killing insects. Instead, Jainism became a religion of city dwellers and traders. Mahavira's teachings were transmitted orally for nearly a millennium before being compiled into writing by followers in the fifth century CE.

Buddha and Buddhism The most direct challenge to traditional Brahmanic thinking came from Siddhartha Gautama (c. 563–483 BCE), a contemporary of Mahavira and Confucius. Later known as the **Buddha** (Enlightened One), Gautama objected to Brahmanic beliefs, their rituals and sacrifices, and their preference for kingship that kept the priestly class in power. His axial age teachings provided the peoples of South Asia and elsewhere with alternatives to established traditions.

Gautama was born into a comfortable life, the son of a highly respected Kshatriya warrior, in a small oligarchic community nestled in the foothills of the Himalayas. Yet, at the age of twenty-nine, he walked away from everything, leaving behind his father, wife, and newborn son. Family and friends wept as he donned a robe and shaved his head and beard, symbols of the ascetic life that he intended to pursue. Gautama struggled with the belief that the life that he and most others were destined to live would consist of little more than endless episodes of suffering, which began with the pain of childbirth, followed by aging, illness, disease, and death, after which reincarnated beings would experience more of the same.

For six years, Gautama lived as an ascetic wanderer before a forty-nine-day meditation led him to the enlightened moment in which he realized that *nirvana* (spiritual contentment) could be achieved by finding a middle ground between self-indulgence and self-denial. He expressed this new credo as the Four Truths: (1) life, from birth to death, is full of suffering; (2) all sufferings are caused by desires; (3) the only way to rise above suffering is to renounce desire; and (4) the only way to rid oneself of desire is through adherence to the Noble Eightfold Path, which includes wisdom (right views and right intentions), ethical behavior (right conduct, right speech, and right livelihood), and mental discipline (right effort, right thought, and right meditation). This teaching represented a dramatic shift in thinking about humanity and correct behavior. Like the teachings of Mahavira, the Buddha's doctrines left no space for Brahmanic deities to dictate human lives. Buddha's logical explanation of human suffering and his guidelines for renouncing desire appealed to many people for their simplicity, accessibility, and challenge to the Vedic hierarchies. (See **Current Trends in World History: Prophets and the Founding Texts**.)

Like other dissident thinkers of this period, the Buddha delivered his message in a vernacular dialect of Sanskrit that all could understand. His many followers soon formed a community of monks called a *sangha* ("gathering"). The Buddha

Brahman Recluse When Buddhists started to tell stories in sculptures and paintings, Brahmans were included when appropriate. This character in Gandharan Buddhist art probably represents a Brahman who lived as a recluse, instead of as a priest. He is not shaved or dressed, but his expression is passionate.

Current Trends in World History

Prophets and the Founding Texts: Comparing Confucius and the Buddha

World history offers many opportunities to compare one society with another, and this chapter, with its emphasis on teachers, prophets, and intellectuals, in what we have called an axial age, provides an unparalleled moment to contrast the lives and the ideals of central figures whose teachings shaped spiritual movements, legal and political systems, and long-lasting traditions. In Confucianism and Buddhism, we find key leaders who inspired belief systems that were subsequently named for them.

 Confucius (Kong Fuzi, 551–479 BCE) was one of the ancient world's great innovators. A government official in Zhou-era China, he elaborated a code of behavior that valued individual performance of traditional rituals and governmental morality based on correct social relationships, sincerity, and justice. Seeing division and war among rival states, he wished to restore order by promoting education, moral behavior, and the performance of rituals.

Over the centuries, the method and substance of his teaching, with many revisions, became the mainstream value system of imperial China. His idea of modeling the state on the patriarchal family—that is, the ruler should respect heaven as if it were his father and protect his subjects as if they were his children—became the foundation of Chinese political theory. Confucius wanted people to perform the rituals bequeathed by the early Zhou and to emulate the sages who had ordered the world according to principles of civility and culture.

Chinese philosophers did not always agree on how to interpret Confucius's ideas. Representing one school of Confucianists, Mencius (372–289 BCE) held that while recognizing the tendency of people to be led astray by worldly appetites and ambitions, he still believed in the inherent goodness of human nature. To recover that innate goodness required moral training. But according to Xunzi (310–237 BCE), Confucius saw humans as evil and lacking an innate moral sense. They therefore had to be controlled by education, ritual, and custom.

Nevertheless, both Mencius and Xunzi embraced Confucius's dictum that people were perfectible through education and the practice of proper conduct. All Confucians, whether pessimists or optimists, viewed moral cultivation through education as the heart of the civilizing process, and they ensured that his ideas remained a vital force throughout Chinese history.

The teachings of the Buddha (Siddhartha Gautama, c. 563–483 BCE), like those of Confucius, had far-reaching influence. The two thinkers were roughly contemporary, and both formulated their ideas in response and his followers wandered from one city to another on the Ganges plain, where they found large audiences as well as the alms needed to sustain the expanding *sangha*. The Buddha's most influential patrons were urban merchants. In struggles between oligarchs and kings, the Buddha sided with the oligarchs, reflecting his upbringing in an oligarchic republic. He inevitably aroused opposition from the Brahmans, who favored monarchical government. While the Buddha himself did not seek to erase the Vedic hierarchies, Buddhism provided an escape from its oppressive aspects and the prestige that it afforded the Brahmans. Together with Jainism, Buddhism's challenge to Brahmanic thinking appealed particularly in the new urban contexts of South Asia and to those who felt disadvantaged by prevailing Vedic hierarchies in the first millennium BCE.

The Mediterranean World

COMPARISON

EXPLAIN the relationship between axial age thinkers across Afro-Eurasia, and the political and social situations to which they were responding.

Political, economic, and social changes also stimulated new thinking in the Mediterranean world. The violent upheavals that tore through the borderland areas of the northern Levant, the coastal lands of Anatolia, the islands of the Aegean and Mediterranean seas, and mainland Greece in the few centuries after 1000 BCE freed the people in these regions from the domination of Assyria and Persia (Chapter 4). These borderland communities encircling the Mediterranean basin also created second-generation societies that developed new social and political methods of organization and explored new axial age ideas.

to social chaos and degeneration. The Buddha presented a vision of society that challenged the Brahmanic order. Buddhism shaped the views of life and death and the scheme of time and space of the universe in South Asia. It also had a profound impact on peoples outside the region and even replaced Confucianism as the dominant religion in China for a few hundred years.

The Buddha offered a logical approach in the form of a unified system underlying the universe, instead of invoking divine intervention, to understand the universe and social life at a time of rapid political development. He believed that the universe and individual lives go through eternal cycles of birth, death, and rebirth, and he elaborated the concept of *karma* ("fate" or "action"), a universal principle of cause and effect. The birth of every living being, human or animal, reflects actions taken in his or her past lives. Karma embodies the sins and merits of each individual, establishing his or her status in the current life. In turn, deeds in the current life affect that karma and thus determine suffering and happiness in the next life. Buddhist believers therefore focused on the consequences of their actions: through their own behavior, they could attain better future lives.

Confucianism and Buddhism, much like the Vedic, Brahmin, and Judaic faiths discussed in Chapter 4, emerged in times of great turmoil. All the faiths were first transmitted orally; later, adherents created a written record to spread them more widely. But Buddhism and Confucianism stand out in that they have founders whose identification with their belief systems remains their most defining characteristic: the Buddha as an enlightened one, and Confucius as a sage teacher. We will see this phenomenon again with the rise of Christianity (from the teachings of Jesus) and Islam (from the teachings of Muhammad) as we continue our discussion of universalizing religions.

QUESTIONS FOR ANALYSIS

- What is the reward for good moral behavior for Confucius? For Buddha?
- What are the major similarities and differences between these two traditions?

Explore Further

David Schaberg, A *Patterned Past: Form and Thought in Early Chinese Historiography* (2002).

Karen Armstrong, *Buddha* (2001).

Lothar von Falkenhausen, *Chinese Society in the Age of Confucius (1000–250 BC): The Archaeological Evidence* (2006).

Phoenicians, Greeks, Cretans, Cypriots, Lydians, Etruscans, and many others exchanged not only trade goods but also ideas about the virtues of self-sufficient cities whose inhabitants shared power more widely than before. (See Map 5.4.)

FORMATION OF NEW CITY-STATES

In the ninth and eighth centuries BCE, as order returned to the eastern Mediterranean and the population rebounded, peoples who were clustered in more concentrated settlements formed city-states. Unlike the city-states of earlier Mesopotamia, which were governed by semidivine monarchs, or the great urban centers of Southwest Asian empires run by elite scribes, high priests, and monarchs, the Mediterranean city-states were governed by their citizens. These self-governing city-states were a new political form that profoundly influenced the Mediterranean region. This new urban entity—known first by the Phoenicians as a *qart*, then by the Greeks as a *polis*, and the Romans as a *civitas*—multiplied throughout the Mediterranean by the sixth century BCE.

The new principles of rulership were revolutionary. Ordinary residents, or "citizens," of these cities—such as Carthage and Gadir (modern-day Cádiz in Spain) among the western Phoenicians; Athens, Thebes, Sparta, and Corinth among the Greeks; Rome and Praeneste among the early Latins—governed themselves and selected their leaders. Their self-government took various forms, including tyranny (rule by a popularly approved individual), oligarchy (rule by the few), and democracy (rule by all free adult males).

MAP 5.4 | The Mediterranean World

Phoenician and Greek city-states, as well as the colonies they founded, dotted the coastline of both the Mediterranean and Black seas.

• What were the main goods traded in the Mediterranean world in this period?

• What is the relationship between the sites of cities in areas of colonization and the resources and trade routes?

• What areas did the Greeks and Phoenicians control, and what was their main settlement pattern?

The new cities of the Mediterranean basin included adult male citizens, other free persons (including women, who could not vote or hold office), foreign immigrants, and large numbers of unfree persons (including slaves and people tied to the land who could not vote or fight for the polis). The small family unit, or household, was the most important social unit of the city-state and the city-state was seen as a natural outgrowth of the household. Thus, the free adult male was fully entitled to engage in the city's public affairs. In contrast, adult women of free birth remained enclosed within the private world of the family and had no standing to debate policy in public, vote, or hold office. Those enjoying full citizenship rights—the adult freeborn males—in each community decided what tasks, from warfare to public works, the city-state would undertake and what kind of government and laws it would adopt.

City-states were competitive places. Their histories relate rivalries between individuals, social classes, and other groups. Competition for honor and prestige was a value that shaped behavior in the city-states. This extreme competitive ethic found a benign outlet in organized sporting events. Almost from the moment that Greek city-states emerged, athletic contests sprang up. The greatest of these competitions were the Olympic Games, which began in 776 BCE at Olympia in southern Greece. The competitive spirit among communities also took the destructive form of armed conflicts over borderlands, trade, valuable resources, religious shrines, and prestige. The incessant battles among city-states fueled new developments in military equipment, such as the heavy armor that gave its name to the hoplites, or infantry-men, and in tactics, such as the standard block-like configuration (which the Greeks called a *phalanx*) in which the regular rank and file fought. These wars were so destructive that they threatened to destabilize the city-states' world. The most famous conflicts were the Pelopon-nesian War (431–404 BCE) between Athens and Sparta, and their respective allies, and the ongoing rivalry between the city-states of Rome and Phoenician Carthage (from c. 500 BCE onward). Despite the destabilizing effects of warfare, city-states prospered, and economic innovations facilitated trade and exchange throughout the Mediterranean.

ECONOMIC INNOVATIONS

Without an elaborate top-down bureaucratic and administrative structure, residents of the new cities devised other ways to run their commercial affairs. They developed open trading markets and a system of money that enabled buyers and sellers to know the precise value of commodities so that exchanges were efficient. At their center, the new city-states had a marketplace (*agora*), a large open area where individuals bought and sold commodi-ties. These increasingly complex transactions required money, rather than barter or gift exchange. Like the states in Eastern Zhou China and Vedic South Asia, by the end of the fifth century BCE the Greek city-states were also issuing a striking variety of coins, and other peoples such as the Phoenicians, Etruscans, and Persians were using them. Coins bought services, as well, perhaps at first to hire mercenary soldiers. In the absence of large bureaucracies, Mediterranean cities relied on money to connect the producers and buyers of goods and services, especially as city-states became more far-flung.

The Agora The agora, or central open marketplace, was one of the core defining features of Mediterranean city-states. At its center, each city had one of these open-air plazas, the heart of its commercial, religious, social, and political life. When a new city was founded, the agora was one of the first places that the colonists measured out. The large, rectangular, open area in this picture is the agora of the Greek colonial city of Cyrene (in modern-day Libya).

Mediterranean Coins From the sixth century BCE onward, money in the form of precious metal coins began spreading through the city-states of the Mediterranean, beginning with the Greek city-states in the western parts of what is today Turkey, then spreading to the other Greek *poleis* and beyond. On the left here is the classic tetradrachm (four-drachma piece) coin of Athens with its owl of the goddess Athena; on the right is a silver coin of shekel weight produced by the city of Carthage in the western Mediterranean.

Indeed, the search for silver, iron, copper, and tin drove traders westward across the Mediterranean. By about 500 BCE the Phoenicians, Greeks, and others from the eastern Mediterranean had planted new city-states around the shores of the western Mediterranean and the Black Sea. Once established, these colonial communities became completely independent and transformed the coastal world. City-based life was common from southern Spain and western Italy to the Crimea on the Black Sea. With amazing speed, seaborne communications spread a Mediterranean-wide urban culture that bolstered the region's wealthy and powerful elites. Found among the local elites of Tartessos in southern Spain, the Gallic chiefs in southern France, and the Etruscan and Roman nobles of central Italy, a new aristocratic culture featured similar public displays of wealth: richly decorated chariots, elaborate armor and weapons, fine dining ware, elaborate houses, and public burials. From the western end of the Mediterranean to the Black Sea, the city-state communities developed a culture founded on market-based economies and private property.

In contrast to the privilege enjoyed by these elites was the traffic in human flesh: slavery. Treating men, women, and children as objects of commerce, to be bought and sold in markets, created a new form of commercial slavery called chattel slavery. When dangerous and exhausting tasks such as mining and farming required extra labor, freeborn citizens purchased slave laborers. These slaves were mainly war captives. In some city-states, slaves may have constituted up to a quarter of the population. In every one of the new city-states, slaves provided manual and technical labor of all kinds and produced the agricultural surpluses that supported the urban population.

NEW IDEAS

New ways of thinking about the world emerged from the competitive atmosphere that the Greek city-states fostered. In the absence of monarchical or priestly rule, ideas were free to arise, circulate, and clash. Individuals argued publicly about the nature of the gods, the best state, what is good, and whether to wage war. There was no final authority to give any particular idea a final stamp of approval and force its acceptance. New ideas emerged in science and the arts, and Greek philosophers proposed theories on human society and many other topics.

Naturalistic Science and Realistic Art In this competitive marketplace of ideas, some daring thinkers developed novel ways of perceiving the cosmos and representing the environment. Rather than seeing everything as the handiwork of all-powerful deities, they took a naturalistic view of humans and their place in the universe. This new thinking was evident in their art, which idealized the natural world. Artists increasingly represented humans, objects, and landscapes not in abstract, idealized, or formal ways but in "natural" ways, as they appeared to the human eye. Even their portrayals of gods became more humanlike. Later, these objective and natural views of humans and nature became the new ideals, the highest of which was the unadorned human figure: the nude became the centerpiece of Greek art. Individual artists—such as the vase painter Exekias, the sculptor Praxiteles, and the poet Sappho—began to sign their works in a clear manifestation of the new sense of the individual being freed from the restraints of an autocratic state or a controlling religious system.

New Thinking and Greek Philosophers Axial age thinkers in city-states such as Miletus and Ephesus in western Anatolia did not accept traditional explanations of how and why the universe worked. Each thinker competed to outdo his peers in offering persuasive and comprehensive explanations of the cosmos, and their theories became ever more radical. For instance, Thales (c. 636–546 BCE) believed that water was the primal substance from which all other things were created. Xenophanes (c. 570–480 BCE) doubted the very existence of gods as they had been portrayed, asserting instead that only one general divine aura suffused all creation but that ethnic groups produced images of gods in their own likeness. Democritus (c. 460–370 BCE) claimed that everything was comprised of small and ultimately indivisible particles, which he called *atoma* ("uncuttables"). Pythagoras (c. 570–495 BCE), who devoted himself to the study of numbers, held that a wide range of physical phenomena, like musical sounds, were in fact based in numbers. This rich competition among ideas led to a more aggressive mode of public thinking, which the Greeks called *philosophia* ("love of wisdom").

In the fifth century BCE **Greek philosophers** (wisdom-lovers) were focusing on humans and their place in society. Some of these professional thinkers tried to describe an ideal state, characterized by harmonious relationships and free from corruption and political decline. One such thinker was Socrates (469–399 BCE), a philosopher who frequented the agora at Athens and encouraged people to reflect on ethics and morality, even as the Peloponnesian War raged on. (See **Analyzing Global Developments: Axial Age Thinkers and Their Ideas**.) He stressed the importance of honor and integrity as opposed

The Human Form The human body as it appeared naturally, without any adornment, became the ideal set by Greek art. Even gods were portrayed in the same natural nude human form. This statue by Praxiteles is of the god Dionysus and the child Hermes. Such bold nude portraits of humans and gods were sometimes shocking to other peoples.

Analyzing Global Developments

Axial Age Thinkers and Their Ideas

In the mid-twentieth century, the German philosopher Karl Jaspers invented the term "axial age" to describe the importance of ideas that originated in the first millennium BCE. These thinkers and their ideas are characterized as "axial" because: 1) they were a pivot point, or axis, that seemed to turn the world in a new direction, 2) they occurred along an East-West axis stretching from the Mediterranean to East Asia, and 3) they are central to ethical thought even down to the present day. These axial age philosophers were both the product of, and a challenge to, the societies from which they came—in other words, they were spurred by complex social and political contexts to develop their new ideas, but these new ideas in many ways critiqued and offered alternatives to the status quo. The chart below does not represent every axial age tradition, but is meant to draw into relief the relationship between the innovative thinkers, their historical context, and the tenets of the new belief systems.

QUESTIONS FOR ANALYSIS

- What connections, if any, can be made between the geopolitical situation of a society and the axial age philosophy that sprang from that region? In what ways does each philosopher support or challenge the status quo?
- Jaspers was particularly impressed that societies he understood as being disconnected from one another would develop philosophical ideas so similar. How might the temporal and geographic relationship of the philosophers listed on the chart be explained? How do connections with other regions, or lack thereof, impact the development of these ideas? What might account for similarities and differences in these axial age philosophies?
- What are the similarities and differences in how these philosophers' ideas were transmitted through time?

THINKER	PHILOSOPHY	CORE TEXT	HISTORICAL CONTEXT	CENTRAL TENET	EXEMPLARY SAYINGS
Zoroaster, a.k.a. Zarathustra (1000–600 BCE)	Zoroastrianism	Avesta, the most sacred part of which is the Gathas, seventeen Middle Persian hymns purportedly written by Zoroaster himself	Southwest Asia, based in eastern Iranian nomadic culture, eventually becoming the central religion of Persian Empire	**Dualistic ethical system,** a world order based on the cosmic struggle between Ahura Mazda, the god of light (good), and Ahriman, the god of destruction (evil). Humans must choose between good and evil with reward or retribution doled out in the afterlife	**On dualism:** "There [are] . . . two spirits [present] in the primal [stage of one's existence], twins who have . . . [manifested themselves as] the two [kinds] of dreams, . . . thoughts and words, . . . [and] actions, the better and the evil." (30.3) **On rewards:** "Brilliant things . . . will be for the person who comes to the truthful one. But a long period of darkness, foul food, and the word 'woe'—to such an existence your religious view will lead you, O deceitful ones, of your own actions." (31.20)
Ezekiel (sixth century BCE), Isaiah (mid-6th century BCE), among other Jewish writers and prophets	Judaism	The Hebrew Bible, whose second part, Nevi'im, contains the writings of the prophets	Southwest Asia, with origins in Mesopotamian tribal cultures, eventually spreading to the early empires of Egypt and the Levant	A strict monotheistic tradition which dictates that its followers are the chosen people and have entered a **covenant,** or contractual relationship, with their god	**On monotheism:** "I am the first and I am the last; besides me there is no god." (Isaiah 44:6) **On the convenant:** "[. . .] I will make a new covenant . . . not like the covenant which I made with their fathers . . . to bring them out of the land of Egypt, my covenant which they broke, though I was their husband, says the Lord." (Jeremiah 31:31–32) **On individual responsibility:** "The righteousness of the righteous shall be upon himself, and the wickedness of the wicked shall be upon himself." (Ezekiel 18:20)

Sources: H. Humbach and I. Ichaporia, *The Heritage of Zarathustra* (Heidelberg, 1994); Helmut Humbach "Gathas, i. Texts," *Encyclopedia Iranica* (2000) vol. X, fasc. 3, pp. 321–27; William W. Malandra, "Gathas, ii. Translations," *Encyclopedia Iranica* (2000) vol. X, fasc. 3, pp. 327–30; Thomas G. West and Grace Starry West, *Four Texts on Socrates* (Cornell, 1984); D. C. Lau's translation of *Analects* in H. James, ed., *Norton Anthology of World Literature, vol. 1* (Norton, 2002), pp. 820–30; *The Dhammapada*, translated by Juan Mascaro (Penguin, 1973); *New Oxford Annotated Bible with Apocrypha*, Revised Standard Version (Oxford).

THINKER	PHILOSOPHY	CORE TEXT	HISTORICAL CONTEXT	CENTRAL TENET	EXEMPLARY SAYINGS
Siddhartha Gautama, later known as Buddha (c. 563–483 BCE)	Buddhism	Dhammapad, verse sayings of the Buddha, which were recorded in the third century BCE	India, as a challenge to Kshatriya oligarchy and the hierarchical system of the Vedic society	An ethical system governed by the **Four Noble Truths:** 1. Life is suffering 2. Suffering is rooted in attachment 3. Escape suffering by escaping attachment 4. Escape attachment via the **Eight-fold Path** of right view, intention, speech, action, livelihood, effort, mindfulness, and concentration	**On the Eight-fold Path:** The best of the paths is the path of eight. The best of the truths, the four sayings. The best of states, freedom from passions. The best of men, the one who sees. (*Dhammapada*, 273) **On extremes:** "He who lives not for pleasures, and whose soul is in self-harmony, who eats and fasts with moderation, and has faith and the power of virtue—this man is not moved by temptations, as a great rock is not shaken by the wind (8)
Kong Fuzi, also known as Confucius (551–479 BCE)	Confucianism	*Analects*, Confucius's dialogues with state leaders and students that were most likely recorded centuries later	China, during political turmoil toward the end of the Spring and Autumn period (722–481 BCE)	The code of moral behavior, as exemplified in the *junzi* (gentleman or superior man), centered on: *ren* (benevolence) *li* (proper ritual) *xiao* (filial piety)	**On virtue:** "The rule of virtue can be compared to the Pole Star which commands the homage of the multitude of stars without leaving its place." (II.1) **On respect:** "Duke Ai asked: 'What must I do before the common people will look up to me?' Confucius answered: 'Raise the straight and set them over the crooked and the common people will look up to you.'" (II.19)
Socrates (469–399 BCE)	Greek Philosophy	Dialogues recorded in the contemporary work of his students, especially Plato, and a collection of his sayings published later on	Greece, during a period of Greco-Perisan conflict and inter-city-state wars	Ethical code that encourages self-discovery through knowledge, the recognition of the limits to one's own faculties, and the questioning of authority to find truth	**On self-discovery:** "The unexamined life is not worth living for a human being." (*Apology* 38a) **On wisdom:** "I am wiser than this human being, for probably neither of us knows anything noble and good; but he supposes he knows something, when he does not know; while I, just as I do not know, do not even suppose that I do." (*Apology* 21d)
Jesus (6/4 BCE– ca. 30 CE)	Christianity	Sayings later known through canonical and noncanonical Christian Gospels, first put in writing in the late first century CE	Levant, specifically in Judea under Roman imperial rule, later spreads throughout the Indo-Mediterranean	God's personal relationship with humanity mediated by His son, Jesus, whose suffering expiates human sins and grants eternal life to believers	**On ethical thought:** "Blessed are you poor, for yours is the kingdom of God; Blessed are you that hunger now, for you shall be satisfied . . . Love your enemies, do good to those who hate you. . . ." (Luke 6:20–38) **On Judaism:** "'Love the Lord your God . . . ' This is the first . . . commandment. And the second is like it: 'Love your neighbor as yourself.' All the Law and the Prophets hang on these two commandments." (Matthew 22:37–40)

to wealth and power (just as Confucius had done in Eastern Zhou China and the Buddha in Vedic South Asia). Plato (427–347 BCE), a student of Socrates, presented Socrates's philosophy in a series of dialogues (much as Confucius's students had written down his thoughts). In *The Republic,* Plato envisioned a perfect city that philosopher-kings would rule. He thought that if fallible humans could imitate this model city more closely, their states would be less susceptible to the decline that was affecting the Greek city-states of his own day.

Plato's most famous pupil answered the same questions about nature and the acquisition of knowledge differently. Deeply interested in the natural world, Aristotle (384–322 BCE) believed that by collecting and studying all the facts one could about a given thing, one could achieve a better understanding. His main idea was that the interested inquirer can find out more about the world by collecting as much evidence as possible about a given thing and then making deductions from these data about general patterns. This was in stark contrast to Plato's claim that everything a person observes is in fact only a flawed copy of the "real" thing that exists in a thought-world of abstract patterns accessible only by pure mental meditation—completely the opposite of Aristotle's method. This competition of ideas raged on for centuries, with the new thinking of these Mediterranean axial age philosophers at times fueling the aspirations of the city-states and at other times challenging them.

Common Cultures in the Americas and Sub-Saharan Africa

COMPARISON

COMPARE the political, cultural, and social developments across Afro-Eurasia with those occurring in the Americas and sub-Saharan Africa.

During what we have termed the axial age in Eurasia and North Africa, peoples living in the Americas and most of sub-Saharan Africa built complex, urban-based societies for the first time. These regions did not have immense cities, elaborate written texts, domesticated animals, and the other ingredients that underlay the radical new ideas of this era. Nonetheless, among the Chavín of the Andes, the Olmecs of Mesoamerica, the peoples of Nubia, and the West African Nok, exciting new developments were taking place in the first millennium BCE. Since the written record from these communities is limited, however, knowledge of their societies and beliefs is based largely in archaeological remains.

THE CHAVÍN IN THE ANDES

Around 1400 BCE, as the **Chavín** peoples began to share a common belief system, they also began to organize their societies vertically along the steep mountainsides and deep fertile valleys of the Andes. (See Map 5.1.) Valley floors yielded tropical and subtropical produce; the mountains supported maize and other crops; and in the highlands, potatoes became a staple and llamas produced wool and dung (used as fertilizer and fuel) and, eventually, served as beasts of burden. Llamas could not transport humans, however, so the Chavín migratory and political reach remained limited. While most necessities were available nearby thanks to the ecological diversity of the region, the Chavín did undertake some long-distance trade— mainly in dyes and precious stones, such as obsidian. By 900 BCE, the Chavín were erecting elaborate stone carvings, using advanced techniques to weave fine cotton textiles, and making gold, silver, and copper metal goods. Scholars have found evidence that by 400 BCE trade in painted textiles, ceramics, and gold objects spanned the Pacific coast, the Andean highlands, and the watershed eastward to the tropical rainforests of the Amazon basin.

What unified the fragmented Chavín communities was a shared artistic tradition manifested in their devotion to powerful deities. Their spiritual capital was the central temple complex of Chavín de Huántar, in modern Peru's northeastern highlands. The temple boasted

El Lanzón The Chavín excelled at elaborate stone carvings with complex images of their deities. This image of El Lanzón is a good example. At the center of one of the Chavín peoples' greatest temples is a massive gallery with this giant monument in the middle, etched with images of snakes, felines, and humans combined into one hybrid supernatural form. Observe the hands and feet with claws and the eyebrows that turn into serpents. The rendering on the right makes it easier to see the details on the actual object.

a U-shaped platform whose opening to the east surrounded a sunken, circular plaza. From its passageways and underground galleries, priests—whom the Chavín believed were transformed into jaguars through their consumption of hallucinogenic drugs—could make dramatic entrances during ceremonies. Pilgrims brought tribute to Chavín de Huántar, where they worshipped and feasted together. The Chavín drew on influences from as far away as the Amazon and the Pacific coast as they created devotional cults that revered wild animals as representatives of spiritual forces. Carved stone jaguars, serpents, and hawks, baring their large fangs and claws to remind believers of nature's powers, dominated the spiritual landscape. The Chavín cult gave way around 400 BCE to local cultural heirs, but some elements of it survived in successor religions adopted by stronger states to the south.

THE OLMECS IN MESOAMERICA

Further to the north, the first complex society in Mesoamerica emerged around 1500 BCE between the highland plateaus of central Mexico and the Gulf Coast around modern-day Veracruz. (See Map 5.5.) The **Olmecs** are an example of a first-generation community that created new political and economic institutions while contemplating profound questions about the nature of humanity and the world beyond. The culture of the Olmecs—a name meaning "inhabitants in the land of rubber," one of their staples—sprang up from local village roots. The region's peoples formed a loose confederation of villages scattered from the coast to the highlands, mainly nestling in river valleys and along the shores of swampy lakes. Their residents traded with one another, shared a common language, and worshipped the same gods. Around 1500 BCE, the residents of hundreds of hamlets began to develop a single culture and to spread their beliefs, artistic achievements, and social structure far beyond their heartland.

At the core of Olmec culture were its decentralized villages, which housed hundreds—possibly thousands—of households apiece. In these settlements productive subsistence

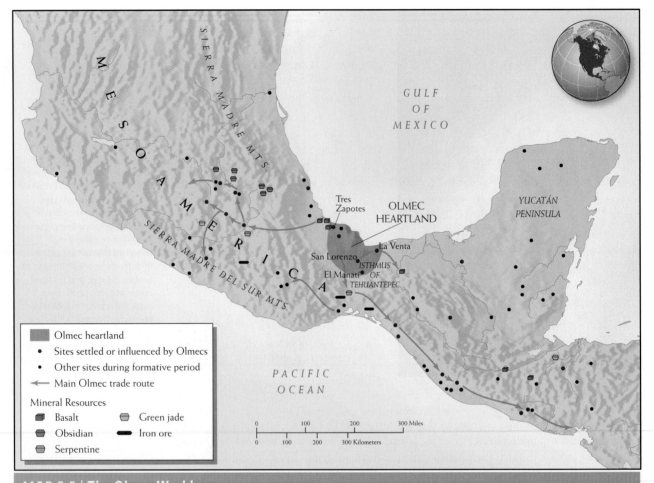

MAP 5.5 | The Olmec World

The Olmecs had a strong impact on Mesoamerica's early cultural integration.

• According to this map, how did they influence people living beyond the Olmec heartland?

• What geographical factors limited the extent of Olmec influence?

• What is the relationship between resources, trade routes, and Olmec settlements?

farmers cultivated most of the foodstuffs their communities needed (especially maize, beans, squash, and cacao), while shipping lightweight products including ceramics and precious goods (such as jade, obsidian, or quetzal feathers, used to create masks and ritual figurines) to other villages. Most of the precious objects were for religious purposes rather than everyday consumption. Despite their dispersed social landscape, the Olmec peoples created shared belief systems, a single language, and a priestly class who ensured that villagers and residents of the new urban centers followed highly ritualized practices.

Cities as Sacred Centers The primary Olmec cities, including San Lorenzo, La Venta, and Tres Zapotes, were small compared with the urban centers of Afro-Eurasia, but they served as devotional and secular hubs. The cities featured specialized structures that included massive earthen mounds, platforms, palaces, capacious plazas, and large stone monuments (colossal heads, jaguar sculptures, and basalt thrones). Beneath the mounds of the devotional centers, archaeologists have found axes, knives of sharpened obsidian, other tools, and jade figurines, buried as tokens for those who dwelled in the supernatural world. Olmec devotional art depicted natural and supernatural entities—not just snakes, jaguars, and crocodiles, but also certain humans called shamans, whom the Olmecs believed could commune with the supernatural and transform themselves wholly or partly into beasts. A common figurine is the "were-jaguar," a being that was part man, part animal. Shamans representing jaguars invoked the Olmec rain god, a jaguar-like being, to bring rainfall and secure the land's fertility.

A range of agriculture-linked devotional activity thrived in the Olmecs' major cities. Noble players competed in a complex ball game to honor the rain god, as fans cheered on. Olmec archaeological sites are filled with the remains of game equipment and trophies, some of which were entombed with dead rulers so they could play ball with the gods in the otherworld. It is likely that athletics and human sacrifice were blended in the same rituals. Many monuments depict a victorious and costumed ballplayer (sporting a jaguar headdress or a feathered serpent helmet) atop a defeated, bound human, though scholars are not sure whether the losers were literally executed. Nevertheless, rainmaking rites did include human sacrifice, which involved executing and dismembering captives. The Olmecs believed that the gods defined calendric passages, and thus the seasons and crucial rainfall patterns. Priests, charting celestial movements, devised a complex calendar that marked the passage of seasons and generations. Indeed, Olmecs' ceremonial life—from ball games to human sacrifice to calendars—was focused on agricultural and rainfall cycles.

A World of Social Distinctions Unlike many decentralized agrarian cultures that were simple and egalitarian, the Olmecs developed an elaborate cultural system marked by many tiers of social rankings. Daily labor kept village-focused Olmecs busy. The vast majority worked the fertile lands as part of household units, with children and parents toiling in the fields with wooden tools, fishing in streams with nets, and hunting turtles and other small animals. Most Olmecs juggled the needs of their immediate families, their village neighbors, and the taxes imposed by rulers.

The priestly class, raised and trained in the palaces at La Venta, San Lorenzo, and Tres Zapotes, directed the exchanges of sacred ritual objects among farming communities. Alongside the priestly elite emerged a secular elite composed of chieftains who supervised agrarian transactions, oversaw artisans, and accepted villagers' tribute. The highest-ranking chieftains commanded villages scattered over a large territory. The chieftains set up workshops, managed by foremen, where craftworkers created pots, painted, sculpted, and wove. Some of their work featured stones and gems imported from surrounding villages.

It is likely that a merchant class also developed to facilitate trade throughout Olmec territories and beyond. As the Olmecs' arts expanded, so did their demand for imported obsidian and jade, seashells, plumes, and other precious goods. The Olmecs exported rubber, cacao, pottery, ceramics, figurines, jaguar pelts, and crocodile skins throughout Mesoamerica. They also conveyed their belief system to neighbors—if not to convert them, at least to influence them and reinforce a sense of superiority.

The Loss of Centers The breakdown of the Olmec culture around the middle of the first millennium is shrouded in mystery. The decline was abrupt in some centers and drawn out in others. At La Venta, the altars and massive basalt heads were defaced and buried, indicating a dramatic shift. Yet there is little evidence of a spasm of war, a peasant uprising, a population shift, or conflict within the ruling classes. Indeed, in many parts of the heartland, the religious centers that had been the hubs of the Olmec world were abandoned but not destroyed. As the bonds between rulers and subjects weakened, so did the exchange of ritual objects that had enlivened the Olmec centers and made them magnets for obedience and piety. Although Olmec hierarchies collapsed, much of the Olmec hinterland remained heavily populated and highly productive. While it lasted, the Olmec combination of an integrated culture, a complex hierarchical social structure, and urban-centered devotional practice offered a degree of cohesion unprecedented in the Americas.

COMMON CULTURES IN SUB-SAHARAN AFRICA

In Africa, too, widespread common cultures emerged in a number of favorable locations. Africa's most significant climate-related historical development in the first millennium BCE was the continued drying up of the northern and central landmass and the sprawl of the great Sahara Desert. (See Map 5.6.) Large areas that had once supported abundant plant and animal life, including human settlements, now became sparsely populated. As a result, the African peoples began to coalesce in a few locations. Most important was the Nile Valley, which may have held more than half of the entire population of Africa at this time.

Climatic change divided Africa from the equator northward to the Sahara Desert into four zones. The first zone was the Sahara itself, which never completely emptied out despite its extreme heat and aridity. Its oases supported pastoral peoples, who raised livestock and promoted contacts between the northern and western parts of the landmass. South of the Sahara was the Sahel, literally the "coast" (Arabic *sahil*) of the great ocean of sand, which saw no city of great size in this period. The next zone was the Sudanic savanna, an area of high grasslands stretching from present-day Senegal along the Atlantic Ocean in the west to the Nile River and the Red Sea in the east. Many of West Africa's kingdoms later emerged there because the area was free of the tsetse fly, which was as lethal to animals as to humans, killing off cattle, horses, and goats. The fourth zone comprised the western and central African rain forests, a sparsely populated region characterized by small-scale societies.

Although there was contact across the Sahara, Africa below the Sahara differed markedly from North Africa and Eurasia. It did not develop plow agriculture; instead, its farmers depended on hoes. Also, except in densely populated regions, land was held communally and never carried as much value as labor, which was in short supply. African peoples could always move into new locations. They had more difficulty finding workers to turn the soil. In the savanna, millet and sorghum were the primary food crops; in the rain forests, yams and other root crops predominated. Relatively large populations inhabited the Sudanic savanna, the sole area for which substantial historical records exist. Here, in fact, a way of life that historians call Sudanic began to crystallize.

These Sudanic peoples were not completely dependent on their feet to get around (in contrast to their llama-reliant counterparts in the Americas). They had domesticated several animals, including cattle and goats, and even possessed small horses. Although their communities were scattered widely across this region of Africa, they had much in common. For example, they all possessed religious beliefs dominated by a high god, polities led by sacred kings, and burial customs of interring servants alongside dead rulers to serve them in the afterlife. Sudanic peoples were skilled cultivators and weavers of cotton, which they had domesticated. Archaeologists and historians used to believe that the Sudanic peoples borrowed their institutions, notably their sacred kingships, from their Egyptian neighbors; but linguistic evidence and their burial customs indicate that the Sudanic communities developed these practices independently.

Nubia: Kush and Meroe One of the most highly developed locations of common culture in sub-Saharan Africa was Nubia, a region lying between the first Nile cataract (a large waterfall) and the sixth, just north of where the Blue and White Niles come together. From at least the fourth millennium BCE onward, peoples in this region had contact with both the northern and southern parts of the African landmass. It was one of the few parts of sub-Saharan Africa known to the Eurasian world during this period.

By the second and first millennia BCE, complex societies formed and developed into states in Nubia. The first of the important Nubian states was Kush. It flourished between 1700 and 1500 BCE between the first and third cataracts, and had its capital at Kerma. Because of its proximity to Egypt, it adopted many Egyptian cultural and political practices, even as it was under constant pressure from the northern powerhouse. Its successor

Nubia
Kush
Nok
Mediterranean colonies
Persia
• City
NOK State
← Trans-Saharan trade route
▲ Spread of iron making from 6th century BCE to the 2nd century BCE
/// Sudanic savannah
\\\ Rainforest

MAP 5.6 | Africa, 500 BCE

The first millennium BCE was a period of cultural, economic, and political integration for North and sub-Saharan Africa.

- According to this map, what effect did the Mediterranean colonies have on Africa? What main factor integrated Kush, Nubia, and Egypt?

- Does the map reveal a relationship between the rise of Sudanic culture and the spread of iron working? If so, what is it?

states had to move farther south, up the Nile, to keep free from the powerful Egyptians; the kingdom's capitals were repeatedly uprooted and relocated upriver.

Nubia was Egypt's corridor to sub-Saharan Africa, a source of ivory, gold, and slaves; and an area that Egyptian monarchs wanted to dominate. To the Egyptians, the land of Kush and its people were there to be exploited, not conquered, as Egyptians had no desire to live there. Ramses II left his mark with his magnificent monuments at the Nubian site Abu Simbel around 1250 BCE.

Building on the foundations of earlier kings who had ruled Nubia, the **Meroe** kingdom arose in the fourth century BCE and flourished until 300 CE. Its rulers were influenced by the pharaonic culture, adapting hieroglyphs, erecting pyramids in which to bury their rulers, viewing their kings as divine, and worshipping the Egyptian god Amun. Meroe became a thriving center of production and commerce. Its residents were especially skilled in iron smelting and the manufacture of textiles, and their products circulated widely throughout Africa. However, Meroe was equally a part of the Sudanic savanna way of life—as evidenced by the distinctiveness of the language and the determination of its inhabitants to retain political autonomy from Egypt, including, if necessary, moving farther south, out of the orbit of Egypt and more into the orbit of Sudanic polities. Although they called their kings pharaohs, the influential leaders of Meroe selected them from among the many members of the royal family, attempting to ensure that their rulers were men of proven talents. In addition, the Nubian states had close commercial contacts with other merchants and commercial hubs in Sudanic Africa.

West African Kingdoms Complex societies also thrived in West Africa. The most spectacular West African culture of the first millennium BCE was the Nok culture, which arose in the sixth century BCE in an area that is today the geographical center of Nigeria. Though slightly south of the savanna lands of West Africa, the area was (and still is) in regular contact with that region. At Taruga, near the present-day village of Nok, early

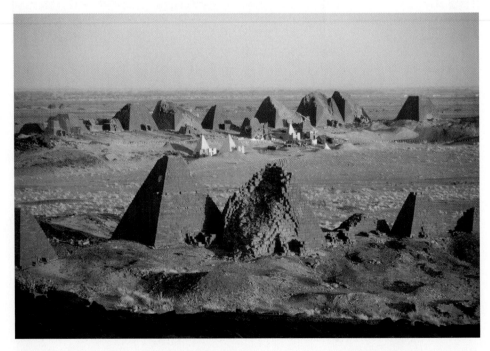

Nubian pyramids at Meroe In imitation of Egyptian pharaohs more than a millennium ago, Meroitic royalty constructed pyramids for their burials. Smaller and steeper than Egyptian pyramids, they were decorated with reliefs on their interior walls and filled with grave goods from the Mediterranean world.

iron smelting occurred in 600 BCE. Taruga may well have been the first place in western Africa where iron ores were smelted. Ironworking was significant for the Nok peoples, who moved from using stone materials directly to iron, bypassing bronze and copper. They made iron axes and hoes, iron knives and spears, and luxury items for trade. The Nok achieved historical fame not for their iron-smelting prowess but for their magnificent terra-cotta figurines, discovered in the 1940s in the tin-mining region of central Nigeria. These naturalistic figures date to at least 500 BCE. They were likely altarpieces for a cult associated with the land's fertility. Placed next to new lands that were coming into cultivation, they were believed to bless the soil and enhance its productivity.

The Nok were not the only culture developing in this region. Peoples living in the Senegal River basin and Mande peoples around the western branch of the Niger River also began to establish large settlements, in which artisans smelted iron ore and wove textiles, and merchants engaged in long-distance trade. West Africa was also home to the Bantu-speaking peoples destined to play a major role in the history of the landmass. Around 300 BCE, small Bantu groups began to migrate southward into the equatorial rain forests, where they cleared land for farming; from there, some moved on to southern Africa. (See Chapter 8 for a discussion of the Bantu peoples.) As impressive as the iron working, figurines, and trade of West Africa were, these cultures were not yet producing—or at least there is no record of—the type of axial age developments that were happening in much of Eurasia.

Conclusion

Afro-Eurasia's great river-basin areas—the Nile, the Tigris-Euphrates, the Indus—were still important in the first millennium BCE, but their time as centers of world cultures was passing. Now they yielded some of their leadership to regions that had been on the fringes, whether the Mediterranean in the west or the Ganges in the east. Within the territorial states in China, the kingdoms and oligarchies in urbanizing South Asia, and the city-states in the Mediterranean world, great social and intellectual dynamism occurred.

During this axial age across much of Eurasia, influential thinkers came to the fore with perspectives quite different from those of the earlier river-basin civilizations and other contemporary developments elsewhere in worlds apart. In China, the political instability of the Warring States period propelled scholars such as Confucius to engage in political debate, where they stressed respect for social hierarchy. In South Asia, dissident thinkers challenged the Brahmanic spiritual and political order, and the Buddha articulated a religious belief system that was much less hierarchical than its Vedic predecessor. Mediterranean Greek philosophers offered new views about nature, their political world, and human relations and values—based primarily on secular rather than religious ideas.

Even where contacts with other societies were less intense, innovations occurred as first complex societies began to arise in the Americas and in sub-Saharan Africa. In the Americas, the Olmecs developed a worldview in which mortals had to appease angry gods through human sacrifice, and built elaborate temples where many peoples could pay homage to the same deities. In West Africa, the Nok peoples promoted interregional trade and cultural contact as they expanded their horizons. In sub-Saharan Africa, settled pockets devised complex cultural foundations for community life. One spectacular example of sub-Saharan and Egyptian synthesis was the Nubian culture of Meroe. As the world was coalescing into culturally distinct regions, many of the ideas newly forged in Eurasia, the Americas, and sub-Saharan Africa had a continuing impact on societies that followed.

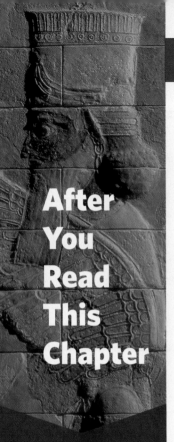

After You Read This Chapter

Go to **INQUIZITIVE** to see what you've learned—and learn what you've missed—with personalized feedback along the way.

FOCUS ON: *Innovative Societies*

CHINA

- Multistate system emerges from warfare, revolutionizing society and thought.

- Confucius and Master Lao outline new ideals of governing and living.

SOUTH ASIA

- Small monarchies and urban oligarchies emerge after the Vedic peoples' migrations and rule over societies organized around the varna system.

- Dissident thinkers like Mahavira and the Buddha challenge Brahman priests and the caste system.

THE MEDITERRANEAN WORLD

- Independent city-states emerge from social destruction and facilitate revolutionary principles in rulership, commerce, and thought.

- Thinkers like Socrates, Plato, and Aristotle challenge conventions and encourage public discourse about the role of the individual in society and the way the universe works.

THE AMERICAS

- Chavín peoples and the Olmecs produce increasingly hierarchical societies and connect villages via trade.

- Large-scale common cultures emerge.

SUB-SAHARAN AFRICA

- Expansion of the Sahara Desert and population migrations cause people to coalesce in a few locations.

- Early signs of a common culture appear across the Sudanic savanna.

CHRONOLOGY

EAST ASIA	
SOUTH ASIA	
THE MEDITERRANEAN	
THE AMERICAS	Olmec culture emerges and diffuses through Mesoamerica 1500–400 BCE
	Chavín culture flourishes in Central Andes of South America 1400–400 BCE
SUB-SAHARAN AFRICA	

1600 BCE   **1400 BCE**   **1200 BCE**

- *Thinking about Transformation & Conflict and the Axial Age* In the first millennium BCE across Afro-Eurasia, axial age thinkers developed radical new ideas in response to their respective political and cultural situations. In what ways did axial age thinkers in East Asia (Confucius and Master Lao), South Asia (Mahavira and the Buddha), and the Mediterranean (naturalist philosophers and Socrates) address the unique transformations and conflicts that were taking place where they lived? How do Zoroaster of Persia and the Jewish prophets of Israel, discussed in Chapter 4, fit this model?

- *Thinking about* Worlds Together, Worlds Apart *and the Axial Age* From the mid-second through the mid-first millennium BCE, "second-generation" societies developed in Eastern Zhou China, the Ganges plain of South Asia, and the Mediterranean, while parts of South America, Mesoamerica, and sub-Saharan Africa birthed their first complex societies. What are the differences between the second-generation societies of Afro-Eurasia and the first complex societies elsewhere, and what might account for these very different, yet contemporary, developments across the globe?

- *Thinking about Changing Power Relationships and the Axial Age* Axial age thinkers in East Asia, South Asia, and the Mediterranean offered challenges to both political and social traditions. How did the innovative ideas of thinkers such as Confucius, the Buddha, and Socrates contest and help to reshape power relationships ranging from the political to the familial?

1. What specific problems faced Eastern Zhou China in the Spring and Autumn period (722–481 BCE) and Warring States period (403–221 BCE)? How did **Confucius** and Master Lao's **Daoism** address these issues?

2. How did urbanization influence the Vedic belief system of South Asia in the first millennium BCE? In what ways, and to whom, would Vedic beliefs as compared with **Jainism** and the ideas of **Buddha** have been appealing, especially considering the hierarchies (*varnas* and *jatis*) of South Asian society and urban versus rural contexts?

3. What forces shaped Mediterranean developments in the first millennium BCE, and how did innovative **Greek philosophers** address some of those forces?

4. What are some of the distinctive features of the Andean **Chavín** and the Mesoamerican **Olmecs**? In what ways were these complex societies in the Americas fragmented and in what ways were they unified?

5. How do sub-Saharan developments in Nubia, such as Kush and **Meroe**, compare and contrast with those taking place in West Africa?

6. What are some of the defining qualities of **axial age** thought and the innovative thinkers who inspired these ideas?

7. What is it about **second-generation societies** that seems to foster an environment in which the **axial age** develops?

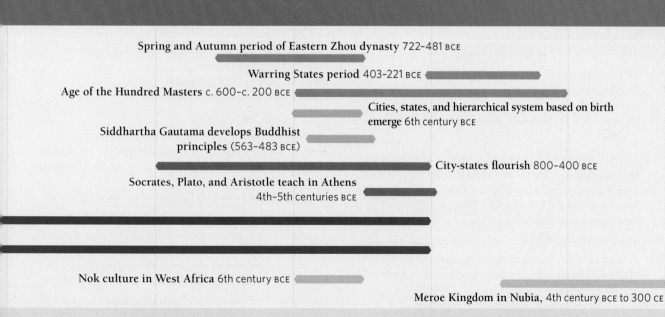

Spring and Autumn period of Eastern Zhou dynasty 722–481 BCE

Warring States period 403–221 BCE

Age of the Hundred Masters c. 600–c. 200 BCE

Cities, states, and hierarchical system based on birth emerge 6th century BCE

Siddhartha Gautama develops Buddhist principles (563–483 BCE)

City-states flourish 800–400 BCE

Socrates, Plato, and Aristotle teach in Athens 4th–5th centuries BCE

Nok culture in West Africa 6th century BCE

Meroe Kingdom in Nubia, 4th century BCE to 300 CE

| 0 BCE | 800 BCE | 600 BCE | 400 BCE | 200 BCE |

Competing Perspectives

Axial Age Ideas

This chapter has emphasized the radical challenge that axial age thinkers posed to their communities. The documents in this section allow us to explore these ideas further.

Zoroaster, in the *Gathas*, outlines a philosophy in which opposing forces of light and truth battle those of darkness and lies. These hymns, which are addressed by Zoroaster to the god of light Ahura Mazda, praise the god and seek his guidance. Initially a challenge to the spirit-focused tradition of the pastoral nomadic culture from which the Persians came, Zoroaster's ideas were eventually adopted by kings to undergird the Persian state and justify their rule.

In China, Confucius engaged in philosophical dialogues with his students in the transitional period of the 480s BCE, from the Spring and Autumn period to the Warring States period. Confucius's teachings about what it meant to be a superior gentleman (*junzi*), following the principles of practicing benevolence toward others (*ren*), proper ritual observance (*li*), and filial piety toward elders and ancestors (*xiao*)—as presented in the second document here—became the foundation for Chinese government and society for thousands of years.

Siddhartha Gautama, later called the Buddha, offers his own wisdom in a text recorded by his followers in the third century BCE and known as the *Dhammapada*. The Buddha's ideas about suffering, desire, and how to escape both offered a distinct challenge to the prevailing hierarchies of the *varna* system.

The ideas of the Greek philosopher Socrates, recorded in dialogues and a speech called the *Apology* (in defense of his influence on youth), call on Athenians to look within, to question, and to reason for themselves, as we see in the final excerpt here. As a citizen of democratic Athens, Socrates was a full participant in the political system and in the Peloponnesian War (431–404 BCE), as well as an influential teacher. Each of these axial age thinkers and his ideas was a product of, and a challenge to, his sociopolitical context.

PRIMARY SOURCE 5.1

The Gathas *from* The Hymns of Zoroaster (1000-600 BCE)

33.1 In accordance with the Primeval Laws of this existence,
The Ratu (Judge) shall deal perfect justice to all;
To the good who chose the Truth,
To the evil who chose Falsehood,
And to those in whom good and evil are mixed . . .

33.3 He who is most good to the righteous,
Be he a noble, or a peasant, or a dependent,
He who zealously makes the good living creation flourish,
He shall come to dwell with Truth in the realm of the Good Mind.

33.4 I [Zarathustra] am he who by devotion and prayer shall
Keep disobedience and the Evil Mind far from Thee, O Mazda,
Keep insolent heresy away from the nobles,
The distrust spread by slanderers, from the community,
And the evil of destruction from the pastures of cattle . . .

33.6 I, who as Thy steadfast priest, have learned the straight path of Asha (Truth and Righteousness),
And would learn from the Best Mind how best to do what should be done,

Therefore I ask of Thee, My Lord,
Bless me with Thy Vision and grant me a consultation with Thee!

33.7 Come hither to me, in Thine own self, O Mazda!
Come unmistakably, O Thou Best One, with
The Spirit of Truth and The Good Mind!
Let my message be heard beyond the limits of the community of adherents.
Let the brilliant offerings of reverential prayers be manifest to all . . .

33.9 And with the blessings of these comrade Spirits of Perfection and Immortality,
Let all advance to Thee, O Mazda!
Let all promote the cause of Truth! . . .

33.12 Arise for me, O Ahura!
Through my devotion give me steadfastness of purpose,
Through Thy Most Bounteous Spirit make me pure in goodness,
Through the Spirit of Righteousness grant me the courage of spiritual might,
And through the Good Mind give me the trust of the people.

33.14 To the Lord Mazda, as an offering,
Zarathustra dedicates the works of his life, even his very self.
The noblest essence of his Good Thought.
To Truth, he consecrates obedience to its principles
In word and deed, and all the might of his spiritual authority.

Source: "Yasna 33," *The Gathas: The Hymns of Zarathushtra*, ed. and trans. K. D. Irani (Mumbai: K. R. Cama Oriental Institute, 1999) 47–50.

The Analects (c. 400 BCE), Confucius

1.2. Master You said: "A man who respects his parents and his elders would hardly be inclined to defy his superiors. A man who is not inclined to defy his superiors will never foment a rebellion. A gentleman works at the root. Once the root is secured, the Way unfolds. To respect parents and elders is the root of humanity."

1.3. The Master said: "Clever talk and affected manners are seldom signs of goodness."

1.4. Master Zeng said: "I examine myself three times a day. When dealing on behalf of others, have I been trustworthy? In intercourse with my friends, have I been faithful? Have I practiced what I was taught?"

1.5. The Master said: "To govern a state of middle size, one must dispatch business with dignity and good faith; be thrifty and love all men; mobilize the people only at the right times."

1.6. The Master said: "At home, a young man must respect his parents; abroad, he must respect his elders. He should talk little, but with good faith; love all people, but associate with the virtuous. Having done this, if he still has energy to spare, let him study literature."

1.7. Zixia said: "A man who values virtue more than good looks, who devotes all his energy to serving his father and mother, who is willing to give his life for his sovereign, who in intercourse with friends is true to his word—even though some may call him uneducated, I still maintain he is an educated man."

1.8. The Master said: "A gentleman who lacks gravity has no authority and his learning will remain shallow. A gentleman puts loyalty and faithfulness foremost; he does not befriend his moral inferiors. When he commits a fault, he is not afraid to amend his ways."

1.9. Master Zeng said: "When the dead are honored and the memory of remote ancestors is kept alive, a people's virtue is at its fullest."

1.10. Ziqin asked Zigong: "When the Master arrives in another country, he always becomes informed about its politics. Does he ask for such information, or is it given him?"

Zigong replied: "The Master obtains it by being cordial, kind, courteous, temperate, and deferential. The Master has a way of enquiring which is quite different from other people's, is it not?" . . .

1.16. The Master said: "Don't worry if people don't recognize your merits; worry that you may not recognize theirs."

Source: Confucius, The Analects, trans. Simon Leys, ed. Michael Nylan, A Norton Critical Edition (New York: W. W. Norton & Company, 2014), 3–4.

The Dhammapada (3rd century BCE), Buddha

Long is the night for the sleepless. Long is the road for the weary. Long is samsara (the cycle of continued rebirth) for the foolish, who have not recognized the true teaching.   60

If on one's way one does not come across one's better or an equal, then one should press on resolutely alone. There is no companionship with a fool.   61

"I've got children," "I've got wealth." This is the way a fool brings suffering on himself. He does not even own himself, so how can he have children or wealth?   62

A fool who recognises his own ignorance is thereby in fact a wise man, but a fool who considers himself wise—that is what one really calls a fool.   63

Even if a fool lived with a wise man all his life, he would still not recognise the truth, like a wooden spoon cannot recognise the flavour of the soup.   64

Even if a man of intelligence lives with a wise man only for a moment, he will immediately recognise the truth, like one's tongue recognises the flavour of the soup.   65

Stupid fools go through life as their own enemies, doing evil deeds which have bitter consequences.   66

A deed is not well done if one suffers after doing it, if one bears the consequences sobbing and with tears streaming down one's face.   67

But a deed is well done if one does not suffer after doing it, if one experiences the consequences smiling and contented.   68

. . .

Better than a thousand pointless words is one saying to the point on hearing which one finds peace.   100

Better than a thousand pointless verses is one stanza on hearing which one finds peace.   101

Better than reciting a hundred pointless verses is one verse of the teaching (one dhammapada) on hearing which one finds peace.   102

Though one were to defeat thousands upon thousands of men in battle, if another were to overcome just one—himself, he is the supreme victor.   103

. . .

Though one were to perform sacrifices by the thousand month after month for a hundred years, if another were to pay homage to a single inwardly perfected man for just a moment, that homage is better than the hundred years of sacrifices.   106

Source: "The Fool," The Dhammapada, trans. John Richards (Pembrokeshire, England: Electronic Buddhist Archives, 1993). Copyright © 1993 John Richards, Pembrokeshire (UK), jhr@elidor.demon.co.uk, CompuServe ID 100113,1250.

The Apology of Socrates (c. 400 BCE), Plato

19a–e: Let us consider, then, from the beginning, what the accusation is, from which the prejudice against me arose. . . . What precisely did the accusers say when they accused me? . . . "Socrates is guilty of meddling, of inquiring into things under the earth and in the heavens, of making the weaker speech the stronger and of teaching these very things"—something like this. . . . I call on the majority of you as witnesses, and I expect you to teach and inform one another, those of you who have ever heard me in discussion—and this includes many of you. Inform one another if any of you heard me ever discussing such things, either a lot or a little. And from this you will realize that the same is true of the other things that the many say about me, when really none of this is the case. And if you have heard from anyone that I endeavor to teach people and make money, this is certainly not true. Though again, I think that it is a fine thing if an individual is able to teach people. . . .

21 c–d: I went to one of the people who are thought to be wise. . . . Scrutinizing this fellow—there's no need to refer to him by name, he was one of the politicians with whom I experienced something of the following sort when examining him, men of Athens—in talking with him it seemed to me that while this man was considered to be wise both by many other people and especially by himself, he was not. And so I tried to show him that he took himself to be wise, but was not. As a result I became hated by this man and by many of those present. And so, as I was going away, I was thinking to myself, "I am at least wiser than this man. It's likely that neither of us knows anything worthwhile, but whereas he thinks he knows something when he doesn't know it, I, when I don't know something, don't think I know it either. It's likely, then, that by this I am indeed wiser than him in some small way that I don't think myself to know what I don't know." Next, I went to another one of the people thought to be wiser than him and things seemed the same to me, and so I made an enemy of him as well as of many others.

Source: Plato, *Socrates' Defense* (*The Apology of Socrates*), trans. Cathal Woods and Ryan Pack (Cathal Woods, 2012), 2–4.

QUESTIONS FOR ANALYSIS

1. What elements of each axial age thinker's ideas, as outlined in this chapter, do you find in these excerpts?

2. Given the political context from which each thinker comes, what is so radical about the ideas in each excerpt?

3. What are some of the similarities and differences among these axial age ideas? What do you think accounts for the similarities and differences?

4. The teachings of each of these thinkers were recorded not by the thinker himself, but by his students. What evidence in the excerpts suggests transmission of these ideas by disciples? Why do you think the axial age thinkers did not write down their own ideas?

Interpreting Visual Evidence

Elsewhere in the Axial Age

During the time that the axial age thinkers such as Confucius, the Buddha, and Socrates were sharing their radical ideas with disciples who recorded them in written texts, other major developments were taking place in preliterate societies. Some of the complex civilizations that formed in this period, like the Nok (in sub-Saharan Africa) and the Olmecs (in Meso-america), apparently did not leave written records, so historians rely on artwork—as well as many other sources, such as oral traditions and linguistic analysis—to learn about these peoples.

For example, although the Nok left no written texts that would tell us of their thinking, they did leave behind intriguing figurines. The Nok figurines were shaped from terra-cotta. Their impressive craftsmanship, with finely sculpted poses and carefully shaped hair, clothing, jewelry, and facial features, conveys the artistic tastes of these African peoples dating back to the mid-first millennium BCE. Who these figurines represent, however, is not clear, nor is their purpose. The second Nok terra-cotta pictured here offers a glimpse of everyday life with its scenes of the harvest and mothers caring for their children.

The Olmecs, who thrived on the other side of the world in first-millennium-BCE Mesoamerica, constructed ceremonial centers and also produced a wide range of artifacts, many of which provide evidence of their religious beliefs. The *Young Lord*, a two-foot-tall jade figurine, shows Olmec artisans' delicate skill and their ability to convey deep meaning. Incisions on the figure indicate the bloodletting rituals of many Mesoamerican peoples. Wearing a mask that resembles classic Olmec shamanic images—like a jaguar's snarling mouth (see fourth image) and an eagle's beak—these figurines suggests the shape-shifting powers of a shaman. Even without written texts from these first-millennium-BCE peoples, artifacts like these help us reconstruct their ideas.

Nok figurine.

Nok terracotta.

Olmec Young Lord.

Olmec jaguar.

QUESTIONS FOR ANALYSIS

1. Compare the Nok and Olmec figurines with the depictions of the axial age thinkers on the first page of this chapter. What do these depictions suggest about what matters to the people who produced them?

2. Looking at Map 5.6, what connection might the Nok have had with the Mediterranean in the first millennium BCE? How might transregional exchange, not just of goods but also of ideas, have impacted both the Mediterranean and the sub-Sahara?

3. Looking at Map 5.5, how might trade in Mesoamerica in raw materials such as jade and obsidian have influenced the creation of objects such as the *Young Lord* and jaguar figurines?

4. Given that the Nok and Olmec cultures were sophisticated and expressed their beliefs through artworks like these, why do you think there is no evidence of singular axial age thinkers (like Confucius, Buddha, or Socrates) among the Nok and the Olmecs?

Before You Read This Chapter

GLOBAL STORYLINES

- Conquests by Alexander the Great and the influence of his successor states spread Hellenism across Southwest Asia and into South Asia.
- The Mauryan Empire accelerates the integration of South Asia and helps Buddhism spread throughout that region and beyond.
- "Silk Roads," both overland and by sea, facilitate the movement of commodities (spices, metals, and silks) and ideas (especially Buddhism and Hellenism) across Afro-Eurasia.

CORE OBJECTIVES

- **DESCRIBE** Hellenism and **EXPLAIN** its impact across Afro-Eurasia.
- **ANALYZE** the political changes that shaped central and South Asia in the aftermath of Alexander's incursion on the region.
- **EVALUATE** the forces that influenced the spread of Buddhism in this period.
- **TRACE** the early routes of the "Silk Roads" and **ASSESS** their importance in connecting Afro-Eurasia.

Shrinking the Afro-Eurasian World

350–100 BCE

In the blistering August heat of 324 BCE, at a town on the Euphrates River that the Greeks called Opis (not far from modern Baghdad), Alexander the Great's experienced Macedonian troops declared that they had had enough. They had been fighting far from their homeland for more than a decade. They had marched eastward from the Mediterranean, forded wide rivers, traversed great deserts, trudged over high mountain passes, and slogged through rain-drenched forests. Along the way they had defeated massive armies, including those armed with fearsome war elephants. Some had taken wives from the cities and tribes they vanquished, so the army had become a giant swarm of ethnically mixed families. This was an army like no other. It did more than just defeat neighbors and rivals—it forcefully connected entire worlds, bringing together diverse peoples and lands.

Conquering in the name of building a new world, however, was not what the soldiers had bargained for. They loved their leader, but many thought he had gone too far. They had lost companions and grown weary of war. Some had mutinied at a tributary of the Indus, halting Alexander's advance into South Asia. Now they threatened to desert him altogether. Summoning up their courage, they voiced these resentments to their supreme commander. Alexander's response was immediate and inspired. In order to persuade his troops not to desert him, he evoked the astounding military triumphs and historic achievement they had accomplished: establishing his rule from Macedonia to the Indus Valley. This far-reaching political vision came to a sudden end with Alexander's death a year later, when he was thirty-two years old. Even in his short lifetime, though, he set in motion cultural and economic forces that would transform Afro-Eurasia.

In the aftermath of Alexander's conquests and the political developments that followed, two broad cultural movements came to link diverse populations across wide expanses of the Afro-Eurasian landmass: Hellenism and Buddhism. Buddhism, as an axial-age philosophy, was introduced in the previous chapter. Hellenism, briefly defined, was a shared Greek identity that spread throughout the lands in which Greeks settled and was expressed in their language, art, architecture, politics, and more. New empires—namely Alexander's successor states of the Mediterranean and the Mauryan Empire in South Asia—and broad new trade routes created the circuits through which Hellenism and Buddhism flowed. Imperial conquests and long-distance trade laid the foundations for widespread cultural systems that were far more enduring than the empires themselves.

One consequence of these developments was the emergence of the Silk Roads, a system of routes that for nearly a thousand years constituted the primary commercial network linking East Asia and the Mediterranean world. This system of trade routes, along which many different types of precious commodities were exchanged, extended over 5,000 miles and took its name from the huge quantities of precious silk that passed along it. Merchants, monks, and administrators helped to connect widespread parts of Afro-Eurasia, as the busy sea-lanes and Silk Roads flourished. Merely a few centuries after the conquests of Alexander and Mauryan kings, the world looked very different from the realms their armies had traversed.

Alexander and the Emergence of a Hellenistic World

COMPARISON

DESCRIBE Hellenism and **EXPLAIN** its impact across Afro-Eurasia.

The armed campaigns of the Macedonians led by Alexander the Great (356–323 BCE) began a drive for empire from the west that connected distant regions and spread a Hellenistic culture throughout the conquered lands. (See Map 6.1.) Alexander came from the frontier state of Macedonia to the north of Greece and commanded a highly mobile force armed with advanced military technologies that had developed during the incessant warfare among Greek city-states in the fifth and fourth centuries BCE. Under Alexander's predecessors—especially his father, Philip II—Macedonia had become a large ethnic and territorial state. Philip had unified Macedonia and then gone on to conquer neighboring states. Macedonia boasted gold mines that could finance Philip's new military technology and his disciplined army. Philip's troops included heavily armored infantry that maneuvered in closely arrayed units called phalanxes as well as large-scale cavalry formations for shock tactics. These infantry and cavalry forces were supported by income not only from Macedonian gold mines but also from the slave trade that passed through Macedonia. By the early 330s BCE, Philip had crushed the Greek city-states to the south, including Athens.

After Philip's assassination, his son Alexander used this new military machine in a series of daring attacks on the Persian Empire. Alexander owed much of his success to a readiness to take risks. In his initial forays into Southwest Asia he outpaced, outflanked, and outthought his adversaries. Through these rapid assaults he brought under the rule of his Greek-speaking elites all the lands of the former Persian Empire, extending from Egypt and the eastern Mediterranean to the Indus River valley.

The result of this expansion was hardly an empire, given that Alexander did not live long enough to establish institutions to hold the distant lands together. But his military campaigns continued a process that the Persians had already set in motion of smashing barriers that had separated peoples on the eastern and western ends of Afro-Eurasia. The conqueror saw himself as a new universal figure, a bridge connecting distant cultures.

Alexander's conquests increased exposure of formerly Persian lands to the commodities of the Mediterranean and to cultural ideas associated with the Greek city-states. Alexander founded dozens of new cities named after himself, the most famous of which was Alexandria in Egypt,

Battle of Issus Mosaic of the Battle of Issus between Alexander the Great of Macedon and Darius, the king of Persia (found in a house at Pompeii in southern Italy). Alexander is the bareheaded figure to the far left; Darius is the figure to the right, gesturing with his right hand. The men represent two different types of warfare. On horseback, Alexander leads the cavalry-based shock forces of the Macedonian Greeks, while Darius directs his army from a chariot in the style of the great kings of Southwest Asia.

but also Iskandariya and Khandahar in modern-day Iraq and Afghanistan. Alexander seized the accumulated wealth that the Persian kings stored in their immense palaces, especially at Persepolis, and dispersed it into the money economies of the Mediterranean city-states. This massive redistribution of wealth fueled a widespread economic expansion in the Mediterranean and beyond.

ALEXANDER'S SUCCESSORS AND THE TERRITORIAL KINGDOMS

Alexander died in Babylon at age thirty-two, struck down by overconsumption of alcohol and other excesses that matched his larger-than-life personality and reflected the war culture of Macedonian warriors. His death in 323 BCE brought on the collapse of the regime he had personally held together. The conquered lands fragmented into large territories over which his generals squabbled for control.

Alexander's successors—his generals Seleucus, Antigonus, Ptolemy, Lysimachus, and others—thought of themselves not as citizens of a Greek city-state, but rather as absolute rulers over large blocks of territory, modeling themselves on the regional rulers they had defeated. One effect of powerful families controlling whole kingdoms was that some women could now hold great power, an unthinkable prospect in the democracies of the city-states. Queens in Macedonia, Syria, and Egypt—whether independent or as co-regents with their husbands—established new public roles for women. For example, Berenice of Egypt (c. 320–280 BCE) was the first in a series of powerful women who helped rule the kingdom of the Nile, a line that ended with the famous Cleopatra VII in the 30s BCE.

Three large territorial states stood out in the new Hellenistic world: the Seleucid Empire (established by Seleucus), stretching from Syria to present-day

Berenice Portrait head of Berenice, wife and consort of Ptolemy I, the first Macedonian king of Egypt after its conquest by Alexander the Great. Berenice was one of the women who, as queens of huge empires, wielded power and commanded wealth in their own right.

MAP 6.1 | **Afro-Eurasia in 250 BCE**

Alexander of Macedonia did not live long enough to create one large politically unified empire, but his conquests integrated various Afro-Eurasian worlds culturally and economically. Trace the pathways that Alexander followed on his conquests.

• What were the names and locations of the Hellenistic successor states? What did these states have in common?

• Which states on the map did Greeks *not* rule? How did the spread of Hellenism affect them?

Afghanistan; Macedonia, ruled by the Antigonids (established by Antigonus); and Egypt, ruled by the Ptolemies (established by Ptolemy). In areas between these larger states, middle-sized kingdoms emerged. The old city-states of the Mediterranean, such as Athens and Corinth, still thrived, but now they functioned in a world dominated by these much larger power blocs. On mainland Greece, larger confederations of previously independent city-states formed.

Competition in war remained an unceasing fact of life, but the wars among the kingdoms of Alexander's successors were broader in scope and more complex in organization than ever before. Since the successor kingdoms were nearly equal in strength and employed the same advanced military technology, however, the near-constant state of wars between the new kings never achieved much. After battles that killed tens of thousands, and severely injured and wounded hundreds of thousands more, the three major kingdoms—and even the minor ones—remained largely unchanged.

The great powers therefore settled into a centuries-long game of watching one another and balancing threats with alliances. What emerged was a fierce competition that dominated international relations, in which diplomacy and treaty making sometimes replaced actual fighting. This equilibrium was reminiscent of the first age of international relations in the second millennium BCE (see Chapter 3). Long periods of peace began to grace the intervals between the new kingdoms' violent and destructive wars.

HELLENISTIC CULTURE

The unification of large blocks of territory under Alexander's successors helped spread a common Hellenistic culture. Following existing commercial networks, Hellenism was a shared Greek culture that extended across the entire Mediterranean basin and into Southwest Asia. Hellenistic culture included philosophical and political thinking, secular disciplines ranging from history to biology, popular entertainment in theaters, exercising and socializing in gymnasia, competitive public games, and art in many forms. Despite pockets of resistance, Hellenism was remarkably successful.

Common Language The core element of Hellenism was a common language known as *koine*, or "common," Greek. It replaced the city-states' numerous dialects with an everyday form that people anywhere could understand. ***Koine* Greek** quickly became the international language of its day. Peoples in Egypt, Judea, Syria, and Sicily, who all had distinct languages and cultures, could now communicate more easily with one another, and enjoy the same dramatic comedies and new forms of art and sculpture.

Cosmopolitan Cities Individuals were no longer citizens of a particular city (*polis*); instead they were the first **cosmopolitans**, that is, citizens (*polites*) belonging to the whole world or universe (*kosmos*). Much as Athens had been the model city of the age of the Greek city-state, Alexandria in Egypt became exemplary in the Hellenistic age. Whereas fifth-century BCE city-states had zealously maintained their exclusive civic identities (as Athenians, Spartans, or Corinthians, for example), Alexandria was a multiethnic city built by immigrants, who rapidly totaled half a million as they streamed in from all over the Mediterranean and Southwest Asia seeking new opportunities. Members of Alexandria's dynamic population, representing dozens of Greek and non-Greek peoples, communicated in the common language that supplanted their original dialects. Soon a new urban culture emerged to meet the needs of so diverse a population.

Hellenistic entertainment in this more connected world had to appeal to broad audiences and a wide variety of people. Plays were now staged in any city touched by Greek influence and had to translate to any environment. Consequently, the distinctive regional

The Theater at Syracuse
The great theater in the city-state of Syracuse in Sicily was considerably refurbished and enlarged under the Hellenistic kings. It could seat 15,000 to 20,000 persons. Here the people of Syracuse attended plays written by playwrights who lived on the far side of their world, but whose works they could understand as if the characters were from their own neighborhood. In the common culture of the Hellenistic period, plays deliberately featured typecast characters and situations, thereby broadening their audience.

humor and local characters of fifth-century Greek city-state drama gave way to dramas populated by the stock characters of standard sit-coms with which any audience could identify: the greedy miser, the old crone, the jilted lover, the golden-hearted whore, the boastful soldier, the befuddled father, the cheated husband, the rebellious son. At performances throughout the Mediterranean basin, laughter would be just as loud in Syracuse on the island of Sicily as in Scythopolis in the Jordan Valley of Judea.

A new political style of distant, almost godlike kings developed, in part due to the size of the territories over which they ruled. Instead of being accessible, which was not possible when Hellenistic kingdoms and states were so enormous, Hellenistic leaders became larger-than-life figures. Individuals related to political leaders primarily through the personality of the kings and their families. Rulership was personality, and personality could unite large numbers of subjects. For example, Demetrius Poliorcetes, the ruler of Macedonia, stood out in his high-platform shoes and heavy makeup, and he decorated his elaborate, flowing cape with images of the sun, the stars, and the planets. In the presence of a powerful sun-king like Demetrius, ordinary individuals felt small and inconsequential.

Philosophy and Religion Hellenistic religion and philosophy increasingly focused on the individual and his or her place in the larger world. This growing concern with the individual found expression in many new philosophical schools that proposed a range of ideas, including self-sufficiency (Cynicism), detachment (Epicureanism), and involvement (Stoicism). For instance, the Athenian Diogenes (c. 412–323 BCE), an early proponent of the Cynic school of philosophy, sought freedom from society's laws and customs, rejecting cultural norms as human-made inventions not in tune with nature and therefore false. Similarly turning thoughts to the self, Epicurus (c. 341–279 BCE), the founder of a school in Athens that he called The Garden, envisioned an ideal community of adherents regardless of their gender and social status, centered on his school. Seeking out pleasure and avoiding pain, these Epicureans contemplated the answer to the question "What is the good life?" and struggled to develop a sense of "not caring" (*ataraxia*) about their worries. More widespread than Diogenes's Cynicism and Epicurus's philosophy was Zeno's Stoicism. Zeno (c. 334–262 BCE), from the island of Cyprus, initiated it, and other cosmopolitan figures across the Hellenistic world—from Babylon in Mesopotamia to Sinope on the Black Sea—developed its beliefs. Named after the *Stoa Poikilē*, the roofed colonnade in the Athenian agora in which Zeno first presented his ideas, Stoicism argued that everything was grounded in nature. Stoicism regarded cities and kingdoms as human-made things, important but transient. Being in tune with nature and living a good life required understanding the rules of the natural order and being in control of one's passions, and thus indifference to pleasure and pain. Stoicism, Epicureanism, and Cynicism offered the individual a range of philosophical responses to the Hellenistic world developing all around.

Long-established religions were also shaped by Hellenism, and then reexported throughout the Mediterranean. For example, Greeks in Egypt drew on the indigenous cult of Osiris and his consort, Isis, to fashion a new narrative about Osiris's death and rebirth that represented personal salvation from death. Isis became a supreme goddess whose "supreme virtues" encompassed the powers of dozens of other Mediterranean gods and goddesses. Believers experienced personal revelations and out-of-body experiences (*exstasis,* "ecstasy"). A ritual of dipping in water (*baptizein,* "to baptize") marked the transition of believers, "born again" into lives devoted to a "personal savior" who delivered an understanding of a new life by direct revelation. These new beliefs, like the worship of Isis, emphasized the spiritual concerns of humans as individuals, rather than the collective worries of towns or cities. Other Hellenistic adaptations from earlier Greek religion, including cults of Demeter and Dionysus, similarly focused on the salvation of the individual as they spread throughout the Hellenistic world.

PLANTATION SLAVERY AND MONEY-BASED ECONOMIES

Ironically, philosophical and religious innovations focused on the self were accompanied by the rise of plantation slavery—the ultimate devaluing of an individual—as an engine of the Hellenistic economy. Large numbers of slaves were used in agricultural production—especially in Italy, Sicily, and North African regions close to Carthage. Alexander's conquests and Rome's political rise had produced unprecedented wealth for a small elite. These men and women used their riches to acquire huge tracts of land and to purchase slaves (either kidnapped individuals or conquered peoples) on a scale and with a degree of managerial organization never seen before. The slave plantations, wholly devoted to producing surplus crops for profit, helped to drive a new Mediterranean economy. The estates created vast wealth for their owners—though at a heavy price to others, as reliance on slave labor now left the free peasants who used to work the fields with no option but to move into overcrowded cities, where employment was hard to find.

The circulation of money reinforced the effects of forced labor. With more cash in the economy, wealthy landowners, urban elites, and merchants could more easily do business. The increasing use of Greek-style coins to pay for goods and services (in place of barter) promoted the importation of commodities such as wine from elsewhere in the Mediterranean. As coined money became even more available, it led to even more commercial exchanges. The forced transfer of precious metals to the Mediterranean from Southwest Asia by Alexander's conquests was so large that it actually caused the price of gold to fall.

In the west, Carthage began to mint its own coins—at first mainly in gold, but later in other metals. Rome moved to a money economy at the same time. By the 270s and 260s BCE, the Romans were issuing coins on a large scale under the pressures of their first war with Carthage (264–241 BCE). By the end of the third century, even borderland peoples such as the Gauls had begun to mint coins, imitating the galloping-horse images found on Macedonia's gold coins. So, too, did kingdoms in North Africa, where the coins of

Numidian kings bore the same Macedonian royal imagery. By around 100 BCE, inhabitants of the entire Mediterranean basin and surrounding lands were using coins to buy and sell all manner of commodities.

To pay for the goods that satisfied their newly acquired tastes, Celtic chieftains in the regions encompassing modern-day France began selling their own people in the expanding slave markets of the Mediterranean. Slavery and slave trading also became central to the economies of the Iberian Peninsula—especially in the hinterlands of large river valleys like the Ebro, where local elites founded urban centers imitating Greek styles.

Hellenistic Adaptation and Resistance The new high Greek culture spread far and wide, though it was not fully accepted everywhere in the Mediterranean. It appealed particularly to elites who sought to enhance their position by embracing Hellenistic culture over local values. Syrian, Jewish, and Egyptian elites in the eastern Mediterranean adopted this attitude, as well as Roman, Carthaginian, and African elites in the western Mediterranean.

The Hellenistic influences reached sub-Saharan Africa, where the kingdom of Meroe (see Chapter 5), already influenced by pharaonic forms, now absorbed characteristics of Greek culture as well. It is not surprising that Greek influences were extensive at Meroe, because continuous interaction with the Egyptians also exposed its people to the world of the Mediterranean. Both Meroe and its rival, Axum, located in the Ethiopian highlands, used Greek-style stelae (inscribed stone pillars) to boast of their military exploits. Citizens of Meroe worshipped Zeus and Dionysus. The rulers of Meroe, understanding the advantages of the Greek language, employed Greek scribes to record their accomplishments on the walls of Greek-Egyptian temples. In this way, Meroe developed a mix of Greek, Egyptian, and African cultural and political elements.

Not every community succumbed to the allure of Hellenism. The Jews in Judea offer a striking case of resistance and accommodation to its universalizing forces. Having been released from their Babylonian exile by the Persian monarch Cyrus in 538 BCE, the Jews returned to Judea—now a Persian province—and began rebuilding Jerusalem. While the Persians tolerated local customs and beliefs (see Chapter 4), the Hellenism brought by the Seleucid successor state that took Persia's place after Alexander's conquest brought a shock to Judaism. While some among the Jewish ruling elite began to adopt Greek ways—to wear Greek clothing, to participate in the gymnasium with its cult of male nudity, to produce images of gods as art—others rejected the push. Those who spurned assimilation rebelled against the common elements of Hellenism—its language, music, gymnasia, nudity, public art, and secularism—as being deeply immoral and threatening to their beliefs. Ultimately, this resistance to Hellenism led to full-scale armed revolt, headed up by the family of the Maccabees. In 167 BCE, the Seleucids provoked the Maccabees by forbidding the practice of Judaism (by outlawing worship and circumcision) and profaning the Jews' temple (by erecting an altar to Zeus in the sanctuary of the temple and sacrificing pigs on it). Though the Maccabees succeeded in establishing an independent Jewish state centered on the temple in Jerusalem, they did not entirely overcome the impact of the new universal culture on Judaism. A huge Jewish community in the Hellenistic city of Alexandria in Egypt embraced the new culture. Scholars there produced a version of the Hebrew scriptures in *koine* Greek, and historians (such as Jason of Cyrene) and philosophers (such as Philo of Alexandria) wrote in Greek, imitating Greek models.

Similar resistance and accommodation were taking place elsewhere. In the 330s and 320s BCE, when Alexander was uniting the eastern Mediterranean, the city-state of Rome took the first critical military actions to unify Italy. Rather than beginning as a kingdom like Macedonia, Rome went from being a city-state to flourishing as a large territorial state. During this transformation it adopted significant elements of Hellenistic culture: Greek-style temples, elaborately decorated Greek-style pottery and paintings, and an alphabet based on that of the Greeks. Many Roman elites saw immersion in Hellenistic ideals as a way to appear to the rest of the world as "civilized," while others resisted Greek ways as being overly luxurious and contrary to Roman ideals of manliness. The conservative Roman senator Cato the Elder (234–149 BCE) struggled with the tensions that Hellenism introduced to Roman ways. Although he was devoted to the Roman past, the Latin language, and the ideal of small-scale Roman peasant farmers and their families, Cato embraced many Hellenistic influences. He wrote a standard manual for the new economy of slave plantation agriculture, invested in shipping and trading, learned Greek rhetoric (both speaking and writing the language), and added the genre of history to Latin literature. Cato blended an extreme devotion to Roman tradition with bold Hellenistic innovations in most aspects of daily life.

Rome's long-time rival, the Phoenician colony of Carthage, also adopted Hellenism but with less internal conflict than at Rome. Carthaginian culture took on important elements of Hellenistic culture. For example, some Carthaginians went to Athens to become philosophers. Innovative ideas on political theory and warfare came from the Greek city-states. The design of their sanctuaries, temples, and other public buildings reveals a mix of Greek-style pediments and columns, Carthaginian designs and measurements, and local North African motifs and structures. Carthaginian women adorned themselves with jewelry that reflected styles from Egypt, such as ornate necklaces of gold and earrings of lapis lazuli.

Already well integrated into the Mediterranean economy, Carthage welcomed the increased communication and exchange that Hellenism facilitated. Carthaginian merchants traded with other Phoenician colonies in the western Mediterranean, with the towns of the Etruscans and the Romans in Italy, with the Greek trading city of Massilia (modern Marseilles) in southern France, and with Athens in the eastern Mediterranean. In addition, the Carthaginians expanded their commercial interests into the Atlantic, moving north along the coast of Iberia and south along the coast of West Africa, even establishing a trading post at the island of Mogador more than 600 miles down the Atlantic coast of Africa. Profoundly shaped by Alexander's conquests, Hellenism spread even further across Afro-Eurasia with Alexander's successors.

Converging Influences in Central and South Asia

COMPARISON

ANALYZE the political changes that shaped Central and South Asia in the aftermath of Alexander's incursion on the region.

During this period, tighter political organization in South Asia helped to spread new influences, like Hellenism and Buddhism, across the region. The high mountains of modern-day Afghanistan were a major geographical barrier to east-west exchange, but not impassable. Mountain passes—pinched like the narrow neck of an hourglass between the high plateau of Iran to the west and the towering ranges of Tibet to the east—offer the shortest route through the formidable Hindu Kush range. By crossing these passes, Alexander's armies expanded the routes between the eastern and western portions of Afro-Eurasia and brought about massive political and cultural changes in central and South Asia. Conquerors moved from west to east (like Alexander), from east to west (like the later nomads from central Asia) and from north to south, through the mountains, into the rich plains of the Indus and Ganges river valleys. At the same time, South Asian trade and religious influences, especially Buddhism, moved northward toward routes running west to east along what became known as the Silk Roads.

CHANDRAGUPTA AND THE MAURYAN EMPIRE

Alexander's brief occupation of the Indus Valley (327–325 BCE) paved the way for one of the largest empires in South Asian history, the Mauryan Empire. Before the arrival of Alexander's forces, South Asia had been a conglomerate of small warring states. This political instability came to an abrupt halt when, in 321 BCE, an ambitious young man named Chandragupta Mori (or Maurya), inspired by Alexander, ascended the throne of the Magadha kingdom and launched a series of successful military expeditions in what is now northern India.

The Magadha kingdom, located on the lower Ganges plain, held great strategic advantages over other states. For one thing, it contained rich iron ores and fertile rice paddies. Moreover, on the northeast Deccan plateau ample woods supported herds of elephants, a mainstay of the powerful Magadha mobile military forces, which used elephants to charge down and to terrify the enemy.

The Mori family, or Mauryans, did not start out as a distinguished ruling family, but economic strength and military skill elevated them over their rivals. Chandragupta (r. 321–297 BCE), though of lowly origins, probably from the Vaishya *varna*, grew up in the Punjab region of the Indus Valley observing Alexander's onslaught and aspiring to be an equally powerful military and political leader. When Alexander withdrew his forces from northern India, Chandragupta inserted himself into the political vacuum created by the Greek withdrawal.

Chandragupta's **Mauryan Empire** (321–184 BCE) constituted South Asia's first empire and served as a model for later Indian empire builders. After supplanting Magadha's Nanda monarchic dynasty, which had been in place for just over a century, Chandragupta used his military resources to reach westward beyond the Ganges plain into the area where four tributaries join the Indus. Here he pushed up to the border with the Seleucid kingdom, the largest successor kingdom of Alexander's empire, based in Mesopotamia.

Alexander's eastern successor, the Seleucid king Seleucus Nicator (358–281 BCE), responded by invading Mauryan territory—only to face Chandragupta's impregnable defenses. Soon thereafter, a treaty between the two powers gave a large portion of Afghanistan to the Mauryan Empire. One of the daughters of Seleucus went to the Mauryan court, accompanied by a group of Greek women. Seleucus also sent to Chandragupta's court an ambassador named Megasthenes, who lived in South Asia for years. In return for these gifts and diplomacy, the Mauryans sent Seleucus many South Asian valuables, including hundreds of elephants, which the Greeks soon learned to use in battles.

The Seleucid ambassador Megasthenes gathered his observations while at the Mauryan court into a book entitled *Indica,* after the Greek term for this region. Megasthenes's *Indica* depicted a well-ordered and highly stratified society divided into seven groups: philosophers, farmers, soldiers, herdsmen, artisans, magistrates, and councilors. People respected the boundaries between groups and honored rituals that reinforced their identities: members of different groups did not intermarry or even eat together. Megasthenes also noted the ways in which rulers integrated the region—for example, connecting major cities with extensive tree-lined roads, complete with mile markers. These roads facilitated both trade and the movement of troops. (See **Current Trends in World History: Building Roads**.) Contrary to Greek expectations of a military closely integrated into civil society, Megasthenes reported that soldiers in India were a profession separate from the rest of the population. Mauryan troops did not pursue any other occupation, but stood ready to obey their commander. This military force was huge, boasting cavalry divisions of mounted horses, war elephants, and scores of infantry.

Building Roads: Early Highways for Communication, Trade, and Control

World historians have become fascinated with the history of roads because they provide insight into the way nations and empires functioned, and they allow us to study transnational forces that cross borders, like trade, migration, and the spread of ideas. Indeed, reliable communications and regular trade were among the most important forces that enabled the great regions of the world to be linked. If rivers and seas offered natural waterways to meet this demand, roads were the manmade answer that enabled soldiers, traders, and travelers to cross great stretches of land or go around high mountain ranges more quickly. Road building required huge financial and labor resources. Only empires had the incentives and resources to build large-scale roads and the networks that fed into them; these roads would aid in the empire's rule over their domain and in gathering the revenue that came from transregional trade.

The Persian empire was the largest state in the Afro-Eurasian world, which necessitated efficient communications over vast distances and terrain that was varied and forbidding. The problems were overcome by the construction of many "great" or "royal" roads across the empire to connect the royal capitals where the king resided from time to time. One of the best-known great roads connected the far western coast at Sardis in Asia Minor (present-day Turkey) with the heartland of the Persian empire around Susa (southern Iran) in the east, more than 1,700 miles away. The great roads featured way stations, supply depots, relays of horses and other pack animals, and state personnel, all to enable the local governors or satraps of the emperor to dispatch men and missions to the King of Kings.

If the royal Persian road communications system was a marvel of its age, the roads of the Roman Empire are rightly renowned for their extent and quality of construction.

At its height, the empire boasted about 250,000 miles of roads; about 55,000 miles were of the formal stone-paved quality that most impresses us today. They were formally called "public roads" and were open to travel by anyone. Provincial, city, and municipal officials were in charge of upkeep. High standards of construction were imposed for the main paved highways—land was leveled and roadbeds were built up of layers of hard-packed sand and gravel, with careful gradients that allowed for drainage. The top layer was paved with heavy flagstones that provided long life.

It is easy to underestimate the amount of hard work and engineering required to construct the roadbeds, drainage, and bridges. The work and materials required to construct one major road in Italy, the Via Appia (the "Appian Way"), would be several times that required to build the great pyramids in Egypt. The major roads were marked with milestones that informed the traveler about the distance from the point of departure or to the next major town (5,000 or so of these have

---

The Regime of Aśoka The Mauryan Empire reached its height during the reign of its third king, Aśoka (r. 268–231 BCE), Chandragupta's grandson. Aśoka's lands comprised almost all of South Asia; only the southern tip of the peninsula remained outside his control. In 261 BCE, Aśoka launched the conquest of Kalinga, a kingdom on the east coast of the South Asian peninsula. The Mauryan army triumphed, but at a high price: about 100,000 soldiers died in battle, many more perished in its aftermath, and some 150,000 people endured forcible relocation. Aśoka was appalled and shamed by the brutal devastation his army had wrought. He vowed to cease inflicting pain on his people and pledged to follow the peaceful doctrines of Buddhism, issuing a famous edict that renounced brutal ways.

In this Kalinga edict Aśoka proclaimed his intention to rule according to the Indian concept of *dhamma*, a vernacular form of the Sanskrit word *dharma*, understood widely in Mauryan lands to mean tolerance of others, obedience to the natural order of things, and respect for all of earth's life forms. *Dhamma* was to apply to everyone, including the priestly Brahmans, Buddhists, members of other religious sects, and even Greeks. *Dhamma* became an all-encompassing moral code that all religious sects in South Asia accepted. With *dhamma* as a unifying symbol, Aśoka required all people, whatever their religious practices and cultural customs, to consider themselves his

Roman Road System Coursing through Afro-Eurasia, the Roman road system is shown in all its complexity and glory in the only surviving copy of the ancient *Tabula Peutingeriana*. The icon of a seated ruler represents Rome.

survived). The English word "mile" comes from the Roman *milia passuum* (slightly less than our mile in length). The system of roads allowed the Roman state to maintain a public relay service called the *cursus publicus* along which imperial officials and units of the army, as well as information, could move efficiently and predictably from one part of the empire to another.

One of the singular achievements of the Qin dynasty was the building of a road system to create sufficient infrastructure to unify its far-flung empire. The Qin network of roads connected the capital at Xianyang to every part of the country. The Qin used peasants, soldiers, and some slaves as forced laborers to build new roads and widen existing ones, so that troops could move quickly and easily to put down revolts anywhere in the empire. These roads were expanded under the succeeding Han dynasty to facilitate travel not only for the military, but also for merchants and commoners.

The road system of Qin and Han China paralleled the Persian royal roads and the Roman road network in scale and magnitude. By 100 BCE, many roads were wide, surfaced with stone, and lined with trees; steep mountains were traversed by stone-paved stairways with broad treads and low steps. By the end of the sixth century CE, the internal road network, not counting the Silk Road from the Han and Tang capital of Chang'an to central Asia, had grown to encompass some 25,000 miles. This ingeniously engineered system of roads helped the Chinese—like other empires—to control an empire spanning a vast, geographically diverse area.

QUESTIONS FOR ANALYSIS

- What political and geographical motives did empires have to build road systems?
- What sort of people benefited most from these road systems? Who actually built the roads?

Explore Further

Xinru Liu, *The Silk Road in World History* (2010).

Wood, Francis, *The Silk Road: Two Thousand Years in the Heart of Asia* (2004).

subjects, to respect him as their father, and to conform to his moral code—starting with the precept that people of different religions or sects should get along with each other. He also praised the benefits of agrarian progress and banned large-scale cattle sacrifice as detrimental to agriculture. Meanwhile, he warned the "forest people," the hunters and gatherers living beyond the reach of government, to avoid making trouble.

To disseminate the ideals of *dhamma*, Aśoka regularly issued decrees, which he had chiseled on stone pillars and boulders in every corner of his domain, selecting locations where people were likely to congregate and where they could hear the words as read to them by the few who were literate. Occasionally he also issued edicts to explain his Buddhist faith. All were inscribed in local languages, including Sanskrit, as well as Greek and Aramaic in the Hellenistic- and Persian-influenced northwest.

The Mauryan Empire at its height encompassed 3,000,000 square miles, including all of what is today Pakistan, much of what is Afghanistan, the southeastern part of Iran, and the whole of the Indian subcontinent except for the lands at the southern tip. Its extraordinarily diverse geography consisted of jungles, mountains, deserts, and floodplains, and its equally disparate population of 50 to 60 million inhabitants was made up of pastoralists, farmers, forest dwellers, merchants, artisans, and religious leaders. Aśoka's promotion of

Aśoka Buddhist legend claims that Aśoka placed relics of the Buddha in the many stupas he had built. The stupa at Sarnath (*left*) is the best-preserved one from the time of Aśoka. Aśoka had his edicts carved on pillars like the one on the right all over India. The majestic lion at the top of the pillar shows the influence of Persian art, in which the lion was the symbol of royalty.

the Buddhist tenet of *dhamma* and his elaborate administrative structure were not enough to hold together his empire, which did not last long after his death in 231 BCE. The proliferation of Buddhism made possible by Aśoka's adoption and wholehearted sponsorship of the faith, however, was a lasting impact of his reign.

GREEK INFLUENCES IN CENTRAL ASIA

Hellenistic influences shaped politics and culture in the regimes that succeeded direct Greek control in central Asia. Alexander's military had thrust into Asia and reached as far as the Punjab. There he defeated several rulers of Gandhara in 326 BCE. In the course of this campaign he planted many garrison towns—especially in eastern Iran, northern Afghanistan, and in the Punjab, where he needed to protect his easternmost territorial acquisition. These garrison towns were originally stations for soldiers, but they soon became centers of Hellenistic culture. Many of these outposts displayed the characteristic features of a Greek city-state: a colonnaded main street lined by temples to patron gods or goddesses, a theater, a gymnasium for education, an administrative center, and a marketplace. Following Alexander's death, Seleucus Nicator built more of these Greek garrison towns before he concluded peace with Chandragupta and withdrew from the region.

The garrison towns founded by Alexander and Nicator remained and grew into Hellenistic centers. Once the Greek soldiers who had been stationed in them realized they would be spending their lives far from their homeland, they married local women and started families. Bringing their Hellenistic customs to the local populations, the soldiers established institutions familiar to them from the Greek city-states. *Koine* Greek was the official language; but because locals used their own languages in daily life, subsequent generations were bilingual. For centuries, traditional Greek institutions—especially Greek language and writing—survived many political changes and much cultural assimilation, providing a common basis of engagement in a long zone stretching from the Mediterranean to South Asia.

Hellenistic influences were even more pronounced in the regimes that succeeded Seleucid control in central Asia in the late third century BCE. The Seleucid state had taken over the entirety of the former Persian empire, including its central Asian and South Asian territory. The Hellenistic kingdom of **Bactria** broke away from the Seleucids around 200 BCE to establish a strong state that included the Gandhara region in modern Pakistan. As Mauryan power receded from the northwestern part of India, the Bactrian rulers extended their conquests into this area. Because the cities that the Bactrian Greeks founded included many Indian residents, they have been called "Indo-Greek." Those in Gandhara incorporated familiar features of the Greek polis, but inhabitants still revered Indian gods and goddesses.

Hellenistic Bactria served as a bridge between South Asia and the Greek world of the Mediterranean. Among the goods that the Bactrians sent west were elephants, which were vital to the Greek armies there. Not only did the Bactrian Greeks revive the cities in India left by Alexander but they also founded new Hellenistic cities in the Gandhara region. The Greek king Demetrius, who invaded India around 200 BCE, entrusted the extension of his empire in the northern region of India to his generals, many of whom became independent rulers after his death. Sanskrit literature refers to these Greek rulers as the Yavana kings—a word derived from "Ionia," a region whose name applied to all those who spoke Greek or came from the Mediterranean.

Aï Khanoum, on the Oxus River (now the Amu) in present-day Afghanistan, was the site of an administrative center, possibly the capital of the Bactrian state. Unearthed by archaeologists in the 1960s, Aï Khanoum had avoided the devastations that befell so many other Hellenistic cities in this region. Greek-style architecture and inscriptions indicate that the original residents of Aï Khanoum were soldiers from Greece. Following the typical pattern, they married local women and established the basic institutions of a Greek polis. Aï Khanoum's characteristic Greek structures included a palace complex, a gymnasium, a theater, an arsenal, several temples, and elite residences. Featuring marble columns with Corinthian capitals, the palace contained an administrative section, storage rooms, and a library. A main road divided the city into lower and higher parts, with the main religious buildings located in the lower city. Though far from Greece, the elite Greek residents read poetry and philosophy and staged Greek dramas

Two Coins *Top*: Wearing an elephant cap, Demetrius of Bactria titled himself the king of Indians as well as Greeks. On the other side of the coin is Hercules. *Bottom*: Another central Asian ruler, the Scythian king Maues used Greek to assert his position as "King of Kings" on one side of his coin. On the other side, the goddess Nike is surrounded by Kharoshthi letters.

in the theater. Grape cultivation supported a wine festival associated with the god Dionysius. The remains of various statues indicate that the residents not only revered the Greek deity Athena and the demigod Heracles but also paid homage to the Persian Zoroastrian religion.

Perhaps the most adept ruler at mingling Greek and Indian influences was Menander (also known as Milinda), a Yavana city-state king of the mid-second century BCE. Using images and legends on coins to promote both traditions among his subjects, Menander claimed legitimacy as an Indian ruler who also cultivated Greek cultural forms. The face of his coins bore his regal image surrounded by the words "King, Savior, Menander," in Greek. The reverse side featured the Greek goddess Athena and the king's title in the local Pakrit language. This mixed Indo-Greek identity was not confined to coins. In his discussions with a Buddhist sage, King Menander debated the nature of the Buddha (was he human or divine?) and showed a keen interest in South Asian religious influences even as he embraced Hellenism. These "Indo-Greek" legacies persisted long after the Hellenistic regimes collapsed, because they remained essential to communication and trade around the rim of the Indian Ocean.

The Transformation of Buddhism

COMPARISON

EVALUATE the forces that influenced the spread of Buddhism in this period.

During this time of political and social change, South Asia also experienced upheavals in the religious sphere, as Hellenism and other east-west connections transformed Buddhism. Impressed by Hellenistic thought, South Asian peoples blended it with their own ethical and religious traditions. Beginning among the Yavana city-states in the northwest, where Buddhism's sway was most pronounced, this blended Buddhism rapidly spread to other regions that were experiencing the same changes. In addition to Hellenism, other layers of influence came together in South Asia through increased seafaring and interactions with nomadic peoples. This cultural fusion profoundly transformed and enriched Buddhism.

INDIA AS A SPIRITUAL CROSSROADS

Many land and sea routes now converged in India, rendering the region a melting pot of ideas and institutions. Improved mastery of the monsoon trade winds in this period opened the Indian Ocean to commerce and made India the hub for long-distance ocean traders and travelers. Another major influence on Buddhism was the Kushans, a horse-riding nomadic group who stabilized east-west connectivity through central Eurasia in the first century CE. With Kushan patronage and the thriving commerce their stability brought to the region, Buddhist communities grew so rich that monks began to live in elegant monastic complexes. (We will discuss the Kushans and their role in Silk Road trade later in this chapter.) The center of each monastic community was a stupa, with its Buddhist relics and sculptures depicting the Buddha's life and teachings. Such monasteries provided generously for the monks, furnishing them with halls where they gathered and worshipped and rooms where they meditated and slept. Buddhist monasteries were also open to the public as places for worship.

Stupa Staircase The risers from the staircase of a large stupa in the Gandhara region display scenes from Buddhist stories. The upper one shows men in nomads' clothing playing music, including the Greek-style lyre. On the middle one, men and women in Greek clothing drink and make merry. The pictures are Buddhist versions of performances in a Greek theater.

THE NEW BUDDHISM: THE MAHAYANA SCHOOL

This mixing of new ways—nomadic, Hellenistic, and Persian—with traditional Buddhism produced a spiritual and religious synthesis: **Mahayana** ("Great Vehicle") **Buddhism**. In the first two centuries of the Common Era, Mahayana Buddhists resolved a centuries-long dispute over whether the Buddha was a god or a wise human. They affirmed: the Buddha was indeed a deity. However, Mahayana Buddhism was accommodating; it offered a spiritual pluralism that incorporated outside influences and positioned Indian believers as a cosmopolitan people.

Mahayana Buddhism appealed especially to foreigners and immigrants who traded or settled in India because it made the Buddha easier to understand. The Buddha's preaching had stressed life's suffering and the renunciation of desire to end suffering and achieve nirvana. Newcomers to the region and to Buddhism—such as migrants or traders—saw no attraction in a belief that life consisted of painful cycles of birth, growth, death, and rebirth. This sharp dichotomy between a real world of hardship and the Buddha's abstract world of nirvana gave way to the Mahayana Buddhists' vision that **bodhisattvas**—enlightened demigods, ready to reach nirvana—delayed doing so in order to help others attain it. These bodhisattvas prepared spiritual halfway points to welcome deceased devotees not yet ready to release their desires and enter nirvana. The universe of the afterlife in Mahayana Buddhism presented an array of alternatives to the harsh real existence of worldly living. With its bodhisattvas, Mahayana Buddhism enabled all individuals—the poor and powerless as well as the rich and powerful—to move from a life of suffering into a happy existence.

NEW IMAGES OF BUDDHA IN LITERATURE AND ART

Just as Buddhism absorbed outside influences and became more appealing, it also inspired literature and art that appealed to diverse peoples. A new genre of literature dealing with the Buddha and the bodhisattvas emerged. Buddhist texts written in Sanskrit disseminated the life of the Buddha and his message far and wide, reaching far corners of Asia. Aśvaghosa (c. 80–c. 150 CE), a great Buddhist thinker and the first known Sanskrit writer, wrote a biography of the Buddha, which set the Buddha's life story within the commercial urban environment of the Kushan Empire (instead of in the rural Shakya republic in the Himalaya foothills, where he had actually lived). Aśvaghosa's largely fictive version of the Buddha's life story spread rapidly throughout India and beyond, introducing Buddha and his teachings to many potential converts.

The colorful images of Sanskrit Buddhist texts of the first centuries CE gave rise to a large repertoire of Buddhist sculptural art and drama. On Buddhist stupas and shrines, artisans carved scenes of the Buddha's life, figures of bodhisattvas, and statues of patrons and donors. Buddhist sculptures from the northern Kushan territory, fashioned from gray schist rock, are called **Gandharan art**. Those from the central region of India, created mainly from local red sandstone, are called Mathuran art. Gandharan Buddhist art shows strong Greek and Roman influences, whereas the Mathuran style evolved from the carved idols of South Asian folk gods and goddesses.

Despite their stylistic differences, the schools shared themes and cultural elements. Inspired by Hellenistic art and religious tradition, both took the bold step of sculpting the Buddha and bodhisattvas in realistic human, rather than symbolic, form (such as a bodhi tree, which symbolizes Buddha's enlightenment). Though the Buddha wore no decorations because he had cut off all links to the world, bodhisattvas were dressed as princes because they were still in this world, generously helping others. What was important was bringing the symbolic world of Buddhism closer to the people.

Buddhas The bronze Buddha on the left often strikes viewers as a Christlike figure. Greco-Roman influence on the iconography of Buddha was probably responsible for the Gandharan-style attire and facial expression of Buddhas and bodhisattvas. The Mathuran Buddha of the later Gupta period (*right*) is more refined than the Buddhas of the Kushan era. The robe is so transparent that the artist must have had very fine silk in mind when sculpting it.

Buddhist art reflected a spiritual system that appealed to people of diverse cultural backgrounds. Consider the clothes of the patron figures. For male and female figures alike, the garments were simple and well adapted to tropical climates. Those indigenous to the semitropical land had nude upper bodies and a wrapping like the modern *dhoti*, or loincloth, on their lower bodies. Jewelry adorned their headdresses and bodies. By contrast, the nomadic patron figures wore traditional cone-shaped leather hats, knee-length robes, trousers, and boots. Figures with Greek clothing demonstrate continuing Hellenistic influence, and those wearing Roman togas reveal imperial Rome's influence. The jumble of clothing styles illustrates that Buddhist devotees could share a faith while retaining their ethnic or regional differences.

COMPARISON

TRACE the early routes of the "Silk Roads" and **ASSESS** their importance in connecting Afro-Eurasia.

The Formation of the Silk Roads

In the first century BCE, trade routes stretching from China to central Asia and westward had merged into one big intertwined series of routes, famously referred to as the **Silk Roads** even though caravans transported many other precious commodities, such as incense, gemstones, and metals. Traders traveled segments of the route, passing their goods on to others who took them farther along the road and, in turn, passed them on again. The Silk Roads owed much to earlier overland routes through which merchants had exchanged frankincense and myrrh from the Arabian Peninsula for copper, tin, iron, gemstones, and textiles. (See Map 6.2.) During this period, seaborne trade also created closer connections between Afro-Eurasian worlds.

The effects of these long-distance exchanges altered the political geography of Afro-Eurasia. Egypt and Mesopotamia faded as sources of innovation and knowledge, becoming instead crossroads for peoples on either side of them. The former borderlands emerged as new imperial centers. What we now call the Middle East literally became a commercial middle ground between the Mediterranean and India. East Asia, principally China, finally connected indirectly with the Mediterranean via central and South Asia. Through China, whose traders reached Bali and other islands now in Indonesia, connections developed with Japan, Korea, and Southeast Asia. China, insulated from the west by the Himalayas and Pamir Mountains, remained politically and culturally a mysterious land to those from the Mediterranean. Yet products made from silk revealed to the Greeks and Romans that an advanced society lay far to the east.

NOMADS AND TRADE ROUTES

The horse-riding nomads of Inner Eurasia made long-distance trade possible. These scattered nomadic peoples already for centuries had linked entire regions and facilitated trade and interactions between distant communities. Responding to the drying out of their homelands in the second millennium BCE, they moved southward (see Chapter 3). Moving from place to place and being in close contact with their animals, the nomads were exposed to—and acquired resistance to—a greater variety of microbes than settled peoples did. Their relative immunity to disease made them ideal agents for linking distant settled communities. Nomads also raced into political vacuums and installed new regimes that linked northwest China and the Iranian plateau. Among the most important of these nomadic peoples were the Xiongnu (Hsiung-nu) pastoralists, originally from the eastern part of the Asian steppe in modern Mongolia. By the third century BCE their mastery of bronze technology made them the most powerful nomadic community in the area.

When Xiongnu power waned, a new empire, that of the Kushans, arose in their place around 50 CE. The Yuezhi, a nomadic group to the west of the Qin, unified the region's tribes, migrated southwestward, and established this Kushan empire in Afghanistan and the Indus River basin. The Kushans' empire embraced a large and diverse territory and was critical in the formation of the Silk Roads. The Kushans had been an illiterate people, but they adopted Greek as their official language. Kushan coinage, like the Indo-Greek coinage discussed earlier, blended Greek and Indian elements. Mediterranean traders arriving in the Kushan markets to purchase silks from China, as well as Indian gemstones and spices, conducted their transactions in Greek. The coins they used—struck to Roman weight standards (themselves derived from Greek coinage) and inscribed in Greek—served their needs perfectly. Kushan rule stabilized the trading routes through central Asia that stretched from the steppes in the east to the Parthian Empire in the west. This territory became a major segment of the Silk Roads.

CARAVAN CITIES AND THE INCENSE TRADE

As nomads moved southwestward, they produced a new kind of commercial hub: the caravan city. Established at strategic locations (often at the edges of deserts or in oases or

NORTH SEA

ROMAN EMPIRE

SCYTHIANS

URAL MTS.

BLACK SEA

CASPIAN SEA

ARAL SEA

from the West to India and China:

Rome

ANATOLIA

Bukhara

Merv

Oxus R.

Athens

Antioch

PARTHIAN EMPIRE

Carthage

Dura Europos

Palmyra

Tigris R.

Euphrates R.

ZAGROS MTS.

IRANIAN PLATEAU

MEDITERRANEAN   SEA

Alexandria

Petra

Persepolis

Persian Gulf

from India to the West:
A/D

EGYPT

NABATAEAN KINGDOM

ARABIAN

from Arabia to India:

Myos Hormos

Berenice

DESERT

from Arabia, Ethiopia and East Africa to the West:
I ○ ⬚ ● LF

from Arabia and Ethiopia to India and China:
I

NUBIA

Nile R.

RED SEA

Meroe

ARABIAN STATES

ARABIAN

from the West to India and Southeast Asia:
○ ○ G ⬚ LT

AXUMITE KINGDOM

Lake Victoria

INDIAN

Bhapta

MADAGASCAR

Legend

— Silk Road
— Incense trade route
— Other trade routes
SCYTHS Nomad group
— Boundary of empires, states, and kingdoms
• Port/trading town
⬭ Buddhist heartland
← Spread of Buddhism
○ Buddhist centers
⛬ Buddhist rock-carved temples
▲ Sacred Buddhist mountains

Traded Goods

A/D	Aromatics and drugs	○	Jewelry and cut gems
Cu	Copper	▬	Lacquerware
○	Coral	LF	Luxury foods
	Everyday textiles	LT	Luxury textiles
	Fine cotton/garments	●	Peacocks
	Fine stone and metal vessels	○	Pearls
⧓	Furs		Silk
G	Glassware	⬡	Slaves
⬢	Gems	S	Spices
⬚	Gold	⬙	Statuary
Y	Grain	Sn	Tin
H	Horses	●	Tortoiseshell
I	Incense	⬗	Wine
○	Ivory	⬥	Wood

from Ferghana to China: **H LF**

from Central Asia to the West via China and Silk Road towns: **H⌛**

from Central Asian nomads to China: **H⌛**

from China to Central Asia (Xiongnu) as bribes:

from China to India and the West:

from India to Arabia and Ethiopia:

from India to Southeast Asia:

from India to the West: **A/D** ◯ **S** ◯ **LF**

from Southeast Asia to India and the West: **Cu** ☐ **S Sn** ● **LF**

EASTERN SCYTHS

WUSUN

TIAN SHAN MTS

Turfan

Jade Gates Pass

Dunhuang

Loulan

Kashgar

PAMIR MTS

TAKLAMAKAN DESERT

Bactra

Khotan

Niya

WESTERN REGIONS PROTECTORATE

XIONGNU

GOBI DESERT

Lake Baikal

Datong

Yellow R.

Chang'an

Luoyang

HAN EMPIRE c. 150 CE

Yangzi R.

SEA OF JAPAN

KOREA

JAPAN

KUSHAN EMPIRE

Taxila

HIMALAYA MTS

Indus R.

Mathura

Ganges R.

Buddhist Heartland

Barbarikon

Barygaza

Tamluk

BAY OF BENGAL

SEA

Mekong R.

SOUTH CHINA SEA

PACIFIC OCEAN

OCEAN

INDONESIA

Bali

AUSTRALIAN ABORIGINES

MAP 6.2 | Afro-Eurasian Trade, c. 150 CE

During the period covered in this chapter, trade increasingly brought Afro-Eurasian worlds together. This map highlights important commercial linkages among societies.

• Where did mariners develop ocean-based commercial links?

• What was the relationship between land routes and sea routes?

• What types of goods were flowing to the east? What goods flowed to the west? What might those flows suggest about the balance of trade in this period? Based on the location of various Buddhist sites on this map, how were Buddhism and trade interrelated?

0   500   1000 Miles

0   500   1000 Kilometers

at the end points of major trade arteries), these cities became locations where vast trading groups assembled before beginning their arduous journeys. Some caravan cities originating as Greek garrison towns became centers of Hellenistic culture, displaying such staples of the polis as public theaters. **Caravan cities** were among the most spectacular and resplendent urban centers of this era.

One of the most striking of these caravan cities was the Nabatean capital at Petra. The Nabateans were an Arabic-speaking people, primarily sheepherders who eked out a living in the Sinai Desert and the northwestern Arabian Peninsula. They also facilitated the movement of frankincense, myrrh, and other spices along what was sometimes called the Incense or Spice Road, linking the Arabian peninsula and Indian Ocean with the Mediterranean where Greeks and Romans used these goods to make perfumes and incense. Because the Greeks and later the Romans needed large quantities of incense to burn in worshipping their gods, the trade passing through this region was extremely lucrative. Although originating in Nabatean herders' practice of carving shelter and cisterns for catching rainwater out of the solid stone of the forbidding landscape, the magnificent "Rock City" of Petra (*petros* in Greek means rock) was made possible by the wealth accumulated from the spice trade. Houses, shrines, tombs, and even the vast theater—carved entirely from the sandstone terrain to seat 6,000–10,000 spectators—manifested Hellenistic influences. Petra's power and wealth lasted from the mid-second century BCE to the early second century CE. The caravan traders, the ruling elite of the rock city, controlled the supply of spices and fragrances from Arabia and India to the ever-expanding Roman Empire. Nabataean traders based in Petra traveled throughout the eastern Mediterranean, erecting temples wherever they established trading communities.

With Petra's decline during the Roman period, Palmyra became the most important caravan city at the western end of the Silk Roads. Rich citizens of Rome relied on the Palmyran traders to procure luxury goods for them, importing Chinese silks for women's clothing and incense for religious rituals, as well as gemstones, pearls, and many other precious items. Palmyran traders handled nonsilken textiles as well, including cotton from India and cashmere wool from Kashmir or the nearby central Asian highlands. Administered by the chiefs of local tribes, Palmyra maintained considerable autonomy even under formal Roman control. Although the Palmyrans used a Semitic dialect in daily life, for state affairs and business they used Greek, a reminder of the continued influence of Hellenism. Their merchants had learned Greek when the region came under Seleucid rule, and it remained useful when doing business with caravans from afar, long after the political influences of Hellenism had waned.

Palmyrans built a splendid marble city in the desert. A colonnade, theater, senate house, agora, and major temples formed the metropolitan area. Complexes of hostels, storage houses, offices, and temples served the needs of traders who passed through. The Palmyrans worshipped many deities, both local and Greek, and seemed concerned about their own afterlife. Like Petra, Palmyra had a cemetery as big as its residential area, with marble sculptures on the tombs depicting city life. Many tombs showed the master or the master and his wife reclining on Greek-style couches, holding drinking goblets. Sculptures of camel caravans and horses tell us that the deceased were caravan traders in this world who anticipated continuing their rewarding occupation in the afterlife.

Caravan cities such as Petra, and later Palmyra, linked the Mediterranean with the silk and incense routes that traversed Afro-Eurasia by land and sea. Goods came into the caravan cities via land routes from China, across the Iranian plateau and the Syrian desert, as well as through Afghanistan, the Indus, India's west coast, and across the Indian Ocean to the Red Sea.

Palmyran Tomb Sculpture This tombstone relief sculpture shows a wealthy young Palmyran, attended by a servant—probably a household slave. Palmyra was at the crossroads of the major cultural influences traversing Southwest Asia at the time. The style of the clothing—the flowing pants and top—and the couch and pillows reflect the trading contacts of the Palmyran elite, in this case with India to the east. The hairstyle and mode of self-presentation signal influences from the Mediterranean to the west.

CHINA AND THE SILK ECONOMY

China's flourishing economy owed much to the fact that Chinese silks were the most sought-after commodity in long-distance trade. As thousands of precious silk bales made their way to Indian, central Asian, and Mediterranean markets, silk became the ultimate prestige commodity of the regions' ruling classes. Over time, the exchange between eastern and western portions of the Silk Road was increasingly mediated by Persian, Xiongnu, Kushan, and other middlemen at the great oases and trading centers that grew up in central Asia. Local communities took profitable advantage of the silk trade from China based on their increased knowledge and contacts.

Silk was not only China's most valuable export, but it also served as a tool in diplomacy with the nomadic kingdoms on China's western frontiers and in funding the Chinese armies. The country's rulers used silk to pay off neighboring nomads and borderlanders, buying both horses and peaceful borders with the fabric. During the Zhou dynasty, it served as a precious medium of exchange and trade.

People valued silk as a material for clothing; as a filament made by spinning the protein fibers extracted from the cocoons of silkworms, it is smooth yet strong. Whereas cloth spun from hemp, flax, and other fibers tends to be rough, silk looks and feels rich. Moreover, it is cool against the skin in hot summers and warm in the winter. Silk also has immense tensile strength, being useful for bows, lute strings, and fishing lines. Artisans even wove it into a tight fabric to make light body armor or light bags for transporting liquids (particularly useful for traders crossing arid expanses). Before the Chinese invented paper, silk was a popular writing material that was more durable than bamboo or wood. Texts written on silk often joined other funerary objects in the tombs of aristocratic lords and wealthy individuals.

As the long-distance silk trade grew, commerce within China also expanded. Because of reforms in the Warring States period, economic life in China after 300 BCE centered increasingly on independent farmers producing commercial crops for the marketplaces along land routes as well as rivers, canals, and lakes. As this market economy grew, merchants organized themselves based on family lineages and occupational guilds. Power now shifted away from agrarian elites and into the hands of urban financiers and traders. The traders benefited from the improvement in roads and waterways, which eased the transportation of grain, hides, horses, and silk from the villages to the new towns and cities. Bronze coins of various sizes and shapes, as well as cloth and silk used in barter, spurred long-distance trade. By the second century BCE, wealthy merchants were ennobled as local magnates and wore clothing that marked their official status. As commerce further expanded, regional lords opened local customs offices along land routes and waterways to extract a share of the money and products for themselves.

Though China still had little intellectual interaction with the rest of Afro-Eurasia, its long-distance commercial exchanges skyrocketed due to the Silk Road trade. Southern silk was only the first of many Chinese commodities that reached the world beyond the Taklamakan Desert. China also became an export center for lacquer, hemp, and linen. From Sichuan came iron, steel, flint, hard stone, silver, and animals, while jade came from the northwest. At the same time, China was importing Mediterranean, Indian, and central Asian commodities.

Despite its early development of commerce, China still had no major ports that could compare to the caravan cities of Petra and Palmyra. Most cities in the landlocked north were administrative centers where farmers and traders gathered under the regional states' political and military protection. The larger cities had gates that closed between sunset and sunrise; during the night, mounted soldiers patrolled the streets. Newer towns along the southeastern seacoast still looked upriver to trade

Silk Texts Before the invention of paper, silk was widely used as writing material because it was more portable and durable than bamboo or wood for correspondence, maps, illustrations, and important texts included as funerary objects in the tombs of aristocrats. The Mawangdui silk texts shown here are from a Hunan tomb that was closed in 168 BCE and opened in 1973.

with inland agrarian communities, which also produced silk for export. Facilitating oceanic trade became more of a concern for the state during this period, and merchant ships now enjoyed the protection of military boats. However, internal, interregional trade predominated, and it fed into the Silk Roads through decentralized networks.

THE SPREAD OF BUDDHISM ALONG THE TRADE ROUTES

In addition to silk traders, monks traveled along Afro-Eurasian trade arteries to spread the word of new religions. While Christians would later take advantage of these trade routes to spread their faith (see Chapter 8), Buddhism was the chief expansionist faith in this period. Under Kushan patronage during the first centuries CE, Buddhism reached out from India to China and central Asia, following the Silk Road. Monks from the Kushan Empire accompanied traders traveling to China. There they translated Buddhist texts into Chinese and other languages, aided by Chinese converts. Buddhist ideas were slow to gain acceptance everywhere they proselytized. It took several centuries, and a new wave of nomadic migrations, for Buddhism to take root in China.

Buddhism fared less well when it followed the commercial arteries westward. The religion never became established on the Iranian plateau and made no further headway toward the Mediterranean. The main barrier was Zoroastrianism, which had been a state religion in the Persian Empire during the fifth and fourth centuries BCE (see Chapter 4); by the time Buddhism began to spread, Zoroastrianism had long been established in Iran. Iranian Hellenism had done little to weaken the power of Zoroastrianism, whose adherents formed city-based religious communities affiliated primarily with traders. These Zoroastrian traders continued to adhere to their own faith while traveling along the Silk Roads and did nothing to help Buddhism spread westward.

COMMERCE ON THE RED SEA AND INDIAN OCEAN

Using new navigational techniques and larger ships, seafarers eventually expanded the transport of Silk Road commodities via the Red Sea and the Indian Ocean. Although land routes were the tried-and-true avenues for migrants, traders, and wayfarers, they carried only what could be borne on the backs of humans and animals. Travel on them was slow, and they were vulnerable to marauders. With time, some risk takers found ways of traversing waterways—eventually on an unprecedented scale and with an ease unimaginable to earlier merchants. These risk takers were Arabs, from the commercial middle ground of the Afro-Eurasian trading system.

Arab traders had long carried such spices as frankincense and myrrh to the Egyptians, who used them in religious and funerary rites, and later to the Greeks and Romans. Metals such as bronze, tin, and iron passed along overland routes from Anatolia, as did gold, silver, and chlorite from the Iranian plateau. Gold, ivory, and other goods from the northern part of India passed through Taxila (the capital of Gandhara) and the Hindu Kush Mountains into Persia as early as the sixth century BCE. Following the expansion of the Hellenistic world, however, ships increasingly conducted long-distance trade. Mastering the monsoons over time, they sailed down the Red Sea and across the Indian Ocean as they carried goods between the tip of the Arabian Peninsula and the ports of the Indian landmass.

Arab seafarers led the way into the Indian Ocean, forging links that joined East Africa, the eastern Mediterranean, and the Arabian Peninsula with India, Southeast Asia,

Analyzing Global Developments

The Cosmopolitan World of the *Periplus Maris Erythraei*

*P*eriplus Maris Erythraei, or *Periplus of the Red Sea*, was a first-century-BCE handbook that offered advice to merchants traveling and trading along two major, connected routes: one that scaled the African coast from the Red Sea ports of Egypt and the other that traveled eastward to India in the Arabian Sea. A shrewd trader, keen observer, and experienced navigator, the author catalogued the navigable routes, listed marketable goods at each port, and even recorded anthropological insights on the inhabitants of the far-flung regions he encountered.

The author's voyage began in the Red Sea port of Berenice and moved southward to the tribal countries of modern-day Sudan and Eritrea. To the east, he found the placid waters of the Gulf of Aden and the frankincense of the Arabian coast. Though Indian products like rice and ghee were widely sold in Arabian market towns, the Indian port of Barygaza remained the most sought-after port of the time, despite its rugged coast, uneven sea bottom, and tidal waves. An important node in the Afro-Eurasian trade network, Barygaza proved to be a curious mix of the exotic and the familiar in the author's eyes, with its vendors hawking everything from Chinese silks to old Greek coins. Pragmatic in tone, the *Periplus* and its display of economic opportunity cannot help but dazzle even modern readers. The following table gives an overview of a few important ports in the *Periplus*, as well as a taste of the ancient world.

QUESTIONS FOR ANALYSIS

- What might these commodities imply about the socioeconomic status of the Greek trader and the status of the consumers of the goods that moved along these routes?

- What are some apparent patterns or commonalities in the goods that these market towns import and export? What goods exported at some of these ports are imported at other ports listed in the *PME*'s itinerary? What does that suggest about the nature of trade along this overseas route?

- Imagine that you are a merchant planning your first overseas venture. Based on the table, where should you stock up on supplies for your crew? With what ports would you want to trade and why? How would you come up with the capital investment needed to launch such a venture?

- What other types of evidence might help you interpret the nature of the trade that took place on these overseas routes? In what ways might that evidence add complexity to, or even complete the snapshot of trade offered by a *periplus* such as this one for Red Sea trade?

Source: Lionel Casson. *The Periplus Maris Erythraei: Text with Introduction, Translation, and Commentary* (Princeton, NJ: Princeton University Press, 1989).

and East Asia. Such voyages involved longer stays at sea and were far more dangerous than sailing in the Mediterranean. Yet by the first century CE, Arab and Indian sailors were transporting Chinese silks, central Asian furs, and fragrances from Himalayan trees across the Indian Ocean. The city of Alexandria in Egypt soon emerged as a key transit point between the Mediterranean Sea and the Indian Ocean. Boats carried Mediterranean exports of olives and olive oil, wine, drinking vessels, glassware, linen and wool textiles, and red coral up the Nile, stopping at Koptos and other port cities from which camel caravans took the goods to ports on the Red Sea. For centuries, Mediter-

	PORT	EXPORTS	IMPORTS	GIFTS FOR RULERS
Southern Arabia	Muza (Sect. 24)	myrrh, white marble, stacte (sweet spice for ancient Hebrew incense)	purple cloth; Arab-sleeved clothing, with no adornment, with checks, or interwoven with gold thread; herbs cyperus and saffron; blankets, with traditional local adornment or none; girdles with shaded stripes; ungent; money, considerable amount; wine; grain	horses, pack mules, expensive clothing, goldware, embossed silverware, copperware
East Africa	Opone (Sect. 13)	cinnamon, frankincense, cassia (Chinese cinnamon), better-quality slaves, tortoise shell	grain, rice, ghee, sesame oil, *monache* and *sagmatogene* (India cotton cloth), girdles, Indian cane sugar	
Persia	Omana, Apologos (Sect. 36)	purple cloth; native clothing; slaves; wine; dates; *madarate* (local sewn boats); pearls, in quantity but inferior to Indian	copper, teakwood beams, saplings, logs of sissoo (rosewood), ebony, frankincense from Kane	
Western India	Barygaza (Sect. 14, 47-8)	grain, rice, ghee, sesame oil, *monache* and *sagmatogene* (Indian cotton cloth), girdles, cane sugar, onyx, agate, molochinon, nard, costus, bedellium, ivory, lykion, Chinese [sc. silk] cloth, long pepper	Italian, Laodicean, and Arabian wine; copper, tin, lead; coral, peridot; printed and plain clothing; multicolored girdles, eighteen inches wide; storax, yellow sweet clover; raw glass; Roman money (gold and silver) commands an exchange at some profit against the local currency; inexpensive ungent	slave musicians, beautiful girls for concubinage, precious silverware, fine wine, expensive clothing with no adornment, choice ungent
Eastern India	Ganges (Sect. 63-4)	malabathron; Gangetic nard; pearls; cotton garments of the very finest quality, the so called Gangetic; *kaltis* (gold coins); finest tortoise shell; silk floss; yarn		

ranean merchants had considered the Arabian Peninsula to be the end of the Spice Road. But after Alexander's expedition and the establishment of colonies between Egypt and Afghanistan, they began to value the wealth and opportunities that lay along the shores of the Indian Ocean.

Arab sailors who ventured into the Indian Ocean benefited from new navigational techniques, especially celestial bearings (using the position of the stars to determine the position of the ship and the direction to sail). They used large ships called *dhows*, whose sails were rigged to easily capture the wind; these forerunners of modern cargo vessels were capable of long hauls in rough waters. Beginning about 120 BCE, mariners came to understand the seasonal rain-filled monsoon winds, which blow from the southwest between October and April and then from the northeast between April and October—knowledge that propelled the maritime trade connecting the Mediterranean with the Indian Ocean. Mariners accumulated the new sailing knowledge in books—each called a ***periplus*** ("sailing around")—in which sea captains recorded the landing spots and ports between their destinations, as well as their precious cargoes. (See **Analyzing Global Developments: The Cosmopolitan World of the *Periplus Maris Erythraei*.**) The revolution in navigational techniques and knowledge dramatically reduced the cost of long-distance shipping and multiplied the ports of call around large bodies of water. Some historians have argued that there were now two Silk Roads: one by land and oneby sea.

Conclusion

Alexander's territorial gains were awesome in their scale, but his empire was as transitory as it was huge. Though it crumbled upon his death, Alexander's conquest had effects more profound than those of any military or political regime before. Alexander's armies ushered in an age of thinking and practices that transformed Greek achievements into a common culture—Hellenism—whose influences, both direct and indirect, touched far-flung societies for centuries thereafter.

Hellenism offered a common language, both literally and figuratively, which linked culture, institutions, and trade. However, many Greek-speaking peoples and their descendants in parts of Southwest and central Asia integrated local cultural practices with their own ways, creating diverse and rich cultures. Thus the influences of culture flowed both ways. The economic story is equally complex. Following pathways forged by previous empires and kingdoms, Alexander's successors strengthened and expanded existing trade routes and centers of commercial activity, which ultimately led to the creation of the Silk Road.

Although the effects of this Hellenistic age lasted longer than most cultural systems and had a wider appeal than previous philosophical and spiritual ideas, they did not overwrite everything that came before. Some, like the Jewish people of Judea and elsewhere, like Alexandria, either fought against Hellenism with all their might or accommodated to it. Others, like the Romans and Carthaginians, took from the new common culture what they liked and discarded the rest.

In South Asia, the immediate successor to Alexander's military was the Mauryan Empire, which established its dominion over much of South Asia and even some of central Asia for close to a century and a half. Once Mauryan control receded, South Asia was opened up even more than before to currents moving swiftly across Afro-Eurasia, including the institutions and cultures of steppe nomads, seafarers, and Hellenists. The most telling South Asian responses occurred in the realm of spiritual and ethical norms, where Buddhist doctrines began to evolve toward a full-fledged world religious system.

Greater political integration helped fashion highways for commerce and enabled the spread of Buddhism. Nomads, like the Kushans, left their steppe lands and exchanged wares across great distances. As they found greater opportunities for business, their trade routes shifted farther south. Eventually merchants, rather than the trading nomads, seized the opportunities provided by new technologies, especially in sailing and navigation, and by thriving caravan cities. These commercial transformations connected distant parts of Afro-Eurasia. The Silk Roads and new sea-lanes connected ports and caravan cities from North Africa to South China, created new social classes, produced new urban settings, supported powerful new polities, and transported Hellenism and Buddhism well beyond their points of origin.

After You Read This Chapter

Go to INQUIZITIVE to see what you've learned—and learn what you've missed—with personalized feedback along the way.

FOCUS ON: *Forces that Unify Afro-Eurasia*

THE MEDITERRANEAN WORLD

- The spread of Hellenism around the Mediterranean via Alexander's conquests leads to a common language, cosmopolitan cities, new types of philosophy and religion, plantation slavery, and money-based economies.

CENTRAL AND SOUTH ASIA

- Alexander's withdrawal from the Indus Valley leads to the creation of the Mauryan Empire, which integrates the northern half of India.

- The Seleucid and Bactrian kingdoms further solidify the spread of Hellenism into central Asia.

THE TRANSFORMATION OF BUDDHISM

- The combined influences of Hellenism, nomadism, and Indian Ocean seafaring transform Buddhism into a world religion.

FORMATION OF SILK ROADS

- Nomadic warriors from central Asia complete the final links of the overland Silk Roads, strengthening the ties that joined peoples across Afro-Eurasia.

- Overland traders carry spices, transport precious metals, and convey Buddhist thought along the Silk Roads into China.

- Seafaring traders use new navigation techniques and larger ships called *dhows* to expand the transport of Silk Road commodities to the Mediterranean world via the Indian Ocean.

CHRONOLOGY

SOUTHWEST ASIA AND EGYPT	Conquests of Alexander the Great 334–323 BCE			
THE MEDITERRANEAN				
CENTRAL AND SOUTH ASIA		Transformation of Buddhism begins 3rd century BCE		
EAST ASIA			Growth of market economy 3rd century–1st century BCE	
	400 BCE	350 BCE	300 BCE	250 BCE

- *Thinking about Crossing Borders and Shrinking the Afro-Eurasian World* Alexander's conquests and the resulting Hellenistic kingdoms of his successors brought about a never-before-seen cultural unity across huge swaths of Afro-Eurasia. To what extent was this cultural diffusion—comparable in some ways to the globalization or "Americanization" of culture around the world in modern times—a positive development? In what ways might it have been seen by those living through it as a negative development?

- *Thinking about Transformation & Conflict and Shrinking the Afro-Eurasian World* Alexander and his successors brought about unity initially by brutal conquest, then later through diplomatic strategies and the spread of Hellenistic ideas. Likewise, as the Kalinga War demonstrated, Aśoka brutally conquered territories before his change of heart and promotion of *dhamma*. Compare and contrast the role of military conflict and cultural movements (like Hellenism and *dhamma*) in bringing unity to the Hellenistic world and South Asia.

- *Thinking about Worlds Together, Worlds Apart and Shrinking the Afro-Eurasian World* The long-distance trade routes known as the Silk Roads, and sometimes the Incense Roads, brought intensified interactions among societies across Afro-Eurasia in the last centuries BCE. Which societies were closely involved in this exchange? Which appear to have been less involved? What accounts for these regions' involvement, or lack thereof, in Silk Road exchange?

1. In what ways did Alexander's conquests, his successors, and Hellenism have an impact on Afro-Eurasia? In particular, how did **koine Greek, cosmopolitan** identity, new ways of thinking, and slavery shape the Hellenistic world?

2. In what ways did the **Mauryan Empire** bring continuity and change to South Asia? What role did *dhamma* play in Aśoka's uniting of South Asia?

3. Describe the long-term impact of Greek influence in central and South Asia. Consider garrison towns, the region of **Bactria**, and Yavana kings in your answer.

4. How did interregional contacts transform Buddhism in the aftermath of Hellenism and the Mauryan Empire? Consider the development of **Mahayana Buddhism**, the role of **bodhisattvas** in it, and the depictions of the Buddha in **Gandharan art** and Mathuran art.

5. To what extent were the **Silk Roads** a new development in this period 350 BCE –100 CE? What role did **caravan cities** and, later, the Kushans play in the development of these exchange routes? What new developments in interregional exchange do texts like the *Periplus* demonstrate?

Mauryan Empire 321–184 BCE

Expansion of Rome and clash with Carthage 330–146 BCE

Spread of plantation and money-based economies 250–40 BCE

Mauryan Empire 321–184 BCE

Kushan State 3rd–1st centuries BCE

Warring States period 401–223 BCE

200 BCE   150 BCE   100 BCE   50 BCE

Competing Perspectives

Spread of Ideas

In the aftermath of Alexander's conquests, Hellenistic successor states flourished in western Afro-Eurasia, Indo-Greek Bactrian states reigned in central Eurasia, the Mauryans developed the first "Indian" empire in South Asia, and a web of trade routes through each of these regions joined together to form the Silk Roads. Two powerful movements, Hellenism and Buddhism, thrived as a result of this connectivity and consolidation. The sources in this section offer a glimpse into this connected world.

In the first passage, the Greek geographer Strabo describes the thriving Egyptian port city of Alexandria, which had become an enormous transshipment center (or entrepôt). A different view of exchange is presented in Aśoka's Kalinga Edict. After his vicious conquest of the region of Kalinga (261 BCE), the Mauryan emperor Aśoka issued this edict to express his regret over the miseries his conquest had caused and explain Aśoka's conversion to Buddhism. His intent to rule by *dhamma* and to extend Buddhism's influence through his realm is preserved in rock edicts found at Dhauli and Jaugada in northeastern India. In the *Questions of Menander*, the Indo-Greek king Menander, before raising questions into the divine nature of Buddha, describes his kingdom in the country of Yonakas, focusing on the trading city of Sâgala.

PRIMARY SOURCE 6.1

"The Ancient City of Alexandria" (early 1st Century CE), Strabo

As for the Great Harbor at Alexandria, it is not only wonderfully well closed in and protected by artificial levees and by nature, it is also so deep that even the largest ships can be moored right at the stairs along its quayside. This Great Harbor is divided up into several minor harbors. . . . Even more exports are handled than imports. Anyone who might happen to be at Alexandria and at Dichaiarchia [the large Italian port on the Bay of Naples] would easily see for himself that the cargo ships sailing from here are bigger and more heavily laden. . . . The city itself is crisscrossed by streets that are wide enough for riding horses and driving chariots, and intersected by two main roads very much broader than the others. Its streets and avenues cut across each other at right angles. The city also boasts exceedingly beautiful public parks and its royal quarters take up a quarter, perhaps even a third of the whole city. . . . In earlier times, not even twenty ships would dare to go as far as the Arabian Gulf and manage to get a look outside its straits. But now large fleets of ships are sent out as far as India and to the furthest lands of the Ethiopians, from which the most valuable cargoes are brought to Egypt and then sent out again to other regions of the world. Double charges are collected on these shipments—both when they come in and when they go out—and the duties are especially high on luxury goods . . . for Alexandria alone does not just receive trade goods of this kind from all over the world, but it also furnishes supplies to the whole of the world outside.

Source: Strabo, *Geography* 17.1.6, 7, 8, 13; translated by Brent Shaw.

PRIMARY SOURCE 6.2

The Kalinga Edict (261 BCE), Aśoka

[Certainly] the slaughter, death and deportation of men which take place in the course of the conquest of an unconquered country are now considered extremely painful and deplorable by the Beloved of the Gods. But what is considered even more deplorable by the Beloved of the Gods is the fact that injury to or slaughter or deportation of the beloved ones falls to the lot of the Brahmans, *śramanas*, the adherents of other sects and the householders, who live in that country and among whom are established such virtues as obedience to superior personages, obedience to mother and father, obedience to elders and proper courtesy and firm devotion to friends, acquaintances, companions and relatives as well as to slaves and servants. And if misfortune befalls the friends, acquaintances, companions and relatives of persons who are full of affection towards the former, even though they are themselves well provided for, the said misfortune as well becomes an injury to their own selves. In war, this fate is shared by all classes of men and is considered deplorable by the Beloved of the Gods.

Excepting [among the Greeks], there is no country where . . . the Brahmans and the *śramanas* do not exist; and there is no place in any country where men are not indeed sincerely devoted to one sect or the other. Therefore, the slaughter, death or deportation of even a hundredth or thousandth part of all those people who were slain or who died or were carried away captive at that time in Kalinga, is now considered very deplorable by the Beloved of the Gods.

Now the Beloved of the Gods thinks that, even if a person should wrong him, the offense would be forgiven if it was possible to forgive it. And the forest [tribes] who live in the dominions of the Beloved of the Gods, even them he entreats and exhorts in regard to their duty. It is hereby explained to them that, in spite of his repentance, the Beloved of the Gods possesses power enough to punish them for their crimes, so that they should turn from evil ways and would not be killed for their crimes. [Certainly] the Beloved of the Gods desires the following in respect of all creatures[:] non-injury to them, restraint in dealing with them, and impartiality in the case of crimes committed by them.

So, what is conquest through *Dhamma* is now considered to be the best conquest by the Beloved of the Gods. And such a conquest has been achieved by the the Beloved of the Gods not only here in his own dominions but also in the territories bordering on his dominions, as far away as . . . six hundred *yojanas* [about 1,500 miles], where the [Greek] king named Antiochus is ruling and where, beyond the kingdom of the said Antiochus, four other kings named Ptolemy, Antigonus, Magas, and Alexander are also ruling, and, towards the south, where the Colas and Pa⁻ndyas living as far as Ceylon. Likewise here in the dominion of His Majesty, the Beloved of the Gods—in the countries of the [Greeks] and the Kambojas, the Na⁻bhakas and Na⁻bhapanktis, the Bhojas and Pitinikas, the Andhras and Pa⁻rindas, everywhere the people are conforming to the instructions in *Dhamma* imparted by the Beloved of the Gods.

Even where the envoys of the Beloved of the Gods have not penetrated, there too men have heard of the practices of *Dhamma* and the ordinances issued and the instructions in *Dhamma* imparted by the Beloved of the Gods, and are conforming to *Dhamma* and will continue to conform to it.

[W]hatever conquest is achieved in this way, [certainly] that conquest creates an atmosphere of satisfaction everywhere both among the victors and the vanquished. In the conquest through *Dhamma*, satisfaction is derived by both the parties. But that satisfaction is indeed of little consequence. Only happiness of the people in the next world is what is regarded by the Beloved of the Gods as a great thing resulting from such a conquest.

And this record relating to *Dhamma* has been written on stone for the following purpose, [namely] that my sons and great-grandsons should not think of a fresh conquest by arms as worth achieving, that they should adopt the policy of forbearance and light punishment towards the vanquished even if they conquer a people by arms, and that they should regard the conquest through *Dhamma* as the true conquest. Such a conquest brings happiness to all concerned both in this world and in the next. And let all their intense joys be what is pleasure associated with *Dhamma*.

For this brings happiness in this world as well as in the next.

Source: Aśoka, "Rock Edicts," *Inscriptions of Aśoka*, trans. D. C. Sircar (New Delhi, India: Publications Division, Ministry of Information & Broadcasting, Government of India, 1967), 57–59.

PRIMARY SOURCE 6.3

"Sâgala: City of the Gods" (c. 150–130 BCE) from The Questions of King Menander

Thus hath it been handed down by tradition—There is in the country of the Yonakas a great centre of trade, a city that is called Sâgala, situated in a delightful country well watered and hilly, abounding in parks and gardens and groves and lakes and tanks, a paradise of rivers and mountains and woods. Wise architects have laid it out, and its people know of no oppression, since all their enemies and adversaries have been put down. Brave is its defence, with many and various strong towers and ramparts, with superb gates and entrance archways; and with the royal citadel in its midst, white walled and deeply moated. Well laid out are its streets, squares, cross roads, and market places. Well displayed are the innumerable sorts of costly merchandise with which its shops are filled. It is richly adorned with hundreds of almshalls of various kinds; and splendid with hundreds of thousands of magnificent mansions, which rise aloft like the mountain peaks of the Himâlayas. Its streets are filled with elephants, horses, carriages, and foot-passengers, frequented by groups of handsome men and beautiful women, and crowded by men of all sorts and conditions, Brahmans, nobles, artificers, and servants. They resound with cries of welcome to the teachers of every creed, and the city is the resort of the leading men of each of the differing sects. Shops are there for the sale of Benares muslin, of Kotumbara stuffs and of other cloths of various kinds; and sweet odours are exhaled from the bazaars, where all sorts of flowers and perfumes are tastefully set out. Jewels are there in plenty, such as men's hearts desire, and guilds of traders in all sorts of finery display their goods in the bazaars that face all quarters of the sky. So full is the city of money, and of gold and silver ware, of copper and stone ware, that it is a very mine of dazzling treasures. And there is laid up there much store of property and corn and things of value in warehouses—foods and drinks of every sort, syrups and sweetmeats of every kind. In wealth it rivals Uttara-kuru, and in glory it is as Âlakamandâ, the city of the gods.

Source: *The Questions of King Milinda*, translated by T. W. Rhys Davis (1890; reprint, Delhi: Motilal Banarsidass, 1975), 2–3.

QUESTIONS FOR ANALYSIS

1. What evidence of exchange of goods and/or ideas do you see in each passage?

2. In what ways are Hellenism and/or Buddhism a factor in each text? What does that suggest to you about the potential influence of these two movements in this period?

3. In what ways does each text contribute to your understanding of the Silk Roads, and the potential for the spread of Hellenism and Buddhism along the routes that were shrinking the Afro-Eurasian world in the late first millennium BCE?

Interpreting Visual Evidence

Coinage

The minting of coins was one of the many ways that rulers asserted their identity and conveyed propaganda about their rule. While minting coins was a statement of political authority, rulers often wanted to suggest not only the new ideals of their rule but also a cultural continuity. They chose for their coins words and images that blended the new with the old and the imported with the local.

The well-preserved gold octadrachm coin pictured below displays the image of Berenice II of Egypt (r. 246–221 BCE), one of the many female Egyptian rulers of this period. The coin's flip-side shows a cornucopia brimming with fruit and the words Berenike Basileia (Queen Berenice). The next coin shown here was minted by King Menander (r. circa 165–130 BCE), known for his discussions with Indian sages on the nature of the Buddha. Menander stamped his own image on a silver coin, along with his name and his title (Basileus Soter; King Savior). On the other side of the coin, the Greek goddess Athena is surrounded by an Indian writing known as Kharoshthi script.

Several examples of coins from points farther east look a little different than these Hellenistic examples, but express similarly complex messages of identity and continuity. The bronze, rectangular coin displayed below was minted at Pushkalavati (c. 220–185 BCE), near modern-day Lahore, Pakistan, a site situated along the Silk Roads. Its elephant on one side and horse on the other signaled both contemporary and Vedic values. The knife-shaped coin with Chinese characters on it dates to 250–221 BCE and comes from northeastern China. It shows just how diverse coin types could be; even though the practice of government-issued coins was taking hold in many places, there was no one way to mint them. Even within China, coin types varied. The last coin pictured here is a bronze *ban liang* and was minted under the authority of Qin ruler King Huiwen (r. 338–311 BCE) an ancestor of Shi Huangdi who later established the short-lived Qin Dynasty in 221 BCE (see Chapter 7).

Gold octadrachm.

Bronze karshapana.

Menander coin.

Bronze jimo.

Bronze ban liang.

QUESTIONS FOR ANALYSIS

1. Compare these coins with one another. To what extent do you think the "shrinking Afro-Eurasian world," described in this chapter, may have influenced their similarities and differences?

2. What messages might the images and words on the coins have conveyed to those who may have used them?

3. Coins of high value (like Berenice's gold octadrachm) are usually far better preserved than lower-value coins (like the bronze coin from Pushkalavati). Why do you think that is the case?

Before You Read This Chapter

7

Han Dynasty China and Imperial Rome

300 BCE–300 CE

In third-century-BCE China, the Eastern Zhou state of Qin absorbed the remaining Warring States (see Chapter 5) and set the stage for the Han dynasty. The chief minister of the Qin state, Li Si, urged his king to seize the opportunity presented by the disarray of his opponents: by combining his fearsome armies and his own personal virtues, the king could sweep away his rivals as if dusting ashes from a kitchen hearth. "This is the one moment in ten thousand ages," Li Si whispered to the man who would become Qin Shi Huangdi. The king listened carefully. He followed the advice and laid the foundations for a mighty empire. Although Shi Huangdi's Qin Empire collapsed in 207 BCE after a mere two decades, his political innovations set the stage for the much more powerful Han Empire (206 BCE–220 CE), which became one of the most successful dynasties in Chinese history. Following the Qin model, the Han defeated other regional groups and established a Chinese empire that would last for four centuries.

At the other end of Afro-Eurasia another great state, imperial Rome, also met its rivals in war, emerged victorious, and consolidated its power into a vast empire. The Romans achieved this feat by using violent force on a scale hitherto unseen in their part of the globe. The result was a state of huge size, astonishingly unified and stable. Living in the Roman Empire in the mid-70s CE, Pliny the Elder wrote glowingly about the unity of the imperial Roman state. In his eyes, all the benefits that flowed from Rome's extensive reach derived from the greatness of a peace that joined diverse peoples under one benevolent emperor. In this chapter we will examine and compare the growth, politics, economies, and societies of the Han and Roman empires.

Globalizing Empires: The Han Dynasty and Imperial Rome

The Han and the Roman states became truly **globalizing empires**: they covered immense amounts of territory, included huge, diverse populations, and exerted influence far beyond their own borders. Their major innovation was not that they found new ways to plow resources into big armies and civil bureaucracies or because rulers gave new justifications for their rule. Rather, what distinguished the Romans and the Han from their predecessors was their commitment to integrating conquered neighbors and rivals into their worlds—by extending laws, offering systems of representation, exporting belief systems, colonizing lands, and promoting trade within and beyond their empires. Subject peoples became members of empires, not just the vanquished. Those who resisted not only waved away the benefits of living under imperial rule but also became the targets for military retribution.

In this period, an estimated one out of every four human beings in Afro-Eurasia fell directly under the authority of China or Rome. Their control shaped the identity of those living within their respective realms. To be "Han Chinese" meant that elites shared a common written language based on the Confucian classics, which qualified them for public office. It also meant that commoners from all walks of life shared the elites' belief system based on ancestor worship, ritual practices stressing appropriate decorum and dress for each social level, and a view that the agrarian-based Han Empire was a small-scale model of the entire cosmos. Those who lived beyond the realm of the Han were considered uncivilized.

What it meant to be "Roman" changed over time as Rome's imperial reach expanded. In the fifth century BCE, being Roman meant being a citizen of the city of Rome, speaking Latin (the regional language of central Italy), and eating and dressing like Latin-speaking people. By the late second century BCE, the concept of citizenship expanded to include not only citizens of the city but also anyone who had formal membership in the larger territorial state that the Romans were building. By the beginning of the third century CE, being Roman meant simply being a subject of the Roman emperors. This Roman identity became so deeply rooted that when the western parts of the empire disintegrated two centuries later, the inhabitants of the surviving eastern parts—who had no connection with Rome, did not speak Latin, and did not dress or eat like the original Romans—still considered themselves "Romans" in this broader sense.

The two empires reflected different patterns of development, types of public servants, and ideals for the best kind of government. For example, the civilian magistrate and the bureaucrat were typical of the Han Empire, whereas the citizen, the soldier, and the military governor were at the heart of the Roman Empire. In China, dynastic empires fashioned themselves according to the models of past empires. By contrast, Rome began as a collectively ruled city-state and pursued its road to domination as if creating something new. Nonetheless, like the Chinese, Romans were strongly traditional and also idealized their ancestors. Both new empires united huge landmasses and extraordinarily diverse populations.

While both China and Rome participated in Silk Road exchange, both economies were primarily agrarian-based; yet in China, free peasants worked the land, while a huge enslaved population worked the fields of the Roman Empire. At its height, the Han Empire included around 59 million inhabitants and covered 3 million square miles in China proper and, for a while, another 1 million square miles in central Asia. The Roman Empire governed an area and a population nearly as great as those of Han China.

Both empires left indelible legacies; following their collapses, both survived as models. Successor states in the Mediterranean sought to become the second Rome, and after the Han dynasty fell, the Chinese people identified themselves and their language simply as "Han." Both empires raised life to a new level of bureaucratic and military complexity and offered a common identity on a grander scale than ever before. It was a vision that would never be lost.

The Han Dynasty (206 BCE–220 CE)

The Han dynasty (206 BCE–220 CE) oversaw an unprecedented blossoming of peace and prosperity. Although supporters of the Han dynasty boasted of the regime's imperial uniqueness, in reality it owed much to its predecessor, the Qin state, which contributed vital elements of political unity and economic growth to its more powerful successor regime. (See Map 7.1.) Together, the Qin and Han created the political, social, economic, and cultural foundations that characterized imperial China thereafter.

COMPARISON

DESCRIBE the development of the Han dynasty from its beginnings through the third century CE.

THE QIN DYNASTY (221–207 BCE): A CRUCIAL FORERUNNER

Although it lasted only fourteen years, the Qin dynasty integrated much of China and made important administrative and economic innovations. The Qin were but one of many militaristic regimes during the Warring States period. What enabled the Qin to prevail over rivals was their expansion into the Sichuan region, which was remarkable for its rich mineral resources and fertile soils. There, a merchant class and the silk trade spurred economic growth, and public works fostered increased food production. These strengths enabled the Qin by 221 BCE to defeat the remaining warring states and unify an empire that covered roughly two-thirds of modern China.

Supported by able ministers and generals, a large conscripted army, and a system of taxation that financed all-out war, the Qin ruler King Zheng assumed the mandate of heaven from the Zhou. Declaring himself **Shi Huangdi**, or "First August Emperor" in 221 BCE, Zheng harkened back to China's mythical emperors of great antiquity. Forgoing the title of king (*wang*), which had been used by leaders of the Zhou and warring states, Zheng instead took the title of emperor (*di*), a term that had meant "ancestral ruler" for the Shang and Zhou.

Shi Huangdi centralized the administration of the empire. He forced the defeated rulers of the warring states and their families to move to Xianyang, the Qin capital—where they would be unable to gather rebel armies. The First August Emperor then parceled out the territory of his massive state into thirty-six provinces, called **commanderies** (*jun*). Each commandery had a civilian and a military governor, as well as an imperial inspector. Regional and local officials answered directly to the emperor, who could dismiss them at will. Civilian governors did not serve in their home areas, thus preventing them from building up power for themselves. These reforms provided China with a centralized bureaucracy and a hereditary emperor that later dynasties, including the Han, inherited.

The chief minister of the Qin Empire, Li Si, subscribed to the principles of Legalism developed during the Warring States period. This philosophy valued written law codes, administrative regulations, and inflexible punishments more highly than rituals and ethics (which the Confucians emphasized) or spontaneity and the natural order (which the Daoists stressed). Determined to bring order to a turbulent world, Li Si advocated strict laws and harsh punishments that included beheading, mutilation, and loss of rank and office.

MAP 7.1 | East Asia, 206 BCE–220 CE

Both the Qin and the Han dynasties consolidated much of East Asia into one large regional empire.

• According to the map, what physical features imposed a limit to this territorial expansion?

• Why was the Great Wall so long and why was it placed facing north?

• What impact did the pastoral Xiongnu have on each empire's effort to consolidate a large territorial state?

• According to your reading, why did the Han expand their influence farther west than the Qin?

Other methods of control further facilitated Qin rule. Registration of the common people at the age of sixteen provided the basis for taxation and conscription both for military service and public works projects. The Qin emperor established standard weights and measures, as well as a standard currency. The Qin also improved communication systems and administrative efficiency by constructing roads radiating out from their capital to all parts of the empire. Just as crucial was the Qin effort to standardize writing. Banning regional variants of written characters, the Qin required scribes and ministers throughout the empire to adopt the "small seal script," which later evolved into the less complicated style of bureaucratic writing known as "clerical script" that became prominent during the Han dynasty. In 213 BCE, a Qin decree ordered officials to confiscate and burn all books in private possession, except for technical works on medicine, divination, and agriculture. Education and learning were now under the exclusive control of state officials.

The agrarian empire of the Qin yielded wealth that the state could tax. Increased tax revenues meant more resources for imposing order. The government issued rules on working the fields, taxed farming households, and conscripted laborers to build irrigation systems and canals so that even more land could come under cultivation. The Qin and later the Han dynasties relied on free farmers and conscripted their able-bodied sons into their huge armies. Working their own land and paying a portion of their crops in taxes, peasant families were the economic bedrock of the Chinese empire. Long-distance commerce thrived, as well. In the dynamic regional market centers of the cities, merchants peddled foodstuffs as well as weapons, metals, horses, dogs, hides, furs, silk, and salt—all produced in different regions and transported on the improved road system. Taxed both in transit and in the market at a higher rate than agricultural goods, these trade goods yielded even more revenue for the imperial government.

Intellectual Censorship This seventeenth-century painting depicts the infamous "Burning of the Books and Burying of the Scholars," edict enacted by Shi Huangdi at the suggestion of his advisor, Li Si. Unfortunately, even the state-approved texts were destroyed a mere six years later, during the fall of the Qin dynasty and sack of the capital.

The Qin grappled with the need to expand and defend their borders, extending those boundaries in the northeast to the Korean Peninsula, in the south to present-day Vietnam, and in the west into central Asia. Relations between the settled Chinese and the nomadic Xiongnu to the north and west (see Chapter 6) teetered in a precarious balance until 215 BCE, when the Qin Empire pushed north into the middle of the Yellow River basin, seizing pasturelands from the Xiongnu and opening the region up for settlement. Qin officials built roads into these areas and employed conscripts and criminals to create a massive defensive wall that covered a distance of 3,000 miles along the northern border (the beginnings of the Great Wall of China—though north of the current wall, which was constructed more than a millennium later). In 211 BCE the Qin settled 30,000 colonists in the steppe lands of Inner Eurasia.

Despite its military power, the Qin dynasty collapsed quickly, due to constant warfare and the heavy taxation and exhausting conscription that war required. When conscripted workers mutinied in 209 BCE, they found allies in descendants of Warring States nobles, local military leaders, and influential merchants. The rebels swept up thousands of supporters with their call to arms against the "tyrannical" Qin. Shortly before Shi Huangdi died in 210, even the educated elite joined former lords and regional vassals in revolt. The second Qin emperor committed suicide in 207, and his weak successor surrendered to the leader of the Han forces later that year. The resurgent Xiongnu confederacy also reconquered their old pasturelands as the dynasty fell.

Qin Archer and Crossbow This kneeling archer was discovered in the tomb of the First Emperor. Notice his breastplate; its overlapping plates would have enhanced maneuverability. The wooden bow he was holding has disintegrated, but a replica appears above. The bronze arrowhead and trigger mechanism in this reproduction were found with the terra-cotta army.

BEGINNINGS OF THE WESTERN HAN DYNASTY

The civil war that followed the collapse of Qin rule opened the way for the formation of the Western Han dynasty. A commoner and former policeman named Liu Bang (r. 206–195 BCE) declared himself prince of his home area of Han. In 202 BCE, Liu proclaimed himself the first Han emperor. Claiming the mandate of heaven, the Han portrayed the Qin as evil; yet at the same time they adopted the Qin's bureaucratic system. In reality, Qin laws had been no crueler than those of the Han. Under Han leadership, China's armies swelled with some 50,000 crossbowmen who brandished mass-produced weapons made from bronze and iron. Armed with the crossbow, foot soldiers and mounted archers extended Han imperial lands in all directions. Following the Qin practice, the Han also relied on a huge conscripted labor force for special projects such as building canals, roads, and defensive walls.

The first part of the Han dynasty is known as the Western (or Former) Han dynasty (206 BCE–9 CE). The Han brought economic prosperity and the expansion of empire. This was especially the case under **Emperor Wu**, known also as Han Wudi, who presided over one of the longest and most eventful reigns in Chinese history (r. 140–87 BCE). Although called the "Martial Emperor" because of the state's many military campaigns, Emperor Wu rarely inspected his military units and never led them in battle. Wu followed the Daoist principle of *wuwei* (noninterference), striving to remain aloof from day-to-day activities and permitting the empire to function on its own as if it did not require intervention. Still, he used a stringent penal code to eliminate powerful officials who got in his way. In a single year, his court system prosecuted over a thousand such cases.

HAN POWER AND ADMINISTRATION

Undergirding the Han Empire was the tight-knit alliance between the imperial family and the new elite—the scholar-gentry class—who shared a determination to impose order on the Chinese population. Although the first Han emperors had no choice but to compromise with the aristocratic groups who had helped overthrow the Qin, in time the Han created the most highly centralized bureaucracy in the world. No fewer than 130,000 individuals staffed the central and local governments. That structure became the source of its enduring power. As under the Qin, the Han bureaucracy touched everyone because all males had to register, pay taxes, and serve in the military.

The Han court moved quickly to tighten its grip on regional administration. First it removed powerful princes, crushed rebellions, and took over the areas controlled by regional lords. According to arrangements instituted in 106 BCE by Emperor Wu, the empire consisted of thirteen provinces under imperial inspectors. Commanderies, each administered by a civilian and a military official, covered vast lands inhabited by countless ethnic groups totaling millions of people. These officials maintained political stability and ensured the efficient collection of taxes. However, given the immense numbers under their jurisdiction and the heavy duties they bore, in many respects the local administrative staff was still inadequate to the tasks facing them.

Han Coin After the Qin created the first standard imperial currency in China, the copper wuzhu coin was issued by Emperor Xuandi during the Western Han dynasty, 73–49 BCE. *Wuzhu*, which means "five grains," refers to the weight of the coin (1 wuzhu = 5 grains = 4 grams). The wuzhu was in circulation until 621 CE.

Government schools that promoted the scholar-official ideal became fertile sources for recruiting local officials. In 136 BCE, Emperor Wu founded what became the **Imperial University**, a college for classical scholars that supplied the Han need for well-trained bureaucrats. By the second century CE, the university boasted 30,000 students and faculty. Apart from studying the classics, Han scholars were naturalists and inventors. They made important medical discoveries, dealing with rational diagnoses of the body's functions and the role of wind and temperature in transmitting diseases. They also invented the magnetic compass and developed high-quality paper. Local elites encouraged their sons to master the classical teachings. This practice could secure future entry into the ruling class and firmly planted the Confucian classics at the heart of the imperial state.

Confucian thought slowly became the ideological buttress of the Han Empire. Under Emperor Wu, the bureaucracy deemed people's welfare to be the essential purpose of legitimate rule. By 50 BCE, the *Analects* containing Confucius's sayings was widely disseminated and three Confucian ideals reigned as the official doctrine of the Han Empire: honoring tradition, respecting the lessons of history, and the emperor's responsibility to heaven. Scholars used Confucius's words to tutor the princes. By embracing Confucian political ideals, Han rulers established an empire based on the mandate of heaven and crafted a careful balance in which the officials provided a counterweight to the emperor's autocratic strength. When the interests of the court and the bureaucracy clashed, however, the emperor's will was paramount.

ECONOMY AND THE NEW SOCIAL ORDER

Part of the Han leaders' genius was their ability to win the support of diverse social groups that had been squabbling for centuries. The basis of their success was their ability to organize daily life, create a stable social order, promote economic growth, and foster a state-centered religion. One important element in promoting political and social stability was how the Han allowed surviving Qin aristocrats to reacquire some of their former power. The Han also urged enterprising peasants who had worked the nobles' lands to become local leaders in the countryside. Successful merchants won permission to extend their influence in cities, and in local areas scholars found themselves in the role of masters when the state removed their lords.

Out of a massive agrarian base flowed a steady stream of tax revenues and labor for military forces and public works. The Han court drew revenues from many sources: state-owned imperial lands, mining, and mints; tribute from outlying domains; household taxes on the nobility; and taxes on surplus grains from wealthy merchants. Emperor Wu established state monopolies in salt, iron, and wine to fund his expensive military campaigns. His policies encouraged silk and iron production—especially iron weapons and everyday tools—and controlled profiteering through price

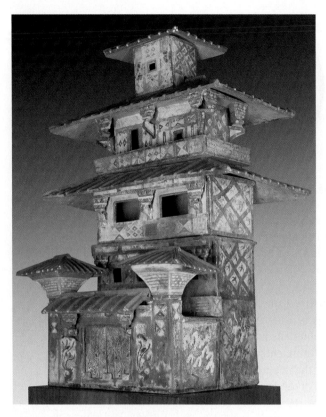

Model of a Han House Elite families in Chang'an and other Han cities typically lived in two-story houses with carved crossbeams and rafters and enclosed courtyards. The floors were covered with embroidered cushions, wool rugs, and mats for sitting. Screens were used for privacy. Women and children were cloistered in the inner quarters.

controls. He also minted standardized copper coins and imposed stiff penalties for counterfeiting.

Han cities were laid out in an orderly grid. Bustling markets served as public areas. Carriages transported rich families up and down wide avenues (and they paid a lot for the privilege: keeping a horse required as much grain as a family of six would consume). Court palaces became forbidden inner cities, off-limits to all but those in the imperial lineage or the government. Monumental architecture in China announced the palaces and tombs of rulers.

Domestic Life Daily life in Han China included new luxuries for the elite and reinforced traditional ideas about gender. Wealthy families lived in several-story homes with richly carved crossbeams and rafters and floors cushioned with embroidered pillows, wool rugs, and mats. Fine embroideries hung as drapes, and screens in the rooms secured privacy. Domestic space reinforced male authority as women and children stayed cloistered in inner quarters, preserving the sense that the patriarch's role was to protect them from a harsh society. Nonetheless, some elite women, often literate, enjoyed respect as teachers and managers within the family while their husbands served as officials away from home. Women who were commoners led less protected lives, working in the fields or even joining entertainment troupes.

Silk was abundant and available to all classes, though in winter only the rich wrapped themselves in furs while everyone else stayed warm in woolens and ferret skins. The rich also wore distinctive slippers lined with leather or silk. Wine and cooked meat came to the dinner tables of the wealthy on vessels fashioned with silver inlay or golden handles. Entertainment for those who could afford it included gambling, performing animals, tiger fights, foreign dancing girls, and even live music in private homes, performed by orchestras in the families' private employ. Although events like these had occurred during the Zhou dynasty, they had marked only public ritual occasions.

Social Hierarchy At the base of Han society was a free peasantry of farmers who owned and tilled their own land. The Han court upheld an agrarian ideal—which Confucians and Daoists supported—honoring the peasants' productive labors, while subjecting merchants to a range of controls (including regulations on luxury consumption) and belittling them for not doing physical labor. Confucians envisioned scholar-officials as working hard for the ruler to enhance a moral economy, which minimized profiteering by greedy merchants.

In reality, however, the first century of Han rule perpetuated the power of elites. At the apex were the imperial clan and nobles, followed, in order, by high-ranking officials and scholars, great merchants and manufacturers, and a regionally based class of local magnates. Below these elites, lesser clerks, medium and small landowners, free farmers, artisans, small merchants, poor tenant farmers, and hired laborers eked out a living. The more destitute became government slaves and relied on the state for food and clothing. At the bottom were convicts and private slaves.

Between 100 BCE and 200 CE, scholar-officials linked the imperial center with local society. At first, their political clout and prestige complemented the power of landlords and

Han Entertainment Han entertainment included dancing, particularly by foreign girls (*top left*), and acrobatics, for which the Chinese remain famous today (*bottom left*). Music was often played at the homes of rich families, who kept their own orchestras complete with bells and drums. Musical events became so popular, for both the entertainers (note the face in the Han statue on the right) and the entertained, that performances ceased being only somber ritual occasions.

large clans, but over time their autonomy grew as they gained wealth by acquiring private property. Following the fall of the Han, they emerged as the dominant aristocratic clans.

In the long run, the imperial court's struggle to limit the power of local lords and magnates failed. Rulers had to rely on local officials to enforce their rule, but those officials could rarely stand up to the powerful men they were supposed to be governing. And when central rule proved too onerous for local elites, they could rebel. Local uprisings against the Han that began in 99 BCE forced the court to relax its measures and left landlords and local magnates as dominant powers in the provinces. Below these privileged groups, powerless agrarian groups turned to Daoist religious organizations that crystallized into potent cells of dissent.

Religion and Omens Under Emperor Wu, Confucianism took on religious overtones. One treatise portrayed Confucius not as a humble teacher but as an uncrowned monarch, and even as a demigod and a giver of laws, which differed from the portrait in the *Analects* of a more modest, accessible, and very human Confucius.

Although Confucians at court championed classical learning, many local communities practiced forms of a remarkably dynamic popular Chinese religion. Imperial cults, magic, and sorcery reinforced the court's interest in astronomical omens—such as the appearance of a supernova, solar halos, meteors, and lunar and solar eclipses. Unpredictable celestial events, as well as earthquakes and famines, could be taken to mean that the emperor had lost the mandate of heaven. Powerful ministers exploited these occurrences to intimidate their ruler. People of high and low social position alike believed that witchcraft could manipulate natural events and interfere with the will of heaven. Religion in its many forms, from philosophy to witchcraft, was an essential feature of Han society from the elite to the poorer classes.

MILITARY EXPANSION AND THE SILK ROADS

The Han military machine was effective at expanding their borders and enforcing stability around the borderlands. Peace was good for business, specifically for creating stable conditions that allowed the safe transit of goods over the Silk Roads. Emperor Wu did much to transform the military forces. Following the Qin precedent, he made military service compulsory, resulting in a huge force: 100,000 crack troops in the Imperial Guard stationed in the capital and more than a million in the standing army.

Expanding Borders Han forces were particularly active along the borders. During the reign of Emperor Wu, Han control extended from southeastern China to northern Vietnam. When pro-Han Koreans appealed for Han help against rulers in their internal squabbles, Emperor Wu's expeditionary force defeated the Korean king and four Han commanderies sprang up in northern Korea. While incursions into Sichuan and the southwestern border areas were less successful due to mountainous terrain and malaria, a commandery nonetheless took root in southern Sichuan in 135 BCE, and soon it opened trading routes to Southeast Asia.

The Han Empire's most serious military threat, however, came from the Xiongnu and other nomadic peoples in the north. The Han inherited from the Qin a symbiotic relationship with these proud, horse-riding nomads: Han merchants brought silk cloth and thread, bronze mirrors, and lacquerware to exchange for furs, horses, and cattle. After humiliating defeats at the hands of the Xiongnu, the Han under Emperor Wu successfully repelled Xiongnu invasions around 120 BCE and ultimately penetrated deep into Xiongnu territory. The Xiongnu tribes were split in two, with the southern tribes surrendering and the northern tribes moving west, ultimately threatening Roman territory.

The Chinese Peace and the Silk Roads The retreat of the Xiongnu and other nomadic peoples introduced a glorious period of internal peace and prosperity some scholars have referred to as a ***Pax Sinica*** ("Chinese Peace," 149–87 BCE). During this period, long-distance trade flourished, cities ballooned, standards of living rose, and the population surged. As a result of their military campaigns, Emperor Wu and his successors enjoyed tribute from distant subordinate states, only intervening in their domestic policy if they rebelled. The Han instead relied on trade and markets to incorporate outlying lands as prosperous satellite states within the tribute system. The Xiongnu nomads even became key middlemen in Silk Road trade.

When the Xiongnu were no longer a threat from the north, the Han expanded westward. (See Map 7.2.) By 100 BCE, Emperor Wu had extended the northern defensive wall from the Tianshan Mountains to the Gobi Desert. Along the wall stood signal beacons for sending emergency messages, and its gates opened periodically for trading fairs. The westernmost gate was called the Jade Gate, since jade from the Taklamakan Desert passed through it. Wu also built garrison cities at oases to protect the trade routes. Soldiers at these oasis garrison cities settled with their families on the frontiers. When its military power expanded beyond the Jade Gate, the Han government set up a similar system of oases on the rim of the Taklamakan Desert. With irrigation, oasis agriculture attracted many more settlers. Trade routes passing through deserts and oases now were

MAP 7.2 | *Pax Sinica*: The Han Empire in the First Century BCE

Agriculture, commerce, and industry flourished in East Asia under Han rule.

- According to the map, what were the main commodities that passed among the empire's regions?
- What type of administrative infrastructure integrated the vast domain?
- What other features united and/or marked off Han territory?

safer and more reliable—until fierce Tibetan tribes threatened them at the beginning of the Common Era—than the steppe routes, which they gradually replaced.

SOCIAL UPHEAVAL AND NATURAL DISASTER

The strain of military expenses and the tax pressures those expenditures placed on small landholders and peasants were more than the Han Empire could bear. By the end of the first century BCE, heavy financial expenditures drained the Chinese empire. A devastating chain of events exacerbated the empire's troubles: natural disasters led to crop failures, which led to landowners being unable to pay taxes based not on crop yield but on size of landholding. Taking advantage of landowners' financial distress, free peasants became tenant farmers, and large landowners had to sell their farms to their slaves. In desperation, dispossessed peasants rebelled. Wang Mang (r. 9–23 CE), a former Han minister and regent to a child emperor, took advantage of the crisis. Believing that the Han had lost the mandate of heaven, Wang Mang took over the throne in 9 CE and established a new dynasty. He designed reforms to help the poor and to foster economic activity by confiscating gold from wealthy landowners and merchants. By redistributing excess land, he hoped that all families would work their own parcels and share in cultivating a communal plot whose crops would become tax surplus for the state.

Wang Mang's regime, and his idealistic reforms, failed miserably. Violent resistance from peasants and large landholders, as well as the Yellow River changing its course in 11 CE, contributed to his demise. When the Yellow River, appropriately called "China's Sorrow," changed course—as it has many times in China's long history—tremendous floods caused mass death, vast migrations, peasant impoverishment, and revolt. The floods of 11 CE likely affected half the Chinese population. Rebellious peasants, led by Daoist clerics, used this far-reaching disaster as a pretext to march on Wang's capital at Chang'an. The peasants painted their foreheads red in imitation of demon warriors and called themselves Red Eyebrows. By 23 CE, they had overthrown Wang Mang. The natural disaster was attributed by Wang's rivals to his unbridled misuse of power, and soon Wang became the model of the evil usurper.

THE EASTERN HAN DYNASTY

After Wang Mang's fall, social, political, and economic inequalities fatally weakened the power of the emperor and the court. As a result, the Eastern (or Later) Han dynasty (25–220 CE), with its capital at Luoyang on the North China plain, followed a hands-off economic policy under which large landowners and merchants amassed more wealth and more property. Decentralizing the regime was also good for local business and long-distance trade, as the Silk Roads continued to flourish. Chinese silk became popular as far away as the Roman Empire. In return, China received glass, jade, horses, precious stones, tortoiseshells, and fabrics.

By the second century CE, landed elites enjoyed the fruits of their success in manipulating the Later Han tax system. It granted them so many land and labor exemptions that the government never again firmly controlled its human and agricultural resources as Emperor Wu had. As the court refocused on the new capital in Luoyang, local power fell into the hands of great aristocratic families. These elites acquired even more privately owned land and forced free peasants to become their rent-paying tenants, then raised their rents higher and higher.

Such prosperity bred greater social inequity—among large landholders, tenant farmers, and peasants working their small parcels—and a renewed source of turmoil. Simmering tensions between landholders and peasants boiled over in a full-scale rebellion in 184 CE. Popular religious groups championed new ideas among commoners and elites for whom the Daoist sage Master Laozi, the voice of naturalness and spontaneity, was an exemplary model. Daoist masters challenged Confucian ritual conformity and they advanced their ideas in the name of a divine order that would redeem all people, not just elites. Officials, along with other political outcasts, headed strong dissident groups and eventually formed local movements. Under their leadership, religious groups such as the Yellow Turbans—so called because they wrapped yellow scarves around their heads—championed Daoist millenarian movements across the empire. (A millenarian movement is a broad, popular upheaval calling for a just and ideal society, sometimes based on the restoration of a bygone moral age, led by charismatic spiritual prophets.) Their message received a warm welcome from a population that was increasingly hostile to Han rule.

Proclaiming the Daoist millenarian belief in a future "Great Peace," the Yellow Turbans demanded fairer treatment by the Han state and equal distribution of all farm lands. As agrarian conditions worsened, a widespread famine ensued. It was a catastrophe that, in the rebels' view, demonstrated the emperor's loss of the mandate of heaven. The economy disintegrated when people refused to pay taxes and provide forced labor, and internal wars engulfed the dynasty. After the 180s CE, three competing states replaced the Han: the Wei in the northwest, the Shu in the southwest, and the Wu in the south. A long-lasting unified empire did not return for several centuries.

The Roman Empire

At the other end of Afro-Eurasia from Han China, in a centuries-long process, Rome became a great power that ruled over as many as 60 million subjects. The Roman Empire at its height encompassed lands from the highlands of what is now Scotland in Europe to the lower reaches of the Nile River in modern-day Egypt and part of Sudan, and from the borders of the Inner Eurasian steppe in Ukraine and the Caucasus to the Atlantic shores of North Africa. (See Map 7.3.) Whereas the Han Empire dominated an enormous and unbroken landmass, the Roman Empire dominated lands around the Mediterranean Sea. Like Han China, though, the Romans acquired command over their world through violent military expansion. By the first century CE, almost unceasing wars against their neighbors had enabled the Romans to forge an unparalleled number of ethnic groups and minor states into a single, large political state. (See **Analyzing Global Developments: Great Empires Compared**.)

COMPARISON

EXPLAIN the process by which Rome transitioned from a minor city-state to a dominating Mediterranean power.

FOUNDATIONS OF THE ROMAN EMPIRE

Three major factors influenced the beginnings of Rome's imperial expansion: migrations of foreign peoples and Rome's military and political innovations.

Population Movements Between 450 and 250 BCE, migrations from northern and central Europe brought large numbers of Celts to settle in lands around the Mediterranean Sea. They convulsed the northern rim of the Mediterranean, staging armed forays into lands from what is now Spain in the west to present-day Turkey in the east. One of these migrations involved Gallic peoples from the region of the Alps and beyond launching a series of violent incursions into northern Italy that ultimately—around 390 BCE—led to the seizure of Rome. The important result for the Romans was not their city's capture, which was traumatic yet temporary, but rather the permanent dislocation that the invaders inflicted on the city-states of the Etruscans. These Etruscans, themselves likely a combination of indigenous people and migrations from Asia Minor centuries before, spoke their own language and were centered in what is now Tuscany. Before the Gallic invasions, the Etruscans had dominated the Italian peninsula. While the Etruscans with great difficulty drove the invading Gauls back northward, their cities never recovered nor did their ability to dominate other peoples in Italy, including their fledgling rival, the Romans. Thus the Gallic migrations removed one of the most formidable roadblocks to Roman expansion in Italy.

NORTH SEA

BALTIC SEA

BRITANNIA

⊙ Londinium

ATLANTIC OCEAN

GERMANIA INFERIOR

GERMANI

BELGICA

GALLIA LUGDUNENSIS

AGRI DECUMATES

IUTHUNGI

Rhine R.

GALLIA AQUITANIA

GERMANIA SUPERIOR

RAETIA

NORICUM

Danube R.

PANNONIA

GALLIA NARBONENSIS

DALMATIA

LUSITANIA

TARRACONENSIS

ITALIA

ADRIATIC SEA

CORSICA

⊙ Rome

⊙ Corduba

SARDINIA

BAETIA

MEDITERRANEAN

MAURETANIA TINGITANA

SICILIA

MAURETANIA CAESARIENSIS

⊙ Carthage

Syracuse

NUMIDIA

AFRICA

GAETULI

GARAMANTES

Legend:

→ Mediterranean Sea current
Roman expansion to 201 BCE
Roman expansion 201–100 BCE
Roman expansion 100–44 BCE
Roman expansion 44 BCE–14 CE
Roman expansion 14–96 CE
Roman expansion 96–106 CE
GALLIA Roman province
GAETULI Border peoples
⊙ Roman provincial capital

MAP 7.3 | Roman Expansion to 120 CE

Roman expansion continued for several centuries before reaching its peak in the second century CE.

- According to the map, what were the first provinces to fall under Rome's power? What were the last two?
- Why did the Romans not expand their empire farther into eastern Europe or Southwest Asia?
- What were the geographic limits to Rome's expansion?

IAZYGES

GOTHI

SCYTHI

CASPIAN SEA

DACIA

MOESIA SUPERIOR

MOESIA INFERIOR

BLACK SEA

IBERI

ARMENIA

THRACIA

MACEDONIA

BITHYNIA AND PONTUS

CAPPADOCIA

PARTHIAN EMPIRE

AEGEAN SEA

ASIA

GALATIA

MESOPOTAMIA

Tigris R

ACHAEA

Corinth

LYCIA AND PAMPHYLIA

CILICIA

Antioch

Euphrates R

RHODES

CYPRUS

SYRIA

CRETE

Caesarea

ARABI

SEA

JUDAEA

CYRENAICA

Alexandria

AEGYPTUS

Jerusalem

ARABIA

Nile R.

RED SEA

Analyzing Global Developments

Great Empires Compared: The Han, the Roman, the Qing, and the British Empires after World War I

The Roman and Han empires were the most powerful and extensive empires that the world had known at the time, and they remained part of the European and Chinese historical traditions. Even the British imperialists of the nineteenth and early twentieth centuries who, as the following table demonstrates, ruled over much larger populations than the Romans and the Han Chinese, though with smaller military forces, often compared their empire to that of the Romans. We have added the Qing Empire at its height at the end of the nineteenth century because it rivaled the British Empire in so many respects.

While working with these population figures, it is important to keep in mind that the numbers for the early periods are based on conjecture rather than precise information. Although censuses were conducted in both the early Roman Empire and the Han dynasty, what they tabulated was different: Rome counted male citizens over the age of sixteen and China counted households. For instance, in an inscription boasting of his accomplishments over his forty-four-year reign, the Roman emperor Augustus claimed to have conducted censuses that counted over 4,063,000 citizens in 28 BCE, 4,233,000 in 8 BCE, and 4,937,000 in 14 CE. Assuming these reported census figures were correct, the modern demographer still must estimate how many people are represented by a male Roman citizen (wife, children, and slaves) and, in the case of the Han documents, a Chinese household (wife and children). Determining how many people lived in the rest of Afro-Eurasia is again based on conjecture and highly disputed. Nonetheless, these rough estimates offer some fascinating opportunities for comparison of empires.

QUESTIONS FOR ANALYSIS

- If you compare the modern-day British Empire with the empires of the Romans and the Han Chinese, what differences stand out in terms of land area and total population? How can we explain some of these differences?
- Can you explain why the Han Empire and the Qing Empire had much larger armies than the Roman and British empires?
- What does the population data on cities suggest about the place of cities in early world history versus modern world history?
- Given that these population figures, especially for the early period, are so conjectural and disputed, what is to be gained by estimating these numbers?

MAXIMUM LAND AREA

Roman Empire	2,500,000 square miles, mainly land based
Han Empire	4,000,000 square miles, mainly land based
British Empire	1,800,000 square miles, mainly sea-borne
Qing Empire	4,500,000 square miles, mainly land based

TOTAL POPULATION

Roman Empire	c. 60,000,000
Han Empire	c. 59,000,000
British Empire	459,307,735
Qing Empire	450,000,000

SIZE OF THE MILITARY FORCES

Roman Empire	400,000
Han Empire	1,000,000
British Empire	330,000
Qing Empire	1,000,000

LARGEST CITIES

Roman Empire		British Empire in 1920 (CONT.)	
Rome	1,100,000	Bombay	1,176,000
Alexandria	600,000	Glasgow	1,052,000
Carthage	400,000	Birmingham	922,000
Athens	300,000	Cairo	791,000
Antioch	250,000	**Qing Empire in 1910**	
Han Empire		Beijing	1,100,000
Chang'an City	400,000	Guangzhou	739,000
Luoyang City	1,000,000	Yangzhou	567,300
British Empire in 1920		Shanghai	444,318
London	7,488,000	Suzhou	252,800
Calcutta	1,328,000	Hangzhou	120,000

Sources: Ping-Ti Ho, *Studies on the Population of China, 1368–1953* (1959); Susan Naquin, *Peking: Temples and City Life, 1400–1900* (2000); Tim Cornell and John Matthews, *Atlas of the Roman World* (1982); Greg Woolf, *Rome: An Empire's Story* (2012).

Military Manpower and the War Ethos The Romans achieved unassailable military power by organizing the communities that they conquered in Italy into a system that generated manpower for their army. This development began around 340 BCE, when the Romans faced a concerted attack by their fellow Latin city-states. By then, the other Latins viewed Rome not as an ally in a system of mutual defense, but as a growing threat to their own independence. After overcoming these nearby Latins, the Romans charged onward to defeat one community after another in Italy. Demanding from their defeated enemies a supply of men for the Roman army every year, Rome amassed a huge reservoir of military manpower.

In addition to their overwhelming advantage in manpower, the Romans cultivated an unusual war ethos. A heightened sense of honor drove Roman men to push themselves into battle again and again, and never to accept defeat. Guided by the example of great warriors and shaped by a regime of training and discipline, in which minor infractions of duty were punishable by death, the Roman army trooped out to war in annual spring campaigns beginning in the month—still called March today—dedicated to and named for the Roman god of war, Mars.

By 265 BCE, Rome controlled the Italian peninsula. It next entered into three great **Punic Wars** with Carthage, which had begun as a Phoenician colony and was now the major power centered in the northern parts of present-day Tunisia (see Chapters 4 and 5). The First Punic War (264–241 BCE) was a prolonged naval battle over the island of Sicily. With their victory, the Romans acquired a dominant position in the western Mediterranean. The Second Punic War (218–201 BCE), however, revealed the real strength and might of the Roman army. The Romans drew on their reserve force of nearly 750,000 men to ultimately repulse—with huge casualties and dramatic losses—the Carthaginian general Hannibal's invading force of 20,000 troops and their war elephants. They took the war to enemy soil, winning the decisive battle at Zama near Carthage in late 202 BCE. In a final war of extermination, waged between 149 and 146 BCE, the Romans used their overwhelming advantage in manpower, ships, and other resources to bring the five-centuries-long hegemony of Carthage in the western Mediterranean to an end.

With an unrelenting drive to war, the Romans continued to draft, train, and field extraordinary numbers of men for combat. Soldiers, conscripted at age seventeen or eighteen, served for up to ten years at a time. With so many young men devoted to war for such long spans of time, the war ethos became deeply embedded in the ideals of every generation. After 200 BCE, the Romans unleashed this successful war machine on the kingdoms of the eastern Mediterranean. In 146 BCE, the Romans annihilated what was left of Carthage—killing all its adult males and selling all its women and children into slavery—and obliterated the great Greek city-state of Corinth. Their monopoly of power over the entire Mediterranean basin was now unchallenged.

Roman military forces served under men who knew they could win not just glory and territory for the state, but also enormous rewards for themselves. They were talented men driven by burning ambition, from Scipio Africanus in the 200s BCE, the conqueror of Carthage, to Julius Caesar, the great general of the 50s BCE. Julius Caesar's eight-year-long cycle of Gallic wars resulted in the deaths of more than 1 million Gauls and the enslavement of another million. Western Afro-Eurasia had never witnessed war on this scale; it had no equal anywhere, except in China.

Political Institutions and Internal Conflict The conquest of the Mediterranean placed unprecedented power and wealth into the hands of a few men in the Roman social elite. The rush of battlefield successes had kept Romans and their Italian allies preoccupied with the demands of army service overseas. Once this process of territorial expansion slowed, social and political problems that had been lying dormant began to resurface.

Following the traditional date of its founding in 509 BCE, the Romans had lived in a state that they called the "public thing" or **res publica** (hence the modern word "republic"). In this state, policy issued from the Senate—a body of permanent members, 300 to 600 of Rome's

Roman Farmers and Soldiers
In the late Republic most Roman soldiers came from rural Italy, where small farms were being absorbed into the landholdings of the wealthy and powerful. In the empire, soldiers were recruited from rural provincial regions. They sometimes worked small fields of their own and sometimes worked the lands of the wealthy—like the domain in the Roman province of Africa (in modern-day Tunisia) that is depicted in this mosaic.

most powerful and wealthy citizens—and from popular assemblies of the citizens. Every year the citizens elected the officials of state, principally two consuls who held power for a year and commanded the armies. In addition, the people annually elected ten men who, as tribunes of the plebs ("the common people"), had the special task of protecting the common people's interests against those of the rich and the powerful. In severe political crises, the Romans sometimes chose one man, a dictator, whose words, *dicta*, were law and who held absolute power over the state for no longer than six months. These institutions, originally devised for a city-state, were problematic for ruling a Mediterranean-sized empire.

By the second century BCE, Rome's power elite were exploiting the wealth from its Mediterranean conquests to acquire huge tracts of land in Italy and Sicily. They then imported enormous numbers of slaves from all around the Mediterranean to work this land. Free citizen farmers, the backbone of the army, were driven off their lands and into the cities. The result was a severe agrarian and recruiting crisis. In 133 and 123–121 BCE, two tribunes, the brothers Tiberius and Gaius Gracchus, tried—much as Wang Mang would in China more than a century later—to address these inequalities. The Gracchi brothers attempted to institute land reforms guaranteeing to all of Rome's poor citizens a basic amount of land that would qualify them for army service. But political enemies assassinated both men.

Thereafter, poor Roman citizens looked not to state institutions but to army commanders, to whom they gave their loyalty and support, to provide them with land and income. These generals became increasingly powerful and started to compete with one another, ignoring the Senate and the traditional rules of politics. As generals sought control of the state and their supporters took sides, a long series of civil wars began that lasted from 90 BCE to the late 30s BCE. The Romans now turned inward on themselves the tremendous resources built up during the conquest of the Mediterranean.

EMPERORS, AUTHORITARIAN RULE, AND ADMINISTRATION

Julius Caesar's adopted son, Octavian (63 BCE–14 CE) ultimately reunited the fractured empire and emerged as undisputed master of the Roman world. Octavian's authoritarian one-man

COMPARISON

COMPARE Han China with Imperial Rome in terms of their respective political authority, economy, cultural developments, and military expansion.

rule marked the beginning of the **Pax Romana** ("Roman Peace," 25 BCE–235 CE). This peace depended on the power of one man with enough authority to enforce an orderly competition among Roman aristocrats.

Octavian concentrated immense wealth and the most important official titles and positions of power in his own hands. Signaling the transition to a new political order in which he alone controlled the army, the provinces, and the political processes in Rome, Octavian assumed a new title, **Augustus** ("the Revered One")—comparable to Qin Shi Huangdi's title—as well as the traditional republican roles of *imperator* (commander in chief, or emperor), *princeps* (first man), and *Caesar* (a name connoting his adoptive heritage, but which over time became a title assumed by imperial successors).

Rome's subjects tended to see these emperors as heroic or even semidivine beings in life, and to think of the good ones as becoming gods on their death. Yet emperors were always careful to present themselves as civil rulers whose power ultimately depended on the consent of Roman citizens and the might of the army. They contrasted themselves with the image of "king," a role the Romans had learned to detest from the monarchy they themselves had long ago overthrown to establish their Republic in 509 BCE. Nonetheless, the emperors' powers were immense.

Being a Roman emperor required finesse and talent, and few succeeded at it. Of the twenty-two emperors who held power in the most stable period of Roman history (between the first Roman emperor, Augustus, and the early third century CE), fifteen met their end by murder or suicide. As powerful as he might be, no individual emperor alone could govern an empire of such great size and population, encompassing a multitude of languages and cultures. He needed institutions and competent people to help him. In terms of sheer power, the most important institution was the army. So the emperors systematically transformed the army into a full-time professional force. Men now entered the imperial army not as citizen volunteers but as paid experts who enlisted for life and swore loyalty to the emperor and his family. It was part of the emperor's image to present himself as a victorious battlefield commander, inflicting defeat on the "barbarians" who threatened the empire's frontiers.

For most emperors, however, governance was largely a daily chore of listening to complaints, answering petitions, deciding court cases, and hearing reports from civil administrators and military commanders. At its largest in the second century CE, the Roman Empire encompassed more than forty administrative units, called provinces. As in Han China, each had a governor appointed or approved by the emperor; but unlike Han China, which had its formal Confucian-trained bureaucracy with ranks of senior and junior officials, the Roman Empire of this period was relatively understaffed in terms of central government officials. The emperor and his provincial governors depended very much on local help, sometimes aided by elite slaves and freedmen (former slaves) serving as government bureaucrats. With a limited staff of full-time assistants and an entourage of friends and acquaintances, each governor was expected to guarantee peace. For some essential tasks, though, the state had to rely on private companies, as with the collection of imperial taxes, where the profit motives of the publicans (the men in the companies that took up government contracts) were at odds with the expectations of fair government among the empire's subjects.

A Roman Town Roman towns featured many of the standard elements of modern towns and cities. Streets and avenues crossed at right angles; streets were paved; sidewalks ran between streets and houses. The houses were often several stories high and had wide windows and open balconies. All these elements can be seen in this street from Herculaneum, nicely preserved by the pyroclastic flow that ran down the slopes of nearby Mount Vesuvius when its volcano erupted in August of 79 CE, burying the town and its inhabitants.

TOWN AND CITY LIFE

Due to the conditions of peace and the wealth it generated, urban settlements were clustered in core areas of the empire—central Italy, southern Spain, northern Africa, and the western parts of present-day Turkey. The towns, whose municipal charters echoed Roman forms of government, provided the backbone of local administration for the empire. Towns often were walled, and inside those walls the streets and avenues ran at right angles. A large, open-air, rectangular area called the *forum* dominated the town center. Around it clustered the main public buildings: the markets, the main temples of principal gods and goddesses, and the building that housed city administrators. Residential areas featured regular blocks of houses, close together and fronting on the streets. Larger towns contained large apartment blocks that were not much different from the four- and five-story buildings in any modern city. In the smaller towns, sanitary and nutritional standards were reasonably good.

The imperial metropolis of Rome was another matter. With well over a million inhabitants, it was larger than any other urban center of its time; Xianyang and Chang'an—the Qin and Han capitals, respectively—each had a population of between 300,000 and 500,000. While Rome's inhabitants were privileged in terms of their access to government doles of wheat and aqueduct-supplied water, their living conditions could be appalling, with people jammed into ramshackle high-rise apartments prone to collapse in a fire. Apart from crime and violence, poor sanitary conditions and the diseases that accompany them were constant threats to the population.

Towns large and small tended to have two major entertainment venues: a theater, adopted from Hellenistic culture and devoted to plays, dances, and other popular events, and an amphitheater, a Roman innovation with a much larger seating capacity that surrounded the oval performance area at its center. In the amphitheaters, Romans could stage exotic beast hunts and gladiatorial matches for the enjoyment of huge crowds of appreciative spectators. These public entertainment facilities of Roman towns stressed the importance of citizens in civic life, as compared with the largely private entertainment of Han elite.

Deadly Roman Entertainment The huge amphitheater (left) is in the remains of the Roman city of Thysdrus in North Africa (the town of el-Jem in modern-day Tunisia). The wealth of the Africans under the empire enabled them to build colossal entertainment venues that competed with the one at Rome in scale and grandeur. Roman gladiators would fight, sometimes to the death, in such venues. In the brilliant mosaic from Rome (right), we see two gladiators at the end of a full combat in which Astacius has killed Astivus. The Greek letter theta, or "th" (the circle with crossbar through it) beside the names of Astivus and Rodan indicates that these men are dead—*thanatos* being the Greek word for "death."

SOCIAL AND GENDER RELATIONS

In Rome's civil society, laws and courts governed formal relationships, including those based on patronage and the family. By the last century BCE, the Roman state's complex legal system featured a rich body of written law, courts, and well-trained lawyers. Deeply entrenched throughout the empire, this legal infrastructure long outlasted the Roman Empire. Also firmly embedded in Roman society was a system of personal relationships that linked the rich and powerful with the mass of average citizens. Men and women of wealth and high social status acted as patrons, protecting and supporting dependents or "clients" from the lower classes. From the emperor at the top to the local municipal man at the bottom, the bonds between these groups in each city found formal expression in legal definitions of patrons' responsibilities to clients; at the same time, this informal social code raised expectations that the wealthy would be civic benefactors, sponsoring the construction of public libraries, bathhouses, and even theaters.

While patronage was important, the family was at the very foundation of the Roman social order. Legally speaking, the authoritarian *paterfamilias* ("father of the family") had nearly total power over his dependents, including his wife, children, grandchildren, and the slaves whom he owned. Despite this patriarchal system, Roman women, even those of modest wealth and status, had much greater freedom of action and much greater control of their own wealth and property when compared with women in most Greek city-states. As in Han China, some women in the Roman world could be well educated, literate, well connected, and in control of their own lives—despite what the laws and ideas of Roman males might suggest.

ECONOMY AND NEW SCALES OF PRODUCTION

Rome achieved staggering transformations in agriculture and mining. The area of land surveyed and cultivated rose steadily throughout this period, as Romans reached into arid lands on the periphery of the Sahara Desert to the south and opened up heavily forested regions in present-day France and Germany to the north. Roman agriculture and mining relied on chattel slaves—human beings purchased as private property (see Chapter 6). The massive concentration of wealth and slaves at the center of the Roman world led to the first large-scale commercial plantation agriculture and the first technical handbooks on how to run such operations for profit; it also led to dramatic slave rebellions, such as the Sicilian Revolt (135–132 BCE) and the Spartacus uprising (73–71 BCE), although the latter began among slaves in a school for gladiators. Slave-worked estates specialized in products destined for the big urban markets: wheat, grapes, and olives, as well as cattle and sheep. An impressive road system connected the far-flung parts of their empire. Milestones marked most of these roads and complex itineraries mapped major roads and distances between towns. (See Map 7.4.)

Rome mined copper, tin, silver, and gold—out of which the Roman state produced the most massive coinage system known in western Afro-Eurasia before early modern times. Public and private demand for metals was so great that traces of the air pollution generated by their

Coin Hoard The use of coins for a wide spectrum of economic exchanges became common in the Roman Empire. Looking at the batches buried for safekeeping gives us an idea of the range of coins in circulation at any one time. This coin hoard was found near Didcot in Oxfordshire, England. Buried about 165 CE, it contained about 125 gold coins minted between the 50s and 160s CE and represents the equivalent of about eleven years' pay for a Roman soldier. Gold coins were used for expensive transactions or to store wealth. Most ordinary purchases or payments were made with silver or brass coins.

MAP 7.4 | *Pax Romana*: The Roman Empire in the Second Century CE

The Roman Empire enjoyed remarkable peace and prosperity in the second century CE. Economic production increased, and Roman culture expanded throughout the realm.

- According to the map, what commodities were traded most widely?
- With what groups did Romans trade beyond their empire, and for what commodity in particular?
- Given what you know from your reading about the eastern Mediterranean origins of Christianity, how did the features of the *Pax Romana* shown on this map promote the spread of Christianity to the west?

mining operations remain in ice core samples taken from Greenland today. Rome's standardized currency facilitated taxation and the increased exchange of commodities and services. The economy functioned more efficiently due to this production of coins, which was paralleled only by the coinage output of Han dynasty China and its successors.

THE RISE OF CHRISTIANITY

Over centuries, Roman religion had cultivated a dynamic world of gods, spirits, and demons that was characteristic of earlier periods of Mediterranean history. **Christianity** took shape in this richly pluralistic world. Its foundations lay in a direct confrontation with Roman imperial authority: the trial of Jesus. After preaching the new doctrines of what was originally a sect of Judaism, Jesus was found guilty of sedition and executed by means of crucifixion—a standard Roman penalty—as the result of a typical Roman provincial trial overseen by a Roman governor, Pontius Pilatus.

No historical reference to Jesus survives from his own lifetime. Shortly after the crucifixion, Paul of Tarsus, a Jew and a Roman citizen from southeastern Anatolia, claimed to have seen Jesus in full glory outside the city of Damascus. Paul and the Mediterranean communities to whom he preached between 40 and 60 CE referred to Jesus as the Anointed One (the Messiah, in keeping with Jewish expectations) or the Christ—*ho Christos* in Greek (still the dominant language of the eastern Mediterranean region thanks to Hellenism). Only many decades later did accounts that came to be called the Gospels—such as Matthew, Mark, Luke, and John—describe Jesus's life and record his sayings. Jesus's preaching drew not only on Jewish models, but also on the Egyptian and Mesopotamian image of the great king as shepherd of his people (see Chapter 3). With Jesus, this image of the good shepherd took on a new, personal closeness. Not a distant monarch but a preacher, Jesus had set out on God's behalf to gather a new, small flock.

Through the writings of Paul and the Gospels, both written in Greek, this image of Jesus rapidly spread beyond Palestine (where Jesus had preached only to Jews and only in the local language, Aramaic) and entered the religious bloodstream of the Mediterranean. Core elements of Jesus's message, such as the responsibilities of the well-off for the poor and the promised eventual empowerment of "the meek," appealed to many ordinary people in the wider Mediterranean world. But it was the apostle Paul who was especially responsible for reshaping this message for a wider audience. While Jesus directed his teachings to villagers and peasants, Paul's message spoke to a world divided by religious identity, wealth, slavery, and gender differences: "There is neither Jew nor Greek, there is neither slave nor free, there is neither male nor female; for you are all one in Christ Jesus." This new message, universal in its claims and appeal, was immediately accessible to the dwellers of the towns and cities of the Roman Empire.

Just half a century after Jesus's crucifixion, the followers of Jesus saw in his life not merely the wanderings of a Jewish charismatic teacher, but a head-on collision between "God" and "the world." Jesus's teachings came to be understood as the message of a divine being—who, for thirty years had moved (largely unrecognized) among human beings. Jesus's followers formed a church: a permanent gathering committed to the charge of leaders chosen by God and by their fellow believers. For these leaders and their followers, death offered a defining testimony for their faith. Christians hoped for a Roman trial and the opportunity to offer themselves as witnesses (*martyrs*) for their faith.

Persecutions of Christians were sporadic and responses to local concerns. Not until the emperor Decius, in the mid-third century CE, did the state direct an empire-wide attack on Christians. But Decius died within the year, and Christians interpreted their persecutor's death as evidence of the hand of God in human affairs. By the last decades of the third century, Christian communities of various kinds, reflecting the different strands of their movement through the Mediterranean as well as the local cultures in which they settled, were present in every society in the empire.

THE LIMITS OF EMPIRE

The limitations of Roman force were a pragmatic factor in determining who belonged in, and was subject to, the empire as opposed to who was outside it and therefore excluded. The Romans pushed their authority in the west to the shores of the Atlantic Ocean, and to the south they drove it to the edges of the Sahara Desert. In both cases, there was little additional useful land available to dominate. (See Map 7.5.) Roman power was blocked, however, to the east

MAP 7.5 | Population of Roman World in 362 CE

Roman frontiers at the northern and eastern limits of the empire were persistent sources of anxiety and concern for imperial leaders. While not as densely populated as the Roman Empire, these regions contained large population centers as well.

• Name some of the major groups of peoples that lived just beyond Roman rule in the areas of eastern Europe and Southwest Asia.

• What were the geographical limits of the Roman Empire?

• According to your reading, why were Roman armies never able to subdue these neighboring peoples?

by the Parthians and then the Sasanians and to the north by the Goths and other Germanic peoples. (See **Current Trends in World History: Empires, Allies, and Frontiers**.)

The Parthians On Rome's eastern frontiers, powerful Romans such as Marcus Crassus in the mid-50s BCE and Mark Antony in the early 30s BCE wished to imitate the achievements of Alexander the Great and conquer the arid lands lying east of Judea and Syria. They failed miserably, stopped by the Parthian Empire and its successor the Sasanian Empire. The Parthian people had moved south from present-day Turkmenistan and settled in the region comprising the modern states of Iraq and Iran. Unlike the Persians before them, the Parthian social order was founded on nomadic pastoralism and a war capability based on technical advances in mounted horseback warfare. Reliance on horses made their style of fighting highly mobile and ideal for warfare on arid plains and deserts. They perfected the so-called Parthian shot: the arrow shot from a bow with great accuracy at long distance and from horseback at a gallop. On the flat, open plains of Iran and Iraq, the Parthians had a decisive advantage over slow-moving, cumbersome mass infantry formations that had been developed for war in the Mediterranean. Eventually the expansionist states of Parthia and Rome became archenemies: they confronted each other in Mesopotamia for nearly four centuries.

The Sasanians expanded the technical advances in mounted horseback warfare that the Parthians had used so successfully in open desert warfare against the slow-moving Roman mass infantry formations. King Shapur I (Shabuhr), their greatest monarch, exploited the weaknesses of the Roman Empire in the mid-third century, even capturing the Roman emperor Valerian. (See Chapter 8 for more on the Sasanians.) As successful as the Parthians and the Sasanians were in fighting the Romans, however, they could never challenge Roman sway over Mediterranean lands. Their decentralized political structure limited their coordination and resources, and their horse-mounted style of warfare was ill suited to fight around the more rocky and hilly environments of the Mediterranean world.

German and Gothic "Barbarians" In the lands across the Rhine and Danube, to the north, environmental conditions largely determined the limits of empire. The long and harsh winters, but excellent soil and growing conditions, produced hardy, dense population clusters scattered across vast distances. These illiterate, kin-based agricultural societies had changed little since the first millennium BCE.

As the Roman Empire fixed its northern frontiers along the Rhine and Danube rivers, two factors determined its relationship with the Germans and Goths on the rivers' other side. First, these small societies had only one big commodity for which the empire was willing to pay: human bodies. So the slave trade out of the land across the Rhine and Danube became immense: gold, silver, coins, wine, arms, and other luxury items flowed across the rivers in one direction in exchange for slaves in the other. Second, their wars were unremitting, as every emperor faced the expectation of dealing harshly with these so-called barbarians. Ironically, internal conflicts within the Roman Empire ultimately prompted increasing use of "barbarians" as soldiers and even as officers who served the empire.

While the Han Empire had fallen by 220 CE, the Roman Empire in the west continued to exist politically for 250 years, in which its history became intertwined with the rise of Christianity, one of the world's universalizing religions.

Soldier versus Barbarian On the frontiers of the Roman Empire, the legionary soldiers faced the non-Roman "barbarians" from the lands beyond. In this piece of a stone-carved picture from the northwestern frontier, we see a civilized and disciplined Roman soldier, to the left, facing a German "barbarian"—hair uncut and unkempt, without formal armor, his house a thatched hut. Frontier realities were never so clear-cut, of course. Roman soldiers, often recruited from the "barbarian" peoples, were a lot more like them than was convenient to admit, and the "barbarians" were influenced by and closer to Roman cultural models than this picture indicates.

Conclusion

China and Rome both constructed empires of unprecedented scale and duration, yet they differed in fundamental ways. Starting out with a less numerous and less dense population than China, Rome relied on slaves and "barbarian" immigrants to expand and diversify its workforce. While less than 1 percent of the Chinese population were slaves, more than 10 percent were slaves in the Roman Empire. The Chinese rural economy was built on a huge population of free peasant

Current Trends in World History

Empires, Allies, and Frontiers

Both the Han and the Roman empires faced threats on their frontiers and used allies as well as their own military prowess to counter such threats. Keeping good relations with frontier allies was essential to the statecraft of empires. It could also yield important intelligence for rulers in capitals.

THE HAN

Consider how the Han dealt with their enemies, the Xiongnu. Emperor Wu sent a special envoy to the Yuezhi, whom he thought would be willing to ally with him against the Xiongnu. His emissary was Zhang Qian, who had volunteered to undertake the journey into the dangerous steppe. In 139 BCE, Zhang set out with a group of 100 people; one was a former slave from the steppe, Ganfu, who guided the travelers and used his bow to kill wild animals when they ran out of food. Aware of the envoy's purpose, the Xiongnu chief detained the group when they tried to pass through his territory. The

Xiongnu kept Zhang Qian for ten years, during which time he married a Xiongnu woman and had children. Zhang learned much of steppe life and geography, but he did not forget his mission; together with Ganfu, he eventually managed to escape. At last, they reached the Yuezhi camp on the northern bank of the Oxus River.

Unfortunately, Zhang Qian did not succeed in enlisting the support of the Yuezhi. Their surviving leaders had little inclination to return to the steppe to again battle the fierce Xiongnu, especially as they could see before them the fertile Bactrian plain dotted with Hellenistic cities (see Chapter 6). Zhang Qian accompanied the Yuezhi court in touring the land of Bactria. After consuming a year in futile negotiations with the Yuezhi leaders, Zhang set out for home, bearing much information about the cultures and products of Bactria and regions beyond, including India and Persia. He finally reached Chang'an, the Han capital, thirteen years after beginning his expedition. Although he had failed in his diplomatic mission, Zhang had collected invaluable information for Wudi about the frontier areas in central Asia.

THE ROMANS

The Romans also had to deal with their frontiers. To the north they contended with "barbarians," and to the east they ran up against the powerful kingdoms of the Parthians and the Sasanians. But the Romans did have occasional contacts with kingdoms far to the east. For example, in the reign of Augustus (r. 30 BCE–14 CE) an embassy came from Poros, a king in India. In a letter that his ambassadors carried, Poros described himself as the king over 600 other kings, and he offered any help that the emperor Augustus might want of him. With the letter came gifts carried by eight slaves, naked except for their scented loincloths: a "freak," a number of large snakes, a huge turtle, and a partridge larger than a vulture.

Although embassies of this sort did bring information from far afield, Rome knew little of communities outside the empire to the east except for the peoples and provinces of the Parthian and Sasanian empires, which were closest to its frontiers. Most of this knowledge was very local in nature, gained not through formal channels but in contacts between the two states over

farmers; this enormous labor pool, together with a remarkable bureaucracy, enabled the Han to achieve great political stability. In contrast, the millions of peasant farmers who formed the backbone of rural society in the Roman Empire were much more loosely integrated into the state structure. They never unified to revolt against their government and overthrow it, as did the mass peasant movements of Later Han China. In comparison with their counterparts in China, the peasants in the Roman Empire were not as well connected in their proximity or density, or as united in purpose. Here, too, the Mediterranean environment accented separation and difference.

By Chinese standards, the Roman Empire was relatively fragmented and underadministered. Moreover, no single philosophy or religion ever underpinned the Roman state in the way that Confucianism buttressed the dynasties of China. Both empires, however, benefited from the spread of a uniform language and imperial culture. The process was more comprehensive in China, which possessed a single language that the elites used, than in Rome, where officially a two-language world existed: Latin in the western Mediterranean, Greek in the east. Both states fostered a common imperial culture across all levels of society. Once entrenched, these cultures and languages lasted well after the end of empire.

military or territorial problems or from merchants and other travelers. Diplomacy did exist, but the Roman Empire had no centralized office to manage intelligence reports.

More important than statecraft were exchanges along the Silk Road that brought news, rumors, and impressions of distant empires. The Chinese were the source of the most expensive item in the Roman Empire: the highly valued commodity silk. But in Roman eyes, the Chinese were still very remote and unknown. As Pliny the Elder wrote, "Though mild in character, the Chinese still resemble wild animals in that they shun the company of the rest of humankind, and wait for trade to come to them." Although connected, the two empires that so dominated their own worlds were still worlds apart.

Zhang Qian This painting shows Zhang Qian crossing the Yellow River during his journey to the Yuezhi. Although he failed to forge an alliance for Emperor Wu, he returned home with valuable information about frontier areas of central Asia.

QUESTIONS FOR ANALYSIS

- Compare the ways in which the Han Chinese and Romans dealt with enemies on the fringes of their respective empires.
- What makes frontier zones useful for the study of world history?

Explore Further

Michael Loewe, *The Government of Qin and Han Empires: 221 BCE–220 CE* (2006).

Peter S. Wells, *The Barbarians Speak: How the Conquered Peoples Shaped Roman Europe* (1999).

Differences in human resources, languages, and ideas led the Roman and Han states to evolve in unique ways. In both places, however, the faiths of outsiders—Christians and Buddhists—eclipsed the classical and secular traditions that grounded their states' foundational ideals. Transmission of these new faiths benefited from expanded communications networks. The new religions added to the cultural mix that succeeded the Roman Empire and the Han dynasty.

At their height, both states surpassed their forebears by translating unprecedented military power into the fullest form of state-based organization. Each state's complex organization involved the systematic control, counting, and taxing of its population. In both cases, the general increase of the population, the growth of huge cities, and the success of long-distance trade contributed to the new scales of magnitude, making these the world's first two long-lasting global empires. The Han were not superseded in East Asia as the model empire until the Tang dynasty in the seventh century CE. In western Afro-Eurasia, the Roman Empire was not surpassed in scale or intensity of development until the rise of powerful European nation-states more than a millennium later.

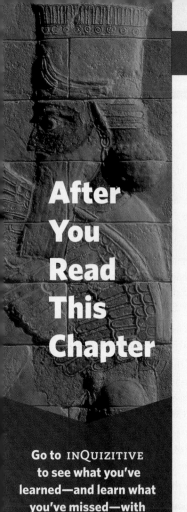

After You Read This Chapter

Go to INQUIZITIVE to see what you've learned—and learn what you've missed—with personalized feedback along the way.

FOCUS ON: *Comparing Han China and Imperial Rome*

- Han China and imperial Rome assimilate diverse peoples to their ways and regard outsiders as uncivilized.

- Both empires develop professional military elites, codify laws, and value the role of the state (not just the ruler) in supporting their societies.

- Both empires serve as models for successor states in their regions.

- The empires differ in their ideals and the officials they value: Han China values civilian bureaucrats and magistrates; Rome values soldiers and military governors.

CHRONOLOGY

EAST ASIA

Qin Empire of Shi Huangdi 221-207 BCE

Emperor Wu expands Han Empire 140-87 BCE

THE MEDITERRANEAN

Roman state expands through Italian peninsula 350-265 BCE

Rome eliminates Carthage (Punic Wars) 264-146 BCE

Tiberius and Gaius Gracchus attempt agrarian reforms 133-121 BCE

| 300 BCE | 200 BCE | 100 BCE |

- *Thinking about* **Worlds Together, Worlds Apart** *and Globalizing Empires* In the six centuries between 300 BCE and 300 CE, the Han dynasty and imperial Rome united huge populations and immense swaths of territory not only under their direct control but also under their indirect influence. In what ways did this expansive unity at each end of Afro-Eurasia have an impact on the connections between these two empires? In what ways did these two empires remain worlds apart?

- *Thinking about* **Changing Power Relationships** *and Globalizing Empires* Both the Han dynasty and the Roman Empire developed new models for heightened authoritarian control placed in the hands of a single ruler. In what ways did this authoritarian control at the top shape power relationships at all levels of these two societies? What were some potential challenges to this patriarchal, centralized control?

- *Thinking about* **Transformation & Conflict** *and Globalizing Empires* Both the Han dynasty and the Roman Empire faced intense threats along their borders. In what ways did Han interactions with nomadic groups like the Xiongnu and Roman interactions with Parthians to the east and Germans and Goths to the north impact these globalizing empires?

1. What are the characteristics of a **globalizing empire** and how do the Han dynasty and the Roman Empire fit that model?

2. How did developments begun under **Shi Huangdi**, such as **commanderies** and other Qin innovations, lay the foundations for the Han dynasty?

3. In what ways did **Emperor Wu** contribute to the creation of the Han dynasty?

4. What role did Confucianism and the **Imperial University** play in shaping the Han bureaucracy? What role did millenarian movements play in the demise of the Han dynasty?

5. What was the Roman war ethos and what role did it play in Roman imperialist endeavors, such as the **Punic Wars**?

6. What political features were central to the Roman *res publica* and in what ways did **Augustus** incorporate and challenge those in his formation of a model for empire?

7. Describe how hierarchies, such as the patron-client system and family structure, governed Roman life and in what ways **Christianity** challenged those structures.

8. Explain how Han and Roman leaders promoted long periods of peace—the *Pax Sinica* and *Pax Romana*, respectively. What were some of the results of that long-lasting peace and what were the threats to preserving that peace?

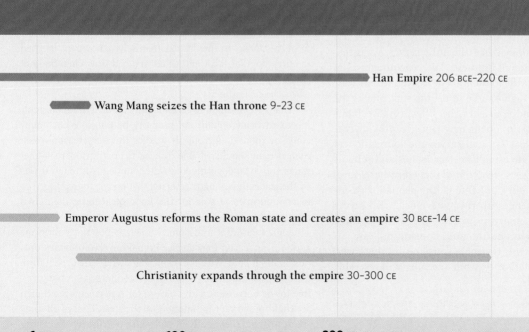

Han Empire 206 BCE–220 CE

Wang Mang seizes the Han throne 9–23 CE

Emperor Augustus reforms the Roman state and creates an empire 30 BCE–14 CE

Christianity expands through the empire 30–300 CE

1 CE   **100 CE**   **200 CE**   **300 CE**

Competing Perspectives

Maintaining Political and Domestic Order

The four passages included here offer views from the Han Chinese and the Romans on how to maintain order within their respective empires. The first two philosophical treatises, on rulership, provide a male point of view on legitimate political authority in each empire. Reflecting a different perspective, the other two philosophical discussions (one written by a woman) describe how to bring harmony to the most basic unit of society in both the Han dynasty and the Roman Empire—the household.

In the first excerpt, the second-century BCE Han Chinese scholar Dong Zhongshu integrates a Confucian rationale into the justification for the legitimacy of Han rule. In the second text, Marcus Tullius Cicero, a leading Roman politician from the 60s through the 40s BCE, presents his view on the responsibilities of political officeholders in the Roman state.

While Dong Zhongshu and Cicero were elite men and part of the power structure, writers from other backgrounds offer different ideas of what brings harmony to a community. For instance, in Han China an exceptional woman named Ban Zhao, whose father and brother were court historians writing the *Book of Han*, finalized the text herself following their deaths. Widowed at a young age, Ban Zhao was able to devote her attentions to literary and philosophical pursuits. One of these was her *Lessons for Women*, which is excerpted below. No exact parallel of Ban Zhao's text survives from the Roman Empire. While there are literary fragments, short handwritten notes, and possibly epitaphs (funeral inscriptions) composed by Roman women, we must turn to a male writer for a text that gives a Roman perspective on domestic life comparable to the *Lessons* of Ban Zhao in China. The excerpt included here comes from the philosophical works associated with the first-century CE Stoic philosopher Musonius Rufus.

PRIMARY SOURCE 7.1

Dong Zhongshu on Responsibilities of Han Rulership (2000 BCE)

One who is an enlightened master and worthy ruler believes such things [i.e. that the way to transform the people and administer the state is through reverence for "the foundation" of all living things, namely Heaven, Earth, and humankind]. For this reason he respectfully and carefully attends to the three foundations. He reverently enacts the suburban sacrifice, dutifully serves his ancestors, manifests filial and brotherly love, encourages filial conduct, and serves the foundation of Heaven in this way. He takes up the plough handle to till the soil, plucks the mulberry leaves and nourishes the silkworms, reclaims the wilds, plants grain, opens new lands to provide sufficient food and clothing, and serves the foundation of Earth in this way. He establishes academies and schools in towns and villages to teach filial piety, brotherly love, reverence, and humility, enlightens [the people] with education, moves [them] with rites and music, and serves the foundation of humanity in this way. If these three foundations [Heaven, Earth, and humankind] are all served, the people will resemble sons and brothers who do not dare usurp authority, while the ruler will resemble fathers and mothers.

Source: Dong Zhongshu, "Responsibilities of Han Rulership" from *Sources of Chinese Tradition, Volume 1*, eds. Wm. Theodore de Bary and Irene Bloom © 1999 Columbia University Press.

PRIMARY SOURCE 7.2

The Role of the Roman State (44 BCE), Cicero

That man who undertakes responsibility for public office in the state must make it his first priority to see that every person can continue to hold what is his and that no inroads are made into the goods or property of private persons by the state. It was a bad policy when Philippus, when he was tribune of the plebs [about 104 BCE], proposed an agrarian reform law. When his law was defeated, he took the defeat well and was moderate in his response. In the debates themselves, however, he tried to curry popular favor and acted in a bad way when he said, "In our community there are not more than two thousand men who have real property."

That speech ought to be condemned outright for attempting to advocate equality of property holdings. What policy could be more dangerous? It was for this very reason—that each person should be able to keep his own property—that states and local governments were founded. Although it was by the leadership of nature herself that men gathered together in communities, it was for the hope of keeping their own property that they sought the protection of states. . . .

Some men want to become known as popular politicians and for this reason they engage in making revolutionary proposals about land, with the result that owners are driven from their homes and money lent out by creditors is simply given free to the borrowers with no need for repayment. Such men are shaking the very foundations of the state. First of all, they are destroying that goodwill and sense of trust which can no longer exist when money is simply taken from some people and given to others [by the state]. And then they take away fairness, which is totally destroyed if each person is not permitted to keep what is his own. For, as I have already said, it is the peculiar function of the state and of local government to make sure that each person should be able to keep his own things freely and without any worry.

Source: *De Officiis (On Duties)*, 2.21.73, 22.78; translated by Brent Shaw.

PRIMARY SOURCE 7.3

Lessons for Women (c. 100 CE), Ban Zhao

The Way of husband and wife is intimately connected with *yin* and *yang*, and relates the individual to gods and ancestors. Truly it is the great principle of Heaven and Earth, and the great basis of human relationships. Therefore the *Record of Rites* honors union of man and woman; and in the *Book of Odes* the First Ode manifests the principle of marriage. For these reasons the relationship cannot but be an important one. If a husband be unworthy, then he possesses nothing by which to control his wife. If a wife be unworthy, she possesses nothing with which to serve her husband. If a husband does not control his wife, then the rules of conduct manifesting his authority are abandoned and broken. If a wife does not serve her husband, then the proper relationship (between men and women) and the natural order of things are neglected and destroyed. As a matter of fact the purpose of these two (the controlling of women by men, and the serving of men by women) is the same.

Now examine the gentlemen of the present age. They only know that wives must be controlled, and that a husband's rules of conduct manifesting his authority must be established. They therefore teach their boys to read books and (study) histories. But they do not in the least understand that husbands and masters must (also) be served, and that the proper relationship and the rites should be maintained.

Yet only to teach men and not to teach women—is that not ignoring the essential relation between them? According to the *Record of Rites*, it is the rule to begin to teach children to read at the age of eight years, and by the age of fifteen years they ought then be ready for cultural training. Only why should it not be (that girls' education as well as boys' be) according to this principle?

Source: Translated in Robin Wang, *Images of Women in Chinese Thought and Culture* (Indianapolis: Hackett Publishing, 2003), pp. 180–81.

PRIMARY SOURCE 7.4

On Women in Rome (first century CE), Musonius Rufus

(4) If a man knows something about a particular skill, and a woman doesn't, or if the reverse is true, this shows that there is no difference in their education. Only about all the important things do not let one know and the other not, but let them both know the same. If someone asks me, which doctrine requires such an education, I would answer him that without philosophy no man and no woman either can be well educated. I do not mean to say that women need to have clarity with or facility in argument, because they will use philosophy as women use it. But I do not recommend these skills particularly in men. My point is that women ought to be good and noble in their characters, and that philosophy is nothing other than the training for that nobility.

(13a) [Musonius Rufus] said that a husband and wife come together in order to lead their lives in common and to produce children, and that they should consider all their property to be common, and nothing private, not even their bodies. For the birth of a human being that such a union produces is a significant event, but it is not sufficient for the husband, because it could have come about without marriage, from some other conjunction, as in the case of animals. In marriage there must be complete companionship and concern for each other on the part of both husband and wife, in health and in sickness and at all times, because they entered upon the marriage for this reason as well as to produce offspring. When such caring for one another is perfect, and the married couple provide it for one another, and each strives to outdo the other, then this is marriage as it ought to be and deserving of emulation, since it is a noble union. [12] But when one partner looks to his own interests alone and neglects the others, or (by Zeus) the other is so minded that he lives in the same house, but keeps his mind on what is outside it, and does not wish to pull together with his partner or to cooperate, then inevitably the union is destroyed, and although they live together their common interests fare badly, and either they finally get divorced from one another or they continue on in an existence that is worse than loneliness.

Source: M. Lefkowitz and M. Fant, *Women's Life in Greece and Rome*, 3rd edition (Baltimore: Johns Hopkins, 2005), p. 53–54 (also online at http://www.stoa.org/diotima/anthology/wlgr/wlgr-philosophers.shtml).

QUESTIONS FOR ANALYSIS

1. According to these texts, what are the characteristics of a good ruler? What are the traits of a good husband? A good wife?

2. According to these texts, what brings political and domestic harmony? What brings discord?

3. What, from these texts, suggests that they offer an elite, primarily male, perspective? To what extent do the ideas presented in these texts extend beyond elite men to women, children, and non-elites?

4. What do these texts suggest about the similarities and differences in ideas about political and domestic harmony in Han China and late republican and imperial Rome?

Interpreting Visual Evidence

Images of Power

While their empires were gained and maintained largely through military force, Shi Huangdi and Octavian Augustus also expressed their power through elaborate construction projects. Both men commissioned elaborate mausoleums in which they were buried. Shi Huangdi's massive mausoleum, located in Chang'an (modern-day Xi'an), contained not only the emperor's tomb but also as many as 8,000 life-sized terra-cotta warriors, their horses, and chariots. One ancient Chinese historian reported that the emperor's concubines and the craftsmen who designed the tomb were buried alive with the emperor, though the tomb itself has not been excavated. Augustus's mausoleum was constructed on the Field of Mars just outside the city walls of Rome and was meant to entomb him and his close relatives upon their deaths. While his mausoleum is much more modest than Shi Huangdi's, Augustus's burial site was just one component of his elaborate building program at Rome, which included a forum with its temple to Mars the Avenger, as well as an Altar of Peace, and a massive sundial.

Power and authority could also be conveyed through portraiture. The so-called Prima Porta statue of Augustus, pictured here, depicts him as a triumphant general. The statue's iconography suggests several messages: for example, the breastplate shows his adopted son and heir, Tiberius, receiving back the military standards lost to the Parthians, and the Cupid on a dolphin calls to mind Augustus's divine ancestry reaching back to Venus. While there is no statue or other image from the Qin or Han period showing what Shi Huangdi looked like, the standard picture, dating to a much later period, shows him with an elaborate head-covering, draped in a robe with a dragon on it, and with a sword at his waist.

Shi Huangdi's terra-cotta army in Xi'an.

Emperor Augustus's mausoleum in Rome (top, aerial view; bottom, entrance).

Augustus of Prima Porta.

Portrait of Shi Huangdi.

QUESTIONS FOR ANALYSIS

1. Compare the mausoleums of Shi Huangdi and Augustus. What do you think each ruler was attempting to convey through his burial monument?
2. Looking at the images of these two rulers, what in the representations gives a visual cue of their authority?

Why do you think there are no contemporary images of Shi Huangdi, but so many of Augustus?

3. What do these images of Shi Huangdi and Augustus and their burial monuments suggest about the nature of power in the Roman and Chinese worlds?

Before You Read This Chapter

GLOBAL STORYLINES

- Universalizing religions—notably Christianity and Buddhism—appeal to diverse, widespread populations and challenge the power of secular rulers and thinkers.
- Across Afro-Eurasia, these universalizing religions offer continuity even as powerful empires, specifically the Roman Empire in the west and the Han dynasty in China, fall away.
- Along the Silk Roads, the merchants and rulers of Sasanian Persia, Sogdiana, and South Asia profoundly influence the exchange of goods, people, and ideas between east and west.
- In the "worlds apart," common cultural beliefs help unify newly organized polities in Mesoamerica and new communities of Bantu-speakers in sub-Saharan Africa.

CORE OBJECTIVES

- **DESCRIBE** the characteristics of universalizing religions, and **EXPLAIN** why universalizing religions developed to varying degrees in Afro-Eurasia but did not develop elsewhere in the world.
- **ANALYZE** the relationship between empires and universalizing religions across Afro-Eurasia in this period.
- **ASSESS** the connections between political unity and religious developments in sub-Saharan Africa and Mesoamerica in the fourth to sixth centuries CE.
- **COMPARE** the unifying political and cultural developments in sub-Saharan Africa and Mesoamerica with those that took place across Eurasia in this period.

The Rise of Universal Religions

300–600 CE

A round 180 CE, twelve Christians, seven men and five women, stood trial before the provincial governor at Carthage. Their crime was refusal to worship the gods of the Roman Empire. While the governor argued for the simplicity of his religion with its devotion to "the protecting spirit of our lord the emperor," one Christian retorted that his own lord was "the king of kings and emperor of all nations." This distinction was an unbridgeable gap between the governor and the Christians. The governor condemned them all. "Thanks be to God!" cried the Christians, and straightaway they were beheaded. As the centuries unfolded, the governor's old Roman ideas of the supremacy of an emperor-lord would give way to the martyrs' devotion to their Lord God as emperor over all. As with Christianity's claim of an "emperor of all nations," a religion's capacity for universalizing—particularly its broad appeal across diverse peoples and cultures—became ever more important to its success.

From 300 to 600 CE, the entire Afro-Eurasian landmass experienced a surge of religious activity. In the west, Christianity became the state faith of the Roman Empire. In India, Vedic religion (Brahmanism) evolved into a more formal spiritual system called Hinduism. Buddhism spread across northern India, central Asia, and China.

Around the same time, the peoples living in sub-Saharan Africa reached beyond their local communities, creating common cultures across wider geographical areas. The Bantu-speaking peoples, residing in the southeastern corner of present-day Nigeria, began to spread their way of life throughout the entire southern half of the landmass. Similarly, across the Atlantic Ocean, the Mayans established political and cultural institutions over a large portion of Mesoamerica. Across much of the world, spiritual concerns integrated scattered communities into shared faiths (see Map 8.1).

This integration was facilitated in Afro-Eurasia in part by the spread of what we might call universalizing religions. Two faiths in this era—Christianity and Buddhism—fit the model for this type of religion particularly well. Six main features characterize **universalizing religions**: their appeal to diverse populations (men and women, freeborn and slaves, rich and poor); their adaptability as they moved from one cultural and geographical area to another; their promotion of universal rules and principles to guide behavior that transcended place, time, and specific cultural practices; their proselytizing of new believers by energetic and charismatic missionaries; the deep sense of community felt by their converts despite, and perhaps because of, their many demands on followers; and—in the case of Christianity, though to a lesser extent Buddhism—the support given to them by powerful empires. Even as the Roman Empire and the Han dynasty began to crumble, these universalizing traditions continued to flourish.

Across Afro-Eurasia, universal religions were on the move (see Map 8.2). Religious leaders carrying written texts (books, scrolls, or tablets of wood or palm leaf) traveled widely. Christians from Persia went to China. Buddhists journeyed from South Asia to Afghanistan and used the caravan routes of central Asia to reach China. Voyages, translations, long-distance pilgrimages, and sweeping conversion campaigns remapped the spiritual landscape of the world. New religious leaders were the brokers of more universal but also more intolerant worldviews, premised on a distinct relationship between gods and their subjects. Religions and their brokers profoundly integrated societies. But they also created new ways to drive them apart.

Religious Change and Empire in Western Afro-Eurasia

By the fourth century CE in western Afro-Eurasia, the Roman Empire was hardly the political and military juggernaut it had been 300 years earlier. Surrounded by peoples who coveted its wealth while resisting its power, Rome was fragmenting. So-called barbarians eventually overran the western part of the empire, but in many ways those areas still felt "Roman." Rome's endurance was a boon to the new religious activity that thrived in the turmoil of the immigrations and contracting political authority of the empire. Romans and so-called barbarians alike looked to the new faith of Christianity to maintain continuity with the past, eventually founding a central church in Rome to rule the remnants of empire.

THE APPEAL OF CHRISTIANITY

The spread of new religious ideas, including Christianity, in the Roman Empire changed the way people viewed their existence. Believing implied that an important otherworld

COMPARISON

DESCRIBE the characteristics of universalizing religions.

COMPARISON

ANALYZE the relationship between empires and universalizing religions in the Roman and Sasanian empires, and the Gupta and Wei dynasties.

loomed beyond the world of physical matter. Feeling contact with that other world gave worshippers a sense of worth; it guided them in this life, and they anticipated someday meeting their guides and spiritual friends there. No longer were the gods understood by believers as local powers to be placated by archaic rituals in sacred places. Many gods became omnipresent figures whom mortals could touch through loving attachment. As ordinary mortals now could hope to meet these divine beings in another, happier world, the sense of an afterlife glowed more brightly.

Christians' emphasis on obedience to their Lord God, rather than to a human ruler, sparked a Mediterranean-wide debate on the nature of religion. Christians, like the Jews from whose tradition their sect had sprung, possessed divinely inspired scriptures that told them what to believe and do, even when those actions went against the empire's laws. (See **Analyzing Global Developments: One God, Two Communities**.) Christians spoke of their scriptures as "a divine codex." Bound in a compact volume or set of volumes, this was the definitive code of God's law that outlined proper belief and behavior.

Another central feature of early Christianity was the figure of the **martyr**. Martyrs were women and men whom the Roman authorities executed for persisting in their Christian beliefs instead of submitting to emperor worship, as we saw in this chapter's opening story of the twelve Scillitan martyrs—so-called for the town in North Africa from which they came. While other religions, including Judaism and later Islam, honored martyrs who died for their faith, Christianity claimed to be based directly on "the blood of martyrs," in the words of the North African Christian theologian Tertullian (writing around 200 CE).

The story of Vibia Perpetua, a well-to-do mother in her early twenties, offers a striking example of martyrdom. Refusing to sacrifice to the Roman gods, Perpetua and her maidservant Felicitas, along with their companions, were condemned in 203 CE to face wild beasts in the amphitheater of Carthage, a venue small enough that the condemned and the spectators would have had eye contact with one another throughout the fatal encounter. The prison diary that Perpetua dictated before her death offered to Christians and potential converts a powerful religious message that balanced heavenly visions and rewards with her concerns over responsibility to her father, brother, and infant son. The remembered heroism of women martyrs like Perpetua and Felicitas offset the increasingly all-male leadership—bishops and clergy—of the institutionalized Christian church.

Christian Martyrs This detail from a mosaic found in a Roman circus in North Africa shows a criminal tied to a stake and being pushed on a little cart toward a lunging leopard. Christian martyrs were treated much the same as criminals: they were executed, sometimes thrown to wild animals. How might the treatment of martyrs like criminals have influenced those watching such "entertainment"?

Constantine: From Conversion to Creed Crucial in spurring Christianity's spread was the transformative experience of Constantine (c. 280–337 CE). Born near the Danubian frontier, he belonged to a class of professional soldiers whose careers took them far from the Mediterranean. Constantine's troops proclaimed him emperor after the death of his father, the emperor Constantius. In the civil war that followed, Constantine looked for signs from the gods. Before the decisive battle for Rome, which took place at a strategic bridge in 312 CE, he supposedly had a dream in which he saw an emblem bearing the words "In this sign

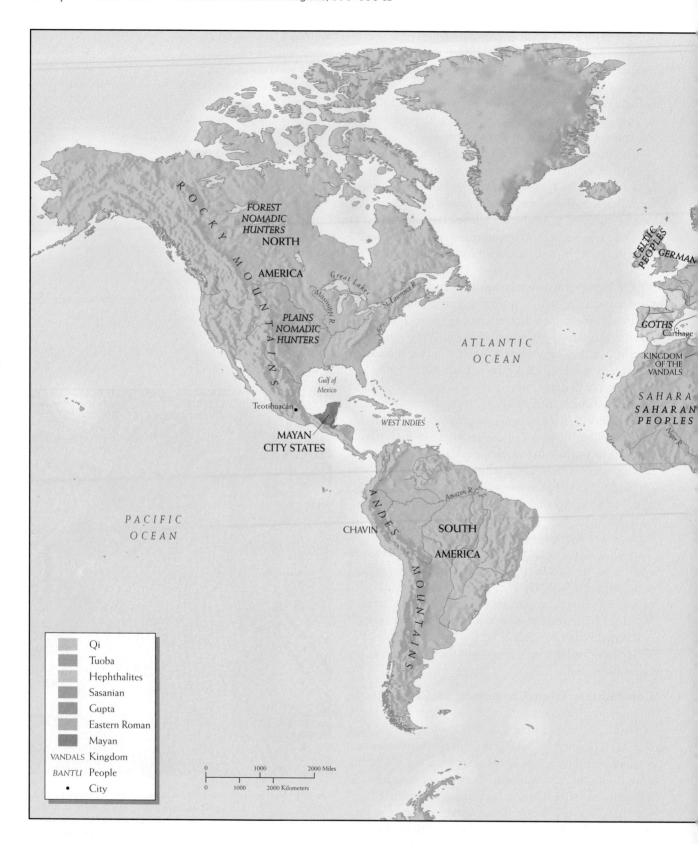

FOREST
NOMADIC
HUNTERS
NORTH

AMERICA

Great Lakes

Mississippi R.

St. Lawrence R.

R O C K Y   M O U N T A I N S

PLAINS
NOMADIC
HUNTERS

ATLANTIC
OCEAN

*Gulf of
Mexico*

Teotihuacán

WEST INDIES

MAYAN
CITY STATES

CELTIC
PEOPLES

GERMAN

GOTHS   Carthage

KINGDOM
OF THE
VANDALS

S A H A R A
SAHARAN
PEOPLES

Niger R.

PACIFIC
OCEAN

Amazon R.

CHAVIN   SOUTH

AMERICA

A N D E S   M O U N T A I N S

	Qi
	Tuoba
	Hephthalites
	Sasanian
	Gupta
	Eastern Roman
	Mayan
VANDALS	Kingdom
BANTU	People
•	City

0   1000   2000 Miles

0   1000   2000 Kilometers

The following labels appear on the map:

ARCTIC OCEAN

FINNO-UGRIANS

TURKIC

OPLES
GOTHS
Rome
BLACK SEA
Constantinople
ARAL
SEA
EMPIRE OF THE
HEPHTHALITES
TAKLAMAKAN
DESERT
GOBI DESERT
SEA
OF
JAPAN
EASTERN ROMAN
EMPIRE
CASPIAN SEA
Merv
Bactra
Taxila
HIMALAYA MTS.
TUOBA
EMPIRE
Luoyang
Changan
YELLOW
SEA
MEDITERRANEAN
SEA
Jerusalem
Tigris R.
PERSIAN
SASANIAN
EMPIRE
Indus R.
Euphrates R.
Ctesiphon
Persian Gulf
GUPTA
EMPIRE
Ganges R.
Yangzi R.
QI
EMPIRE
DESERT
ARABS
RED SEA
ARABIAN
SEA
Mekong R.
SOUTH
CHINA
SEA
PACIFIC
OCEAN
Lake
Chad
Nile R.
BANTUS
Congo R.
Lake
Victoria
Lake
Tanganyika
INDIAN
OCEAN
KALAHARI
DESERT
AUSTRALIAN ABORIGINES

MAP 8.1 | Empires and Universalizing Religions from 300 to 600 CE

The period from 300 to 600 CE was a time of tumultuous political change accompanied by the spread of adaptable and accessible universalizing faiths.

- Comparing this map with those in Chapters 6 and 7, which polities are new? Which polities have disappeared? Which ones have expanded or contracted?
- Where on the map are the world's empires located? How are peoples organized outside those empires?
- Looking at Map 8.2, what seems to be the relationship between these empires and religions or philosophies such as Christianity, Buddhism, Judaism, Hinduism, and Confucianism?

conquer." The "sign," which he then placed on his soldiers' shields, was the first two letters of the Greek *christos*, a title for Jesus meaning "anointed one." Constantine's troops won the ensuing battle and, thereafter, Constantine's visionary sign became known all over the Roman world. Constantine showered imperial favor on this once-persecuted faith, issuing an edict praising the work of Christian bishops and granting them significant tax exemptions.

By the time that Constantine embraced Christianity, it had already made considerable progress within the Roman Empire. It had prevailed in the face of stiff competition and periodically intense persecution from the imperial authorities. Apart from the new imperial endorsement, Christianity's success could be attributed to the sacred aura surrounding its authoritative texts, the charisma of its holy men and women, the fit that existed between its doctrines and popular preexisting religious beliefs and practices, and its broad, universalizing appeal to rich and poor, city dwellers and peasants, slaves and free people, young and old, and men and women.

In 325 CE, hoping to bring unity to the diversity of belief within Christian communities, Constantine summoned all bishops to Nicaea (modern Iznik in western Turkey) for a council to develop a statement of belief, or **creed** (from the Latin *credo,* "I believe"). The resulting Nicene Creed balanced three separate divine entities—God "the father," "the son," and "the holy spirit"—as facets of one supreme being. Also at Nicaea the bishops agreed to hold Easter, the day on which Christians celebrate Christ's resurrection, on the same day in every church of the Christian world. Writing near the end of Constantine's reign, an elderly bishop in Palestine named Eusebius noted that the Roman Empire of his day would have surprised the martyrs of Carthage, who had willingly died rather than recognize any "empire of this world."

Christianity in the Cities and Beyond After 312 CE, the large churches built in every major city, many with imperial funding, signaled Christianity's growing strength. These gigantic meeting halls were called basilicas, from the Greek word *basileus*, meaning king. They were modeled on Roman law-court buildings and could accommodate over a thousand worshippers. Inside a basilica's vast space, oil lamps shimmered on marble and brought mosaics to life. Rich silk hangings, swaying between rows of columns, increased the sense of mystery and directed the eye to the far end of the building—a splendidly furnished semicircular apse. Under the dome of the apse, which represented the dome of heaven, and surrounded by priests, the bishop sat and preached from his special throne, or *cathedra*.

These basilicas became the new urban public forums, ringed with spacious courtyards where the city's poor would gather. In return for the tax exemptions that Constantine had granted them, bishops cared for the metropolitan poor. Bishops also became judges, as Constantine turned their arbitration process for disputes between Christians into a kind of small claims court. Offering the poor shelter, quick justice, and moments of unearthly splendor in grand basilicas, Christian bishops perpetuated "Rome" for centuries after the empire had disappeared.

The spread of Christianity outside the cities and into the hinterlands of Africa and Southwest Asia required the

Basilica Interior The interior of a basilica was dominated by rows of ancient marble columns and was filled with light from upper windows, so that the eye was led directly to the apse of the church, where the bishop and clergy would sit under a dome, close to the altar.

MAP 8.2 | The Spread of Universal Religions in Afro-Eurasia, 300–600 CE

The spread of universal religions and the shifting political landscape were intimately connected.

- Where did Hinduism, Buddhism, and Christianity emerge, and where did they spread?
- Along what routes did each religion spread?
- How did the rise and fall of empires affect the expansion of universal religions?

breaking of language barriers. In Egypt, Christian clergy replaced hieroglyphics with Coptic, a more accessible script based on Greek letters, in an effort to bridge the linguistic and cultural gap between town and countryside. In the crucial corridor that joined Antioch to Mesopotamia, Syriac, an offshoot of the Semitic language Aramaic, became a major Christian language. As Christianity spread farther north, to Georgia in the Caucasus and to Armenia, Christian clergy created written languages that are still used in those regions.

Analyzing Global Developments

One God, Two Communities: Comparing the Structures of Christianity and Judaism, 600 CE

Christianity emerged from Judaism in the first and second centuries ce and continues to share the same God and many of the same scriptures to this very day. Yet, despite these fundamental commonalities, what arose were two distinct religious communities, each with its own notions of God in relation to humanity. The following diagrams illustrate the major impact that Christian and Jewish understandings of the same God had upon the structures of their early religious institutions and their ability to grow and become universalizing.

Looking at the diagram, Judaism's institutional structure is flatter and simpler, and Christianity's is more hierarchical. One would think the more direct connection to God found in Judaism, with rabbis being the primary teachers of the Torah and overseeing most of the responsibilities at the synagogue, would make it more appealing and universalizing than Christianity, with its church's hierarchical structure composed of bishops, priests, monks, and nuns—but this was not the case.

QUESTIONS FOR ANALYSIS

- Based on your reading in the text, what factors more generally made religions like Christianity and Buddhism more appealing and universalizing than Judaism and Hinduism?

- The diagram suggests that the people of Israel had a direct connection to God. What does the diagram suggest about the relationship of Christians to the same God? Why is this relationship important in understanding the structures of the two religions and their universalizing appeal?

- Martyrs, like Perpetua (discussed in the chapter), played a big role in both Christianity and Judaism (e.g., rabbis resisting Rome c. 100 CE). Where would you place martyrs on this diagram, and why? What role might martyrdom have played in the universalizing appeal of Christianity as opposed to Judaism?

- Based on your reading, what were the origins of the hierarchical structure of Christianity, and why would it actually aid in the growth of the religion?

THE "FALL" OF ROME IN THE WEST

By the third and fourth centuries CE, the political and economic fabric of the old Roman world was unraveling (see Map 8.3). The so-called barbarian invasions of the late fourth and fifth centuries CE further contributed to that demise. These "invasions" were less an assault, and more a violent and chaotic immigration of young fighting men from the

MAP 8.3 | Western Afro-Eurasia: War, Immigration, and Settlement in the Roman World, 375–450 CE

Invasions and migrations brought about the reconstitution of the Roman Empire at this time.

• Using the map, identify the people who migrated to or invaded the Roman Empire. Where were they from, and where did they go?

• How did these migrations and invasions reshape the political landscape of western Afro-Eurasia?

• Considering these effects, to what extent was the Roman depiction of these groups as "barbarians" a fair assessment?

frontiers of the empire. Today the term *barbarian* implies uncultivated or savage, but its meaning in antiquity was "foreigner" (with overtones of inferiority). Inhabitants of the empire's western provinces had become accustomed to non-Roman soldiers from across the frontiers, and for them *barbarian* was synonymous with "soldier." The popular image of bloodthirsty barbarian hordes streaming into the empire bears little resemblance to reality.

The Goths It was the Romans' need for soldiers that drew the barbarians in. The process reached a crisis point when tribes of Goths petitioned the emperor Valens (r. 365–378 CE) to let them immigrate into the empire. These Goths were no strangers to Roman influence: in fact, many had been evangelized into an anti-Nicene version of Christianity by the

Gothic bishop Ulfilas, who had even translated the Bible into the Gothic language using an alphabet he developed for that purpose.

Valens, desperate for manpower, encouraged the Goths' entrance into Roman territory but mistreated these new immigrants. A lethal combination of famine and anger at the breakdown of supplies—not innate bloodlust—turned the Goths against Valens. When he marched against them at Adrianople in the hot August of 378 CE, Valens was not seeking to halt a barbarian invasion but rather intending to teach a lesson in obedience to his new recruits. The Gothic cavalry, however, proved too much for Valens's imperial army, and the Romans were trampled to death by the men and horses they had hoped to hire. As the pattern of disgruntled "barbarian" immigrants, civil war, and overextension continued, the Roman Empire in western Europe crumbled.

Rome's maintenance of its northern borders required constant efforts and high taxes. But after 400 CE the western emperors could no longer raise enough taxes to maintain control of the provinces. In 418 CE, the Goths settled in southwest Gaul as a kind of local militia to fill the absence left by the contracting Roman authority. Ruled by their own king, who kept his military in order, the Goths suppressed alarmingly frequent peasant revolts. Roman landowners of Gaul and elsewhere anxiously allied themselves with the new military leaders rather than face social revolution and the raids of even more dangerous armies. Although they practiced a different, "heretical" version of Christianity, the Goths came as Christian allies of the aristocracy, not as godless enemies of Rome.

The Huns Romans and non-Romans also drew together to face a common enemy: the Huns. Led by their king Attila (406–453 CE) for twenty years, the Huns threatened both Romans and Germanic peoples (like the Goths). While the Romans could hide behind their walls, the Hunnish cavalry regularly plundered the scattered villages and open fields in the plains north of the Danube.

Attila intended to be a "real" emperor of a warrior-aristocracy. Having seized (perhaps from the Chinese empire) the notion of a "mandate of heaven"—in his case, a divine right to rule the tribes of the north—he fashioned the first opposing empire that Rome ever had to face in northern Europe. Rather than selling his people's services to Rome, Attila extracted thousands of pounds of gold coins in tribute from the Roman emperors who hoped to stave off assaults by his brutal forces. Drained both militarily and economically by this Hunnish threat, the Roman Empire in the west disintegrated only twenty years after Attila's death. In 476 CE, the last Roman emperor of the west, a young boy named Romulus Augustulus (namesake of both Rome's legendary founder and its first emperor), resigned to make way for a so-called barbarian king in Italy.

The political unity of the Roman Empire in the west now gave way to a sense of unity through the church. The Catholic Church (*Catholic* meaning "universal," centered in the bishops' authority) became the one institution to which all Christians in western Europe, Romans and non-Romans alike, felt that they belonged. The bishop of Rome became the symbolic head of the western churches. Rome became a spiritual capital instead of an imperial one. By 700 CE, the great Roman landowning families of the Republic and early empire had vanished, replaced by religious leaders with vast moral authority.

CONTINUITY OF ROME IN THE EAST: BYZANTIUM

Elsewhere the Roman Empire was alive and well. From the borders of Greece to the borders of modern Iraq, and from the Danube River to Egypt and the borders of Saudi Arabia, the empire survived undamaged. The new Roman Empire of the east—to which historians gave the name **Byzantium**—had its own New Rome, Constantinople. Founded in 324 CE by its namesake Constantine, on the Bosporus straits separating Europe from Asia, this strategically located city was well situated to receive taxes in gold and to control the sea-lanes of the eastern Mediterranean.

Constantinople was one of the most spectacularly successful cities in Afro-Eurasia, soon boasting a population of over half a million and 4,000 new palaces. Every year, more than 20,000 tons of grain arrived from Egypt, unloaded on a dockside over a mile long. A gigantic hippodrome echoing Rome's Circus Maximus straddled the city's central ridge, flanking an imperial palace whose opulent enclosed spaces stretched down to the busy shore. As they had for centuries before in Rome, emperors would sit in the imperial box, witnessing chariot races as rival teams careened around the stadium. The hippodrome also featured displays of eastern imperial might, as ambassadors came from as far away as central Asia, northern India, and Nubia.

Similarly, the future emperor Justinian came to Constantinople as a young man from an obscure Balkan village, to seek his fortune. When he became emperor in 527 CE, he considered himself the successor of a long line of forceful Roman emperors—and he was determined to outdo them. Most importantly, Justinian reformed the Roman laws. Within six years a commission of lawyers had created the *Digest,* a massive condensation and organization of the preexisting body of Roman law. Its companion volume was the *Institutes,* a teacher's manual for schools of Roman law. These works were the foundation of what later ages came to know as "Roman law," followed in both eastern and western Europe for more than a millennium.

Reflecting the marriage of Christianity with empire was the church of the Hagia Sophia, grandly rebuilt by Justinian on the site of two earlier basilicas. The basilica of Saint Peter in Rome, the largest church built by Constantine two centuries earlier, would have reached only as high as the lower galleries of Hagia Sophia. Walls of multicolored marble, gigantic columns of green and purple granite, audaciously curved semicircular niches placed at every corner, and a spectacular dome lined with gleaming gold mosaics inspired awe in those who entered its doors. Hagia Sophia represented the flowing together of Christianity and imperial culture that for another 1,000 years would mark the eastern Roman Empire centered in Constantinople.

Contacts between east and west, as well as internal discord, intensified during Justinian's reign. Not only did Justinian quell riots at the heart of Byzantium, he also undertook wars to reclaim parts of the western Mediterranean and to hold off the threat from Sasanian Persia in the east (see next section). Perhaps the most grisly reminder of this increased connectivity was a sudden onslaught in 541–542 CE of the bubonic plague from the east. One-third of the population of Constantinople died within weeks. Justinian himself survived, but thereafter he ruled

Hagia Sophia The domed ceiling of Justinian's Hagia Sophia soared high above worshippers. Intricate mosaics decorated many of the walls and ceilings. The mosaic adorning the eastern apse, shown here, depicts Jesus sitting in the lap of the Virgin Mary.

an empire whose heartland was decimated. Nonetheless, Justinian's contributions—to the law, to Christianity, to the maintenance of imperial order—helped Byzantium last almost for nearly a millennium after Rome in the west had fallen away.

The Silk Roads

Although exchange along the Silk Roads had been taking place for centuries (see Chapter 6), the sharing of knowledge between the Mediterranean world and China began in earnest

MAP 8.4 | Exchanges Across Afro-Eurasia, 300–600 CE

Southwest Asia remained the crossroads of Afro-Eurasia in a variety of ways. Trade goods flowing between west and east passed through this region, as did universal religions. The question mark in eastern Africa indicates scholars' uncertainty about the origination of the plague.

- Using your finger, trace the principal trade routes and maritime routes. What were the areas of major religious influence? What was the relationship between trade routes and the areas of major religious influence?
- Then point out each area of religious influence. How did religious geography correspond to political geography?
- How was Southwest Asia affected by other regions, such as sub-Saharan Africa and central Asia, and how did it shape developments in these regions?

during this period. Wending their way across the difficult terrains of central Asia, a steady parade of merchants, scholars, ambassadors, missionaries, and other travelers transmitted commodities, technologies, and ideas between the Mediterranean worlds and China, and across the Himalayas into northern India, exploiting the commercial routes of the Silk Roads. Ideas, including the beliefs of the universalizing religions described in this chapter, traveled along with goods on these exchange routes. Christianity spread through the Mediterranean and beyond and, as we shall see later in this chapter, Buddhism and the Vedic religion (Brahmanism) also continued to spread.

The great oasis cities of central Asia played a crucial role in the effective functioning of the Silk Roads. While the Sasanians controlled the city of Merv in the west, nomadic rulers became the overlords of Sogdiana and Tukharistan and extracted tribute from the cities of Samarkand and Panjikent in the east. The tribal confederacies in this region maintained the links between west and east by patrolling the Silk Road between Iran and China. They also joined north to south as they passed through the mountains of Afghanistan into the plains of northern India. As a result, central Asia between 300 and 600 CE was the hub of a vibrant system of religious and cultural contacts covering the whole of Afro-Eurasia (see Map 8.4).

SASANIAN PERSIA

Beginning at the Euphrates River and stretching for eighty days of slow travel across the modern territories of Iraq, Iran, Afghanistan, and much of central Asia, the Sasanian Empire of Persia encompassed all the land routes of western Asia that connected the Mediterranean world with East Asia. In the early third century CE, the Sasanians had replaced the Parthians as rulers of the Iranian plateau and Mesopotamia. The Sasanian ruler called himself the "King of Kings of Iranian and non-Iranian lands," a title suggestive of the Sasanians' aspirations to universalism. The ancient, irrigated fields of what is modern Iraq became the economic heart of this empire. Its capital, Ctesiphon, arose where the Tigris and the Euphrates rivers come close, only twenty miles south of modern Baghdad.

Symbolizing the king's presence at Ctesiphon was the 110-foot-high vaulted Great Arch of Khusro, named after Justinian's rival, Khusro I Anoshirwan (Khusro of the Righteous Soul). As his name implied, Khusro Anoshirwan (r. 531–579 CE) exemplified the model ruler: strong and just. His image in the east as an ideal monarch was as glorious as that of Justinian in the west as an ideal Christian Roman emperor. For both Persians and Arab Muslims of later ages, the Arch of Khusro was as awe-inspiring as Justinian's Hagia Sophia was to Christians. (See **Current Trends in World History: Religious Conflict in Imperial Borderlands**.)

The Sasanian Empire controlled the trade crossroads of Afro-Eurasia and posed a military threat to Byzantium. Their Iranian armored cavalry was a fighting machine adapted from years of competition with the nomads of central Asia. These fearless horsemen fought covered from head to foot in flexible armor (small plates of iron sewn onto leather) and chain mail, riding "blood-sweating horses" draped in thickly padded cloth. Their lethal swords were light and flexible owing to steel-making techniques imported from northern India. With such cavalry, Khusro in 540 CE sacked Antioch, a city of great significance to early Christianity. The campaign was a warning, at the height of Justinian's glory, that Mesopotamia could reach out once again to conquer the eastern Mediterranean shoreline. Under Khusro II the confrontation between Persia and Rome escalated into the greatest war that had been seen for centuries. Between 604 and 628 CE, Persian forces under Khusro II conquered Egypt and Syria and even reached Constantinople before being defeated in northern Mesopotamia.

Politically united by Sasanian control, Southwest Asia also possessed a cultural unity. Syriac was the dominant language. While the Sasanians themselves were devout Zoroastrians (see Chapter 4), Christianity and Judaism enjoyed tolerance in Mesopotamia. Nestorian Christians—so named by their opponents for their acceptance of a hotly contested understanding of Jesus's divine and human nature, promoted by a former bishop of Constantinople named Nestorius—exploited Sasanian trade and diplomacy to spread their faith as far as Chang'an in China and the western coast of southern India. Protected by the Sasanian King of Kings, the Jewish rabbis of Mesopotamia compiled the monumental Babylonian Talmud at a time when their western peers, in Roman Palestine, were feeling cramped under the Christian state. The Sasanian court also embraced offerings from northern India, including the *Pancantantra* stories (moral tales played out in a legendary kingdom of the animals), polo, and the game of chess. In this regard Khusro's was truly an empire of crossroads, where the cultures of central Asia and India met that of the eastern Mediterranean.

THE SOGDIANS AS LORDS OF THE SILK ROADS

The Sogdians, who controlled the oasis cities of Samarkand and Panjikent, served as human links between the two ends of Afro-Eurasia. Their religion was a blend of Zoroastrian

Current Trends in World History

Religious Conflict in Imperial Borderlands

World historians often study borderland areas because it is in these zones that they can see most clearly the effects of cultural interaction. One example is the borderlands of the Sasanian Empire, which through the Persian Gulf reached out to control the trade on the Indian Ocean. This effort brought Persians into conflict with Roman merchants, who strove to reach India from the Red Sea. As a result, the entire region bounded by present-day Ethiopia (at the western end of the Red Sea), Yemen (in southern Arabia), and the Persian Gulf became a field of conflict between the Roman and Sasanian empires.

Their clash took religious as well as commercial and political form. Both Axum (modern-day Ethiopia) and Himyar (modern-day Yemen) had embraced monotheism, expressed in the worship of a Most High God known as al-Rahmānān (the Merciful One). In Axum, this monotheism was Christian: Christ was the protector of its kings, and the Cross of Christ was their talisman in battle. In contrast, the leaders of Himyar and the southern coast of Arabia were Jewish, and they dismissed Jesus as a crucified sorcerer.

The kings of Axum occupied the African side of the southern end of the Red Sea, looking down from the foothills of the well-watered and populous mountains of Ethiopia. Their formidable warrior-kingdom stretched as far as the Nile to the northwest, south into equatorial Africa, and eastward across the Red Sea to southern Arabia and Yemen. Axum's rulers, who became Christian around 340 CE, celebrated their victories on gigantic granite obelisks; they were monuments to a God that was very much a god of battles. Faced by the aggressive Christian kingdom of Axum, the Sasanians reached out to support the kings of Himyar, who since 380 CE had been Jewish. Thus, two monotheisms faced each other across the narrow southern opening of the Red Sea. Each was associated with a rich and aggressive kingdom. Each was backed by a great power—Axum by Christian Rome and Himyar by the Persians.

---

and Mesopotamian beliefs, touched with Brahmanic influences. Their language was the common tongue of the early Silk Roads, and their shaggy camels bore the commodities that passed through their entrepôts (transshipment centers). Moreover, their splendid mansions (excavated at Panjikent) show strong influences from the warrior-aristocracy culture of Iran. The palace walls display gripping frescoes of armored riders, reflecting the revolutionary change to cavalry warfare from Rome to China. The Sogdians were known as merchants as far away as China.

Through the Sogdians, products from western Asia and North Africa found their way to the eastern end of the landmass. Carefully packed for the long trek on jostling camel caravans, Persian and Roman goods rode side by side. Along with Sasanian silver coins and gold pieces minted in Constantinople, these exotic products found eager buyers as far east as China and Japan.

BUDDHISM ON THE SILK ROADS

South of the Hindu Kush Mountains, in northern India, nomadic groups made the roads into central Asia safe to travel, enabling Buddhism to spread northward and eastward via the mountainous corridor of Afghanistan into China. Buddhist monks were the primary missionary agents, the bearers of a universal message who traveled across the roads of central Asia, carrying holy books, offering salvation to commoners, and establishing themselves more securely in host communities than did armies, diplomats, or merchants.

At Bamiyan, a valley of the Hindu Kush—two gigantic statues of the Buddha, 121 and 180 feet in height, were carved from a cliffside during the fourth and fifth centuries CE (and stood there for 1,500 years until dynamited by the Taliban in 2001). Travelers found

Between 522 and 530 CE, a Jewish king of Himyar popularly known as Dhu Nuwas (the Man with the Forelock) drove the Ethiopian Christian garrisons out of southern Arabia. He turned churches into synagogues (just as, in the Christian empire far to the north, many synagogues had been turned into churches). In 523 CE, the Christians of the oasis city of Najran were ordered to become Jewish. Those who refused to do so Dhu Nuwas burned on pyres of brushwood piled into a deep trench.

Swept by these rivalries, the Arabian Peninsula was no longer a world apart, shut off from "civilization" by its cruel deserts and by its inhabitants' nomadic lifestyle. Far from it—Arabia had become a giant soundboard that amplified claims about the pros and cons of Judaism and Christianity, argued over with unusual intensity for an entire century. The "nonaligned" Arabs of the intermediate regions (between southern Arabia and Mesopotamia) still worshipped their ancestral tribal gods. But they had heard much, of late, about Jews and Christians, Romans and Persians. Arab tribes around Yathrib (modern Medina) adopted Judaism and remained in touch with the rabbis of Galilee along the caravan routes of northern Arabia. Here was a new kind of borderland between empires and between religions. In fact, it would be from this borderland that a new religion and a new prophet would emerge. His name was Muhammad.

QUESTIONS FOR ANALYSIS

- How did the geographical features of the Arabian Peninsula shape its religious development?
- What about borderlands makes them useful locations of analysis for world historians?

Explore Further

Fowden, Garth, *Empire to Commonwealth: The Consequences of Monotheism in Late Antiquity* (1993).

Yarshater, Ehsan, *Encyclopedia Iranica* (1982).

 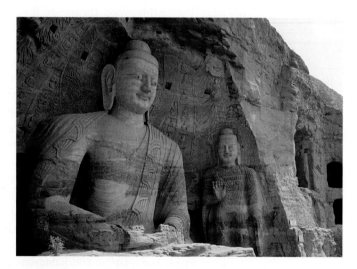

Bamiyan and Yungang Buddhas Compare the Buddhas at Bamiyan and Yungang. Note the Gandharan dress and standing pose of the Bamiyan Buddha, whose majesty and ornamentation the pilgrim Xuanzang described in the mid-seventh century CE. The Buddha in Yungang, one of five created under the emperors of the Northern Wei, sits at the foothills of the Great Wall, marking the eastern destination of the central Asian Silk Roads.

welcoming cave monasteries here and at oases all along the way from the Taklamakan Desert to northern China where—2,500 miles from Bamiyan—travelers also encountered five huge Buddhas carved from cliffs in Yungang, China. (See Interpreting Visual Evidence: Representations of Holiness.) While those at Bamiyan stood tall with royal majesty, the Buddhas of Yungang sat in postures of meditation. In the cliff face and clustered around the feet of the Bamiyan Buddhas various elaborately carved cave chapels housed intricate paintings with Buddhist imagery. Surrounding the Yungang Buddhas, over fifty caves sheltered more than 50,000 statues representing Buddhist deities and patrons. The Yungang Buddhas, seated just inside the Great Wall, welcomed travelers to the market in China and marked the eastern end of the central Asian Silk Road (see Map 8.5). The Bamiyan and Yungang Buddhas are a reminder that by the fourth century CE religious ideas were creating world empires of the mind, transcending kingdoms of this world and bringing a universal message contained in their holy scriptures.

Political and Religious Change in South Asia

COMPARISON

ANALYZE the relationship between empires and universalizing religions in South Asia and China.

South Asia, especially the area of modern India, enjoyed a surge of religious enthusiasm during the Gupta dynasty, the largest political entity in South Asia from the early fourth to the mid-sixth century CE. Its kings facilitated commercial and cultural exchange, much as the Roman Empire had done in the west. Chandragupta (r. c. 320–335 CE, not to be confused with Chandragupta Maurya from Chapter 6), calling himself "King of Kings, Great King," and his son expanded Gupta territory to the entire northern Indian plain and made a long expedition to southern India. The development of Hinduism out of the *varna*-bound Vedic Brahmanic religion and the continued spread of Buddhism helped unify a diverse region and the diverse peoples who lived there.

THE HINDU TRANSFORMATION

During this period, the ancient Brahmanic Vedic religion spread widely in South Asia. Because Buddhism and Jainism had many devotees in cities and commercial communities (see Chapter 5), conservative Brahmans turned their attention to rural India and brought their religion into accord with rural life and agrarian values. This refashioned Brahmanic religion emerged as the dominant faith in Indian society in the form of what we today call **Hinduism**.

In the religion's new, more accessible form, believers became vegetarians, abandoning the animal sacrifices that had been important to their earlier rituals. Their new rituals were linked to self-sacrifice—denying themselves meat rather than offering up slaughtered animals to the gods, as they had done previously. Three major deities—Brahma, Vishnu, and Shiva—formed a trinity representing the three phases of the universe—birth, existence, and destruction, respectively—and the three expressions of the eternal self, or *atma*. Vishnu was the most popular of the three and was thought by believers to reveal himself through various avatars (or incarnations).

Poets during the reign of Chandragupta, a generous patron of the arts, expressed the religious sentiments of the age. Working with the motifs and episodes from two early epics, *Mahabharata* and *Ramayana* (see Chapter 4), these poets addressed new problems and praised new virtues. What had once been lyric dramas and narrative poems written to provide entertainment now served as collective memories of the past and underscored Brahmanic religious beliefs about ideal behavior. The heroes and deeds that the poets praised in classical Sanskrit served as models for kings and their subjects.

A central part of the *Mahabharata* revolves around the final battle between two warring confederations of Vedic tribes. The hero Arjuna, the best warrior of one of these confederations, is unwilling to fight against his enemies because many of them are his cousins. At a crucial moment on the battlefield, Krishna—an avatar of Vishnu, who was Arjuna's charioteer and religious teacher—intervenes, commanding Arjuna to slay his

MAP 8.5 | Buddhist Landscapes, 300–600 CE

Buddhism spread from its heartland in northern India to central and East Asia at this time.

- Using your finger, trace the red lines of trade routes and then the red arrows showing the spread of Buddhism.
- According to the map, what role did increasingly extensive trade routes play in pushing this movement?
- What was the relationship among Buddhist centers and rock-carved temples, trade routes, and the spread of this universal faith?
- How did the travels of Xuanzang symbolize growing connections between East and South Asia?

foes, even those related to him. Krishna reminds Arjuna that he belongs to the Kshatriya *varna*, the warriors put on earth to govern and to fight against the community's enemies. The *Bhagavad Gita*, which preserves this tale of Krishna and Arjuna, became part of the authoritative literature of Hindu spirituality. It prescribed religious and ethical teachings and behaviors, called *dharma* in Hinduism, for people at every level of society.

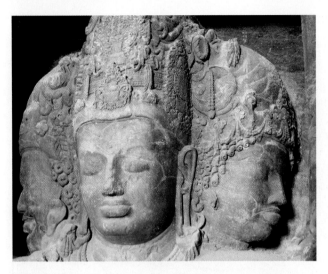

Hindu Statue This huge statue of a three-headed god in a cave on a small island near Mumbai (Bombay) represents the theology of Hinduism. Brahma, the creator; Vishnu, the keeper; and Shiva, the destroyer are all from one *atma,* or the single soul of the universe.

Hindus also adopted the deities of other religions, even regarding the Buddha as an avatar of Vishnu. Thus the Hindu world of gods became larger and more accessible than the earlier Vedic one, enabling more believers to share a single faith. Hindus did not wish to approach the gods only through the sacrificial rituals at which Brahmans alone could officiate. Individuals, therefore, also developed an active relationship with particular gods through personal devotion, in a practice called *bhakti*. This individualized, personal *bhakti* devotion attracted Hindus of all social strata, while the mythological literature wove the deities into a heavenly order presided over by the trinity of Brahma, Vishnu, and Shiva as universal gods. During this period Hinduism lived side by side with Buddhism, competing for followers by building ornate temples and sculptures of gods and by holding elaborate rituals and festivals.

While the stories of human-divine interaction, the larger number of gods, and the development of *bhakti* devotion made Hinduism more personal than the old Vedic Brahmanism had been, Hinduism was still very much rooted in the hierarchical *varna* system. While Hinduism was more accessible to a wider audience than Brahmanism had been, there were limits to how universalizing this tradition could be since the *varna* system, with which it was closely intertwined, did not extend outside South Asia.

THE TRANSFORMATION OF THE BUDDHA

During the Gupta period, the two main schools of Buddhism—the Mahayana (Greater Vehicle) school and the Hinayana (Lesser Vehicle) school—acquired universalizing features that were different from what the Buddha had preached centuries earlier. The historical Buddha was a sage who was believed to enter *nirvana*, ending the pain of consciousness. In the earliest Buddhist doctrine, god and supernatural powers were not a factor (see Chapter 5). But by 200 CE a crucial transformation had occurred: his followers started to view the Buddha as a god. Mahayana Buddhism not only recognized Buddha as a god, but extended worship to the many bodhisattvas who bridged the gulf between the Buddha's perfection and the world's sadly imperfect peoples (see Chapter 6). It was especially in the Mahayana school that Buddhism became a universal religion, whose adherents worshipped divinities, namely the Buddha and the bodhisattvas, rather than recognizing them merely as great men.

Some Buddhists fully accepted the Buddha as god but could not accept the divinity of bodhisattvas; these adherents belonged to the more monkish school of old-fashioned **Hinayana Buddhism**, later called Theraveda in Ceylon and Southeast Asia. Rejecting Sanskrit authoritative scripture on the supernatural power of bodhisattvas, they remained loyal to the early Buddhist texts, which were probably based on the words of the Buddha himself. Hinayana temples barred all colorful idols of the bodhisattvas and other heavenly beings; they only contained images of the Buddha. Buddhism, with its vibrant competing Mahayana and Hinayana schools, spread along the Silk Roads far beyond its South Asian point of origin.

CULTURE AND IDEOLOGY INSTEAD OF AN EMPIRE

Unlike China and Rome, India did not have a centralized empire that could establish a code of laws and an overarching administration. Instead, what emerged to unify South Asia was a distinctive form of cultural synthesis—called by scholars the **Sanskrit cosmopolis**—based on Hindu spiritual beliefs and articulated in the Sanskrit language.

Spearheading this development from 300 to 1300 CE were priests and intellectuals well versed in the Sanskrit language and literary and religious texts. As Sanskrit spread, it stepped beyond religious scriptures and became the public language of politics, although local languages retained their prominence in day-to-day administration and everyday life. Kings and emperors used Sanskrit to express the ideals of royal power and responsibility. Rulers issued inscriptions in it, recording their genealogies and their prestigious acts. Poets celebrated ruling dynasties and recorded important moments in the language.

The emergence of Sanskrit as the common language of the elites in South and Southeast Asian societies also facilitated the spread of Brahmanism. Possessing an unparalleled knowledge of the language, Brahmans circulated their ideals on morality and society in Sanskritic texts, the most influential of which was the **Code of Manu**. This document records a discourse given by the sage, Manu, to a gathering of wise men seeking answers on how to organize their communities after the destruction wrought by a series of floods. The text lays out a set of laws designed to address the problems of assimilating strangers into expanding towns and refining the hierarchical Brahmanic order as the agricultural frontier expanded. Above all, the laws of Manu offered guidance for living within the *varna* and *jati* system, including whom to marry, which profession to follow, and even what to eat. The laws of Manu provided mechanisms for absorbing new groups into the system of *varnas* and *jatis*, thus propelling Hinduism into every aspect of life, far beyond the boundaries of imperial control.

During this period, settlers from northern India pushed southward into lands formerly outside the domain of the Brahmans. In these territories Brahmans encountered Buddhists and competed with them to win followers. The mixing of these two groups and the intertwining of their ideas and institutions ultimately created a common "Indic" culture organized around a shared vocabulary addressing concepts such as the nature of the universe and the cyclical pattern of life and death. Much of this mixing of ideas took place in schools, universities, and monasteries. The Buddhists already possessed large monasteries, such as Nalanda in northeast India, where 10,000 residential faculty and students assembled, and more than 100 smaller establishments in southeast India housing at least 10,000 monks. In these settings Buddhist teachers debated theology, cosmology, mathematics, logic, and botany. Brahmans also established schools where similar intellectual topics were discussed and where Buddhist and Brahmanic Hindu ideas were fused.

The resulting Indic cultural unity covered around 1 million square miles (an area as great as the extent of the Roman Empire) and a highly diverse population. Although India did not have a single governing entity like China and did not adhere to one religious system as in the Christian Roman Empire, it was developing a distinctive culture based on the intertwining of two shared, accessible, and—to varying degrees—universalizing religious traditions.

Political and Religious Change in East Asia

With the fall of the Han dynasty, China experienced a period of political disunity and a surge of new religious and cultural influences. In the first century CE, Han China was the largest state in the world, with as great a population as the Roman Empire had at its height. Its emperor extracted an annual income of millions of pounds of rice and bolts of cloth and conscripted millions of workers whose families paid tribute through their labor. Later Chinese regarded the end of the Han Empire as a disaster just as great as western Europeans regarded the end of the Roman Empire. In post-Han China, new influences arrived via the Silk Roads through contact with nomadic "barbarians" and the proselytizing of Buddhist monks and new forms of Daoism responded to a changing society.

THE WEI DYNASTY IN NORTHERN CHINA

After the fall of the Han in 220 CE, several small kingdoms—at times as many as sixteen of them—competed for control. Civil wars raged for roughly three centuries, a time called the Six Dynasties period, when no single state was able to conquer more than half of China's territory. The most successful regime was that of the Tuoba, a people originally from Inner Mongolia. In 386 CE the Tuoba founded the Northern Wei dynasty, which lasted 150 years and administered part of the Han territory. Although technically Mongolian "barbarians," the Northern Wei had lived for generations within the Chinese orbit as tributary states.

The Northern Wei maintained many Chinese traditions of statecraft and court life: they taxed land and labor on the basis of a census, conferred official ranks and titles, practiced court rituals, preserved historical archives, and promoted classical learning and the use of classical Chinese for record keeping and political discourse. Though they were nomadic warriors, they adapted their large standing armies to city-based military technology, which required drafting huge numbers of workers to construct dikes, fortifications, canals, and walls.

Among the challenges facing the Northern Wei rulers was the need to consolidate authority over their own highly competitive nomadic people. One strategy was to make their own government more "Chinese." Under Emperor Xiaowen (r. 471–499 CE), for example, the Tuoba royal family adopted the Chinese family name of Yuan and required all court officials to speak Chinese and wear Chinese clothing. However, the Tuoba warrior families resisted these policies. Xiaowen also rebuilt the old Han imperial capital of Luoyang based on classical architectural models dating from the Han dynasty (see Chapter 7) and made it the seat of his government.

Wei rulers sought stronger relationships with the Han Chinese families of Luoyang that had not fled south. The Wei offered them political power as officials in the Wei bureaucracy and more land. For example, the Dowager Empress Fang (regent for Xiaowen from 476–490 CE) attempted progressive land reforms that offered land to all young men—whether Han or Wei—who agreed to cultivate it. But even this plan failed to bridge the cultural divides between the "civilized" Han Chinese of Luoyang and the "barbarian" Tuoba Wei, because the latter showed no interest in farming.

Members of the Wei court supported Buddhist temples and monumental cave sites in an appeal to their Tuoba roots while also honoring Confucian traditions dating to the ancient Zhou period. Emperor Xiaowen's death cut short his efforts to unify the north. Several decades of intense fighting among military rulers followed, leading ultimately to the downfall of the Northern Wei dynasty.

CHANGING DAOIST TRADITIONS

Daoism, a popular Chinese religion under the Han and a challenge to the Confucian state and its scholar-officials (see Chapters 5 and 7), lost its political edge and adapted to the new realities in this period of disunity. Two new traditions of Daoist thought flourished in this era of self-doubt. The first was organized and community oriented, and involved heavenly masters who as mortals guided local religious groups or parishes. Followers sought salvation through virtue, confession, and ceremonies, including a mystical initiation rite. A second Daoist tradition was more individualistic, attempting to reconcile Confucian classical learning with Daoist religious beliefs in the occult and magic. It used trance and meditation to control human physiology. Through such mental and physical efforts, a skilled practitioner could accumulate enough religious merit to prolong his life. The concept of religious merit and demerit in Daoist circles echoed the Buddhist notion of karmic retribution (the cosmic assessment of one's acts in this life that determines one's rebirth into a better or worse next life; see Chapter 5). For the Daoists, however, eternal life was the ultimate goal, and not the Buddhists' ideal of release from the cycle of life, death, and rebirth.

BUDDHISM IN CHINA

Buddhism's universalizing message appealed to many people living in the fragmented Chinese empire. By the third and fourth centuries CE, travelers from central Asia who had converted to Buddhism had become frequent visitors in the streets and temples of the competing capitals: Chang'an, Luoyang, and Nanjing. Spreading the faith required intermediaries, endowed with texts and explanations, to convey its message. Kumarajiva (344–413 CE), a renowned Buddhist scholar and missionary, was the right man, in the right place, at the right time to spread Buddhism in China—where it already coexisted with other faiths.

Kumarajiva's influence on Chinese Buddhist thought was critical. Not only did he translate previously unknown Buddhist texts into Chinese, but he also clarified Buddhist terms and philosophical concepts. He and his disciples established a Mahayana branch known as **Madhyamika (Middle Way) Buddhism**, which used irony and paradox to show that reason was limited. For example, they contended that all reality was transient because nothing remained unchanged over time. They sought enlightenment by means of transcendental visions and spurned experiences in the material world of sights and sounds.

Kumarajiva represented the beginning of a profound cultural shift. After 300 CE Buddhism began to expand in northwestern China, taking advantage of imperial disintegration and the decline of Daoism and state-sponsored Confucian classical learning. The Buddhists stressed devotional acts, such as daily prayers and mantras, which included seated meditations in solitude requiring mind and breath control, as well as the saving power of the Buddha and the saintly bodhisattvas who postponed their own salvation for the sake of others. They even encouraged the Chinese to join a new class—the clergy. The idea that persons could be defined by faith rather than kinship was not new in Chinese society (see Chapter 7), but it had special appeal in a time of serious crisis like that of the turbulent Six Dynasties period. In the south, the immigrants from the north found that membership in the Buddhist clergy and monastic orders offered a way to restore their lost prestige.

Even more important, in the northern states—now part Chinese, part "barbarian"—Buddhism provided legitimacy. With Buddhists holding prominent positions in government, medicine, and astronomy, the Wei ruling houses could espouse a philosophy that was just as legitimate as that of the Han Chinese. As a Tuoba who ruled at the height of the Northern Wei in the early sixth century, Emperor Xuanwu was an avid Buddhist who made Mahayana Buddhism the state religion during his reign.

In 643 CE, the Chinese Buddhist Xuanzang brought back to Chang'an (then the world's largest city) an entire library of Buddhist scriptures—527 boxes of writings and 192 birch-bark tablets—that he had collected on a pilgrimage to Buddhist holy sites in South Asia. He lodged them in the Great Wild Goose Pagoda and immediately began to translate every line into Chinese. Although the importation of these texts from India was prfoundly important, Buddhism did not seek to be the same in all places and at all times. On the contrary, as the expression of a cosmic truth as timeless and varied as the world itself,

Xuanzang This painting, c. 900 CE, which survives in the caves of Dunhuang along the Silk Roads, portrays the Chinese pilgrim Xuanzang accompanied by a tiger on his epic travels in South Asia to collect important Buddhist scriptures.

Amitabha This exquisite tapestry is an illustration for the *Amitabha Sutra,* the "Sutra of the Western Pure Land." Since the text was translated into Chinese by Kumarajiva in the fourth century CE, Amitabha has been one of the most popular bodhisattvas in China. A devotee who invokes the name of Amitabha ten times before death would be saved to this Western Pure Land, where the Seven Treasures decorated the quiet landscape.

Buddhism showed a high level of adaptability, easily absorbing the gods and the wisdom of every country it touched.

By 400 CE China had more than 1,700 Buddhist monasteries and about 80,000 monks and nuns. By contrast, in 600 CE (after two centuries of monastic growth), Gaul and Italy—the two richest regions of western Europe—had, altogether, only 320 monasteries, many with fewer than 30 monks. Yet, in the two ends of Afro-Eurasia the principal bearers of the new religions were monks. Set apart from "worldly" affairs in their refuges, they enjoyed the pious support of royal courts and warriors whose lifestyles differed sharply from their own. Through their devoted faith in the divine and the support of secular rulers, these two universalizing religions—Buddhism and Christianity—would continue to grow, flourish, and revitalize themselves.

Faith and Cultures in the Worlds Apart

COMPARISON

ASSESS the connections between political unity and religious developments in sub-Saharan Africa and Mesoamerica in the fourth to sixth centuries CE.

In most areas of sub-Saharan Africa and Mesoamerica, it was not easy for ideas, institutions, peoples, and commodities to circulate broadly. Thus we do not see the development of universalizing faiths. Rather, belief systems and their associated deities remained local. Nonetheless, sub-Saharan Africans and peoples living in Mesoamerica revered prophetic figures who, they believed, communicated with deities and brought to humankind divinely prescribed rules of behavior. Peoples in both regions honored beliefs and rules that were passed down orally across generations. These unifying spiritual traditions guided behavior and established social customs.

BANTUS OF SUB-SAHARAN AFRICA

Today, most of Africa south of the equator is home to peoples who speak some variant of more than 400 Bantu languages. Although scholars using oral traditions and linguistic

MAP 8.6 | Bantu Migrations

The migration of Bantu speakers throughout much of sub-Saharan Africa in the first millennium CE dramatically altered the cultural landscape.

- According to the map, where did the Bantu speakers originate? Into which areas did the Bantu speakers migrate?
- What skills did they have that enabled them to dominate the peoples already living there?
- According to your reading, did the Bantu migrations create a common culture below the Sahara Desert during this time?

evidence can trace a clear narrative of the Bantu people no further back than 1000 CE, it appears that the first Bantu speakers lived in the southeastern part of modern Nigeria, where about 4,000 or 5,000 years ago they likely shifted from hunting, gathering, and fishing to practicing settled agriculture. Preparing just one acre of tropical rain forest for farming required removing 600 tons of moist vegetation. To accomplish this arduous task, Bantus used mainly machetes, billhooks, and controlled burning. Bantus cultivated woodland plants such as yams and mushrooms, as well as palm oils and kernels. Yet the difficulties in preparing the land for settled agriculture did not keep the Bantus from being the most expansionist of African peoples (see Map 8.6).

Bantu Migrations Following riverbeds and elephant trails, Bantu migrants traveled out of West Africa in two great waves. One wave moved across the Congo forest region to East Africa. Their knowledge of iron smelting enabled them to deploy iron tools for agriculture. Because their new habitats supported a mixed economy of animal husbandry and sedentary agriculture, this group became relatively prosperous. A second wave of migrants moved southward through the rain forests in present-day Congo, eventually reaching the Kalahari Desert. The tsetse fly–infested environment did not permit them to rear livestock, so they were limited to subsistence farming. These Bantus learned to use iron later than those who had moved to the Congo region in the east.

Precisely when these **Bantu migrations** began is unclear, but once under way, the travelers moved rapidly. Genetic and linguistic evidence reveals that they absorbed most of the hunting-and-gathering populations who originally inhabited these areas. What enabled the Bantus to prevail and prosper was their skill as settled agriculturalists. They adapted their farming techniques and crops to widely different environments, including the tropical rain forests of the Congo River basin, the savanna lands of central Africa, the high grasslands around Lake Nyanza, and the highlands of Kenya.

For the Bantu of the rain forests of Central Africa (the Western Bantu), the introduction of the banana plant from tropical South and Southeast Asia was decisive. Linguistic evidence suggests that it first arrived in the Upper Nile region and then traveled into the rest of Africa with small groups migrating from one favorable location to another; the earliest proof of its presence is a record from the East African coast dating to 525 CE. The banana adapted well to the equatorial rain forests, withstanding the heavy rainfalls, requiring less clearing of rain forests, reducing the presence of the malaria-carrying anopheles mosquito, and providing more nutrients than the indigenous yam crop. Exploiting banana cultivation, the Western Bantu filled the equatorial rain forests of central Africa between 500 and 1000 CE.

Bantu Cultures, East and West The widely different ecological zones into which the Bantu-speaking peoples spread made it difficult to establish the same political, social, and cultural institutions. In the Great Lakes area of the East African savanna lands and the savanna lands of Central Africa, where communication was relatively easy, the Eastern Bantu speakers developed centralized polities whose kings ruled by divine right. They moved into heavily forested areas similar to those they had left in southeastern Nigeria. These locations supported a way of life that remained fundamentally unaltered until European colonialism in the twentieth century.

The Western Bantu-speaking communities of the lower Congo River rain forests formed small-scale societies based on family and clan connections. They organized themselves socially and politically into age groups, the most important of which were the ruling elders. Within these age-based networks, individuals who demonstrated talent in warfare, commerce, and politics provided leadership. Certain rights and duties were imposed on different social groups based mainly on their age. Males moved from child to warrior to ruling elder and females transitioned from child to married child-bearer. Bonds among age groups were powerful, and movement from one to the next was marked by meaningful and well-remembered rituals. So-called big men, supported by followers attracted by their valor and wisdom as opposed to inheritance, promoted territorial expansion. Individuals who could attract a large community of followers, marry many women, and sire many children could lead their bands into new locations and establish dominant communities.

These rain-forest communities held a common belief that the natural world was inhabited by spirits, many of whom were their own heroic ancestors. These spiritual beings intervened in mortals' lives and required constant appeasement. Diviners helped men and women understand the spirits' ways, and charms warded off the misfortune that aggrieved spirits might wish to inflict. Diviners and charms also protected against the injuries that living beings—witches and sorcerers—could inflict. In fact, much of the misfortune that occurred in the Bantu world was attributed to these malevolent forces. The Bantu migrations ultimately filled up more than half the African landmass. They spread a political and social order based on family and clan structures that rewarded

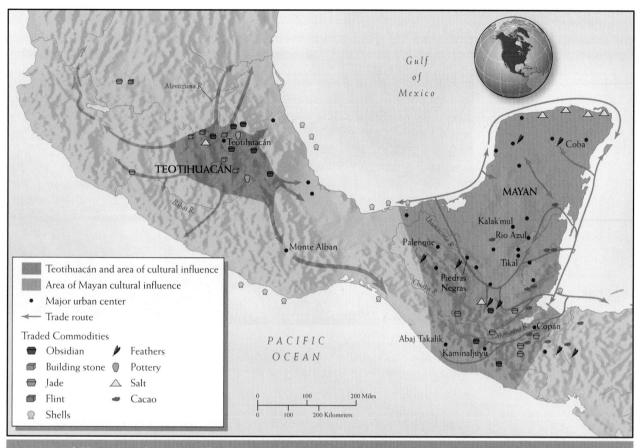

MAP 8.7 | Mesoamerican Worlds, 200–700 CE

At this time, two groups dominated Mesoamerica: one was located at the city of Teotihuacán in the center, and the other—the Mayans—was in the south.

- What commodities did these cultures trade? Look at the symbols for Traded Commodities in the map key, and find them all on the map.
- Judging by what you see, how did each group create a common culture in surrounding regions?
- To what extent do you believe the people of the Teotihuacán and Mayan worlds influenced each other?

individual achievement—and maintained an intense relationship to the world of nature that they believed was imbued with supernatural forces.

MESOAMERICANS

As in sub-Saharan Africa, the process of settlement and expansion in Mesoamerica differed from that in the large empires of Afro-Eurasia. Mesoamerica had no integrating artery of a giant river and its floodplain, and so it lacked the extensive resources that a state could harness for monumental ambitions. Nonetheless, some remarkable polities developed in the region, ranging from the city-state of Teotihuacán to the more widespread influence of the Mayans (see Map 8.7).

Teotihuacán Around 300 BCE, people in the central plateau and the southeastern districts of Mesoamerica where the dispersed villages of Olmec culture had risen and fallen (see Chapter 5) began to gather in larger settlements. Soon, political and social integration

COMPARISON

COMPARE the unifying political and cultural developments in sub-Saharan Africa and Mesoamerica with those that took place across Eurasia in this period.

Teotihuacán The ruins of Teotihuacán convey the importance of monumental architecture to its culture. In the foreground is the Plaza of the Moon leading to the Street of the Dead, with the Pyramid of the Sun to the left. These massive structures were meant to confirm the importance of spiritual affairs in urban life.

led to city-states. Teotihuacán, in the heart of the fertile valley of central Mexico, became the largest center of the Americas before the Aztecs almost 500 years later.

Fertile land and ample water from the valley's marshes and lakes fostered high agricultural productivity despite the inhabitants' technologically rustic methods of cultivation. The local food supply sustained a metropolis of between 100,000 and 200,000 residents, living in more than 2,000 apartment compounds lining the city's streets. At one corner rose the massive pyramids of the sun and the moon—the focus of spiritual life for the city dwellers. Marking the city's center was the huge royal compound; the grandeur and refinement of its stepped stone pyramid, the Temple of the Feathered Serpent, were famous throughout Mesoamerica.

The feathered serpent was the anchor for their spiritual lives. It was a symbol of fertility that governed reproduction and life. The feathered serpent's temple was the core of a much larger structure. From it radiated the awesome promenade known as the Street of the Dead, which culminated in the hulking Pyramid of the Moon, where foreign warriors and dignitaries were mutilated, sacrificed, and often buried alive to consecrate the holy structure.

Teotihuacán was a powerful city-state that flexed its military muscle to overtake its rivals. By 300 CE, Teotihuacán controlled the entire basin of the Valley of Mexico. It dominated its neighbors and demanded gifts, tribute, and humans for ritual sacrifice. Its massive public architecture displayed art that commemorated decisive battles, defeated neighbors, and captured fighters. While the city's political influence beyond the basin was limited, its cultural and economic diffusion were significant. Making use of porters, Teotihuacán's merchants traded their ceramics, ornaments of marine shells, and all sorts of decorative and valued objects (especially of green obsidian) far and wide. At the same time, Teotihuacán imported pottery, feathers, and other goods from distant lowlands.

This kind of expansion left much of the political and cultural independence of neighbors intact, with only the threat of force keeping them in check. In the fifth century CE, however, invaders burned Teotihuacán and smashed the carved figurines of the central temples and palaces, targeting Teotihuacán's institutional and spiritual core.

The Mayans In the Caribbean region of the Yucatán and its interior, the Mayan people flourished from about 250 CE to their zenith in the eighth century. The Mayans lived in an inhospitable region—hot, infertile, lacking navigable river systems, and vulnerable to hurricanes. Yet the Mayans achieved greatness without founding a single great central metropolis. Instead, they established hundreds, possibly thousands, of agrarian villages scattered across the diverse ecological zones of present-day southern Mexico to western El Salvador. Villages were linked by a shared Mayan language and through tribute payments, chiefly from lesser settlements to sacred towns. At their peak the Mayans may have numbered as many as 10 million.

Mayan Political and Social Structure The Mayans established a variety of kingdoms around major ritual centers—such as Palenque, Copán, and Piedras Negras—and their hinterlands. Such hubs were politically independent but culturally and economically interconnected through commerce. Some larger settlements, such as Tikal and Kalak'mul, became sprawling centers with dependent provinces. Ambitious rulers in these larger states frequently engaged in hostilities with one another.

Mayan culture encompassed about a dozen kingdoms that shared many features. Highly stratified, with an elaborate class structure, each kingdom was topped by a shamanistic king who legitimated his position via his lineage, reaching back to a founding father and, ultimately, the gods. The vast pantheon of gods included patrons of each subregion, as well as a creator god and deities for rain, maize, war, and the sun. Gods were neither especially cruel nor benevolent; but rather focused on the dance that sustained the axis connecting the underworld and the skies. What humans had to worry about was making sure that the gods got the attention and reverence they needed.

This was the job of Mayan rulers. Kings sponsored elaborate public rituals to reinforce their divine heritages, including ornate processions down their cities' main boulevards to honor gods and their descendants, the rulers. Lords and their wives performed ritual

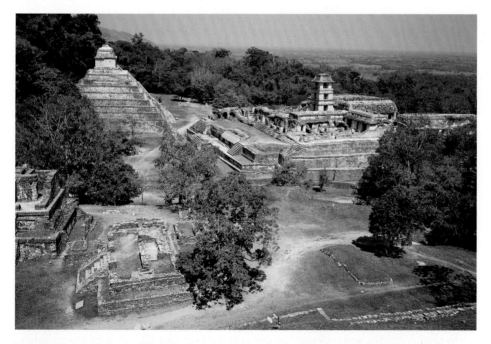

Palenque Deep in the Lacandon jungle of present-day Mexico lies the ruin of the Mayan city of Palenque. Its pyramid, on the left, overlooks the site; on the right, the Tower of the Palace shadows a magnificent courtyard where religious figures and nobles gathered. There is no mistaking how a city like Palenque could command its hinterland with religious authority.

Wood Tablet This detail of a carved-wood tablet from a temple in the city of Tikal (c. 741 CE) is a fine example of the ornate form of scribal activity, which combined images and portraits with glyphs that tell a narrative.

blood sacrifice to feed their ancestors. A powerful priestly elite, scribes, legal experts, military advisers, and skilled artisans were vital to the hierarchy.

Most of the Mayan people remained tied to the land, which could sustain a high population only through dispersed settlements. Poor soil quality and limited water supply prevented large-scale agriculture: major rivers or irrigation systems were lacking. Through terraces, the draining of fields, and slash-and-burn agriculture, Mayans managed a subsistence economy of diversified agrarian production. Villagers cultivated maize, beans, and squash, rotating them to prevent the depletion of soil nutrients. Farmers supplemented these staples with root crops such as sweet potato and cassava. Cotton—the basic fiber used for clothing—frequently grew amid rows of other crops as part of a diversified mix.

Mayan Writing, Mathematics, and Architecture

A common set of beliefs, codes, and values connected the dispersed Mayan villages. Sharing a similar language, Mayans developed writing and an important class of scribes who were vital to the society's integration. Rulers rewarded scribes for writing grand epics about dynasties and their founders, major battles, marriages, deaths, and sacrifices. Such writings offered to Mayans shared common histories, beliefs, and gods—always associated with the narratives of ruling families.

The best-known surviving text is the *Popol Vuh*, a "Book of Community." It narrates one community's creation myth, extolling its founders (twin heroes) and the experiences—wars, natural disasters, human ingenuity—that enabled a royal line to rule the Quiché Kingdom. The text begins with the gods' creation of the earth and ends with the rituals the kingdom's tribes must follow to avoid a descent into social and political anarchy, which had occurred several times throughout their history.

The Mayans also had skilled mathematicians, who devised a calendar and studied astronomy. They accurately charted regular celestial movements and marked the passage of time by precise lunar and solar cycles. The Mayans kept sacred calendars, by which they rigorously observed their rituals at the proper times. Each change in the cycle had particular rituals, dances, performances, and offerings to honor the gods with life's sustenance.

Cities reflected a ruler's ability to summon his subjects to contribute to the kingdom's greatness. Plazas, ball courts, terraces, and palaces sprawled out from neighborhoods. Activity revolved around grand royal palaces and massive ball courts, where competing teams treated enthusiastic audiences to contests that were more religious ritual than game. The Mayans also excelled at building monumental structures. In Tikal, for instance, surviving buildings include six massive, steep funerary pyramids featuring elaborately carved and painted masonry walls, vaulted ceilings, and royal burial chambers; the tallest temple soars more than 220 feet high (forty feet higher than Justinian's Hagia Sophia).

Mayan Bloodletting and Warfare Mayan elites were obsessed with spilling blood as a way to honor rulers and ancestors as well as gods. This gory rite led to frequent warfare, especially among rival dynasties, the goal of which was to capture victims for the bloody rituals. Rulers also would shed their own blood at intervals set by the calendar. Royal wives drew blood from their tongues and men had their penises perforated. Such bloodletting by means of elaborately adorned and sanctified instruments was reserved for those of noble descent. Carvings and paintings portray blood cascading from rulers' mutilated bodies.

Internal warfare doomed the Mayans, especially after devastating confrontations between Tikal and Kalak'mul during the fourth through seventh centuries CE. With each outbreak, rulers drafted larger armies and sacrificed greater numbers of captives. Crops perished. People fled. After centuries of misery, it must have seemed as if the gods themselves were abandoning the Mayan people. The cycle of violence destroyed the cultural underpinnings of elite rule that had held the Mayan world together. There was no single catastrophic event, no great defeat by a rival power. The Mayan people simply abandoned their spiritual centers, and cities became ghost towns. As populations declined, jungles overtook temples. Eventually, the hallmark of Mayan unity—the ability to read a shared script—vanished. While vibrant religious traditions thrived in sub-Saharan Africa and in Mesoamerica, they served more to reinforce the political and social situations from which they came rather than to spread a universalizing message far beyond their original context.

Conclusion

The breakdown of two imperial systems—Rome around the Mediterranean, and Han China in East Asia—introduced an era in which religion and shared culture rather than military conquest and political institutions linked large areas of Afro-Eurasia.

The Roman Empire gave way to a new religious unity, first represented by Christian dissenters and then co-opted by the emperor Constantine. In western Europe, the sense of unity unlimited by imperial frontiers gave rise to a universal, or "Catholic," church—the "true" Christian religion that believers felt all peoples should share. In the eastern Mediterranean, where the Roman Empire survived, Christianity and empire coalesced to reinforce one another. Christians here held that beliefs about God and Jesus found their most correct expression within the eastern Roman Empire and in its capital, Constantinople.

Similarly, in East Asia, the weakening of the Han dynasty enabled Buddhism to dominate Chinese culture. Without a unified state in China, Confucian officials lost their influence, while Buddhist priests and monks enjoyed patronage from regional rulers, local warriors, and commoners. In India, Brahman elites exploited population movements beyond the reach of traditional rulers as they established ritual forms for daily life on every level of society, while melding aspects of their own Vedic faith with those of Buddhism to create a new Hindu synthesis.

Not all regions felt the spread of universalizing religions, however. In most of sub-Saharan Africa belief systems were much more localized. Similarly in Mesoamerica, where long-distance transportation was harder and political authority more diffuse, religion was a unifying force but nothing like the widespread universalizing religions of Afro-Eurasia. Nevertheless, spiritual life was no less profound. Here, a strong sense of a shared worldview, a shared sense of purpose, and a shared sense of faith enabled common cultures to develop. Indeed, the Bantus and Mayans became large-scale common cultures—but ruled at the local level.

Thus, the period 300–600 CE saw the emergence of three great cultural units in Afro-Eurasia, each defined in religious terms: Christianity in the Mediterranean and parts of Southwest Asia, Hinduism in South Asia, and Buddhism in East Asia. They illustrate the ways in which peoples were converging under larger religious tents, while also becoming more distinct. Universalizing religions, whether Christian or Buddhist, and codes of behavior, such as the Brahmanic Code of Manu, gave people a new way to define themselves and their loyalties.

COMPARISON

EXPLAIN why universalizing religions developed to varying degrees in Afro-Eurasia but did not develop elsewhere in the world.

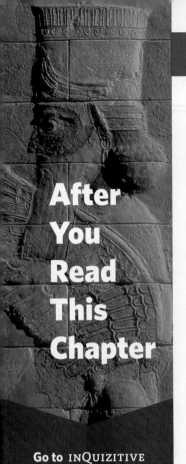

After You Read This Chapter

Go to INQUIZITIVE to see what you've learned—and learn what you've missed—with personalized feedback along the way.

FOCUS ON: *Religions and Regions*

EUROPE AND SOUTHWEST ASIA

- Christianity moves from a minority, persecuted faith to a state religion in the Roman Empire.

- The Sasanian state in Iran provides fertile ground for a tolerant mixture of Zoroastrianism, Nestorian Christianity, Judaism, Buddhism, and Brahmanic religion.

SUB-SAHARAN AFRICA AND MESOAMERICA

- Large parts of Africa and the Americas develop common cultures based on religious beliefs shared by large, widely dispersed groups.

SOUTH ASIA AND EAST ASIA

- Brahmanism, or Hinduism, becomes the dominant religion among the Vedic peoples of South Asia.

- Buddhism spreads out of South Asia along the Silk Roads through central Asia and into East Asia.

CHRONOLOGY

THE MEDITERRANEAN AND SOUTHWEST ASIA	Sasanian Empire flourishes in Iran and Mesopotamia 3rd–6th century CE				
	Emperor Constantine legalizes Christianity in Roman Empire 313 CE ◆				
	"Barbarian" invasions of Roman Empire 4th and 5th centuries CE				
CENTRAL ASIA					
SOUTH ASIA	Transformation of Brahmanism into Hinduism begins 1st or 2nd century CE				
EAST ASIA	Six Dynasties period 220–589 CE				
SUB-SAHARAN AFRICA	Bantu migrations from western Africa to south, central, and east				
MESOAMERICA	Maya culture dominates Yucatán Peninsula and surrounding area 3rd–9th century CE				
	City of Teotihuacán dominates Valley of Mexico 4th–5th century CE				

| 1 CE | 100 CE | 200 CE | 300 CE | 400 CE |

- **Thinking about Crossing Borders and Universalizing Religions** Why did borders seem to infuse vitality into Christianity and Buddhism from the fourth through the sixth centuries CE? Which religions in this period did not seem to cross borders and why? What effect did this have on those religions?

- **Thinking about Changing Power Relationships and Universalizing Religions** Universalizing religions, like Christianity and Buddhism, were successful in part because of their diverse personalized appeal to men and women, rich and poor, and the upper and lower classes. How might this diverse appeal enable a universalizing religion like Christianity to undermine and alter traditional power relationships? In what ways did Buddhism do the same? Hinduism?

- **Thinking about Worlds Together, Worlds Apart and Universalizing Religions** Why did universalizing religions like Christianity and Buddhism develop in some parts of the world but not in others in the period 300 to 600 CE? How did these universalizing religions allow for continuity in Eurasia, even as empires fell away? In the "worlds apart," how might the lack of universalizing religion have influenced continuity, as political entities rose and fell over time?

1. What are the major characteristics of a **universalizing religion**, for the period from 300 to 600 CE? In what specific ways do Christianity, Buddhism, and other religious developments in this period fit this model? What traditions do *not*?

2. What factors contributed to the "fall" of the Roman Empire in the west? How do Christianity and the rise of **Byzantium** challenge the notion that Rome "fell"?

3. Explain the role of the Sasanians and the Sogdians in fostering connections along the Silk Roads.

4. What forces contributed to the development of **Hinduism** out of Brahmanism?

5. In what ways does the concept of the **Sanskrit cosmopolis** help to explain the nature of cultural unity in South Asia in this period?

6. What are some of the ways in which Buddhism universalized in this period, and what impact did this have on South Asia and East Asia?

7. In what specific ways did the Northern Wei dynasty attempt to fill the void left by the collapse of the Han dynasty?

8. What was the impact of the **Bantu migrations** on sub-Saharan Africa? What helped to unite the Bantu peoples?

9. In what ways did Teotihuacán and later the Mayans bring a degree of unity to parts of Mesoamerica? What factors impeded them?

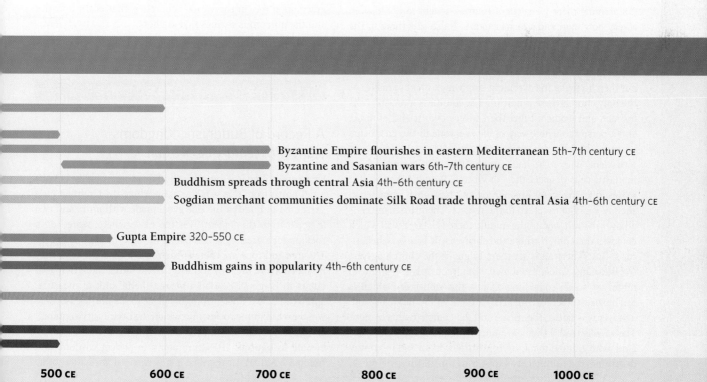

Byzantine Empire flourishes in eastern Mediterranean 5th-7th century CE
Byzantine and Sasanian wars 6th-7th century CE
Buddhism spreads through central Asia 4th-6th century CE
Sogdian merchant communities dominate Silk Road trade through central Asia 4th-6th century CE

Gupta Empire 320-550 CE

Buddhism gains in popularity 4th-6th century CE

500 CE   600 CE   700 CE   800 CE   900 CE   1000 CE

Competing Perspectives

Pilgrimage and Universalizing Religions

Religious tourism, or pilgrimage, went hand in hand with the spread of universalizing religions along the trade routes that stretched across Eurasia. Christians, Buddhists, and Hindus traveled the religious geography of their faith, visiting sacred sites and relics and hearing stories of holy women and men. The first passage included here is excerpted from the travel diary kept by a woman named Egeria, who was likely a nun from Spain. Around 400 CE, Egeria journeyed to holy sites across the eastern Mediterranean, recording the places she visited and her experiences at each location. At roughly the same time Egeria was traveling, an elderly Chinese Buddhist monk named Faxian was making his way from Chang'an in China to South Asia to look for Buddhist scriptures and to visit sites sacred to Buddhism. The description of his travels offers a view into the varied worship practices within different schools of Buddhism as well as the many different regions—from China, to India, to Sri Lanka, and back again—where Buddhism flourished. The third passage comes from the *Bhagavata Purana*, a sacred text of Hinduism that exemplifies the *bhakti* devotion to Krishna, a human incarnation of the Hindu god Vishnu. Although this passage describes the travels of Vidura, a major character in the *Mahabharata* whose legendary storyline extends back to 1000 BCE, this purana is thought to have been recorded in Sanskrit in the mid–first millennium CE as *bhakti* Hinduism became increasingly popular. While the pilgrimages of Egeria and Faxian demonstrate many of the universalizing elements within Christianity and Buddhism, the account of Vidura's pilgrimage in the *Bhagavata Purana* shows the development of personalized *bhakti* devotion in the context of nearly 2,000 years of hierarchical Vedic belief.

PRIMARY SOURCE 8.1

Diary of a Pilgrimage (*late fourth century CE*), Egeria

On arriving there [Seleucia of Isauria], I went to the bishop, a very holy man and a former monk. I also saw there in the same city a very beautiful church. Since it is around fifteen hundred feet from the city to the shrine of Saint Thecla, which lies beyond the city on a rather flat hill, I thought it best to go out there to make the overnight stop which I had to make. At the holy church there is nothing but countless monastic cells for men and women. I met there a very dear friend of mine, and a person to whose way of life everyone in the East bears witness, the holy deaconess Marthana, whom I had met in Jerusalem, where she had come to pray. She governs these monastic cells of *aputactitae*, or virgins. Would I ever be able to describe how great was her joy and how great mine when she saw me? But to return to the subject: There are many cells all over the hill, and in the middle there is a large wall which encloses the church where the shrine is. It is a very beautiful shrine. The wall is set there to guard the church against the Isaurians, who are evil men, who frequently rob and who might try to do something against the monastery which is established there. Having arrived there in the name of God, a prayer was said at the shrine and the complete Acts of Saint Thecla was read. I then gave unceasing thanks to Christ our God, who granted to me, an unworthy woman and in no way deserving, the fulfillment of my desires in all things. And so,

after spending two days there seeing the holy monks and the *aputactitae*, both men and women, who live there, and after praying and receiving Communion, I returned to Tarsus and to my journey. [Egeria makes her way to Constantinople] . . . After arriving [in Constantinople], I did not cease giving thanks to Jesus our God, who had deigned to bestow His grace upon me, in the various churches, that of the apostles and the numerous shrines that are here. . . .

Source: Egeria, *Ancient Christian Writers: Diary of a Pilgrimage*, trans. George E. Gringras (Mahwah, New Jersey: The Newman Press, 1970), p. 87–88.

PRIMARY SOURCE 8.2

A Record of Buddhistic Kingdoms (*early fifth century CE*), Faxian

Chapter 31. Two *le* [Chinese unit of measure, roughly 1/3 of a mile] north from this was the place where the Gramika girls presented to Buddha the rice gruel made with milk; and two *le* north from this (again) was the place where, seated on a rock under a great tree, and facing the east, he ate (the gruel). The tree and rock are there at the present day. The rock may be six cubits in breadth and length, and rather more than two cubits in height. . . . Half a yojana [Vedic unit of measure, approximately 8 miles] from this place to the north-east there was a cavern in the rocks, into which the Bodhisattva entered, and sat cross-legged with his face to the west. (As he did so), he said to himself, 'If I am to attain to perfect wisdom (and become Buddha), let there be a supernatural attestation of it.'

[The text describes various signs that lead him to the tree under which the Buddha attained enlightenment] . . . At the place mentioned above . . . men subsequently reared topes and set up images, which all exist at the present day . . . At the place where Buddha attained to perfect Wisdom, there are three monasteries, in all of which there are monks residing. The families of their people around supply the societies of these monks with an abundant sufficiency of what they require, so that there is no lack or stint. The disciplinary rules are strictly observed by them. The laws regulating their demeanor in sitting, rising, and entering when the others are assembled are those which have been practiced by all the saints since Buddha was in the world down to the present day. . . .

Chapter 36. Faxian's original object had been to search for copies of the Vinaya. In the various kingdoms of North India, however, he had found one master transmitting orally (the rules) to another, but no written copies he could transcribe. He had therefore travelled far and come on to Central India. Here in the mahayana monastery, he found a copy of the Vinaya, containing the Mahasanghika rules—those which were observed in the first Great Council, while Buddha was still in the world.

Source: Faxian, *A Record of Buddhistic Kingdoms, Being an Account by the Chinese Monk Fa-Hsien of his Travels in India and Ceylon* (A.D. 399–414) *in Search of the Buddhist Books of Discipline*, trans. James Legge (Oxford at the Clarendon Press, 1886), pp. 87–88, 98.

PRIMARY SOURCE 8.3

Bhagavata Purana (recorded c. 500 CE)

SB 3.1.17 By his piety, Vidura achieved the advantages of the pious Kauravas. After leaving Hastināpura, he took shelter of many places of pilgrimages, which are the Lord's lotus feet. With a desire to gain a high order of pious life, he traveled to holy places where thousands of transcendental forms of the Lord are situated. (18) He began to travel alone, thinking only of Krṣṇa [i.e. Krishna], through various holy places like Ayodhyā, Dvārakā and Mathurā [all cities in India]. He traveled where the grove, hill, orchard, river and lake are all pure and sinless and where the forms of the Unlimited decorate the temples. Thus he performed the pilgrim's progress. (19) While so traversing the earth, he simply performed duties to please the Supreme Lord Hari. His occupation was pure and independent. He was constantly sanctified by taking his bath in holy places, although he was in the dress of a mendicant and had no hair dressing nor a bed on which to lie. Thus he was always unseen by his various relatives. (20) Thus, when he was in the land of Bhāratavarṣa [i.e. India] traveling to all the places of pilgrimage, he visited Prabhāsakṣetra. At that time Mahārāja Yudhiṣthira was the emperor and held the world under one military strength and one flag. . . . After this he proceeded west, where the river Sarasvatī flows. (22) On the bank of the river Sarasvatī there were eleven places of pilgrimage, namely (1) Trita, (2) Uśanā, (3) Manu, (4) Pṛthu, (5) Agni, (6) Asita, (7) Vāyu, (8) Sudāsa, (9) Go, (10) Guha and (11) Śrāddhadeva. Vidura visited all of them and duly performed rituals. (23) There were also many other temples of various forms of the Supreme Personality of Godhead Viṣṇu, established by great sages and demigods. These temples were marked with the chief emblems of the Lord, and they reminded one always of the original Personality of Godhead, Lord Krṣṇa. (24) Thereafter he passed through very wealthy provinces like Surat, Sauvīra and Matsya and through western India, known as Kurujāṅgala. At last he reached the bank of the Yamunā, where he happened to meet Uddhava, the great devotee of Lord Krṣṇa [Vidura asks Uddhava to give him updates on various family members of Lord Krishna. Vidura offers a profession of faith regarding the incarnation of Vishnu and asks Uddhava:] (45) O my friend, please, therefore, chant the glories of the Lord, who is meant to be glorified in the places of pilgrimage. He is unborn, and yet He appears by His causeless mercy upon the surrendered rulers of all parts of the universe. Only for their interest did He appear in the family of His unalloyed devotees the Yadus.

Source: *Śrīmad Bhāgavatam*: Third Canto, "The Status Quo" (Part One—Chapters 1–16), trans. His Divine Grace A. C. Bhaktivedanta Sawmi Prabhupāda (Los Angeles: The Bhaktivedanta Book Trust, 1988), pp. 18, 21–26, 28, 53–54.

QUESTIONS FOR ANALYSIS

1. What do these pilgrims—Egeria, Faxian, and Vidura—see and do when they visit a holy site? What are some of the threats, explicit and implicit, they face as they travel?

2. How might their travel (where they go, what they do, how and to whom they report their experiences, etc.) indicate the extent to which theirs was a universalizing faith?

3. What appears to be the role of storytelling in pilgrimage? What do these excerpts suggest about the relationship between monasteries and holy sites? Between pilgrims and written text?

4. In what ways do these passages highlight the universalizing aspects of Christianity and Buddhism? What evidence do you see in the *Bhagavata Purana* of the accessibility of *bhakti* devotion? What evidence do you see of the arguably less universalizing components of Hinduism?

Interpreting Visual Evidence

Representations of Holiness

One of the features of universalizing religions discussed in this chapter is that they offered individuals a more personal connection with the divine. This accessibility is visible in the religious art from the period.

As the images here show, artists expressed what it means to be holy in various ways. The Yungang Caves in northeastern China were situated at the eastern end of the Silk Roads. The large statues and interior painting and carvings pictured here were created during the Northern Wei dynasty (c. 450–525 CE). Many different Buddhas reside in individual niches on the walls surrounding the large central Buddha statue. Thousands of miles away, in the crumbling western Roman Empire, the Archbishop's Chapel from Ravenna (c. 500 CE) in northern Italy preserved depictions of martyrs and other religious figures, notably Perpetua and Felicitas. These women appear here not as violently bloodied witnesses to their faith but rather as a serenely modest matron and her humble servant.

The two relief sculptures pictured here provide additional perspectives on sacred subjects. The Hindu relief depicts the Kalyanasundara, or "beautiful marriage," of Parvati and Shiva (the Hindu god of destruction and rejuvenation). This particular relief was carved in the mid-sixth century CE in Cave 1 at Elephanta on an island in the harbor of modern-day Mumbai. Its imagery recurs in numerous versions throughout the ancient Hindu temples of India and beyond. In this carving, Parvati, a reincarnation of Shiva's first wife, Sati, is married to Shiva as a reward for her patient devotion. The final image is a limestone relief from Yaxchilan, Mexico, and shows a royal Mayan bloodletting ritual. In the image (dated by the glyphs to October 26, 709 CE), the queen pierces her tongue with a thorny rope in a reenactment of the bloodletting by the gods in the Mayan creation narrative.

Yungang Caves.

Perpetua and Felicitas.

Kalyanasundara of Parvati and Shiva.

Royal bloodletting ritual.

QUESTIONS FOR ANALYSIS

1. Compare these visual representations of what it means to be holy. To what extent do they convey a message that is particular to their tradition?

2. What might account for the similarities in these depictions of what it means to be holy?

3. Given what you know about the features of these universalizing traditions, what in these images might suggest human access to holiness or the possibility of a personal connection to the divine?

4. How does the location of these images (where they were created and displayed) contribute to an understanding of how universalizing these traditions were?

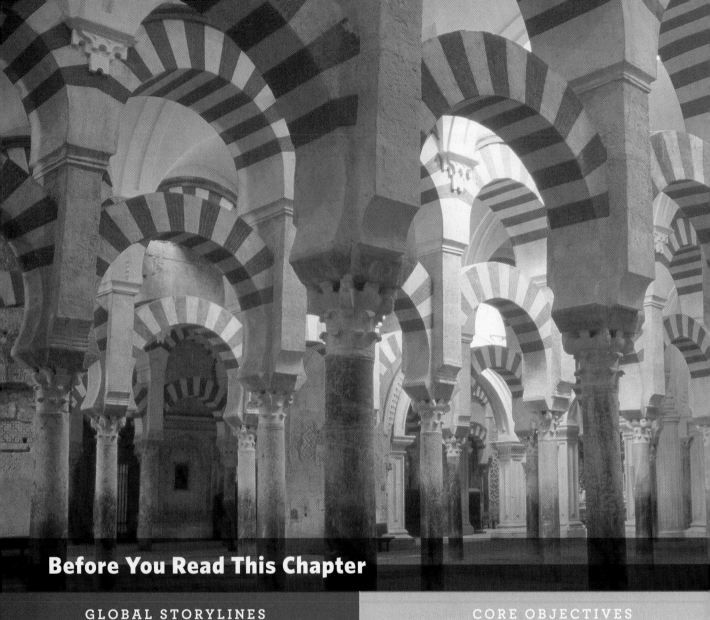

Before You Read This Chapter

GLOBAL STORYLINES

- The universalizing religion of Islam, based on the message of the prophet Muhammad, originates on the Arabian Peninsula and spreads rapidly across Afro-Eurasia.

- The expanding Tang dynasty in East Asia consolidates its bureaucracy, struggles with religious pluralism, and extends its influence into Korea and Japan.

- Christianity splits over religious and political differences, leading to a divide between Roman Catholicism in the west and Greek Orthodoxy in the east.

CORE OBJECTIVES

- **DESCRIBE** and **EXPLAIN** the spread of Islam, Buddhism, and Christianity from 600 to 1000 CE.

- **COMPARE** the organizational structures of the Abbasids, Tang China, and Christendom.

- **COMPARE** the internal divisions within the Islamic, Tang, and Christian worlds.

- **EVALUATE** the relationships between religion, empire, and commercial exchange across Afro-Eurasia during this period.

New Empires and Common Cultures

600–1000 CE

I n 754 CE al-Mansur, ruler of the new Muslim Abbasid dynasty, decided to relocate his capital city from Damascus (the capital of Islam's first dynasty) closer to the Abbasids' home region on the Iranian plateau. Islam was barely a century old, yet it flourished under this second dynasty. The caliph al-Mansur chose, for both practical and symbolic reasons, to build his capital near an unimposing village called Baghdad. Not only did the site lie between Mesopotamia's two great rivers, at the juncture of the canals that linked them, but it was also close to the ancient capital of the earlier Sasanian Empire and the site of ancient Sumerian and Babylonian power. By building at Baghdad, al-Mansur could reaffirm Mesopotamia's centrality in the world and promote the universalizing ambitions of Islam.

Al-Mansur's choice had enduring effects. Baghdad became a vital crossroads for commerce. Overnight, the city exploded into a bustling world entrepôt. Chinese goods arrived by land and sea; commodities from Inner Eurasia flowed in over the Silk Roads; and cargo-laden camel caravans wound across Baghdad's western desert, linking the capital with Syria, Egypt, North Africa, and southern Spain. The unity that the Abbasids imposed from Baghdad intensified the movement of peoples, ideas, innovations, and commodities.

While Islam was gaining ground in central Afro-Eurasia, Chinese might was surging in East Asia under the Tang dynasty. Yet, Islam and Tang China were clearly different worlds. The Islamic state had a universalizing religious mission: to bring humankind under the authority of the religion espoused by the Prophet Muhammad. In contrast, the Tang state had no such grandiose religious goals; the ruling elite supported religious variety within China, and they did not use Buddhism to expand their control into areas outside China. Instead, the Tang rulers expected that their neighbors would copy Chinese institutions and pay tribute as symbols of respect to the greatness of the Tang Empire. Though not as expansive as Islam and the Tang Empire, Christianity also strived in this period to extend its domain and add to its converts. With Islam's warriors, traders, and scholars crossing into Europe, Chinese influences taking deeper root in East Asia, and Christendom extending itself across Europe, religion and empire once again intertwined to serve as the social foundation across much of Afro-Eurasia.

The Origins and Spread of Islam

COMPARISON

DESCRIBE and **EXPLAIN** the spread of Islam, Buddhism, and Christianity from 600 to 1000 CE.

Islam began inside Arabia. Despite its remoteness and sparse population, by the sixth century CE Arabia was brushing up against exciting outside currents: long-distance trade, religious debate, and imperial politics. The Hijaz—the western region of Arabia bordering the Red Sea—knew the outside world through trading routes reaching up the coast to the Mediterranean. Mecca, located in the Hijaz, was an unimposing village of simple mud huts. Mecca's inhabitants included both merchants and the caretakers of a revered sanctuary called the kaaba, a dwelling place of deities. In this remote region, one of the world's major prophets emerged, and the universalizing faith he founded soon spread from Arabia through the trade routes stretching across Southwest Asia and North Africa.

Mecca At the great mosque at Mecca, which many consider the most sacred site in Islam, hundreds of thousands of worshippers gather for Friday prayers. Many are performing their religious duty to go on a pilgrimage to the holy places in the Arabian Peninsula.

A VISION, A TEXT, A NEW COMMUNITY

Born in Mecca around 570 CE into a well-respected tribal family, Muhammad enjoyed only moderate success as a trader. Then came a revelation that would convert him into a proselytizer of a new faith. In 610 CE, while Muhammad was on a month-long spiritual retreat in the hills near Mecca, he believed that God came to him in a vision and commanded him to recite a series of revelations.

The early revelations were short and powerful, emphasizing a single, all-powerful God (Allah), and instructions for Muhammad's fellow Meccans to carry this message to nonbelievers. Muhammad's early preaching had a clear message. He urged his small band of followers to act righteously, to set aside false deities, to submit themselves to the one and only true God, and to care for the less fortunate—for the Day of Judgment was imminent. Muhammad's most insistent message was the oneness of God, a belief that has remained central to the Islamic faith ever since.

These teachings, compiled into an authoritative version after the Prophet's death, constituted the foundational text of Islam: the Quran. Accepted as the word of God, the Quran's verses were understood to have flowed flawlessly through God's perfect instrument, the Prophet Muhammad. Muhammad believed that he was a prophet in the tradition of Moses, other Hebrew prophets, and Jesus, and that he communicated with the same God that they did. The Quran and Muhammad proclaimed the tenets of a new faith to unite a people and to expand its spiritual frontiers. Its message already had universalizing elements, though how far it was to be extended, whether to the tribesmen living in the Arabian Peninsula or well beyond, was not at all clear at first.

In 622 CE, Muhammad and a small group of followers, opposed by Mecca's leaders because of their radical religious beliefs and their challenge to the ruling elite's authority, escaped to Yathrib (later named Medina). The perilous 200-mile journey, known as *the hijra* ("breaking off of relations" or "departure"), yielded a new form of communal unity: the *umma* ("band of the faithful"). So significant was this moment that Muslims date the beginning of the Muslim era from this year.

Medina became the birthplace of a new faith called Islam ("submission"—in this case, to the will of God) and a new community called Muslims ("those who submit"). The city of Medina had been facing tribal and religious tensions, and by inviting Muhammad and his followers to take up residence there, its elders hoped that his leadership and charisma would bring peace and unity to their city. Early in his stay Muhammad put forth the Constitution of Medina, which required the community's people to refer all disputes to God and him. Now the residents were expected to replace traditional family, clan, and tribal affiliations with loyalty to Muhammad as the last and the truest Prophet of God.

Over time, the core practices and beliefs of every Muslim would crystallize as the **five pillars of Islam**. Muslims were expected to (1) *proclaim* the phrase "there is no God but God and Muhammad is His Prophet"; (2) *pray* five times daily facing Mecca; (3) *fast* from sunup until sundown during the month of Ramadan; (4) *travel* on a pilgrimage to Mecca at least once in a lifetime if their personal resources permitted; and (5) *pay* alms in the form of taxation that would alleviate the hardships of the poor. These clear-cut expectations gave the imperial system that soon developed a doctrinal and legal structure and a broad appeal to diverse populations.

MUHAMMAD'S SUCCESSORS AND THE EXPANDING *DAR AL-ISLAM*

In 632 CE, in his early sixties, the Prophet passed away; but Islam remained vibrant thanks to the energy of its early followers—especially Muhammad's first four successors, the "rightly guided caliphs" (the Arabic word *khalīfa* means successor). These caliphs ruled

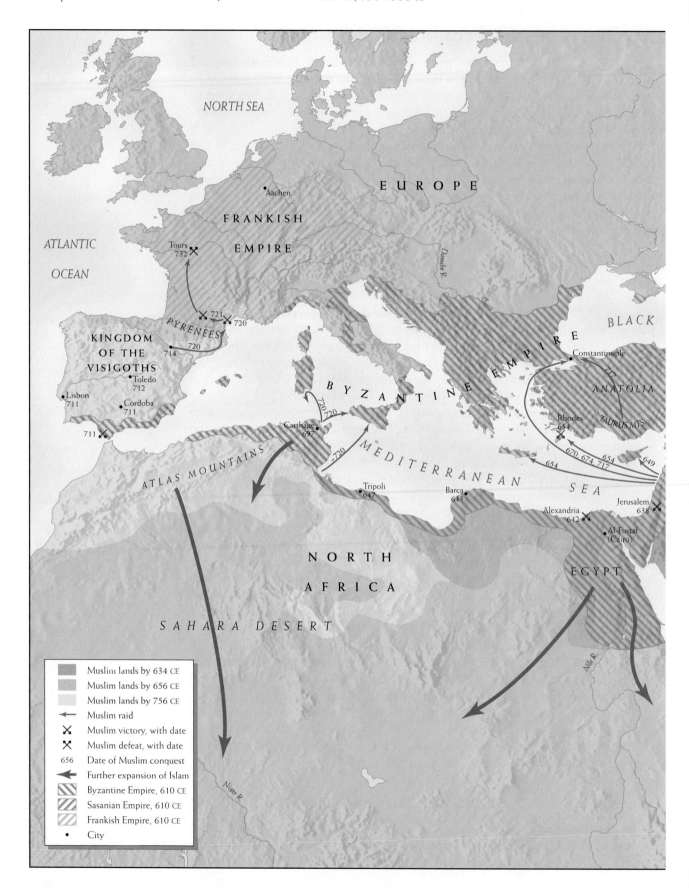

NORTH SEA

EUROPE

FRANKISH

Aachen

EMPIRE

ATLANTIC

OCEAN

Tours
732

PYRENEES
721
720

KINGDOM
OF THE
VISIGOTHS

714

720

Toledo
712

Lisbon
711

Cordoba
711

711

Danube R.

BLACK

BYZANTINE EMPIRE

Constantinople

ANATOLIA

TAURUS MTS

Rhodes
654

670 674 717
654

649

654

CARTHAGE
697

ATLAS MOUNTAINS

MEDITERRANEAN

SEA

720

Tripoli
647

Barca
643

Alexandria
642

Jerusalem
638

Al-Fustat
(Cairo)

NORTH

AFRICA

EGYPT

SAHARA DESERT

Nile R.

Niger R.

	Muslim lands by 634 CE
	Muslim lands by 656 CE
	Muslim lands by 756 CE
←	Muslim raid
✕	Muslim victory, with date
✗	Muslim defeat, with date
656	Date of Muslim conquest
←	Further expansion of Islam
▨	Byzantine Empire, 610 CE
▨	Sasanian Empire, 610 CE
▨	Frankish Empire, 610 CE
•	City

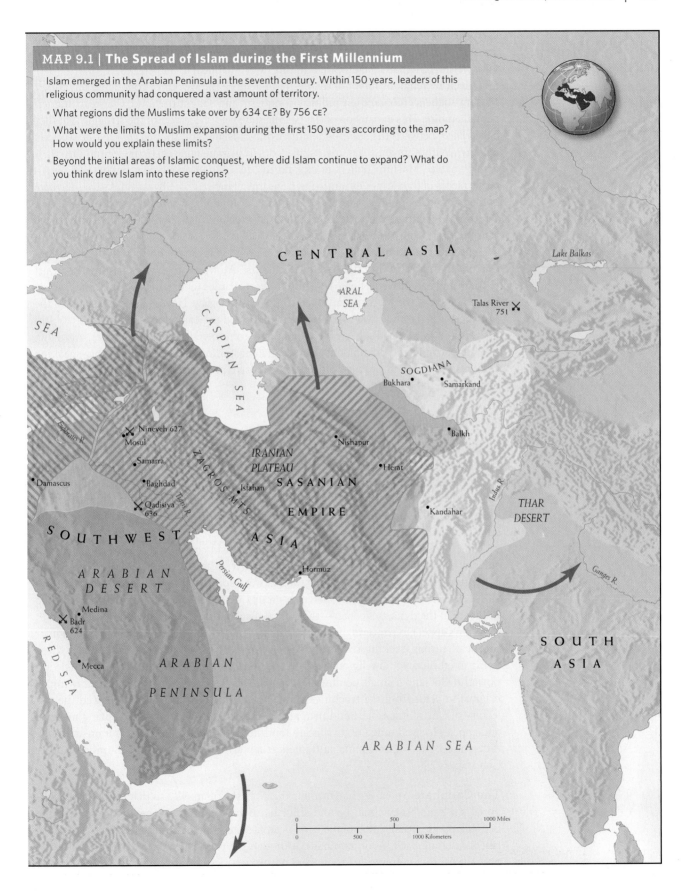

MAP 9.1 | The Spread of Islam during the First Millennium

Islam emerged in the Arabian Peninsula in the seventh century. Within 150 years, leaders of this religious community had conquered a vast amount of territory.

- What regions did the Muslims take over by 634 CE? By 756 CE?
- What were the limits to Muslim expansion during the first 150 years according to the map? How would you explain these limits?
- Beyond the initial areas of Islamic conquest, where did Islam continue to expand? What do you think drew Islam into these regions?

CENTRAL ASIA

Lake Balkas

SEA

ARAL
SEA

CASPIAN SEA

Talas River
751

SOGDIANA

Bukhara •Samarkand

•Balkh

Nineveh 627
Mosul

Nishapur

Samarra

IRANIAN
PLATEAU

ZAGROS MTS.

Herat

Damascus

Baghdad

Isfahan

SASANIAN

Indus R.

THAR
DESERT

Qadisiya
636

EMPIRE

Tigris R.

Kandahar

SOUTHWEST

ASIA

ARABIAN
DESERT

Persian Gulf

Hormuz

Ganges R.

SOUTH
ASIA

Medina
Badr
624

ARABIAN

Mecca

PENINSULA

RED SEA

ARABIAN SEA

| 0 | | 500 | | 1000 Miles |
| 0 | 500 | | 1000 Kilometers | |

over Muslim peoples and the expanding state. They institutionalized the new faith. They set the new religion on the pathway to imperial greatness by linking religious uprightness with territorial expansion, empire building, and an appeal to all peoples.

Driven by religious fervor and a desire to acquire the wealth of conquered territories, Muslim soldiers embarked on military conquests and sought to found a far-reaching territorial empire. This expansion of the Islamic state was one aspect of the struggle that they called *jihad,* between the *dar al-Islam* (the world of Islam) and the *dar al-harb* (the world of warfare). Within fifteen years, their skill in desert warfare and their inspired military leadership enabled Muslim soldiers to expand the *dar al-Islam* into Syria, Egypt, and Iraq—centerpieces of the former Byzantine and Sasanian empires. The Byzantines saved the core of their empire by pulling back to the highlands of Anatolia, where they could defend their frontiers. In contrast, the Sasanians hurled their remaining military resources against the Muslim armies, only to be annihilated.

A political vacuum opened in the new and growing Islamic empire with the assassination of Ali, the last of the "rightly guided caliphs." Ali was arguably the first male convert to Islam and had proved a fierce leader in the early battles for expansion. The Umayyads, a branch of one of the Meccan clans, laid claim to Ali's legacy. Having been governors of the province of Syria under Ali, the Umayyads relocated the capital to the Syrian city of Damascus and introduced a hereditary monarchy to resolve leadership disputes. Although tolerant of conquered populations, Umayyad dynasts did not permit non-Arabic-speaking converts to hold high political offices, an exclusive policy that contributed to their ultimate demise.

THE ABBASID REVOLUTION

As the Umayyads spread Islam beyond Arabia, some peoples resisted what they experienced as Arab Umayyad repression and religious impurity. A new coalition emerged under the Abbasi family, which claimed descent from the Prophet. Disgruntled provincial authorities and their military allies, as well as non-Arab converts, joined the movement. These individuals had embraced Islam and learned Arabic, only to discover that they were still second-class citizens.

After amassing a sizable military force, the Abbasid coalition trounced the Umayyad ruler in 750 CE. The center of the Muslim state then shifted to Baghdad in Iraq (as we saw at the start of this chapter), signifying the eastward sprawl of the faith and its empire. This shift represented a success for non-Arab groups within Islam without eliminating Arab influence at the dynasty's center—the capital, Baghdad, in Arabic-speaking Iraq.

Islam's appeal to converts during the Abbasid period was diverse. Some turned to it for practical reasons, seeking reduced taxes or enhanced power. Others, particularly those living in ethnically and religiously diverse regions, welcomed the message of a single all-powerful God and a single community united by a clear code of laws. Islam, drawing its original impetus from the teachings and actions of a prophetic figure, followed the trajectory of Christianity and Buddhism and became a faith with a universalizing message and appeal. It owed much of its success to its ability to merge the contributions of vastly different geographic, economic, and intellectual territories into a rich yet unified culture (see Map 9.1).

The Caliphate An early challenge for the Abbasid rulers was to determine how traditional, or "Arab," they could be and still rule so vast an empire. They chose to keep the bedrock political institution of the early Islamic state—the **caliphate** (the line of political rulers reaching back to Muhammad). Although the caliphs exercised political authority over the Muslim community, they were not understood to have inherited Muhammad's prophetic powers or any authority in religious doctrine. That power was reserved for religious scholars, called *ulama*.

Abbasid rule borrowed practices from successful predecessors in its mixture of Persian absolute authority and the royal seclusion of the Byzantine emperors who lived in palaces far removed from their subjects. This blend of absolute authority and decentralized power involved a delicate and ultimately unsustainable balancing act. As the empire expanded it became increasingly decentralized politically, enabling wily regional governors and competing caliphates in Spain and Egypt to grab power. Even as Islam's political center diffused, though, its spiritual center remained fixed in Mecca, where many of the faithful gathered to fulfill their pilgrimage obligation.

The Army The Abbasids, like all rulers, relied on force to integrate their empire. Yet they struggled with what the nature of that military force should be: a citizen-conscript, all-Arab force or a professional, even non-Arab, army. In the early stages, leaders conscripted military forces from local Arab populations, creating citizen armies. Ultimately, however, the Abbasids recruited professional soldiers from Turkish-speaking communities in central Asia, and from the non-Arab, Berber-speaking peoples of North Africa and West Africans. Their reliance on foreign—that is, non-Arab—military personnel represented a major shift in the Islamic world. Not only did the change infuse the empire with dynamic new populations, but soon these groups gained political authority. Having begun as an Arab state and then incorporated strong Persian influence, the Islamic empire now embraced Turkish elements from the pastoral belts of central Asia.

Islamic Law (The *Sharia*) and Theology Islamic law, or the **sharia**, began to take shape in the Abbasid period. The work of generations of religious scholars, the *sharia* covers all aspects of practical and spiritual life, providing legal principles for marriage contracts, trade regulations, and religious prescriptions such as prayer, pilgrimage rites, and ritual fasting. The most influential early scholar of the *sharia* was an eighth-century Palestinian-born Arab, al-Shafi'i, who insisted that Muhammad's laws as laid out in the Quran, in addition to his sayings and actions as written in later reports (*hadith*), provided all the legal guidance that Islamic judges needed. This shift gave *ulama* (Muslim scholars) a central place in Islam since only their spiritual authority, and not the political authority of the caliphs, was qualified to define religious law. The *ulama*'s ascendance opened a sharp division within Islam: between the secular realm of the caliphs and the religious sphere of religious judges, experts on Islamic law, teachers, and holy men.

Gender in Early Islam Pre-Islamic Arabia was one of the last regions in Southwest Asia where patriarchy had not triumphed. Instead, men still married into women's families and moved to those families' locations, as was common in tribal communities. Some women engaged in a variety of occupations and, if they became wealthy, even married more than one husband. But contact with the rest of Southwest Asia, where men's power over women prevailed, was already altering women's status in the Arabian Peninsula before the birth of Muhammad.

Muhammad's relations with women reflected these changes. As a young man, he married a woman fifteen years his senior—Khadija, an independent trader—and took no other wives before she died. It was Khadija to whom he went in fear following his first revelations. She wrapped him in a blanket and assured him of his sanity. She was also his first convert. Later in life, however, he took younger wives, some of whom were widows of his companions, and insisted on their veiling (partly as a sign of their modesty and privacy). He married his favorite wife, Aisha, when she was only nine or ten years old. As a major source for collecting Muhammad's sayings, Aisha became an important figure in early Islam.

By the time Islam reached Southwest Asia and North Africa, where strict gender rules and women's subordinate status were entrenched, the new faith was adopting a patriarchal outlook. Muslim men could divorce freely; women could not. A man could take four wives and numerous concubines; a woman could have only one husband. Well-to-do women, always veiled, lived secluded from male society. Still, the Quran did offer women some protections. Men had to treat each wife with respect if they took more than one. Women could inherit property (although only half of what a man inherited). Marriage dowries went directly to the bride rather than to her guardian, indicating women's independent legal standing; and while a woman's adultery drew harsh punishment, its proof required eyewitness testimony. The result was a legal system that reinforced men's dominance over women but empowered magistrates to oversee the definition of male honor and proper behavior.

THE BLOSSOMING OF ABBASID CULTURE

COMPARISON

EVALUATE the relationships between religion, empire, and commercial exchange across Afro-Eurasia during this period.

The arts flourished during the Abbasid period, a blossoming that left its imprint throughout society. Within a century of Abbasid rule, Arabic had superseded Greek as the Muslim world's preferred language for poetry, literature, medicine, science, and philosophy. Arabic spread beyond native speakers to become the language of the educated classes. Arabic scholars preserved and extended Greek and Roman thought, in part through the transmission of treatises by Aristotle, Hippocrates, Galen, Ptolemy, and Archimedes, among others. To house such manuscripts, patrons of the arts and sciences—including the caliphs—opened magnificent libraries.

The Muslim world absorbed scientific breakthroughs from China and other areas: they incorporated the use of paper from China, adopted siege warfare from China and Byzantium, and assimilated knowledge of plants from the ancient Greeks. From Indian sources, scholars borrowed a numbering system based on the concept of zero and units of ten—what we today call Arabic numerals. Arab mathematicians were pioneers in arithmetic, geometry, algebra, and trigonometry. Since much of Greek science had been lost in the West and later was reintroduced via the Muslim world, the Islamic contribution to the West was of immense significance. Thus, this intense borrowing, translating, storing, and diffusing of ideas brought worlds together.

ISLAM IN A WIDER WORLD

As Islam spread and decentralized, it generated dazzling and often competitive dynasties in Spain, North Africa, and points farther east. Each dynastic state revealed the Muslim talent for achieving high levels of artistry far from its heartland. But growing diversity led to a problem: Islam fragmented politically. No single political regime could hold its widely dispersed believers together (see Map 9.2).

Cities in Spain One extraordinary Muslim state arose in Spain under Abd al-Rahman III (r. 912–961 CE), the successor ruler of a Muslim kingdom founded there over a century earlier. Abd al-Rahman brought peace and stability to a violent frontier region where civil conflict had disrupted commerce and intellectual exchange. His evenhanded governance promoted amicable relations among Muslims, Christians, and Jews, and his diplomatic relations with Christian potentates as far away as France, Germany, and Scandinavia generated impressive commercial exchanges between western Europe and North Africa. He expanded and beautified the capital city of Cordoba, and his successor made the Great Mosque of Cordoba one of Spain's most stunning sites. In the nearby city Madinat al-Zahra, Abd al-Rahman III surrounded the city's administrative offices and mosque

The Great Mosque of Cordoba The great mosque of Cordoba was built in the eighth century by the Umayyad ruler Abd al-Rahman I and added to by other Muslim rulers. Built on the site of a Gothic church, which had been placed on the site of an earlier Roman temple, the mosque's most striking features were alternating red and white arches, made of jasper, onyx, marble, and granite and fashioned from materials from the Roman temple and other buildings in the vicinity. Around the doors and across the walls Arabic calligraphy proclaimed Muhammad's message and asserted the superiority of Arabic as God's chosen language.

with verdant gardens of lush tropical and semitropical plants, tranquil pools, fountains that spouted cooling waters, and sturdy aqueducts that carried potable water to the city's inhabitants.

Talent in Central Asia In the eastern regions of the Islamic empire, Abbasid rulers in Baghdad surrounded themselves with learned men from Sogdiana, the central Asian territory where Greek learning had flourished. The Barmaki family, who for several generations held high administrative offices under the Abbasids, came from the central Asian city of Balkh. Loyal servants of the caliph, the Barmakis made sure that wealth and talent from the crossroads of Asia were funneled into Baghdad. Devoted patrons of the arts, the Barmakis promoted and collected Arabic translations of Persian, Greek, and Sanskrit manuscripts. They also encouraged central Asian scholars to enhance their learning by moving to Baghdad. These scholars included the Islamic cleric al-Bukhari (d. 870 CE), who was a renowned collector of *hadith*; the mathematician al-Khwarizmi (c. 780–850 CE), who modified Indian digits into Arabic numerals and wrote the first book on algebra; and the philosopher al-Farabi (d. 950 CE), from a Turkish military family, who also made his way to Baghdad, where he studied eastern Christian teachings and promoted the Platonic ideal of a philosopher-king. Even when the Abbasid caliphate began to decline, intellectual vitality continued under the patronage of local rulers. The best example of this is, perhaps, the polymath Ibn Sina (known in the West as Avicenna, 980–1037), whose *Canon of Medicine* stood as the standard medical text in both Southwest Asia and Europe for centuries.

Trade in Sub-Saharan Africa Islam also crossed the Sahara Desert and penetrated well into Africa, carried by traders and scholars (see Map 9.3), where merchants exchanged weapons and textiles for gold, salt, and slaves. Trade did more than join West Africa to North Africa. It generated prodigious wealth, which allowed centralized political kingdoms to develop. The most celebrated was Ghana, which lay at the terminus of North Africa's major trading routes and was often hailed in Arab sources for its gold, as well as its pomp and power. Seafaring Muslim traders carried Islam into East Africa via the Indian Ocean. As early

MAP 9.2 | Political Fragmentation in the Islamic World, 750–1000 CE

By 1000 CE, the Islamic world was politically fractured and decentralized. The Abbasid caliphs still reigned in Baghdad, but they wielded very limited political authority. Looking at the map, first point to Baghdad and then point out all the areas under Abbasid control.

- What are the regions where major Islamic powers emerged?
- What areas were Sunni? Which were Shiite?
- Why were the Abbasids unable to sustain political unity in the Islamic world?

as the eighth century CE, coastal trading communities in East Africa were exporting ivory and possibly slaves. By the tenth century, the East African coast featured a mixed African-Arab culture. The region's evolving Bantu language absorbed Arabic words and before long gained a new name, Swahili (derived from the Arabic plural of the word meaning "coast").

OPPOSITION WITHIN ISLAM: SHIISM AND THE FATIMIDS

Islam's whirlwind rise generated internal tensions from the start. It is hardly surprising that a religion that extolled territorial conquests and created a large empire in its first decades would also spawn dissident religious movements that challenged the existing imperial structures. Muslims shared a reverence for a basic text and a single God, but often had little else in common. Religious and political divisions only grew deeper as Islam spread into new corners of Afro-Eurasia.

Sunnis and Shiites Early division within Islam was fueled by disagreements about who should succeed the Prophet, how the succession should take place, and who should lead Islam's expansion into the wider world. **Sunnis** (from the Arabic word meaning

The Jenne Mosque and the Al-Azhar Mosque The Jenne Mosque *(left)* arose in the kingdom of Mali when that kingdom was at the height of its power. The mosque speaks to the depth and importance of Islam's roots in the Malian kingdom. The mosque of al-Azhar *(right)* is Cairo's most important ancient mosque. Built in the tenth century by the Fatimid conquerors and rulers of Egypt, it quickly became a leading center for worship and learning, frequented by Muslim clerics and admired in Europe.

"tradition") accept that the political succession from the Prophet to the four "rightly guided caliphs" and then to the Umayyad and Abbasid dynasties was the correct one. The vast majority of Muslims today are Sunni. Dissidents, like the Shiites, contest the Sunni understanding of political and spiritual authority. **Shiites** ("members of the party of Ali") felt that the proper successors should have been Ali, who had married the Prophet's daughter Fatima, and then his descendants. Ali was one of the early converts to Islam and one of the band of Meccans who had migrated with the Prophet to Medina. The fourth of the "rightly guided caliphs," he ruled over the Muslim community from 656 to 661 CE, dying at the hands of an assassin who struck him down as he was praying in a mosque in Kufa, Iraq. Shiites believe that Ali's descendants, whom they call *imams,* have religious and prophetic power as well as political authority—and thus should be spiritual leaders.

Shiism appealed to regional and ethnic groups whom the Umayyads and Abbasids had excluded from power; it became Islam's most potent dissident force and created a permanent divide within Islam. Shiism was well established in the first century of Islam's existence, and over time the Sunnis and Shiites diverged even more than these early political disputes over succession might have indicated. Both groups had their own versions of the *sharia,* their own collections of *hadith,* and their own theological tenets.

The Fatimids Repressed in what is present-day Iraq and Iran, Shiite activists made their way to North Africa, where they joined with dissident Berber groups to topple several rulers. In 909 CE, a Shiite religious and military leader, Abu Abdallah, overthrew the Sunni ruler there. Thus began the Fatimid regime.

After conquering Egypt in 969 CE, the Fatimids set themselves against the Abbasid caliphs of Baghdad, refusing to acknowledge their legitimacy and claiming to speak for the whole Islamic world. The Fatimid rulers established their capital at al-Qahira (or Cairo). Early on they founded al-Azhar mosque, which attracted scholars from all over Afro-Eurasia and spread Islamic learning outward. They also built other elegant mosques and centers of learning. The Fatimid regime lasted until the late twelfth century, though its rulers made little headway in persuading the Egyptian population, most of whom remained Sunnis, to embrace their Shiite beliefs.

MAP 9.3 | Islam and Trade in Sub-Saharan Africa, 700–1000 CE

Islamic merchants and scholars, not Islamic armies, carried Islam into sub-Saharan Africa. Trace the trade routes in Africa, being sure to follow the correct direction of trade.

- According to the map key and icons, what commodities were Islamic merchants seeking below the Sahara?

- What were the major trade routes and the direction of trade in Africa?

- How did trade and commerce lead to the geographic expansion of the Islamic faith?

By 1000 CE Islam, which had originated as a radical religious revolt in a small corner of the Arabian Peninsula, had grown into a vast political and religious empire. It had become the dominant force in the middle regions of Afro-Eurasia. Like its rival in this part of the world, Christianity, it aspired to universality. But unlike Christianity, it was linked from its outset to political power. Muhammad and his early followers created an empire to facilitate the expansion of their faith, while their Christian counterparts inherited an empire when Constantine embraced the new faith. A vision of a world under the jurisdiction of Muslim caliphs, adhering to the dictates of the *sharia,* drove Muslim armies, merchants, and scholars to territories thousands of miles away from Mecca and Medina. Yet as Islam's reach stretched thin, political fragmentation within the Muslim world meant that Islam's reach could not extend to much of western Europe and China.

The Tang State

The rise of the powerful Tang Empire (618–907 CE) in China paralleled Islam's explosion out of Arabia and its impact throughout Afro-Eurasia. Once again the landmass had two centers of power, as Islam replaced the Roman Empire in counterbalancing the power and wealth of China. Like the Umayyads and the Abbasids, the Tang dynasty promoted a cosmopolitan culture. Under Tang rule Buddhism, medicine, and mathematics from India gave China's chief cities an international flavor. China became a hub for East Asian integration, and spread its influence to Korea and Japan.

COMPARISON

COMPARE the organizational structures of the Abbasids, Tang China, and Christendom.

TERRITORIAL EXPANSION UNDER THE TANG DYNASTY

The Tang dynasty expanded the boundaries of the Chinese state and reestablished its dominance in East and central Asia. After the fall of the Han, China had faced a long period of political fragmentation (see Chapter 8). As had happened several times before, yet another sudden change in the course of the Yellow River caused extensive flooding on the North China plain and set the stage for the emergence of the Tang dynasty. Revolts ensued as the population faced starvation. Li Yuan, the governor of a province under the short-lived Sui dynasty (589–618 CE) marched on Chang'an and took the throne in 618. He promptly established the Tang dynasty and began building a strong central government by increasing the number of provinces and doubling the number of government offices. By 624 CE the initial steps of establishing the Tang dynasty were complete; but Li Yuan's ambitious son, Li Shimin, forced his father to abdicate and took the throne in 627 CE.

An expanding Tang state required a large and professionally trained army, capable of defending far-flung frontiers and squelching rebellious populations. Toward these efforts the Tang built a military organization of aristocratic cavalry and peasant soldiers. The cavalry regularly clashed on the northern steppes with encroaching nomadic peoples, who also fought on horseback; at its height the Tang military had 700,000 horses. At the same time, between 1 and 2 million peasant soldiers garrisoned the south and toiled on public works projects.

Much like the Islamic forces, the Tang's frontier armies increasingly relied on pastoral nomadic soldiers from the Inner Eurasian steppe. Notable were the Uighurs, Turkish-speaking peoples who had moved into western China and by 750 CE constituted the empire's most potent military force. These warriors mobilized fearsome cavalries, fired longbows at distant range, and wielded steel swords and knives in hand-to-hand combat. The Tang military also pushed the state into Tibet, the Red River valley in northern Vietnam, Manchuria, and Bohai (near Korea).

At the empire's height, Tang armies controlled more than 4 million square miles of territory (see Map 9.4)—an area as large as the entire Islamic world in the ninth and tenth centuries. Once the Tang administrators brought South China's rich farmlands under

MAP 9.4 | The Tang State in East Asia, 750 CE

The Tang dynasty, at its territorial peak in 750 CE, controlled a state that extended from central Asia to the East China Sea.

- What foreign areas are under Tang control? What areas were heavily influenced by Tang government and culture?
- How can we tell from the map that China was undergoing an economic revolution during the Tang period?
- How did the Tang maintain order and stability in such a large, dynamic realm?

cultivation (by draining swamps, building an intricate network of canals and channels, and connecting lakes and rivers to the rice lands), the state was able to collect taxes from roughly 10 million families, representing 57 million individuals. Most of these taxes took the form of agricultural labor, which propelled the expansion of cultivated frontiers throughout the south.

ORGANIZING THE TANG EMPIRE

The Tang Empire emulated the Han in many ways, but its rulers also introduced new institutions. The heart of the agrarian-based Tang state was the magnificent capital city of Chang'an, the population of which reached 1 million, half of whom lived within its impressive city walls. The outer walls enclosed a thirty-square-mile area. Internal security arrangements made it one of the safest urban locales for its age. Its more than 100 quarters were separated from each other by interior walls with gates that were closed at night, after which no one was permitted on the streets. Horsemen patrolled the streets until the gates reopened in the morning. Chang'an had a large foreign population, estimated at one-third of its total, and a diverse religious life. Zoroastrian fires burned as worshippers sacrificed animals and chanted temple hymns. Nestorian Christians from Syria found a welcoming community, and Buddhists could boast ninety-one of their own temples in Chang'an in 722 CE.

Confucian Administrators Despite the Tang's reliance on the fruits of agriculture and a military force, the day-to-day control of the empire required an efficient and loyal civil service. Entry into the Tang ruling group required knowledge of Confucian ideas and all of the commentaries on the Confucian classics. It also required skill in the intricate classical Chinese language, in which this literature was written.

The Tang state introduced the world's first fully written **civil service examinations**, which tested sophisticated literary skills and knowledge of the Confucian classics. The Tang also allowed the use of Daoist classics as texts for the exams, believing that the early Daoists represented another important stream of ancient wisdom. Candidates for office, whom local elites recommended, gathered in the capital triennially to take qualifying exams. They had been trained since the age of three in the classics and histories, either by their families or in Buddhist temple schools. Most failed, but those who were successful underwent further trials to evaluate their character and determine the level of their appointments. New officials were selected from the pool of graduates on the basis of social conduct, eloquence, skill in calligraphy and mathematics, and legal knowledge.

Although official careers were in theory open to anyone of proven talent, in practice they were closed to certain groups. Women were not permitted to serve, nor were sons of merchants, nor those who could not afford a classical education. Over time, though, Tang civil examinations forced aristocrats to compete with commoner southern families, whose growing wealth gave them access to educational resources that made them the equals of the old elites. Through examinations, this new elite eventually outdistanced the sons of the northern aristocracy in the Tang government in effect by out-studying them.

The system underscored education as the primary avenue for success. Even impoverished families sought the best classical education they could afford for their sons. Although few succeeded in the civil examinations, many boys and even some girls learned the fundamentals of reading and writing. The Buddhists played a crucial role in extending education across society: as part of their charitable mission, their temple schools introduced many children to primers based on classical texts. Many Buddhist monks, in fact, entered the clergy only after not qualifying for or failing the civil examinations.

China's Female Emperor Not all Tang power brokers were men. The wives and mothers of emperors wielded influence in the court—usually behind the scenes, but sometimes publicly. The most striking example is the Empress Wu.

Born into a noble family, Wu Zhao played music and mastered the Chinese classics as a young girl. Because she was witty, intelligent, and beautiful, Wu was recruited before age thirteen to Li Shimin's court and became his favorite concubine. When Li Shimin died, his son assumed power and became the Emperor Gaozong. Wu became the new emperor's favorite concubine and gave birth to the sons he required to succeed him. As the mother of the future emperor, Wu enjoyed heightened political power. Subsequently, she took the place of Gaozong's Empress Wang by accusing her of killing Wu's newborn daughter.

After Gaozong suffered a stroke, Wu became administrator of the court, a position equal to the emperor's. She created a secret police force to spy on her opposition, and she jailed or killed those who challenged her. Following her husband's death, she made

The Tang Court This tenth-century painting of elegant ladies of the Tang imperial court enjoying a feast and music (*left*) tells us a great deal about the aesthetic tastes of elite women in this era. It also shows the secluded "inner quarters," where court ladies passed their daily lives far from the hurly-burly of imperial politics. Castrated males, known as eunuchs (*right*), guarded the women and protected the royal family of Tang emperors. By the late eighth century, eunuchs were fully integrated into the government and wielded a great deal of military and political power.

herself Empress Wu (r. 684–705 CE). She expanded the military and recruited her administrators from the civil examination candidates to oppose her enemies at court.

Wu ordered scholars to write biographies of famous women, and she empowered her mother's clan by assigning high political posts to her relatives. Later, she moved her court from Chang'an to Luoyang, where she tried to establish a new "Zhou dynasty," seeking to imitate the widely admired era of Confucius. Empress Wu elevated Buddhism over Daoism as the favored state religion, invited the most gifted Buddhist scholars to her capital at Luoyang, built Buddhist temples, and subsidized spectacular cave sculptures. In fact, Chinese Buddhism achieved its highest officially sponsored development in this period.

Eunuchs Tang rulers protected themselves, their possessions, and especially their women, with loyal and well-compensated **eunuchs** (men surgically castrated as youths and thus sexually impotent). By the late eighth century, more than 4,500 eunuchs were fully entrenched in the Tang Empire's institutions, wielding significant power not only within the imperial household but at the court and beyond. For instance, the Chief Eunuch controlled the military. Through him, the military power of court eunuchs extended to every province and garrison station in the empire, forming an all-encompassing network. This eunuch bureaucracy mediated between the emperor and the provincial governments.

Under Emperor Xianzong (r. 806–820 CE), eunuchs acted as a third pillar of the government, working alongside the official bureaucracy and the imperial court. Yet by 838 CE, the delicate balance of power among throne, eunuchs, and civil officials had evaporated. Eunuchs became an unruly political force in late Tang politics, and their competition for influence produced political instability.

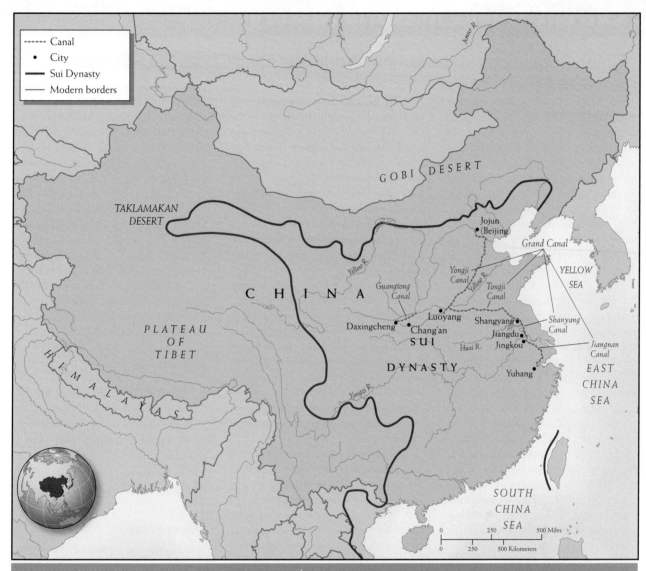

MAP 9.5 | The Sui Dynasty Canals

China, like the Islamic world, experienced a population explosion during this period.

• Where are the Sui dynasty canals on the map and the two areas showing population concentration?

• Why do you think the population concentrations are located along the canals? What major cities did the canals connect and what role did the canals play in integrating China under the Sui dynasty and its successor state, the Tang Empire?

AN ECONOMIC REVOLUTION

At its height, Tang China's economic achievements included agricultural production based on an egalitarian land allotment system, an increasingly fine handicrafts industry, a diverse commodity market, and a dynamic urban life. The earlier short-lived Sui dynasty had started this economic progress by reunifying China and building canals, especially the Grand Canal linking the north and south (see Map 9.5). The Tang continued by centering their efforts on the Grand Canal and the Yangzi River, which flows from west to east. These waterways aided communication and transport throughout the empire. The south grew richer, largely through the backbreaking labor of immigrants from the north.

Current Trends in World History

Green Revolutions in the Islamic World and Tang China, 300–600 CE

World historians often focus on the more famous Columbian Exchange to talk about how the sharing of foods between regions of the world created revolutions in diet. The Afro-Eurasian world underwent a food revolution of its own between 300 and 600 CE. New crops, especially food crops, leaped across political and cultural borders during this period, offering expanding populations more diverse and nutritious diets and the ability to feed increased numbers. Such was true of the Islamic world and Tang China in the eighth century. Now, however, it was India that replaced Mesopotamia as the source of a dazzling array of new cultigens. Most of them originated in Southeast Asia, made their way to India, and dispersed throughout the Muslim world and into China. These crops included new strains of rice, taro, sour oranges, lemons, limes, and most likely coconut palm trees, sugarcane, bananas, plantains, and mangoes. Sorghum and possibly cotton and watermelons arrived from Africa. Only the eggplant was indigenous to India. Although these staples spread quickly to East Asia, their westward movement was slower. Not until the Muslim conquest of Sindh in northern India in 711 CE did territories to the west fully discover the crop innovations pioneered in Southeast Asia.

India fascinated the Arabs, and they exploited its agricultural offerings to the hilt. Soon a revolution in crops and diet swept through the Muslim world. Sorghum supplanted millet and the other grains of antiquity because it was hardier, had higher yields, and required a shorter growing season. Citrus trees added flavor to the diet and provided refreshing drinks during the summer heat. Increased cotton cultivation led to a greater demand for textiles.

For over three hundred years, farmers from northwest India to Spain, Morocco, and West Africa made impressive use of the new crops. They increased agricultural output, slashed fallow periods, and grew as many as three crops on lands that formerly had yielded one (see Map 9.6). As a result farmers could feed larger communities; even as cities grew, the countryside became more densely populated and even more productive.

The same agricultural revolution that was sweeping through South Asia and the Muslim world also took East Asia by storm. China received the same crops that Muslim cultivators were carrying westward. Rice was critical. New varieties entered from the south, and groups migrating from the north (after the collapse of the Han Empire) eagerly took them up. Soon Chinese farmers became the world's

most intensive wet-field rice cultivators. Early- and late-ripening seeds supported two or three plantings a year. Champa rice, introduced from central Vietnam, was especially popular for its drought resistance and rapid ripening.

Because rice needs ample water, Chinese hydraulic engineers went into the fields to design water-lifting devices, which peasant farmers used to construct hillside rice paddies. They also dug more canals, linking rivers and lakes (see Map 9.6) and even drained swamps, alleviating the malaria that had long troubled the region. Their efforts yielded a booming and constantly moving rice frontier.

QUESTIONS FOR ANALYSIS

- Historians think of the eighteenth century as having produced an agricultural revolution. To what extent is the same term appropriate for this earlier period?
- How did the new crops change diets and contribute to population growth?

Explore Further

Andrew Watson, *Agricultural Innovation in the Early Islamic World: The Diffusion of Crops and Farming Techniques, 700–1100* (1983).

Fertile land along the Yangzi became China's new granary, and areas south of the Yangzi became its demographic center.

Chinese merchants took full advantage of the Silk Roads to trade with India and the Islamic world; when rebellions in northwest China and the rise of Islam in central Asia jeopardized the land route, the "silk road by sea" became the avenue of choice. From all over Asia and Africa, merchant ships arrived in South China ports bearing spices, medicines, and jewelry in exchange for Chinese silks and porcelain. (See **Current Trends in World History: Green Revolutions in the Islamic World and Tang China, 300–600 CE**.)

In the large cities of the Yangzi delta, workshops produced rich brocades (silk fabrics), fine paper, intricate wood-block prints, unique iron casts, and exquisite porcelains. Art collectors all across Afro-Eurasia especially valued Tang "tricolor pottery," decorated with brilliant hues. Chinese artisans transformed locally grown cotton into highest-quality

MAP 9.6 | Agricultural Diffusion in the First Millennium

The second half of the first millennium saw a revolution in agriculture throughout Afro-Eurasia. Agriculturalists across the landmass increasingly cultivated similar crops.

- Where did most of the crops originate? In what direction and where did most of them flow?
- What role did the spread of Islam and the growth of Islamic empires (see Map 9.1) play in the process?

Legend:

Original Source Areas of Staple Crops
- Bananas
- Sugarcane
- Cotton
- Sorghum

Spread of Staple Crops
- Bananas
- Sugarcane
- Cotton
- Sorghum

Areas to Which Crops Had Spread by 1500
- Bananas
- Sugarcane
- Cotton
- Sorghum

clothing. Painting and dyeing technology improved and the resulting superb silk products generated significant tax revenue. These Chinese luxuries dominated the trading networks that reached Southwest Asia, Europe, and Africa via the Silk Roads and the Indian Ocean. (See **Analyzing Global Developments: Islam and the Silk Trade**.)

ACCOMMODATING WORLD RELIGIONS

The early Tang emperors tolerated remarkable religious diversity. Nestorian Christianity, Zoroastrianism, and Manichaeanism (a radical Christian sect) had entered China from Persia during the time of the Sasanian Empire. Islam came later. These spiritual impulses—together with Buddhism and the indigenous teachings of Daoism and Confucianism—spread throughout the Tang Empire and at first were widely used to enhance state power.

Analyzing Global Developments

Islam and the Silk Trade: Adapting Religion to Opulence

Although the Silk Roads emerged from the industries and commercial networks of the Han, Kushan, Parthian, and Roman empires in the first century BCE, it was not until centuries later, after the collapse of these states, that the golden age of Eurasian trade arose with new, powerful players. Tang China inherited the Han monopoly on silk production, while the Byzantine Empire utilized its Roman resources to develop its own silk weaving industry. Yet, a major threat to these monopolies appeared in the seventh century CE, when the first Islamic empire, the Umayyad caliphate (661–750 CE), built a vast, state-run textile industry to exert influence over its newly conquered cities. Not only did the establishment of textile factories throughout the empire keep the working classes in line, but the luxury textiles produced were incentives for the elite of newly conquered territories (many of which were wealthy and were more sophisticated than the Arab tent culture of early Islamic caliphs) to submit to Muslim rule.

Tensions arose between this opulent lifestyle and the Muslim way of life, which prohibited its adherents from wearing silk. The political, social, and religious authority that the Islamic silk trade lent the caliphate, however, was crucial to its unity and longevity. What's more, the Islamic silk industry was rapidly expanding, with no limits in sight, unlike Byzantine and Tang silks, which were restricted by their respective emperors. And so this textile-centered culture proliferated in an unbridled fashion, eventually infiltrating even religious rituals. The Abbasid caliphate (749–1258 CE) became one of the wealthiest medieval states, and its capital, Baghdad, the most cosmopolitan. To illustrate the sheer extent of the impact that the Islamic silk trade had upon the values of its people, the following table is a record of the goods that caliph Harun al-Rashid, upon whom several *Arabian Nights* stories are based, left behind upon his death in 809 CE.

QUESTIONS FOR ANALYSIS

- Looking back at Map 6.2 (see p. 217) and assuming that the exports of each region remained relatively constant throughout the history of the Silk Roads, with which cities and empires did the Abbasid Empire conduct most of its trade? The least? What might account for these differences?

- What can this list tell us about the values and activities of a caliph c. 800 CE? What, if anything, does the inventory reveal about the values and activities of the nonelite or working classes?

- What kind of evidence from contemporary Tang China or Western Christendom would allow you to draw comparable conclusions to arguments that can be constructed from al-Rashid's inventory?

Textiles: Silk Items	
4,000	silk cloaks, lined with sable and mink
1,500	silk carpets
100	silk rugs
1,000	silk cushions and pillows
1,000	cushions with silk brocade
1,000	inscribed silk cushions
1,000	silk curtains
300	silk brocade curtains

Everyday Textile Items	
4,000	small tents with their accessories
150	marquees (large tents)

Source: Xinru Liu, *The Silk Road in World History* (New York: Oxford University Press, 2010).

The Growth of Buddhism Buddhism, in particular, thrived under Tang rule. Initially, Emperor Li Shimin distrusted Buddhist monks because they avoided serving the government and paying taxes. Yet after Buddhism gained acceptance as one of the "three ways" of learning—joining Daoism and Confucianism—Li endowed huge monasteries, sent emissaries to India to collect texts and relics, and commissioned Buddhist paintings and statuary. Caves along the Silk Roads, such as those at Dunhuang, provided ideal venues for monks to paint the inside walls where religious rites and meditation took place.

Luxury Textile Items	
4,000	embroidered robes
500	pieces of velvet
1,000	Armenian carpets
300	carpets from Maysan (present-day eastern Iraq)
1,000	carpets from Darabjird (present-day Darab, Iran)
500	carpets from Tabaristan (southern coast of the Caspian sea)
1,000	cushions from Tabaristan

Fine Cotton Items and Garments	
2,000	drawers of various kinds
4,000	turbans
1,000	hoods
1,000	capes of various kinds
5,000	kerchiefs of different kinds
10,000	caftans (long robes)
4,000	curtains
4,000	pairs of socks

Fur and Leather Items	
4,000	boots lined with sable and mink
4,000	special saddles
30,000	common saddles
1,000	belts

Metal Goods	
500,000	dinars (cash)
2,000	brass objects of various kinds
10,000	decorated swords
50,000	swords for the guards and pages (*ghulam*)
150,000	lances
100,000	bows
1,000	special suits of armor
10,000	helmets
20,000	breastplates
150,000	shields
300	stoves

Aromatics and Drugs	
100,000	mithqals of musk (1 mithqual = 4.25 grams)
100,000	mithqals of ambergris (musky perfume ingredient)
	many kinds of perfume
1,000	baskets of India aloes

Jewelry and Cut Gems	
	jewels valued by jewelers at 4 million dinars
1,000	jeweled rings

Fine Stone and Metal Vessels	
1,000	precious china vessels
1,000	ewers

Anti-Buddhist Campaigns By the mid-ninth century, however, the growing influence of China's hundreds of thousands of Buddhist monks and nuns threatened Confucian and Daoist leaders, who responded by arguing that Buddhism's values conflicted with native traditions. One Confucian-trained scholar-official, Han Yu, even attacked Buddhism as a foreign doctrine of barbarian peoples who were different in language, culture, and knowledge. Although Han Yu was exiled for his objections, two decades later the state began suppressing Buddhist monasteries and confiscating their wealth, fearing that religious loyalties would undermine political ones. Increasingly intolerant Confucian

One of the Four Sacred Mountains This monastery on Mount Song is famous because in 527 CE an Indian priest, Bodhidharma, arrived there to initiate the Zen school of Buddhism in China.

scholar-administrators argued that the Buddhist monastic establishment threatened the imperial order.

By the mid-ninth century CE, the Tang state openly persecuted Buddhism. Emperor Wuzong (814–846 CE), for instance, closed more than 4,600 monasteries and destroyed 40,000 temples and shrines. More than 260,000 Buddhist monks and nuns endured a forced return to secular life, after which the state parceled out monastery lands to taxpaying landlords and peasant farmers. To expunge the cultural impact of Buddhism, classically trained literati revived ancient prose styles and the teachings of Confucius and his followers. Their efforts reversed some of the early Buddhist successes in China.

Although Buddhism remained important, the Tang era represented the triumph of homegrown ideologies (Confucianism and Daoism) over a foreign universalizing religion (Buddhism). In addition, by permanently dismantling huge monastic land holdings, the Tang ensured that no religion would rival its power. Successor dynasties continued to keep religious establishments weak and fragmented, although Confucianism maintained a more prominent role within society as the basis of the ruling classes' ideology and as a quasi-religious belief system for a wider portion of the population. The result was persistent religious diversity within China.

TANG INTERACTIONS WITH KOREA AND JAPAN

While China was opening up to the cultures of its western regions, its own culture was reaching out to the east—to Korea and, eventually, to Japan (see Map 9.7). Chinese influence, both indirect and direct, had reached into Korea for more than a millennium, and later into Japan; but not without local resistance and the flourishing of entirely indigenous and independent political and religious developments.

Early Korea Interactions with China played a fundamental role in the history of the Korean peninsula. Unification in 668 CE under the Silla—one of three rival states in

MAP 9.7 | Borderlands: Korea and Japan, 600–1000 CE

The Tang dynasty held great power over emerging Korean and Japanese states, although it never directly ruled either region.

- Based on the map, what connections do you see between Korea and Japan and the Tang Empire?
- What, if any, relationship do you see between the proliferation of Buddhist temples and Shinto shrines?

Korea—enabled Koreans to establish an autonomous government, but their opposition to the Chinese did not deter them from modeling their government on the Tang imperial state. The Silla rulers dispatched annual emissaries bearing tribute payments to the Chinese capital and regularly sent students and monks. As a result, literary Chinese—not their own dialect—became the written language of Korean elites. Chinese influence extended to the way in which the Silla state organized its court and bureaucracy and to the construction of the Silla capital city of Kumsong, which imitated the Tang capital of Chang'an. Silla's fortunes became entwined with the Tang's to such an extent, however, that once the Tang declined, Silla also began to fragment.

Early Japan Like Korea, Japan also felt influences emanating from China, and it responded by thwarting and accommodating them at the same time. But Japan enjoyed added autonomy: it was an archipelago of islands, separated from the mainland although internally fragmented. In the mid-third century, a warlike group had arrived by sea from Korea and imposed military and social control over southern Japan. These conquerors—known as the "Tomb Culture" because of their elevated burial sites—unified Japan by extolling their imperial ancestors and maintaining their social hierarchy. In time, the complex aristocratic society that had developed within the Tomb Culture gave rise to a Japanese state on the Yamato plain in the region now known as Nara. In becoming the ruling faction in this area, the Yamato clan incorporated native Japanese as well as Korean migrants.

After 587 CE the Soga kinship group—originally from Korea but by 500 CE a minor branch of the Yamato imperial family—became Japan's leading family and controlled the Japanese court through intermarriage. Soon they were attributing their cultural innovations to their own Prince Shotoku (574–622 CE), of Soga and Yamato descent. Contemporary Japanese scribes claimed that Prince Shotoku, rather than Korean immigrants, introduced Buddhism to Japan and that his illustrious reign sparked Japan's rise as an exceptional island kingdom. Shotoku promoted both Buddhism and Confucianism, thus enabling Japan, like its neighbor China, to accommodate numerous religions.

Indeed, religious influences flowed into Japan, contributing to spiritual diversity while bolstering the Yamato rulers. Although Prince Shotoku and later Japanese emperors turned to Confucian models for government, they also dabbled in occult arts and Daoist purification rituals. In addition, governmental edicts promoted Buddhism as the state religion of Japan. Association with Buddhism gave the Japanese state extra status by lending it the prestige of a universal religion whose appeal stretched to Korea, China, and India. State-sponsored spiritual diversity led native Shinto cults—which believed that after death a person's soul (or spirit) became a Shinto *kami*, or local deity, provided that it was nourished and purified through proper rituals and festivals—to formalize a creed of their own. The introduction of Confucianism and Buddhism motivated Shinto adherents to assemble their diverse religious practices into a well-organized belief system. Shinto priests now collected ancient liturgies, and Shinto rituals (such as purification rites to ward off demons and impurities) gained recognition in the state's official Department of Religion.

Horyuji Temple The main hall of the Horyuji Temple in Nara, Japan (*left*), built in the seventh century CE. The fresco (*right*) from the Horyuji Temple depicts gauze-draped celestial beings (known as *apsara* or *tennin* in Japanese Buddhism), flying above the Buddha's Pure Land burning incense.

Political integration under Prince Shotoku did not mean political stability, however. In 645 CE, the Nakatomi kinship group seized the throne and eliminated the Soga and their allies. Via intermarriage with the imperial clan, the Nakatomi became the new spokesmen for the Yamato tradition. Thereafter Nakatomi no Kamatari (614–669 CE) enacted a series of reforms that reflected Confucian principles of government allegedly enunciated by Shotoku. These reforms enhanced the power of the ruler, no longer portrayed simply as an ancestral kinship group leader but now depicted as an exalted "emperor" (*tenno*) who ruled by the mandate of heaven, as in China, and exercised absolute authority.

THE FALL OF TANG CHINA

Hence, at the eastern end of Afro-Eurasia, the Tang, as well as the Silla of Korea and the Yamato state of Japan, interacted with one another and blended both religious and political authority to maintain stability. The peak of Chinese power in East Asia occurred just as the Abbasids were expanding into Tang portions of central Asia. Yet, despite the Abbasid Empire's spread, China in 750 CE was still the most powerful and best-administered empire in the world. When Muslim forces drove the Tang from Turkistan in 751 CE at the battle of Talas River, however, their success emboldened groups such as the Sogdians and Tibetans to challenge the Tang and even take their capital. As a result, the Tang gradually retreated into the old heartlands along the Yellow and Yangzi rivers. Thereafter misrule, court intrigues, economic exploitation, and popular rebellions weakened the empire, but the dynasty held on for over a century more until northern invaders toppled it in 907 CE.

The Emergence of European Christendom

Although western Europe lacked a highly developed political empire like that of the Abbasids or the Tang dynasty, Christianity increasingly unified the peoples of Europe. In fifth-century western Europe, the mighty Roman military machine gave way to a multitude of warrior leaders whose principal allegiances were local. The political ideal of the Roman Empire certainly influenced western Europeans, but the true inheritor of Rome in the west was the Roman Catholic Church, with its priests, missionaries, and monks. In northern Europe, a frontier mentality and the Viking threat shaped Christianity. In eastern Europe and Byzantium, a form of Christianity known as Greek Orthodoxy had become dominant by 1000 CE. Together, these two major strands of the faith—the western Roman Catholic Church and eastern Greek Orthodoxy—constituted the realm of Christendom, the entire portion of the world in which Christianity prevailed as a unifying institution (see Map 9.8).

COMPARISON

COMPARE the internal divisions within the Islamic, Tang, and Christian worlds.

CHARLEMAGNE'S FLEDGLING EMPIRE

Far removed from the old centers of high culture, Charlemagne (r. 768–814 CE), ruler of the Franks, expanded his western European kingdom through constant warfare and plunder. In 802 CE, Harun al-Rashid, the Abbasid ruler of Baghdad, sent the gift of an elephant to Charlemagne, already the king of the Franks for three decades and recently crowned by the pope in Rome as "Holy Roman Emperor" (on Christmas Day in 800 CE). While the Franks interpreted the caliph's gift as an acknowledgment of Charlemagne's power, al-Rashid more likely sent the rare beast as a gracious reminder of his own formidable sway. In al-Rashid's eyes, Charlemagne's "empire" was a minor principality. Although Charlemagne claimed the lofty title of emperor and ultimately controlled much of western Europe, compared with the Islamic world's rulers and vast domain he was a political lightweight.

MAP 9.8 | Christendom, 600–1000 CE

The end of the first millennium saw much of Europe divided between two versions of Christianity, each with different traditions. On the map, locate Rome and Constantinople, the two seats of power in Christianity.

- According to the map, what were the two major regions where Christianity held sway?
- In what directions did Roman Catholic Christianity and Greek Orthodox Christianity spread?
- The map suggests that missionaries played important roles in spreading Roman Catholicism and Greek Orthodoxy. Why do you think that this was the case?

Charlemagne's empire had a population of less than 15 million; he rarely commanded armies larger than 5,000; and his tax system was rudimentary. At a time when the caliph's palace at Baghdad covered nearly 250 acres, Charlemagne's palace at Aachen was merely 330 by 655 feet. Baghdad itself was almost forty square miles in area, whereas there was no "town" outside the palace at Aachen. The palace was essentially a large country house set in open countryside, where Charlemagne and his Franks hunted wild boar from horseback.

Charlemagne and his men were representatives of the warrior class that dominated post-Roman western Europe. After Roman control faded away, war became once again the duty and joy of the aristocrats. Although the Franks vigorously engaged in trade, even that trade was based on war. Europe's principal export at this time was Europeans, and the massive sale of prisoners of war, in markets at Alexandria, Tunis, and southern Spain, financed the Frankish empire. The main victims of this trade were Slavic-speaking peoples, tribal hunters and cultivators from eastern Europe. This trade in Slavs gives us the modern term "slave."

Yet Charlemagne's seemingly uncivilized and inhospitable empire offered fertile ground for Christianity to sink down roots. As Christianity grew in western and northern Europe, the rough frontier mentality fueled its expansionist ambitions.

CHRISTIANITY IN WESTERN EUROPE

Christians of the west, including those in northern Europe, felt that theirs was the one truly universal religion. Their goal was to bring rival groups into a single **Roman Catholic Church** that was replacing a political unity lost in western Europe when the Roman Empire fell. Drawing on the ideas of Augustine of Hippo (c. 410 CE), the western Christians believed that the "city of God" would take earthly shape in the form of the Catholic Church, and that the Catholic Church was not just for Romans—it was for all times and for all peoples.

Charlemagne's Palace and Chapel Though not large by Byzantine or Islamic standards, Charlemagne's palace and chapel were heavy with symbolic meaning. A royal hall for banqueting in Frankish, "barbarian" style was linked by a covered walkway to the imperial domed chapel, which was meant to look like a miniature version of the Hagia Sophia of Constantinople. Outside the chapel was a courtyard, like that outside the shrine of Saint Peter at Rome.

The arrival of Christianity in northern Europe provoked a cultural revolution. Preliterate societies now encountered a sacred text—the Bible—in a language that seemed utterly strange. Latin had become a sacred language, and books themselves were vehicles of the holy. The bound codex, which had replaced the clumsy scroll, was still messy: it had no divisions between words, no punctuation, no paragraphs, no chapter headings. Readers who knew Latin as a spoken language could understand the script. But Irishmen, Saxons, and Franks could not, for they had never spoken Latin. Consequently, great care was lavished on the few parchment texts—like the Gospels in the Book of Kells (c. 800 CE)—that were prepared with words separated, sentences correctly punctuated and introduced by uppercase letters, and chapter headings.

Those producing these stunning Bibles were starkly different from ordinary men and women. They were monks and nuns. Christian **monasticism** had originated in Egypt, but it suited well the missionary tendencies of Christianity in northern Europe. The root of "monastic" and "monk" is the Greek *monos,* "alone": a man or a woman who chose to live alone, without the support of marriage or family. In Muslim (and Jewish) communities, religious leaders emphasized what they had in common with those around them. Many Islamic scholars, theologians, and mystics were married men, even merchants and courtiers. In the Christian West, the opposite was true: warrior societies honored small groups of monks and nuns who were utterly unlike themselves: unmarried, unfit for warfare, and intensely literate in an incomprehensible tongue.

Monasticism appealed to a deep sense that the very men and women who had little in common with ordinary people were best suited to mediate between believers and God. Laypersons (common believers, not clergy) gave gifts to the monasteries and offered them protection. In return, they gained the prayers of monks and nuns and the reassurance that

Monasticism The great monasteries of the age of Charlemagne, such as the St. Gallen Monastery (*left*), were like Roman legionary settlements. Placed on the frontiers of Germany, they were vast stone buildings, around which entire towns would gather. Their libraries, the largest in Europe, were filled with parchment volumes, carefully written out and often lavishly decorated in a "northern," Celtic style. Monasticism was also about the lonely search for God at the very end of the world, which took place in these Irish monasteries (*right*) on the Atlantic coast. The cells, made of loose stones piled in round domes, are called "beehives."

although they themselves were warriors and men of blood, the monks' and nuns' interventions on their behalf would keep them from going to hell. Payment for human sin, the atoning power of Jesus's crucifixion, and the efficacy of monastic prayers were significant theological emphases for western Roman Catholics.

The Catholic Church of northern Europe was a religion of monks, whose communities represented an otherworldly alternative to the warrior societies of the time. By 800 CE, most regions of northern Europe held great monasteries, many of which were far larger than the local villages. Supported by thousands of serfs donated by kings and local warlords, the monasteries became powerhouses of prayer that kept the regions safe.

Northern Christianity also gained new ties to an old center: the city of Rome. The Christian bishop of Rome had always enjoyed much prestige, but often took second place to other bishops in Carthage, Alexandria, Antioch, and Constantinople. Though people spoke of him with respect as *papa* ("the grand old man"), many others shared that title.

By the ninth century, this picture had changed. Believers from the distant north saw only one *papa* left in western Europe: Rome's pope. New Christians in northern borderlands wanted to find a religious leader for their hopes, and the Catholic Church of western Europe united behind the symbolic center of Rome and its popes. Charlemagne fed this desire when, in 800 CE, he went out of his way to celebrate Christmas Day by visiting the shrine of Saint Peter at Rome. There, Pope Leo III acclaimed him as the new "emperor" of the west. A "modern" Rome—inhabited by popes, famous for shrines of the martyrs, and protected by a "modern" Christian monarch from the north—was what Charlemagne's subjects wanted.

VIKINGS AND CHRISTENDOM

Vikings from Scandinavia exposed the weakness of Charlemagne's Christian empire. When al-Rashid's elephant died in 813 CE, the Franks viewed it as an omen of coming disasters. The great beast keeled over when his handlers marched him out to confront a Viking army from Denmark. Charlemagne died the next year. In the next half century, Charlemagne's empire of borderland peoples met its match on the wide border between the European landmass and the Atlantic (see Map 9.9).

The Emergence of European Christendom | **331**

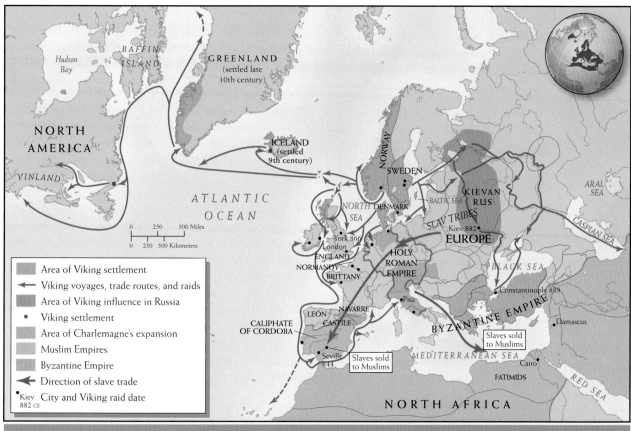

MAP 9.9 | The Age of Vikings and the Slave Trade, 800–1000 CE

Vikings from Scandinavia dramatically altered the history of Christendom.

- In what directions did the Vikings carry out their voyages, trade routes, and raids?
- What were the geographic limits of the Viking explorations in each direction?
- In what direction did the slave trade move, and what role did the Vikings and the Holy Roman emperors play in expanding the slave trade?

The **Vikings**' motives were announced in their name, which derives from the Old Norse *vik*, "to be on the warpath." The Vikings sought to loot the now-wealthy Franks and replace them as the dominant warrior class of northern Europe. They succeeded in their plundering and enslaving because of a deadly technological advantage: ships of unparalleled sophistication. Light and agile, Viking ships traveled far up the rivers of northern Europe and could even be carried overland from one river system to another. Under sail, the same boats could tackle open water and cross the North Atlantic. In the ninth century, the Vikings set their ships on both courses. They sacked the great monasteries along the coasts of Ireland and Britain and overlooking the Rhine and Seine rivers. At the same time, Norwegian adventurers colonized the uninhabited island of Iceland, and then Greenland. By 982 CE, they had even reached continental North America and established a settlement at L'Anse aux Meadows on the Labrador coast.

More long-lasting than their settlements in North America was the Viking incursion into eastern Europe. The Vikings sailed east along the Baltic and then turned south, edging up the rivers that crossed the watershed of central Russia. Here the Dnieper, the Don, and the Volga rivers flow south into the Black Sea and the Caspian. Consequently, the Vikings created an avenue of commerce that linked Scandinavia and the Baltic directly to

Oseberg Ship The Viking ship was a triumph of design. It could be rowed up the great rivers of Europe, or its sails could take it across the Atlantic.

Constantinople and Baghdad. Muslim geographers bluntly called this route "The Highway of the Slaves" because so much of the trade was in human cargo.

In 860 CE, more than 200 Viking long ships gathered ominously beneath the walls of Constantinople in the straits of the Bosporus. What they found was not poorly defended monasteries or Charlemagne's rustic Aachen, but a city with a population exceeding 100,000 protected by well-engineered late-Roman walls. For nearly two centuries, Constantinople had resisted almost yearly campaigns launched by the successive Islamic empires of Damascus and later Baghdad. These campaigns were deflected by Constantinople's highly professional generals, a line of skillfully constructed fortresses that controlled the roads across Anatolia, and a deadly technological advantage in naval warfare: Greek fire. This combination of petroleum and potassium, when sprayed from siphons, would explode in a great sheet of flame on the water. The experience and weaponry of Byzantium were too much for the Vikings, and their raid of the most significant city in eastern Christendom was a spectacular failure. Despite their inability to take Byzantium, the Vikings asserted an enduring influence through their forays across the North Atlantic, their brutal interactions with Christian communities in northern Europe, and their expansion into eastern Europe, especially the slave trade they facilitated there.

GREEK ORTHODOX CHRISTIANITY

Outlasting so many military emergencies bolstered the morale of the eastern Christians and led to a flowering of Christianity in this region. Not just Constantinople but Justinian's Hagia Sophia—its heart—had survived significant threats. That great building and the solemn Greek divine liturgy that reverberated within its domed spaces symbolized the branch of Christian belief that dominated in the east: **Greek Orthodoxy**. Greek Orthodox theology held that Jesus became human, less to atone for humanity's sins (as emphasized in Roman Catholicism) and more to facilitate *theosis* (a transformation of humans into divine beings). This was a truly distinct message from that which prevailed in the Roman Catholicism of the west.

In the tenth century CE, as Charlemagne's empire collapsed in western Europe, large areas of eastern Europe became Greek Orthodox, not Roman Catholic. In addition, Greek Christianity gained a spiritual empire in Southwest Asia. The conversion of Russian peoples, Balkan Slavs, and Arab peoples to Greek Orthodox Christianity was a complex process. It reflected a deep admiration for Constantinople on the part of Russians, Bulgarians, Arabs, and Slav princes. It was an admiration as intense as that of any western Catholic for the Roman popes.

By the year 1000 CE, then, there were two Christianities: the new and confident "borderland" Roman Catholicism of western Europe, and an ancient Greek Orthodoxy. Western Roman Catholics believed that their church was destined to expand everywhere. Greek Orthodox Christians were less euphoric but believed that their church would forever survive the regular ravages of invasion. This was a significant difference in attitude; Greek Orthodox Christians considered the Franks barbarous and grasping, and western Roman Catholics contemptuously called the eastern Christians "Greeks" and condemned them for "Byzantine" cunning.

Thus, like Islam, the Christian world was divided, with differences in heritage, theology, customs, and levels of civilization. At that time, the Orthodox world was considerably more ancient and more cultured than the world of the Catholic west. And each dealt with Islam differently. At Constantinople, eastern Christianity held off Muslim forces that constantly threatened the great city and its Christian hinterlands. In the west, by contrast, Muslim expansionism reached all the way to the Iberian Peninsula. Western Christendom, led by the Roman papacy, set about spreading Christianity to pagan tribes in the north, and it began to contemplate retaking lands from the Muslims. Yet in spite of their deep political, ethnic, and theological differences, the two regions of Christianity conducted a brisk trade in commodities and ideas.

Conclusion

Despite the intermixing of peoples, ideas, and goods across Afro-Eurasia, new political and cultural boundaries were developing that would split this landmass in ways previously unimaginable. The most important dividing force was religion, as Islam challenged and slowed the spread of Christianity and as Buddhism challenged the ruling elite of Tang China. As a consequence, Afro-Eurasia's major cultural zones began to compete in terms of religious and cultural doctrines. The Islamic Abbasid Empire pushed back the borders of the Tang Empire. But the conflict grew particularly intense between the Islamic and Christian worlds, where the clash involved faith as well as frontiers.

Jelling Stone Carved on the side of this great stone, Christ appears to be almost swallowed up in an intricate pattern of lines. For the Vikings, complicated interweaving like serpents or twisted gold jewelry was a sign of majesty: hence, in this, the first Christian monument in Denmark, Christ is part of an ancient pattern of carving, which brought good luck and victory to the king.

The Tang Empire revived Confucianism, insisting on its political and moral primacy as the foundation of a new imperial order, and it embraced the classical written language as another unifying element. By doing so the Tang counteracted universalizing foreign religions—notably Buddhism but also Islam—spreading into the Chinese state. The same adaptive strategies influenced new systems on the Korean peninsula and in Japan.

In some circumstances, faith followed empire and relied on rulers' support or tolerance to spread the word. This was the case especially in East Asia. At the opposite extreme, empire followed faith—as in the case of Islam, whose believers endeavored to spread their empire in every direction. The Islamic empire and its successors represented a new force: expanding political power backed by one God whose instructions were to spread his message. In the worlds of Christianity, a common faith absorbed elements of a common culture (shared books, a language for the learned classes). But in the west, political rulers never overcame inhabitants' intense allegiance to local authority.

While universalizing religions expanded and common cultures grew, debate raged within each religion over foundational principles. In spite of the diffusion of basic texts in "official" languages, regional variations of Christianity, Islam, and Buddhism proliferated as each belief system spread. The period from 600 to 1000 CE demonstrated that religion, reinforced by prosperity and imperial resources, could bring peoples together in unprecedented ways. But it could also, as the next chapter will illustrate, drive them apart in bloody confrontations.

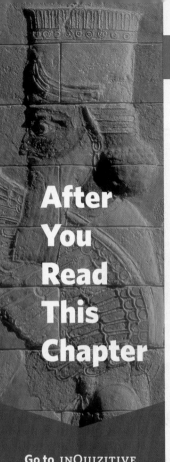

After You Read This Chapter

Go to INQUIZITIVE to see what you've learned—and learn what you've missed—with personalized feedback along the way.

FOCUS ON: *Faith and Empire*

THE ISLAMIC EMPIRE

- Warriors from the Arabian Peninsula defeat Byzantine and Sasanian armies and establish an Islamic empire stretching from Morocco to South Asia.

- The Abbasid state takes over from the Umayyads, crystallizes the main Islamic institutions of the caliphate and Islamic law, and promotes cultural achievements in religion, philosophy, and science.

- Disputes over Muhammad's succession lead to a deep and enduring split between Sunnis and Shiites.

TANG CHINA

- The Tang dynasty dominates East Asia and exerts a strong influence on Korea and Japan.

- Tang rulers balance Confucian and Daoist ideals with Buddhist thought and practice.

- A common written language and shared philosophy, rather than a universalizing religion, integrate the Chinese state.

CHRISTIAN EUROPE

- Monks, nuns, and Rome-based popes spread Christianity throughout western Europe.

- Constantinople-based Greek Orthodoxy survives the spread of Islam.

CHRONOLOGY

THE ISLAMIC WORLD	Life of Muhammad 570-632 CE Umayyad caliphate 661-750 CE
EAST ASIA	Prince Shotoku initiates reforms in Japan 574-622 CE Tang dynasty in China 618-906 CE Silla unify Korean state 668-935 CE
EUROPE	Arab armies conquer much of Byzantine Empire but the empire survives 632-661 CE

600 CE   **700 CE**

- **Thinking about Crossing Borders and Faith & Empire** As Islam spread outside its initial Arabian context, the faith underwent a range of developments. As Christianity and Buddhism continued to spread, these traditions underwent changes as well. Compare the shifts that took place within Islam as it expanded (600–1000 CE) with those within Buddhism and Christianity, not only in their earlier periods (see Chapter 8) but also during the period from 600 to 1000 CE.

- **Thinking about Changing Power Relationships and Faith & Empire** As each of the empires discussed in this chapter matured, divisions developed within the faiths that initially had helped to bring unity to their respective regions. In the Abbasid world, a split developed between Sunni and Shiite Muslims. In Tang China, Buddhism and Confucianism vied for political influence. Christendom divided into the Roman Catholic west and the Greek Orthodox east. What was the exact nature of each religious disagreement? How do these divisions compare in terms of the root of the internal rifts and their impact in the political realm?

- **Thinking about Worlds Together, Worlds Apart** The empires described in this chapter reached across wide swaths of territory and interacted with vibrant societies on their margins. The peoples of Europe struggled with the onslaught of the fierce Vikings. The peoples of Tang China interacted with neighboring Korea and Japan. How does the interaction of Europe and the Vikings compare with the relations of the Tang and the external influences that they experienced? To what extent did the Abbasids contend with similar exchanges?

1. Describe the origins and basic beliefs of Islam, including Muhammad, the Quran, and the **five pillars of Islam.** To what extent does this tradition fit the model for a universalizing religion (as described in Chapter 8)?

2. Trace the process, including jihad, by which Islam expanded from a new, localized religious tradition on the Arabian Peninsula to a dominant political power in western Afro-Eurasia. How did that expansion require a balancing act between political powers (such as the **caliphate** and religious authority (such as the *ulama* and **sharia** law)?

3. Although the Abbasid dynasty brought a great degree of integration across western Afro-Eurasia, what were some of the regional distinctions (in Spain, central Eurasia, and Africa) as well as internal divisions (such as between **Sunnis** and **Shiites**)?

4. How did the Tang Dynasty establish its control over East Asia? What role did the army, **civil service examinations**, and **eunuchs** play in Tang political organization?

5. How did the Tang interact with foreign ideas (including Zoroastrianism, Christianity, and Buddhism) and influence other polities (as in Korea and Japan)?

6. Identify some of the distinctive features of Christendom in western, northern, and eastern Europe. Compare the **Roman Catholic Church** and **Greek Orthodoxy.**

7. Explain the role of **monasticism** within Christian Europe. How does that compare with the role of monasticism in Tang China?

8. Analyze the impact of the **Vikings** in this period of world history, both in Europe and beyond.

Abbasid caliphate 750–1250 CE

Fatimid Shiite regime founded in Egypt 969 CE ◆

Catholic Church based in Rome begins converting much of northern Europe into Christian communities 8th century CE

Charlemagne unites much of western Europe into a short-lived Christian kingdom 768–814 CE

Vikings raid much of Europe and establish strong commercial links across eastern Europe 9th and 10th centuries CE

800 CE   **900 CE**   **1000 CE**

Competing Perspectives

Women, Faith, and Empire

The role of women within the community was of great concern as the new empires discussed in this chapter spread their common cultures. As the Abbasid dynasty extended its reach from Southwest Asia across North Africa and into Spain, Muslim ideas about women and family became more widespread. Surah 4 of the Quran ("On Women"), excerpted below, outlines rules about marriage, inheritance, and the treatment of orphans, among other family-oriented topics. Recorded in the seventh century CE, the Quran, along with the *hadith* (the sayings of Muhammad), was the basis for the *sharia* regulating community matters.

The Christian text excerpted here, the *Law of Adamnan*, demonstrates how both lay leaders and the Christian clergy had to come to terms with the brutal realities of tribal warfare as their faith expanded into Ireland. In response to those realities and to protect noncombatants, such as women, children, and the clergy, a monk named Adamnan at Iona created the *Cáin Adamnáin* (or Law of Adamnan) around 700 CE. This text describes how Adamnan, inspired by his mother and an angel, developed a law protecting noncombatants that was then signed by kings, nobles, and religious authorities.

During this period Tang authorities vacillated in their endorsement of Buddhism, but the importance of Confucian thought in political and social matters never waned. In the late eighth century CE, two young women, Song Ruoxin and Song Ruozhao, in attendance at the court of the Tang emperor, composed their *Analects for Women*. This text, which in some ways expands on Ban Zhao's ideas from almost 700 years earlier (see Chapter 7, Competing Perspectives), adapted Confucian thought in a set of advice for women living around 800 CE. From Western Christendom through Abbasid Islam and into the Tang realm, religious and philosophical ideals influenced the realities that governed women's lives.

PRIMARY SOURCE 9.1

Surah 4, An-Nisa' ("On Women"), from the Quran (seventh century CE)

1. O mankind! Be careful of your duty to your Lord who created you from a single soul and from it created its mate and from two has spread abroad a multitude of men and women. Be careful of your duty toward God in whom you claim (your rights) of one another . . . God has been a watcher over you. . . .

3. . . . [M]arry of the women, who seem good to you, two or three or four; and if you fear that you cannot do justice (to so many) then one (only) or (the captives) that your right hands possess. . . .

4. And give to the women (whom you marry) free gift of their marriage portions; but if they of their own accord remit to you any part of it, then you are welcome to absorb it (in your wealth).

23. Forbidden to you are your mothers, and your daughters, and your sisters, and your father's sisters, and your mother's sisters, and your brother's daughters and your sister's daughters, and your foster-mothers, and your foster-sisters, and your mothers-in-law, and your step-daughters who are under your protection (born) of your women to whom you have gone in. . . .

25. And whoever is not able to afford to marry free, believing women, let them marry from the believing slave girls whom your right hands possess. . . . This is for him among you who fears to commit sin. But to have patience would be better for you. God is forgiving, merciful. . . .

34. Men are in charge of women, because God has made the one of them to excel the other, and because they spend of their property (for the support of women). So good women are the obedient, guarding in secret what God has guarded. As for those from whom you fear rebellion, admonish them and banish them to beds apart, and scourge them. Then if they obey you, do not seek a way against them. God is ever high exalted, great.

Source: "Sura 4," *The Norton Anthology of World Religions: Judaism, Christianity, Islam*, Vol. 2, ed. Dammen McAuliffe, trans. Marmaduke Pickthall (New York: W. W. Norton & Company, 2014), pp. 45–48.

PRIMARY SOURCE 9.2

Law of Adamnan *(700 CE), Adamnan*

33. After fourteen years Adamnan obtained this Law of God, and this is the cause. On Pentecost eve a holy angel of the Lord came to him, and again at Pentecost after a year, and seized a staff, and struck his side and said to him: "Go forth into Ireland, and make a law in it that women be not in any

manner killed by men, through slaughter or any other death, either by poison, or in water, or in fire, or by any other beast, or in a pit, or by dogs, but that they shall die in their lawful bed. Thou shalt establish a law in Ireland and Britain for the sake of the mother of each one, because a mother has borne each one, and for the sake of Mary mother of Jesus Christ, through whom all are. . . . For whoever slays a woman shall be condemned to a twofold punishment, that is, his right hand and his left foot shall be cut off before death, and then he shall die, and his kindred shall pay seven full *cumals*, and one-seventh part of the penance. If, instead of life and amputation, a fine has been imposed, the penance is fourteen years, and fourteen *cumals* shall be paid. But if a host has done it, every fifth man up to three hundred shall be condemned to that punishment; if few, they shall be divided into three parts. The first part of them shall be put to death by lot, hand and foot having been first cut off; the second part shall pay fourteen full *cumals*; the third shall be cast into exile beyond the sea, under the rule of a hard regimen; for the sin is great when any slays the mother and sister of Christ's mother and the mother of Christ, and her who carries a spindle and who clothes every one. . . .

34. The enactment of this Law of Adamnan is a perpetual law on behalf of clerics and women and innocent children until they are capable of slaying a man, and until they take their place in the tribe, and their (first) expedition is known.

Source: Adamnan, *Anecdota Oxoniensia: Cáin Adamnáin, an Old-Irish Treatise on the Law of Adamnan*, ed. and trans. Kuno Meyer (Oxford at the Clarendon Press, 1905), pp. 23–25.

PRIMARY SOURCE 9.3

Analects for Women (800 CE), Song Ruoxin and Song Ruozhao

Book One: On Deportment

The first thing for any woman to learn is the principle of deportment: that of purity and chastity. If you are pure, then chastity will follow; if you are chaste, then you will be honored. . . . Indoors or out, men and women should be in separate groups. . . . Hide your face when watching something. When going outside you must cover yourself.

Book Eleven: On Conciliation and Yielding

The rules for managing a household for a wife are to prize harmony and filial piety above all else. When your mother-in-law rebukes you, don't feel hurt. When your father-in-law has any criticism, listen to it quietly. In the upper rooms, and in the lower chambers, with nephews and nieces, you should behave harmoniously. Whether [disagreements are] right or wrong, don't get involved. [Whether an issue involves] good or bad, don't argue. Shameful family matters should never be exposed to the public. Be as good as you can in etiquette to neighbors both to the east and west. Greet them as they come and go, and behave cordially to them; [offer] a cup of tea or water, exchange pleasantries joyfully; say only what needs to be said; do whatever needs to be done. Idle talk of right or wrong should not enter your door. Don't learn from those stupid women who gossip in vile language without knowing the truth of the matter, thus offending and insulting the venerable elders. I venture to advise women to look to the past and to think ahead.

Book Twelve: On Preserving Chastity

. . . The bonds of the first marriage weigh more than a thousand pieces of gold. If there occurs the misfortune of the husband dying at a young age, wear mourning clothes for three years, and remain firm in your will to preserve your chastity. Protect your family and manage your property. Clean and sweep your husband's tomb. In life or in death, it is one life shared.

This essay "Book of Analects" discusses all topics exhaustively. Women from now on should follow this, day after day and month after month, remembering it always, taking unquestioned guidance from it. If you persist in this, you will enjoy boundless happiness.

Source: Song Ruoxin and Song Ruozhao, "Book of Analects for Women: Consort Song (Tang)," trans. Heying Jenny Zhan and Roger Bradshaw, *Journal of Historical Sociology* 9, no. 3 (Oxford, U.K.: Blackwell Publishers Ltd., 1996), pp. 261, 267–268.

QUESTIONS FOR ANALYSIS

1. What are some of the rules having to do with women in these texts? What do the rules appear to govern: women's behavior or men's behavior with respect to women? Why might that distinction matter when it comes to women's choices?

2. What is the punishment for breaking these rules, and what is the higher authority (implied or stated) to which these rules appeal?

3. How do these rules concerning women fit your understanding of the Abbasid, Christian, and Tang worlds, based on your reading of this chapter? How do they challenge your impression of women in this historical context?

Interpreting Visual Evidence

Transmission of Religious Knowledge

A major development in the period from 600 to 1000 CE was the production of authoritative versions of religious texts. The images gathered here show the variety of forms these texts took—ranging from scroll to codex, handwritten manuscript to printed text—and the diverse materials used in making them.

The Lindisfarne Gospel was created around 700 CE by a Christian monk named Eadfrith on a remote island off of England. A beautifully "illuminated" (decorated) page opens each Gospel, followed by Latin text, to which a monk named Aldred in the tenth century CE added an Old English translation between the lines. Pictured here are two pages: one showing the beginning of the Gospel of Matthew and the other showing the last page of the codex, on which Aldred added some information about the gospels.

The "Diamond Sutra," shown in the next image, was printed in 868 CE, during the Tang dynasty, in Dunhuang, China. Using carved wooden blocks, this text with illustrations was printed on separate sheets of paper, then glued onto a scroll nearly sixteen feet long. It is the oldest surviving printed text that has a date on it. In this text, written in Chinese, the Buddha instructs an elderly student that one must cut through, as with a diamond, the illusion that masks all perception.

The fragmentary early Islamic manuscript of the Quran, pictured here, can be dated to the ninth century CE by its Abbasid-style Arabic script. It records the opening of Surah 52, which reads "In the name of God, Most Gracious, Most Merciful. By the mount, and by a Book inscribed, in a parchment spread open. . . ."

From a world apart, the Mayan Dresden Codex dates to around 1100 CE but records a text originally written perhaps 300 years before. It includes astronomical tables and ritual instructions on both sides of the bark paper, which is nearly twelve feet long. As many as six different scribes used around 350 glyphs and numerical symbols in composing this text.

Finally, the palm-leaf manuscript pictured here dates to 1139 and preserves a copy of the Śivadharma corpus from the sixth century CE. This Hindu text, which contains rituals honoring and ideas about the deity Shiva, was written in Sanskrit in ink on palm-leaves that were then stacked between wooden slats and strung together.

 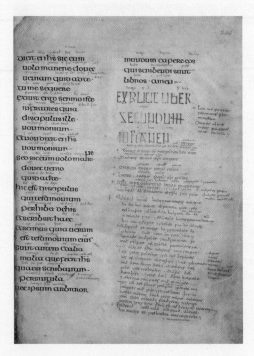

The Lindisfarne Gospel (700 CE, with tenth-century-CE interlinear comments).

The "Diamond Sutra" (868 CE).

Ninth-century Quran.

The Śivadharma (1139).

The Dresden Codex (c. 1100).

QUESTIONS FOR ANALYSIS

1. Compare the various texts. What are the similarities and differences in terms of content, form, and decoration, and what do you think accounts for them?

2. Consider the language in which these texts are written. What role does translation seem to play in the transmission of these texts and the preservation of the ideas they contained?

3. Given what you know from this chapter about the Abbasid Caliphate, Tang China, Charlemagne's Europe, and the Vikings, what role do you think empires played in the preservation, or destruction, of religious texts?

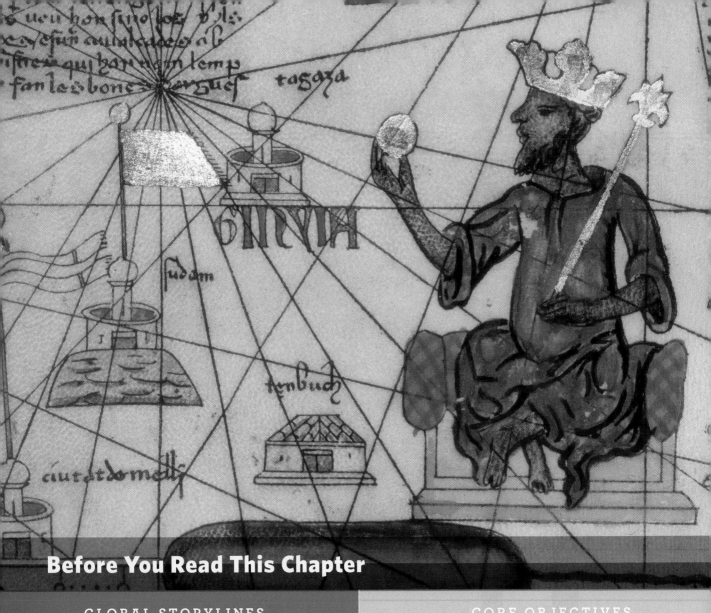

Before You Read This Chapter

GLOBAL STORYLINES

- Advances in maritime technology lead to increased sea trade, transforming coastal cities into global trading hubs and elevating Afro-Eurasian trade to unprecedented levels.
- Intensified trade and religious integration shape four major cultural "spheres": the Islamic world, India, China, and Europe.
- Sub-Saharan Africa is drawn into Eurasian exchange resulting in a true Afro-Eurasia–wide network, while the Americas experience more limited political, economic, and cultural integration.
- The Mongol Empire integrates many of the world's major cultural spheres.

CORE OBJECTIVES

- **IDENTIFY** technological advances of this period, especially in ship design and navigation, and **EXPLAIN** how they facilitated the expansion of Afro-Eurasian trade.
- **DESCRIBE** the varied social and political forces that shaped the Islamic world, India, China, and Europe, and **EVALUATE** the degree to which these forces integrated cultures and geographic areas.
- **COMPARE** both the internal integration and external interactions of sub-Saharan Africa with those of the Americas.
- **ASSESS** the impacts that the Mongol Empire had on Afro-Eurasian peoples and places.

Becoming "The World"

1000–1300 CE

In the late 1270s two Christian monks, Bar Sāwmā and Markōs, voyaged into the heart of the Islamic world. They were not Europeans. They were Uighurs, a Turkish people of central Asia, many of whom had converted to Christianity centuries earlier. The monks hoped to make pilgrimage to Jerusalem in order to visit the tombs of the martyrs.

On their journey westward, Bar Sāwmā and Markōs traveled a world bound together by economic and cultural exchange. The two monks lingered at the magnificent trading hub of Kashgar in what is now western China, where caravan routes converged in a market for jade, exotic spices, and precious silks. Unable to continue on to Jerusalem due to the route's dangers (including murderous robbers), at Baghdad the monks parted ways. Bar Sāwmā was appointed an ambassador by the Buddhist Mongol il-Khan of Persia to drum up support among European leaders for an attack on Jerusalem to wrest it from Muslim control. He visited Constantinople (where the Byzantine emperor gave him gold and silver), Rome (where he met with the pope at the shrine of Saint Peter), and Paris (where he saw that city's vibrant university). In the end, neither monk ever reached Jerusalem or returned to China. Bar Sāwmā ended his days in Baghdad and Markōs became patriarch of the Nestorian branch of Christianity, centered in modern-day Iran.

Yet their voyages exemplified the crisscrossing of people, money, goods, and ideas along the trade routes and sea-lanes that connected the world's regions.

Three related themes dominate the period from 1000 to 1300 CE. First, trade along sea-based routes increased and coastal trading cities began to expand dramatically. Second, greater trade and religious integration generated the world's four major cultural "spheres," whose inhabitants were linked by shared institutions and beliefs: the Islamic world, India, China, and Europe. During this period sub-Saharan Africa and the Americas also thrived; however, they remained more fragmented, experiencing more limited political and economic integration. Third, the Mongol Empire, stretching from China to Persia and as far as eastern Europe, ruled over huge swaths of land in many of the world's major cultural spheres. Each of these three themes contributes to an understanding of how Afro-Eurasia became a "world" unified through trade, migration, and even religious conflict.

COMPARISON

IDENTIFY technological advances of this period, especially in ship design and navigation, and **EXPLAIN** how they facilitated the expansion of Afro-Eurasian trade.

Development of Maritime Trade

By the tenth century CE, sea routes were becoming more important than land networks for long-distance trade. Improved navigational aids, better mapmaking, refinements in shipbuilding, and new political support for shipping made seaborne trade easier and slashed its cost. These developments also fostered the growth of maritime commercial hubs (called anchorages), which further facilitated the expansion of maritime trade.

A new navigational instrument spurred this boom: the magnetic needle compass. This Chinese invention initially identified promising locations for houses and tombs, but eleventh-century sailors from Guangzhou (Canton) used it to find their way on the high seas. The use of this device eventually spread among navigators. Not only did the compass allow sailing under cloudy skies, but it also improved mapmaking.

An array of new ship types—dhows, junks, and cogs—allowed for more impressive mastery of the seas. Maximizing monsoon trade winds on the Arabian Sea and the wider Indian Ocean were dhows, ships with triangular sails, called lateens. Sailing the South China seas were junks, large, flat-bottomed ships with internal sealed bulkheads, stern-mounted rudders, as many as four decks, six masts with a dozen sails, and the space to carry as many as 500 men. And, in the Atlantic, cogs, with their single mast and square sail, linked Genoa to locations as distant as the Azores and Iceland. The numbers testify to the power of the maritime revolution: while a porter could carry about 10 pounds over long distances, and animal-drawn wagons could move 100 pounds of goods over small distances, the Arab dhows could transport up to 5 tons of cargo, Atlantic cogs as much as 200 tons, and Chinese junks more than 500 tons.

Maritime traders enjoyed the protection of political authorities such as the Song rulers in China, who maintained a standing navy that protected traders and lighthouses that guided trading fleets in and out of harbors. The Fatimid

Antique Chinese Compass Chinese sailors from Canton started to use magnetic needle compasses in the eleventh century. By the thirteenth century, magnetic needle compasses were widely used on ships in the Indian Ocean and were starting to appear in the Mediterranean.

Dhow This modern dhow in the harbor of Zanzibar displays the characteristic triangular sail. The sail can make good use of the trade monsoon and thus has guided dhows on the Arabian Sea since ancient times.

caliphate in Egypt profited from maritime trade and defended merchant fleets from pirates, using armed convoys of ships to escort commercial fleets and regulate the ocean traffic. The system of protection soon spread to North Africa and southern Spain.

Long-distance trade spawned the growth of commercial cities. These cosmopolitan **entrepôts** where ships could drop anchor served as transshipment centers, located between borders or in ports, where traders exchanged commodities and replenished supplies. Beginning in the late tenth century CE, several regional centers became major anchorages of the maritime trade: in the west, the Egyptian port city of Alexandria on the Mediterranean (and Cairo, just up the Nile); near the tip of the Indian subcontinent, the port of Quilon (now Kollam); in the Malaysian Archipelago, the city of Melaka; and in the east, the Chinese city of Quanzhou (see Map 10.1) These hubs thrived under the political stability of powerful rulers who recognized that trade would generate wealth for their regimes.

Cairo and Alexandria were the Mediterranean's main maritime commercial centers. Cairo was home to numerous Muslim and Jewish trading firms, and Alexandria was their lookout post on the Mediterranean. The Islamic legal system prevalent in Egypt promoted a favorable business environment. Through Alexandria, Europeans acquired silks from China, especially the coveted *zaytuni* (satin) fabric from Quanzhou. But the Egyptian anchorage handled much more: from the Mediterranean, olive oil, glassware, flax, corals, and metals; from India, gemstones and aromatic perfumes; and from elsewhere, minerals and chemicals for dyeing or tanning, and raw materials such as timber and bamboo. Paper and books (including hand-copied Bibles, Talmuds, and Qurans) traveled along this network as well.

In south India during the tenth century CE, the Chola dynasty supported the port of Quilon, which was the nerve center of maritime trade between China and the Red Sea and the Mediterranean. Trade through Quilon continued to flourish long after the Chola golden age passed away. Personal relationships were key to trade at this anchorage as elsewhere; for instance, when striking a deal with a local merchant, a Chinese trader would mention his Indian neighbor in Quanzhou and that family's residence in Quilon. At Quilon, dhows arrived laden not only with goods from the Red Sea and Africa but

MAP 10.1 | Afro-Eurasian Trade, 1000–1300

During the early second millennium, Afro-Eurasian merchants increasingly turned to the Indian Ocean to transport their goods. Locate the global hubs of Quilon, Alexandria, Cairo, Melaka, and Quanzhou on this map.

- What regions do each of these global hubs represent?
- Based on the map, why would sea travel have been preferable to overland travel?
- According to the text, what revolutions in maritime travel facilitated this development?

also with traders, sojourners, and fugitives. Chinese junks unloaded silks and porcelain, and picked up passengers and commodities for East Asian markets. Muslims, the largest foreign community in Quilon, lived in their own neighborhoods and shipped horses from Arab countries to India and the southeast islands, where kings viewed them as symbols of royalty. There was even trade through Quilon in elephants and cattle from tropical countries, though the most common goods were spices, perfumes, and textiles.

East of Quilon, across the Bay of Bengal, Melaka became a key cosmopolitan entrepôt because of its strategic location and proximity to Malayan tropical produce. Indian, Javanese, and Chinese merchants and sailors spent months in such ports selling their goods, purchasing return cargo, and waiting for the winds to change so they could reach their next destination. During peak season, Southeast Asian ports were crowded with colorfully dressed foreign sailors, local Javanese artisans who produced finely textured batik handicrafts, and traders eager for profit. The traders converged from all over Asia to flood the markets with their merchandise and to search for pungent herbs, aromatic spices, and agrarian staples such as quick-ripening strains of rice to ship out.

In China, the Song government set up offices of seafaring affairs in its three major ports: Quanzhou, Guangzhou (Canton), and a third near present-day Shanghai. In return for a portion of the taxes, these offices registered cargoes, sailors, and traders, while guards kept a keen eye on the traffic. All foreign traders in Song China were guests of the governor, who doubled as the chief of seafaring affairs. Every year, the governor conducted a wind-calling ritual. Traders of every origin—Arabs, Persians, Jews, Indians, and Chinese—witnessed the ceremony, then joined together for a sumptuous banquet. Although most foreign merchants did not reside apart from the rest of the city, they did maintain buildings for religious worship according to their faiths. A mosque from this period still stands on a busy street in Quanzhou. Hindu traders living in Quanzhou worshipped in a Buddhist shrine where statues of Hindu deities stood alongside those of Buddhist gods. Each bustling port teemed with a cosmopolitan mix of peoples, goods, and ideas that flowed through the growing maritime networks thanks to improved ships and better navigational tools.

COMPARISON

DESCRIBE the varied social and political forces that shaped the Islamic world, China, and Europe, and **EVALUATE** the degree to which these forces integrated cultures and geographic areas.

The Islamic World in a Time of Political Fragmentation

While the number of Muslim traders began to increase in commercial hubs from the Mediterranean to the South China Sea, it was not until the ninth and tenth centuries CE that Muslims became a majority within their own Abbasid Empire (see Chapter 9), and even then rulers struggled to unite the diverse Islamic world. From the outset, Muslim rulers and clerics dealt with large non-Muslim populations, even as these groups were converting to Islam. Rulers accorded non-Muslims religious toleration as long as the non-Muslims accepted Islam's political dominion. Jewish, Christian, and Zoroastrian communities within Muslim lands were free to choose their own religious leaders and to settle internal disputes in their own religious courts. They did, however, have to pay a special tax, the *jizya*, and defer to their rulers. While tolerant, Islam was an expansionist, universalizing faith. Intense proselytizing—especially by Sufi missionaries—carried the sacred word to new frontiers and, in the process, reinforced the spread of Islamic institutions that supported commercial exchange.

POLITICAL DIVISIONS

As the Islamic faith increased its reach across Afro-Eurasia, its political institutions had begun to fragment. From 950 to 1050, it appeared that Shiism would be the vehicle for uniting the Islamic world. The Fatimid Shiites had established their authority over Egypt and much of North Africa (see Chapter 9), and the Abbasid state in Baghdad was controlled by a Shiite family, the Buyids. Each group created

Slave Market Slaves were a common commodity in the marketplaces of the Islamic world. Turkish conquests during the years from 1000 to 1300 put many prisoners on the slave market.

MAP 10.2 | The Islamic World, 900–1200

The Islamic world experienced political disintegration in the first centuries of the second millennium.

- According to the map key, what were the two major types of Muslim states in this period and what were the two major empires?
- What were the sources of instability in this period according to the map?
- As Islam continued to expand in this period, what challenges did it face?

universities, in Cairo and Baghdad respectively, ensuring that leading centers of higher learning were Shiite. But divisions also sapped Shiism, as Sunni Muslims began to challenge Shiite power and establish their own strongholds. In Baghdad, the Shiite Buyid family surrendered to a group of Sunni strongmen in 1055. A century later, the last of the Shiite Fatimid rulers gave way to a new Sunni regime in Egypt (see Map 10.2).

The new strongmen were mainly Turks. Their people had been migrating into the Islamic heartland from the Asian steppes since the eighth century CE, bringing superior military skills and an intense devotion to Sunni Islam. Once established in Baghdad, they founded outposts in Syria and Palestine, and then moved into Anatolia after defeating Byzantine forces in 1071. But this Turkish state also crumbled, as tribesmen quarreled for preeminence.

By the thirteenth century the Islamic heartland had fractured into three regions. In the east (central Asia, Iran, and eastern Iraq), the remnants of the old Abbasid state persevered, with a succession of caliphs claiming to speak for all of Islam yet deferring to their Turkish military commanders. In the core of the Islamic world—Egypt, Syria, and the Arabian Peninsula—where Arabic was the primary language, military men of non-Arab origin held the reins of power. Farther west in North Africa, Arab rulers prevailed, but the influence of Berbers, some from the northern Sahara, was extensive. Islam was a vibrant faith, but its polities were splintered.

THE SPREAD OF SUFISM

Even in the face of this political splintering, Islam's spread was facilitated by a popular form of the religion, highly mystical and communal, called **Sufism.** The term *Sufi* comes from the Arabic word for wool (*suf*), which many of the early mystics wrapped themselves in to mark their penitence. Seeking closer union with God, Sufis performed ecstatic rituals such as repeating over and over again the name of God. In time, groups of devotees gathered to read aloud the Quran and other religious tracts. Sufi mystics' desire to experience God's love found ready expression in poetry. Most admired of Islam's mystical love poets was Jalal al-Din Rumi (1207–1273), spiritual founder of the Mevlevi Sufi order that became famous for the ceremonial dancing of its whirling devotees, known as dervishes.

Although many *ulama* (scholars) despised the Sufis and loathed their seeming lack of theological rigor, the movement spread with astonishing speed and offered a unifying force within Islam. Sufism's emotional content and strong social bonds, sustained in Sufi brotherhoods, added to its appeal for many. Sufi missionaries carried the universalizing faith to India, to Southeast Asia, across the Sahara Desert, and to many other distant locations. It was from within these brotherhoods that Islam became truly a religion for the people. As trade increased and more converts appeared in the Islamic lands, urban and peasant populations came to understand the faith practiced by the political, commercial, and scholarly upper classes even while they remained attached to their Sufi brotherhood ways. Over time, Islam became even more accommodating, embracing Persian literature, Turkish ruling skills, and Arabic-language contributions in law, religion, literature, and science.

WHAT WAS ISLAM?

Buoyed by Arab dhows on the high seas and carried on the backs of camels, following commercial networks, Islam had been transformed from Muhammad's original goal of creating a religion for Arab peoples. By 1300, its influence spanned Afro-Eurasia and reached multitudes of non-Arab converts (see Map 10.3). While Arabic remained the primary language of religious devotion, Persian became the language of Muslim philosophy and art and Turkish the language of law and administration. Islam attracted city dwellers and rural peasants alike, as well as its original audience of desert nomads. As other cities joined Cairo and Baghdad as centers of Islamic learning, Islam's extraordinary universal appeal generated an intense cultural flowering around 1000 CE.

That cultural blossoming in all fields of high learning was marked by diversity in both language and ideas. Representing the new Persian ethnic pride was Abu al-Qasim Firdawsi (920–1020), a devout Muslim who believed in the importance of pre-Islamic Sasanian traditions. In the epic poem *Shah Namah,* or Book of Kings, he celebrated the origins of Persian culture and narrated the history of the Iranian highland peoples from the dawn of time to the Muslim conquest. Indicative of the enduring prominence of the Islamic faith and the Arabic language in thought was the legendary Ibn Rushd (1126–1198), known as Averroës in the western world. Steeped in the writings of Aristotle, Ibn Rushd's belief that faith and reason were compatible even influenced the thinking of the Christian world's leading philosopher and theologian, Thomas Aquinas (1225–1274).

During this period, the Islamic world became one of the four cultural spheres that would play a major role in world history, laying the foundation for what would become

MAP 10.3 | Islamic and Hindu States and the Byzantine Empire, 1200–1300

Islam continued to expand during the thirteenth century.

• Where were Islam's largest and most important gains according to the map?

• What are some of the internal divisions within the Islamic world?

• What other religious communities existed under Islamic rule in this period? Based on the map, what might account for the location where these communities prospered?

known as the Middle East up through the middle of the twentieth century. Islam became the majority religion of most of the inhabitants of Southwest Asia and North Africa, Arabic language-use became widespread, and the Turks began to establish themselves as a dominant force, ultimately creating the Ottoman Empire, which would last into the twentieth century. The Islamic world became integral in transregional trade and the creation and transmission of knowledge.

India as a Cultural Mosaic

With its pivotal location along land- and sea-based trade routes, India became an intersection for the trade, migration, and culture of Afro-Eurasian peoples. With 80 million inhabitants in 1000 CE, it had the second-largest population in the region, not far behind China's 120 million. (See **Analyzing Global Developments: Growth in the World Population to 1340**.) Turks ultimately spilled into India as they had into the Islamic heartlands, bringing their newfound Islamic beliefs. But the Turkish newcomers encountered an ethnic and religious mix of which they were just one part (see Map 10.4).

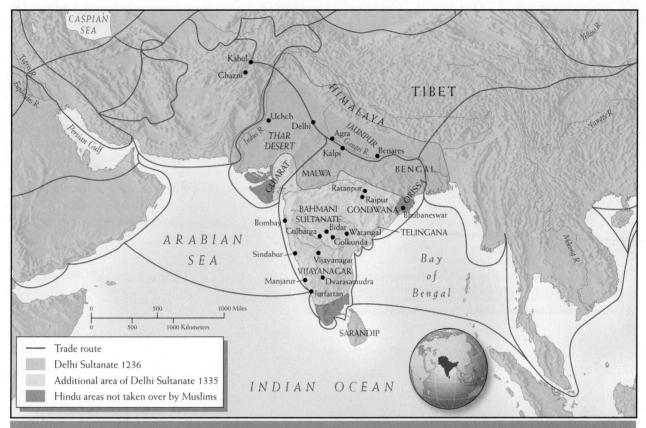

MAP 10.4 | South Asia in 1300

As the fourteenth century began, India was a blend of many cultures. Politically, the Turkish Muslim regime of the Delhi Sultanate dominated the region. Use the map key to identify the areas dominated by the Delhi Sultanate.

• How do you suppose the trade routes helped to spread the Muslims' influence in India?

• Now use the key to find the Hindu areas. Based on your reading, what factors accounted for Hinduism's continued appeal despite the Muslims' political power?

Before the Turks arrived, India was splintered among rival chiefs called *rajas*. These leaders gained support from Brahmans by doling out land grants to them. Since much of the land was uncultivated, the Brahmans first built temples, then converted the indigenous hunter-gatherer peoples to the Hindu traditions, and finally taught the converts how to cultivate the land. In this way, Brahmans simultaneously spread their faith and expanded the agrarian tax base for themselves and the rajas. They also repaid the rajas' support by compiling elaborate genealogies for them and endowing them with lengthy and legitimizing ancestries. In return, the rajas demonstrated that they, too, were well versed in Sanskrit culture, including equestrian skills and courtly etiquette, and were prepared to patronize artists and poets.

When the Turkish warlords began entering India, the rajas had neither the will nor resources to resist them after centuries of fighting off invaders. For example, Mahmud of Ghazna (971–1030) launched many expeditions from the Afghan heartland into northern India and, eager to win status within Islam, made his capital, Ghazni, a center of Islamic learning. Later, in the 1180s, Muhammad Ghuri led another wave of Islamic Turkish invasions from Afghanistan across the Delhi region in northern India. Wars raged between

Analyzing Global Developments

Growth in the World Population to 1340

The world experienced considerable human population growth during the first millennium of the Common Era in spite of occasional downturns, such as in Asia and Europe between 200 and 600 CE that were the result of climate change, movement of peoples, and the decline of the Roman and Han empires. Overall, however, an upward trajectory occurred though it averaged out to a mere .06 percent per year. For the period from 1750 to 1950 that percentage has increased to a little more than 0.5 percent per year, and since 1950 the number has risen to 1.75 percent per year. Even so, as we will see in the next chapter,

the major populations in the Afro-Eurasian landmass were terrified by the loss of life that accompanied the spread of the Black Death across this immense area. Since the Afro-Eurasian recovery from the Black Death, the world's population has been on a steady increase, spectacularly so in the twentieth century, the result of more abundant food supplies, more accurate knowledge of the spread of diseases and a resulting control of epidemic diseases, and a general rise in the standards of living.

QUESTIONS FOR ANALYSIS

- Why was the rate of population growth so limited in premodern times?
- Comparing the population size of the regions in 1340, what do the numbers tell us about where the largest share of wealth and power resided? How does this compare to earlier moments in the chart?
- Why was the population of the Americas in 1340 so small considering its large territorial size?
- How do changes in global population relate to the developments tracked in this chapter: a maritime revolution; a more integrally connected Africa; a thriving Abbasid caliphate; and an expanding Mongol Empire?

REGIONAL HUMAN POPULATION (IN MILLIONS)						
YEAR	ASIA	EUROPE	AFRICA	AMERICAS	OCEANIA	WORLD
	97	30	17	8	1	**153**
1 CE	172	41	26	12	1	**252**
200	160	55	30	11	1	**257**
600	136	31	24	16	1	**208**
1000	154	41	39	18	1	**253**
1200	260	64	48	26	2	**400**
1340	240	88	80	32	2	**442**

Source: Massimo Livi-Bacci, *A Concise History of World Population* (2012), p. 25.

the Indus and Ganges rivers until, one by one, all the way to the lower Ganges valley, the fractured kingdoms of the rajas toppled. The Turks introduced their own customs while accepting local social structures, such as the hierarchical *varna* system The Turks constructed grand mosques and built impressive libraries where scholars could toil and share their wisdom with the court.

The most powerful and enduring of the Turkish Muslim regimes of northern India was the **Delhi Sultanate** (1206–1526), whose rulers brought political integration but also strengthened the cultural diversity and tolerance that were already a hallmark of the Indian social order. Sultans recruited local artisans for numerous building projects, and palaces and mosques became displays of Indian architectural tastes adopted by Turkish newcomers. But Islam never fully dominated South Asia because the sultans did not force their subjects to convert. Nor did they display much interest in the flourishing commercial life along the Indian coast. The sultans permitted these areas to develop on their own: Persian Zoroastrian traders settled on the coast around modern-day Mumbai (Bombay) while farther south, Arab traders controlled the Malabar coast. The Delhi Sultanate was a rich and powerful regime that brought political integration but did not enforce cultural homogeneity.

Hindu Temple When Buddhism started to decline in India, Hinduism was on the rise. Numerous Hindu temples were built, many of them adorned with ornate carvings like this small tenth-century temple in Bhubaneshwar, east India.

WHAT WAS INDIA?

During the eleventh, twelfth, and thirteenth centuries India became the most diverse and, in some respects, most tolerant region in Afro-Eurasia. India in this era arose as an impressive but fragile mosaic of cultures, religions, and ethnicities. When the Turks arrived, the local Hindu population, having had much experience with foreign invaders and immigrants, assimilated these intruders as they had done earlier peoples. Before long, the newcomers thought of themselves as Indians who, however, retained their Islamic beliefs and steppe ways. They continued to wear their distinctive trousers and robes and flaunted their horse-riding skills. At the same time, the local population embraced some of their conquerors' ways, donning the tunics and trousers that characterized Central Asian peoples.

Diversity and cultural mixing became most visible in the multiple languages that flourished in India. Although the sultans spoke Turkish languages, they regarded Persian literature as a high cultural achievement and made Persian their courtly and administrative language. Meanwhile, most of their Hindu subjects spoke local languages, adhered to the regulations of the *varna* system of hierarchies, and practiced diverse forms of Hindu worship. The rulers in India did what Muslim rulers in Southwest Asia and the Mediterranean did with Christian and Jewish communities living in their midst: they collected the *jizya* tax and permitted communities to worship as they saw fit and to administer their own communal law. Ultimately, Islam proved in India that it did not have to be an intolerant conquering religion to prosper.

Although Buddhism had been in decline in India for centuries, it, too, became part of the cultural intermixing of these centuries. As Vedic Brahmanism evolved into Hinduism (see Chapter 8), it had absorbed many Buddhist doctrines and practices, such as nonviolence (*ahimsa*) and vegetarianism. The two religions became so similar in India that Hindus simply considered the Buddha to be one of their deities—an incarnation of the great god Vishnu. Many Buddhist moral teachings mixed with and became Hindu stories. Artistic motifs reflected a similar process of adoption and adaptation. Goddesses, some beautiful and others fierce, appeared alongside Buddhas, Vishnus, and Shivas as their consorts.

The Turkish invaders' destruction of major monasteries in the thirteenth century deprived Buddhism of local spiritual leaders. Lacking dynastic support, Buddhists in India were more easily assimilated into the Hindu population or converted to Islam.

Once the initial disruptive effects of the Turkish invasions were absorbed, India remained a highly diverse and tolerant region during this period. Most importantly, India also emerged as one of the four major cultural spheres, enjoying a tremendous level of integration as Turkish-Muslim rulership and their traditions and practices were successfully intermixed with the native Hindu society, leading to a more integrated and peaceful India.

Song China: Insiders versus Outsiders

The preeminent world power in 1000 CE was still China, despite its recent turmoil. In 907 CE the Tang dynasty splintered into regional kingdoms, mostly led by military generals. In 960 CE one of these generals, Zhao Kuangyin, ended the fragmentation, reunified China, and assumed the mandate of heaven for the Song dynasty (960–1279). The following three centuries witnessed many economic and political successes, but northern nomadic tribes kept the Song dynasty from completely securing their reign (see Map 10.5 and Map 10.6). Ultimately, one of those nomadic groups, the Mongols, would bring the Song dynasty to an end; but not before Song influence had fanned out into Southeast Asia, helping to create new identities in the polities that developed there.

ECONOMIC AND POLITICAL DEVELOPMENTS

Chinese merchants, like those from India and the Islamic world, participated in Afro-Eurasia's powerful long-distance trade. Yet China's commercial successes could not have occurred without the country's strong agrarian base—especially its vast wheat, millet, and rice fields, which fed a population that reached 120 million. Crop cultivation benefited from breakthroughs in metalworking that produced stronger iron plows, which Song farmers harnessed to sturdy water buffalo to extend the agricultural frontier.

Manufacturing also flourished. With their piston-driven bellows to force air into furnaces, Song iron production in the eleventh century equaled that of European iron production in the early eighteenth century. In the early tenth century, Chinese alchemists mixed saltpeter with sulfur and charcoal to produce a product that would burn and could be deployed on the battlefield: gunpowder. Song entrepreneurs were soon inventing a remarkable array of incendiary devices that flowed from their mastery of techniques for controlling explosions and high heat. At the same time, artisans were producing increasingly light, durable, and exquisitely beautiful porcelains. Before long, their porcelain was the envy of all Afro-Eurasia (hence the modern term "china" for fine dishes). Also flowing from the artisans' skillful hands were vast amounts of clothing and handicrafts, made from the fibers grown by Song farmers. In effect, the Song Chinese oversaw the world's first manufacturing revolution, producing finished goods on a large scale for consumption far and wide.

Expanding commerce transformed the role of money and its wide circulation. By now the Song government was annually minting nearly 2 million strings of currency, each containing 1,000 copper coins. As the economy grew, the supply of metal currency could not match the demand, which fueled East Asia's desire for gold from East Africa. At the same time, merchant guilds in northwestern Shanxi developed the first letters of exchange, or paper money, which they called **flying cash**. These letters linked northern traders with their colleagues in the south. Before long, printed money became more common than minted coins for trading purposes. Eventually, the Song dynasty began to issue more notes to pay its bills—a practice that ultimately contributed to runaway inflation.

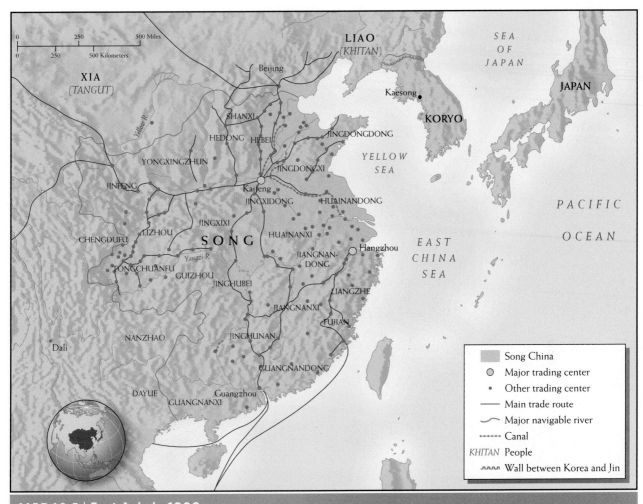

MAP 10.5 | East Asia in 1000

MAP 10.5 | East Asia in 1000

Several states emerged in East Asia between 1000 and 1300, but none were as strong as the Song dynasty in China. Using the key to the map, try to identify the factors that contributed to the Song state's economic dynamism.

• What external factors kept the Song dynasty from completely securing their reign?

• What factors drove the Chinese commercial revolution in this period?

Song emperors built on Tang political institutions by expanding a central bureaucracy of scholar-officials chosen even more extensively through competitive civil service examinations. Zhao Kuangyin, or Emperor Taizu (r. 960–976 CE), himself administered the final test for all who had passed the highest-level palace examination. In subsequent dynasties, the emperor was the nation's premier examiner, symbolically demanding oaths of allegiance from successful candidates. By 1100 these ranks of learned men had accumulated sufficient power to become China's new ruling elite. This expansion of the civil service examination system was crucial to a shift in power from the still significant hereditary aristocracy to a less wealthy but more highly schooled class of scholar officials.

CHINA'S NEIGHBORS: NOMADS, JAPAN, AND SOUTHEAST ASIA

China's prosperity influenced its neighbors and its interactions with them. As Song China flourished, nomads on the outskirts eyed the Chinese successes closely. To the north, nomadic

COMPARISON

DESCRIBE the social and political forces that shaped Song China, and **EVALUATE** the degree to which they integrated the cultures of East Asia.

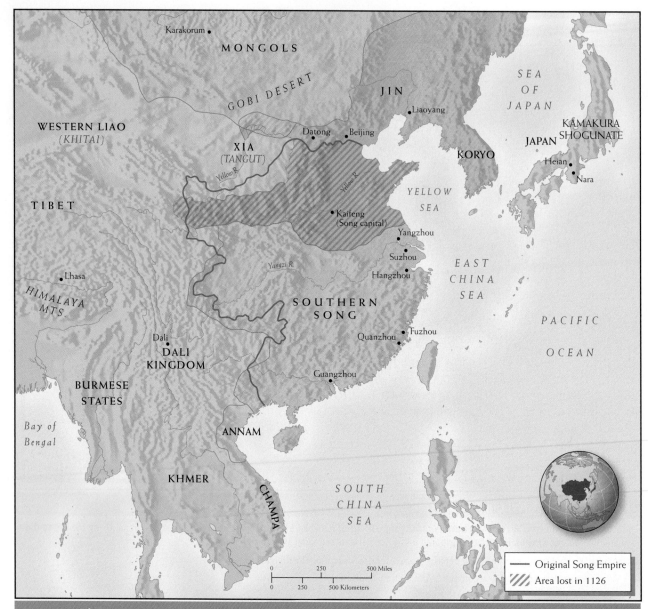

MAP 10.6 | East Asia in 1200

The Song dynasty regularly dealt with "barbarian" neighbors. What were the major "barbarian" tribes during this period?

• Approximately what percentage of Song China was lost to the Jin in 1126?

• How did the "barbarian" tribes affect the Chinese identity in this period?

societies formed their own dynasties and adopted Chinese institutions. Located within the "greater China," as defined by the Han and Tang dynasties, these non-Chinese nomads sought both to conquer and to copy China proper. Despite their sophisticated weapons, the Song army could not match their enemies on the steppe when the nomads united against them. Steel tips improved the arrows that Song soldiers shot from their crossbows, and flame throwers and "crouching tiger" catapults sent incendiary bombs streaking into their enemies' ranks. But none of these breakthroughs was secret. Warrior neighbors on the steppe mastered the new arts of war more fully than did the Song military. Consequently, China drew on its economic success (and the innovation of paper money) to "buy off" the borderlanders. This short-term solution, however, led to economic instability (particularly inflation) and military weakness, especially as the Song forces were cut off from their supply, via the steppe nomads, of horses for warfare purposes.

Feeling the pull of China's economic and political gravity, cultures around China consolidated their own internal political authority and defined their own identities in order to keep from being swallowed up by China. At the same time, they increased their commercial transactions with China. In Japan, for instance, leaders distanced themselves from Chinese influences, but they also developed a strong sense of their islands' distinctive identity. Even so, the long-standing dominance of Chinese ways remained apparent at virtually every level of Japanese society, and was most pronounced at the imperial court in the capital city of Heian (present-day Kyoto), which was modeled after the Chinese capital city of Chang'an. Outside Kyoto, however, a less China-centered way of life existed and began to impose itself on the center. Here, local notables, mainly military leaders and large landowners, began to challenge the imperial court for dominance. This challenge was accompanied by the arrival of an important new social group in Japanese society—samurai warriors. By the beginning of the fourteenth century, Japan had multiple sources of political and cultural power: an imperial family with prestige but little authority; an endangered and declining aristocracy; powerful landowning notables based in the provinces; and a rising and increasingly ambitious class of samurai.

Chinese and Barbarian After losing the north, the Han Chinese grew resentful of outsiders. They drew a dividing line between their own agrarian society and the nomadic warriors, calling them "barbarians." Such identities were not fixed, however. Chinese and so-called barbarians were mutually dependent.

During the Song period, Southeast Asia became a crossroads of Afro-Eurasian influences. The Malay Peninsula became home to many entrepôts for traders shuttling between India and China, because it connected the Bay of Bengal and the Indian Ocean with the South China Sea (see Map 10.7). Consequently, Southeast Asia was characterized by a fusion of religio-cultural influences: Vedic Brahmanism in Bali and other islands, Islam in Java and Sumatra, and Mahayana Buddhism in Vietnam and other parts of mainland Southeast Asia. Important Vedic and Buddhist kingdoms emerged in Southeast Asia. The most powerful and wealthy of these kingdoms was the Khmer Empire (889–1431), with its capital at Angkor, in present-day Cambodia. Public works and magnificent temples

Angkor Wat Mistaken by later European explorers for a remnant of Alexander the Great's conquests, the enormous temple complexes built by the Khmer people in Angkor borrowed their intricate layout and stupa (a mound-like structure containing religious relics) architecture from the Brahmanist Indian temples of the time. As the capital, Angkor was a microcosm of the world for the Khmer, who aspired to represent the macrocosm of the universe in the magnificence of Angkor's buildings and their geometric layout.

MAP 10.7 | Southeast Asia, 1000–1300

Cross-cultural influences affected Southeast Asian societies during this period.

• What makes Southeast Asia unique geographically compared to other regions of the world?

• Based on the map, why were the kingdoms of Southeast Asia exposed to so many cross-cultural influences?

• How does the system of regional kingdoms in Southeast Asia compare with that in India (Map 10.4)?

dedicated to the revived Vedic gods from India went hand in hand with the earlier influence of Indian Buddhism. One of the greatest temple complexes in Angkor—Angkor Wat—exemplified the Khmers' heavy borrowing from Vedic Indian architecture and the revival of the Hindu pantheon within the Khmer royal state. Kingdoms like the Khmer Empire functioned as political buffers between the strong states of China and India and brought stability and further commercial prosperity to the region.

WHAT WAS CHINA?

Paradoxically, the increasing exchange between outsiders and insiders within China hardened the lines that divided them and gave residents of China's interior a highly developed sense of themselves as a distinctive people possessing a superior culture. Exchanges with outsiders nurtured a "Chinese" identity among those who considered themselves true insiders and referred to themselves as Han. Song Chinese grew increasingly suspicious and resentful toward the outsiders living in their midst. They called these outsiders "barbarians" and treated them accordingly.

Print culture crystallized the distinct Chinese identity. Of all Afro-Eurasian societies in 1300, the Chinese were the most advanced in their use of printing and book publishing and circulation. Their books established classical Chinese as the common language of educated classes in East Asia. The Song government used its plentiful supply of paper to print books, especially medical texts, and to distribute calendars. The private publishing industry expanded and printing houses throughout the country produced Confucian classics, works on history, philosophical treatises, and literature—all of which figured in the civil examinations. Buddhist publications, too, were available everywhere.

China's huge population base coupled with a strong agrarian base and manufacturing innovations made it the wealthiest of the four major cultural spheres, and its common language and Confucian civil service system, which enabled a transfer of power from hereditary aristocrats to Confucian scholars, made it the most unified. China's influence on the surrounding region was tremendous.

Christian Europe

Europe, from 1000–1300, was a region of strong contrasts. Intensely localized power was balanced by a shared sense of Europe's place in the world, especially with respect to Christian identity. Some inhabitants even began to believe in the existence of something called "Europe" and increasingly referred to themselves as "Europeans" (see Map 10.8), especially in contrast to the world of Islam to the east and south.

LOCALIZATION OF POWER

From the agriculture-based manors of western Europe to the cities of Russia, power structures were localized. For example, in western Europe of the eleventh and twelfth centuries, the Franks became the unchallenged rulers after the collapse of Charlemagne's empire, yet they oversaw a somewhat fragmented manor-based economy and social structure. The peasantry's subjugation to this knightly class was at the heart of a system scholars have called feudalism (emphasizing the power of the local lords over the peasantry); but a more accurate term for the system is **manorialism**, which emphasizes instead the manor's role as the basic unit of economic power. The manor comprised the lord's fortified home (or castle), the surrounding fields controlled by the lord but worked by peasants (as free tenants or as serfs tied to the land), and the village in which those peasants lived. Although manorialism was driven by agriculture, limited manufacturing and trade augmented the manor economy. This system harnessed agrarian energy and helped western Europe shed its identity as a somewhat "barbarian" appendage of the Mediterranean.

Between 1100 and 1200, as many as 200,000 pioneering peasants emigrated from the regions of Belgium, Holland, and northern Germany to the frontiers of Europe (now Poland, the Czech Republic, Hungary, and the Baltic states). Despite the harsh climate and landscape, the area offered the promise of freedom from feudal lords' arbitrary justice and the imposition of forced labor that the peasants had experienced in western Europe. In a fragile balance between the native elites and liberty-seeking newcomers, castles and villages echoing the landscape of manorial France now replaced local economies that had been based on gathering honey, hunting, and the slave trade. For a thousand miles along the Baltic Sea, forest clearings dotted with new farmsteads and small towns edged inward from the coast up the river valleys.

COMPARISON

COMPARE the role that religions and migration played in forging unified identities in Europe, India, and the Islamic worlds.

1
Spread of Latin Christianity into Eastern Europe and Baltic Regions through conquest and migration

2
Spread of Latin Christianity through Spanish Reconquista

3
Spread of Latin Christianity through Norman Conquest of Sicily

4
Spread of Latin Christianity through Crusades

Areas and direction of expansion of Latin Christendom with annotations
• Cities over 50,000 population
• Important cities with less than 50,000
■ University

MAP 10.8 | Latin Christendom in 1300

Catholic Europe expanded geographically and integrated culturally during this era.

• According to this map, into what areas did Western Christendom successfully expand?

• What factors contributed to the growth of a widespread common culture and shared ideas?

• How did long-distance trade shape the history of the region during this time?

Russian lands modeled themselves after Byzantium, not Rome or western Europe. A giant borderland between the steppes of Eurasia and the booming centers of Europe, Russia's cities lay at the crossroads of overland trade and migration. These cities were not agrarian centers, but hubs of expanding long-distance trade. Kiev became one of the region's greatest urban centers, a small-scale Constantinople with its own miniature Hagia Sophia. Russian Christians looked not to the Roman Catholic faith associated with the popes in Rome, but rather to Byzantium's Hagia Sophia and the Orthodoxy of the east as the source of religious authority. Russian Christianity remained that of a borderland—vivid oases of high culture set against the backdrop of vast forests and widely scattered settlements. Like the agricultural manors of western Europe, these Russian cities demonstrate the highly localized nature of power in Europe in this period.

WHAT WAS CHRISTIAN EUROPE?

Christianity in this era—primarily the Roman Catholicism of the west, but also the Orthodoxy of the east—became a universalizing faith that transformed the region becoming known as "Europe." The Christianity of post-Roman Europe had been a religion of monks, and its most dynamic centers were great monasteries. Members of the laity were expected to revere and support their monks, nuns, and clergy, but not to imitate them. By 1200, all this had changed. The internal colonization of western Europe—the clearing of woods and founding of villages—ensured that parish churches arose in all but the wildest landscapes. Now the clergy reached more deeply into the private lives of the laity. Marriage and divorce, previously considered family matters, became the domain of the church.

New understandings of religious devotion and innovative institutions for learning developed in the west. For instance, the followers of Francis of Assisi (1182–1226) emerged as an order of preachers who brought a message of repentance. Franciscans encouraged the laity—from the poorest to the elite—to feel remorse for their wrongdoings, to confess their sins to local priests, and to strive to be better Christians. At nearly the same time, intellectuals were beginning to gather in Paris to form the first European university, a sort of trade guild of scholars. These professional thinkers endeavored to prove that Christianity was the only religion that fully addressed the concerns of all rational human beings. Such was the message of Thomas Aquinas, who wrote *Summa contra Gentiles* (Summary of Christian Belief against Non-Christians) in 1264. The growing number of churches, new religious orders, and universities began to change what it meant to live in a "Christian Europe."

RELATIONS WITH THE ISLAMIC WORLD

In the late eleventh century, western Europeans launched the Crusades, a wave of attacks against the Muslim world. The First Crusade began in 1095, when Pope Urban II appealed to the warrior nobility of France to put their violence to good use: they should combine their role as pilgrims to Jerusalem with that of soldiers, in order to free Jerusalem from Muslim rule. Such a just war, the clergy proposed, was a means for absolution, not a source of sin.

Starting in 1097, an armed host of around 60,000 men set out from northwestern Europe to seize Jerusalem. Crusading forces included knights in heavy armor, as well as people drawn from Europe's impoverished masses, who joined the movement to help besiege cities and construct a network of castles as the Christian knights drove their frontier forward. The fleets of Venice, Genoa, and Pisa helped transport later Crusaders and supplied the kingdoms they created as they moved eastward. Later Crusaders, especially those from the upper class, brought their wives, who found a degree of autonomy away from their homeland. There are even accounts of a children's crusade (1212), inspired by the visions of a boy. Over time, the Crusades drew together a range of peoples from varied walks of life in common purpose.

Crusader Kneeling, this Crusader promises to serve God (as he would serve a feudal lord) by going to fight on a Crusade (as he would fight for any lord to whom he had sworn loyalty). The two kinds of loyalty—to God and to one's lord—were deliberately confused in Crusader ideas. Both were about war. But fighting for God was unambiguously good, while fighting for a lord was not always so clear-cut.

The Crusades from Dual Perspectives

World history promotes comparative historical study, and when two cultures come together, as they did in the European crusades, their meeting offers unique opportunities to see how different societies view one another, and it provides a clear sense for their own self-identity. Such a confrontation took place during the crusades between European Christians and Muslims between 1095 and 1272.

In 1095, Pope Urban II called for the First Crusade in the following words:

Oh, race of Franks, race from across the mountains, race chosen and beloved by God, as shines forth in very many of your works, set apart from all nations by the situation of your country, as well as by your Catholic faith and the honor of the Holy Church! To you our discourse is addressed, and for you our exhortation is intended. We wish you to know what a grievous cause has led us to your country, what peril, threatening you and all the faithful, has brought us.

The "grievous cause" was the occupation of the Holy City of Jerusalem by the Islamic empire. Formed within the complex relationship between the Byzantine Empire and the western Christian papacy and kingdoms of Europe, the religious motivation behind the Crusades became the subject of many literary renditions of the tumultuous events. It also generated emotionally stirring and argumentative writing, depicting either a Muslim or Christian enemy (depending on the work's author).

These written attacks are often passionate, harsh, and emotional. They also inspire and reinforce the conviction of fellow believers, with little concern for accuracy. Thus, some authors in the time of the Crusades were usually too biased or too misinformed to present accurate portraits of their enemies. But occasionally, firsthand accounts in the form of chronicles and histories offer us unique glimpses into Christian-Muslim relations in the age of the Crusades.

Consider Usāmah ibn Munqidh (1095–1188), the learned ruler of the city of Shaizar in western Syria. Skirmishes, truces, and the ransoming of prisoners were part of his daily life, and Usāmah socialized with his Frankish neighbors as much as he fought with them. He offers a dismissive opinion of his enemies. Basically, they struck him as "animals possessing the virtues of courage and fighting, but nothing else." In particular, their medical practice appalled him. More strange, the Franks allowed their wives to walk about freely and to talk to strangers unaccompanied by male guardians. How could men be at once so brave and yet so lacking in a proper, Arab sense of honor, which would lead a man to protect his women? Unlike other Muslim authors of his time, however, Usāmah does not refer to the Franks in derogatory terms such as "infidels" or "devils." In fact, he occasionally refers to some of them as his companions and writes of a Frank who called him "my brother."

No fewer than nine Crusades were fought over the two centuries that followed Urban II's call; but none of the coalitions, in the end, created lasting Christian kingdoms in the lands they "reconquered." Most knights returned home, their epic pilgrimage completed. The remaining fragile network of Crusader lordships barely threatened the Islamic heartland. The real prosperity and the capital cities of Muslim kingdoms lay inland, away from the coast—at Cairo, Damascus, and Baghdad. The assaults' long-term effect was to harden Muslim feelings against the Franks and the millions of nonwestern Christians who had previously lived peacefully in Egypt and Syria (see **Current Trends in World History: The Crusades from Dual Perspectives**).

Other campaigns of Christian expansion, like the Iberian efforts to drive out the Muslims, were more successful. Beginning with the capture of Toledo in 1061, the Christian kings of northern Spain slowly pushed back the Muslims. Eventually they reached the heart of Andalusia in southern Iberia and conquered Seville, adding more than 100,000 square miles of territory to Christian Europe. Another force, from northern France, crossed Italy to conquer Muslim-held Sicily, ensuring Christian rule in the strategically located mid-Mediterranean island. Unlike the Crusaders' fragile foothold at the edge of the Middle East, these two conquests

Christian authors had similar interests in documenting the customs of their enemies in battle. Jean de Joinville (1224/1225–1317) was a chronicler of medieval France. During one crusade, while in the service of the king, Joinville had occasion to note the Muslims' social behavior:

> Whenever the Sultan was in the camp, the men of the personal Guard were quartered all round his lodging, and appointed to guard his person. At the door of the Sultan's lodging there was a little tent for the Sultan's door-keepers, and for his musicians, who had Arabian horns and drums and kettledrums; and they used to make such a din at daybreak and at nightfall that people near them could not hear one another speak, and that they could be heard plainly all through the camp. The musicians never dared sound their instruments in the daytime unless by the order of the Chief of the Guard. Thus it was, that whenever the Sultan had a proclamation to make he used to send for the Chief of the Guard, and give him the order; and then the Chief would cause all the Sultan's instruments to be sounded; and thereupon all the host would come to hear the Sultan's commands.

Although scholars regard such literary renditions with caution, they are useful for gleaning personal details that other types of works omit. The colorful accounts by authors such as Usāmah ibn Munqidh and Joinville are invaluable resources for the social history of the Crusaders.

Jean de Joinville Joinville offering his history, in which he described the Seventh Crusade, to Louis X of France (r. 1314–1316).

QUESTIONS FOR ANALYSIS

- What customs or practices of their opponents did the Muslim and the Christian writers select to write about? Why?

- What aspects of the other side's customs does the writer seem to see as good or praiseworthy? What does that tell us about their perceptions of the strangers that they encountered?

- If a historian uses polemical written sources like this to analyze societies from the past, what can he or she say that is trustworthy about them?

Explore Further

Natasha, Hodgson, *Women, Crusading and the Holy Land in Historical Narrative* (2007).

Amin Maalouf, *The Crusades Through Arab Eyes*, trans. Jon Rothschild (1984).

Edward Peters (ed.), *The First Crusade: The Chronicle of Fulcher of Chartres and Other Source Materials* (1971).

were a turning point in relations between Christian and Muslim power in the Mediterranean. Christianity—and in particular the rise of the Roman Catholic Church, the spread of universities, and the fight against the Muslims in their native and spiritual homelands—were forces that helped create a cultural sphere known as Europe, whose peoples would become known as European, at the western end of the Afro-Eurasian landmass during this period.

Worlds Coming Together: Sub-Saharan Africa and the Americas

From 1000 to 1300, sub-Saharan Africa and the Americas became far more internally integrated—culturally, economically, and politically—than before. Islam's spread and the growing trade in gold, slaves, and other commodities brought sub-Saharan Africa more fully into the exchange networks of the Eastern Hemisphere; yet the Americas remained isolated from Afro-Eurasian networks for several more centuries.

COMPARISON

COMPARE both the internal integration and external interactions of sub-Saharan Africa with those of the Americas.

SUB-SAHARAN AFRICA COMES TOGETHER

During this period sub-Saharan Africa's relationship to the rest of the world changed dramatically. While sub-Saharan Africa had never been a world entirely apart before 1000 CE, now its integration with Eurasia became much stronger. Increasingly, interior hinterlands found themselves touched by the commercial and migratory impulses emanating from the Indian Ocean and Arabian Sea transformations (see Map 10.9).

West Africa and the Mande-Speaking Peoples Once trade routes bridged the Sahara Desert (see Chapter 9), the flow of commodities and ideas linked sub-Saharan Africa to North Africa and Southwest Asia. As the savanna region became increasingly connected to developments in Eurasia, Mande-speaking peoples became the primary agents for integration within and beyond West Africa. Exploiting their expertise in commerce and political organization, the Mande edged out rivals. The Mande homeland was a vast area, 1,000 miles wide between the bend in the Senegal River to the west and the bend of the Niger River to the east, stretching more than 2,000 miles from the Senegal River in the north to the Bandama River in the south.

By the eleventh century, Mande-speaking peoples were spreading their cultural, commercial, and political hegemony from the high savanna grasslands southward into the woodlands and tropical rain forests stretching to the Atlantic Ocean. Those dwelling in the rain forests organized small-scale societies led by local councils, while those in the savanna lands developed centralized forms of government under sacred kingships. Mande-speakers believed that their kings had descended from the gods and that they enjoyed the gods' blessing.

As the Mande broadened their territory to the Atlantic coast, they gained access to tradable items that residents of Africa's interior were eager to have—notably kola nuts and malaguetta peppers, for which the Mande exchanged iron products and manufactured textiles. Mande-speaking peoples, with their far-flung commercial networks and highly dispersed populations, dominated trans-Saharan trade in salt from the northern Sahel, gold from the Mande homeland, and slaves. By 1300 the Mande-speaking merchants had followed the Senegal River to its outlet on the coast and then pushed their commercial frontiers farther inland and down the coast. Thus, even before European explorers and traders arrived in the mid-fifteenth century, West African peoples had created dynamic networks linking the hinterlands with coastal trading hubs.

The Empire of Mali In the early thirteenth century, the empire of **Mali** became the Mande successor state to the kingdom of Ghana (see Chapter 9). The origins of the Mali Empire and its legendary founder are enshrined in *The Epic of Sundiata*. Sundiata's triumph, which occurred in the first half of the thirteenth century, marked the victory of new cavalry forces over traditional foot soldiers. Horses—which had always existed in some parts of Africa—now became prestige objects of the savanna peoples, symbols of state power.

Under the Mali Empire, commerce was in full swing. With Mande trade routes extending to the Atlantic Ocean and spanning the Sahara Desert, West Africa was no longer an isolated periphery of the central Muslim lands. The Mali king Mansa Musa (r. 1312–1332), made a celebrated hajj, or pilgrimage to Mecca, in 1325–1326, traveling through Cairo and impressing crowds with the size of his retinue—including soldiers, wives, consorts, and as many as 12,000 slaves—and his displays of wealth, especially many dazzling items made of gold. Mansa Musa's stopover in Cairo, one of Islam's primary cities, astonished the Egyptian elite and awakened much of the world to the fact that Islam had spread far below the Sahara and that a sub-Saharan state could mount such an impressive display of power and wealth.

MAP 10.9 | Sub-Saharan Africa, 1300

Increased commercial contacts influenced the religious and political dimensions of sub-Saharan Africa at this time. Compare this map to Map 9.3 (p. 314).

- Where had strong Islamic communities emerged by 1300?

- According to this map, what types of activity were affecting the Mande homeland?

- To what extent had sub-Saharan Africa "come together"?

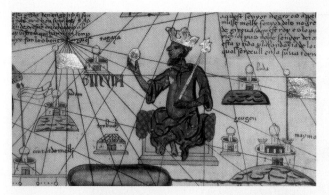

West African Asante Gold This picture from the 1375 Catalan Atlas shows Mansa Musa, the king of Mali, on his throne, surrounded by images of gold. When Mansa Musa traveled on pilgrimage to Mecca (1324–1325), his entourage included soldiers, wives, consorts, and as many as 12,000 slaves, many wearing rich brocades woven of Persian silk. His caravan brought immense quantities of gold—nearly 100 camels each bearing 300-pound sacks of gold—and Mansa Musa distributed it lavishly. Preceding his retinue as it crossed the desert were 500 slaves, each carrying a golden staff.

The Mali Empire boasted two of West Africa's largest cities. Jenne, an entrepôt dating back to 200 BCE, was a vital assembly point for caravans laden with salt, gold, and slaves preparing for journeys west to the Atlantic coast and north over the Sahara. More spectacular was the city of Timbuktu; founded around 1100 as a seasonal camp for nomads, it grew in size and importance under the patronage of various Malian kings. By the fourteenth century it was a thriving commercial, intellectual, and religious center famed for its three large mosques, which are still standing.

Trade Between East Africa and the Indian Ocean

Africa's eastern and southern regions were also integrated into long-distance trading systems. Because of monsoon winds, East Africa was a logical end point for much of the Indian Ocean trade. Swahili peoples living along that coast became brokers for trade from the Arabian Peninsula, the Persian Gulf territories, and the western coast of India. Merchants in the city of Kilwa on the coast of present-day Tanzania brought ivory, gold, slaves, and other items from the interior and shipped them to destinations around the Indian Ocean.

Shona-speaking peoples grew rich by mining the gold ore in the highlands between the Limpopo and Zambezi rivers. By the year 1000 CE, the Shona had founded up to fifty small religious and political centers, each one erected from stone to display its power over the peasant villages surrounding it. Around 1100, one of these centers, Great Zimbabwe, stood supreme among the Shona. Built on the fortunes made from gold, its most impressive landmark was a massive elliptical building made of stones fitted so expertly that they needed no grouting.

African slaves were as valuable as African gold in shipments to Indian Ocean as well as Mediterranean markets. Although the Quran attempted to mitigate the severity of slavery, requiring Muslim slave owners to treat their slaves kindly and praising those who freed their slaves, nonetheless the African slave trade flourished under Islam. Africans became slaves either taken as prisoners of war or as criminals sold into slavery as punishment. Slaves might work as soldiers, seafarers on dhows, domestic servants, and plantation workers. One instance of plantation labor on agricultural estates of lower Iraq was so oppressive that it led, in the ninth century CE, to one of the largest slave wars documented in world history (the Zanj rebellion). Yet in this era plantation-slave labor, like that which later became prominent in the Americas in the nineteenth century, was the exception, not the rule.

THE AMERICAS

During this period, the Americas were untouched by the connections reverberating across Afro-Eurasia. Apart from limited Viking contacts in North America (see Chapter 9), navigators still did not cross the large oceans that separated the Americas from other lands. Yet, here, too, commercial and expansionist impulses fostered closer contact among peoples who lived there.

Andean States of South America Growth and prosperity in the Andean region gave rise to South America's first empire. The **Chimú Empire** developed in the early second millennium in the fertile Moche Valley bordering the Pacific Ocean (see Map 10.10). Ultimately the Moche people expanded their influence across numerous valleys and ecological zones, from pastoral highlands to rich valley floodplains to the fecund fishing grounds of the Pacific Coast. As their geographical reach grew, so did their wealth.

The Chimú economy was successful because it was highly commercialized. Agriculture was its base, and complex irrigation systems turned the arid coast into a string of fertile oases capable of feeding an increasingly dispersed population. Cotton became a lucrative export to distant markets along the Andes. Parades of llamas and porters lugged these commodities up and down the steep mountain chains that are the spine of South America. A well-trained bureaucracy oversaw the construction and maintenance of canals, with a hierarchy of provincial administrators watching over commercial hinterlands.

The Chimú Empire's biggest city, Chan Chan, held a core population of 30,000 inhabitants. A sprawling walled metropolis, covering nearly ten square miles with extensive roads circulating through neighborhoods, Chan Chan boasted ten huge palaces at its center. Protected by thick walls thirty feet high, these opulent residence halls symbolized the rulers' power. Within the compound, emperors erected burial complexes for storing their accumulated riches: fine cloth, gold and silver objects, splendid *Spondylus* shells, and other luxury goods. Around the compound spread neighborhoods for nobles and artisans; farther out stood rows of commoners' houses. The Chimú regime, centered at Chan Chan, lasted until Incan armies invaded in the 1460s and incorporated the Pacific state into their own immense empire.

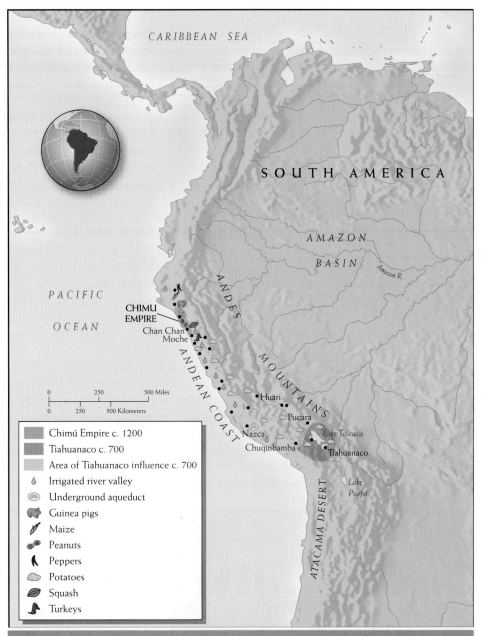

MAP 10.10 | Andean States

Although the Andes region of South America was isolated from Afro-Eurasian developments before 1500, it was not stagnant. Indeed, political and cultural integration brought the peoples of this region closer together.

- Where are the areas of the Chimú Empire and Tiahuanaco influence on the map?
- What kinds of ecological niches did they govern?
- According to your reading, how did each polity encourage greater cultural and economic integration?

Chan Chan The image shows what remains of Chan Chan. The city covered fifteen square miles and was divided into neighborhoods for nobles, artisans, and commoners, with the elites living closest to the hub of governmental and spiritual power.

Toltecs in Mesoamerica Additional hubs of regional trade developed farther north. By 1000 CE, Mesoamerica had seen the rise and fall of several complex societies, including Teotihuacán and the Mayans (see Chapter 8). Caravans of porters bound the region together, working the intricate roads that connected the coast of the Gulf of Mexico to the Pacific, and the southern lowlands of Central America to the arid regions of modern Texas (see Map 10.11). The **Toltecs** filled the political vacuum left by the decline of Teotihuacán and tapped into the commercial network radiating from the rich valley of central Mexico.

The Toltecs were a combination of migrant groups, farmers from the north and refugees from the south fleeing the strife that followed Teotihuacán's demise. These migrants settled northwest of Teotihuacán as the city waned, making their capital at Tula. They relied on a maize-based economy supplemented by beans, squash, and dog, deer, and rabbit meat. Their rulers made sure that enterprising merchants provided them with status goods such as ornamental pottery, rare shells and stones, and precious skins and feathers.

Tula was a commercial hub, a political capital, and a ceremonial center. While its layout differed from Teotihuacán's, many features revealed borrowings from other Mesoamerican peoples. Temples consisted of giant pyramids topped by colossal stone soldiers, and ball courts where subjects and conquered peoples alike played their ritual sport were found everywhere. The architecture and monumental art reflected the mixed and migratory origins of the Toltecs: a combination of Mayan and Teotihuacáno influences. At its height, the Toltec capital teemed with 60,000 people, a huge metropolis by contemporary European standards (if small, by Song Chinese and Abbasid Islamic world standards).

Toltec Temple Tula, the capital of the Toltec Empire, carried on the Mesoamerican tradition of locating ceremonial architecture at the center of the city. The Pyramid of the Morning Star cast its shadow over all other buildings. And above them stood columns of the Atlantes, carved Toltec god-warriors, the figurative pillars of the empire itself. The walls of this pyramid were likely embellished with images of snakes and skulls. The north face of the pyramid has the image of a snake devouring a human.

Cahokians in North America As in South America (Chan Chan of the Chimú) and Mesoamerica (Tula of the Toltecs), cities took shape at the hubs of trading networks across North America, as well. The largest was **Cahokia**, along the Mississippi River near modern-day East St. Louis. A city of about 15,000, it approximated the size of London at the time. Farmers and hunters had settled in the region around 600 CE, attracted by its rich soil, its woodlands for fuel and game, and its access to trade via the Mississippi. Eventually, fields of maize and other crops fanned out toward the horizon. The hoe replaced the trusty digging stick, and satellite towns erected granaries to hold the growing harvests.

Cahokia became a commercial center for regional and long-distance trade. The hinterlands produced staples for Cahokia's urban consumers, and in return its crafts rode inland on the backs of porters and to distant markets in canoes. Woven fabrics and ceramics from Cahokia were exchanged for mica from the Appalachian Mountains, seashells and sharks' teeth from the Gulf of Mexico, and copper from the upper Great Lakes. Cahokia became more than an

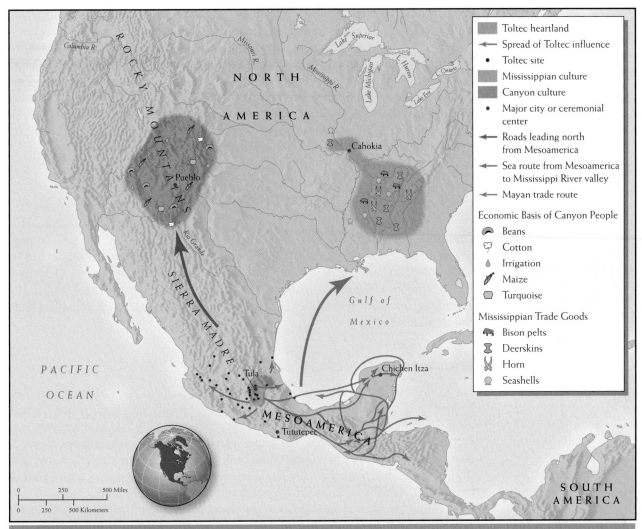

MAP 10.11 | Commercial Hubs in Mesoamerica and North America, 1000

Both Cahokia and Tula were commercial hubs of vibrant regional trade networks.

- Where are Cahokia and Tula on the map?
- According to the map, what kinds of goods circulated through these cities?
- How important do cities appear to be in North America and Mesoamerica?

importer and exporter: it was the exchange hub for an entire regional network trading in salt, tools, pottery, woven stuffs, jewelry, and ceremonial goods.

Dominating Cahokia's urban landscape were enormous earthen mounds of sand and clay (thus the Cahokians' nickname of "mound people"). It was from these artificial hills that the people honored spiritual forces. Building these types of structures without draft animals, hydraulic tools, or even wheels was labor-intensive, so the Cahokians recruited neighboring people to help. A palisade around the city protected the metropolis from marauders.

Ultimately Cahokia's success bred its downfall. As woodlands fell to the axe and soil lost nutrients, timber and food became scarce. In contrast to the sturdy dhows of the Arabian Sea and the bulky junks of the China Sea, Cahokia's river canoes could carry only limited cargoes. Cahokia's commercial networks met their limits. When the creeks that fed its water system could not keep up with demand, engineers changed their course, but to no avail. By 1350 the city was practically empty. Cahokia represented the growing networks of trade and migration, and the ability of North Americans to organize vibrant commercial societies.

Two forces contributed to greater integration in sub-Saharan Africa and the Americas, from 1000 to 1300: commercial exchange (salt, gold, ivory, and slaves in sub-Saharan Africa, and shells, pottery, textiles and metals in the Americas) and urbanization (at Jenne, Timbuktu, and Great Zimbabwe in sub-Saharan Africa, and Chan Chan, Tula, and Cahokia in the Americas). By 1300, trans-Saharan and Indian Ocean exchange had brought Africa into full-fledged Afro-Eurasian networks of exchange and, as we will see in Chapter 12, transatlantic exchange would soon bring the Americas into a global network.

The Mongol Transformation of Afro-Eurasia

COMPARISON

ASSESS the impacts that the Mongol Empire had on Afro-Eurasian peoples and places.

Commercial networks were clearly one way to integrate the world. But just as long-distance trade connected people, so could conquerors. The Inner Eurasian steppes had already unleashed horse-riding warriors such as the Kushans and Xiongnu (see Chapters 6 and 7). Now, the Mongols created an empire that straddled east and west (see Map 10.12), expanding their reach not only through brutal conquest but also through intensified trade and cultural exchange.

WHO WERE THE MONGOLS?

The Mongols were a combination of forest and prairie peoples. Residing in circular, felt-covered tents, which they shared with some of their animals, they lived by hunting and livestock herding. They changed campgrounds with the seasons. Life on the steppes was such a constant struggle that only the strong survived. Their food, primarily animal products, provided high levels of protein, which built up their muscle mass and their strength. Always on the march, their society resembled a perpetual standing army with bands of well-disciplined military units led by commanders chosen for their skill.

Wielding heavy compound bows made of sinew, wood, and horn, Mongol archers were deadly accurate at over 200 yards—even at full gallop. Their small but sturdy horses, capable of withstanding extreme cold, bore saddles with high supports in front and back, enabling the warriors to maneuver at high speeds. With their feet secure in iron stirrups, the archers could rise in their saddles to aim their arrows without stopping. These expert horsemen often remained in the saddle all day and night, even sleeping while their horses continued on. Each warrior kept many horses, replacing tired mounts with fresh ones so that the armies could cover up to seventy miles per day.

Mongol tribes solidified their conquests by extending kinship networks, building an empire out of an expanding confederation of familial tribes. Women were a vital link in those networks. Households sealed alliances by the exchange of daughters in marriage. In addition to their role in linking kinship networks, women in Mongol society were responsible for child-rearing, shearing and milking livestock, and processing pelts for clothing. But they also took part in battles. Although women could be bought and sold, Mongol wives had the right to own property and to divorce. Elite women, such as the mother and wife of the Mongol ruler Kubilai Khan, even played important political roles.

CONQUEST AND EMPIRE

The Mongols' need for grazing lands contributed to their desire to conquer the distant fertile belts and rich cities. The Mongols depended on settled peoples for grain and manufactured

Mongol Warriors This miniature painting is one of the illustrations for *History* by Rashid al Din, the most outstanding scholar under the Mongol regimes. Note the relatively small horses and strong bows used by the Mongol soldiers.

goods, including iron for tools, wagons, weapons, bridles, and stirrups. Their first expansionist forays followed caravan routes.

The Mongol expansion began in 1206 under a united cluster of tribes. These tribes were unified by a gathering of clan heads who chose one of those present as Chinggis (Genghis) Khan, or Supreme Ruler. This Chinggis (c. 1155–1227) launched a series of conquests southward across the Great Wall of China, and westward to Afghanistan and Persia. The Mongols even invaded Korea in 1231. The armies of Chinggis's sons reached both the Pacific Ocean and the Adriatic Sea. Chinggis's grandsons founded dynasties in Persia, in China, and on the southern Eurasian steppes. Thus, a realm took shape that touched all four of Afro-Eurasia's main worlds.

Mongols in Abbasid Baghdad In the thirteenth century, Mongol tribesmen were streaming out of the steppes, crossing the whole of Asia and entering the eastern parts of Europe. Mongke Khan, a grandson of Chinggis, made clear the Mongol aspiration for world domination: he commanded his brother, Hulagu, to conquer Iran, Syria, Egypt, Byzantium, and Armenia, and he appointed another brother, Kubilai, to rule over China, Tibet, and the northern parts of India.

When Hulagu reached Abbasid Baghdad in 1258, he encountered a feeble foe and a city that was a shadow of its former glorious self. Merely 10,000 horsemen faced his army of 200,000 soldiers, who were eager to acquire the booty of a wealthy city. Even before the battle had taken place, Baghdadi poets were composing elegies for their dead and mourning the defeat of Islam. The slaughter was vast. Hulagu himself boasted of taking the lives of at least 200,000 people. The Mongols hunted their adversaries in wells, latrines, and sewers and followed them into the upper floors of buildings, killing them on rooftops until, as an Iraqi Arab historian observed, "blood poured from the gutters into the streets. . . . The same happened in the mosques." In a few weeks of sheer terror, the Abbasid caliphate was demolished. Hulagu's forces showed no mercy to the caliph himself, who was rolled up in a carpet and trampled to death by horses. With Baghdad crushed, the Mongol armies pushed on to Syria, slaughtering Muslims along the way.

BALTIC SEA

POLAND

Leigritz

KHANATE OF THE GOLDEN HORDE

Moscow

URAL MOUNTAINS

RUSSIAN
PRINCIPALITIES

Kiev

Buda Pest

UKRAINE

New Sarai

Old Sarai

Lake Balkas

ARAL
SEA

BLACK SEA

CAUCASUS MTS.

CASPIAN SEA

KHANATE OF THE

Constantinople

Samarkand

BYZANTINE
EMPIRE

Tabriz

Balkh

HINDU KUSH MTS.

Aleppo

MEDITERRANEAN SEA   Damascus

Baghdad

Herat

IL-KHANATE

HIMALAYA

Jerusalem

RED SEA

ARABIA

SULTANATE
OF DELHI

INDIAN   OCEAN

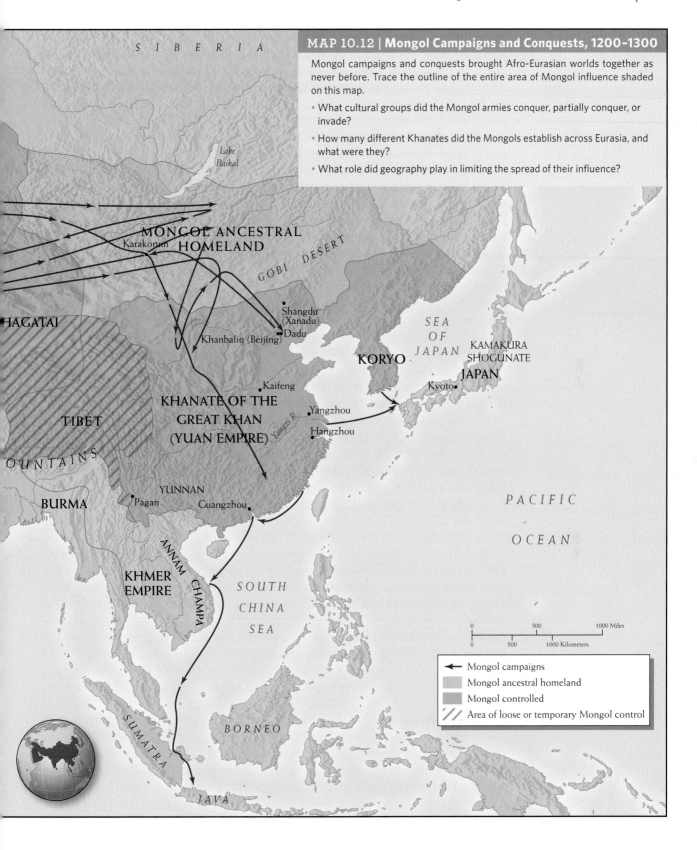

MAP 10.12 | Mongol Campaigns and Conquests, 1200–1300

Mongol campaigns and conquests brought Afro-Eurasian worlds together as never before. Trace the outline of the entire area of Mongol influence shaded on this map.

- What cultural groups did the Mongol armies conquer, partially conquer, or invade?
- How many different Khanates did the Mongols establish across Eurasia, and what were they?
- What role did geography play in limiting the spread of their influence?

Map labels: SIBERIA · Lake Baikal · MONGOL ANCESTRAL HOMELAND · Karakorum · GOBI DESERT · CHAGATAI · Shangdu (Xanadu) · Dadu · Khanbaliq (Beijing) · SEA OF JAPAN · KAMAKURA SHOGUNATE · KORYO · JAPAN · Kyoto · TIBET · Kaifeng · KHANATE OF THE GREAT KHAN (YUAN EMPIRE) · Yangzi R. · Yangzhou · Hangzhou · MOUNTAINS · YUNNAN · Guangzhou · PACIFIC OCEAN · BURMA · Pagan · ANNAM · CHAMPA · KHMER EMPIRE · SOUTH CHINA SEA · SUMATRA · BORNEO · JAVA

Legend:
- ← Mongol campaigns
- Mongol ancestral homeland
- Mongol controlled
- Area of loose or temporary Mongol control

Mongols in China In the east, Mongol forces under Chinggis Khan had entered northern China at the beginning of the thirteenth century, defeating the Jin army that was no match for the Mongols' superior cavalry on the North China plain. Despite some serious setbacks from the climate (including malaria for the men and the death of horses from the heat), Chinggis's grandson Kubilai Khan (1215–1294) seized southern China from the Song dynasty beginning in the 1260s. The southern Song army fell before his warriors brandishing the latest gunpowder-based weapons, which the Mongols had borrowed from Chinese inventors and now used against them.

Hangzhou, the last Song capital, fell in 1276. Kubilai Khan's most able commander, Bayan, led his crack Mongol forces in seizing town after town, ever closer to the capital, while the Empress Dowager tried to buy them off, proposing substantial tribute payments, but Bayan was uncompromising. Once conquered, the Empress Dowager and Hangzhou were treated well by the Mongols. In fact, Hangzhou was still one of the greatest cities in the world when it was visited by the Venetian traveler Marco Polo in the 1280s and by the Muslim traveler Ibn Battuta in the 1340s. Both men agreed that neither Europe nor the Islamic world had anything like it.

Kubilai Khan founded his Yuan dynasty, with a capital at Dadu, present-day Beijing. The Mongol conquest both north and south changed the political and social landscape. But Mongol rule did not impose rough steppe-land ways on the "civilized" urbanite Chinese. While non-Chinese outsiders took political control, they were a conquering elite that ruled over a vast Han majority. The result was a divided ruling system in which incumbent Chinese elites governed locally, while newcomers managed the unifying central dynasty and collected taxes for the Mongols.

Southeast Asia also felt the whiplash of Kubilai Khan's conquest. Circling Song defenses in southern China, the Mongols galloped southwest and conquered states in Yunnan and in Burma. From there, in the 1270s, the armies headed directly back east into the soft underbelly of the Song state. In this sweep, portions of mainland Southeast Asia became annexed to China for the first time. Kubilai Khan used the conquered Chinese fleets to push his expansionism onto the high seas—meeting with failure during the unsuccessful 1274 and 1281 invasions of Japan from Korea. An ill-fated Javanese expedition to extend Mongol reach beyond the South China Sea in 1293 was Kubilai Khan's last.

In the end, the Mongol Empire reached its outer limits. In the west, the Egyptian Mamluks stemmed the advancing Mongol armies and prevented Egypt from falling into their hands. In the east, the waters of the South China Sea and the Sea of Japan foiled Mongol expansion into Java and Japan. Better at conquering than governing, the Mongols struggled to rule their vast possessions in makeshift states. Bit by bit, they yielded control to local administrators and rulers who governed as their surrogates. There was also frequent feuding among the Mongol rulers themselves. In China and in Persia, Mongol rule collapsed in the fourteenth century. Ultimately, the Mongols would meet a deadly adversary even more brutal than they were—the plague of the fourteenth century (see Chapter 11).

Mongol conquest reshaped Afro-Eurasia's social landscape. Islam would never again have a unifying authority like the caliphate or a powerful center like Baghdad. China, too, was divided and changed by the Mongols' introduction of Persian, Islamic, and Byzantine influences into China's architecture, art, science, and medicine. The Yuan policy of benign tolerance brought elements from Christianity, Judaism, Zoroastrianism, and Islam into the Chinese mix. The Mongol thrust also facilitated the flow of fine goods, traders, and technology from China to the rest of the world. Finally, the Mongol conquests encouraged an unprecedented Afro-Eurasian interconnectedness, surpassing even the Hellenistic connections that Alexander's conquests had brought in the late fourth century BCE (see Chapter 6).

Out of Mongol conquest and warfare would come centuries of trade, migration, and increasing contacts among Africa, Europe, and Asia.

Conclusion

Between 1000 and 1300, Afro-Eurasia was forming large cultural spheres. As trade and migration spanned longer distances, these spheres prospered and became more integrated. In central Afro-Eurasia, Islam was firmly established, and its merchants, scholars, and travelers acted as commercial and cultural intermediaries joining the landmass together, as they spread their universalizing faith. As seaborne trade expanded, India, too, became a commercial crossroads. Merchants in its port cities welcomed traders arriving from Arab lands to the west, from China, and from Southeast Asia. China also boomed, pouring its manufactures into trading networks that reached throughout Afro-Eurasia and even into Africa. Christian Europe had two centers—at Rome and at Constantinople— both of which were at war with Islam.

Neither sub-Saharan Africa nor the Americas saw the same degree of integration, but trade and migration in these areas had profound effects. Certain African cultures flourished as they encountered the commercial energy of trade on the Indian Ocean. Africans' trade with one another linked coastal and interior regions in an ever more integrated world. American peoples also built cities that dominated cultural areas and thrived through trade. American cultures shared significant features: reliance on trade, maize, and the exchange of goods such as shells and precious feathers. And larger areas honored the same spiritual centers.

By 1300, trade, migration, and conflict were connecting Afro-Eurasian worlds in unprecedented ways. When Mongol armies swept into China, into Southeast Asia, and into the heart of Islam, they applied a thin coating of political integration to these widespread regions and built on existing trade links. At the same time, most people's lives remained quite localized, driven by the need for subsistence and governed by spiritual and governmental representatives acting at the behest of distant authorities.

Still, locals noticed the evidence of cross-cultural exchanges everywhere—in the clothing styles of provincial elites, such as Chinese silks in Paris or Quetzal plumes in northern Mexico; in enticements to move (and forced removals) to new frontiers; in the news of faraway conquests or advancing armies. Worlds were coming together within themselves and across territorial boundaries, while remaining apart as they sought to maintain their own identity and traditions. In Afro-Eurasia especially, as the movement of goods and peoples shifted from ancient land routes to sea-lanes, these contacts were more frequent and far-reaching. Never before had the world seen so much activity connecting its parts. Nor within them had there been so much shared cultural similarity. By the time the Mongol Empire arose, the regions composing the globe were those that we now recognize as the cultural spheres of today's world.

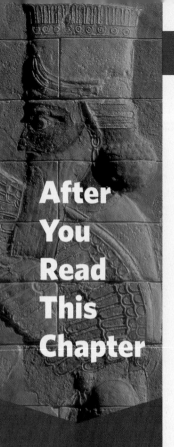

After You Read This Chapter

Go to INQUIZITIVE to see what you've learned—and learn what you've missed—with personalized feedback along the way.

FOCUS ON: *Foundational Cultural Spheres*

THE ISLAMIC WORLD

- The Islamic world undergoes a burst of expansion, prosperity, and cultural diversification but remains politically fractured.

- Arab merchants and Sufi mystics spread Islam over great distances and make it more appealing to other cultures, helping to transform Islam into a foundational world.

- Islam travels across the Sahara Desert; the powerful gold- and slave-supplying empire of Mali arises in West Africa.

CHINA

- The Song dynasty reunites China after three centuries of fragmented rulership, reaching into the past to reestablish a sense of a "true" Chinese identity as the Han, through a widespread print culture and denigration of outsiders.

- Agrarian success and advances in manufacturing—including the production of both iron and porcelain—fuel an expanding economy, complete with paper money.

INDIA

- India remains a mosaic under the canopy of Hinduism despite cultural interconnections and increasing prosperity.

- The invasion of Turkish Muslims leads to the Delhi Sultanate, which rules over India for three centuries, strengthening cultural diversity and tolerance.

CHRISTIAN EUROPE

- Roman Catholicism becomes a "mass" faith and helps to create a common European cultural identity.

- Feudalism organizes the elite–peasant relationship, while manorialism forms the basis of the economy

- Europe's growing confidence is manifest in the Crusades and the reconquering of Iberia, an effort to drive Islam out of Christian lands.

CHRONOLOGY

	900	1000	1100
SUB-SAHARAN AFRICA			Kingdom of Mali emerges (King Mansa Musa 1312–1332) 1100 CE ◆ Great Zimbabwe flourishes 1100 CE ◆
THE AMERICAS	Cahokia flourishes as a commercial hub in North America ◆ 1000 CE ◆ Moche people found city of Chan Chan in South America 900 CE Toltecs dominate valley of Mexico 900-1100 CE		
THE ISLAMIC WORLD		Turkish migrants and armies spread into Islamic world's heartland 1000 CE ◆	
SOUTH ASIA		◆ Central Asian invasions begin 1000 CE	
EAST ASIA	Song dynasty in China 906-1279 CE		
SOUTHEAST ASIA			
EUROPE	Reconquering of the Iberian Peninsula 1061-1492 CE		

- *Thinking about* **Worlds Together, Worlds Apart** From 1000 to 1300 CE, a range of social and political developments contributed to the consolidation of four cultural spheres that still exist today: Europe, the Islamic world, India, and China. In what ways did these spheres interact with one another? In what ways was each sphere genuinely distinct from the others? To what extent were sub-Saharan Africa and the Americas folded into these spheres and with what result?

- *Thinking about* **Transformation & Conflict and Becoming the World** As the four cultural spheres of Afro-Eurasia consolidated, shocking examples of conflict between them began to take place. Whether Pope Urban II's call in 1095 to reclaim the "holy land" from Muslims or the Mongol Hulagu's brutal sack of Baghdad in 1258, this period was marked by large-scale warfare between rival cultural spheres. To what extent was such conflict inevitable? In what ways did conflict transform the groups involved?

- *Thinking about* **Crossing Borders and Becoming the World** Major innovations facilitated economic exchange in the Indian Ocean and in Song China. The magnetic needle compass, better ships, and improved maps shrank the Indian Ocean to the benefit of traders. Similarly, paper money in Song China changed the nature of commerce. How did these developments shift the axis of Afro-Eurasian exchange? What evidence suggests that bodies of water and the routes across them became more significant than overland exchange routes in binding together Afro-Eurasia? What might be the longer-term implications of these developments?

1. How did technological advances, such as the magnetic needle compass, junks, and dhows, fuel the maritime revolution in 1000–1300?

2. What political forces contributed to the fragmentation of the Islamic world in this period? What cultural forces provided a unifying force within Islam?

3. Compare raja-ruled India with that of Muslim-Turkish regimes such as the **Delhi Sultanate**.

4. How did economic and manufacturing developments, coupled with political developments, cement the power of the Song dynasty? How did Song interactions with nomads and neighbors lead to distinctive identities for both the Song and their neighbors?

5. How did developments such as **manorialism**, universities, and the Crusades contribute to Europe's identity as a fragmented yet distinctive cultural sphere?

6. Compare the trans-Saharan trade of the Mande-speaking peoples of West Africa and later **Mali** Empire that developed there with the Indian Ocean trade of the Shona-speaking peoples of East Africa. What goods were traded and what was the impact of that trade on these two regions of Africa?

7. Compare the degrees of integration in various regions of the Americas: South America (**Chimú Empire**), Mesoamerica (**Toltecs**), and North America (**Cahokia**).

8. What enabled the Mongols to conquer such huge swaths of territory across Eurasia? Contrast the expansion of Hulagu into the west with that of Kubilai Khan in the east?

Chimú Empire in South America 1000–1460

◆ Sufism spreads through Islamic world

◆ Mongol forces sack Baghdad and end Abbasid caliphate 1258

Delhi Sultanate 1206–1526

Mongol Yuan dynasty 1279–1368

Khmer state 899–1431

Crusades 1095–1272

Competing Perspectives

"World" Travelers

The maritime revolution described in this chapter, along with the Silk Roads across Inner Eurasia, facilitated travel for trade, diplomacy, and religious pilgrimage on a scale previously unseen. Some travelers who moved between the worlds of Afro-Eurasia in this period left records of their stunning journeys.

As we saw at the start of this chapter, Bar Sāwmā traveled primarily along land routes from Yuan dynasty China all the way to modern-day France. A Nestorian Christian monk, Bar Sāwmā appears to have made his journeys with both diplomacy and religious pilgrimage in mind. The excerpt here describes his travels with his companions, which were recorded in a Syriac text shortly after his death in Baghdad in 1294.

The Venetian merchant Marco Polo was traveling at nearly the same time in the opposite direction. Long after his voyages were completed, Marco Polo recounted his twenty-four years of travel (1271–1295), including his time in the Mongol court of China. As the passage here shows, he wrote in detail about the wonders and dangers of the worlds through which he traveled.

The North African Muslim scholar Ibn Battuta traveled a combination of land and sea routes through much of Africa, Southwest Asia, Southeast Asia, and East Asia between 1325 and 1354. Writing after his travels were completed, Battuta offered details about the places he visited and their customs, as well as the hardships of travel. Battuta was particularly interested in the role and practice of Islam in each place.

The final "world" traveler represented here is the Chinese naval commander Zheng He, whose voyages came later (1405–1433; see Chapter 11) but can be usefully compared with those of Bar Sāwmā, Marco Polo, and Ibn Batutta. In a series of expeditions, Zheng He's fleet sailed from China through Southeast Asia, to Sri Lanka, into the northern Indian Ocean, and even to the Persian Gulf and the Red Sea, leaving stone inscriptions at many of the sites he visited. A trilingual inscription (in Chinese, Persian, and Tamil) was set up in 1411 by Zheng He and his companions at Sri Lanka. Included here is a translation of the Chinese portion of that inscription, which records an offering to Buddha.

PRIMARY SOURCE 10.1

Pilgrimage to Jerusalem (c. 1300), Bar Sāwmā

Chapter 3. One day they meditated, saying, "It would be exceedingly helpful to us if we were to leave this region and set out for the West, for we could then [visit] the tombs of the holy martyrs and Catholic Fathers and be blessed [by them]. And if Christ, the Lord of the Universe, prolonged our lives, and sustained us by His grace, we could go to Jerusalem, so that we might receive complete pardon for our offences, and absolution for our sins of foolishness. Now although Rabban Sâwmâ opposed Rabban Mark, and [tried to] frighten him with the toil of the journey, and the fatigue of travelling, and the terror of the ways, and the tribulations that would beset him in a foreign country, Rabban Mark burned to set out on the road. . . . And they arrived in Baghdad, and thence they went to the Great Church of Kôkê. . . . And they went to the monastery of Mâr Mârî, the Apostle, and received a blessing from the sepulchers (or relics?) of that country. And from there they turned back and came to the country of Bêth Garmai, and they received blessings from the shrine (or tomb) of Mâr Ezekiel [the prophet, near

Dâkôk], which was full of helps and healings. And from there they went to Arbîl, and thence to Mâwsil (i.e., Môsul on the Tigris). And they went Shîgar (Sinjâr), and Nisibis, and Merdâ (Mardîn); and were blessed by the shrine [containing] the bones of Mâr Awgîn, the second Christ. And thence they went . . . and they were blessed by all the shrines and monasteries, and the religious houses, and monks, and the Fathers (i.e., Bishops) in their dioceses. . . . [W]hen they arrived there they heard from the inhabitants of the country that the road was cut because of the murders and robberies which had taken place along it.

Chapter 4. And the two monks turned back and came to Mâr Catholicus, who rejoiced [at the sight of] them, and said unto them, "This is not the time for a journey to Jerusalem. The roads are a disturbed state, and the ways are cut. Now behold, ye have received blessings from all the Houses of God, and the shrines (or relics?) which are in them, and it is my opinion that when a man visits them with a pure heart, the service thus paid to them is in no way less than that of a pilgrimage to Jerusalem.

Source: Rabban Bar Sâwmâ. *The Monks of Kublai Khan, Emperor of China, or The History of the Life and Travels of Rabban Sâwmâ,* trans. E. A. Wallis Budge (London: Religious Tract Society, 1928), pp. 141–43, 145–46.

Mongol Divination (c. 1300), Marco Polo

Chapter 45. Chingis-khan commanded his astrologers and magicians to declare to him which of the two armies, in the approaching conflict, should obtain the victory. Upon this they took a green reed, and dividing it lengthways into two parts, they wrote upon one the name of their master, and upon the other the name of Un-khan. They then placed them on the ground, at some distance from each other, and gave notice to the king that during the time of their pronouncing their incantations, the two pieces of reed, through the power of their idols, would advance towards each other, and that the victory would fall to the lot of that monarch whose piece should be seen to mount upon the other. The whole army was assembled to be spectators of this ceremony, and whilst the astrologers were employed in reading their books of necromancy, they perceived the two pieces begin to move and to approach, and after some small interval of time, that inscribed with the name of Chingis-khan to place itself upon the top of its adversary. Upon witnessing this, the king and his band of Tartars marched with exultation to the attack of the army of Un-khan, broke through its ranks and entirely routed it. Un-khan himself was killed, his kingdom fell to the conqueror, and Chingis-khan espoused his daughter. After this battle he continued during six years to render himself master of additional kingdoms and cities; until at length, in the siege of a castle named Thaigin, he was struck by an arrow in the knee, and dying of the wound, was buried in the mountain of Altaï.

Source: Marco Polo, *The Travels of Marco Polo, The Venetian: The Translation of Marsden Revised, with a Selection of His Notes*, ed. Thomas Wright (London: Henry G. Bohn, York Street, Convent Garden, 1854) pp. 124–25.

The Sacred Mosque of Jerusalem (c. 1360), Ibn Battuta

We then reached Jerusalem (may God ennoble her!), third in excellence after the two holy shrines of Mecca and Madína and the place whence the Prophet was caught up into heaven. Its walls were destroyed by the illustrious King Saladin and his successors, for fear lest the Christians should seize it and fortify themselves in it. The sacred mosque is a most beautiful building, and is said to be the largest mosque in the world. Its length from east to west is put at 752 "royal" cubits and its breadth at 435. . . . The entire mosque is an open court and unroofed, except the mosque al-Aqsá, which has a roof of most excellent workmanship, embellished with gold and brilliant colours. Some other parts of the mosque are roofed as well. The Dome of the Rock is a building of extraordinary beauty, solidity, elegance, and singularity of shape. It stands on an elevation in the centre of the mosque and is reached by a flight of marble steps. It has four doors. The space round it is also paved with marble, excellently done, and the interior likewise. Both outside and inside the decoration is so magnificent and the workmanship so surpassing as to defy description. The greater part is covered with gold so that the eyes of one who gazes on its beauties are dazzled by its brilliance, now glowing like a mass of light, now flashing like lightning. In the centre of the Dome is the blessed rock from which the Prophet ascended to heaven, a great rock projecting about a man's height, and underneath it there is a cave the size of a small room, also of a man's height, with steps leading down to it. Encircling the rock are two railings of excellent workmanship, the one nearer the rock being artistically constructed in iron, and the other of wood.

Source: Ibn Battúta, *Ibn Battúta: Travels in Asia and Africa, 1325–1354*, trans. and ed. H. A. R. Gibb (London: George Routledge & Sons, Ltd., 1929), pp. 55–56.

The Galle Trilingual Stone Inscription (1411), Zheng He

His Majesty, the Emperor of the Great Ming dynasty has despatched the eunuchs Ching-Ho [Zheng He], Wang Ch'ing-Lien, and others to set forth his utterance before Buddha, the World Honoured one, as follows:

"Deeply do we reverence you, Merciful and Honoured One, whose bright perfection is wide-embracing, and whose way of virtue passes all understanding, whose law enters into all human relations, and the years of whose great Kalpa (period) are like the sand of the river in number, you whose controlling influence ennobles and converts, whose kindness quickens, and whose strength discerns, whose mysterious efficacy is beyond compare! Whereas Ceylon's mountainous isle lies in the south of the ocean, and its Buddhist temples are sanctuaries of your gospel, where your miraculous responsive power imbues and enlightens. Of late, we have dispatched missions to announce our mandate to foreign nations, and during their journey over the ocean they have been favoured with the blessing of your beneficent protection. They escaped disaster or misfortune and journeyed in safety to and fro. In everlasting recognition of your supreme virtue, we, therefore, bestow offerings in recompense, and do now reverently present before Buddha, the Honoured One, oblations of gold and silver, gold embroidered jewelled banners of variegated silk, incense burners, and flower vases, silks of many colours in lining and exterior, lamps and candles with other gifts, in order to manifest the high honour of our worship. Do you, Lord Buddha, bestow on them, your regard!"

List of Alms bestowed at the shrine of the Buddhist temple in the Mountain of Ceylon as offerings:

1000 pieces of gold; 5000 pieces of silver; fifty rolls of embroidered silk in many colours; fifty rolls of silk taffeta in many colours; four pairs of jewelled banners, gold embroidered, and of variegated silk; two pairs of the same picked in red; one pair of the same in yellow; one pair in black; five antique brass incense burners; five pairs of antique brass flower vases picked in gold on lacquer, with gold stands; five pairs of yellow brass candle-sticks, picked in gold on lacquer, with gold stand; five yellow brass lamps picked in gold on lacquer, with gold stands; five incense vessels in vermilion red, lacquered gold picked on lacquer, with gold stands; six pairs of golden lotus flowers; 2500 catties of scented oil; ten pairs of wax candles; ten sticks of fragrant incense.

The date being the seventh year of Yung-Lo (1410 A.D.) marked Chi ch'ou in the sixty years' cycle, on the Chia Hsu day of the sixty days cycle in the second moon, being the first day of the month. A reverent oblation.

Source: "Appendix I. Translation of the Chinese Inscription," trans. Edmund Backhouse, in "The Galle Trilingual Stone," *Spolia Zeylanica* 8 (Issued from the Colombo Museum; Ceylon: H. M. Richards, Acting Government Printer, 1913).

QUESTIONS FOR ANALYSIS

1. Based on these excerpts, what sorts of details seem to interest each traveler? How does the form of each text (life of revered holy figure, post-trip travelogues, inscription) influence the reliability of the account?

2. What sorts of dangers are explicitly mentioned, or implied, in these texts?

3. What in the texts suggests the exchange of goods and ideas?

4. Apart from the fact that these individuals were traveling such great distances, what evidence do these texts offer for connected worlds?

Interpreting Visual Evidence

Imagining the World

During this period when Afro-Eurasia was "Becoming the World," cartographers began producing "world" maps. In 1154 al-Idrisi, a Muslim cartographer sponsored by King Roger II of Sicily, produced his *Tabula Rogeriana*. Al-Idrisi's map was accompanied by a commentary that contained information about the ten regions (numbered west to east; but note the map was drawn so that the south is at the top) and seven climate zones (numbered south to north and following the scheme set forth by the second-century-CE Greco-Roman geographer Ptolemy). In 1375, a Jewish mapmaker named Abraham Cresques, from the island of Majorca off the east coast of Spain, produced the second map included here, which is known as the *Catalan Atlas*. Cresques's map is a mixture of practical information and storytelling. The crisscrossed lines that marked compass bearings, suggestive of a nautical chart, reflect the influence of the compass on European mapmaking beginning around 1300. The ornate depictions of the Malian king Mansa Musa and the caravan of Marco Polo offer historical information. In 1459, a monk named Fra Mauro, from Venice, created his *Mappa Mundi* (Map of the World), the third map pictured here. Fra Mauro's map is striking in its detail and information. Not only does Fra Mauro's map carefully mark out shorelines, rivers, cities, and other geographical features, it also includes banners with detailed information and even drawings of the different types of ships (such as the North Atlantic cogs, Chinese junks, and Arabian dhows, discussed in this chapter) that sailed the different seas.

Al-Idrisi's Tabula Rogeriana.

Fra Mauro's Mappa Mundi.

Cresques's Catalan Atlas.

QUESTIONS FOR ANALYSIS

1. Compare these maps, in terms of their representations of land, water, perspective, and other features. What accounts for the maps' similarities and differences?

2. Based on the features and information on the maps, where did cartographers get the data to create the maps? How might these maps have been used and by whom?

3. What do these maps suggest about how these cartographers and their patrons understood the known world? Why are certain parts of the world emphasized and others left off?

Before You Read This Chapter

GLOBAL STORYLINES

- The spread of the Black Death and the collapse of the Mongol Empire sets off crises across Afro-Eurasia, with major demographic, political, economic, and cultural consequences.
- Across Afro-Eurasia, continuity in religious beliefs and cultural institutions accompanies changes in political structures in Europe, the Muslim world, and China.
- In central Eurasia, new rulers—most notably the Ottomans—rebuild dynasties in place of the Mongols, using a blend of religion, military expansion, administrative control, and cultural tolerance.
- In Western Christendom, new monarchies establish political order, and the Renaissance brings a cultural rebirth to societies devastated by plague.
- In East Asia, the Ming dynasty replaces the Mongol Yuan dynasty, using an elaborate Confucian bureaucracy to oversee infrastructure and long-distance exchange.

CORE OBJECTIVES

- **DESCRIBE** the nature and origins of the crises spanning Afro-Eurasia during the fourteenth century and **ASSESS** the magnitude of the crises' effects, locally and trans-regionally.
- **EXPLAIN** the continuities of religious belief systems from the fourteenth through the fifteenth century.
- **COMPARE** the ways in which regional rulers in post-plague Afro-Eurasia attempted to construct unified states and **ANALYZE** the extent and nature of their successes.
- **EXAMINE** the ways in which the art and/or architecture of different regions reflected political realities, and **DESCRIBE** the specific themes that communicate these messages to viewers.
- **COMPARE** the means by which the Iberian kingdoms, the Ottoman Empire, the Ming Dynasty, and European polities each extended their territory and regional influence.

Crises and Recovery in Afro-Eurasia

1300–1500

W hen Mongol armies besieged the Genoese trading outpost of Caffa on the Black Sea in 1346, they not only damaged trading links between East Asia and the Mediterranean but also unleashed a devastating disease: the bubonic plague. Defeated Genoese merchants and soldiers withdrew, unknowingly taking the germs with them aboard their ships. By the time they arrived in Messina, Sicily, half the passengers were dead. The rest were dying. People waiting on shore for the ships' trade goods were horrified at the sight and turned the ships away. Desperately, the captains went to the next port, only to face the same fate. Despite these efforts at isolation, Europeans could not keep the plague (called the Black Death) from reaching their shores. As it spread from port to port, it eventually contaminated all of Europe, killing more than half of the population.

This story illustrates the disruptive effects of the Mongol invasions and the long-distance trade routes that the Mongol invasions foisted on Afro-Eurasian societies. In the thirteenth and early fourteenth centuries, Mongol armies swept into and took control of vast regions of Afro-Eurasia. Although the invasions ushered in an age of intensified cultural and political contact, the channels of exchange—the land trails and sea-lanes of human voyagers—became accidental conduits for deadly microbes. These germs devastated societies far more decisively than did Mongol warfare. They were the real "murderous hordes" of world history, infecting people from every community, class, and culture they encountered. So staggering was the Black Death's toll that population densities did not recover for 200 years. The most severely affected regions were those that the Mongols had brought together: settlements and commercial hubs along the old Silk Road and around the Mediterranean Sea and the South China Sea. While segments of the Indian Ocean trading world experienced death and disruption, South Asian societies, which had escaped the Mongol conquest, also escaped the dying and political disruptions associated with the Black Death.

This chapter explores the ways in which Afro-Eurasian peoples restored what they thought was valuable from old traditions while discarding what they thought had failed them, in favor of radically new institutions and ideas. Much of the recovery across Afro-Eurasia had striking similarities, as societies reaffirmed their most deeply held and long-standing beliefs. Chinese rulers looked to Confucian thought and well-known dynastic institutions to provide guidance going forward. In the Muslim heartland a small band of Turkish-speaking warriors—the Ottomans—channeled the energies of a revived Islam to expand their own territory and the Muslim world. Europeans also invoked their traditions. In the Iberian Peninsula political elites used a resurgent Catholicism to spread their political power and drive Muslim communities out of Europe. Europeans also created new dynastic monarchies and looked to their distant past in Greek and Roman culture for inspiration.

Radically new institutions and ideas appeared across Afro-Eurasia in the aftermath of the Black Death. Notable among these was the outburst of cultural activity that took place in western Europe. Historians have called this flourishing the Renaissance ("rebirth"), for during this era Europeans rediscovered their Greek and Roman pasts and used their inspiration drawn from classical antiquity to bring about far-reaching innovations in art, architecture, thought, and political and financial institutions. While recognizing significant changes to institutions and ideas in this period, this chapter stresses continuities. Considering how grievously people suffered and how many died, it is surprising how much of the old—particularly religious beliefs and institutions—survived the aftermath of Mongol rule and the Black Death. Rulers altered but did not transform their inherited traditions.

Collapse and Consolidation

COMPARISON

DESCRIBE the nature and origins of the crises spanning Afro-Eurasia during the fourteenth century.

Although the Mongol invasions overturned political systems, the plague devastated society itself. The pandemic killed millions, disrupted economies, and threw communities into chaos. Rulers could explain to their people the assaults of "barbarians," but it was much harder to make sense of an invisible enemy. Nonetheless, in response to the upheaval, new ruling groups moved to reorganize their states. By making strategic marriages and building powerful armies, these rulers enlarged their territories, formed alliances, and built dynasties.

THE BLACK DEATH

The spread of the Black Death was the fourteenth century's most significant historical development (see Map 11.1). Originating in Inner Asia, the disease afflicted peoples from China to Europe and killed 25 to 65 percent of infected populations.

How did the **Black Death** move so far and so fast? One explanation may lie in climatic changes. A cooler climate—scholars refer to a "Little Ice Age"—may have weakened populations and left them vulnerable to disease. In Europe, for instance, beginning around 1310, harsh winters and rainy summers shortened the growing seasons and ruined harvests. Exhausted soils no longer supplied the resources required by growing urban and rural populations, while nobles squeezed the peasantry in an effort to maintain their luxurious lifestyle. The ensuing famine lasted from 1315 to 1322, during which time millions of Europeans died of starvation or of diseases against which the malnourished population had little resistance. This climate change and famine laid the groundwork for the Black Death that soon followed. Another climate-related factor in the spread of the plague lay in the drying up of the central Asian steppe borderlands, where bubonic plague had existed for centuries. This drought may have forced rodents out of their usual dwelling places and pressed pastoral peoples, who carried the infectious strains, to move closer to settled agricultural communities. Fleas transmitted plague from rodent to rodent, and to humans. The resulting epidemic was terrifying, for its causes were unknown at the time. Infected victims died quickly—sometimes overnight—and in agony, coughing up blood and oozing pus and blood from black sores the size of eggs.

But it was the trading network that spread the germs across Afro-Eurasia into famine-struck western Europe. This wider Afro-Eurasian population was vulnerable because its members had no immunities to the disease. The first outbreak in a heavily populated region occurred in the 1320s in south-western China. From there, the disease spread through China and then took its death march along the major trade routes. Many routes terminated at the Italian port cities, where ships with dead and dying people aboard arrived in 1347. From there, what Europeans called the Pestilence or the Great Mortality engulfed the western end of the landmass. In China, the Muslim world, and Europe, societies suffered the disastrous effects of the Black Death.

Plague Victim The plague was highly contagious and quickly led to death. Here the physician and his helper cover their noses to avoid the unbearable stench emanating from the patient. What strategies, other than medical, do you see the individuals in this image using against the plague?

Plague in China China was ripe for the plague's pandemic. Its population had increased under the Song dynasty (960 CE–1279) and subsequent Mongol rule. But by 1300, hunger and scarcity spread as resources were stretched thin. The weakened population was especially vulnerable. For seventy years, the Black Death ravaged China, reduced the size of the already small Mongol population, and shattered the Mongols' claim to a mandate from heaven. In 1331, plague may have killed 90 percent of the population in Bei Zhili (modern Hebei) province. From there it spread throughout other provinces, reaching Fujian and the coast at Shandong. By the 1350s, most of China's large cities suffered severe outbreaks.

COMPARISON

COMPARE the impact of the Black Death on China, Islam, and Europe.

SCANDINAVIA
•1349

Novgorod

NORTH SEA

Edinburgh
(1350)

Moscow
MUSCOVY
•1351

Dublin
(1349)
BRITAIN

Lübeck
(1349)
Danzig

BALTIC SEA

Oxford
(1348)
Bremen
(1349)
Cologne
(1349)

London
(1348)
Amiens
(1348)
Paris
(1348)
EUROPE

Cracow

Kiev

KHANATE OF THE
GOLDEN HORDE

Buda
(1349)

Rostov
New Sarai

ARAL
SEA

Bordeaux
(1348)
Venice
(1347)
Genoa
(1347)

Avignon
(1347)
Florence
(1347)
Pisa
(1347)
Siena
(1347)

BLACK
SEA
Caffa
(1346)

CASPIAN
SEA

Barcelona
(1348)
Marseille

Constantinople
(1347)

Naples

Trebizond

Bukhara
Samar

Lisbon
(1349)
SPAIN
•1348

Madrid

Palermo
(1347)

Messina
(1347)

Athens
(1347)

ANATOLIA

Tabriz

Maraghah

Silk route

Ceuta
Fez

Algiers
Tunis

Aleppo
(1347)

PERSIA
IL-KHANATE

MEDITERRANEAN
SEA

Damascus
(1347)

Baghdad
(1347)

Isfahan

Marrakesh
(1349)

Tripoli
(1348)

Alexandria
(1347)
Cairo
(1347)
Jerusalem
(1347)

Basra

Shiraz

Hormuz

Persian Gulf

AFRICA

Medina

Mecca
(1348)

ARABIA

RED SEA

ARABIAN
SEA

Aden
(1351)

Mogadishu

INDIAN

ATLANTIC

OCEAN

Progress of bubonic plague

Trade routes

• Known areas of major outbreaks

∗ Modern Chinese provincial names for
regions affected by outbreak of plague

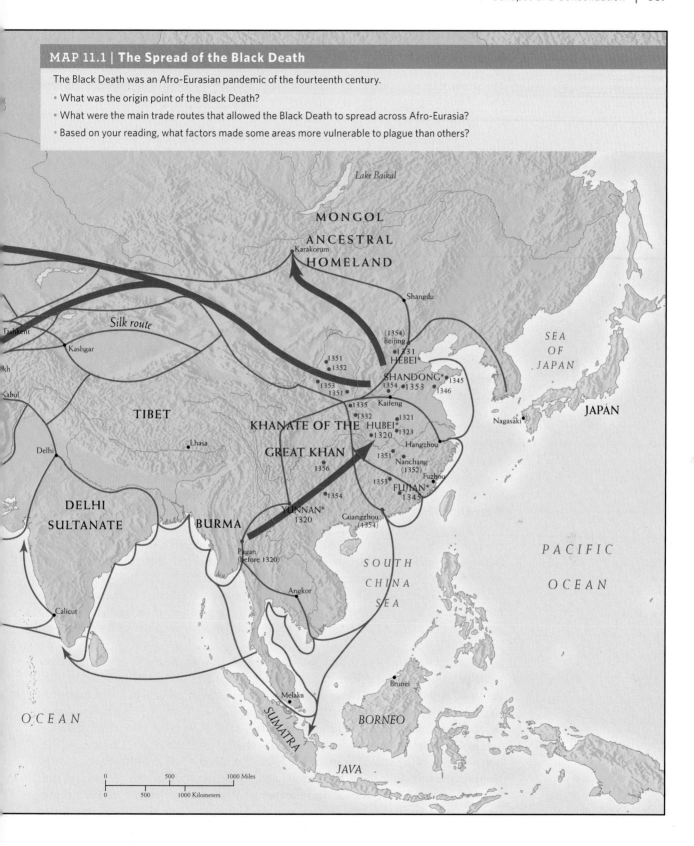

MAP 11.1 | The Spread of the Black Death

The Black Death was an Afro-Eurasian pandemic of the fourteenth century.

- What was the origin point of the Black Death?
- What were the main trade routes that allowed the Black Death to spread across Afro-Eurasia?
- Based on your reading, what factors made some areas more vulnerable to plague than others?

Even as the Black Death was engulfing China, bandit groups and dissident religious sects were undercutting the power of the last Yuan Mongol rulers. Popular religious movements warned of impending doom. Most prominent was the **Red Turban Movement**, which blended China's diverse cultural and religious traditions, including Buddhism, Daoism, and other faiths. Its leaders emphasized strict dietary restrictions, penance, and ceremonial rituals, and made proclamations that the world was drawing to an end.

Plague in the Islamic World The plague devastated parts of the Muslim world as well. The Black Death reached Baghdad by 1347. By the next year, the plague overtook Egypt, Syria, and Cyprus, with as many as 1,000 deaths a day according to a Tunisian report. Animals, too, were afflicted. One Egyptian writer commented: "The country was not far from being ruined. . . . One found in the desert the bodies of savage animals with the bubos under their arms. It was the same with horses, camels, asses, and all the beasts in general, including birds, even the ostriches." In the eastern Mediterranean, plague left much of the Islamic world in a state of near political and economic collapse. The great Arab historian Ibn Khaldun (1332–1406), who lost his mother and father and a number of his teachers to the Black Death in Tunis, underscored the desolation: "Cities and buildings were laid waste, roads and way signs were obliterated, settlements and mansions became empty, dynasties and tribes grew weak," he wrote. "The entire world changed."

Plague in Europe In Europe, the Black Death first ravaged the Italian Peninsula; then it seized France, the Netherlands, Belgium, Luxembourg, Germany, and England in its deathly grip. Overcrowded and unsanitary cities were particularly vulnerable. All levels of society—the poor, craftspeople, aristocrats—were at risk, although flight to the countryside offered some protection from infection. Nearly 50 million of Europe's 80 million perished between 1347 and 1351. After 1353, the epidemic waned, but the plague returned every seven years or so for the rest of the century, and sporadically through the fifteenth century. Consequently, the European population continued to decline, until by 1450 many areas had only one quarter the number of a century earlier.

In the face of the Black Death, some Europeans turned to debauchery, determined to enjoy themselves before they died. Others, especially in urban settings in Flanders, the Netherlands, and parts of Germany, claimed to find God's grace outside what they saw as a corrupt Church. Semimonastic orders like the Beghards held that a good layman could perform sacraments as well as a priest and that people should trust their own "interior instinct" more than the Gospel as then preached. By contrast, the Flagellants were so convinced that man had incurred God's wrath that they whipped themselves to atone for human sin.

For many who survived the plague, disappointment with the clergy smoldered. Famished peasants resented priests and monks for living lives of luxury. In addition, they despaired at the absence of clergy when they were so greatly needed. While many clerics had perished attending to their parishioners during the Black Death, others had fled to rural retreats far from the ravages of the plague, leaving their followers to fend for themselves.

The Black Death wrought devastation throughout Afro-Eurasia. The Chinese population plunged from around 115 million in 1200 to 75 million or less in 1400, the result of the Mongol invasions of the thirteenth century and the disease and disorder of the fourteenth century (see **Analyzing Global Developments: Population Changes in Fourteenth-Century Afro-Eurasia**). Over the course of the fourteenth century, Europe's population shrank by more than 50 percent. In the most densely settled Islamic territory—Egypt—a population that had totaled around 6 million in 1400 was cut in half. When farmers fell ill with the plague, food production collapsed. Famine followed and killed off the survivors.

Bubonic Plague and the Destruction of Society Bubonic plague devastated the countries of Western Christendom. Here, in Pieter Bruegel the Elder's *The Triumph of Death* (1562), we see skeletons murdering indiscriminately, rich and poor alike. Notice the role of religious imagery in this painting. Notice also the representation of social class. How does the artist convey distinctions of rank and status?

Worst afflicted were the crowded cities, especially coastal ports. Some cities lost up to two-thirds of their population. Refugees from urban areas fled their homes, seeking security and food in the countryside. The shortage of food and other necessities led to rapidly rising prices, work stoppages, and unrest. Political leaders added to their unpopularity by repressing the unrest. Everywhere, regimes trembled and collapsed. The Mongol empire, which had held so much of Eurasia together commercially and politically, disintegrated. Thus, the way was prepared for experiments in state building, religious beliefs, and cultural understandings.

REBUILDING STATES

Starting in the late fourteenth century, Afro-Eurasians began the task of reconstructing both their political order and their trading networks. By then the plague had died down, though it continued to afflict peoples for centuries. However, the rebuilding of military and civil administrations—no easy task—also required political legitimacy. With their

Analyzing Global Developments

Population Changes in Fourteenth-Century Afro-Eurasia

Famine, warfare, and disease led to vast population declines all across Afro-Eurasia in the fourteenth century. The Mongols were instrumental players in spreading disease across the landmass starting in China and moving westward along land- and sea-based trading routes towards the Mediterranean world and, ultimately, northern Europe (see Map 11.1). While the effects of these destructive forces were felt across the Afro-Eurasian landmass, some states and regions were less affected than others. The population data below come from the best historical studies of the last forty years and are based on painstaking archival research. They serve as one of the best ways for us to gain historical insight into this tumultuous century.

QUESTIONS FOR ANALYSIS

- Identify the regions or cities where population loss seems to have been lower or higher. Why might those variations in death rates have occurred?
- Compare the losses in urban areas with the losses in the region where those urban areas are located. What might that comparison suggest about the impact of fourteenth-century disasters on urban versus other populations?
- Explain why population decline was more severe and widespread in Europe than in Asia.
- Explain how the great loss of population in Europe and China marked a turning point in their histories.

LOCATION	POPULATION FIGURES	ACROSS THE 14TH CENTURY	% CHANGE
By Regions			
Europe	80M in 1346	30M in 1353	−60%
Asia	230M in 1300	235M in 1400	+2%
Islam	(regional data are not available)		
By Countries			
Spain	6M in 1346	2.5M in 1353	−60%
Italy	10M in 1346	4.5M in 1363	−55%
France	18M in 1346	7.2M in 1353	−60%
England	6M in 1346	2.25M in 1353	−62.5%
China	115M in 1200 85M in 1300	75M in 1400	−35% overall
Japan	9.75M in 1300	12.5M in 1400	+28%
Korea	3M in 1300	3.5M in 1400	+17%
India	91M in 1300	97M in 1400	+6.5%
By Cities			
London	100,000 in 1346	37,000 in 1353	−62.5%
Florence	92,000 in 1346	37,250 in 1353	−59.5%
Sienna	50,000 in 1346	20,000 in 1353	−60%
Bologna	50,000 in 1346	27,500 in 1353	−45%
Cairo	500,000 in 1300	300,000 in 1400	−40%
Damascus	80,000 in 1300	50,000 in 1400	−37%

Sources: Ole J. Benedictow, *The Black Death, 1346–1353: The Complete History* (Woodbridge, England, 2004); Michael Dols, *The Black Death in the Middle East* (Princeton, 1974): Colin McEvedy and Richard Jones, *Atlas of World Population History* (Hammondsworth, England, 1978); Ping-ti Ho, *Studies on the Population of China, 1368–1953* (Cambridge, MA, 1959).

people deeply shaken by the extraordinary loss of life, rulers needed to revive confidence in themselves and their regimes, which they did by fostering beliefs and rituals that confirmed their legitimacy and by increasing their control over subjects.

The basis for power was a political institution well known to Afro-Eurasians for centuries, the **dynasty**—the hereditary ruling family that passed control from one generation to the next. As in the past, the new dynasties sought to establish their legitimacy in three ways. First, ruling families insisted that their power derived from a divine calling: Ming emperors in China claimed for themselves what previous dynastic rulers had asserted—the "mandate of heaven"—while European monarchs claimed to rule by "divine right." From their base in Anatolia, Ottoman warrior-princes asserted that they now carried the banner of Islam. In these ways, ruling households affirmed that God or the heavens intended for them to hold power. Second, leaders prevented squabbling among potential heirs by establishing clear rules about succession to the throne. Many European states tried to standardize succession by passing titles to the eldest male heir, thus ensuring political stability at a potential time of crisis, but in practice there were countless complications and quarrels. In the Islamic world, successors could be designated by the current ruler or elected by the community; here, too, struggles over succession were frequent. Third, ruling families elevated their power through conquest or alliance—by ordering armies forcibly to extend their domains, or by marrying their royal offspring to rulers of other states or members of other elite households, a technique widely practiced in Europe. Once it established legitimacy, the typical royal family would consolidate power by enacting coercive laws and punishments and sending emissaries to govern distant territories. A ruling family would also establish standing armies and new administrative structures to collect taxes and to oversee building projects that proclaimed royal power.

As we will see in the next three sections of this chapter, the innovative state building that occurred in the wake of the plague's devastation would not have been as successful had it not drawn on older traditions. In Europe, a cultural flourishing based largely on ancient Greek and Roman models gave rise to thinkers who proposed new views of governance. The peoples of the Islamic world held fiercely to their religion as successor states, notably the Ottoman Empire, absorbed numerous Turkish-speaking groups. The Ming, having failed in their attempts to control northern Vietnam and Korea, renounced the Mongol expansionist legacy and emphasized a return to Han rulership consolidating control of Chinese lands and concentrating on internal markets rather than overseas trade. Many of these regimes lasted for centuries, promoting political institutions and cultural values that became deeply embedded in the fabric of their societies.

The Islamic Heartland

The devastation of the Black Death followed hard on the heels of the Mongol destruction of Islam's most important city, Baghdad, and Islam's old political order. Nonetheless, these two catastrophes prepared the way for new Islamic states to emerge. The old, Arabic-speaking Islamic world remained vital, still at the heart of Islam geographically, but it now had to yield authority to new rulers and religious men. These societies now included large Turkish- and Persian-speaking populations as well. The new Islamic world occupied a vast geographical triangle. It stretched from Anatolia in the west to the Khurasan region of Persia and Afghanistan in the east and to the southern point at Baghdad.

The Ottomans, the Safavids, and the Mughals emerged as the dominant states in the old Islamic world in the early sixteenth century. They exploited the rich agrarian resources of the Indian Ocean regions and the Mediterranean Sea basin, and they benefited from a brisk seaborne and overland trade. By the mid-sixteenth century the Mughals controlled the northern Indus River valley; the Safavids occupied Persia; and the Ottomans ruled Anatolia, the Arab world, and much of southern and eastern Europe. Here we will explore in depth the Ottoman Empire, which emerged first and endured the longest of the three. (See Chapter 12 for a fuller discussion of the Mughals and Chapter 14 for more on the Safavids.)

THE OTTOMAN EMPIRE

The rise of the **Ottoman Empire** owed as much to innovative administrative techniques and religious tolerance as to military strength. Although the Mongols considered Anatolia to be a borderland region of little economic importance, their military forays in the late thirteenth century opened up the region to new political forces. The ultimate victors here were the Ottoman Turks. They transformed themselves from warrior bands roaming the borderlands between Islamic and Christian worlds into rulers of a settled state and, finally, into sovereigns of a far-flung highly bureaucratic empire (see Map 11.2). Under their chief, Osman (r. 1299–1326), the Turkish Ottomans formalized a stern and disciplined warrior ethos. They triumphed over their rivals by adapting the techniques of administration from their neighbors and by attracting these groups to their rule. In time, not only did the Ottoman state win the favor of Islamic clerics, but it also became the champion of Sunni Islam throughout the Islamic world.

MAP 11.2 | The Ottoman Empire, 1300–1566

This map charts the expansion of the Ottoman state from the time of its founder, Osman, through the reign of Suleiman, the empire's most illustrious ruler. Identify the earliest part of the empire under Osman. Then identify all the areas of conquest under Suleiman.

• Against whom did the Ottomans fight between the years 1326 and 1566?

• What were the geographic limits of the empire?

• According to your reading, how did Ottoman rulers promote unity among such a diverse population?

By the mid-fourteenth century, the Ottomans had expanded into the Balkans, becoming the most powerful force in the eastern Mediterranean and western Asia. By the early sixteenth century, the state controlled a vast territory, stretching in the west to the Moroccan border, in the north to Hungary and Moldavia, in the south through the Arabian Peninsula, and in the east to the Persian border. What was impressive and new within the Islamic world was the Ottomans' elaborate administrative hierarchy, atop which stood the sultan. Below him was a military and civilian bureaucracy, whose task was to demand obedience and revenue from subjects. The bureaucracy's discipline enabled the sultan to expand his realm, which in turn forced him to invest in an even larger bureaucracy.

The empire's spectacular expansion was primarily a military affair. To recruit followers, the Ottomans promised wealth and glory to new subjects. This was an expensive undertaking, but territorial expansion generated vast financial and administrative rewards. Moreover, by spreading the spoils of conquest and lucrative administrative positions, rulers bought off potentially unhappy subordinates. Still, without military might, the Ottomans would not have enjoyed the successes associated with the brilliant reigns of Murad II (r. 1421–1451) and his appropriately named successor, Mehmed the Conqueror (r. 1451–1481).

Mehmed's most spectacular triumph was the conquest of Constantinople, an ambition for Muslim rulers ever since the birth of Islam. Mehmed left no doubt that this was his primary goal: shortly after his coronation he vowed to capture the capital of the Byzantine Empire, a city of immense strategic and commercial importance, which had withstood Muslim efforts at conquest for centuries. First he built a fortress of his own to prevent European vessels from reaching the capital. Then, by promising his soldiers free access to booty and portraying the city's conquest as a holy cause, he amassed a huge army that outnumbered the defending force of 7,000 by more than ten times. For forty days his troops bombarded Constantinople's massive walls with artillery that included enormous cannons built by Hungarian and Italian engineers. On May 29, 1453, Ottoman troops overwhelmed the surviving soldiers and took the ancient Roman and Christian capital of Byzantium—which Mehmed promptly renamed Istanbul.

The Tools of Empire Building

The Ottomans adopted Byzantine administrative practices to unify their enlarged state and incorporated many of Byzantium's powerful families into it. Their dynastic power was, however, not only military; it also rested on a firm religious foundation. At the center of this empire were the sultans, who combined a warrior ethos with an unwavering devotion to Islam. Describing themselves as the "shadow of God" on earth, they claimed to be caretakers for the welfare of the Islamic faith. Throughout the empire, the sultans devoted substantial resources to the construction of elaborate mosques and to the support of Islamic schools. As self-appointed defenders of the faithful, the sultans assumed the role of protectors of the holy cities on the Arabian Peninsula and of Jerusalem, while working to unite the realm's diverse lands and peoples and constantly striving to extend the borders of Islam. During the reign of Suleiman (r. 1520–1566), the Ottomans reached the height of their territorial expansion. Under his administration, the Ottoman state ruled over 20 to 30 million people. By the time Suleiman died, the Ottoman

The Fall of Constantinople The use of heavy artillery in the forty-day siege of Constantinople was instrumental to the Ottoman victory. At the center of this Turkish miniature is one such cannon, possibly of Hungarian origin, which required hundreds of men and oxen to transport and secure outside the city walls.

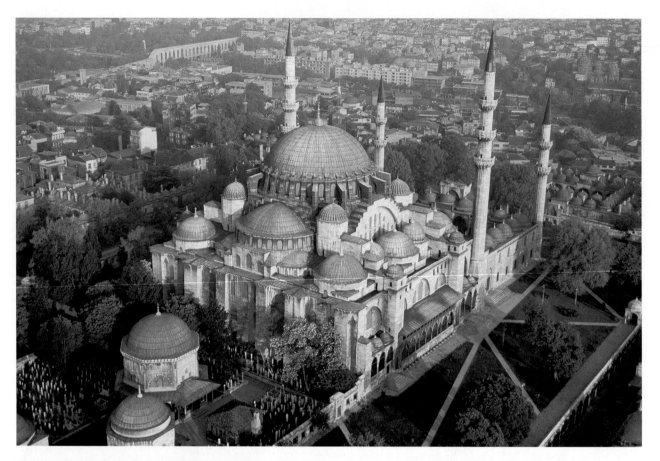

The Suleymaniye Mosque Built by Sultan Suleiman in the mid-sixteenth century to crown his achievements, the Suleymaniye Mosque was designed by the architect Sinan to dominate the city. What message do you think Suleiman was attempting to convey in building the mosque across a park from the Hagia Sophia, a formerly Christian basilica built in the sixth century by Justinian upon foundations going back 200 years earlier to the time of Constantine and his sons?

Empire bridged Europe and the Arab world. Istanbul by then was a dynamic imperial hub, dispatching bureaucrats and military men to oversee a vast domain.

Istanbul's **Topkapi Palace** exhibited the Ottomans' view of governance, the sultans' emphasis on religion, and the continuing influence of Ottoman familial traditions. Laid out by Mehmed II, the palace complex projected a vision of Istanbul as the center of the world. As a way to promote the sultan's magnificent power, architects designed the complex so that the buildings containing the imperial household were nestled behind layers of outer courtyards, in a mosaic of mosques, courts, and special dwellings for the sultan's harem. The harem had its own hierarchy of thousands of women, from the sultan's mother and consorts to the slave women who waited on them, and it became a formidable political force at the heart of Ottoman power.

The growing importance of Topkapi Palace as the command post of empire represented a crucial transition in the history of Ottoman rulers. Not only was the palace the place where future bureaucrats received their training; it was also the place where the chief bureaucrat, the grand vizier, carried out the day-to-day running of the empire. Whereas the early sultans had led their soldiers into battle personally and had met face-to-face with their kinsmen, the later rulers withdrew into the sacredness of the palace, venturing out only occasionally for grand ceremonies. Still, every Friday, subjects lined up outside the palace to introduce their petitions, ask for favors, and seek justice. If they were lucky, the

The Topkapi Palace A view of the inner courtyard of Topkapi's seraglio (sequestered living space), where the sultan and his harem lived. What does this image suggest about how the sultan used the palace to run his empire?

sultans would be there to greet them—but they did so behind grated glass, issuing their decisions by tapping on the window. The palace thus projected a sense of majestic, distant wonder, a home fit for semidivine rulers.

Diversity and Control The fact that the Ottoman Empire endured into the twentieth century owed much to the ruling elite's ability to gain the support and employ the talents of exceedingly diverse populations. After all, neither conquest nor conversion eliminated cultural differences in the empire's distant provinces. Thus, for example, the Ottomans' language policy was one of flexibility and tolerance. Although Ottoman Turkish was the official language of administration, Arabic was the primary language of the Arab provinces, the common tongue of street life. Within the empire's European corner, many people spoke their own languages. From the fifteenth century onward, the Ottoman Empire was perhaps more multilingual than any of its rivals.

In politics, as in language, the Ottomans showed flexibility and tolerance. The imperial bureaucracy permitted extensive regional autonomy. In fact, Ottoman military cadres perfected a technique for absorbing newly conquered territories into the empire by parceling them out as revenue-producing units among loyal followers and kin. Regional appointees could collect local taxes, part of which they earmarked for Istanbul and part of which they pocketed for themselves. (This was a common administrative device for many world dynasties ruling extensive domains.)

Like other empires, the Ottoman state was always in danger of losing control over its provincial rulers. Local potentates—the group that the imperial center allowed to rule in their distant regions—found that great distances enabled them to operate independently from central authority. These authorities kept larger amounts of tax revenues than Istanbul deemed proper. So, to limit their autonomy, the Ottomans established the janissaries, a corps of infantry soldiers and bureaucrats who owed direct allegiance to the sultan. The system at its high point involved a conscription of Christian youths from the empire's European lands. This conscription, called the ***devshirme***, required each village to hand over a certain number of males between the ages of eight and eighteen. Uprooted from their families and villages, selected for their fine physiques and good looks, these young men were converted to Islam and sent to farms to build up their bodies and learn Turkish. A select few were moved on to Topkapi Palace to learn Ottoman military, religious, and administrative techniques. Some of these men later enjoyed exceptional careers in the arts and sciences—such as the architect Sinan, who designed the Suleymaniye Mosque. Recipients of the best education available in the Islamic world, and trained in Ottoman ways, instructed in the use of modern weaponry, and deprived of family connections, the *devshirme* recruits were prepared to serve the sultan (and the empire as a whole) rather than the interests of any particular locality or ethnic group.

Thus, the Ottomans established their legitimacy via military skill, religious backing, and a loyal bureaucracy. They artfully balanced the decentralizing tendencies of the outlying regions with the centralizing forces of the imperial capital. Relying on a careful mixture of religious faith, imperial patronage, and cultural tolerance, the sultans curried loyalty and secured political stability. Indeed, the Ottoman Empire was so strong and stable that it dominated the coveted and highly contested trading crossroads between Europe and Asia for many centuries. Thus, its consolidation had powerful consequences for European efforts to rebuild their societies after the plague; above all, it closed off traditional overland trade routes to India and China.

Western Christendom

No region suffered more from the Black Death than Western Christendom, and no region made a more spectacular comeback. From 1100 to 1300, Europe had enjoyed a surge in population, rapid economic growth, and significant technological and intellectual innovations, only to see these achievements halted in the fourteenth century by famine and the Black Death. Europeans responded by creating new political and cultural forms. New dynastic states arose, competing with one another, and a movement called the Renaissance revived Europe's connections with its Greek and Roman past and produced masterpieces of art, architecture, and other forms of thought.

THE CATHOLIC CHURCH, STATE BUILDING, AND ECONOMIC RECOVERY

In the aftermath of famine and plague, the peoples of Western Christendom, like those in the Muslim world, looked to their religious beliefs and institutions as foundations for recovery. The faith of many had been severely tested, and religious authorities had to struggle to reclaim their power. To begin with, the late medieval western church found itself divided at the top (at one point during this period there were three popes) and challenged from below, both by individuals pursuing alternative kinds of spirituality and by increasing demands on the clergy and church administration. Disappointment with the clergy smoldered. The peasantry despaired at the absence of clergy when they were so greatly needed during the famines and Black Death. With groups like the Beghards challenging the clergy's right to define religious doctrine and practices, the church fought back, identifying all that was suspect and demanding strict obedience to the true faith. This entailed the persecution of heretics, Jews, Muslims in the Iberian Peninsula, homosexuals, prostitutes, and "witches." During this period the church expanded its charitable and bureaucratic functions, providing alms to the urban poor and registering births, deaths, and economic transactions. Crucially, faced with challenges to its authority, the church associated itself with secular rulers, lending moral authority to kings who claimed to rule "by divine right."

Europe's political rulers aligned themselves with church leaders to rebuild their states and consolidate their power. One royal family, the Habsburgs, drew on their Catholic religious traditions and established a powerful, long-lasting dynasty that would rule large parts of central Europe for centuries to follow. Habsburg leaders were elected to head the

COMPARISON

COMPARE the role religious belief systems played in rebuilding Europe and Islam in the fourteenth and fifteenth centuries.

federation of states known as the Holy Roman Empire almost continuously from 1438 to 1806, and for a time they ruled Spain and its New World colonies. Yet even at the height of its power in the early sixteenth century, the Habsburg monarchy never succeeded in restoring an integrated empire to western Europe.

In 1450 Western Christendom had no central government, no official tongue, and only a few successful commercial centers, mostly in the Mediterranean basin (see Map 11.3).

MAP 11.3 | Western Christendom, 1400–1500

Europe was a region divided by dynastic rivalries during the fifteenth century. Locate the most powerful regional dynasties on the map: Portugal, Castile, Aragon, France, Burgundy, England, and the Holy Roman Empire.

▫ Which areas witnessed the greatest warfare during this period?

▫ On the basis of this map and the reading, why do you think that was the case?

▫ Contrast the size of political units in this map with those in Maps 11.2 and 11.4. Explain the significance of the differences.

Joan of Arc: A Charismatic Leader in a Time of Social Turmoil

The immense historical impact of a French peasant girl, Joan of Arc, demonstrates the importance of charismatic individuals—even women in male-dominated societies—during periods of social turmoil. As Europe endured plagues, famines, and war, its people sought help through the special talents of women, even in areas like warfare. Indeed, if not for Joan of Arc, the country we know today as France might not exist. Gender is also a useful approach to study the relations between men and women in a society. World historians use it as a comparative theme across cultures and time, which makes it an even more useful lens for historical analysis.

Appearing on the scene in 1429, as the English seemed to be winning the Hundred Years' War, she rallied the French against the English occupiers and turned the tide of the war. By giving religious sanction, as well as military succor, to the Valois monarch Charles VII, she made possible the consolidation of France and left Europe an inspiring image of the female warrior-saint.

The world of Joan's childhood was a chaotic one, in which English lords were laying claim to various French-speaking principalities. By 1420, Valois authority had been greatly eroded, and English armies were conquering more and more French towns. In 1428, the English laid siege to Orléans, a large town in north-central France. To contemporaries, it seemed a symbolic battle: as Orléans went, they thought, so the war would go—and so would God wish it to go.

This is the point at which the paths of a seventeen-year-old peasant girl and the monarch of France crossed. Beginning at about age thirteen, the shy girl had received visions of saints who instructed her to rescue Orléans and bring France's ruler to be crowned king at Reims Cathedral. (He had not been crowned there, in the tradition of all French kings, because the English armies controlled Reims, Paris, and northern France.) For five years Joan resisted, but at last she obeyed her celestial advisers. Granted an audience with Charles VII in 1429, Joan impressed him with her piety and her passionate devotion to the Valois crown. He concluded that God really had sent her to serve France's cause—and his own. Joan won command of 7,000 to 8,000 men; then, wearing a suit of armor and brandishing a sword, she marched to relieve Orléans. Joan directed the assault with brilliance and inspired the French forces; her charisma came not only from a tradition of female Christian "seers," but also from the peculiarity of her appearance (a young woman in male attire) and her appeal to French speakers who resented rule by English "outsiders." After driving the English from Orléans, she then pressed on to Reims; here, thanks to her military victories, Charles VII was crowned, fulfilling her visions. He was now king of France—and though the war continued, the tide now turned in favor of the French.

The tide for Joan, however, turned for the worse. Although she continued to direct the troops with remarkable savvy, she failed to force open the gates of Paris, and jealous courtiers around Charles began to question her divine authority. She was wounded, then taken prisoner. After a year in English captivity she faced the

The feudal system of a lords' control over the peasantry (see Chapter 10), which was now in decline, left a legacy of political fragmentation and enduring elite privileges, which made the consolidation of a unified Christian Europe even more difficult to achieve. Europe's linguistic diversity reflected its political fragmentation. No single ruler or language united peoples, even when they shared a religion. Latin lost ground as rulers chose various regional dialects (e.g., French, Spanish, English) to be their official state language, whereas the written literary Chinese script remained a key administrative tool for China's dynasts, and in the Islamic world Arabic was the common language of faith and Turkish the language of administration.

Those who sought to rule the emerging states faced numerous obstacles. For example, rival claimants to the throne financed threatening private armies. Also, the clergy demanded and received privileges in the form of access to land and relief from taxation; they often meddled in politics themselves, and the church became a formidable economic

Inquisition and was found guilty of heresy, on the grounds that her visions were false and misleading. On May 30, 1431, she was burned at the stake in the marketplace in the town of Rouen. Since that time she has stood as a heroic and charismatic martyr, and the French have often invoked her name to awaken patriotism against foreign threats.

The fact that this young, illiterate woman played such an important role in the history of European warfare and state formation testifies to the fact that male aristocrats, intellectuals, and clerics were not the only important actors. At the right place, at the right time, a woman could use courage, faith, and intelligence to make her visions prevail.

QUESTIONS FOR ANALYSIS

- What other heroic figures, male or female, does Joan of Arc remind you of and why?
- Why do you think Charles VII failed to rescue Joan of Arc from her English prison?

Explore Further

Régine Pernoud and Marie-Véronique Clin, *Joan of Arc: Her Story*, trans. Jeremy Adams (1999).

powerhouse. And once the printing press became available in Europe in the 1460s, printers circulated anonymous pamphlets criticizing the court and the clergy. Some states had consultative political bodies—such as the Estates General in France, the Cortes in Spain, and Parliament in England—in which princes formally asked representatives of their people for advice and, in the case of the English Parliament, for consent to new forms of taxation. Such political bodies gave no voice to common men and no representation to women. But they did allow the collective expression of grievances against overbearing policies.

Out of the chaos of famine, disease, and warfare, the diverse peoples of Europe found a political way forward. This path involved the formation of centralized dynastic monarchies. A **monarchy** is a political system in which one individual holds supreme power and passes that power on to his or her next of kin. Often in competition with the new monarchies, a handful of European city-states, in which a narrow group of wealthy and influential voters selected their leaders, survived right up to the nineteenth century and in some cases into the twentieth. Consolidation of these states occurred sometimes through strategic marriages but more often through warfare, both between princely families and with local aristocratic allies and foreign mercenaries (see **Current Trends in World History: Joan of Arc**). Political stabilization was swiftest in southern Europe, where economies rebounded through seaborne trade with Southwest Asia. The stabilization of Italian city-states such as Venice and Florence, and of monarchical rule in Portugal and Spain, led to an economic and cultural flowering known as the Renaissance. In northern and western Europe, the process took longer. In England and France, in particular, internal feuding, regional warfare, and religious fragmentation delayed recovery for decades (see Chapter 12).

POLITICAL CONSOLIDATION AND TRADE IN THE IBERIAN PENINSULA

War and overseas trade played a central role in the emergence of new dynasties in Portugal and Spain. Through the fourteenth century, Portuguese Christians devoted themselves to fighting the Moors, who were Muslim occupants of North Africa, the western Sahara, and the Iberian Peninsula. After the Portuguese crossed the Strait of Gibraltar and seized the Moorish fortresses at Ceuta, in Morocco, their ships could sail between the Mediterranean and the Atlantic without Muslim interference. With that threat diminished, the Portuguese perceived their neighbor, Castile (part of which is now Spain), as their chief foe. Under João I (r. 1385–1433) Portugal defeated the Castilians, becoming the dominant power on the Iberian peninsula. No longer preoccupied with Castilian competition, the Portuguese sought new territories and trading opportunities in the North Atlantic and along the West African coasts. João's son Prince Henrique, known later as Henry the Navigator, further expanded the royal family's domain by supporting expeditions down the coast of Africa and offshore to the Atlantic islands of the Madeiras and the Azores. The west and central coasts of Africa and the islands of the North and South Atlantic, including the Cape Verde Islands, São Tomé, Principe, and Fernando Po, soon became Portuguese ports of call.

Portuguese monarchs granted the Atlantic islands to nobles as hereditary possessions on condition that the grantees colonize them, and soon the colonizers were establishing lucrative sugar plantations. In gratitude, noble families and merchants threw their political weight behind the king. Subsequent monarchs continued to cultivate local aristocrats' support for monarchical authority, thus ensuring smooth succession to the crown for members of the royal family.

In Spain, a new dynasty also emerged, though the road was difficult. Medieval Spain comprised rival kingdoms that quarreled ceaselessly. Within those kingdoms, several religions coexisted: Muslims, Jews, and Christians lived side by side in relative harmony, and Muslim armies still occupied strategic posts in the south. Over time, marriages and the formation of kinship ties among nobles and between royal lineages yielded a new political order. One by one, the major houses of the Spanish kingdoms intermarried, culminating in the wedding of Isabella of Castile and Ferdinand of Aragon (1469). This marriage linked Castile, wealthy and populous, to Aragon, which enjoyed an extended trading network in the Mediterranean. Together, the monarchs brought unruly nobles and distant towns under their control. They topped off their achievements by marrying their children into other European royal families—especially the Habsburgs, central Europe's most powerful dynasty.

Thus, Spain's two most important provinces were joined, and Spain later became a state to be reckoned with.

The new Spanish rulers sent Christian armies south to push Muslim forces out of the Iberian Peninsula. By the mid-fifteenth century only Granada, a strategic linchpin overlooking the straits between the Mediterranean and the Atlantic, remained in Muslim hands. After a long and costly siege, Christian forces captured the fortress there in 1492. This was a victory of enormous symbolic importance, as joyous as the fall of Constantinople was depressing (for Christians).

The Inquisition and Westward Exploration Isabella and Ferdinand sought to drive all non-Catholics out of Spain. Terrified by Ottoman incursions into Europe, they launched the **Inquisition** in 1481, taking aim especially against *conversos*—converted Jews

Ferdinand and Isabella Entering Granada This altar relief, sculpted by Felipe Vigarny in the early sixteenth century, depicts the triumphant entrance of King Ferdinand and Queen Isabella into the city of Granada after their conquest of this last Muslim stronghold in Spain. Why would such an image be depicted on an altar? In what ways does the image show power and distinction among the individuals depicted?

and Muslims, whom they suspected were Christians only in name. When Granada fell, the crown ordered the expulsion of all Jews from Spain. After 1499, a more tolerant attempt to convert the Moors (Muslims) by persuasion gave way to forced conversion—or emigration. All told, almost half a million people were forced to flee the Spanish kingdoms. This lack of tolerance meant that Spain, like other European states in this era, became increasingly homogeneous. With fewer groups vying for influence within their territories, rulers turned their attention outward, fueling rivalries between the various European states.

So strong was the tide of Spanish fervor by late 1491 that the monarchs listened now to a Genoese navigator whose pleas for patronage they had previously rejected. Christopher Columbus promised them unimaginable riches that could finance their military campaigns and bankroll a crusade to liberate Jerusalem from Muslim hands. Off he sailed with a royal patent that guaranteed the monarchs a share of all he discovered. Soon the Spanish economy was reorienting itself toward the Atlantic, and Spain's merchants, missionaries, and soldiers were preparing for conquest and profiteering in what had been, just a few years before, a blank space on the map.

THE RENAISSANCE

Just as the Ming harkened back to Han Chinese traditions and the Ottomans looked to Sunni Islam to point the way forward, so European elites looked to their own traditions for guidance as they rebuilt after the devastation of the plague. They found inspiration in ancient Greek and Roman institutions and ideas. Europe's extraordinary political and economic revival also involved a powerful outpouring of cultural achievements, led by Italian scholars and artists and financed by bankers, churchmen, and nobles. Much later, scholars coined the word **Renaissance** to characterize the cultural flourishing of the Italian city-states, France, the Netherlands, England, and the Holy Roman Empire in the period 1430–1550. What was being "reborn" was ancient Greek and Roman art and learning—knowledge that could help people understand an expanding world and support the rights of secular individuals to exert power in it. Although the Renaissance was largely funded by popes and Christian kings, it challenged the authority of traditional religious elites, breaking the medieval church's monopoly on answers to the big questions. The movement emphasized secular forms of learning rather than just Christian doctrine and a more human-centered understanding of the cosmos.

The Renaissance was all about new exposure to the old—to classical texts and ancient art and architectural forms. Although some Greek and Roman texts were known in Europe and the Islamic world, the use of the printing press made others accessible to western scholars for the first time. Scholars now realized that the pre-Christian Greeks and Romans had developed powerful means of representing and caring for the human body. Having studied the world directly, without the need to square their observations with biblical information, the ancients had much to teach about geography, astronomy, and architecture and about how to govern states and armies. For Renaissance scholars it was no longer enough to understand Christian doctrine and to concern themselves with the next world. One had to go back to the original, classical sources in order to understand the human condition. This in turn required the learning of languages and history. Scholarship that attempted to return to Greek and Roman sources became known as **humanism**.

Because political and religious powers were not united in Europe (as they were in China and the Islamic world), scholars and artists seeking sponsors for their work could play one side against the other, or, alternatively, could suffer both clerical and political

COMPARISON

COMPARE the way art and architecture reflected the political realities of Europe and Islam after the Black Death.

Renaissance Masterpieces Leonardo da Vinci's *The Last Supper* (*left*) depicts Christ's disciples reacting to his announcement that one of them will betray him. Michelangelo's *David* (*right*) stands over thirteen feet high and was conceived as an expression of Florentine civic ideals. In what ways do these Renaissance masterpieces draw on the principles of humanism and reflect a return to western "classics" of the Greco-Roman world?

persecution. Michelangelo (1475–1564), a leading painter, sculptor, architect, and engineer of the age, completed commissions for the famous Florentine bankers and political leaders of the Medici family, for the Florentine Wool Guild, and for Pope Julius II. Peter Paul Rubens painted for the courts of France, Spain, England, and the Netherlands, as well as selling paintings on the open market. These two painters, renowned for showing a great deal of flesh, frequently offended conservative church officials. Most support for the arts, however, came either from the church or individual clergymen, and virtually all secular donors were devout believers who commissioned works with religious themes. The Dutch scholar Desiderius Erasmus ridiculed corrupt popes and the clergy with the patronage of English, Dutch, and French supporters, while remaining a Catholic, an ordained cleric, and an opponent of Reformation doctrines. Conflicts within the Catholic Church, between the church and secular leaders, and among secular leaders and wealthy private citizens enabled artists to present challenging images and ideas with an unusual independence.

Gradually, a network of educated men and women took shape that was not wholly dependent on either the church or the state or a single princely patron. Classical knowledge gave individuals the means to challenge political, clerical, and aesthetic authority. Moreover, rivalries between Europe's relatively small states and city-states allowed many of these scholars to dodge the authorities by fleeing to neighboring communities. Of course, they could also use their learning to defend the older elites: for example, numerous lawyers and scholars continued to work for the popes in defending the papacy. At the same time, in contrast, men like Erasmus and later Martin Luther (the leading figure of the Reformation in the sixteenth century) looked to secular princes to support their critical scholarship. In Florence, Niccolò Machiavelli wrote the most famous treatise on authoritarian power, *The Prince* (1513). Machiavelli argued that political leadership required mastering the rules of modern statecraft, even if in some cases this meant disregarding moral imperatives. Holding and exercising power were vital ends in themselves, he claimed; traditional ideas of civic virtue should not deter rulers, like those of the Medici family, from maintaining control over society.

With Renaissance ideas challenging traditional authority and rulers facing a range of internal and external obstacles, the new monarchies of Europe were not all immediately successful in consolidating power and unifying peoples. In France and England, for example, the great age of monarchy had yet to dawn. Even when stable states did arise in Europe, they were fairly small compared to the Ottoman and Ming empires. In the mid-sixteenth century, Portugal and Spain, Europe's two most expansionist states, had populations of 1 million and 9 million, respectively. England, excluding Wales, was a mere 3 million in 1550. Only France, with 17 million, had a population close to the Ottoman Empire's 25 million. And these numbers paled in comparison with Ming China's population of nearly 200 million in 1550. But in Europe, small could be advantageous. Portugal's relatively small population meant that the crown had fewer groups to control. In the world of finance, the most successful merchants were those inhabiting the smaller Italian city-states and, a bit later, the cities of the northern Netherlands. The Florentines developed sophisticated banking techniques, created extensive networks of agents throughout Europe and the Mediterranean, and served as bankers to the popes. At the same time, the Renaissance—which flourished in the city-states and newly stabilized monarchies—made elite European culture more cosmopolitan and independent from government authority, even if it could not unify the states and peoples who cultivated it.

Ming China

Like the Europeans, the Chinese saw their stable worldview and political order crumble under the catastrophes of human and bacterial invasions. Moreover, like the Europeans, people in China had long regarded outsiders as "barbarians" and balked at being ruled by outsiders. Together, the Mongols and the Black Death upended the political and intellectual foundations of what had appeared to be the world's most integrated society. The Mongols brought the Yuan dynasty to power; then the plague devastated China and prepared the way for the emergence of the Ming dynasty. The Ming dynasty, ruled by ethnically Han Chinese, defined itself against its foreign predecessors. Ming emperors sought to reinforce everything Chinese. In particular, they supported China's vast internal agricultural markets in an attempt to minimize dependence on merchants and foreign trade.

RESTORING ORDER

In the chaotic fourteenth century, as plague and famine ravaged China and the Mongol Yuan dynasty collapsed, only a strong military movement capable of overpowering other groups could restore order. That intervention began at the hands of a poor young man who had trained in the Red Turban Movement: Zhu Yuanzhang.

It soon became clear that Zhu had a much grander design for China than the ambitions of most warlords. When he took Nanjing in 1356, he renamed it Yingtian ("In response to Heaven"). Lifted by subsequent successful military campaigns, Zhu (r. 1368–1398) took the imperial title of Hongwu ("expansive and martial") Emperor and proclaimed the founding of the Ming ("brilliant") dynasty in 1368. Soon thereafter, his troops met little resistance when they seized the Yuan capital of Beijing, causing the Mongol emperor to flee to his homeland in the steppe. It would, however, take Hongwu almost another twenty years to reunify the entire country.

CENTRALIZATION UNDER THE MING

Hongwu and successive Ming emperors had to rebuild a devastated society from the ground up. Although in the past China had experienced natural catastrophes, wars, and social dislocation, the plague's legacy was devastation on an unprecedented scale. It left the new rulers with the formidable challenge of rebuilding the great cities, restoring respect for ruling elites, and reconstructing the bureaucracy.

Imperial Grandeur and Kinship The rebuilding began with the Hongwu Emperor, whose capital at Nanjing reflected imperial grandeur. When the dynasty's third emperor, the Yongle ("perpetual happiness") Emperor, relocated the capital to Beijing, he flaunted an even more grandiose style, employing around 100,000 artisans and 1 million laborers to build this new capital, including its Forbidden City. The city had three separate walled enclosures. Inside the outer city walls sprawled the imperial city; within its walls lay the palace city, the Forbidden City. Traffic within the walled sections navigated through broad boulevards leading to the different gates, above which imposing towers soared. The palace compound, where the imperial family resided, had more than 9,000 rooms. Anyone standing in the front courts, which measured more than 400 yards on a side and boasted marble terraces and carved railings, would gasp at the sense of awesome power. That was precisely the effect the Ming emperors wanted, just as the Ottoman sultans did in building Topkapi Palace.

Marriage and kinship buttressed the power of the Ming imperial household, much like the dynastic strategies of Europe. The Ming dynasty's founder married the adopted daughter of a leading Red Turban rebel (her father, according to legend, was a convicted murderer), thereby consolidating his power and eliminating a threat. Empress Ma, as she was known, became Hongwu's principal wife and was praised for her compassion. Emerging as the kinder face of the regime, she tempered the harsh and sometimes cruel disposition of her spouse. He had numerous other consorts as well, including Korean and Mongol women, who bore him twenty-six sons and sixteen daughters (similar to, although on smaller scale than, the sultan's harem at Ottoman Topkapi).

COMPARISON

COMPARE the ways rulers rebuilt unified states and their levels of success in China, Islam, and Europe.

The Forbidden City The Yongle Emperor relocated the capital to Beijing, where he began the construction of the Forbidden City, or imperial palace, in the early fifteenth century. The palace was designed to inspire awe in all who saw it. In what ways do the partitions of space and the activities of people within that space appear to support imperial grandeur?

Building a Bureaucracy Faced with the challenge of reestablishing order out of turmoil, Hongwu initially sought to rule through his kinsmen—by giving imperial princes generous stipends, command of large garrisons, and significant autonomy in running their domains. However, when the princes' power began to threaten the court, Hongwu slashed their stipends, reduced their privileges, and took control of their garrisons. No longer dependent on these men, he established an imperial bureaucracy beholden only to him and to his successors. These officials won appointments through their outstanding performance on a reinstated civil service examination.

In addition, Hongwu took other steps to install a centralized system of rule. He assigned bureaucrats to oversee the manufacture of porcelain, cotton, and silk products, as well as tax collection. He reestablished the Confucian school system as a means of selecting a cadre of loyal officials (not unlike the Ottoman janissaries and administrators). He also set up local networks of villages to rebuild irrigation systems and to supervise reforestation projects to prevent flooding—with the astonishing result that the amount of land reclaimed nearly tripled within eight years. For water control, over 40,000 reservoirs underwent repairs or new construction. Historians estimate that Hongwu's reign oversaw the planting around Nanjing of about 1 billion trees, which were later used in building a maritime expedition fleet in the early fifteenth century.

The imperial palace not only projected the image of a power center, it *was* the center of power. Every official received his appointment by the emperor through the Ministry of Personnel. Hongwu eliminated the post of prime minister (he executed the man who held the post) and ruled directly. Ming bureaucrats had to kneel before the emperor. The drawback of this centralized control, of course, was that the Ming emperor had to keep tabs on this immense system. Hongwu constantly moved his bureaucrats around, sometimes fortifying the administration, sometimes undermining it lest it become too autonomous. Over time, Hongwu nurtured a bureaucracy far more extensive than that of the Ottomans. The Ming thus established the most highly centralized system of government of all the monarchies of this period.

Religion under the Ming Just as the Ottoman sultans projected themselves as Muslim rulers, calling themselves the shadow of God, and European monarchs claimed to rule by divine right, so the Ming emperors enhanced their legitimacy by drawing on ancient Chinese religious traditions. Citing the mandate of heaven, the emperor revised and strengthened the elaborate rites and ceremonies that had supported dynastic power for centuries. Official rituals, such as those related to the gods of soil and grain, reinforced political and social classes, portraying the rulers as

Ming Deities A pantheon of deities worshipped during the Ming dynasty, demonstrating the rich religious culture of the period. In what ways does this document show Ming religious beliefs?

the moral and spiritual benefactors of their subjects. In lavish ceremonies, the emperor engaged in sacrificial rites, cultivating his image as mediator between the human and the spiritual worlds. The message was clear: the gods were on the side of the Ming household.

MING RULERSHIP

Conquest and defense helped establish the realm, and bureaucracy kept it functioning. The empire's scale (see Map 11.4) required complex administration. To many outsiders

MAP 11.4 | Ming China, 1500s

The Ming state was one of the largest empires at this time—and the most populous. Using the scale, determine the length of its coastline and its internal borders.

- What were the two Ming capitals and the three main seaport trading cities and how far are they from one another?
- According to the map, where did the Ming rulers expect the greatest threat to their security?
- How did the Ming rulers view foreign contact and exchange during this period?

(especially Europeans, whose region was in a state of constant war), Ming stability and centralization appeared to be political wizardry.

Ming rulers worried in particular about maintaining the support of ordinary people in the countryside. The emperor wished to be seen as the special guardian of his subjects. He wanted their allegiance as well as their taxes and labor. But during hard times, poor farmers were reluctant to provide resources—taxes or services—to distant officials. For these reasons and because the emperor distrusted state bureaucrats, Hongwu preferred to entrust management of the rural world to local leaders, whom he appointed as village chiefs, village elders, or tax captains. A popular Chinese proverb was: "The mountain is high and the emperor is far away." Within these communities, the dynasty created a social hierarchy based on age, sex, and kinship. While women's labor remained critical for the village economy, the government reinforced a gender hierarchy by promoting women's chastity and constructing commemorative arches for widows who honored their husbands by refraining from remarrying.

Like the European and Islamic states, the Ming Empire also faced periodic unrest and rebellion. Rebels often proclaimed their own brand of religious beliefs, just as local elites resented central authority. Outright terror helped stymie threats to central authority. In a massive wave of carnage, Hongwu slaughtered anyone who posed a threat to his authority, from the highest of ministers to the lowliest of scribes. From 1376 to 1393, four of his purges condemned close to 100,000 subjects to execution. Yet, despite the emperor's immense power, the Ming Empire remained undergoverned. Indeed, as the population multiplied, there were too few loyal officials to handle local affairs. By the sixteenth and early seventeenth centuries, for example, some 10,000 to 15,000 officials shouldered the responsibility of managing a population exceeding 200 million people. Nonetheless, Hongwu bequeathed to his descendants a set of tools for ruling that drew on subjects' direct loyalty to the emperor and on the intricate workings of an extensive bureaucracy. His legacy enabled his successors to balance local sources of power with the needs of dynastic rulership.

TRADE AND EXPLORATION UNDER THE MING

COMPARISON

COMPARE the ways that the Ming, Iberian, and Ottoman rulers extended their territories and influence.

In the fourteenth century, China began its economic recovery from the devastation of disease and political turmoil. Gradually, political stability allowed trade to revive. Now the new dynasty's merchants reestablished China's preeminence in long-distance commercial exchange. Chinese silk and cotton textiles, as well as fine porcelains, ranked among the world's most coveted luxuries. When a Chinese merchant ship sailed into port, trading partners and onlookers crowded the docks to watch the unloading of precious cargoes. Although Ming rulers' support for overseas ventures wavered and eventually declined, this period saw important developments in Chinese trade and exploration.

Overseas Trade: Success and Suspicion During the Ming period, Chinese traders based in ports such as Hangzhou, Quanzhou, and Guangzhou (Canton) were as energetic as their Muslim counterparts in the Indian Ocean. These ports were home to prosperous merchants and the point of convergence for vast sea-lanes. Leaving the mainland ports, Chinese vessels carried precious wares to offshore islands, the Pescadores, and Taiwan. From there, they sailed on to the ports of Southeast Asia. As entrepôts for global goods, East Asian ports flourished. Former fishing villages developed into major urban centers.

The Ming dynasty viewed overseas expansion with suspicion, however. Hongwu feared that too much contact with the outside world would cause instability and undermine his rule. In fact, he banned private maritime commerce in 1371. But enforcement was lax, and by the late fifteenth century maritime trade once again surged. Because much of the thriving business took place in defiance of official edicts, it led to constant friction between government officials and maritime traders. Although the Ming government ultimately agreed to issue licenses for overseas trade in the mid-sixteenth century, its policies continued to vacillate. To Ming officials, unlike their counterparts in Portugal and Spain, the sea represented problems of order and control rather than opportunities.

The Expeditions of Zheng He One spectacular exception to the Ming's attitude toward maritime trade was a series of officially sponsored expeditions in the early fifteenth century. It was the ambitious third Ming emperor, the Yongle Emperor, who took the initiative. One of his loyal followers was a Muslim whom the Ming army had captured as a boy. The youth was castrated and sent to serve at the court (as a eunuch, he could not continue his family line and so theoretically owed sole allegiance to the emperor). Given the name **Zheng He** (1371–1433), he grew up to be an important military leader. The emperor entrusted him with venturing out to trade, collect tribute, and display China's power to the world.

From 1405 to 1433, Zheng He commanded the world's greatest armada and led seven naval expeditions. His larger ships stretched 400 feet in length (Columbus's Santa Maria was 85 feet), carried hundreds of sailors on four tiers of decks, and maneuvered with sophisticated rudders, nine masts, and watertight compartments. The first expedition set sail with 28,000 men aboard a flotilla of sixty-two large ships and over 200 lesser ones. Zheng He and his entourage aimed to establish tributary relations with far-flung territories—from Southeast Asia to the Indian Ocean ports, to the Persian Gulf, and to the east coast of Africa (see Map 11.5). These expeditions did not seek territorial expansion, but rather control of trade and tribute. When the Yongle Emperor died in 1424, the expeditions lost their most enthusiastic patron. Moreover, by the mid-fifteenth century, there was a revival of military threats from the north, recalling how the maritime-oriented Song

Zheng He's Ship The largest ship in Zheng He's armada had nine staggered masts and twelve silk sails, all designed to demonstrate the grandeur of the Ming dynasty. How much larger was Zheng He's ship compared to Columbus's *Santa Maria* (pictured in the foreground)? How might the differences in size and construction reflect differences in the capabilities and goals of European and Chinese seafaring?

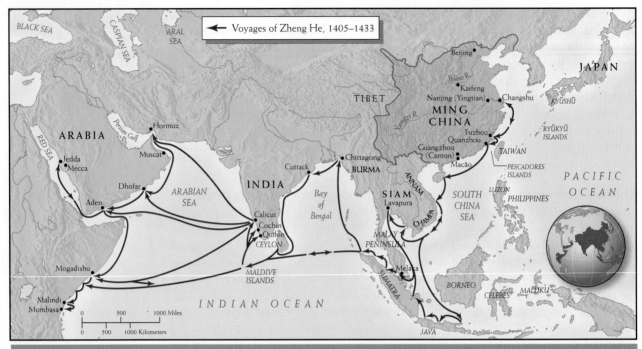

MAP 11.5 | Voyages of Zheng He, 1405–1433

Zheng He's voyages are some of the most famous in world history. Many have speculated about how history might be different if the Chinese emperors had allowed the voyages to continue.

- For how many years did Zheng's voyages go on?
- How far did Zheng go?
- Based on your reading, why did Chinese expeditions not have the same impact as European voyages of exploration toward the end of the fifteenth century, such as those of Columbus?

dynasty had been overrun by invaders from the north (see Chapter 10). Consequently, Ming officials withdrew imperial support for seagoing ventures and instead devoted their energies to overland ventures and defense.

Even though maritime commerce continued without official patronage, the Chinese decision to forgo overseas ventures was momentous. If China remained the wealthiest, most densely settled region of the world with the most fully developed state structures and thriving markets, the empire's wariness of overseas projects deprived merchants and would-be explorers of vital support in an age when others were beginning to look outward and overseas.

Conclusion

The dying and devastation that came with the Black Death caused many transformations, but certain underlying ideals and institutions endured. What changed were mainly the political regimes, which took the blame for the catastrophes. The Yuan dynasty collapsed and regimes in the Muslim world and Western Christendom were replaced by new political forms. In contrast, universal religions and cultural systems persisted even though they underwent vast transformations. A fervent form of Sunni

Islam found its champion in the Ottoman Empire. In Europe, centralizing monarchies appeared in Spain, Portugal, France, and England. The Ming dynasts in China set the stage for a long tenure by claiming the mandate of heaven and stressing China's place at the center of their universe.

The new states and empires had notable differences. These were evident in the ambition of a Ming warlord who established a new dynasty, the military expansionism of Turkish households bordering the Byzantine Empire, and the desire of various European rulers to consolidate power. But interactions among peoples also mattered; this era saw an eagerness to reestablish and expand trade networks, and a desire to convert unbelievers to "the true faith"—be it a form of Islam or an exclusive Christianity.

All of the dynasties surveyed in this chapter faced similar problems. They had to establish legitimacy, ensure smooth succession, deal with religious groups, and forge working relationships with nobles, townspeople, merchants, and peasants. Yet each state developed a distinctive identity; they all combined political innovation, traditional ways of ruling, and ideas borrowed from neighbors. European monarchies achieved significant internal unity, often through warfare with competing states. Ottoman rulers perfected techniques for ruling an ethnically and religiously diverse empire: they moved military forces swiftly, allowed local communities a degree of autonomy, and trained a bureaucracy dedicated to the Ottoman and Sunni Islamic way of life. The Ming fashioned an imperial system based on a Confucian-trained bureaucracy and intense subordination to the emperor so that it could manage a mammoth population. The rising monarchies of Europe and the Ottoman state all blazed with religious fervor and sought to eradicate or subordinate the beliefs of other groups.

The new states displayed unprecedented political and economic powers. All demonstrated military prowess, a desire for stable political and social hierarchies and secure borders, and a drive to expand. Each legitimized its rule via dynastic marriage and succession, state-sanctioned religion, and administrative bureaucracies. Each supported vigorous commercial activity. The Islamic regimes, especially, engaged in long-distance commerce and, by conquest and conversion, extended their holdings.

For Western Christendom, the Ottoman conquests were decisive. They provoked Europeans to establish commercial connections to the east, south, and west. The consequences of their new toeholds would be momentous—just as the Chinese decision to turn away from overseas exploration and commerce meant that China's contact with the outside world would be overland and eastward. As we shall see in Chapter 12, both decisions were instrumental in determining which worlds would come together and which would remain apart.

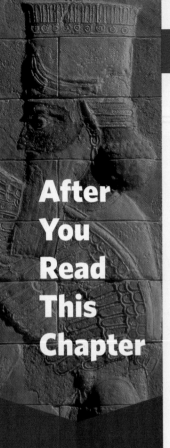

After You Read This Chapter

Go to **INQUIZITIVE** to see what you've learned—and learn what you've missed—with personalized feedback along the way.

FOCUS ON: *Crisis and Recovery in Afro-Eurasia*

COLLAPSE AND CONSOLIDATION

- Bubonic plague originates in Inner Asia and afflicts people from China to Europe.

- Climate change and famine leaves people vulnerable, while commerce facilitates the spread of disease.

- The plague kills 25 to 65 percent of infected populations and leaves societies in turmoil.

ISLAMIC HEARTLAND

- Ottomans overrun Constantinople and become the primary Sunni regime in the Islamic world.

- The Ottomans establish their legitimacy with military prowess, religious backing, and a loyal bureaucracy.

- Sultans manage decentralizing tendencies of outlying provinces with flexibility and tolerance, relying on religious faith, patronage, and bureaucracy.

WESTERN CHRISTENDOM

- New dynastic monarchies that claim to rule by divine right appear in Portugal, Spain, France, and England.

- The Inquisition takes aim against *conversos*—converted Jews and Muslims.

- A rebirth of classical learning, known as the Renaissance, originates in Italian city-states and spreads throughout western Europe.

MING CHINA

- The Ming dynasty replaces the Mongol Yuan dynasty and rebuilds a strong state from the ground up, claiming a mandate from heaven.

- An elaborate, centralized bureaucracy oversees the revival of infrastructure and long-distance trade.

- The emperor and bureaucracy concentrate on developing internal markets and overland trade at the expense of overseas commerce.

CHRONOLOGY

ISLAMIC WORLD	Osman begins Ottoman Empire 1299 ◆	
	The Black Death arrives in Baghdad 1347 ◆	
WESTERN CHRISTENDOM	Black Death reaches Italian port cities 1347 ◆	
EAST ASIA	Black Death begins in China 1320 ◆	
	Hongwu founds Ming dynasty 1368 ◆	
	1200	**1300**

Thinking about Exchange Networks By the fourteenth century, most of the Afro-Eurasian landmass was bound together by multiple exchange networks that functioned on many levels—political, cultural, and commercial. How did these exchange networks facilitate the spread of the plague? In what ways did the spread of the Black Death correspond with and diverge from existing political, cultural, and commercial networks?

Thinking about Changing Power Relationships Fourteenth-century famine, plague, and the accompanying political, economic, and natural crises together triggered powerful, often differing, responses in western Europe, the Ottoman lands, and Ming China. How did men and women at different levels of society respond to the fourteenth-century crises? How did their responses reshape their societies? Pay special attention to the relationships among ordinary men and women, elites, and imperial bureaucracies in all three regions.

Thinking about Environmental Impacts Climatic changes laid the groundwork for the devastation of the Black Death. What environmental developments in Europe, central Asia, and China set the stage for the Black Death?

1. Identify the fourteenth-century crisis that had the greatest impact throughout Afro-Eurasia and explain why: the **Black Death** (and accompanying famine of 1315 and climate change), the Mongol collapse, or political turmoil?

2. Analyze the role of philosophical and religious developments—both elite, like **humanism**, and popular movements, like the **Red Turban Movement** in China—in politics from 1300–1500 and explain how they provided both continuity and change in each society.

3. Explain how the Ottomans employed institutions such as **Topkapi Palace** and the *devshirme* system to consolidate their power?

4. Describe the ways in which regional monarchies and the **Renaissance** responded to the impact of the plague in western Europe? Analyze the role of the **Inquisition** in that process.

5. Explain how the Ming dynasty centralized power in China in the fourteenth and fifteenth centuries? What roles did emperors, bureaucrats, and ordinary people play? Compare Chinese efforts at bureaucratic centralization with those of the Ottomans.

◆ Ottoman armies conquer Constantinople 1453

Suleiman expands and consolidates
Ottoman Empire 1520–1566

◆ Castile and Aragon unite to form Spain 1469

◆ Spain conquers Granada 1492

Zheng He's voyages 1405–1433

Competing Perspectives

Cultural Responses to the Black Death

The devastation of the plague in Afro-Eurasia and the upheaval that followed were unprecedented. People desperately sought explanations, particularly religion-based ones, and responded to the turmoil in many different ways. The three primary sources brought together here exemplify radical responses to the crises of the fourteenth century. Qalandar dervishes sprang up in Damascus, Syria, and in Egypt, and renounced the world, living on alms and engaging in highly individualistic practices such as palm reading. European Flagellants also renounced the world, and whipped themselves in public until bruised, swollen, and bloody. Chinese rebels known as the Red Turbans believed that the Mongol rulers had lost the mandate of heaven and deserved to be replaced.

In the first excerpt Giovan Antonio Menavino, a European observer of Ottoman society, gives an obviously biased account of the Qalandars, whom he called the *torlaks*. In the second reading, Robert of Avesbury describes the actions of Flagellants in England during the reign of King Edward III. Finally, we see in the only surviving document written by the rebels themselves—a communiqué sent to the Koryo court in Korea in 1359—that the Red Turbans adopted the rhetoric of the dynastic authorities to establish their own political legitimacy. As you read these documents, consider not only how the groups' views and practices reflect the turmoil of the period, but also pay close attention to what perspective the authors bring to each account.

Source: Ahmet T. Karamustafa, "Dervish Groups in the Ottoman Empire, 1450–1550" from *God's Unruly Friends: Dervish Groups in the Islamic Later Middle Period, 1200–1550,* pp. 6–7. Oneworld Publications, Oxford, 2006. Reprinted with the permission of Oneworld Publications.

PRIMARY SOURCE 11.1

Qalandar Dervishes in the Islamic World (1548), Menavino

Dressed in sheepskins, the torlaks [Qalandars] are otherwise naked, with no headgear. Their scalps are always clean-shaven and well rubbed with oil as a precaution against the cold. They burn their temples with an old rag so that their faces will not be damaged by sweat. Illiterate and unable to do anything manly, they live like beasts, surviving on alms only. For this reason, they are to be found around taverns and public kitchens in cities. If, while roaming the countryside, they come across a well-dressed person, they try to make him one of their own, stripping him naked. Like Gypsies in Europe, they practice chiromancy [palm reading], especially for women who then provide them with bread, eggs, cheese, and other foods in return for their services.

Amongst them there is usually an old man whom they revere and worship like God. When they enter a town, they gather around the best house of the town and listen in great humility to the words of this old man, who, after a spell of ecstasy, foretells the descent of a great evil upon the town. His disciples then implore him to fend off the disaster through his good services. The old man accepts the plea of his followers, though not without an initial show of reluctance, and prays to God, asking him to spare the town the imminent danger awaiting it. This time-honored trick earns them considerable sums of alms from ignorant and credulous people.

PRIMARY SOURCE 11.2

Flagellants in England (1350s), Robert of Avesbury

In that same year of 1349, about Michaelmas [September 29], more than 120 men, for the most part from Zeeland or Holland, arrived in London from Flanders. These went barefoot in procession twice a day in the sight of the people, sometimes in St Paul's church and sometimes elsewhere in the city, their bodies naked except for a linen cloth from loins to ankle. Each wore a hood painted with a red cross at front and back and carried in his right hand a whip with three thongs. Each thong had a knot in it, with something sharp, like a needle, stuck through the middle of the knot so that it stuck out on each side, and as they walked one after the other they struck themselves with these whips on their naked, bloody bodies; four of them singing in their own tongue and the rest answering in the manner of the Christian litany. Three times in each procession they would all prostrate themselves on the ground, with their arms outstretched in the shape of a cross. Still singing, and beginning with the man at the end, each in turn would step over the others, lashing the man beneath him once with his whip, until all of those lying down had gone through the same ritual. Then each one put on his usual clothes and, always with their hoods on their heads and carrying their whips, they departed to their lodgings. It was said that they performed a similar penance every night.

Source: Robertus de Avesbury, "Flagellants in England" from *The Black Death*, Rosemary Horrox, trans./ed., pp. 153–54. Copyright © Rosemary Horrox 1994. Reprinted with permission of Manchester University Press.

PRIMARY SOURCE 11.3

The Red Turban Movement in China (1359)

Aggrieved that the people have long fallen under the Mongols, we have taken up the righteous cause and raised troops in order to recover the Central Plains. To the east, we have moved beyond the Shandong region; to the west, we have gone beyond Chang'an; to the south, we have passed beyond Fujian and Guandong; to the north, we have reached the Capital Region. All have joined us in good faith, like the starving who receive meat and grain or the ill who happened upon medicine. We have now ordered our generals to strictly prohibit their soldiers from disturbing the people. We will succor those people who join us; we will chastise those who resist in battle.

Source: David M. Robinson, *Empire's Twilight: Northeast Asia under the Mongols* (Cambridge, MA, 2009), p. 147.

QUESTIONS FOR ANALYSIS

1. Interpret the description of clothing in the first two documents. What does clothing tell us about the lifestyles of the dervishes and the Flagellants? What, if anything, can we tell about the authors and their views of these groups from these descriptions?

2. Explain how each of these documents characterizes setbacks within the societies. How do the members of these groups understand the period's crises, and what solutions, if any, do they offer? Pay special attention to the role of social class.

3. Identify and compare the critiques that each of the groups makes of traditional ways of behaving, whether through their own behavior or their words. What do they tell us about existing social norms?

Interpreting Visual Evidence

Marking Boundaries, Inspiring Loyalty

The fourteenth century witnessed the emergence of dynastic states across Afro-Eurasia that endured for centuries. The size of these new states and the ethnic and religious diversity of their populations posed formidable challenges to those in power. Rulers had to distinguish those who belonged to the community—and owed taxes or military service—from those who did not. They used a careful mixture of privilege and punishment to create a sense of unity among their subjects while at the same time justifying their own right to rule and reinforcing traditional social hierarchies. The three images below show different ways rulers approached this problem.

The first painting, from around 1500, is by the Spanish artist Pedro Berruguete. It portrays a scene from two centuries earlier in which Spanish authorities burned people at the stake for their alleged heretical beliefs. Notice in the foreground members of the Dominican Order, who were instrumental in the administration of the Inquisition, and soldiers loyal to the crown. The second image, a miniature painting from 1558, depicts the *devshirme* system in the Ottoman Empire. Authorities took non-Muslim children from their families in Europe as a human tribute in place of cash taxes, which the poor region could not pay. The children would then be educated in Ottoman Muslim ways and prepared for service in the sultan's civil and military bureaucracy. The final image, a painting on silk by Ch'iu Ying, represents a group of Confucian scholars waiting for the results of their civil service examination. Candidates spent three days and two nights taking examinations as they sought to enter the Ming bureaucracy.

Spanish painting by Berruguete.

The devshirme *system.*

Chinese painting by Ch'iu Ying.

QUESTIONS FOR ANALYSIS

1. Assess the combinations of privilege and punishment conveyed by these images. What kinds of assistance or special privileges did leaders grant, to whom did they offer this assistance, and what kinds of punishments did they impose?

2. Describe the original context for these images. Who might have created these images, for whom, and who might have seen them?

3. Interpret the role religion plays in these images. How does the artist present the relationship between religion and social order?

4. Explain how Berruguete's use of the past alters the relationship between royal authorities and traditional elites presented in the first painting, compared to the relationship between rulers and elites shown or implied by the other two images.

Further Readings

CHAPTER 1: BECOMING HUMAN

Arsuaga, Juan Luis, *The Neanderthal's Necklace: In Search of the First Thinkers*, translated by Anthony Klatt (2002). A stimulating overview of prehistory that focuses on the Neanderthals and compares them with *Homo sapiens*.

Lawrence Barham and Peter Mitchell, *The First Africans: African Archaeology from the Earliest Toolmakers to Most Recent Foragers* (2008). New findings on the evolution of hominids in Africa.

Barker, Graeme, *Agricultural Revolution in Prehistory: Why Did Foragers Become Farmers?* (2006). The most recent, truly global, and up-to-date study of this momentous event in world history.

Bellwood, Peter, *First Farmers: The Origins of Agricultural Societies* (2005). A state-of-the-art global history of the origins of agriculture including recent archaeological, linguistic, and microbiological data.

Bogucki, Peter, *The Origins of Human Society* (1999). An authoritative overview of prehistory.

Cauvin, Jacques, *The Birth of the Gods and the Origins of Agriculture*, translated by Trevor Watkins from the original 1994 French publication (2000). An important work on the agricultural revolution of Southwest Asia and the evolution of symbolic thinking at this time.

Cavalli-Sforza, Luigi Luca, *Genes, Peoples, and Languages*, translated by Mark Selestad from the original 1996 French publication (2000). An expert's introduction to the use of gene research for revealing new information about the evolution of human beings in the distant past.

Childe, V. Gordon, *What Happened in History* (1964). A classic work by one of the pioneers in studying the early history and evolution of human beings. Though superseded in many respects, it is still an important place to start one's reading and a work of great power and emotion.

Clark, J. Desmond, and Steven A. Brandt (eds.), *From Hunters to Farmers: The Causes and Consequences of Food Production in Africa* (1984). Excellent essays on the agricultural revolution.

Coon, Carleton Stevens, *The Story of Man: From the First Human to Primitive Culture and Beyond*, 2nd ed. (1962). An important early work on the evolution of humans, emphasizing the distinctiveness of "races" around the world.

Cunliffe, Barry (ed.), *The Oxford Illustrated Prehistory of Europe* (1994). The definitive work on early European history.

Ehrenberg, Margaret, *Women in Prehistory* (1989). What was the role of women in hunting-and-gathering societies, and how greatly were women affected by the agricultural revolution? The author offers a number of stimulating generalizations.

Ehret, Christopher, *The Civilizations of Africa: A History to 1800* (2002). Although this is a general history of Africa, the author, a linguist and an expert on early African history, offers new information and new overviews of African peoples in very ancient times.

Fagan, Brian, *People of the Earth: An Introduction to World Prehistory* (1989). An authoritative overview of early history, widely used in classrooms.

Fage, J. D., and Roland Oliver (eds.), *The Cambridge History of Africa*, 8 vols. (1975–1984). A pioneering work of synthesis by two of the first and foremost scholars of the history of Africa. Volume 1 deals with African prehistory.

Frison, George C., *Survival by Hunting: Prehistoric Human Predators and Animal Prey* (2004). An archaeologist applies his knowledge of animal habitats, behavior, and hunting strategies to an examination of prehistoric hunting practices in the North American Great Plains and Rocky Mountains.

Gebauer, Anne Birgitte, and T. Douglas Price (eds.), *Transition to Agriculture in Prehistory* (1992). Excellent essays on the agricultural revolution, especially those written by the two editors.

Johnson, Donald, Lenora Johnson, and Blake Edgar, *Ancestors: In Search of Human Origins* (1999). A good overview of human evolution, with insightful essays on *Homo erectus* and *Homo sapiens*.

Jones, Steve, Robert Martin, and David Pilbeam (eds.), *The Cambridge Encyclopedia of Human Evolution* (1992). A superb guide to a wide range of subjects, crammed with up-to-date information on the most controversial and obscure topics of human evolution and early history.

Ki-Zerbo, J. (ed.), *Methodology and African Prehistory*, vol. 1 of the UNESCO General History of Africa (1981).

A general history of Africa, written for the most part by scholars of African descent.

Klein, Richard G., and Blake Edger, *The Dawn of Human Culture* (2002). A fine and reliable guide to the tangled history of human evolution.

Leakey, Richard, *The Origin of Humankind* (1994). A readable and exciting account of human evolution, written by the son of the pioneering archaeologists Louis and Mary Leakey, a scholar of equal stature to his parents.

Lewin, Roger, *The Origin of Modern Humans* (1993). Yet another good overview of human evolution, with useful chapters on early art and the use of symbols.

Loewe, Michael, and Edward Shaughnessy (eds.), *The Cambridge History of Ancient China: From the Origins of Civilization to 221 B.C.* (1999). A good review of the archaeology of ancient China.

Mellaart, James, *Çatal Höyük: A Neolithic Town in Anatolia* (1967). A detailed description of one of the first towns associated with the agricultural revolution in Southwest Asia.

Mithen, Steven, *The Prehistory of the Mind: The Cognitive Origins of Art and Science* (1996). A stimulating discussion of the impact of biological and cultural evolution on the cognitive structure of the human mind.

Olson, Steve, *Mapping Human History: Genes, Race, and Our Common Origins* (2003). Using the findings of genetics and attacking the racial thinking of an earlier generation of archaeologists, the author writes powerfully about the unity of all human beings.

Price, T. Douglas (ed.), *Europe's First Farmers* (2000). A discussion of the agricultural revolution in Europe.

Price, T. Douglas, and Anne Birgitte Gebauer (eds.), *Last Hunters–First Farmers: New Perspectives on the Prehistoric Transition to Agriculture*

(1996). An exciting collection of essays by some of the leading scholars in the field studying the transition from hunting and gathering to settled agriculture.

Scarre, Chris (ed.), *The Human Past: World Prehistory and the Development of Human Societies* (2005). An encyclopedia and an overview rolled up into one mammoth volume, written by leading figures in the field of early human history.

Shaw, Thurstan, Paul Sinclair, Bassey Andah, and Alex Okpoko (eds.), *The Archaeology of Africa: Food, Metals, and Towns* (1993). Up-to-date research on the earliest history of human beings in Africa.

Smith, Bruce D., *The Emergence of Agriculture* (1995). How early humans domesticated wild animals and plants.

Stringer, Christopher, and Robin McKie, *African Exodus: The Origins of Modern Humanity* (1996). Detailed data on why Africa was the source of human origins and why *Homo sapiens* is a recent wanderer out of Africa.

Tattersall, Ian, *The Fossil Trail: How We Know What We Think We Know about Human Evolution* (1995). A passionately written book about early archaeological discoveries and the centrality of Africa in human evolution.

——, *The World from Beginnings to 4000 BCE* (2008). A brief up-to-date overview of humanity's early history by a leading authority.

——, *Masters of the Planet: The Search for Our Human Origins* (2012). The most recent survey of human evolution.

Van Oosterzee, Penny, *Dragon Bones: The Story of Peking Man* (2000). Describes how the late-nineteenth-century unearthing of sites in China containing fossils of animals used for medicinal purposes led to the discovery of the fossils of the Peking Man.

Weiss, Mark L., and Alan E. Mann, *Human Biology and Behavior: An Anthropological Perspective* (1996). The authors stress the contribution that biological research has made and continues to make to unravel the mystery of human evolution.

Wrangham, Richard, *Catching Fire: How Cooking Made Us Human* (2009). The author shows how fire made it possible for humans to have a more varied and richer diet but also one that provided energy for the one organ—the brain—that consumes the most energy.

CHAPTER 2: RIVERS, CITIES, AND FIRST STATES, 3500–2000 BCE

Adams, Robert McCormick, *The Evolution of Urban Society* (1966). A classic study of the social, political, and economic processes that led to the development of the first urban civilizations.

Algaze, Guillermo, *The Uruk World System: The Dynamics of Expansion of Early Mesopotamian Civilization* (1993). A compelling argument for the colonization of the Tigris and Euphrates valley by the proto-Sumerians at the end of the fourth millennium BCE.

Andrews, Carol, *Egyptian Mummies* (1998). An illustrated summary of Egyptian mummification and burial practices.

Bagley, Robert, *Ancient Sichuan: Treasures from a Lost Civilization* (2001). Describes the remarkable findings in Southwest China, particularly at Sanxingdui, which have challenged earlier accounts of the Shang dynasty's central role in the rise of early Chinese civilization.

Bar-Yosef, Ofar, and Anatoly Khazanov (eds.), *Pastoralism in the Levant: Archaeological Materials in Anthropological Perspectives* (1992). Classic study of the role of nomads in the development of societies in the Levant during the Neolithic period.

Bruhns, Karen Olsen, *Ancient South America* (1994). The best basic text on pre-Columbian South American cultures.

Butzer, Karl W., *Early Hydraulic Civilization in Egypt: A Study of Cultural Ecology* (1976). The best work on how the Egyptians dealt with the Nile floods and the influence that these arrangements had on the overall organization of society.

Cunliffe, Barry, *Europe Between the Oceans, 9000 BC–AD 1000* (2008). A very up-to-date and spectacularly illustrated account of early Europe.

Habu, Junko, *Ancient Jomon of Japan* (2004). Study of prehistoric Jomon hunter-gatherers on the Japanese archipelago that incorporates several different aspects of anthropological studies, including hunter-gatherer archaeology, settlement archaeology, and pottery analysis.

Jacobsen, Thorkild, *The Treasures of Darkness: A History of Mesopotamian Religion* (1976). Best introduction to the religious and philosophical thought of ancient Mesopotamia.

Kemp, Barry J., *Ancient Egypt: Anatomy of a Civilization* (1989). A synthetic overview of the culture of the pharaohs.

Kramer, Samuel Noah, *The Sumerians: Their History, Culture and Character* (1963). Classic study of the Sumerians and their culture by a pioneer in Sumerian studies.

Pollock, Susan, *Ancient Mesopotamia: The Eden That Never Was* (1999). An analysis of the social and economic development of Mesopotamia from the beginnings of settlement until the reign of Hammurapi.

Possehl, Gregory L., *Indus Age: The Beginnings* (1999). The second of four volumes analyzing the history of the Indus Valley civilization.

Postgate, J. N., *Early Mesopotamia: Society and Economy at the Dawn of History* (1992). A study of the economic and political development of the Sumerian civilization.

Preziosi, Donald, and L. A. Hitchcock, *Aegean Art and Architecture* (1999). One of the best general guides to the figurative and decorative art produced both by the Minoans and Mycenaeans and by related early societies in the region of the Aegean.

Ratnagar, Shereen, *Trading Encounters: From the Euphrates to the Indus in the Bronze Age*, 2nd ed. (2004). A comprehensive presentation of the evidence for the relationship between the Indus Valley and its western neighbors.

——, *Understanding Harappa: Civilization in the Greater Indus Valley* (2001). Harappan site archaeological data of the last century organized into a historical narrative comprehensible to the general audience.

Rice, Michael, *Egypt's Legacy: The Archetypes of Western Civilization, 3000–300 BC* (1997). The author argues for the decisive influence of Egyptian culture on the whole of the Mediterranean and its later historical development.

Roaf, Michael, *Cultural Atlas of Mesopotamia and the Ancient Near East* (1990). A comprehensive compendium of the historical and cultural development of the Mesopotamian civilization from the Neolithic background through the Persian Empire.

Shaw, Ian (ed.), *The Oxford History of Ancient Egypt* (2000). The most up-to-date and comprehensive account of the history of Egypt down to the Greek invasion.

Thorp, Robert, *The Chinese Neolithic: Trajectories to Early States* (2005). Uses the latest archaeological evidence to describe the development of early Bronze Age cultures in North and northwestern China from about 2000 BCE.

CHAPTER 3: NOMADS, TERRITORIAL STATES, AND MICROSOCIETIES, 2000–1200 BCE

Allan, Sarah, *The Shape of the Turtle: Myth, Art and Cosmos in Early China* (1991). Explains the roles of divination and sacrifice in artistic representations of the Shang cosmology.

Allen, James P., *Middle Egyptian: An Introduction to the Language and Culture of Hieroglyphs* (2000). An introduction to the system of writing and its use in Ancient Egypt.

Anthony, David W., *The Horse, the Wheel, and Language: How Bronze-Age Riders from the Eurasian Steppes Shaped the Modern World* (2007). A superb analysis of the origins and spread of the Indo-European peoples.

Arnold, Dieter, *Building in Ancient Egypt: Pharaonic Stone Masonry* (1996). Details the complex construction of monumental stone architecture in ancient Egypt.

Baines, John, and Jaromir Málek, *Atlas of Ancient Egypt* (1980). Useful compilation of information on ancient Egyptian society, religion, history, and geography.

Beal, Richard H., *The Organization of the Hittite Military* (1992). A detailed study based on textual sources of the world's first chariot-based army.

Bogucki, Peter, and Pam J. Crabtree (eds.), *Ancient Europe 8000 BC–AD 1000: Encyclopedia of the Barbarian World*, 2 vols. (2004). An indispensable handbook on the economic, social, artistic, and religious life in Europe during this period.

Bruhns, Karen Olsen, *Ancient South America* (1994). The best basic text on pre-Columbian South American cultures.

Bryant, Edwin, *The Quest for the Origins of Vedic Culture: The Indo-Aryan Migration Debate* (2001). Insight into the highly charged debate on who the Indo-European speakers were, where they originated, and where they migrated to.

Castleden, Rodney, *The Mycenaeans* (2005). One of the best current surveys of all aspects of the Mycenaean Greeks.

Chadwick, John, *The Decipherment of Linear B,* 2nd ed. (1968). Not only a retelling of the story of the decipherment of the Linear B script but also an introduction to the actual content and function of the tablets themselves.

Cline, E. H., *Sailing the Wine-Dark Sea: International Trade and the Late Bronze Age Aegean* (1994). An excellent account of the trade and contacts between the Aegean and other areas of the Mediterranean, Europe, and the Near East during the late Bronze Age.

Cunliffe, Barry, *Facing the Ocean: The Atlantic and Its Peoples, 8000 BC–AD 1500* (2001). An in-depth, highly useful treatment of western Europe during this period.

—— (ed.), *Prehistoric Europe: An Illustrated History* (1997). A state-of-the-art treatment of first farmers, agricultural developments, and material culture in prehistoric Europe.

Davis, W. V., and L. Schofield, *Egypt, the Aegean and the Levant: Interconnections in the Second Millennium BC* (1995). A discussion of the complex interactions in the eastern Mediterranean during the "international age."

Doumas, Christos, *Thera: Pompeii of the Ancient Aegean* (1983). A study of the tremendous volcanic eruption and explosion that destroyed the Minoan settlement on the island of Thera.

Drews, Robert, *Coming of the Greeks: Indo-European Conquests in the Aegean and the Near East* (1988). A good survey of the evidence for the "invasions" or "movements of peoples" that reconfigured the world of the eastern Mediterranean and Near East.

Finley, M. I., *The World of Odysseus,* 2nd rev. ed. (1977; reprint, 2002). The classic work that describes what might be recovered about the social values and behaviors of men and women in the period of the so-called Dark Ages of early Greek history.

Frankfort, Henri, *Ancient Egyptian Religion: An Interpretation* (1948; reprint, 2000). A classic study of Egyptian religion and culture during the pharaonic period.

Keightley, David N., *The Ancestral Landscape: Time, Space, and Community in Late Shang China, ca. 1200-1045 BC* (2000). Provides insights into the nature of royal kinship that undergirded the Shang court and its regional domains.

Kemp, Barry J., *Ancient Egypt: Anatomy of a Civilization* (2006). A definitive presentation of the history, culture, and religion of ancient Egypt.

Klein, Jacob, "The Marriage of Martu: The Urbanization of 'Barbaric' Nomads," in *Mutual Influences of Peoples and Cultures in the Ancient Near East,* ed. Meir Malul (1996).

Kristiansen, Kristian, *Europe before History* (1998). The finest recent survey of all the major developmental phases of European prehistory.

McIntosh, Jane, *Handbook to Life in Prehistoric Europe* (2006). Highlights the archaeological evidence that enables us to re-create the day-to-day life of different prehistoric communities in Europe.

Preziosi, Donald, and L. A. Hitchcock, *Aegean Art and Architecture* (1999). One of the best general guides to the figurative and decorative art produced both by the Minoans and Mycenaeans and by related early societies in the region of the Aegean.

Quirke, Stephen, *Ancient Egyptian Religion* (1992). A highly readable presentation of ancient Egyptian religion that summarizes the roles and attributions of the many Egyptian gods.

Robins, Gay, *The Art of Ancient Egypt* (1997). The most comprehensive survey to date of the art of pharaonic Egypt.

——, *Women in Ancient Egypt* (1993). An interesting survey of the place of women in Ancient Egyptian society.

Romer, John, *Ancient Lives: Daily Life in Egypt of the Pharaohs* (1990). A discussion of the economic and social lives of everyday ancient Egyptians.

Sandars, N. K., *The Sea Peoples: Warriors of the Ancient Mediterranean* (1985). A readable discussion of a very complex period of Levantine history.

Simpson, William Kelly (ed.), *The Literature of Ancient Egypt: An Anthology of Stories, Instructions, and Poetry* (1972). A compilation of the most important works of literature from Ancient Egypt.

Thorp, Robert L., *China in the Early Bronze Age: Shang Civilization* (2005). Reviews the archaeological discoveries near Anyang, site of two capitals of the Shang kings.

Warren, Peter, *The Aegean Civilizations: From Ancient Crete to Mycenae,* 2nd ed. (1989). An excellent textual and pictorial guide to all the basic aspects of the Minoan and Mycenaean societies.

Wilson, John A., *The Culture of Ancient Egypt* (1951). A classic study of the history and culture of pharaonic Egypt.

Yadin, Yigael, *The Art of Warfare in Biblical Lands in the Light of Archaeological Discovery* (1963). A well-illustrated presentation of the machinery of war in the second and first millennia BCE.

CHAPTER 4: FIRST EMPIRES AND COMMON CULTURES IN AFRO-EURASIA, 1250–325 BCE

Ahlström, Gosta W., *The History of Ancient Palestine from the Paleolithic Period to Alexander's Conquests* (1993). An excellent survey of the history of the region by a renowned expert, with good attention to the recent archaeological evidence.

Aubet, Maria Eugenia, *The Phoenicians and the West,* 2nd ed. (2001).

The basic survey of the Phoenician colonization of the western Mediterranean and Atlantic, with special attention to recent archaeological discoveries.

Behringer, Wolfgang, *A Cultural History of Climate*, Translated by Patrick Camiller (2010). A summary view of the place of climate in historical change, written by an expert in historical climatology.

Briant, Pierre, *From Cyrus to Alexander: A History of the Persian Empire*, trans. Peter T. Daniels (2002). A complex and comprehensive history of the Persian Empire by its finest modern scholar.

Bright, John, *A History of Israel,* 4th ed. (2000). An updated version of a classic and still very useful overview of the whole history of the Israelite people down to the end of the period covered in this chapter.

Cook, J. M., *The Persian Empire* (1983). An older but still useful, and highly readable, standard history of the Persian Empire.

Fagan, Brian, *The Long Summer: How Climate Changed Civilization* (2004). An accessible overview of the role of climate in historical change, written by one of the leading historians of ancient history and an individual who has brought together considerable evidence about climatic change and historical development.

Falkenhausen, Lothar von, *Chinese Society in the Age of Confucius (1000–250 BC): The Archaeological Evidence* (2006). A timely reassessment of early Chinese history that compares the literary texts on which it has traditionally been based to the new archaeological evidence.

Frye, Richard N., *The Heritage of Persia* (1963). This classic study of ancient Iran gives the political and literary history of the Persians and their successors.

Grayson, A. K., "Assyrian Civilization," in *Cambridge Ancient History,* vol. 3, pt. 2, pp. 194–228 (1992). The Assyrian and Babylonian empires and other states of the Near East, from the eighth to the sixth century BCE.

Hornung, Erik, *Akhenaten and the Religion of Light*, translated from the German by David Lorton (1999). An important, brief biography of Egypt's most controversial pharaoh.

——, *History of Ancient Egypt: An Introduction*, translated from the German by David Lorton (1999). An accessible overview of the history of ancient Egypt by a leading Egyptologist.

Isserlin, Benedikt J., *The Israelites* (1998). A very well-written and heavily illustrated history of all aspects of life in the regions of the Levant inhabited by the Israelites, equally good on the latest scholarship and the archaeological data.

Keay, John, *India: A History* (2010). A useful, readable overview of the sweep of Indian history.

Lancel, Serge, *Carthage: A History*, trans. Antonia Nevill (1997). By far the best single-volume history of the most important Phoenician colony in the Mediterranean (the first three chapters are especially relevant to materials covered in this chapter).

Lemche, Niels Peter, *Ancient Israel: A New History of Israelite Society* (1988). A quick, readable, and still up-to-date summary of the main phases and themes.

Lewis, Mark Edward, *Writing and Authority in Early China* (1999). A work that traces the changing uses of writing to command assent and obedience in early China.

Markoe, Glenn E., *Phoenicians* (2000). A thorough survey of the Phoenicians and their society as it first developed in the Levant and then expanded over the Mediterranean, with excellent illustrations of the diverse archaeological sites.

Matthews, Victor H., and Don C. Benjamin, *Social World of Ancient Israel, 1350–587 BCE* (1993). A thematic overview of the main occupational groups and social roles that characterized ancient Israelite society.

Oates, Joan, and David Oates, *Nimrud: An Assyrian Imperial City Revealed* (2001). A fine and highly readable summary of the state of our knowledge of the Assyrian Empire from the perspective of the early capital of Assurnasirpal II.

Oded, Bustenay, *Mass Deportations and Deportees in the Neo-Assyrian Empire* (1979). A detailed textual examination of the deportation strategy of the Assyrian kings. Good for in-depth research of the question.

Potts, D. T., *The Archaeology of Elam: Formation and Transformation of an Ancient Iranian State* (1999). The definitive study of the archaeology of western Iran from the Neolithic period through the Persian Empire.

Shaughnessy, Edward L., *Sources of Western Zhou History: Inscribed Bronze Vessels* (1992). Detailed work on the historiography and interpretation of the thousands of ritual bronze vessels discovered by China's archaeologists.

Stein, Burton, *A History of India*, 2nd ed., edited by David Arnold (2010). One of the standard general histories of India, brought up-to-date by a leading historian of the subcontinent.

Tanner, Harold M., *China: A History* (2009). A readable and up-to-date overview of the sweep of Chinese history.

Thapar, Romila, *From Lineage to State* (1984). The only book on early India that uses religious literature historically and analyzes major lineages to reveal the transition from tribal society to state institutions.

Tignor, Robert L., *Egypt: A Short History* (2010). A succinct treatment of the entire history of Egypt from the pharaohs to the present, with three chapters on the ancient period.

Tubb, Jonathan N., *Canaanites* (1998). The best recent survey, well illustrated, of one of the main ethnic groups dominating the culture of the Levant.

CHAPTER 5: WORLDS TURNED INSIDE OUT, 1000–350 BCE

Adams, William Y., *Nubia: Corridor to Africa* (1977). The authoritative historical overview of Nubia, the area of present-day Sudan just south of Egypt and a geographical connecting point between the Mediterranean and sub-Saharan Africa.

Armstrong, Karen, *Buddha* (2001). A readable and impressive account of the life of the Buddha.

Aubet, Maria Eugenia, *The Phoenicians and the West*, 2nd ed. (2001). The basic survey of the Phoenician colonization of the western Mediterranean and Atlantic, with special attention to recent archaeological discoveries.

Barker, Graeme, and Tom Rasmussen, *The Etruscans* (1998). The most up-to-date introduction to this important pre-Roman society in the Italian peninsula, with strong emphasis on broad social and material patterns of development as indicated by the archaeological evidence.

Bruhns, Karen Olsen, *Ancient South America* (1994). A very useful overview of recent debates and conclusions about pre-Columbian archaeology in South America, including both the Andes and the lowland and coastal regions.

Burkert, Walter, *Greek Religion*, trans. John Raffan (1985). The best one-volume introduction to early Greek religion, placing the Greeks in their larger Mediterranean and Near Eastern contexts.

Cartledge, Paul (ed.), *The Cambridge Illustrated History of Ancient Greece* (2002). An excellent history of the Greek city-states down to the time of Alexander the Great.

Chakravarti, Uma, *The Social Dimensions of Early Buddhism* (1987). A description of the life of Buddha drawn from early Buddhist texts.

Cho-yun, Hsu, *Ancient China in Transition* (1965). An account of the political, economic, social, and intellectual changes that occurred during the Warring States period.

Coarelli, Filippo (ed.), *Etruscan Cities* (1975). A brilliantly and lavishly illustrated guide to the material remains of the Etruscans: their cities, their magnificent tombs, and their architecture, painting, sculpture, and other art.

Coe, Michael, et al. (eds.), *The Olmec World: Ritual and Rulership* (1996). A collection of field-synthesizing articles with important illustrations, based on one of the most comprehensive exhibitions of Olmec art in the world.

Confucius, *The Analects (Lun Yü)*, trans. D. C. Lau (1979). An outstanding translation of the words of Confucius as recorded by his major disciples. Includes valuable historical material needed to provide the context for Confucius's teachings.

Falkenhausen, Lothar von, *Chinese Society in the Age of Confucius (1000–250 BC)* (2006). The larger Chinese society under the influence of Confucian thought.

Finley, M. I., and H. W. Pleket, *The Olympic Games: The First Thousand Years* (2005). A fine description of the most famous of the Greek games; it explains how they exemplify the competitive spirit that marked many aspects of the Greek city-states.

Garlan, Yvon, *Slavery in Ancient Greece*, trans. Janet Lloyd (1988). A treatment of the emergence, development, and institutionalization of chattel slavery in the Greek city-states.

——, *War in the Ancient World: A Social History*, trans. Janet Lloyd (1976). A discussion of the emergence of the forms of warfare, including male citizens fighting in hoplite phalanxes and the development of siege warfare, that were typical of the Greek city-states.

Iliffe, John, *Africans: The History of a Continent*, 2nd ed. (2007). A first-rate scholarly survey of Africa from its beginnings, with a strong emphasis on demography.

Kagan, Donald, *The Peloponnesian War* (2004). A vivid description of the war that pitted the major Greek city-states, including Athens and Sparta, against each other over the latter half of the fifth century BCE.

Lancel, Serge, *Carthage: A History*, trans. Antonia Nevill (1997). By far the best single-volume history of the most important Phoenician colony in the Mediterranean.

Lewis, Mark Edward, *Sanctioned Violence in Early China* (1990). An analysis of the use of sanctioned violence as an element of statecraft from the Warring States period to the formation of the Qin and Han empires in the second half of the first millennium BCE.

——, *Writing and Authority in Early China* (1999). A revisionist account of the central role of writing and persuasion in models for the invention of a Chinese world empire.

Ling, Trevor, *The Buddha: Buddhist Civilization in India and Ceylon* (1972). An overview of Buddhism in India and Ceylon.

Lloyd, G. E. R., *Early Greek Science: Thales to Aristotle* (1970). An especially clear and concise introduction to the main developments and intellectuals that marked the emergence of critical secular thinking in the early Greek world.

Lloyd, G. E. R., and Nathan Sivin, *The Way and the Word: Science and Medicine in Early China and Greece* (2002). A comprehensive rethinking of the social and political settings in ancient China and city-state Greece that contributed to the different views of science and medicine that emerged in each place.

Mote, Frederick, *Intellectual Foundations of China* (1971). An early but still useful description of the seminal figures in China's early intellectual life.

Murray, Oswyn, *Early Greece*, 2nd ed. (1993). One of the best introductions to the emergence of the Greek city-states down to the end of the archaic age.

Osborne, Robin, *Archaic and Classical Greek Art* (1998). An outstanding book that clearly explains the main innovations in Greek art, setting them in their historical context.

——, *Greece in the Making, 1200–479 BC* (1999). The standard history of the whole early period of the Greek city-states characterized by an especially fine and judicious mix of archaeological data and literary sources.

Pallottino, Massimo, *The Etruscans*, rev. ed., trans. J. Cremona (1975). A fairly traditional but still classic survey of all aspects of Etruscan history, political and social institutions.

Redford, Donald B., *From Slave to Pharaoh: The Black Experience of Ancient Egypt* (2004). A description of Egypt's twenty-fifth dynasty, which was made up of Sudanese conquerors.

Schaberg, David, *A Patterned Past: Form and Thought in Early Chinese Historiography* (2002). A comprehensive study of the intellectual content of historical anecdotes by the followers of Confucius collected around the fourth century BCE.

Schaps, David, *The Invention of Coinage and the Monetization of Ancient Greece* (2004). A new analysis that offers a broad overview of the emergence of coined money in the Near East and the eastern Mediterranean and its effects on the spread of money-based markets.

Sharma, J. P., *Republics in Ancient India, c. 1500 B.C.–500 B.C.* (1968). Relying on information from early Buddhist texts, this book first revealed that South Asia had not only monarchies but also alternative polities.

Shaw, Thurston, *Nigeria: Its Archaeology and Early History* (1978). An important introduction to the early history of Nigeria by one of that country's leading archaeologists.

Shinnie, P. L., *Ancient Nubia* (1996). An excellent account of the history of the ancient Nubians, who, we are discovering, had great influence on Egypt and on the rest of tropical Africa.

Snodgrass, Anthony, *Archaic Greece: The Age of Experiment* (1981). A good introduction to the archaeological evidence of archaic Greece.

Taylor, Christopher, Richard Hare, and Jonathan Barnes, *Greek Philosophers* (1999). A fine, succinct, one-volume introduction to the major aspects of the three big thinkers who dominated the high period of classical Greek philosophy: Socrates, Plato, and Aristotle.

Torok, Laszlo, *Meroe: Six Studies on the Cultural Identity of an Ancient African State* (1995). A good collection of essays on the most recent work on Meroe.

The Kingdom of Kush: The Napatan and Meroitic Empires (1996). A fine book on these two important Nubian kingdoms.

CHAPTER 6: SHRINKING THE AFRO-EURASIAN WORLD, 350 BCE–250 CE

Bradley, Keith, *Slavery and Rebellion in the Roman World, 140 B.C.–70 B.C.* (1989). A description of the rise of large-scale plantation slavery in Sicily and Italy, and a detailed account of the three great slave wars.

Browning, Iain, *Palmyra* (1979). A narrative of the history of the important desert city that linked eastern and western trade routes.

Casson, Lionel, *The Periplus Maris Erythraei* (1989). An introduction to a typical ancient sailing manual, this one of the Red Sea and Indian Ocean.

——, *Ships and Seamanship in the Ancient World* (1995). The classic account of the ships and sailors that powered commerce and war on the high seas.

Colledge, Malcolm, *The Art of Palmyra* (1976). A well-illustrated introduction to the unusual art of Palmyra with its mixture of eastern and western elements.

Fowler, Barbara H., *The Hellenistic Aesthetic* (1989). How the artists in this new age saw and portrayed their world in new and different ways.

Green, Peter, *Alexander to Actium: The Historical Evolution of the Hellenistic Age* (1990). The best general guide to the whole period in all of its various aspects, and well illustrated.

Habicht, Christian, *Athens from Alexander to Antony*, trans. Deborah L. Schneider (1997). The authoritative account of what happened to the great city-state of Athens in this period.

Holt, Frank L., *Thundering Zeus: The Making of Hellenistic Bactria* (1999). A basic history of the most eastern of the kingdoms spawned by the conquests of Alexander the Great.

Hopkirk, Peter, *Foreign Devils on the Silk Road* (1984). A historiography of the explorations and researches on the central Asian Silk Road of the nineteenth and early twentieth centuries.

Juliano, Annette L., and Judith A. Lerner (eds.), *Nomads, Traders and Holy Men Along China's Silk Road* (2003). A description of the travelers along the Silk Road in human terms, focusing on warfare, markets, and religion.

Lane Fox, Robin, *Alexander the Great* (1973). Still the most readable and in many ways the sanest biography of the world conqueror.

Lewis, Naphtali, *Greeks in Ptolemaic Egypt* (1986). An account of the relationships between Greeks and Egyptians as seen through the lives of individual Greek settlers and colonists.

Liu, Xinru, *Ancient India and Ancient China* (1988). The first work to connect political and economic developments in India and China with the evolution and spread of Buddhism in the first half of the first millennium.

———, *The Silk Road in World History* (2010). A study of the history of the great trade and communications route that connected the different regions of Afro-Eurasia between the third century BCE and the thirteenth century CE.

Long, Antony A., *Hellenistic Philosophy: Stoics, Epicureans, Sceptics*, 2nd ed. (1986). One of the clearest guides to the main new trends in Greek philosophical thinking in the period.

Martin, Luther H., *Hellenistic Religions: An Introduction* (1987). An introduction to the principal new Hellenistic religions and cults that emerged in this period.

Mendels, Doron, *The Rise and Fall of Jewish Nationalism* (1992). A sophisticated account of the various phases of Jewish resistance in Judah to foreign domination.

Miller, James Innes, *The Spice Trade of the Roman Empire, 29 B.C. to A.D. 641* (1969). A first-rate study of the spice trade in the Roman Empire.

Pomeroy, Sarah B., *Women in Hellenistic Egypt: From Alexander to Cleopatra* (1990). A highly readable investigation of women and family in the best-documented region of the Hellenistic world.

Ray, Himanshu P., *The Wind of Change: Buddhism and the Maritime Links of Early South Asia* (1994). Ray's study of Buddhism and maritime trade stretches from the Arabian Sea to the navigations between South Asia and Southeast Asia.

Rosenfield, John, *The Dynastic Art of the Kushans* (1967). Instead of focusing on the Gandharan Buddhist art itself, Rosenfield selects sculptures of Kushan royals and those representing nomadic populations in religious shrines to display the central Asian aspect of artworks of the period.

Rostovtzeff, Michael Ivanovich, *Caravan Cities*, trans. D. and T. Talbot Rice (1932). Though published more than seven decades ago, this small volume contains accurate descriptions of the ruins of many caravan cities in modern Jordan and Syria.

———, *The Social and Economic History of the Hellenistic World* (1941). A monumental achievement. One of the great works of history written in the twentieth century. An unsurpassed overview of all aspects of the politics and social and economic movements of the period. Despite its age, there is still nothing like it.

Schoff, Wilfred H. (ed. and trans.), *The Periplus of the Erythraean Sea* (1912). An invaluable tool for mapping the names and places from the Red Sea to Indian coastal areas during this period.

Shipley, Graham, *The Greek World after Alexander, 323–30 BC* (2000). A more up-to-date survey than Peter Green's work (above), with more emphasis on the historical detail in each period.

Tarn, W. W., *Greeks in Bactria and India* (1984). The most comprehensive coverage of Greek sources on Hellenistic states in Afghanistan and northwest India.

Thapar, Romila, *Ashoka and the Decline of the Mauryas* (1973). Using all available primary sources, including the edicts of Aśoka and Greek authors' accounts, Thapar gives the most authoritative analysis of the first and the most important empire in Indian history.

Vainker, Shelagh, *Chinese Silk: A Cultural History* (2004). A work that traces the cultural history of silk in China from its early origins to the twentieth century and considers its relationship to the other decorative arts. The author draws on the most recent archaeological evidence to emphasize the role of silk in Chinese history, trade, religion, and literature.

Wood, Francis, *The Silk Road: Two Thousand Years in the Heart of Asia* (2004). Illustrated with drawings, manuscripts, paintings, and artifacts to trace the Silk Road to its origins as far back as Alexander the Great, with an emphasis on its importance to cultural and religious movements.

Young, Gary K., *Rome's Eastern Trade: International Commerce and Imperial Policy, 31 BC–AD 305* (2001). This study examines the taxation and profits of eastern trade from the perspective of the Roman government.

CHAPTER 7: HAN DYNASTY CHINA AND IMPERIAL ROME, 300 BCE–300 CE

Bodde, Derk, *China's First Unifier: A Study of the Ch'in Dynasty as Seen in the Life of Li Ssu (280?–208 B.C.)* (1938). A classic account of the key Legalist adviser, Li Si, who formulated the Qin policy to enhance its autocratic power.

Bowman, Alan K., *Life and Letters on the Roman Frontier: Vindolanda and Its Peoples* (1994). An introduction to the exciting discovery of writing tablets at a Roman army base in northern Britain.

Bradley, Keith, *Slavery and Society at Rome* (1994). The best single overview of the major aspects of the slave system in the Roman Empire.

Chevallier, Raymond, *Roman Roads*, trans. N. H. Field (1976). A guide to the fundamentals of the construction, maintenance, administration, and mapping of Roman roads.

Coarelli, Fillipo (ed.), *Pompeii*, trans. Patricia Cockram (2006). A lavishly illustrated large volume that allows the reader to sense some of the wondrous wealth of the buried city of Pompeii.

Colledge, Malcolm A. R., *The Parthians* (1967). A bit dated but still a fundamental introduction to the Parthians, the major power on the eastern frontier of the Roman Empire.

Cornell, Tim, *The Beginnings of Rome: Italy and Rome from the Bronze Age to the Punic Wars, c. 2000 to 264 B.C.* (1995). The single best one-volume history of Rome through its early history to the first war with Carthage.

Cornell, Tim, and John Matthews, *Atlas of the Roman World* (1982). A history of the Roman world; much more than simply an atlas. It is provided not only with good maps and a gazetteer but also with marvelous color illustrations and a text that guides the reader through the basics of Roman history.

Csikszentmihalyi, Mark, *Readings in Han Chinese Thought* (2006). A volume presenting a representative selection of primary sources to illustrate the growth of ideas in early imperial times; a useful introduction to the key strains of thought during this crucial period.

Dixon, Suzanne, *The Roman Family* (1992). The best one-volume guide to the nature of the Roman family and family relations.

Garnsey, Peter, and Richard Saller, *The Roman Empire: Economy, Society, and Culture* (1987). A perceptive and critical introduction to three basic aspects of social life in the empire.

Giardina, Andrea (ed.), *The Romans*, trans. Lydia Cochrane (1993). Individual studies of important typical figures in Roman society, from the peasant and the bandit to the merchant and the soldier.

Goldsworthy, Adrian, *The Roman Army at War: 100 B.C.–A.D. 200* (1996). A summary history and analysis of the Roman army in action during the late Republic and early Empire.

Goodman, Martin, *The Roman World: 44 B.C.–A.D. 180* (1997). A newer basic history text covering the high Roman Empire.

Harris, William, *Ancient Literacy* (1989). A basic survey of what is known about communication in the form of writing and books in the Roman Empire.

Hopkins, Keith, *Death and Renewal: Sociological Studies in Roman History*, vol. 2 (1983). Innovative studies in Roman history, including one of the best on gladiators and another on death and funerals.

——, *A World Full of Gods: Pagans, Jews and Christians in the Roman Empire* (1999). A somewhat unusual but interesting and provocative look at the world of religions in the Roman Empire.

Juliano, Annette L., and Judith A. Lerner (eds.), *Nomads, Traders and Holy Men along China's Silk Road* (2003). A description of the travelers along the Silk Road in human terms, focusing on warfare, markets, and religion.

Kern, Martin, and Michael Hunter (eds.), *The Analects. A Western Han Text?* (2013): Challenges the assumption that the Confucian *Analects* was compiled before the Han Dynasty.

Kraus, Theodore, and Leonard von Matt, *Pompeii and Herculaneum: The Living Cities of the Dead*, trans. Robert E. Wolf (1975). A huge, lavishly illustrated compendium of all aspects of life in the buried cities of Pompeii and Herculaneum as preserved in the archaeological record.

Loewe, Michael, *The Government of the Qin and Han Empires: 221 BCE–220 CE* (2006). A useful overview of the government of the early empires of China. Topics include the structure of central government, provincial and local government, the armed forces, officials, government communications, the laws of the empire, and control of the people and the land.

Millar, Fergus, *The Crowd in the Late Republic* (1998). An innovative study of the democratic power of the citizens in the city of Rome itself.

——, *The Emperor in the Roman World, 31 B.C.–A.D. 337* (1992). Everything you might want to know about the Roman emperor, with special emphasis on his civil role as the administrator of an empire.

Potter, David, *Roman Empire at Bay: A.D. 180–395* (2004). A basic text covering the later Roman Empire, including the critical transition to a Christian state.

Potter, David S., and David J. Mattingly (eds.), *Life, Death, and Entertainment in the Roman Empire* (1999). A good introduction to basic aspects of Roman life in the empire, including the family, feeding the cities, religion, and popular entertainment.

Qian, Sima, *Records of the Grand Historian: Qin Dynasty,* trans. Burton Watson, 3rd ed. (1995). The classic work of Chinese history in a readable --NNGlation. The Han dynasty's Grand Historian describes the slow rise and meteoric fall of the Qin dynasty from the point of view of the succeeding dynasty, which Sima Qian witnessed or heard of during his lifetime.

Southern, Pat, *The Roman Army: A Social and Institutional History* (2006). A fundamental guide to all aspects of the Roman army.

Todd, Malcolm, *The Early Germans*, rev. ed. (2004). A basic survey of the peoples in central and western Europe at the time of the Roman Empire.

Vainker, Shelagh, *Chinese Silk: A Cultural History* (2004). A work that traces the cultural history of silk in China from its early origins to the twentieth century and considers its relationship to the other decorative arts. The author draws on the most recent archaeological evidence to emphasize the role of silk in Chinese history, trade, religion, and literature.

Wells, Peter S., *The Barbarians Speak: How the Conquered Peoples Shaped Roman Europe* (1999). The cultures of the peoples of central and northern Europe at the time of the Roman Empire and their impact on Roman culture.

Wood, Francis, *The Silk Road: Two Thousand Years in the Heart of Asia* (2004). A work illustrated with drawings, manuscripts, paintings, and artifacts to trace the Silk Road to its origins as far back as Alexander the Great. The author stresses the importance of the Silk Road to cultural and religious movements.

Woolf, Greg (ed.), *The Cambridge Illustrated History of the Roman World* (2005). A good guide to various aspects of Roman history, culture, and provincial life.

———, *Rome: An Empire's Story* (2012). An up-to-date narrative of the Roman Empire told according to major themes that are particularly relevant to world history.

CHAPTER 8: THE RISE OF UNIVERSAL RELIGIONS, 300–600 CE

Bowersock, G. W., Peter Brown, and Oleg Grabar (eds.), *Late Antiquity: A Guide to the Postclassical World* (1999). Essays and items for the entire period 150–750 CE. The volume covers the Roman, East Roman, Sasanian, and early Islamic worlds.

Brown, Peter, *The Rise of Western Christendom: Triumph and Diversity, A.D. 200–1000*, 2nd ed. (2003). The rise and spread of Christianity in Europe and Asia, with up-to-date bibliographies on all topics, maps, and time charts.

———, *The World of Late Antiquity: From Marcus Aurelius to Muhammad, AD 150–750* (1989). A social, religious, and cultural history of the late Roman and Sasanian empires, with illustrations and a time chart.

Bühler, G. (trans.), *The Laws of Manu* (1886). The classic translation of one of India's most important historical, legal, and religious texts.

Coe, Michael D., *The Maya*, 6th ed. (1999). A work by the world's most famous Mayanologist, with recent evidence, analyses, and illustrations.

Cowgill, George L., "The Central Mexican Highlands and the Rise of Teotihuacan to the Decline of Tula," in Richard Adams and Murdo Macleod (eds.), *The Cambridge History of the Native Peoples of the Americas*, vol. 2, *Mesoamerica*, Pt. 1 (2000). A thorough review of findings about urban states in central Mexico.

Fash, William L., *Scribes, Warriors and Kings: The City of Copan and the Ancient Maya* (2001). A fascinating and comprehensive study of one of the most elaborate of the Mayan city-kingdoms.

Fowden, Elizabeth Key, *The Barbarian Plain: Saint Sergius between Rome and Iran* (1999). The study of a major Christian shrine and its relations to Romans, Persians, and Arabs.

Fowden, Garth, *Empire to Commonwealth: The Consequences of Monotheism in Late Antiquity* (1993). A study of the relation between empire and world religions in western Asia.

Gombrich, Richard F., and Sheldon Pollack (eds.), *Clay Sanskrit Library* (2005–2006). All major works from the Gupta and post-Gupta periods, in both Sanskrit and English versions. During the Gupta period, classical Sanskrit literature reached its apex, with abundant drama, poetry, and folk stories.

Gordon, Charles, *The Age of Attila* (1960). The last century of the Roman Empire in western Europe, vividly illustrated from contemporary sources.

Harper, Prudence, *The Royal Hunter: The Art of the Sasanian Empire* (1978). The ideology of the Sasanian Empire as shown through excavated hoards of precious silverware.

Heather, Peter, *The Fall of the Roman Empire: A New History of Rome and the Barbarians* (2006). A military and political narrative based on up-to-date archaeological material.

Herrmann, Georgina, *Iranian Revival* (1977). The structure and horizons of the Sasanian Empire as revealed in its monuments.

Hillgarth, Jocelyn (ed.), *Christianity and Paganism, 350–750: The Conversion of Western Europe*, rev. ed. (1986). A collection of contemporary sources.

Holcombe, Charles, *In the Shadow of the Han: Literati Thought and Society at the Beginning of the Southern Dynasties* (1994). A clear and concise account of the evolution of thought in China after the fall of the Han dynasty in 220 CE. The book presents the rise of Buddhism and Daoism as popular religions as well as elite interests in classical learning in a time of political division and barbarian conquest in North and South China.

La Vaissière, Étienne de, *Sogdian Traders: A History*, trans. James Ward (2005). A summary of historical facts about the most important trading community and its commercial networks on the Silk Road, from the early centuries CE to its demise in the ninth century CE.

Little, Lester (ed.), *Plague and the End of Antiquity: The Pandemic of 541–750* (2008). A series of debates over the nature and impact of the first great pandemic attested in global history.

Liu, Xinru, and Lynda Norene Shaffer, *Connections across Eurasia: Transportation, Communication, and Cultural Exchanges on the Silk Roads* (2007). A survey of trade and religious activities on the Silk Road.

Maas, Michael, *Readings in Late Antiquity: A Source Book* (1999). Well-chosen extracts that illustrate the interrelation of Romans and non-Romans, and of Christians, Jews, and pagans.

Maas, Michael (ed.), *The Cambridge Companion to the Age of Justinian*

(2005). A survey of all aspects of the eastern Roman Empire in the sixth century CE.

Moffett, Samuel, *A History of Christianity in Asia*, vol. 1 (1993). Particularly valuable on Christians in China and India.

Munro-Hay, Stuart, *Aksum: An African Civilization of Late Antiquity* (1991). The origins of the Christian kingdom of Ethiopia.

Murdock, George P., *Africa: Its Peoples and Their History* (1959). A vital introduction to the peoples of Africa and their history.

Oliver, Roland, *The African Experience: From Olduvai Gorge to the Twenty-First Century* (1999). An important overview, written by one of the pioneering scholars of African history and one of the leading authorities on the Bantu migrations.

Pregadio, Fabrizio, *Great Clarity: Daoism and Alchemy in Early Medieval China* (2006). An examination of the religious aspects of Daoism. The book focuses on the relation of alchemy to the Daoist traditions of the third to sixth centuries CE and shows how alchemy was integrated into the elaborate body of doctrines and practices of Daoists at that time.

Tempels, Placide, *Bantu Philosophy* (1959). A highly influential effort to argue for the underlying cultural unity of all the Bantu peoples.

Vansina, Jan, *Paths in the Rainforests: Toward a History of Political Tradition in Equatorial Africa* (1990). The best work on Bantu history.

Walker, Joel, *The Legend of Mar Kardagh: Narrative and Christian Heroism in Late Antique Iraq* (2006). Christians and Zoroastrians in northern Iraq and in Iran.

Yarshater, Ehsan, *Encyclopedia Iranica* (1982–). A guide to all aspects of the Sasanian Empire and to religion and culture in the regions between Mesopotamia and central Asia.

Xuanzang, *Faxianzhuan Jiaoxhu*. Text excerpt translated by Xinru Liu.

Zürcher, E., *The Buddhist Conquest of China: The Spread and Adaptation of Buddhism in Early Medieval China*, 3rd ed. (2007). A reissue of the classic account of the assimilation of Buddhism in China during the medieval period, with particular focus on the religious and philosophical success of Buddhism among Chinese elites in South China.

CHAPTER 9: NEW EMPIRES AND COMMON CULTURES, 600-1000 CE

Ahmed, Leila, *Women and Gender in Islam* (1992). A superb overview of the relations between men and women throughout the history of Islam.

Aneirin, *Y Gododdin: Britain's Oldest Heroic Poem,* ed. and trans. A. O. H. Jarman (1988). A sixth-century Welsh text that describes the battle of the last Britons against the invading Anglo-Saxons.

Arberry, Arthur J., introduction to *The Koran Interpreted: A Translation,* trans. Arthur J. Arberry (1986). One of the most eloquent appreciations of this classical work of religion.

Augustine, *The City of God,* trans. H. Bettenson (1976). An excellent translation of Augustine's monumental work of history, philosophy, and religion.

Berkey, Jonathan P., *The Formation of Islam: Religion and Society in the Near East, 600-1800* (2005). A recent overview of the history of Islam before the modern era. It is particularly sensitive to the influence of external elements on the history of the Muslim peoples.

Bol, Peter, *This Culture of Ours: Intellectual Transitions in T'ang and Sung China* (1994). A study tracing the transformation of the shared culture of the Chinese learned elite from the seventh to the twelfth centuries.

Brown, Peter, *The Rise of Western Christendom: Triumph and Diversity, AD 200-1000*, 2nd ed. (2003). A description of the changes in Christianity in northern Europe and the emergence of the new cultures and political structures that coincided with this development.

Bulliet, Richard W., *Conversion to Islam in the Medieval Period: An Essay in Quantitative History* (1979). A study of the rate at which the populations overrun by Arab conquerors in the seventh century CE embraced the religion of their rulers.

Cook, Michael, *The Koran: A Very Short Introduction* (2000). A useful overview of Islam's holy book.

——, *Muhammad* (1983). A brief but careful life of the Prophet that takes full account of the prolific and often controversial preexisting scholarship.

Creswell, K. A. C., *A Short Account of Early Muslim Architecture, Revised and supplemented by James W. Allan* (1992). The definitive treatment of the subject, brought up to date.

Cross, S. H., and O. P. Sherbowitz-Westor, trans., *The Russian Primary Chronicle* (1953). A vivid record of the Viking settlement of Kiev, of the conversion of Kiev, and of the princes of Kiev in the tenth and eleventh centuries.

Donner, Fred M., *The Early Islamic Conquests* (1981). The best account of the Arab conquests in the Persian and Byzantine empires in the seventh century.

Duncan, John, *The Origins of the Chosŏn Dynasty* (2000). A historical account of the early Korean dynasties from 900 to 1400.

Elman, Benjamin, *Precocious China: Civil Examinations, 1400-1900* (2013). Summary of civil exams in China from medieval times.

Fage, J. D., *Ghana: A Historical Introduction* (1966). A brief but authoritative history of Ghana from earliest times to the twentieth century.

Fisher, Humphrey J., *Slavery in the History of Muslim Black Africa* (2001). A general history of the relations between North Africa and black Africa, focusing on one of the most important aspects of contact—the slave trade.

Graham-Campbell, James, *Cultural Atlas of the Viking World* (1994). A positioning of the Vikings against their wider background in both western and eastern Europe.

Hawting, G. R., *The First Dynasty of Islam: The Umayyad Caliphate, A.D. 661–750* (2000). The essential scholarly treatment of Islam's first dynasty.

Herrmann, Georgina, *Iranian Revival* (1977). The structure and horizons of the Sasanian Empire as revealed in its monuments.

Hillgarth, J. N. (ed.), *Christianity and Paganism, 350–750: The Conversion of Western Europe,* rev. ed. (1986). A collection of contemporary sources.

Hodges, Richard, and David Whitehouse, *Mohammed, Charlemagne, and the Origins of Europe* (1983). A spirited comparison of Islam and the rise of Europe.

Hodgson, Marshall G. S., *The Venture of Islam: Conscience and History in a World Civilization,* 3 vols. (1977). A magnificent history of the Islamic peoples. Its first volume, *The Classical Age of Islam,* is basic reading for anyone interested in the history of the Muslim world.

Holdsworth, May, *Women of the Tang Dynasty* (1999). An account of women's lives during the Tang dynasty.

Hourani, Albert, *History of the Arab Peoples* (2002). The best overview of Arab history.

Jones, Gwynn, *The Norse Atlantic Saga* (1986). The Viking discovery of America.

Kennedy, Hugh, *The Prophet and the Age of the Caliphate: The Islamic Near East from the Sixth to the Eleventh Century* (2004). A very good synthesis of the rise and spread of Islam.

Lee, Peter, et al. (eds.), *Sources of Korean Tradition,* vol. 1 (1996). A unique view of Korean history through the eyes and words of the participants or witnesses themselves, as provided in translations of official documents, letters, and policies.

Levtzion, Nehemia, *Ancient Ghana and Mali* (1980). The best introduction to the kingdoms of West Africa.

Levtzion, Nehemia, and Jay Spaulding, *Medieval West Africa: Views from Arab Scholars and Merchants* (2003). An indispensable source book on early West African history.

Lewis, Bernard, *The Middle East: Two Thousand Years of History from the Rise of Christianity to the Present Day* (1995). A stimulating introduction to an area that has seen the emergence of three of the great world religions.

—— (trans.), *Islam from the Prophet Muhammad to the Capture of Constantinople,* vol. 2, *Religion and Society* (1974). A fine collection of original sources that portray various aspects of classical Islamic society.

Lewis, David Levering, *God's Crucible: Islam and the Making of Europe, 570–1215* (2008). An exciting and well-written overview of the high period of Islamic power and cultural attainments.

Middleton, John, *The Swahili: The Social Landscape of a Mercantile Community* (2000). An exciting synthesis of the Swahili culture of East Africa.

Miyazaki, Ichisada, *China's Examination Hell* (1981). A study of China's examination system.

Nurse, Derek, and Thomas Spear, *The Swahili: Reconstructing the History and Language of an African Society, 800–1500* (1984). A work that explores the history of the Muslim peoples who lived along the coast of East Africa.

Peters, F. E., *Muhammad and the Origins of Islam* (1994). A work that explores the early history of Islam and highlights the critical role that Muhammad played in promoting a new religion and a powerful Arab identity.

Pourshariati, Parveneh, *Decline and Fall of the Sasanian Empire* (2008). Fundamental analysis of the end of the Sasanian Empire and the reasons for the success of the Arab/Muslim invasions.

Robinson, Chase F., *The Formation of the Islamic World, Sixth to Eleventh Centuries,* vol. 1 in *The New Cambridge History of Islam* (2010). An authoritative and up-to-date six-volume overview of the history of Islam from the sixth century to the present.

Schirokauer, Conrad, et al., *A Brief History of Japanese Civilization,* 2nd ed. (2005). A balanced account; chapters focus on developments in art, religion, literature, and thought as well as on Japan's economic, political, and social history in medieval times.

Smith, Julia, *Europe after Rome: A New Cultural History, 500–1000* (2005). A vivid analysis of society and culture in so-called Dark Age Europe.

Totman, Conrad, *History of Japan* (2004). A recent and readable summary of Japanese history from ancient to modern times.

Twitchett, Denis, *The Birth of the Chinese Meritocracy: Bureaucrats and Examinations in T'ang China* (1976). A description of the role of the written civil examinations that began during the Tang dynasty.

——, *Financial Administration under the T'ang Dynasty* (1970). A pioneering account—based on rare Dunhuang documents that survived from medieval times in Buddhist grottoes in central Asia—of the political and economic system undergirding the Chinese imperial state.

Whittow, Mark, *The Making of Byzantium, 600–1025* (1996). A study on the survival and revival of the eastern Roman Empire as a major power in eastern Europe and Southwest Asia.

Wood, Ian, *The Missionary Life: Saints and the Evangelization of Europe, 400–1050* (2001). The horizons of Christians on the frontiers of Europe.

CHAPTER 10: BECOMING "THE WORLD," 1000–1300 CE

Allsen, Thomas, *Commodity and Exchange in the Mongol Empire: A Cultural History of Islamic Textiles* (1997). A study that uses golden brocade, the textile most treasured by Mongol rulers, as a lens through which to analyze the vast commercial networks facilitated by the Mongol conquests and control.

——, *Culture and Conquest in Mongol Eurasia* (2001). A work that emphasizes the cultural and scientific exchanges that took place across Afro-Eurasia as a result of the Mongol conquest.

Bartlett, Robert, *The Making of Europe: Conquest, Colonization and Cultural Change, 950–1350* (1993). The modes of cultural, political, and demographic expansion of feudal Europe along its frontiers, especially in eastern Europe.

Bay, Edna G., *Wives of the Leopards: Gender, Politics, and Culture in the Kingdom of Dahomey* (1998). A work that stresses the role of women in an important West African society and dips into the early history of this area.

Beach, D. N., *Shona and Zimbabwe, 900–1850: An Outline of Shona History* (1980). A good place to start for exploring the history of Great Zimbabwe.

Brooks, George E., *Landlords and Strangers: Ecology, Society, and Trade in Western Africa, 1000–1630* (1993). A survey assembled from primary sources of early West African history that stresses transregional connections.

Buzurg ibn Shahriyar of Ramhormuz, *The Book of the Wonders of India: Mainland, Sea and Islands*, ed. and trans. G. S. P. Freeman-Greenville (1981). A collection of stories told by sailors, both true and fantastic; they help us imagine the lives of sailors of the era.

Chappell, Sally A. Kitt, *Cahokia: Mirror of the Cosmos* (2002). A thorough and vivid account of the "mound people"; it explores not just what we know of Cahokia but how we know it.

Christian, David, *A Short History of Russia, Central Asia, and Mongolia*, vol. 1, *Inner Eurasia from Prehistory to the Mongol Empire* (1998). Essential reading for students interested in interconnections across the Afro-Eurasian landmass.

Curtin, Philip, *Cross-Cultural Trade in World History* (1984). A groundbreaking book on intercultural trade with a primary focus on Africa, especially the cross-Saharan trade and Swahili coastal trade.

Dawson, Christopher, *Mission to Asia* (1980). Accounts of China and the Mongol Empire brought back by Catholic missionaries and diplomats after 1240.

Foltz, Richard C., *Religions of the Silk Road: Overland Trade and Cultural Exchange from Antiquity to the Fifteenth Century* (1999). A study of the populations and the cities of the Silk Road as transmitters of culture across long distances.

Franklin, Simon, and Jonathan Shepherd, *The Emergence of Rus: 750–1200* (1996). The formation of medieval Russia between the Baltic and Black seas.

Gibb, Hamilton A. R., *Saladin: Studies in Islamic History*, ed. Yusuf Ibish (1974). A sympathetic portrait of one of Islam's leading political and military figures.

Goitein, S. D., *Letters of Medieval Jewish Traders* (1973). The classic study of medieval Jewish trading communities based on the commercial papers deposited in the Cairo Geniza (a synagogue storeroom) during the tenth and eleventh centuries; it explores not only commercial activities but also the personal lives of the traders around the Indian Ocean basin.

——, *A Mediterranean Society: An Abridgment in One Volume,* rev. and ed. Jacob Lassner (1999). A portrait of the Jewish merchant community with ties across the Afro-Eurasian landmass, based largely on the documents from the Cairo Geniza (of which Goitein was the primary researcher and interpreter).

——, "New Light on the Beginnings of the Karim Merchant," *Journal of Social and Economic History of the Orient* 1 (1958). Goitein's description of Egyptian trade.

Goitein, S. D., and Mordechai A. Friedman, *India Traders of the Middle Ages: Documents from the Cairo Geniza* (2008). Collection of documents (translated into English) and authoritative essays that explore the eleventh- and twelfth-century trade conducted by several prominent Jewish families along the Mediterranean and Indian Ocean routes.

Harris, Joseph E., *The African Presence in Asia: Consequences of the East African Slave Trade* (1971). One of the few books that looks broadly at the impact of Africans and African slavery on the societies of Asia.

Hartwell, Robert, "Demographic, Political, and Social Transformations of China, 750–1550," *Harvard Journal of Asiatic Studies* 42 (1982): 365–442. A pioneering study of the demographic changes that overtook China during the Tang and Song dynasties, which are described in light of political reform movements and social changes in this crucial era.

Historical Relations across the Indian Ocean: Report and Papers of the Meeting of Experts Organized by UNESCO at Port Louis, Mauritius, from 15 to 19 July, 1974 (1980). Excellent essays on the connections of Africa with Asia across the Indian Ocean.

Hitti, Philip, *An Arab-Syrian Gentleman and Warrior in the Period of the Crusades: Memoirs of Usāmah ibn-Munqidh* (1929). The Crusaders seen through Muslim eyes.

Hodgson, Natasha, *Women, Crusading, and the Holy Land in Historical Narrative* (2007). A book dealing with the Crusades and focusing on the place of women in them.

Holt, P. M., *The Age of the Crusades: The Near East from the Eleventh Century to 1517* (1984). The Crusades period as seen from the eastern Mediterranean and through the lens of a leading British scholar of the area.

Hymes, Robert, and Conrad Schirokauer (eds.), *Ordering the World: Approaches to State and Society in Sung Dynasty China* (1993). A collection of essays that traces the intellectual, social, and political movements that shaped the Song state and its elites.

Ibn Battuta, *The Travels of Ibn Battuta*, trans. H. A. R. Gibb (2002). A readable translation of the classic book, originally published in 1929.

Ibn Fadlan, Ahmad, *Ibn Fadlan's Journey to Russia: A Tenth Century Traveler from Baghdad to the Volga River*, trans. with commentary by Richard Frye (2005). A coherent summary of the observations of an envoy who traveled from Baghdad to Russia.

Irwin, Robert, *The Middle East in the Middle Ages: The Early Mamluk Sultanate, 1250–1582* (1986). Egypt under Mamluk rule.

Jeppie, Shamil, and Souleymane Bachir Diagne (eds.), *The Meanings of Timbuktu* (2008). New materials on the ancient Muslim city of Timbuktu by scholars who have been preserving its manuscripts and writing about its historical importance.

Lancaster, Lewis, Kikun Suh, and Chaishin Yu (eds.), *Buddhism in Koryo: A Royal Religion* (1996). A description of Buddhism at its height in the Koryo period, when the religion made significant contributions to the development of Korean culture.

Levtzion, Nehemia, and Randall L. Pouwels (eds.), *The History of Islam in Africa* (2000). A useful general survey of the place of Islam in African history.

Lewis, Bernard (trans.), *Islam: From the Prophet Muhammad to the Capture of Constantinople* (1974), vol. 2, *Religion and Society*. A fine collection of original sources that portray various aspects of classical Islamic society.

Lopez, Robert S., *The Commercial Revolution of the Middle Ages, 950–1350* (1976). An account focusing on the development around the Mediterranean of commercial practices such as the use of currency, accounting, and credit.

Lyons, Malcolm C. and D. E. P. Jackson, *Saladin: The Politics of the Holy War*, Cambridge (1984: reprint, 2001). The fundamental revisionist work on one of the more important historical figures of the time.

Maalouf, Amin, *The Crusades through Muslim Eyes*, trans. Jon Rothschild (1984). The European Crusaders as seen by the Muslim world.

Marcus, Harold G., *A History of Ethiopia* (2002). An authoritative overview of the history of this great culture.

Mass, Jeffrey, *Yoritomo and the Founding of the First Bakufu: The Origins of Dual Government in Japan* (1999). A revisionist account of how the Kamakura military leader Minamoto Yoritomo established the "dual polity" of court and warrior government in Japan.

McDermott, Joseph, *A Social History of the Chinese Book: Books and Literati Culture in Late Imperial China* (2006). The history of the book in China since the Song dynasty, with comparisons to the book's role in other civilizations, particularly the European.

McIntosh, Roderik, *The Peoples of the Middle Niger: The Island of Gold* (1988). A historical survey of an area often omitted from other textbooks.

Moore, Jerry D., *Cultural Landscapes in the Ancient Andes: Archaeologies of Place* (2005). The most recent and up-to-date analysis of findings based on recent archaeological evidence, emphasizing the importance of local cultures and diversity in the Andes.

Niane, D. T. (ed.), *Africa from the Twelfth to the Sixteenth Century*, vol. 4 of *General History of Africa* (1984). The general UNESCO history of Africa's volume on four centuries of African history. This work features the scholarship of Africans.

Oliver, Roland (ed.), *From c. 1050 to c. 1600*, vol. 3 of *The Cambridge History of Africa*, ed. J. D. Fage and Roland Oliver (1977). Another general survey of African history. This volume draws heavily on the work of British scholars.

Peters, Edward, *The First Crusade* (1971). The Crusaders as seen through their own eyes.

Petry, Carl F. (ed.), *Islamic Egypt, 640–1517*, vol. 1 of *The Cambridge History of Egypt*, ed. M. W. Daly (1998). A solid overview of the history of Islamic Egypt up to the Ottoman conquest.

Polo, Marco, *The Travels of Marco Polo*, ed. Manuel Komroff (1926). A solid translation of Marco Polo's famous account.

Popovic, Alexandre, *The Revolt of African Slaves in Iraq in the 3rd/9th Century*, trans. Leon King (1999). The account of a massive revolt against their slave masters by African slaves taken to labor in Iraq's mines and fields.

Scott, Robert, *Gothic Enterprise: A Guide to Understanding the Medieval Cathedral* (2003). The meaning and social function of religious building in medieval cities in northern Europe.

Shaffer, Lynda Norene, *Maritime Southeast Asia to 1500* (1996). A history of the peoples of the southeast fringe of the Eastern Hemisphere, up to the time that they became connected to the global commercial networks of the world.

Shimada, Izumi, "Evolution of Andean Diversity: Regional Formations (500 BCE–CE 600)," in Frank Salomon and Stuart Schwartz (eds.), *South America*, vol. 3 of *The Cambridge History of the Native Peoples of the Americas* (1999), Pt. 1, pp. 350–517. A splendid overview that contrasts the varieties of lowland and highland cultures.

Steinberg, David Joel, et al., *In Search of Southeast Asia: A Modern History* (1987). An account of the emergence of the modern Southeast Asian polities of Cambodia, Burma, Thailand, and Indonesia.

Tyerman, Christopher, *God's War: A New History of the Crusades* (2006). The balance of religious and nonreligious motivations in the Crusades.

Waley, Daniel, *The Italian City-Republics*, 3rd ed. (1988). The structures and culture of the new cities of medieval Italy.

Watson, Andrew, *Agricultural Innovation in the Early Islamic World: The Diffusion of Crops and Farming Techniques, 700–1100* (1983). An impressive study of the spread of new crops throughout the Muslim world.

CHAPTER 11: CRISES AND RECOVERY IN AFRO-EURASIA, 1300–1500

Bois, Guy, *The Crisis of Feudalism: Economy and Society in Eastern Normandy, c. 1300-1550* (1984). A good case study of a French region that illustrates the turmoil in fourteenth-century Europe.

Brook, Timothy, *Praying for Power: Buddhism and the Formation of Gentry Society in Late Ming China* (1994). An analysis of the role of a significant religious force in the political and social developments of the Ming.

Dardess, John, *A Ming Society: T'ai-ho County, Kiangsi, Fourteenth to Seventeenth Centuries* (1996). A work that covers the different changes and developments of a single locality in China through the centuries.

Dols, Michael W., *The Black Death in the Middle East* (1977). One of the few scholarly works to examine the Black Death outside Europe.

Dreyer, Edward, *Early Ming China: A Political History, 1355-1435* (1982). A useful account of the early years of the Ming dynasty.

Finkel, Caroline, *Osman's Dream: The Story of the Ottoman Empire, 1300-1923* (2005). The most authoritative overview of Ottoman history.

Hale, John, *The Civilization of Europe in the Renaissance* (1994). A beautifully crafted account of the politics, economics, and culture of the Renaissance period in western Europe.

Hodgson, Marshall, *The Venture of Islam: Conscience and History in a World Civilization*, vol. 3 (1974). A good volume on the workings of the Ottoman state.

Itzkowitz, Norman, *Ottoman Empire and Islamic Tradition* (1972). Another good book on the Ottoman state.

Jackson, Peter, *The Delhi Sultanate* (1999). A meticulous, highly specialized, political and military history.

Jackson, Peter, and Lawrence Lockhart (eds.), *The Cambridge History of Iran*, vol. 6 (1986). A volume that deals with the Timurid and Safavid periods in Iran.

Jones, E. L., *The European Miracle* (1981). A provocative work on the economic and social recovery from the Black Death.

Kafadar, Cemal, *Between Two Worlds: The Construction of the Ottoman State* (1995). A thorough reconsideration of the origins of one of the world's great land empires.

Karamustafa, Ahmed, *God's Unruly Friends: Dervish Groups in the Islamic Later Middle Period, 1200-1550* (1994). A book that describes the unorthodox Islamic activities that were occurring in the Islamic world prior to and alongside the establishment of the Ottoman and Safavid empires.

Levathes, Louise, *When China Ruled the Seas: The Treasure Fleet of the Dragon Throne, 1405-33* (1994). A book that provides a lively account of the Zheng He expeditions.

Lowry, Heath W., *The Nature of the Early Ottoman State* (2003). New perspectives on the rise of the Ottomans to prominence.

McNeill, William, *Plagues and Peoples* (1976). A pathbreaking work with a highly useful chapter on the spread of the Black Death throughout the Afro-Eurasian landmass.

Morgan, David, *Medieval Persia, 1040-1797* (1988). Contains an informative discussion of the Safavid state.

Peirce, Leslie, *The Imperial Harem: Women and Sovereignty in the Ottoman Empire* (1993). A work that describes the powerful place that imperial women had in political affairs.

Pirenne, Henri, *Economic and Social History of Medieval Europe* (1937). A classic study of the economic and social recovery from the Black Death.

Reid, James J., *Tribalism and Society in Islamic Iran, 1500-1629* (1983). A useful account of how the Mongols and other nomadic steppe peoples influenced Iran in the era when the Safavids were establishing their authority.

Singman, Jeffrey L. (ed.), *Daily Life in Medieval Europe* (1999). An introductory description of the social and material world experienced by Europeans of different walks of life.

Tuchman, Barbara W., *A Distant Mirror: The Calamitous Fourteenth Century* (1978). A book that shows, in a vigorous way, how war, famine, and pestilence devastated Europeans in the fourteenth century.

Wittek, Paul, *The Rise of the Ottoman Empire* (1958). A work that contains vital insights on the emergence of the Ottoman state amid the political chaos in Anatolia.

Glossary

Abd al-Rahman III Islamic ruler in Spain who held a countercaliphate and reigned from 912 to 961 CE.

aborigines Original, native inhabitants of a region, as opposed to invaders, colonizers, or later peoples of mixed ancestry.

absolute monarchy Form of government where one body, usually the monarch, controls the right to tax, judge, make war, and coin money. The term *enlightened absolutists* was often used to refer to state monarchies in seventeenth- and eighteenth-century Europe.

acid rain Precipitation containing large amounts of sulfur, mainly from coal-fired plants.

adaptation Ability to alter behavior and to innovate, finding new ways of doing things.

African National Congress (ANC) Multiracial organization founded in 1912 in an effort to end racial discrimination in South Africa.

Afrikaners Descendants of the original Dutch settlers of South Africa; formerly referred to as Boers.

Agones Athletic contests in ancient Greece.

Ahmosis Egyptian ruler in the southern part of the country who ruled from 1550 to 1525 BCE; Ahmosis used Hyksos weaponry—horse chariots in particular—to defeat the Hyksos themselves.

Ahura Mazda Supreme God of the Persians believed to have created the world and all that is good and to have appointed earthly kings.

AIDS (Acquired Immunodeficiency Syndrome) Virus that compromises the ability of the infected person's immune system to ward off disease. First detected in 1981, AIDS was initially stigmatized as a "gay cancer," but as it spread to heterosexuals, public awareness about it increased. In its first two decades, AIDS killed 12 million people.

Akbarnamah Mughal intellectual Abulfazl's *Book of Akbar,* which attempted to reconcile the traditional Sufi interest in the inner life within the worldly context of a great empire.

Alaric II Visigothic king who issued a simplified code of innovative imperial law.

Alexander the Great (356–323 BCE) Leader who used novel tactics and new kinds of armed forces to conquer the Persian Empire, which extended from Egypt and the Mediterranean Sea to the interior of what is now Afghanistan and as far as the Indus River valley. Alexander's conquests broke down barriers between the Mediterranean world and Southwest Asia and transferred massive amounts of wealth and power to the Mediterranean, transforming it into a more unified world of economic and cultural exchange.

Alexandria Port city in Egypt named after Alexander the Great. Alexandria was a model city in the Hellenistic world. It was built up by a multiethnic population from around the Mediterranean world.

Al-Khwarizmi Scientist and mathematician who lived from 780 to 850 CE and is known for having modified Indian digits into Arabic numerals.

Allied powers Name given to the alliance between Britain, France, Russia, and Italy, who fought against Germany and Austria-Hungary (the Central powers) in World War I. In World War II the name was used for the alliance between Britain, France, and America, who fought against the Axis powers (Germany, Italy, and Japan).

allomothering System by which mothers relied on other women, including their own mothers, daughters, sisters, and friends, to help in the nurturing and protecting of children.

alluvium Area of land created by river deposits.

alphabet A new system of writing using relatively few letters (22) developed by the Phoenicians in the mid–second millennium BCE.

American Railway Union Workers' union that initiated the Pullman Strike of 1894, which led to violence and ended in the leaders' arrest.

Amnesty International Non-governmental organization formed to defend "prisoners of conscience"—those detained for their beliefs, race, sex, ethnic origin, language, or religion.

Amorites Name that Mesopotamian urbanites called the transhumant herders from the Arabian desert. Around 2300 BCE, the Amorites, along with the Elamites, were at the center of newly formed dynasties in southern Mesopotamia.

Amun Once insignificant Egyptian god elevated to higher status by Amenemhet (1991–1962 BCE). *Amun* means "hidden" in Ancient Egyptian; the name was meant to convey the god's omnipresence.

Analects Texts that included the teachings and cultural ideals of Confucius.

anarchism Belief that society should be a free association of its members, not subject to government, laws, or police.

Anatolia Now mainly the area known as modern Turkey; in the sixth millennium BCE, people from Anatolia, Greece, and the Levant took to boats and populated the Aegean. Their small villages endured almost unchanged for two millennia.

Angkor Wat Magnificent Khmer Vaishnavite temple that crowned the royal palace in Angkor. It had statues representing the Hindu pantheon of gods.

Anglo-Boer War (1899–1902) Anticolonial struggle in South Africa between the British and the Afrikaners over the gold-rich Transvaal. In response to the Afrikaners' guerrilla tactics and in order to contain the local population, the British instituted the first concentration camps. Ultimately, Britain won the conflict.

animal domestication Gradual process that occurred simultaneously with or just before the domestication of plants, depending on the region.

annals Historical records. Notable annals are the cuneiform inscriptions that record successful Assyrian military campaigns.

Anti-Federalists Critics of the U.S. Constitution who sought to defend the people against the power of the federal government and insisted on a bill of rights to protect individual liberties from government intrusion.

apartheid Racial segregation policy of the Afrikaner-dominated South African government. Legislated in 1948 by the Afrikaner National Party, it had existed in South Africa for many years.

Arab-Israeli War of 1948–1949 Conflict between Israeli and Arab armies that arose in the wake of a U.N. vote to partition Palestine into Arab and Jewish territories. The war shattered the legitimacy of Arab ruling elites.

Aramaic Dialect of a Semitic language spoken in Southwest Asia; it became the lingua franca of the Persian Empire.

Aristotle (384–322 BCE) Philosopher who studied under Plato but came to different conclusions about nature and politics. Aristotle believed in collecting observations about nature and discerning patterns to ascertain how things worked.

Aryans Nomadic charioteers who spoke Indo-European languages and entered South Asia in 1500 BCE. The early Aryan settlers were herders.

Asante state State located in present-day Ghana, founded by the Asantes at the end of the seventeenth century. It grew in power in the next century because of its access to gold and its involvement in the slave trade.

ascetic One who rejects material possessions and physical pleasures.

Asiatic Society Cultural organization founded by British Orientalists who supported native culture but still believed in colonial rule.

Aśoka Emperor of the Mauryan dynasty from 268 to 231 BCE; he was a great conqueror and unifier of India. He is said to have embraced Buddhism toward the end of his life.

Assur One of two cities on the upper reaches of the Tigris River that were the heart of Assyria proper (the other was Nineveh).

Aśvaghosa First known Sanskrit writer. He may have lived from 80 to 150 CE and may have composed a biography of the Buddha.

Ataturk, Mustafa Kemal (1881–1938) Ottoman army officer and military hero who helped forge the modern Turkish nation-state. He and his followers deposed the sultan, declared Turkey a republic, and constructed a European-like secular state, eliminating Islam's hold over civil and political affairs.

Atlantic system New system of trade and expansion that linked Europe, Africa, and the Americas. It emerged in the wake of European voyages across the Atlantic Ocean.

Atma Vedic term signifying the eternal self, represented by the trinity of deities.

Atman In the Upanishads, an eternal being who exists everywhere. The atman never perishes but is reborn or transmigrates into another life.

Attila Sole ruler of all Hunnish tribes from 433 to 453 CE. Harsh and much feared, he formed the first empire to oppose Rome in northern Europe.

Augustus Title meaning "Revered One," assumed in 27 BCE by the Roman ruler Octavian (63–14 BCE). This was one of many titles he assumed; others included *imperator*, *princeps*, and *Caesar*.

australopithecines Hominid species that appeared 3 million years ago and, unlike other animals, walked on two legs. Their brain capacity was a little less than one-third of a modern human's or about the size of the brain capacity of today's African apes. Although not humans, they carried the genetic and biological material out of which modern humans would later emerge.

Austro-Hungarian Empire Dual monarchy established by the Habsburg family in 1867; it collapsed at the end of World War I.

authoritarianism Centralized and dictatorial form of government, proclaimed by its adherents to be superior to parliamentary democracy and especially effective at mobilizing the masses. This idea was widely accepted in parts of the world during the 1930s.

Avesta Compilation of holy works transmitted orally by priests for millennia and eventually recorded in the sixth century BCE.

axial age Term often used to describe the pivotal period of the first millennium BCE when radical thinkers across the "second-generation societies" of connected Eurasia—including the Greek philosophers of the Mediterranean, Zoroaster in Southwest Asia, Buddha in South Asia, and Confucius and Master Lao in East Asia—offered dramatically new ideas that challenged their times.

Axis powers The three aggressor states in World War II: Germany, Japan, and Italy.

Aztec Empire Mesoamerican empire that originated with a league of three Mexica cities in 1430 and gradually expanded through the Central Valley of Mexico, uniting numerous small, independent states under a single monarch who ruled with the help of counselors, military leaders, and priests. By the late fifteenth century, the Aztec realm may have embraced 25 million people. In 1521, they were defeated by the conquistador Hernán Cortés.

baby boom Post–World War II upswing in U.S. birth rates; it reversed a century of decline.

bactrian camel Two-humped animal domesticated in central Asia around 2500 BCE. The bactrian camel was heartier than the one-humped dromedary and became the animal of choice for the harsh and varied climates typical of Silk Road trade.

Bactria A Hellenistic kingdom that broke away from the Seleucids around 200 BCE to establish a state in the Gandhara region modern Pakistan, which served as a bridge between South Asia and the Mediterranean Greek world.

Baghdad Capital of the Islamic Empire under the Abbasid dynasty, founded in 762 CE (in modern-day Iraq). In the medieval period, it was a center of administration, scholarship, and cultural growth for what came to be known as the Golden Age of Islamic science.

Baghdad Pact (1955) Middle Eastern military alliance between countries friendly with America who were also willing to align themselves with the western countries against the Soviet Union.

Balam Na Stone temple and place of pilgrimage for the Mayan people of Mexico's Yucatan peninsula.

Balfour Declaration Letter (November 2, 1917) by Lord Arthur J. Balfour, British foreign secretary, that promised a homeland for the Jews in Palestine.

Bamboo Annals Shang stories and foundation myths that were written on bamboo strips and later collected.

Bantu Language first spoken by people who lived in the southeastern area of modern Nigeria around 1000 CE.

Bantu migrations Waves of rapid population movement from West Africa into eastern and southern Africa during the first millennium CE that brought advanced agricultural practices to these regions and absorbed most of the preexisting hunting-and-gathering populations.

barbarian Derogatory term used to describe pastoral nomads, painting them as enemies of civilization; the term *barbarian* used to have a more neutral meaning than it does today.

barbarian invasions Violent migration of people in the late fourth and fifth centuries into Roman territory. These migrants had long been used as non-Roman soldiers.

basilicas Early church buildings, based on old royal audience halls.

Battle of Adwa (1896) Battle in which the Ethiopians defeated Italian colonial forces; it inspired many of Africa's later national leaders.

Battle of Wounded Knee (1890) Bloody massacre of Sioux Ghost Dancers by U.S. armed forces.

Bay of Pigs (1961) Unsuccessful invasion of Cuba by Cuban exiles supported by the U.S. government. The invaders intended to incite an insurrection in Cuba and overthrow the communist regime of Fidel Castro.

Bedouins Nomadic pastoralists in the deserts of the Middle East.

Beer Hall Putsch (1923) Nazi intrusion into a meeting of Bavarian leaders in a Munich beer hall; the Nazis were attempting to force support for their cause; Adolf Hitler was imprisoned for a year after the incident.

Beghards (1500s) Eccentric European group whose members claimed to be in a state of grace that allowed them to do as they pleased—from adultery, free love, and nudity to murder; also called Brethren of Free Speech.

bell beaker Ancient drinking vessel, an artifact from Europe, so named because its shape resembles an inverted bell.

Berenice of Egypt Egyptian "queen" who helped rule over the Kingdom of the Nile from 320 to 280 BCE.

Beringia Prehistoric thousand-mile-long land bridge that linked Siberia and North America (which had not been populated by hominids). About 18,000 years ago, *Homo sapiens* edged into this landmass.

Berlin Airlift (1948) Supply of vital necessities to West Berlin by air transport primarily under U.S. auspices. It was initiated in response to a land and water blockade of the city instituted by the Soviet Union in the hope that the Allies would be forced to abandon West Berlin.

Berlin Wall Wall built by the communists in Berlin in 1961 to prevent citizens of East Germany from fleeing to West Germany; torn down in 1989.

Bhakti Religious practice that grew out of Hinduism and emphasizes personal devotion to gods.

bhakti Hinduism Popular form of Hinduism that emerged in the seventh century. The religion stresses devotion (*bhakti*) to God and uses vernacular languages (not Sanskrit) spoken by the common people.

big men Leaders of the extended household communities that formed village settlements in African rain forests.

big whites French plantation owners in Saint-Domingue (present-day Haiti) who created one of the wealthiest slave societies.

Bilad al-Sudan Arabic for "the land of the blacks"; it consisted of the land lying south of the Sahara.

bilharzia Debilitating water-borne illness. It was widespread in Egypt, where it infected peasants who worked in the irrigation canals.

Bill of Rights First ten amendments to the U.S. Constitution; ratified in 1791.

bipedalism Walking on two legs, thereby freeing hands and arms to carry objects such as weapons and tools; one of several traits that distinguished hominids.

Black Death Great epidemic of the bubonic plague that ravaged Europe, East Asia, and North Africa in the fourteenth century, killing large numbers, including perhaps as many as one-third of the European population.

Black Jacobins Nickname for the rebels in Saint-Domingue, including Toussaint L'Ouverture, a former slave who led the slaves of this French colony in the world's largest and most successful slave insurrection.

Black Panthers Radical African American group in the 1960s and 1970s; they advocated black separatism and pan-Africanism.

black shirts Fascist troops of Mussolini's regime; the squads received money from Italian landowners to attack socialist leaders.

Black Tuesday (October 29, 1929) Historic day when the U.S. stock market crashed, plunging the United States and international trading systems into crisis and leading the world into the "Great Depression."

blitzkrieg "Lightning war"; type of warfare in which the Germans, during World War II, used coordinated aerial bombing campaigns along with tanks and infantrymen in motorized vehicles.

Bodhisattvas In Mahayana Buddhism, enlightened demigods who were ready to reach *nirvana* but delayed so that they might help others attain it.

Bolívar, Simón (1783–1830) Venezuelan leader who urged his followers to become "American," to overcome their local identities. He wanted the liberated countries to form a Latin American confederation, urging Peru and Bolivia to join Venezuela, Ecuador, and Colombia in the "Gran Colombia."

Bolsheviks Former members of the Russian Social Democratic Party who advocated the destruction of capitalist political and economic institutions and started the Russian Revolution. In 1918 the Bolsheviks changed their name to the Russian Communist Party.

Book of the Dead Ancient Egyptian funerary text that contains drawings and paintings as well as spells describing how to prepare the jewelry and amulets that were buried with a person in preparation for the afterlife.

bourgeoisie The middle class. In Europe, they sought to be recognized not by birth or title, but by capital and property.

Boxer Protocol Written agreement between the victors of the Boxer Uprising and the Qing Empire in 1901 that placed western troops in Beijing and required the regime to pay exorbitant damages for foreign life and property.

Boxer Uprising (1899–1900) Chinese peasant movement that opposed foreign influence, especially that of Christian missionaries; it was put down after the Boxers were defeated by an army composed mostly of Japanese, Russians, British, French, and Americans.

Brahma One of three major deities that form a trinity in Vedic religion. Brahma signifies birth. *See also* Vishnu *and* Siva.

Brahmans Vedic priests who performed rituals and communicated with the gods. Brahmans provided guidance on how to live in balance with the forces of nature as represented by the various deities. The codification of Vedic principles into codes of law took place at the hands of the Brahmans. They memorized Vedic works and compiled commentaries on them. They also developed their own set of rules and rituals, which developed into a full-scale theology. Originally memorized and passed on orally, these may have been written down sometime after the beginning of the Common Era. Brahmanism was reborn as Hinduism sometime during the first half of the first millennium CE.

British Commonwealth of Nations Union formed in 1926 that conferred "dominion status" on Britain's white settler colonies in Canada, Australia, and New Zealand.

British East India Company *See* East India Company.

bronze Alloy of copper and tin brought into Europe from Anatolia; used to make hard-edged weapons.

brown shirts Troops of German men who advanced the Nazi cause by holding street marches, mass rallies, and confrontations and by beating Jews and anyone who opposed the Nazis.

bubonic plague Acute infectious disease caused by a bacterium that is transmitted to humans by fleas from infected rats. It ravaged Europe and parts of Asia in the fourteenth century. Sometimes referred to as the "Black Death."

Buddha (Siddhartha Gautama; 563–483 BCE) Indian ascetic who founded Buddhism.

Buddhism Major South Asian religion that aims to end human suffering through the renunciation of desire. Buddhists believe that removing the illusion of a separate identity would lead to a state of contentment (*nirvana*). These beliefs challenged the traditional Brahmanic teachings of the time and provided the peoples of South Asia with an alternative to established traditions.

bullion Uncoined gold or silver.

Byzantium Modern term for the eastern Roman Empire (lasting from the fourth to the fifteenth century), centered at its "new Rome," Constantinople (founded by emperor Constantine in 324 on the site of a Greek city, Byzantium).

Cahokia Commercial center for regional and long-distance trade in North America. Its hinterlands produced staples for urban consumers. In return, its crafts were exported inland by porters and to North American markets in canoes. *See also* Mound people.

calaveras Allegorical skeleton drawings by the Mexican printmaker and artist José Guadalupe Posada. The works drew on popular themes of betrayal, death, and festivity.

caliphate Institution that arose as the successor to Muhammad's leadership and became both the political and religious head of the Islamic community. Although the caliphs exercised political authority over the Muslim community and were the head of the religious community, the *ummah*, they did not inherit Muhammad's prophetic powers and were not authorities in religious doctrine.

Calvin, Jean (1509–1564) A French theologian during the Protestant Reformation. Calvin developed a Christianity that emphasized moral regeneration through church teachings and laid out a doctrine of predestination.

Candomblé Yoruba-based religion in northern Brazil; it interwove African practices and beliefs with Christianity.

canton system System officially established by imperial decree in 1759 that required European traders to have Chinese guild merchants act as guarantors for their good behavior and payment of fees.

caravan cities Set of networks at long-distance trade locations where groups of merchants could assemble during their journeys. Several of these developed into full-fledged cities, especially in the deserts of Arabia.

caravans Companies of men who transported and traded goods along overland routes in North Africa and central Asia; large caravans consisted of 600–1,000 camels and as many as 400 men.

caravansarais Inns along major trade routes that accommodated large numbers of traders, their animals, and their wares.

caravel Sailing vessel suited for nosing in and out of estuaries and navigating in waters with unpredictable currents and winds.

carrack Ship used on open bodies of water, such as the Mediterranean.

Carthage City in what is modern-day Tunisia; emblematic of the trading aspirations and activities of merchants in the Mediterranean. Pottery and other archaeological remains demonstrate that trading contacts with Carthage were as far-flung as Italy, Greece, France, Iberia, and West Africa.

cartography Mapmaking.

caste system Hierarchical system of organizing people and distributing labor.

Caste War of Yucatan (1847–1901) Conflict between Mayan Indians and the Mexican state over Indian autonomy and legal equality, which resulted in the Mexican takeover of the Yucatan peninsula.

Castro, Fidel (1926–) Cuban communist leader whose forces overthrew Batista's corrupt regime in early January 1959. Castro became increasingly radical as he consolidated power, announcing a massive redistribution of land and the nationalization of foreign oil refineries; he declared himself a socialist and aligned himself with the Soviet Union in the wake of the 1961 CIA-backed Bay of Pigs invasion.

Çatal Hüyük Site in Anatolia discovered in 1958. It was a dense honeycomb of settlements filled with rooms whose walls were covered with paintings of wild bulls, hunters, and pregnant women. Çatal Hüyük symbolizes an early transition into urban dwelling and dates to the eighth millennium BCE.

cathedra Bishop's seat, or throne, in a church.

Catholic Church Unifying institution for Christians in western Europe after the collapse of the Roman Empire. Rome became the spiritual capital of western Europe and the bishops of Rome emerged as popes, the supreme head of the church, who possessed great moral authority.

Cato the Elder (234–149 BCE) Roman statesman, often seen as emblematic of the transition from a Greek to a Roman world. Cato the Elder wrote a manual for the new economy of slave plantation agriculture, invested in shipping and trading, learned Greek rhetoric, and added the genre of history to Latin literature.

caudillos South American local military chieftains.

cave drawings Images on cave walls. The subjects are most often large game, although a few are images of humans. Other elements are impressions made by hands dipped in paint and pressed on a wall or abstract symbols and shapes.

Celali revolts (1595–1610) Peasant and artisan uprisings against the Ottoman state.

Central powers Defined in World War I as Germany and Austria-Hungary.

Chan Chan City founded between 850 and 900 CE by the Moche people in what is now modern-day Peru. It had a core population of 30,000 inhabitants.

Chan Santa Cruz Separate Mayan community formed as part of a crusade for spiritual salvation and the complete cultural separation of the Mayan Indians; means "little holy cross."

Chandra Gupta II King who reigned in South Asia from 320 to 335 CE. He shared his name with Chandragupta, the founder of the Mauryan Empire.

Chandravamsha One of two main lineages (the lunar one) of Vedic society, each with its own creation myth, ancestors, language, and rituals. Each lineage included many clans. *See* Suryavamsha.

chapatis Flat, unleavened Indian bread.

chariots Horse-driven carriages brought by the pastoral nomadic warriors from the steppes that became the favored mode of transportation for an urban aristocratic warrior class and for other men of power in agriculture-based societies. Control of chariot forces was the foundation of the new balance of power across Afro-Eurasia during the second millennium BCE.

charismatic Person who uses personal strengths or virtues, often laced with a divine aura, to command followers.

Charlemagne Emperor of the West and heir to Rome from 764 to 814 CE.

chartered companies Firms that were awarded monopoly trading rights over vast areas by European monarchs (e.g., Virginia Company, Dutch East India Company).

Chartism (1834–1848) Mass democratic movement to pass the Peoples' Charter in Britain, granting male suffrage, secret ballot, equal electoral districts, and annual parliaments, and absolving the requirement of property ownership for members of the parliament.

chattel slavery Form of slavery that sold people as property, the rise of which coincided with the expansion of city-states. Chattel slavery was eschewed by the Spartans, who also rejected the innovation of coin money.

Chavín A people who lived in what is now northern Peru from 1400 to 200

BCE. They were united more by culture and faith than by a unified political system.

Chernobyl (1986) Site in the Soviet Union (in Ukraine) of the meltdown of a nuclear reactor.

Chiang Kai-shek (1887–1975) Leader of the Guomindang following Sun Yat-sen's death who mobilized the Chinese masses through the New Life movement. In 1949 he lost the Chinese Revolution to the communists and moved his regime to Taiwan.

Chimu Empire South America's first empire; it developed during the first century of the second millennium in the Moche Valley on the Pacific coast.

chinampas Floating gardens used by Aztecs in the 1300s and 1400s to grow crops.

China's Sorrow Name for the Yellow River, which, when it changed course or flooded, could cause mass death and waves of migration.

chinoiserie Chinese silks, teas, tableware, jewelry, and paper; popular among Europeans in the seventeenth and eighteenth centuries.

Christendom Entire portion of the world in which Christianity prevailed.

Christianity Religion that originated at the height of the Roman Empire and in a direct confrontation with Roman imperial authority: the trial of Yeshua ben Yosef (Joshua son of Joseph; we know him today by the Greek form of his name, Jesus). Jesus was condemned for sedition and crucified. His followers believed that he was resurrected and that his teachings were not that of a man, but a god who had walked among human beings. At first, the Roman Empire refused to recognize Christianity and persecuted its followers, but in the fourth century CE Christianity was officially recognized as the Roman state religion.

Church of England Established form of Christianity in England dating from the sixteenth century.

city Highly populated concentration of economic, religious, and political power. The first cities appeared in river basins, which could produce a surplus of agriculture. The abundance of food freed most city inhabitants from the need to produce their own food, which allowed them to work in specialized professions.

city-state Political organization based on the authority of a single, large city that controls outlying territories.

Civil Rights Act (1964) U.S. legislation that banned segregation in public facilities, outlawed racial discrimination in employment, and marked an important step in correcting legal inequality.

civil rights movement Powerful movement for equal rights and the end of racial segregation in the United States that began in the 1950s with court victories against school segregation and nonviolent boycotts.

civil service examinations The world's first written civil service examination system, instituted by the Tang dynasty to recruit officials and bureaucrats. Open to most males, the exams tested a candidate's literary skills and knowledge of the Confucian classics. They helped to unite the Chinese state by making knowledge of a specific language and Confucian classics the only route to power.

Civil War, American (1861–1865) Conflict between the northern and southern states of America; this struggle led to the abolition of slavery in the United States.

clan A social group comprising many households, claiming descent from a common ancestor.

clandestine presses Small printing operations that published banned texts in the early modern era, especially in Switzerland and the Netherlands.

Clovis people Early humans in America who used basic chipped blades and pointed spears in pursuing prey. They extended the hunting traditions they had learned in Afro-Eurasia, such as establishing campsites and moving with their herds. They were known as "Clovis people" because the arrowhead point that they used was first found by archaeologists at a site near Clovis, New Mexico.

Code of Manu Part of the handiwork of Brahman priests; a representative code of law that incorporated social sanctions and practices and provided guidance for living within the caste system.

codex Early form of book, with separate pages bound together; it replaced the scroll as the main medium for written texts. The codex emerged around 300 CE.

cognitive skills Skills such as thought, memory, problem-solving, and—ultimately—language. Hominids were able to use these skills and their hands to create new adaptations, like tools, which helped them obtain food and avoid predators.

Cohong Chinese merchant guild that traded with Europeans under the Qing dynasty.

coins Form of money that replaced goods, which previously had been bartered for services and other products. Originally used mainly to hire mercenary soldiers, coins became the commonplace method of payment linking buyers and producers throughout the Mediterranean.

cold war (1945–1990) Ideological conflict in which the Soviet Union and eastern Europe opposed the United States and western Europe.

colonies Regions under the political control of another country.

colons French settler population in Algeria.

colosseum Huge amphitheater completed by Titus and dedicated in 80 CE. Originally begun by Flavian, the structure is named after a colossal statue of Nero that formerly stood beside it.

Columbian exchange Movements between Afro-Eurasia and the Americas of previously unknown plants, animals, people, diseases, and products that followed in the wake of Columbus's voyages.

commanderies Provinces. Shi Huangdi (First August Emperor) divided China into commanderies (*jun*) to enable the Qin dynasty to rule the massive state effectively. The thirty-six commanderies were then subdivided into counties (*xian*).

Communist Manifesto Pamphlet published by Karl Marx and Friedrich Engels in 1848 at a time when political revolutions were sweeping Europe. It called on the workers of all nations to unite in overthrowing capitalism.

Compromise of 1867 Agreement between the Habsburgs and the peoples living in Hungarian parts of the empire that the Habsburg state would be officially known as the Austro-Hungarian Empire.

concession areas Territories, usually ports, where Chinese emperors allowed European merchants to trade and European people to settle.

Confucian ideals The ideals of honoring tradition, emphasizing the responsibility of the emperor, and respect for the lessons of history, promoted by Confucius, which the Han dynasty made the official doctrine of the empire by 50 BCE.

Confucianism Ethics, beliefs, and practices stipulated by the Chinese philosopher Kong Qiu, or Confucius, which served as a guide for Chinese society up to modern times.

Confucius (551–479 BCE) Influential teacher, thinker, and leader in China who developed a set of principles for ethical living. He believed that coercive laws and punishment would not be needed to maintain order in society if men following his ethics ruled. He taught his philosophy to anyone who was intelligent and willing to work, which allowed men

to gain entry into the ruling class through education.

cong tube Ritual object crafted by the Liangzhu. A cong tube was made of jade and was used in divination practices.

Congo Independent State Large colonial state in Africa created by Leopold II, king of Belgium, during the 1880s, and ruled by him alone. After rumors of mass slaughter and enslavement, the Belgian parliament took the land and formed a Belgian colony.

Congress of Vienna (1814–1815) International conference to reorganize Europe after the downfall of Napoleon. European monarchies agreed to respect each other's borders and to cooperate in guarding against future revolutions and war.

conquistadors Spanish military leaders who led the conquest of the New World in the sixteenth century.

Constantine Roman emperor who converted to Christianity in 312 CE. In 313, he issued a proclamation that gave Christians new freedoms in the empire. He also founded Constantinople (at first called "New Rome").

Constantinople Capital city, formerly known as Byzantium, which was founded as the New Rome by Constantine the Great.

Constitutional Convention (1787) Meeting to formulate the Constitution of the United States of America.

Contra rebels Opponents of the Sandinistas in Nicaragua; they were armed and financed by the United States and other anticommunist countries (1980).

Conversion of Constantine A significant political and religious turning point in the Roman Empire. Before the decisive battle for Rome in 312 CE, Constantine supposedly had a dream in which he was told to place a sign with the opening letters of Christ's name on his soldiers' shields. Constantine won the ensuing battle; he soon issued a proclamation giving privileges to Christian bishops. The edict spread Christianity through the institutions and across the byways of the Roman Empire.

converso Jewish and Muslim converts to Christianity in the Iberian Peninsula and the New World.

Coptic Form of Christianity practiced in Egypt. It was doctrinally different from Christianity elsewhere, and Coptic Christians had their own views of Christology, or the nature of Christ.

Corn Laws Laws that imposed tariffs on grain imported to Great Britain, intended to protect British farming interests. The Corn Laws were abolished in 1846 as part of a British movement in favor of free trade.

cosmology Branch of metaphysics devoted to understanding the order of the universe.

cosmopolitans A development referring to the inhabitants of the multiethnic cities that thrived in the Hellenistic world; literally meaning "citizens belonging to the whole world," as opposed to a particular city-state.

Council of Nicaea Church council convened in 325 CE by Constantine and presided over by him as well. At this council, a Christian creed was articulated and made into a formula that expressed the philosophical and technical elements of Christian belief.

Counter-Reformation Movement to counter the spread of the Reformation; initiated by the Catholic Church at the Council of Trent in 1545. The Catholic Church enacted reforms to attack clerical corruption and it placed a greater emphasis on individual spirituality. During this time, the Jesuits were founded to help revive the Catholic Church.

coup d'état Overthrow of established state by a group of conspirators, usually from the military.

creation narratives Narratives constructed by different cultures that draw on their belief systems and available evidence to explain the origins of the world and humanity.

creed Formal statement of faith or expression of a belief system. A Christian creed or "credo" was formulated by the Council of Nicaea in 325 CE.

creoles Persons of full-blooded European descent who were born in the Spanish American colonies.

Crimean War (1853–1856) War waged by Russia against Great Britain and France. Spurred by Russia's encroachment on Ottoman territories, the conflict revealed Russia's military weakness when Russian forces fell to British and French troops.

crossbow Innovative weapon used at the end of the Warring States period that allowed archers to shoot their enemies with accuracy, even from a distance.

Crusades Wave of attacks launched in the late eleventh century by western Europeans. The First Crusade began in 1095, when Pope Urban II appealed to the warrior nobility of France to free Jerusalem from Muslim rule. Four subsequent Crusades were fought over the next two centuries.

Cuban Missile Crisis (1962) Diplomatic standoff between the United States and the Soviet Union that was provoked by the Soviet Union's attempt to base nuclear missiles in Cuba; it brought the world close to a nuclear war.

cult Religious movement, often based on the worship of a particular god or goddess.

cultigen Organism that has diverged from its ancestors through domestication or cultivation.

cuneiform Wedge-shaped form of writing. As people combined rebus symbols with other visual marks that contained meaning, they became able to record and transmit messages over long distances by using abstract symbols or signs to denote concepts; such signs later came to represent syllables, which could be joined into words. By impressing these signs into wet clay with the cut end of a reed, scribes engaged in cuneiform.

Cyrus the Great Founder of the Persian Empire. This sixth-century ruler (559–529 BCE) conquered the Medes and unified the Iranian kingdoms.

Daimyo Ruling lords who commanded private armies in pre-Meiji Japan.

dan Fodio, Usman (1754–1817) Fulani Muslim cleric whose visions led him to challenge the Hausa ruling classes, whom he believed were insufficiently faithful to Islamic beliefs and practices. His ideas gained support among those who had suffered under the Hausa landlords. In 1804, his supporters and allies overthrew the Hausa in what is today northern Nigeria.

Daoism School of thought developed at the end of the Warring States period that focused on the importance of following the Dao, or the natural way of the cosmos. Daoism emphasized the need to accept the world as it was rather than trying to change it through politics or the government. Unlike Confucianism, Daoism scorned rigid rituals and social hierarchies.

Dar al-Islam Arabic for "the House of Islam"; it describes a sense of common identity.

Darius I (521–486 BCE) Leader who put the emerging unified Persian Empire onto solid footing after Cyrus's death.

Darwin, Charles (1809–1882) British scientist who became convinced that the species of organic life had evolved under the uniform pressure of natural laws, not by means of a special, one-time creation as described in the Bible.

D-Day (June 6, 1944) Day of the Allied invasion of Normandy under General Dwight Eisenhower to liberate western Europe from German occupation.

Dear Boy Nickname of an early human remain discovered in 1931 by a team of archaeologists named the Leakeys. They discovered an almost totally intact skull. Other objects discovered with Dear Boy demonstrated that by the time of Dear Boy, early humans had begun to fashion tools and to use them for butchering animals and possibly for hunting and killing smaller animals.

Decembrists Russian army officers who were influenced by events in revolutionary France and formed secret societies that espoused liberal governance. They were put down by Nicholas I in December 1825.

Declaration of Independence U.S. document stating the theory of government on which America was founded.

Declaration of the Rights of Man and Citizen (1789) French charter of liberties formulated by the National Assembly that marked the end of dynastic and aristocratic rule. The seventeen articles later became the preamble to the new constitution, which the assembly finished in 1791.

decolonization End of empire and emergence of new independent nation-states in Asia and Africa as a result of the defeat of Japan in World War II and weakened European influence after the war.

Delhi Sultanate (1206–1526) Turkish regime of northern India. The regime strengthened the cultural diversity and tolerance that were a hallmark of the Indian social order, which allowed it to bring about political integration without enforcing cultural homogeneity.

democracy The idea that people, through membership in a nation, should choose their own representatives and be governed by them.

Democritus Thinker in ancient Greece who lived from 470 to 360 BCE; he deduced the existence of the atom and postulated that there was such a thing as an indivisible particle.

demotic writing The second of two basic forms of ancient Egyptian writing. Demotic was a cursive script written with ink on papyrus, on pottery, or on other absorbent objects. It was the most common and practical form of writing in Egypt and was used for administrative record keeping and in private or pseudo-private forms like letters and works of literature. *See also* Hieroglyphs.

developing world Term applied to countries collectively called the Third World during the cold war and seeking to develop viable nation-states and prosperous economies.

Devshirme System of taking non-Muslim children in place of taxes in order to educate them in Ottoman Muslim ways and prepare them for service in the sultan's bureaucracy.

Dhamma Moral code espoused by Aśoka in the Kalinga edict, which was meant to apply to all—Buddhists, Brahmans, and Greeks alike.

***Dhimma* system** Ottoman law that permitted followers of religions other than Islam, such as Armenian Christians, Greek Orthodox Christians, and Jews, to choose their own religious leaders and to settle internal disputes within their religious communities as long as they accepted Islam's political dominion.

dhows Ships used by Arab seafarers; the dhow's large sails were rigged to maximize the capture of wind.

Dien Bien Phu (1954) Defining battle in the war between French colonialists and the Viet Minh that secured North Vietnam for Ho Chi Minh and his army and left the south to form its own government to be supported by France and the United States.

Din-I-llahi "House of worship" in which the Mughal emperor Akbar engaged in religious debate with Hindu, Muslim, Jain, Parsi, and Christian theologians.

Diogenes Greek philosopher who lived from 412 to 323 BCE and who espoused a doctrine of self-sufficiency and freedom from social laws and customs. He rejected cultural norms as out of tune with nature and therefore false.

Directory Temporary military committee that took over the affairs of the state of France in 1795 from the radicals and held control until the coup of Napoleon Bonaparte.

divination The interpretation of rituals used to communicate the wishes of gods or royal ancestors to foretell future events. Divination was used to legitimize royal authority and demand tribute.

Djoser Ancient Egyptian king who reigned from 2630 to 2611 BCE. He was the second king of the Third Dynasty and celebrated the Sed festival in his tomb complex at Saqqara.

domestication Bringing a wild animal or plant under human control.

Dominion in the British Commonwealth Canadian promise to keep up the country's fealty to the British crown, even after its independence in 1867. Later applied to Australia and New Zealand.

Dong Zhongshu Emperor Wu's chief minister, who advocated a more powerful view of Confucius by promoting texts that focused on Confucius as a man who possessed aspects of divinity.

double-outrigger canoes Vessels used by early Austronesians to cross the Taiwan Straits and colonize islands in the Pacific. These sturdy canoes could cover over 120 miles per day.

Duma Russian parliament.

Dutch learning Broad term for European teachings that were strictly regulated by the shoguns inside Japan.

dynastic cycle Political narrative in which influential families vied for supremacy. Upon gaining power, they legitimated their authority by claiming to be the heirs of previous grand dynasts and by preserving or revitalizing the ancestors' virtuous governing ways. This continuity conferred divine support.

dynasty Hereditary ruling family that passed control from one generation to the next.

Earth Summit (1992) Meeting in Rio de Janeiro between many of the world's governments in an effort to address international environmental problems.

East India Company (1600–1858) British charter company created to outperform Portuguese and Spanish traders in the Far East; in the eighteenth century the company became, in effect, the ruler of a large part of India.

Eastern Front Battlefront between Berlin and Moscow during World War I and World War II.

Edict of Nantes (1598) Edict issued by Henry IV to end the French Wars of Religion. The edict declared France a Catholic country but tolerated some Protestant worship.

Egyptian Middle Kingdom Period of Egyptian history lasting from about 2040 to 1640 BCE, characterized by a consolidation of power and building activity in Upper Egypt.

Eiffel Tower Steel monument completed in 1889 for the Paris Exposition. It was twice the height of any other building at the time.

eight-legged essay Highly structured essay form with eight parts, required on Chinese civil service examinations.

Ekklesia Church or early gathering committed to leaders chosen by God and fellow believers.

Ekpe Powerful slave trade institution that organized the supply and purchase of slaves inland from the Gulf of Guinea in West Africa.

Elamites A people with their capital in the upland valley of modern Fars who became a cohesive polity that incorporated transhumant people of the Zagros Mountains. A group of Elamites who migrated south and west into Mesopotamia helped conquer the Third Dynasty of Ur in 2400 BCE.

empire Group of states or different ethnic groups under a single sovereign power.

Enabling Act (1933) Emergency act passed by the Reichstag (German parliament) that helped transform Hitler from Germany's chancellor, or prime minister, into a dictator following the suspicious burning of the Reichstag building and a suspension of civil liberties.

enclosure A movement in which landowners took control of lands that traditionally had been common property serving local needs.

encomenderos Commanders of the labor services of the colonized peoples in Spanish America.

encomiendas Grants from European Spanish governors to control the labor services of colonized people.

Endeavor Ship of Captain James Cook, whose celebrated voyages to the South Pacific in the late eighteenth century supplied Europe with information about the plants, birds, landscapes, and people of this uncharted territory.

Engels, Friedrich (1820–1895) German social and political philosopher who collaborated with Karl Marx on many publications, including *The Communist Manifesto*.

English Navigation Act of 1651 Act stipulating that only English ships could carry goods between the mother country and its colonies.

English Peasants' Revolt (1381) Uprising of serfs and free farm workers that began as a protest against a tax levied to raise money for a war on France. The revolt was suppressed but led to the gradual emergence of a free peasantry as labor shortages made it impossible to keep peasants bound to the soil.

enlightened absolutists Seventeenth- and eighteenth-century monarchs who claimed to rule rationally and in the best interests of their subjects and who hired loyal bureaucrats to implement the knowledge of the new age.

Enlightenment Intellectual movement in eighteenth-century Europe stressing natural laws and reason as the basis of authority.

entrepôts Trading stations at the borders between communities, which made exchange possible among many different partners. Long-distance traders could also replenish their supplies at these stations.

Epicurus Greek philosopher who espoused emphasis on the self. He lived from 341 to 279 BCE and founded a school in Athens called The Garden. He stressed the importance of sensation, teaching that pleasurable sensations were good and painful sensations bad. Members of his school sought to find peace and relaxation by avoiding unpleasantness or suffering.

Estates-General French quasi-parliamentary body called in 1789 to deal with the financial problems that afflicted France. It had not met since 1614.

Etruscans A dominant people on the Italian peninsula until the fourth century BCE. The Etruscan states were part of the foundation of the Roman Empire.

eunuchs Loyal and well-paid men who were surgically castrated as youths and remained in service to the caliph or emperor. Both Abbasid and Tang rulers relied for protection on a cadre of eunuchs.

Eurasia The combined area of Europe and Asia.

European Union (EU) International body organized after World War II as an attempt at reconciliation between Germany and the rest of Europe. It initially aimed to forge closer industrial cooperation. Eventually, through various treaties, many European states relinquished some of their sovereignty, and the cooperation became a full-fledged union with a single currency, the euro, and with a somewhat less powerful common European parliament.

evolution Process by which the different species of the world—its plants and animals—make changes in response to their environment that enable them to survive and increase in numbers.

Exclusion Act of 1882 U.S. congressional act prohibiting nearly all immigration from China to the United States; fueled by animosity toward Chinese workers in the American West.

Ezo Present-day Hokkaido, Japan's fourth main island.

Fascism Mass political movement founded by Benito Mussolini that emphasized nationalism, militarism, and the omnipotence of the state.

Fascists Radical right-wing group of disaffected veterans that formed around Mussolini in 1919 and a few years later came to power in Rome.

Fatehpur Sikri Mughal emperor Akbar's temporary capital near Agra.

Fatimids Shiite dynasty that ruled parts of the Islamic Empire beginning in the tenth century CE. They were based in Egypt and founded the city of Cairo.

February Revolution (1917) The first of two uprisings of the Russian Revolution, which led to the end of the Romanov dynasty.

Federal Deposit Insurance Corporation (FDIC) Organization created in 1933 to guarantee all bank deposits up to $5,000 as part of the New Deal in the United States.

Federal Republic of Germany (1949–1990) Country formed of the areas occupied by the Allies after World War II. Also known as West Germany, this country experienced rapid demilitarization, democratization, and integration into the world economy.

Federal Reserve Act (1913) U.S. legislation that created a series of boards to monitor the supply and demand of the nation's money.

Federalists Supporters of the ratification of the U.S. Constitution, which was written to replace the Articles of Confederation.

feminist movements Movements that called for equal treatment for men and women—equal pay and equal opportunities for obtaining jobs and advancement. Feminism arose mainly in Europe and in North America in the 1960s and then became global in the 1970s.

Ferangi Arabic word meaning "Frank," which was used to describe Crusaders.

Fertile Crescent Site of the world's first agricultural revolution; an area in Southwest Asia, bounded by the Mediterranean Sea in the west and the Zagros Mountains in the east.

feudalism System instituted in medieval Europe after the collapse of the Carolingian Empire (814 CE) whereby each peasant was under the authority of a lord.

fiefdoms Medieval economic and political units.

First World Term invented during the cold war to refer to western Europe and North America (also known as the "free world" or the West); Japan later joined this group. Following the principles of liberal modernism, First World states sought to organize the world on the basis of capitalism and democracy.

Five Pillars of Islam The five tenets, or main aspects, of Islamic practice: testification or bearing witness that there is no God other than God (Allah, in Arabic) and that Muhammad is the messenger of God; praying five times a day; fasting from sunup to sundown every day during Ramadan (a month on the Islamic calendar); giving alms; and making a pilgrimage to Mecca.

Five-Year Plan Soviet effort launched under Stalin in 1928 to replace the market with a state-owned and state-managed economy, to promote rapid economic development over a five-year period of time and thereby "catch and overtake" the leading capitalist countries. The First Five-Year Plan was followed by the Second Five-Year Plan (1933–1937), and so on, until the collapse of the Soviet Union in 1991.

Flagellants European social group that came into existence during the bubonic plague in the fourteenth century; they believed that the plague was the wrath of God.

floating population Poor migrant workers in China who supplied labor under Emperor Wu.

Fluitschips Dutch shipping vessels that could carry heavy bulky cargo with relatively small crews.

flying cash Letters of exchange—early predecessors of paper cash instead of coins—first developed by guilds in the northwestern Shanxi. By the thirteenth century, paper money had eclipsed coins.

Fondûqs Complexes in caravan cities that included hostels, storage houses, offices, and temples.

Forbidden City Palace city of the Ming and Qing dynasties.

Force Publique Colonial army used to maintain order in the Belgian Congo; during the early stages of King Leopold's rule, it was responsible for bullying local communities.

Fourierism Form of utopian socialism based on the ideas of Charles Fourier (1772–1837). Fourier envisioned communes where work was made enjoyable and systems of production and distribution were run without merchants. His ideas appealed to the middle class, especially women, as a higher form of Christian communalism.

free labor Wage-paying rather than slave labor.

free markets Unregulated markets.

Free Officers Movement Secret organization of Egyptian junior military officers who came to power in a coup d'état in 1952, forced King Faruq to abdicate, and consolidated their own control through dissolving the parliament, banning opposing parties, and rewriting the constitution.

free trade Domestic and international trade unencumbered by tariff barriers, quotas, and fees.

Front de Libération Nationale (FLN) Algerian anticolonial, nationalist party that waged an eight-year war against French troops, beginning in 1854, that forced nearly all of the 1 million colonists to leave.

Fulani Muslim group in West Africa that carried out religious revolts at the end of the eighteenth and the beginning of the nineteenth centuries in an effort to return to the pure Islam of the past.

fur trade Trading of animal pelts (especially beaver skins) by Indians for European goods in North America.

Gandharan art Buddhist sculptures, particularly from the northern Kushan territory, that show a high degree of Greek and Roman influences.

Gandhi, Mohandhas Karamchand (Mahatma) (1869–1948) Indian leader who led a nonviolent struggle for India's independence from Britain.

garrisons Military bases inside cities; often used for political purposes, such as protecting rulers and putting down domestic revolts or enforcing colonial rule.

garrison towns Stations for soldiers originally established in strategic locations to protect territorial acquisition. Eventually, they became towns. Alexander the Great's garrison towns evolved into cities that served as centers from which Hellenistic culture was spread to his easternmost territories.

gauchos Argentine, Brazilian, and Uruguayan cowboys who wanted a decentralized federation, with autonomy for their provinces and respect for their way of life.

Gdansk shipyard Site of mass strikes in Poland that led in 1980 to the formation of the first independent trade union, Solidarity, in the communist bloc.

gendered relations A relatively recent development that implies roles emerged only with the appearance of modern humans and perhaps Neanderthals. When humans began to think imaginatively and in complex symbolic ways and give voice to their insights, perhaps around 150,000 years ago, gender categories began to crystallize.

genealogy History of the descent of a person or family from a distant ancestor.

Geneva Peace Conference (1954) International conference to restore peace in Korea and Indochina. The chief participants were the United States, the Soviet Union, Great Britain, France, the People's Republic of China, North Korea, South Korea, Vietnam, the Viet Minh party, Laos, and Cambodia. The conference resulted in the division of North and South Vietnam.

Genoa One of two Italian cities (the other was Venice) that linked Europe, Africa, and Asia as nodes of commerce in 1300. Genoese ships linked the Mediterranean to the coast of Flanders through consistent routes along the Atlantic coasts of Spain, Portugal, and France.

German Democratic Republic Nation founded from the Soviet zone of occupation of Germany after World War II; also known as East Germany.

German Social Democratic Party Founded in 1875, the most powerful socialist party in Europe before 1917.

Ghana The most celebrated medieval political kingdom in West Africa.

Ghost Dance American Indian ritual performed in the nineteenth century in the hope of restoring the world to precolonial conditions.

Gilgamesh Heroic narrative written in the Babylonian dialect of Semitic Akkadian. This story and others like it were meant to circulate and unify the kingdom.

Girondins Liberal revolutionary group that supported the creation of a constitutional monarchy during the early stages of the French Revolution.

global warming Release into the air of human-made carbons that contribute to rising temperatures worldwide.

globalization Development of integrated worldwide cultural and economic structures.

globalizing empires Empires, such as the Han and the Roman, that covered immense amounts of territory, included huge, diverse populations, exerted influence beyond their own borders, and worked to integrate conquered peoples.

Gold Coast Name that European mariners and merchants gave to that part of West Africa from which gold was exported. This area was conquered by the British in the nineteenth century and became a British colony; upon independence, it became Ghana.

Goths One of the groups of "barbarian" migrants into Roman territory in the fourth century CE.

government schools Schools founded by the Han dynasty to provide an adequate number of officials to fill positions in the administrative bureaucracy. The Imperial University had 30,000 members by the second century BCE.

Gracchus brothers Two tribunes, the brothers Tiberius and Gaius Gracchus, who in 133 and 123–21 BCE attempted to institute land reforms that would guarantee all of Rome's poor citizens a basic amount of land that would qualify them for army service. Both men were assassinated.

Grand Canal Created in 486 BCE, a thousand-mile-long connector between the Yellow and Yangzi rivers, linking the north and south, respectively.

grand unity Guiding political idea embraced by Qin rulers and ministers, with an eye toward joining the states of the Central Plain into one empire and centralizing administration.

"Greased cartridge" controversy Controversy spawned by the rumor that cow and pig fat had been used to grease the shotguns of the sepoys in the British army in India. Believing that this was a British attempt to defile their religion and speed their conversion to Christianity, the sepoys mutinied against the British officers.

Great Depression Worldwide depression following the U.S. stock market crash on October 29, 1929.

great divide The division between economically developed nations and less developed nations.

Great East Asia Co-Prosperity Sphere Term used by the Japanese during the 1930s and 1940s to refer to Hong Kong, Singapore, Malaya, Burma, and other states that they seized during their run for expansion.

Great Flood One of many traditional Mesopotamian stories that were transmitted orally from one generation to another before being recorded. The Sumerian King List refers to this crucial event in Sumerian memory and identity. The Great Flood narrative assigned responsibility for Uruk's demise to the gods.

Great Game Competition over areas such as Turkistan, Persia (present-day Iran), and Afghanistan. The British (in India) and the Russians believed that controlling these areas was crucial to preventing their enemies' expansion.

Great League of Peace and Power Iroquois Indian alliance that united previously warring communities.

Great Leap Forward (1958–1961) Plan devised by Mao Zedong to achieve rapid agricultural and industrial growth in China. The plan failed miserably and more than 20 million people died.

great plaza at Isfahan The center of Safavid power in the seventeenth century created by Shah Abbas (r. 1587–1629) to represent the unification of trade, government, and religion under one supreme political authority.

Great Proletarian Cultural Revolution (1966–1976) Mass mobilization of urban Chinese youth inaugurated by Mao Zedong in an attempt to reinvigorate the Chinese revolution and to prevent the development of a bureaucratized Soviet style of communism; with this movement, Mao turned against his longtime associates in the communist party.

Great Trek Afrikaner migration to the interior of Africa after the British abolished slavery in the empire in 1833.

Great War (August 1914–November 1918) A total war involving the armies of Britain, France, and Russia (the Allies) against those of Germany, Austria-Hungary, and the Ottoman Empire (the Central Powers). Italy joined the Allies in 1915, and the United States joined them in 1917, helping tip the balance in favor of the Allies, who also drew upon the populations and material of their colonial possessions. Also known as World War I.

Greek Orthodoxy Enduring form of Christianity that used the framework of the "Roman" state inherited from Constantine and Justinian to protect itself from Roman Catholicism and Muslim forces. The Greek Orthodox capital was Constantinople and its spiritual empire included the Russian peoples, Baltic Slavs, and peoples living in southwest Asia.

Greek philosophers "Wisdom-lovers" of the ancient Greek city-states, including Socrates, Plato, Aristotle, and others, who pondered such issues as self-knowledge, political engagement and withdrawal, and the order of the world.

Greenbacks Members of the American political party of the late nineteenth century that worked to advance the interest of farmers by promoting cheap money.

griots Counselors and other officials to the royal family in African kingships. They were also responsible for the preservation and transmission of oral histories and repositories of knowledge.

Group Areas Act (1950) Act that divided South Africa into separate racial and tribal areas and required Africans to live in their own separate communities, including the "homelands."

guerrillas Portuguese and Spanish peasant bands who resisted the revolutionary and expansionist efforts of Napoleon; after the French word *guerre*.

guest workers Migrants looking for temporary employment abroad.

Gulag Administrative name for the vast system of forced labor camps under the Soviet regime; it originated in a small monastery near the Arctic Circle and spread throughout the Soviet Union and to other Soviet-style socialist countries. Penal labor was required of both ordinary criminals (rapists, murderers, thieves) and those accused of political crimes (counter-revolution, anti-Soviet agitation).

Gulf War (1991) Armed conflict between Iraq and a coalition of thirty-two nations, including the United States, Britain, Egypt, France, and Saudi Arabia. It was started by Iraq's invasion of Kuwait, which it had long claimed, on August 2, 1990.

gunpowder Explosive powder. By 1040, the first gunpowder recipes were being written down. Over the next 200 years, Song entrepreneurs invented several incendiary devices and techniques for controlling explosions.

gunpowder empires Muslim empires of the Ottomans, Safavids, and

Mughals that used cannonry and gunpowder to advance their military causes.

Guomindang Nationalist Party of China, founded just before World War I by Sun Yat-sen and later led by Chiang Kai-shek.

Habsburg Empire Ruling house of Austria, which once ruled both Spain and central Europe but came to settle in lands along the Danube River; it played a prominent role in European affairs for many centuries. In 1867, the Habsburg Empire was reorganized into the Austro-Hungarian Dual Monarchy, and in 1918 it collapsed.

Hadith Sayings attributed to the Prophet Muhammad and his early converts. Used to guide the behavior of Muslim peoples.

Hagia Sophia Enormous and impressive church sponsored by Justinian and built starting in 532 CE. At the time, it was the largest church in the world.

Hajj Pilgrimage to Mecca; an obligation for Muslims.

Hammurapi's Code Legal code created by Hammurapi, the most famous of the Mesopotamian rulers, who reigned from 1792 to 1750 BCE. Hammurapi sought to create social order by centralizing state authority and creating a grand legal structure that embodied paternal justice. The code was quite stratified, dividing society into three classes: free men, dependent men, and slaves, each with distinct rights and responsibilities.

Han agrarian ideal Guiding principle for the free peasantry that made up the base of Han society. In this system, peasants were honored for their labors, while merchants were subjected to a range of controls, including regulations on luxury consumption, and were belittled for not engaging in physical labor.

Han Chinese Inhabitants of China proper who considered others to be outsiders. They felt that they were the only authentic Chinese.

Han Fei Chinese state minister who lived from 280 to 223 BCE; he was a proponent and follower of Xunzi.

Han military Like its Roman counterpart, a ruthless military machine that expanded the empire and created stable conditions that permitted the safe transit of goods by caravans. Emperor Wu heavily influenced the transformation of the military forces and reinstituted a policy that made military service compulsory.

Hangzhou City and former provincial seaport that became the political center of the Chinese people in their ongoing struggles with northern steppe nomads. It was also one of China's gateways to the rest of the world by way of the South China Sea.

Hannibal Great Roman general from Carthage whose campaigns in the third century BCE swept from Spain toward the Italian peninsula. He crossed the Pyrenees and the Alps mountain ranges with war elephants. He was unable, however, to defeat the Romans in 217 BCE.

Harappa One of two cities that, by 2500 BCE, began to take the place of villages throughout the Indus River valley (the other was Mohenjo Daro). Each covered an area of about 250 acres and probably housed 35,000 residents.

harem Secluded women's quarters in Muslim households.

Harlem Renaissance Cultural movement in the 1920s that was based in Harlem, a part of New York City with a large African American population. The movement gave voice to black novelists, poets, painters, and musicians, many of whom used their art to protest racism; also referred to as the "New Negro movement."

harnesses Tools made from wood, bone, bronze, and iron for steering and controlling chariot horses. Harnesses discovered by archaeologists reveal the evolution of headgear from simple mouth bits to full bridles with headpiece, mouthpiece, and reins.

Hatshepsut Leader known as ancient Egypt's most powerful woman ruler. Hatshepsut served as regent for her young son, Thutmosis III, whose reign began in 1479 BCE. She remained co-regent until her death.

Haussmannization Redevelopment and beautification of urban centers; named after the city planner who "modernized" mid-nineteenth-century Paris.

Hegira "Emigration" of Muhammad and his followers out of a hostile Mecca to Yathrib, a city that was later called Medina. The year in which this journey took place, 622 CE, is also year 1 of the Islamic calendar.

Heian period Period from 794 to 1185, during which began the pattern of regents ruling Japan in the name of the sacred emperor.

Hellenism Process by which the individuality of the cultures of the earlier Greek city-states gave way to a uniform culture that stressed the common identity of all who embraced Greek ways. This culture emphasized the common denominators of language, style, and politics to which anyone, anywhere in the Afro-Eurasian world, could have access.

hieroglyphs One of two basic forms of Egyptian writing that were used in conjunction throughout antiquity. Hieroglyphs are pictorial symbols; the term derives from a Greek word meaning "sacred carving"—they were employed exclusively in temple, royal, and divine contexts. *See also* Demotic writing.

Hijra Tradition of Islam, whereby one withdraws from one's community to create another, more holy, one. The practice is based on the Prophet Muhammad's withdrawal from the city of Mecca to Medina in 622 CE.

Hinayana (Lesser Vehicle) Buddhism Form of Buddhism that accepted the divinity of Buddha himself but not of demigods, or bodhisattvas.

Hinduism A refashioning of the ancient Brahmanic Vedic religion, bringing it in accord with rural life and agrarian values. It emerged as the dominant faith in Indian society in the third century CE. Believers became vegetarians and adopted rituals of self-sacrifice. Three major deities—Brahma, Vishnu, and Siva—formed a trinity representing the three phases of the universe (birth, existence, and destruction, respectively) and the three expressions of the eternal self, or *atma*.

Hindu revivalism Movement to reconfigure traditional Hinduism to be less diverse and more amenable to producing a narrowed version of Indian tradition.

Hiroshima Japanese port devastated by an atomic bomb on August 6, 1945.

Hitler, Adolf (1889–1945) German dictator and leader of the Nazi Party who seized power in Germany after its economic collapse in the Great Depression. Hitler and his Nazi regime started World War II in Europe and systematically murdered Jews and other non-Aryan groups in the name of racial purity.

Hittites The Hittites were a chariot warrior group of Anatolia, which spread east to northern Syria, though they eventually faced weaknesses in their own homeland. Their heyday was marked by the reign of the king Supiliulimua (1380 to 1345 BCE), who preserved the Hittites' influence on the balance of power in the region between Mesopotamia and the Nile.

Holocaust Deliberate racial extermination of the Jews by the Nazis that claimed around 6 million European Jews.

Holy Roman Empire Enormous realm that encompassed much of Europe and aspired to be the Christian successor state to the Roman Empire. In the time of the Habsburg dynasts, the empire was a loose confederation of principalities that obeyed an emperor elected by elite lower-level sovereigns. Despite its size, the empire never effectively centralized power; it was split into Austrian and Spanish factions when Charles V abdicated to his sons in 1556.

Holy Russia Name applied to Muscovy and then to the Russian Empire by Slavic Eastern Orthodox clerics who were appalled by the Muslim conquest in 1453 of Constantinople (the capital of Byzantium and of eastern Christianity) and who were hopeful that Russia would become the new protector of the faith.

home charges Fees India was forced to pay to Britain as its colonial master; these fees included interest on railroad loans, salaries to colonial officers, and the maintenance of imperial troops outside India.

hominids Humanlike beings who walked erect and preceded modern humans.

Homo A word used by scientists to differentiate between pre-human and "true human" species.

Homo caudatus "Tailed man," believed by some European Enlightenment thinkers to be an early species of humankind.

Homo erectus Species that emerged about 1.5 million years ago and had a large brain and walked truly upright. *Homo erectus* means "Standing man."

Homo habilis Scientific term for "Skillful man." Tool-making ability truly made *Homo habilis* the forerunners, though very distant, of modern humans.

Homo sapiens The first humans; they emerged in a small region of Africa about 200,000 years ago and migrated out of Africa about 100,000 years ago. They had bigger brains and greater dexterity than previous hominid species, whom they eventually eclipsed.

homogeneity Uniformity of the languages, customs, and religion of a particular people or place. It can also be demonstrated by a consistent calendar, set of laws, administrative practices, and rituals.

horses Animals used by full-scale nomadic communities to dominate the steppe lands in western Afro-Eurasia by the second millennium BCE. Horse-riding nomads moved their large herds across immense tracts of land within zones defined by rivers, mountains, and other natural geographical features. In the arid zones of central Eurasia, the nomadic economies made horses a crucial component of survival.

Huguenots French Protestants who endured severe persecution in the sixteenth and seventeenth centuries.

humanism The Renaissance aspiration to know more about the human experience beyond what the Christian scriptures offered by reaching back into ancient Greek and Roman texts.

Hundred Days' Reform (1898) Abortive modernizing reform program of the Qing government of China.

hunting and gathering Lifestyle in which food is acquired through hunting animals, fishing, and foraging for wild berries, nuts, fruit, and grains, rather than planting crops, vines, or trees. As late as 1500, as much as 15 percent of the world's population still lived by this method.

Hyksos A western Semitic-speaking people whose name means "Rulers of Foreign Lands"; they overthrew the unstable Thirteenth Dynasty in Egypt around 1640 BCE. The Hyksos had mastered the art of horse chariots, and with those chariots and their superior bronze axes and composite bows (made of wood, horn, and sinew), they were able to defeat the pharaoh's foot soldiers.

Ibn Sina Philosopher and physician who lived from 980 to 1037 CE. He was also schooled in the Quran, geometry, literature, and Indian and Euclidian mathematics.

ideology Dominant set of ideas of a widespread culture or movement.

Il Duce Term designating the fascist Italian leader Benito Mussolini.

Iliad Epic Greek poem about the Trojan War, composed several centuries after the events it describes. It was based on oral tales passed down for generations.

Il-khanate Mongol-founded dynasty in thirteenth-century Persia.

Imam Muslim religious leader and politico-religious descendant of Ali; believed by some to have a special relationship with Allah.

imperialism Acquisition of new territories by a state and the incorporation of these territories into a political system as subordinate colonies.

Imperial University University founded in 136 BCE by Emperor Wu, where important discoveries such as the rational diagnoses of the body's functions, the magnetic compass, and high-quality paper were developed; significant as a mechanism by which the Han state inculcated Confucian thought into the elite.

Imperium Latin word used to express Romans' power and command over their subjects. It is the basis of the English words *empire* and *imperialism*.

Inca Empire Empire of Quechua-speaking rulers in the Andean valley of Cuzco that encompassed a population of 4 to 6 million. The Incas lacked a clear inheritance system, causing an internal split that Pizarro's forces exploited in 1533.

Indian Institutes of Technology (IIT) Institutions originally designed as engineering schools to expand knowledge and to modernize India, which produced a whole generation of pioneering computer engineers, many of whom moved to the United States.

Indian National Congress Formed in 1885, a political party deeply committed to constitutional methods, industrialization, and cultural nationalism.

Indian National Muslim League Founded in 1906, an organization dedicated to advancing the political interests of Muslims in India.

Indo-Greek Fusion of Indian and Greek culture in the area under the control of the Bactrians, in the northwestern region of India, around 200 BCE.

Indu What we would today call India. Called "Indu" by Xuanzang, a Chinese Buddhist pilgrim who visited the area in the 630s and 640s CE.

indulgences Church-sponsored fundraising mechanism that gave certification that one's sins had been forgiven in return for money.

industrial revolution Gradual accumulation and diffusion of old and new technical knowledge that led to major economic changes in Britain, northwestern Europe, and North America, catapulting these countries ahead of the rest of the world in manufacturing and agricultural output and standards of living.

industrious revolution Dramatic economic change in which households that had traditionally produced for themselves decided to work harder and longer hours in order to produce more for the market, which enabled them to increase their income and standard of living. Areas that underwent the industrious revolution shifted from peasant farming to specialized production for the market.

innovation Creation of a new method that allowed humans to make better adaptations to their environment such as the making of new tools.

Inquisition Tribunal of the Roman Catholic Church that enforced religious orthodoxy during the Protestant Reformation.

internal and external alchemy In Daoist ritual, use of trance and meditation or chemicals and drugs, respectively, to cause transformations in the self.

International Monetary Fund (IMF) Agency founded in 1944 to help restore financial order in Europe and the rest of the world, to revive international trade, and to support the financial concerns of Third World governments.

invisible hand As described in Adam Smith's *The Wealth of Nations*, the idea that the operations of a free market produce economic efficiency and economic benefits for all.

iron Malleable metal found in combined forms almost everywhere in the world; it became the most important and widely used metal in world history after the Bronze Age.

Iron Curtain Term popularized by Winston Churchill after World War II to refer to a rift, or an iron curtain, that divided western Europe, under American influence, from eastern Europe, under the domination of the Soviet Union.

irrigation Technological advance whereby water delivery systems and water sluices in floodplains or riverine areas were channeled or redirected and used to nourish soil.

Islam A religion that dates to 610 CE, when Muhammad believed God came to him in a vision. Islam ("submission"—in this case, to the will of God) requires its followers to act righteously, to submit themselves to the one and only true God, and to care for the less fortunate. Muhammad's most insistent message was the oneness of God, a belief that has remained central to the Islamic faith ever since.

Jacobins Radical French political group that came into existence during the French Revolution and executed the French king and sought to remake French culture.

Jacquerie (1358) French peasant revolt in defiance of feudal restrictions.

jade The most important precious substance in East Asia. Jade was associated with goodness, purity, luck, and virtue, and was carved into such items as ceremonial knives, blade handles, religious objects, and elaborate jewelry.

Jagat Seths Enormous trading and banking empire in eastern India.

Jainism Along with Buddhism, one of the two systems of thought developed in the seventh century BCE that set themselves up against Brahmanism. Its founder, Vardhamana Mahavira, taught that the universe obeys its own everlasting rules that no god or other supernatural being could affect. The purpose of life was to purify one's soul in order to attain a state of permanent bliss, which could be accomplished through self-denial and the avoidance of harming other creatures.

Janissaries Corps of infantry soldiers recruited as children from the Christian provinces of the Ottoman Empire and brought up with intense loyalty to the Ottoman state and its sultan. The Ottoman sultan used these forces to clip local autonomy and to serve as his personal bodyguards.

Jati Social groups as defined by Hinduism's caste system.

Jesuits Religious order founded by Ignatius Loyola to counter the inroads of the Protestant Reformation; the Jesuits, or the Society of Jesus, were active in politics, education, and missionary work.

Jihad Literally, "striving" or "struggle." This word also connotes military efforts or "striving in the way of God." It also came to mean spiritual struggles against temptation or inner demons, especially in Sufi, or mystical, usage.

Jih-pen Chinese for "Japan."

Jim Crow laws Laws that codified racial segregation and inequality in the southern part of the United States after the Civil War.

Jizya Special tax that non-Muslims were forced to pay to their Islamic rulers in return for which they were given security and property and granted cultural autonomy.

jong Large ocean-going vessels, built by Southeast Asians, which plied the regional trade routes from the fifteenth century to the early sixteenth century.

Judah The southern kingdom of David, which had been an Assyrian vassal until 612 BCE, when it became a vassal of Assyria's successor, Babylon, against whom the people of Judah rebelled, resulting in the destruction of Jerusalem in the sixth century BCE.

Julius Caesar Formidable Roman general who lived from 100 to 44 BCE. He was also a man of letters, a great orator, and a ruthless military man who boasted that his campaigns had led to the deaths of over a million people.

junks Trusty seafaring vessels used in the South China Seas after 1000 CE. These helped make shipping by sea less dangerous.

Justinian Roman or Byzantine emperor who ascended to the throne in 527 CE. In addition to his many building projects and military expeditions, he issued a new law code.

Kabuki Theater performance that combined song, dance, and skillful staging to dramatize conflicts between duty and passion in Tokogawa, Japan.

Kamikaze Japanese for "divine winds" or typhoons; such a storm saved Japan from a Mongol attack.

Kanun Highly detailed system of Ottoman administrative law that jurists developed to deal with matters not treated in the religious law of Islam.

Karim Loose confederation of shippers banding together to protect convoys.

karma Literally "fate" or "action," in Confucian thought; this is a universal principle of cause and effect.

Kassites Nomads who entered Mesopotamia from the eastern Zagros Mountains and the Iranian plateau as early as 2000 BCE. They gradually integrated into Babylonian society by officiating at temples. By 1745 BCE, they had asserted order over the region, and they controlled southern Mesopotamia for the next 350 years, creating one of the territorial states.

Keynesian Revolution Post-Depression economic ideas developed by the British economist John Maynard Keynes, wherein the state took a greater role in managing the economy, stimulating it by increasing the money supply and creating jobs.

KGB Soviet political police and spy agency, formed as the Cheka not long after the Bolshevik coup in October 1917. Grew to more than 750,000 operatives with military rank by the 1980s.

Khan Ruler who was acclaimed at an assembly of elites and supposedly descended from Chinngis Khan on the male line; those not descended from Chinggis continually faced challenges to their legitimacy.

Khanate Major political unit of the vast Mongol empire. There were four Khanates, including the Yuan Empire in China, forged by Chinggis Khan's grandson Kubilai.

Kharijites Radical sect from the early days of Islam. The Kharijites seceded from the "party of Ali" (who themselves came to be known as the Shiites) because of disagreements over succession to the role of the caliph. They were known for their strict militant piety.

Khmers A people who created the most powerful empire in Southwest Asia between the tenth and thirteenth centuries in what is modern-day Cambodia.

Khomeini, Ayatollah Ruhollah (1902–1989) Iranian religious leader who used his traditional Islamic education and his training in Muslim ethics to accuse the shah's government of gross violations of Islamic norms. He also identified the shah's ally, America, as the great Satan. The shah fled the country in 1979; in his wake, Khomeini established a theocratic state ruled by a council of Islamic clerics.

Khufu A pyramid, among those put up in the Fourth Dynasty in ancient Egypt (2575–2465 BCE), which is the largest stone structure in the world. It is in an area called Giza, just outside modern-day Cairo.

Khusro I Anoshirwan Sasanian emperor who reigned from 530 to 579 CE. He was a model ruler and was seen as the personification of justice.

Kiev City that became one of the greatest cities of Europe after the eleventh century. It was built to be a small-scale Constantinople on the Dnieper.

Kikuyu Kenya's largest ethnic group; organizers of a revolt against the British in the 1950s.

King, Martin Luther, Jr. (1929–1968) Civil rights leader who borrowed his most effective weapon—the commitment to nonviolent protest and the appeal to conscience—from Gandhi.

Kingdom of Awadh One of the most prized lands for annexation and the fertile, opulent, and traditional vestige of Mughal rule in India.

Kingdom of Jerusalem What Crusaders set out to liberate when they launched their attack.

Kizilbash Mystical, Turkish-speaking tribesmen who facilitated the Safavid rise to power.

Knossos Area in Crete where, during the second millennium BCE, a primary palace town existed.

Koine Greek Common form of Greek that became the international spoken and written language in the Hellenistic world. This was a simpler everyday form of the ancient Greek language.

Koprulu reforms Reforms named after two grand viziers who revitalized the Ottoman Empire in the seventeenth century through administrative and budget trimming as well as by rebuilding the military.

Korean War (1950–1953) Cold war conflict between Soviet-backed North Korea and U.S.- and UN-backed South Korea. The two sides seesawed back and forth over the same boundaries until 1953, when an armistice divided the country at roughly the same spot as at the start of the war. Nothing had been gained. Losses, however, included 33,000 Americans, at least 250,000 Chinese, and up to 3 million Koreans.

Koryo dynasty Leading dynasty of the northern-based Koryo kingdom in Korea. It is from this dynasty that the name "Korea" derives.

Kremlin Once synonymous with the Soviet government; refers to Moscow's walled city center.

Kshatriyas Originally the warrior caste in Vedic society, the dominant clan members and ruling caste who controlled the land.

Ku Klux Klan Racist organization that first emerged in the U.S. South after the Civil War and then gained national strength as a radically traditionalist movement during the 1920s.

Kubilai Khan (1215–1294) Mongol leader who seized southern China after 1260 and founded the Yuan dynasty.

kulak Originally a pejorative word used to designate better-off peasants, the term used in the late 1920s and early 1930s to refer to any peasant, rich or poor, perceived as an opponent of the Soviet regime. Russian for "fist."

Kumarajiva Renowned Buddhist scholar and missionary who lived from 344 to 413 CE. He was brought to China by Chinese regional forces from Kucha, modern-day Xinjiang.

Kushans Northern nomadic group that migrated into South Asia in 50 CE. They unified the tribes of the region and set up the Kushan dynasty. The Kushans' empire embraced a large and diverse territory and played a critical role in the formation of the Silk Roads.

Labour Party Founded in Britain in 1900, the party that represented workers and was based on socialist principles.

laissez-faire The concept that the economy works best when it is left alone—that is, when the state does not regulate or interfere with the workings of the market.

"Land under the Yoke of Ashur" Lands not in Assyria proper, but under its authority; they had to pay the Assyrian Empire exorbitant amounts of tribute.

language System of communication reflecting cognitive abilities. Natural language is generally defined as words arranged in particular sequences to convey meaning and is unique to modern humans.

language families Related tongues with a common ancestral origin; language families contain languages that diverged from one another but share grammatical features and root vocabularies. More than a hundred language families exist.

Laozi Also known as Master Lao; perhaps a contemporary of Confucius, and the person after whom Daoism is named. His thought was elaborated upon by generations of thinkers.

latifundia Broad estates that produced goods for big urban markets, including wheat, grapes, olives, cattle, and sheep.

League of Nations Organization founded after World War I to solve international disputes through arbitration; it was dissolved in 1946 and its assets were transferred to the United Nations.

Legalism Also called Statism, a system of thought about how to live an ordered life. It was developed by Master Xun, or Xunzi (310–237 BCE). It is based on the principle that people, being inherently inclined toward evil, require authoritarian control to regulate their behavior.

Lenin, Nikolai (1870–1924) Leader of the Bolshevik Revolution in Russia and the first leader of the Soviet Union.

Liangzhu Culture spanning centuries from the fourth to the third millennium BCE that represented the last new Stone Age culture in the Yangzi River delta. One of the Ten Thousand States, it was highly stratified and is known for its jade objects.

liberalism Political and social theory that advocates representative government, free trade, and freedom of speech and religion.

limited-liability joint-stock company Company that mobilized capital from a large number of investors, called shareholders, who were not to be held personally liable for financial losses incurred by the company.

Linear A and B Two linear scripts first discovered on Crete in 1900. On the island of Crete and on the mainland areas of Greece, documents of the palace-centered societies were written on clay tablets in these two scripts. Linear A script, apparently written in Minoan, has not yet been deciphered. Linear B was first deciphered in the early 1950s.

"Little Europes" Urban landscapes between 1100 and 1200 composed of castles, churches, and towns in what are today Poland, the Czech Republic, Hungary, and the Baltic States.

Liu Bang Chinese emperor from 206 to 195 BCE; after declaring himself the prince of his home area of Han, in 202 BCE, Liu declared himself the first Han emperor.

llamas Animals similar in utility and function to camels in Afro-Eurasia. Llamas could carry heavy loads for long distances.

Long March (1934–1935) Trek of over 10,000 kilometers by Mao Zedong and his communist followers to establish a new base of operations in northwestern China.

Longshan peoples Peoples who lived in small agricultural and riverine villages in East Asia at the end of the third millennium BCE. They set the stage for the Shang in terms of a centralized state, urban life, and a cohesive culture.

lord Privileged landowner who exercised authority over the people who lived on his land.

lost generation The 17 million former members of the Red Guard and other Chinese youth who were denied education from the late 1960s to the mid-1970s as part of the Chinese government's attempt to prevent political disruptions.

Louisiana Purchase (1803) American purchase of French territory from Napoleon, including much of the present-day United States between the Mississippi River and the Rocky Mountains.

Lucy Relatively intact skeleton of a young adult female australopithecine unearthed in the valley of the Awash River in 1974 by an archaeological team working at a site in present-day Hadar, Ethiopia. The researchers nicknamed the skeleton Lucy. She stood just over three feet tall and walked upright at least some of the time. Her skull contained a brain within the ape size range. Also, her jaw and teeth were humanlike. Lucy's skeleton was relatively complete and at the time, was the oldest hominid skeleton ever discovered.

Luftwaffe German air force.

Luther, Martin (1483–1546) A German monk and theologian who sought to reform the Catholic Church; he believed in salvation through faith alone, the importance of reading Scripture, and the priesthood of all believers. His Ninety-five Theses, which enumerated the abuses by the Catholic Church as well his reforms, started the Protestant Reformation.

Maastricht Treaty (1991) Treaty that formed the European Union, a fully integrated trading and financial bloc with its own bureaucracy and elected representatives.

Ma'at Term used in ancient Egypt to refer to stability or order, the achievement of which was the primary task of Egypt's ruling kings, the pharaohs.

Maccabees Leaders of a riot in Jerusalem in 166 BCE; the riot was a response to a Roman edict outlawing the practice of Judaism.

Madhyamika (Middle Way) Buddhism Chinese branch of Mahayana Buddhism established by Kumarajiva (344–413 CE) that used irony and paradox to show that reason was limited.

madrassas Higher schools of Muslim education that taught law, the Quran, religious sciences, and the regular sciences.

Mahayana (Greater Vehicle) Buddhism School of Buddhist theology that believed that the Buddha was a deity, unlike previous groups that had considered him a wise human being.

Mahdi The "chosen one" in Islam whose appearance was supposed to foretell the end of the world and the final day of reckoning for all people.

maize Grains, the crops that the settled agrarian communities across the Americas cultivated, along with legumes (beans) and tubers (potatoes).

Maji-Maji Revolt (early 1900s) Swahili insurrection against German colonialists; inspired by the belief that those who were anointed with specially blessed water (*maji*) would be immune to bullets. It resulted in 200,000–300,000 African deaths.

Mali Empire West African empire, founded by the legendary king Sundiata in the early thirteenth century. It facilitated thriving commerce, with routes linking the Atlantic Ocean, the Sahara, and beyond.

Mamluks (Arabic for "owned" or "possessed") Military men who ruled Egypt as an independent regime from 1250 until the Ottoman conquest in 1517.

Manaus Opera House Opera house built in the interior of Brazil in a lucrative rubber-growing area at the turn of the twentieth century.

Manchukuo Japanese puppet state in Manchuria in the 1930s.

Manchus Descendants of the Jurchens who helped the Ming army recapture Beijing in 1644 after its seizure by the outlaw Li Zicheng. The Manchus numbered around 1 million but controlled a domain that included perhaps 250 million people. Their rule lasted more than 250 years and became known as the Qing dynasty.

mandate of heaven Ideology established by Zhou dynasts to communicate the moral transfer of power. Originally a pact between the Zhou people and their supreme god, it evolved in the first century BCE into Chinese political doctrine.

Mande A people who lived in the area between the bend in the Senegal River and the bend in the Niger River east to west and from the Senegal River and Bandama River north to south. Also known as the Mandinka. Their civilization emerged around 1100.

Mandela, Nelson (1918–2013) Leader of the African National Congress (ANC) who was imprisoned for more than two decades by the apartheid regime in South Africa for his political beliefs; worldwide protests led to his release in 1990. In 1994 Mandela won the presidency in South Africa's first free mass elections.

Manifest Destiny Belief that it was God's will for the American people to expand their territory and political processes across the North American continent.

manorialism System in which the manor (a lord's home, its associated industry, and surrounding fields) served as the basic unit of economic power; an alternative to feudalism (the hierarchical relationships of king, lords, and peasantry) for thinking about the nature of power in western Europe, 1000–1300.

Mao Zedong (1893–1976) Chinese communist leader who rose to power during the Long March (1934). In 1949, he defeated the Nationalists and established a communist regime in China. Although many of Mao's efforts to transform China, such as the industrialization program of 1958 (known as the Great Leap Forward) and the Cultural Revolution of 1966, failed and brought great suffering to the people, he did instill a new spirit of independence in China and a sense of purpose after many decades of political and economic failure.

maroon community Sanctuary for runaway slaves in the Americas.

Marshall Plan Economic aid package given by the United States to Europe after World War II in hopes of a rapid period of reconstruction and economic gain, thereby securing the countries that received the aid from a communist takeover.

martyrs People executed by the Roman authorities for persisting in their Christian beliefs and refusing to submit to pagan ritual or belief.

Marx, Karl (1818–1883) German philosopher and economist who created Marxism and believed that a revolution of the working classes would overthrow the capitalist order and create a classless society.

Marxism Form of scientific socialism created by Karl Marx and Friedrich Engels that was rooted in a materialist theory of history: what mattered in history were the production of material goods and the ways in which society was organized into classes of producers and exploiters.

mass consumption Increased purchasing power in the early twentieth-century prosperous and mainly middle-class societies, stemming from mass production.

mass culture Distinctive form of popular culture that arose in the wake of World War I. It reflected the tastes of the working and the middle classes, who now had more time and money to spend on entertainment, and relied on new technologies, especially film and radio, which could reach an entire nation's population and consolidate their sense of being a single state.

mass production System in which factories were set up to produce huge quantities of identical products, reflecting the early twentieth-century world's demands for greater volume, faster speed, reduced cost, and standardized output.

Mastaba Word meaning "bench" in Arabic; it refers to a huge flat structure identical to earlier royal tombs of ancient Egypt.

Mau-Mau Revolt (1952–1957) Uprising orchestrated by a Kenyan guerrilla movement; this conflict forced the British to grant independence to the black majority in Kenya.

Mauryan Empire Dynasty extended by the Mauryans from 321 to 184 BCE, from the Indus Valley to the northwest areas of South Asia, in a region previously controlled by Persia. It was the first large-scale empire in South Asia and was to become the model for future Indian empires.

Mawali Non-Arab "clients" to Arab tribes in the early Islamic Empire. Because tribal patronage was so much a part of the Arabian cultural system, non-Arabs who converted to Islam affiliated themselves with a tribe and became clients of that tribe.

Maxim gun European weaponry that was capable of firing many bullets per second; it was used against Africans in the conquest of the continent.

Mayans Civilization that ruled over large stretches of Mesoamerica; it was composed of a series of kingdoms, each built around ritual centers rather than cities. The Mayans engaged neighboring peoples in warfare and trade and expanded borders through tributary relationships. They were not defined by a great ruler or one capital city, but by their shared religious beliefs.

McCarthyism Campaign by Republican senator Joseph McCarthy in the late 1940s and early 1950s to uncover closet communists, particularly in the State Department and in Hollywood.

Meat Inspection Act (1906) Legislation that provided for government supervision of meat-packing operations; it was part of a broader "Progressive" reform movement dedicated to correcting the negative consequences of urbanization and industrialization in the United States.

Mecca Arabian city in which Muhammad was born. Mecca was a trading center and pilgrimage destination in the pre-Islamic and Islamic periods. Exiled in 622 CE because of resistance to his message, Muhammad returned to Mecca in 630 CE and claimed the city for Islam.

Medes Rivals of the Assyrians and the Persians. The Medes inhabited the area from the Zagros Mountains to the modern city of Tehran; known as expert horsemen and archers, they were eventually defeated by the Persians.

megaliths Literally, "great stone"; the word *megalith* is used when describing structures such as Stonehenge. These massive structures are the result of cooperative planning and work.

megarons Large buildings found in Troy (level II) that are the predecessors of the classic Greek temple.

Meiji Empire Empire created under the leadership of Mutsuhito, emperor of Japan from 1868 until 1912. During the Meiji period Japan became a world industrial and naval power.

Meiji Restoration Reign of the Meiji emperor, which was characterized by a new nationalist identity, economic advances, and political transformation.

Mencius Disciple of Confucius who lived from 372 to 289 BCE.

mercantilism Economic theory that drove European empire builders. In this economic system, the world had a fixed amount of wealth, which meant one country's wealth came at the expense of another's. Mercantilism assumed that colonies existed for the sole purpose of enriching the country that controlled the colony.

Mercosur Free-trade pact between the governments of Argentina, Brazil, Paraguay, and Uruguay.

meritocracy Rule by persons of talent.

Meroe Ancient kingdom in what is today Sudan. It flourished for nearly a thousand years, from the fifth century BCE to the fifth century CE.

mestizos Mixed-blood offspring of Spanish settlers and native Indians.

métis Mixed-blood offspring of French settlers and native Indians.

Mexican Revolution (1910) Conflict fueled by the unequal distribution of land and by disgruntled workers; it erupted when political elites split over the succession of General Porfirio Díaz after decades of his rule. The fight lasted over ten years and cost 1 million lives, but it resulted in a widespread reform and a new constitution.

***Mfecane* movement** African political revolts in the first half of the nineteenth century that were caused by the expansionist methods of King Shaka of the Zulu people.

microsocieties Small-scale communities that had little interaction with others. These communities were the norm for peoples living in the Americas and islanders in the Pacific and Aegean from 2000 to 1200 BCE.

migration Long-distance travel for the purpose of resettlement. In the case of early man, the need to move was usually a response to an environmental shift, such as climate change during the Ice Age.

millenarian Believer in the imminent coming of a just and ideal society.

millenarian movement Broad, popular upheaval calling for the restoration of a bygone moral age, often led by charismatic spiritual prophets.

Millets Minority religious communities of the Ottoman Empire.

minaret Slender tower within a mosque from which Muslims are called to prayer.

minbar Pulpit inside a mosque from which Muslim religious speakers broadcast their message to the faithful.

Minoans A people who built a large number of elaborate, independent palace centers on Crete, at Knossos, and elsewhere around 2000 BCE. Named after the legendary King Minos, said to have ruled Crete at the time, they sailed throughout the Mediterranean and by 1600 BCE had planted colonies on many Aegean islands, which in turn became trading and mining centers.

mission civilisatrice Term French colonizers used to refer to France's form of "rationalized" colonial rule, which attempted to bring "civilization" to the "uncivilized."

mitochondrial DNA Form of DNA found outside the nucleus of cells, where it serves as cells' microscopic power packs. Examining mitochondrial DNA enables researchers to measure the genetic variation among living objects, including human beings.

Moche A people who extended their power and increased their wealth at the height of the Chimu Empire over several valleys in what is now Peru.

Model T First automobile, manufactured by the Ford Motor Company of Henry Ford, to be priced reasonably enough to be sold to the masses.

Modernists A generation of exuberant young artists, writers, and scientists in the late nineteenth century who broke with older conventions and sought new ways of seeing and describing the world.

Mohism School of thought in ancient China, named after Mo Di, or Mozi, who lived from 479 to 438 BCE. It emphasized one's obligation to society as a whole, not just to one's immediate family or social circle.

monarchy Political system in which one individual holds supreme power and passes that power on to his or her next of kin.

monasticism Christian way of life that originated in Egypt and was practiced as early as 300 CE in the Mediterranean. The word itself contains the meaning of a person "living alone" without marriage or family.

monetization An economic shift from a barter-based economy to one dependent on coin.

Mongols Combination of nomadic forest and prairie peoples who lived by hunting and livestock herding and were expert horsemen. Beginning in 1206, the Mongols launched a series of conquests that brought far-flung parts of the world together under their rule. By incorporating conquered peoples and adapting some of their customs, the Mongols created a unified empire that stretched from the Pacific Ocean to the shores of the eastern Mediterranean and the southern steppes of Eurasia.

monotheism The belief in only one god.

Moors Term employed by Europeans in the medieval period to refer to Muslim occupants of North Africa, the western Sahara, and the Iberian Peninsula.

mosque Place of worship for the people of Islam.

Mound people Name for the people of Cahokia, since its landscape was dominated by earthen monuments in the shapes of mounds. The mounds were carefully maintained and were the loci from which Cahokians paid respect to spiritual forces. *See also* Cahokia.

Mu Chinese ruler (956–918 BCE) who put forth a formal bureaucratic system of governance, appointing officials, supervisors, and military captains to whom he was not related. He also instituted a formal legal code.

muckrakers Journalists who aimed to expose political and commercial corruption in late-nineteenth- and early twentieth-century America.

Muftis Experts on Muslim religious law.

Mughal Empire One of Islam's greatest regimes. Established in 1526, it was a vigorous, centralized state whose political authority encompassed most of modern-day India. During the sixteenth century, it had a population of between 100 and 150 million.

Muhammad (570–632 CE) Prophet and founder of the Islamic faith. Born in Mecca in Saudi Arabia and orphaned when young, Muhammad lived under the protection of his uncle. His career as a prophet began around 610 CE, with his first experience of spiritual revelation.

Muhammad Ali Ruler of Egypt between 1805 and 1848. He initiated a set of modernizing reforms that sought to make Egypt competitive with the great powers.

mullahs Religious leaders in Iran who in the 1970s led a movement opposing Shah Reza Pahlavi and denounced American materialism and secularism.

multinational corporations Corporations based in many different countries that have global investment, trading, and distribution goals.

Muscovy The principality of Moscow. Originally a mixture of Slavs, Finnish tribes, Turkic speakers, and many others, Muscovy used territorial expansion and commercial networks to consolidate a powerful state and expanded to become the Russian Empire, a huge realm that spanned parts of Europe, much of northern Asia, numerous North Pacific islands, and even—for a time—a corner of North America (Alaska).

Muslim Brotherhood Egyptian organization founded in 1938 by Hassan al-Banna. It attacked liberal democracy as a cover for middle-class, business, and landowning interests and fought for a return to a purified Islam.

Muslim League National Muslim party of India.

Mussolini, Benito (1883–1945) Italian dictator and founder of the fascist movement in Italy. During World War II, he allied Italy with Germany and Japan.

Muwahhidin Term meaning "unitarians"; these were followers of the Wahhabi movement that emerged in the Arabian Peninsula in the eighteenth century.

Mycenaeans Mainland competitors of the Minoans; they took over Crete around 1400 BCE. Migrating to Greece from central Europe, they brought their Indo-European language, horse chariots, and metalworking skills, which they used to dominate until 1200 BCE.

Nagasaki Second Japanese city to be hit by an atomic bomb near the end of World War II.

Napoleon Bonaparte (1769–1821) General who rose to power in a post-Revolutionary coup d'état, eventually proclaiming himself emperor of France. He placed security and order ahead of social reform and created a civil legal code. Napoleon expanded his empire through military action, but after his disastrous Russian campaign, the united European powers defeated Napoleon and forced him into exile. He escaped and reassumed command of his army but was later defeated at the Battle of Waterloo.

Napoleonic Code Legal code drafted by Napoleon in 1804; it distilled different legal traditions to create one uniform law. The code confirmed the abolition of feudal privileges of all kinds and set the conditions for exercising property rights.

National Assembly of France Governing body of France that succeeded the Estates-General in 1789 during the French Revolution. It was composed of, and defined by, the delegates of the Third Estate.

National Association for the Advancement of Colored People (NAACP) Founded in 1910, the U.S. civil rights organization dedicated to ending inequality and segregation for black Americans.

National Recovery Administration (NRA) New Deal agency created in 1933 to prepare codes of fair administration and to plan for public works. It was later declared unconstitutional.

nationalism The idea that members of a shared community called a "nation" should have sovereignty within the borders of their state.

nation-state Form of political organization that derived legitimacy from its inhabitants, often referred to as citizens, who in theory, if not always in practice, shared a common language, common culture, and common history.

native learning Japanese movement to promote nativist intellectual traditions and the celebration of Japanese texts.

native paramountcy British form of "rationalized" colonial rule, which attempted to bring "civilization" to the "uncivilized" by proclaiming that when the interests of European settlers in Africa clashed with those of the African population, the latter should take precedence.

natural rights Belief that emerged in eighteenth-century western Europe and North America that rights fundamental to human nature were discernible to reason and should be affirmed in human-made law.

natural selection Charles Darwin's theory that populations grew faster than the food supply, creating a "struggle for existence" among species. In later work he showed how the passing on of individual traits was also determined by what he

called sexual selection—according to which the "best" mates are chosen for their strength, beauty, or talents. The outcome: the "fittest" survived to reproduce, while the less adaptable did not.

Nazis (National Socialist German Workers Party) German organization dedicated to winning workers over from socialism to nationalism; the first Nazi Party platform combined nationalism with anticapitalism and anti-Semitism.

Neanderthals Members of an early wave of hominids from Africa who settled in western Afro-Eurasia, in an area reaching from present-day Uzbekistan and Iraq to Spain, approximately 150,000 years ago.

needle compass Crucial instrument made available to navigators after 1000 CE that helped guide sailors on the high seas. It was a Chinese invention.

negritos Hunter-gatherer inhabitants of the East Asian coastal islands who migrated there around 28,000 BCE but by 2000 BCE had been replaced by new migrants.

Negritude Statement of the virtues of the black identity and the validation of African culture and the African past, even in a westernizing world. This idea was shaped by African and African American intellectuals like Senegal's first president, Léopold Sédar Senghor.

Nehemiah Jewish eunuch of the Persian court who was given permission to rebuild the fortification walls around the city of Jerusalem from 440 to 437 BCE.

Neo-Assyrian Empire Afro-Eurasian empire that dominated around 950 BCE. The Neo-Assyrians extended their control over resources and people beyond their own borders, and their empire lasted for three centuries.

Nestorian Christians Denomination of Christians whose beliefs about Christ differed from those of the

official Byzantine church. Named after Nestorius, former bishop of Constantinople, they emphasized the human aspects of Jesus.

New Deal President Franklin Delano Roosevelt's package of government reforms that were enacted during the 1930s to provide jobs for the unemployed, social welfare programs for the poor, and security to the financial markets.

New Economic Policy Enacted decrees of the Bolsheviks between 1921 and 1927 that grudgingly sanctioned private trade and private property.

New Negro movement *See* Harlem Renaissance.

New World Term applied to the Americas that reflected the Europeans' view that anything previously unknown to them was "new," even if it had existed and supported societies long before European explorers arrived on its shores.

nirvana Literally, nonexistence; *nirvana* is the state of complete liberation from the concerns of worldly life, as in Buddhist thought.

Nō drama Masked theater favored by Japanese bureaucrats and regional lords during the Tokugawa period.

Noble Eightfold Path Buddhist concept of a way of life by which people may rid themselves of individual desire to achieve *nirvana*. The path consists of wisdom, ethical behavior, and mental discipline.

Nok culture Spectacular culture that arose in what is today Nigeria, in the sixth century BCE. Iron smelting occurred there around 600 BCE. Thus the Nok people made the transition from stone to iron materials.

nomads People who move across vast distances without settling permanently in a particular place. Often pastoralists, nomads and transhumant herders introduced new forms of chariot-based warfare that transformed the Afro-Eurasian world.

non-governmental organizations (NGOs) Term used to refer to private organizations like the Red Cross that play a large role in international affairs.

nonviolent resistance (satyagraha) Moral and political philosophy of resistance developed by Indian National Congress leader Mohandas Gandhi. Gandhi believed that if Indians pursued self-reliance and self-control in a nonviolent way, the British would eventually have to leave.

North American Free Trade Agreement (NAFTA) Treaty negotiated in the early 1990s to promote free trade between Canada, the United States, and Mexico.

North Atlantic Treaty Organization (NATO) International organization set up in 1949 to provide for the defense of western European countries and the United States from the perceived Soviet threat.

Northern Wei dynasty Regime founded in 386 CE by the Tuoba, a people originally from Inner Mongolia, that lasted one and a half centuries. The rulers of this dynasty adopted many practices of the earlier Chinese Han regime. At the same time, they struggled to consolidate authority over their own nomadic people. Ultimately, several decades of intense internal conflict led to the dynasty's downfall.

northwest passage Long-sought marine passageway between the Atlantic and Pacific oceans.

Oceania Collective name for the lands of Australia and New Zealand and the islands of the southwest Pacific Ocean.

Odyssey Composed in the eighth century BCE, an epic tale of the journey of Odysseus, who traveled the Mediterranean back to his home in Ithaca after the siege of Troy.

oikos The word for "small family unit" in ancient Greece, similar to the familia in Rome. Its structure, with men as heads of household over women and children, embodied the fundamental power structure in Greek city-states.

oligarchy Clique of privileged rulers.

Olmecs A people who emerged around 1500 BCE and lived in Mesoamerica. The name means those who "lived in the land of the rubber." Olmec society was composed of decentralized villages. Its members spoke the same language and worshipped the same gods.

Open Door Policy Policy proposed by American Secretary of State John Hay that would give all foreign nations equal access to trade with China. As European imperial powers carved out spheres of trade in late-nineteenth-century China, American leaders worried that the United States would be excluded from trade with China. To prevent this, Hay proposed the Open Door Policy.

Opium War (1839–1842) War fought between the British and Qing China over British trade in opium; resulted in granting to the British the right to trade in five different ports and the ceding of Hong Kong to the British.

oracle bones Animal bones used by Shang diviners. Diviners applied intense heat to the shoulder bones of cattle or to turtle shells, which caused them to crack. The diviners would then interpret the cracks as signs from the ancestors regarding royal plans and actions.

Organization of Petroleum Exporting Countries (OPEC) International association established in 1960 to coordinate price and supply policies of oil-producing states.

orientalism Genre of literature and painting that portrayed the non-western peoples of North Africa and Asia as exotic, sensuous, and economically backward with respect to Europeans.

orientalists Western scholars who specialized in the study of the East.

Orrorin tugenensis Predecessor to hominids that first appeared 6 million years ago.

Ottoman Empire Rulers of Anatolia, the Arab world, and much of southern and eastern Europe in the early sixteenth century. They transformed themselves from nomadic warrior bands who roamed the borderlands between Islamic and Christian worlds in Anatolia into sovereigns of a vast, bureaucratic empire. The Ottomans embraced a Sunni view of Islam. They adapted traditional Byzantine governmental practices but tried new ways of integrating the diverse peoples of their empire.

Pacific War (1879–1883) War between Chile and the alliance of Bolivia and Peru.

pagani Pejorative word used by Christians to designate pagans.

palace Official residence of the ruler, his family, and his entourage. The palace was both a social institution and a set of buildings. It first appeared around 2500 BCE, about a millennium later than the Mesopotamian temple, and quickly joined the temple as a defining landmark of city life. Eventually, it became a source of power rivaling the temple, and palace and temple life often blurred, as did the boundary between the sacred and the secular.

Palace of Versailles The palace complex, eleven miles away from the French capital of Paris, built by Louis XIV in the 1670s and 1680s to house and entertain his leading clergymen and nobles, with the hopes of diverting them from plotting against him.

Palmyra Roman trading depot in modern-day Syria; part of a network of trading cities that connected various regions of Afro-Eurasia.

pan movements Groups that sought to link people across state boundaries in new communities based on ethnicity or, in some cases, religion (e.g., pan-Germanism, pan-Islamism, pan-Slavism).

Pansophia Ideal republic of inquisitive Christians united in the search for knowledge of nature as a means of loving God.

papacy The institution of the pope; the Catholic spiritual leader in Rome.

papal Of, relating to, or issued by a pope.

Parthians Horse-riding people who pushed southward around the middle of the second century BCE and wiped out the Greek kingdoms in Iran. They then extended their power all the way to the Mediterranean, where they ran up against the Roman Empire in Anatolia and Mesopotamia.

pastoral nomadic communities Groups of people that moved their domesticated animals from place to place to meet the animals' demanding grazing requirements. Around 3500 BCE, western Afro-Eurasia witnessed the growth and spread of pastoral nomadic communities.

pastoralism Herding and breeding of sheep and goats or other animals as a primary means of subsistence.

paterfamilias Latin for "Father of the family," which itself was the foundation of the Roman social order.

patria Latin, meaning "fatherland."

patrons In the Roman system of patronage, men and women of wealth and high social status who protected dependents or "clients" of a lower class.

Pax Mongolica Term that refers to the political and especially the commercial stability that the vast Mongol Empire provided for the travelers and merchants of Eurasia during the thirteenth and fourteenth centuries.

Pax Romana Latin for "Roman Peace"; refers to the period between 25 BCE and 235 CE during which conditions in the Roman Empire were settled and peaceful.

Pax Sinica Period of peace (149–87 BCE) during which agriculture, commerce, and industry flourished in East Asia under the rule of the Han.

Peace Preservation Act (1925) Act instituted in Japan that specified up to ten years' hard labor for any member of an organization advocating a basic change in the political system or the abolition of private property.

Pearl Harbor American naval base in Hawaii on which the Japanese launched a surprise attack on December 7, 1941, bringing the United States into World War II.

Peloponnesian War War fought between 431 and 404 BCE between two of Greece's most powerful city-states, Athens and Sparta.

Peninsular War (1808–1814) Conflict in which the Portuguese and Spanish populations, supported by the British, resisted the French invasion under Napoleon of the Iberian Peninsula.

Peninsulars Spaniards who, although born in Spain, resided in the Spanish colonial territories. They regarded themselves as superior to Spaniards born in the colonies (creoles).

Peoples' Charter Document calling for universal suffrage for adult males, the secret ballot, electoral districts, and annual parliamentary elections. It was signed by over 3 million British between 1839 and 1842.

periplus Book that reflected sailing knowledge; in such books captains would record landing spots and ports. The word *periplus* literally means "sailing around."

Persepolis Darius I's capital city in the highlands of Fars; a ceremonial center and expression of imperial identity as well as an important administrative hub.

Peterloo Massacre (1819) The killing of 11 and wounding of 460 following a peaceful demonstration for political reform by workers in Manchester, England.

Petra City in modern-day Jordan that was the Nabataean capital. It profited greatly by supplying provisions and water to travelers and traders. Many of its houses and shrines were cut into the rocky mountains. *Petra* means "rock."

phalanx Military formation used by Philip II of Macedonia, whereby heavily armored infantry were closely arrayed in battle formation.

Philip II of Macedonia Father of Alexander the Great, under whose rule Macedonia developed into a large ethnic and territorial state. After unifying Macedonia, Philip went on to conquer neighboring states.

philosophes Enlightenment thinkers who applied scientific reasoning to human interaction and society as opposed to nature.

philosophia Literally "love of wisdom"; this system of thought originally included speculation on the nature of the cosmos, the environment, and human existence. It eventually came to include thought about the nature of humans and life in society.

Phoenicians Known as the Canaanites in the Bible, an ethnic group in the Levant under Assyrian rule in the seventh century BCE; they provided ships and sailors for battles in the Mediterranean. The word *Phoenician* refers to the purple dye they manufactured and widely traded, along with other commercial goods and services, throughout the Mediterranean. While part of wider Mesopotamian culture, their major contribution was the alphabet, first introduced in the second millennium BCE, which made far-reaching communication possible.

phonemes Primary and distinctive sounds that are characteristic of human language.

piety Strong sense of religious duty and devoutness, often inspiring extraordinary actions.

plant domestication Process of growing plants, harvesting their seeds, and saving some of the seeds for planting in subsequent growing cycles, resulting in a steady food supply. This process occurred as far back as 5000 BCE, when plants began to naturally retain their seeds. Plant domestication was practiced first in the southern Levant and spread from there into the rest of Southwest Asia.

Plato (427–347 BCE) Disciple of the great philosopher Socrates; his works are the only record we have of Socrates's teaching. He was also the author of formative philosophical works on ethics and politics.

plebs In Rome, term that referred to the "common people." Their interests were protected by officials called tribunes.

Pochteca Archaic term for merchants of the Mexicos.

polities Politically organized communities or states.

polyglot communities Societies composed of diverse linguistic and ethnic groups.

popular culture Affordable and accessible forms of art and entertainment available to people at all levels of society.

popular sovereignty The idea that the power of the state resides in the people.

populists Members of a political movement that supported U.S. farmers in late-nineteenth-century America. The term is often used generically to refer to political groups who appeal to the majority of the population.

potassium-argon dating Major dating technique based on the changing chemical structure of objects over time, since over time potassium decays into argon. This method makes possible the dating of objects up to a million years old.

potato famine (1840s) Severe famine in Ireland that led to the rise of radical political movements and the migration of large numbers of Irish to the United States.

potter's wheel Fast wheel that enabled people to mass-produce vessels in many different shapes. This advance,

invented at the city of Uruk, enabled potters to make significant technical breakthroughs.

pottery Vessels made of mud and later clay that were used for storing and transporting food. The development of pottery was a major breakthrough.

Prague Spring (1968) Program of liberalization under a new communist party in Czechoslovakia that strove to create a democratic and pluralist socialism.

predestinarian Belief of many sixteenth- and seventeenth-century Protestant groups that God had foreordained the lives of individuals, including their bad and good deeds.

primitivism Western art movement of the late-nineteenth and early twentieth centuries that drew upon the so-called primitive art forms of Africa, Oceania, and pre-Columbian America.

progressive reformers Members of the U.S. reform movement in the early twentieth century that aimed to eliminate political corruption, improve working conditions, and regulate the power of large industrial and financial enterprises.

proletarians Industrial wage workers.

prophets Charismatic freelance religious men of power who found themselves in opposition to the formal power of the kings, bureaucrats, and priests.

Prophet's Town Indian village that was burned down by American forces in the early nineteenth century.

Protestant Reformation Religious movement initiated by sixteenth-century monk Martin Luther, who openly criticized the corruption in the Catholic Church and voiced his belief that Christians could speak directly to God. His doctrines gained wide support, and those who followed this new view of the Christianity rejected the authority of the papacy and the Catholic clergy, broke away from the Catholic Church, and called themselves "Protestants."

Protestantism Division of Christianity that emerged in western Europe from the Protestant Reformation.

Proto-Indo-European The parent of all the languages in the Indo-European family, which includes, among many others, English, German, Norwegian, Portuguese, French, Russian, Persian, Hindi, and Bengali.

Pullman Strike (1894) American Railway Union strike in response to wage cuts and firings.

Punic Wars Three wars waged between the Romans and Carthage in the third and second centuries BCE that resulted in the defeat of the Carthaginian hegemony in the western Mediterranean and demonstrated the might of the Roman military (army and navy) and the beginnings of Rome's aggressive foreign imperialism.

puppet states Governments with little power in the international arena that follow the dictates of their more powerful neighbors or patrons.

Puritans Seventeenth-century reform group of the Church of England; also known as dissenters or nonconformists.

Qadiriyya Sufi order that facilitated the spread of Islam into West Africa.

Qadis Judges in the Ottoman Empire.

qanats Underground water channels, vital for irrigation, which were used in Persia. Little evaporation occurred when water was being moved through qanats.

Qing dynasty (1644–1911) Minority Manchu rule over China that incorporated new territories, experienced substantial population growth, and sustained significant economic growth.

Questions of King Milanda (Milindapunha) Name of a second-century BCE text espousing the teachings of Buddhism as set forth by Menander, a Yavana king. It featured a discussion between the king and a sophisticated Buddhist sage named Nagasena.

Quetzalcoatl Ancient deity and legendary ruler of Native American peoples living in Mexico.

Quran The scripture of the Islamic faith. Originally a verbal recitation, the Quran was eventually compiled into a book in the order in which we have it today. According to traditional Islamic interpretation, the Quran was revealed to Muhammad by the angel Gabriel over a period of twenty-three years.

radicals Widely used term in nineteenth-century Europe that referred to those individuals and political organizations that favored the total reconfiguration of Europe's old state system.

radiocarbon isotope C¹⁴ Isotope contained by all living things, which plants acquire directly from the atmosphere and animals acquire indirectly when they consume plants or other animals. When living things die, the C^{14} isotope they contain begins to decay into a stable nonradioactive element, C^{12}. The rate of decay is regular and measurable, making it possible to ascertain the date of fossils that leave organic remains for ages of up to 40,000 years.

raj British crown's administration of India following the end of the East India Company's rule after the Rebellion of 1857.

raja "King" in the Kshatriya period in South Asia; could also refer to the head of a family, but indicated the person who had control of land and resources in South Asian city-states.

Ramadan Ninth month of the Muslim year, during which all Muslims must fast during daylight hours.

Rape of Nanjing Attack against the Chinese in which the Japanese slaughtered at least 100,000 civilians and raped thousands of women between December 1937 and February 1938.

Rashtriya Swayamsevak Sangh (RSS) (1925) Campaign to organize Hindus as a militant, modern community in India; translated in English as "National Volunteer Organization."

Rebellion of 1857 Indian uprising against the East India Company to bring religious purification, an egalitarian society, and local and communal solidarity without the interference of British rule.

rebus Probably originating in Uruk, a representation that transfers meaning from the name of a thing to the sound of that name. For example, a picture of a bee can represent the sound "b." Such pictures opened the door to writing: a technology of symbols that uses marks to represent specific discrete sounds.

Reconquista Spanish reconquest of territories lost to the Islamic Empire, beginning with Toledo in 1061.

Red Guards Chinese students who were the shock troopers in the early phases of Mao's Cultural Revolution in 1966–1968.

Red Lanterns Female supporters of the Chinese Boxers who rebelled against foreign intrusions in China at the turn of the twentieth century. Most were teenage girls and unmarried women and dressed in red garments.

Red Turban movement Diverse religious movement in China during the fourteenth century that spread the belief that the world was drawing to an end as Mongol rule was collapsing.

Reds Bolsheviks.

Reich German empire composed of Denmark, Austria, and parts of western France.

Reichstag The German parliament.

Reign of Terror Campaign at the height of the French Revolution in the early 1790s that used violence, including systematic execution of opponents of the revolution, to purge France of its enemies and to extend the revolution beyond its borders; radicals executed as many as 40,000 persons who were judged enemies of the state.

Renaissance Term meaning "rebirth" that historians use to characterize the expanded cultural production of European nations between 1430 and 1550. Emphasized a break from the church-centered medieval world and a new concept of humankind as the center of the world.

republican government Government in which power and rulership rest with representatives of the people—not a king.

Res publica Literally "public thing"; this referred to the Roman republic, in which policy and rules of behavior were determined by the Senate and by popular assemblies of the citizens.

Restoration period (1815–1848) European movement after the defeat of Napoleon to restore Europe to its pre-French revolutionary status and to quash radical movements.

Rift Valley Area of northeastern Africa where some of the most important early human archaeological discoveries of fossils were found, especially one of an intact skull that is 1.8 million years old.

river basin Area drained by a river, including all its tributaries. River basins were rich in fertile soil, water for irrigation, and plant and animal life, which made them attractive for human habitation. Cultivators were able to produce surplus agriculture to support the first cities.

riverine Term denoting an area whose inhabitants depend on irrigation for their well-being and whose populations are settled near great rivers. Egypt was, in a sense, the most riverine of all these cultures, in that it had no hinterland of plains as did Mesopotamia and the Indus Valley. Away from the banks of the Nile, there is only largely uninhabitable desert.

Roman army Military force of the Roman Empire. The Romans devised a military draft that could draw from a huge population. In their encounter with Hannibal, they lost up to 80,000 men in three separate encounters and still won the war.

Roman Catholicism Branch of Christianity established by 1000 CE in western Europe and led by the Roman papacy. In contrast to ancient Greek Orthodoxy, western Catholics believed that their church was destined to expand everywhere, and they set about converting the pagan tribes of northern Europe. Western Catholics contemptuously called the eastern Romans "Greeks" and condemned them for their "Byzantine" cunning.

Roman law Roman legal system, under which disputes were brought to the public courts and decisions were made by judges and sometimes by large juries. Rome's legal system featured written law and institutions for settling legal disputes.

roving bandits Large bands of dispossessed and marginalized peasants who vented their anger at tax collectors in the waning years of the Ming dynasty.

Royal Road A 1,600-mile road from Sardis in Anatolia to Susa in Iran; used by messengers, traders, the army, and those taking tribute to the king.

Russification Programs to assimilate people of over 146 dialects into the Russian Empire.

S.S. (*Schutzstaffel*) Hitler's security police force.

Sack of Constantinople Rampage in 1204 by the Frankish armies on the capital city of Constantinople.

sacred kingships Institutions that marked the centralized politics of West Africa. The inhabitants of these kingships believed that their kings were descendants of the gods.

Sahel region Area of sub-Saharan Africa with wetter and more temperate locations, especially in the upland massifs and their foothills, villages, and towns.

St. Bartholomew's Day Massacre (1572) Roman Catholic massacre of French Protestants in Paris.

St. Patrick Former slave brought to Ireland from Britain who later became a missionary, or the "Apostle of Ireland." He died in 470 CE.

Salt March (1930) A 240-mile trek to the sea in India, led by Mohandas Gandhi, to gather salt for free, thus breaking the British colonial monopoly on salt.

Samurai Japanese warriors who made up the private armies of Japanese daimyos.

Sandinista coalition Left-leaning Nicaraguan coalition of the 1970s and 1980s.

Sanskrit cosmopolis A cultural synthesis based on Hindu spiritual beliefs and articulated in the Sanskrit language that served to unify South Asia in place of a centralized empire.

Santería African-based religion, blended with Christian influences, that was first practiced by slaves in Cuba.

Sargon the Great King of Akkad, a city-state near modern Baghdad. Reigning from 2334 to 2279 BCE, Sargon helped bring the competitive era of city-states to an end and sponsored monumental works of architecture, art, and literature.

Sasanian Empire Empire that succeeded the Parthians in the mid-220s CE in Inner Eurasia. The Sasanian Empire controlled the trade crossroads of Afro-Eurasia and possessed a strong armored cavalry, which made them a powerful rival to Rome. The Sasanians were also tolerant of Judaism and Christianity, which allowed Christians to flourish.

sati Hindu practice whereby a woman was burned to death on the pyre of her dead husband.

satrap Governor of a province in the Persian Empire. Each satrap was a relative or intimate associate of the king.

satyagraha See nonviolent resistance.

scientific method Method of inquiry based on experimentation in nature. Many of its principles were first laid out by the philosopher Sir Francis Bacon (1561–1626), who claimed that real science entailed the formulation of hypotheses that could be tested in carefully controlled experiments.

Scramble for Africa European rush to colonize parts of Africa at the end of the nineteenth century.

scribes Those who wield writing tools; from the very beginning they were at the top of the social ladder, under the major power brokers.

Scythian ethos Warrior ethos that embodied the extremes of aggressive mounted-horse culture, c. 1000 BCE. In part the Scythian ethos was the result of the constant struggle between settlers, hunter-gatherers, and nomads on the northern frontier of Europe.

Sea Peoples Migrants from north of the Mediterranean who invaded the cities of Egypt and the Levant in the second millennium BCE. Once settled along the coast of the Levant, they became known as the Philistines and considerably disrupted the settlements of the Canaanites.

SEATO (Southeast Asia Treaty Organization) Military alliance of pro-American, anticommunist states in Southeast Asia from 1954 to 1977.

Second World Term invented during the cold war to refer to the communist countries, as opposed to the West (or First World) and the former colonies (or Third World).

second-generation societies Societies that expanded old ideas and methods by incorporating new aspects of culture and grafting them onto, or using them in combination with, established norms.

Seleucus Nikator Successor of Alexander the Great who lived from 358 to 281 BCE. He controlled Mesopotamia, Syria, Persia, and parts of the Punjab.

Self-Strengthening movement In the latter half of the nineteenth century, a movement of reformist Chinese bureaucrats that attempted to adopt western elements of learning and technological skill while retaining their core Chinese culture.

Semu Term meaning "outsiders" or non-Chinese people—Mongols, Tanguts, Khitan, Jurchen, Muslims, Tibetans, Persians, Turks, Nestorians, Jews, and Armenians—who became a new ruling elite over a Han majority population in the late thirteenth century.

sepoys Hindu and Muslim recruits of the East India Company's military force.

serfs Peasants who farmed the land and paid fees to be protected and governed by lords under a system of rule called feudalism.

settled agriculture Application of human labor and tools to a fixed plot of land for more than one growing cycle. It entails the changeover from a hunting-and-gathering lifestyle to one based on agriculture, which requires staying in one place until the soil has been exhausted.

Seven Years' War (1756–1763) Worldwide war that ended when Prussia defeated Austria, establishing itself as a European power, and when Britain gained control of India and many of France's colonies through the Treaty of Paris.

sexual revolution Increased freedom in sexual behavior, resulting in part from the advances in contraception, notably the introduction of oral contraception in 1960, which allowed men and women to limit childbearing and to have sex with less fear of pregnancy.

shah Traditional title of Persian rulers.

shamans Certain humans whose powers supposedly enabled them to commune with the supernatural and to transform themselves wholly or partly into beasts.

shamisen Three-stringed instrument, often played by Japanese geisha.

Shandingdong Man A *Homo sapiens* whose fossil remains and relics can be dated to about 18,000 years ago. His physical characteristics were close to those of modern humans, and he had a similar brain size.

Shang state Dynasty in northeastern China that ruled from 1600 to 1045 BCE. Though not as well defined by borders as the territorial states in the southwest of Asia, it did have a ruling lineage. Four fundamental elements of the Shang state were a metal industry based on copper, pottery making, standardized architectural forms and walled towns, and divination using animal bones.

Shanghai School Late-nineteenth-century style of painting characterized by an emphasis on spontaneous brushwork, feeling, and the incorporation of western influences into classical Chinese pieces.

sharecropping System of farming in which tenant farmers rented land and gave over a share of their crops to the land's owners. Sometimes seen as a cheap way for the state to conduct agricultural affairs, sharecropping often resulted in the impoverishment and marginalization of the underclass.

sharia Literally, "the way"; now used to indicate the philosophy and rulings of Islamic law.

Sharpeville Massacre (1960) Massacre of sixty-nine black Africans when police fired upon a rally against the recently passed laws requiring non-white South Africans to carry identity papers.

Shawnees Native American tribe that inhabited the Ohio valley during the eighteenth century.

Shays's Rebellion (1786) Uprising of armed farmers that broke out when the Massachusetts state government refused to offer them economic relief.

Shi Huangdi *See* Zheng.

Shiism One of the two main branches of Islam, practiced in the Safavid Empire. Although always a minority sect in the Islamic world, Shiism contains several subsects, each of which has slightly different interpretations of theology and politics.

Shiites Group of supporters of Ali, Muhammad's cousin and son-in-law, who wanted him to be the first caliph and believed that members of the Prophet's family deserved to rule. The leaders of the Shiite community are known as "Imam," which means "leaders."

Shinto Japan's official religion; it promoted the state and the emperor's divinity. The term means "the way of the gods."

shoguns Japanese military commanders. From 1192 to 1333, the Kamakura shoguns served as military "protectors" of the ruler in the city of Heian.

Shotoku Prince in the early Japanese Yamoto state (574–622 CE) who is credited with having introduced Buddhism to Japan.

shudras Literally "small ones"; workers and slaves from outside the Vedic lineage.

Siddhartha Gautama Another name for the Buddha; the most prominent opponent of the Brahman way of life; he lived from 563 to 483 BCE.

Sikhism Islamic-inspired religion that calls on its followers to renounce the caste system and to treat all believers as equal before God.

Silicon Valley Valley between the California cities of San Francisco and San Jose, known for its innovative computer and high-technology industries.

silk Luxury textile that became a vastly popular export from China (via the Silk Roads) to the cities of the Roman world.

Silk Roads Trade routes linking China with central Asia and the Mediterranean; it extended over 5,000 miles, land and sea included, and was so named because of the quantities of silk that were traded along it. The Silk Roads were a major factor in the development of civilizations in China, Egypt, Persia, India, and even Europe.

Silla One of three independent Korean states that may have emerged as early as the third century BCE. These states lasted until 668 CE, when Silla took control over the entire peninsula.

Silver Islands Term used by European merchants in the sixteenth century to refer to Japan, because of its substantial trade in silver with China.

Sino-Japanese War (1894–1895) Conflict over the control of Korea in which China was forced to cede the province of Taiwan to Japan.

Sipahi Urdu for "soldier."

Siva The third of three Vedic deities, signifying destruction. *See also* Brahma *and* Vishnu.

slave plantations System whereby labor was used for the cultivation of crops wholly for the sake of producing surplus that was then used for profit; slave plantations were a crucial part of the growth of the Mediterranean economy.

small seal script Unified script that was used to the exclusion of other scripts under the Qin, with the aim of centralizing administration; its use led to a less complicated style of clerical writing than had been in use under the Han.

social contract The idea, drawn from the writings of British philosopher John Locke, that the law should bind both ruler and people.

Social Darwinism Belief that Charles Darwin's theory of evolution was applicable to humans and justified the right of the ruling classes or countries to dominate the weak.

social hierarchies Distinctions between the privileged and the less privileged.

Social Security Act (1935) New Deal act that instituted old-age pensions and insurance for the unemployed.

socialism Political ideology that calls for a classless society with collective ownership of all property.

Socrates (469–399 BCE) Philosopher in Athens who encouraged people to reflect on ethics and morality. He stressed the importance of honor and integrity as opposed to wealth and power. Plato was his student.

Sogdians A people who lived in central Asia's commercial centers and maintained the stability and accessibility of the Silk Roads. They were crucial to the interconnectedness of the Afro-Eurasian landmass.

Solidarity The communist bloc's first independent trade union, it was established in Poland at the Gdansk shipyard.

Song dynasty Chinese dynasty that took over the mandate of heaven for three centuries starting in 976 CE. It ruled an era of many economic and political successes, but it eventually lost northern China to nomadic tribes.

Song porcelain Type of porcelain perfected during the Song period that was light, durable, and quite beautiful.

South African War (1899–1902) Conflict between the British and Dutch colonists of South Africa which resulted in bringing two Afrikaner republics under the control of the British. Often called the Boer War.

Soviet bloc International alliance that included the east European countries of the Warsaw Pact as well as the Soviet Union but also came to include Cuba.

Spanish-American War (1898) War between the United States and Spain in Cuba, Puerto Rico, and the Philippines. It ended with a treaty in which the United States took over the Philippines, Guam, and Puerto Rico; Cuba won partial independence.

speciation The formation of different species.

specie Money in coin.

species Group of animals or plants possessing one or more distinctive characteristics.

spiritual ferment Process that occurred after 300 CE in which religion touched more areas of society and culture than before and touched them in different, more demanding ways.

Spring and Autumn period Period between the eighth and fifth centuries BCE, during which China was ruled by the feudal system. Considered an anarchic and turbulent time, there were 148 different tributary states in this period.

Stalin, Joseph (1879–1953) Leader of the communist party and the Soviet Union; sought to create "socialism in one country."

steel A metal more malleable and stronger than iron that became essential for industries like shipbuilding and railways.

stoicism Widespread philosophical movement initiated by Zeno (334–262 BCE). Zeno and his followers sought to understand the role of people in relation to the cosmos. For the Stoics, everything was grounded in nature. Being in love with nature and living a good life required being in control of one's passions and thus indifferent to pleasure or pain.

Strait of Malacca Seagoing gateway to Southeast and East Asia.

Strategic Defense Initiative ("Star Wars") Master plan, championed by U.S. president Ronald Reagan in the 1980s, that envisions the deployment of satellites and space missiles to protect the United States from incoming nuclear bombs.

stupa Dome monument marking the burial site of relics of the Buddha.

Suez Canal Channel built in 1869 across the Isthmus of Suez to connect the Mediterranean Sea with the Red Sea and to lower the costs of international trade.

Sufi brotherhoods Mystics within Islam who were responsible for the expansion of Islam into many regions of the world.

Sufism Emotional and mystical form of Islam that appealed to the common people.

sultan Islamic political leader. In the Ottoman Empire, the sultan combined a warrior ethos with an unwavering devotion to Islam.

Sumerian King List Text that recounts the making of political dynasties. Recorded around 2000 BCE, it organizes the reigns of kings by dynasty, one city at a time.

Sumerian pantheon The Sumerian gods, each of whom had a home in a particular floodplain city. In the Sumerian belief system, both gods and the natural forces they controlled had to be revered.

Sumerian temples Homes of the gods and symbols of Sumerian imperial identity. Sumerian temples also represented the gods' ability to hoard wealth at sites where people exchanged goods and services. In addition, temples distinguished the urban from the rural world.

Sun Yat-sen (1866–1925) Chinese revolutionary and founder of the Nationalist Party in China.

Sunnis Orthodox Muslims. The majority sect of Islam, Sunnis originally supported the succession of Abu Bakr over Ali and supported the rule of consensus rather than family lineage for the succession to the Islamic caliphate. *See also* Shiism.

superior man In the Confucian view, a person of perfected moral character, fit to be a leader.

superpowers Label applied to the United States and the Soviet Union after World War II because of their size, their possession of the atomic bomb, and the fact that each embodied a model of civilization (capitalism or communism) applicable to the whole world.

supranational organizations International organizations such as nongovernmental organizations (NGOs), the World Bank, and the International Monetary Fund (IMF).

survival of the fittest Charles Darwin's belief that as animal populations grew and resources became scarce, a struggle for existence arose, the outcome of which was that only the "fittest" survived.

Suryavamsha The second lineage of two (the solar) in Vedic society. *See* Chandravamsha.

Swadeshi movement Voluntary organizations in India that championed the creation of indigenous manufacturing enterprises and schools of nationalist thought, in order to gain autonomy from Britain.

syndicalism Organization of workplace associations that included unskilled labor.

tabula rasa Term used by John Locke to describe the human mind before it begins to acquire ideas from experience; Latin for "clean slate."

Taiping Heavenly Kingdom (Heavenly Kingdom of Great Peace) Religious sect established by the Chinese prophet Hong Xiuquan in the mid-nineteenth century. Hong Xiuquan believed that he was Jesus's younger brother. The group struggled to rid the world of evil and "restore" the heavenly kingdom, imagined as a just and egalitarian order.

Taiping Rebellion Rebellion by followers of Hong Xiuquan and the Taiping Heavenly Kingdom against the Qing government over the economic and social turmoil caused by the Opium War. Despite raising an army of 100,000 rebels, the rebellion was crushed.

Taj Mahal Royal palace of the Mughal Empire, built by Shah Jahan in the seventeenth century in homage to his wife, Mumtaz.

Tale of Genji Japanese work written by Lady Murasaki that gives vivid

accounts of Heian court life; Japan's first novel (early eleventh century).

talking cures Psychological practice developed by Sigmund Freud whereby the symptoms of neurotic and traumatized patients would decrease after regular periods of thoughtful discussion.

Talmud Huge volumes of oral commentary on Jewish law eventually compiled in two versions, the Palestinian and the Babylonian, in the fifth and sixth centuries BCE.

Talmud of Jerusalem Codified written volumes of the traditions of Judaism; produced by the rabbis of Galilee around 400 CE.

Tang dynasty (608–907 CE) Regime that promoted a cosmopolitan culture, turning China into the hub of East Asia cultural integration, while expanding the borders of their empire. In order to govern such a diverse empire, the Tang established a political culture and civil service based on Confucian teachings. Candidates for the civil service were required to take examinations, the first of their kind in the world.

Tanzimat Reorganization period of the Ottoman Empire in the mid-nineteenth century; modernizing reforms affected the military, trade, foreign relations, and civilian life.

tappers Rubber workers in Brazil, mostly either Indian or mixed-blood people.

Tarascans Mesoamerican society of the 1400s; rivals to and sometimes subjects of the Aztecs.

Tatish Ruler of Chan Santa Cruz during the Mexican Caste War. The term means "father."

Tecumseh (1768–1813) Shawnee who circulated Tenskwatawa's message of Indian renaissance among Indian villages from the Great Lakes to the Gulf Coast. He preached the need for Indian unity, insisting that Indians resist any American attempts to get them to sell more land. In response, thousands of followers renounced their ties to colonial ways and prepared to combat the expansion of the United States.

Tekkes Schools that taught devotional strategies and the religious knowledge for students to enter Sufi orders and become masters of the brotherhood.

temple Building where believers worshipped their gods and goddesses and where some peoples believed the deities had earthly residence.

Tenskwatawa (1768–1834) Shawnee prophet who urged disciples to abstain from alcohol and return to traditional customs, reducing dependence on European trade goods and severing connections to Christian missionaries. His message spread to other tribes, raising the specter of a pan-Indian confederacy.

Teotihuacán City-state in a large, mountainous valley in present-day Mexico; the first major community to emerge after the Olmecs.

territorial state Political form that emerged in the riverine cities of Mesopotamia, which was overwhelmed by the displacement of nomadic peoples. These states were kingdoms organized around charismatic rulers who headed large households; each had a defined physical border.

Third Estate The French people minus the clergy and the aristocracy; this term was popularized in the late eighteenth century and used to exalt the power of the bourgeoisie during the French Revolution.

Third Reich The German state from 1933 to 1945 under Adolf Hitler.

Third World Nations of the world, mostly in Asia, Latin America, and Africa, that were not highly industrialized like First World nations or tied to the Soviet bloc (the Second World).

Thirty Years' War (1618–1648) Conflict begun between Protestants and Catholics in Germany that escalated into a general European war fought against the unity and power of the Holy Roman Empire.

Tiananmen Square Largest public square in the world and site of the pro-democracy movement in 1989 that resulted in the killing of as many as a thousand protesters by the Chinese army.

Tiers monde Term meaning "Third World," coined by French intellectuals to describe countries seeking a "third way" between Soviet communism and western capitalism.

Tiglath Pileser III Assyrian ruler from 745 to 728 BCE. This leader instituted reforms that changed the administrative and social structure of the empire to make it more efficient and introduced a standing army.

Tiwanaku Another name for Tihuanaco, the first great Andean polity, on the shores of Lake Titicaca.

Tlaxcalans Mesoamerican society of the 1400s; these people were enemies of the powerful Aztec Empire.

Tokugawa shogunate Hereditary military administration founded in 1603 that ruled Japan while keeping the emperor as a figurehead; it was toppled in 1868 by reformers who felt that Japan should adopt, not reject, Western influences.

Toltecs A Mesoamerican people who, by 1000 CE, had filled the political vacuum created by the decline of the city of Teotihuacán.

tomb culture Warlike group from northeast Asia who arrived by sea in the middle of the third century CE and imposed their military and social power on southern Japan. These conquerors are known today as the tomb culture because of their elevated necropolises near present-day Osaka.

Topkapi Palace Political headquarters of the Ottoman Empire, located in Istanbul.

total war All-out war involving civilian populations as well as military forces, often used in reference to World War II.

transhumant migrants Nomads who entered settled territories in the second millennium BCE and moved their herds seasonally when resources became scarce.

Trans-Siberian Railroad Railroad built over very difficult terrain between 1891 and 1903 and subsequently expanded; it created an overland bridge for troops, peasant settlers, and commodities to move between Europe and the Pacific.

Treaty of Brest-Litovsk (1918) Separate peace between imperial Germany and the new Bolshevik regime in Russia. The treaty acknowledged the German victory on the Eastern Front and withdrew Russia from the war.

Treaty of Nanjing (1842) Treaty between China and Britain following the Opium War; it called for indemnities, the opening of new ports, and the cession of Hong Kong to the British.

Treaty of Tordesillas (1494) Treaty in which the pope decreed that the non-European world would be divided into spheres of trade and missionary responsibility between Spain and Portugal.

trickle trade Method by which a good is passed from one village to another, as in the case of obsidian among farming villages; the practice began around 7000 BCE. Also called "down-the-line trade."

Tripartite Pact (1940) Pact that stated that Germany, Italy, and Japan would act together in all future military ventures.

Triple Entente Alliance developed before World War I that eventually included Britain, France, and Russia.

Troy Important site founded around 3000 BCE in Anatolia, to the far west. Troy is legendary as the site of the war that was launched by the Greeks (the Achaeans) and that was recounted by Homer in the *Iliad*.

Truman Doctrine (1947) Declaration promising U.S. economic and military intervention, whenever and wherever needed, for the sake of preventing communist expansion.

Truth and Reconciliation Commission Quasi-judicial body established after the overthrow of the apartheid system in South Africa and the election of Nelson Mandela as the country's first black president in 1994. The commission was to gather evidence about crimes committed during the apartheid years. Those who showed remorse for their actions could appeal for clemency. The South African leaders believed that an airing of the grievances from this period would promote racial harmony and reconciliation.

truth commissions Elected officials' inquiries into human rights abuses by previous regimes. In Argentina, El Salvador, Guatemala, and South Africa, these commissions were vital for creating a new aura of legitimacy for democracies and for promising to uphold the rights of individuals.

tsar/czar Russian word derived from the Latin *Caesar* to refer to the Russian ruler of Kiev, and eventually to all rulers in Russia.

Tula Toltec capital city; a commercial hub and political and ceremonial center.

Uitlanders British populations living in Afrikaner republics; they were denied voting rights and subject to other forms of discrimination in the late nineteenth century. The term means "outsiders."

ulama Arabic word that means "learned ones" or "scholars"; used for those who devoted themselves to knowledge of Islamic sciences.

Umayyads Family who founded the first dynasty in Islam. They established family rule and dynastic succession to the role of caliph. The first Umayyad caliph established Damascus as his capital and was named Mu'awiya ibn Abi Sufyan.

Umma Arabic word for "community"; used to refer to the "Islamic polity" or "Islamic community."

Universal Declaration of Human Rights (1948) U.N. declaration that laid out the rights to which all human beings are entitled.

universalizing religions Religions that appeal to diverse populations; are easily adaptable across various cultural and geographical areas; promote universal rules and principles to guide behavior that transcend place, time, and specific cultural practices; are proselytized by energetic and charismatic missionaries; foster a deep sense of community felt by their converts; and are supported by powerful empires.

universitas Term used from the end of the twelfth century to denote scholars who came together, first in Paris. The term is borrowed from the merchant communities, where it denoted the equivalent of the modern "union."

Untouchables Caste in the Indian system whose jobs, usually in the more unsanitary aspects of urban life, rendered them "ritually and spiritually" impure.

Upanishads Vedic wisdom literature collected in the first half of the first millennium BCE. It took the form of dialogues between disciples and a sage.

urban-rural divide Division between those living in cities and those living in rural areas. One of history's most durable worldwide distinctions, the urban-rural divide eventually encompassed the globe. Where cities arose, communities adopted lifestyles based on the mass production of goods and on specialized labor. Those living in the countryside remained close to nature, cultivating the land or tending livestock. They diversified their labor and exchanged their grains and animal products for necessities available in urban centers.

utopian socialism The most visionary of all Restoration-era movements.

Utopian socialists like Charles Fourier dreamed of transforming states, workplaces, and human relations and proposed plans to do so.

Vaishyas Householders or lesser clan members in Vedic society who worked the land and tended livestock.

Vardhamana Mahavira Advocate of Jainism who lived from 540 to 468 BCE; he emphasized interpretation of the Upanishads to govern and guide daily life.

varna Caste system established by the Vedas in 600 BCE.

vassal states Subordinate states that had to pay tribute in luxury goods, raw materials, and manpower as part of a broad confederation of polities under the kings' protection.

Vedas Rhymes, hymns, and explanatory texts composed by Aryan priests; the Vedas became their most holy scripture and part of their religious rituals. They were initially passed down orally, in Sanskrit. Brahmans, priests of Vedic culture, incorporated the texts into ritual and society. The Vedas are considered the final authority of Hinduism.

Vedic people People who came from the steppes of Inner Asia around 1500 BCE and entered the fertile lowlands of the Indus River basin, gradually moving as far south as the Deccan plateau. They called themselves Aryan, which means "respected ones," and spoke Sanskrit, an Indo-European language.

veiling Practice of modest dress required of respectable women in the Assyrian Empire, introduced by Assyrian authorities in the thirteenth century BCE.

Venus figures Representations of the goddess of fertility drawn on the Chauvet Cave in southeastern France. Discovered in 1994, they are probably about 35,000 years old.

Versailles Conference (1919) Peace conference between the victors of World War I; resulted in the Treaty of Versailles, which forced Germany to pay reparations and to give up its colonies to the victors.

Viet Cong Vietnamese communist group committed to overthrowing the government of South Vietnam and reunifying North and South Vietnam.

Viet Minh Group founded in 1941 by Ho Chi Minh to oppose the Japanese occupation of Indochina; it later fought the French colonial forces for independence. Also known as the Vietnamese Independent League.

Vietnam War (1965–1975) Conflict that resulted from concern over the spread of communism in Southeast Asia. The United States intervened on the side of South Vietnam in its struggle against peasant-supported Viet Cong guerrilla forces, who wanted to reunite Vietnam under a communist regime. Faced with antiwar opposition at home and ferocious resistance from the Vietnamese, American troops withdrew in 1973; the puppet South Vietnamese government collapsed two years later.

Vikings A people from Scandinavia who replaced the Franks as the dominant warrior class in northern Europe in the ninth century CE. They used their superior ships to loot other seagoing peoples and sailed up the rivers of central Russia to establish a trade route that connected Scandinavia and the Baltic with Constantinople and Baghdad. The Vikings established settlements in Iceland and Greenland and, briefly, North America.

Vishnu The second of three Vedic deities, signifying existence. *See also* Brahma *and* Siva.

viziers Bureaucrats of the Ottoman Empire.

Vodun Mixed religion of African and Christian customs practiced by slaves and free blacks in the colony of Saint-Domingue.

Voting Rights Act (1965) Law that granted universal suffrage in the United States.

Wafd Nationalist party that came into existence during a rebellion in Egypt in 1919 and held power sporadically after Egypt was granted limited independence from Britain in 1922.

Wahhabism Early eighteenth-century reform movement organized by Muhammad Ibn abd al-Wahhab, who preached the absolute oneness of Allah and a return to the pure Islam of Muhammad.

Wang Mang Han minister who usurped the throne in 9 CE because he believed that the Han had lost the mandate of heaven. He ruled until 23 CE.

war ethos Strong social commitment to a continuous state of war. The Roman army constantly drafted men and engaged in annual spring military campaigns. Soldiers were taught to embrace a sense of honor that did not allow them to accept defeat and commended those who repeatedly threw themselves into battle.

War of 1812 Conflict between Britain and the United States arising from U.S. grievances over oppressive British maritime practices in the Napoleonic Wars.

War on Poverty President Lyndon Johnson's push for an increased range of social programs and increased spending on social security, health, education, and assistance for the disabled.

Warring States period Period extending from the fifth century to 221 BCE, when the regional warring states were unified by the Qin dynasty.

Warsaw Pact (1955–1991) Military alliance between the Soviet Union and other communist states that was established in response to the creation of the North American Treaty Organization (NATO) alliance.

Weimar Republic (1919–1933) Constitutional Republic of Germany that was subverted by Hitler soon after he became chancellor.

Western Front Military front that stretched from the English Channel through Belgium and France to the Alps during World War I.

White and Blue Niles The two main branches of the Nile, rising out of central Africa and Ethiopia. They come together at the present-day capital city of Sudan, Khartoum.

White Lotus Rebellion Series of uprisings in northern China (1790–1800s) inspired by mystical beliefs in folk Buddhism and, at times, the idea of restoring the Ming dynasty.

White Wolf Mysterious militia leader, depicted in popular myth as a Chinese Robin Hood whose mission was to rid the country of the injustices of Yuan Shikai's government in the early years of the Chinese Republic (1910s).

Whites "Counterrevolutionaries" of the Bolshevik Revolution (1918–1921) who fought the Bolsheviks (the "Reds"); included former supporters of the tsar, Social Democrats, and large independent peasant armies.

witnessing Dying for one's faith, or becoming a martyr.

Wokou Supposedly Japanese pirates, many of whom were actually Chinese subjects of the Ming dynasty.

Works Progress Administration (WPA) New Deal program instituted in 1935 that put nearly 3 million people to work building roads, bridges, airports, and post offices.

World Bank International agency established in 1944 to provide economic assistance to war-torn and poor countries. Its formal title is the International Bank for Reconstruction and Development.

World War I *See* Great War.

World War II (1939–1945) Worldwide war that began in September 1939 in Europe, and even earlier in Asia, and pitted Britain, the United States, and the Soviet Union (the Allies) against Nazi Germany, Japan, and Italy (the Axis).

Wu or **Wudi** Chinese leader known as the "Martial Emperor" because of his many military campaigns during the Han dynasty. He reigned from 141 to 87 BCE.

Wu Zhao Chinese empress who lived from 626 to 706 CE. She began as a concubine in the court of Li Shimin and became the mother of his son's child. She eventually gained power equal to that of the emperor, and named herself regent when she finagled a place for one of her own sons after their father's death.

Xiongnu The most powerful and intrusive of the nomadic peoples; originally pastoralists from the eastern part of the Asian steppe in what is modern-day Mongolia. They appeared along the frontier with China in the late Zhou dynasty and by the third century BCE had become the most powerful of all the pastoral communities in that area.

Xunzi Confucian moralist whose ideas were influential to Qin rulers. He lived from 310 to 237 BCE and believed that rational statecraft was more reliable than fickle human nature and that strict laws and severe punishments could create stability in society.

Yalta Accords Results of the meeting between President Roosevelt, Prime Minister Churchill, and Premier Stalin that occurred in the Crimea in 1945 to plan for the postwar order.

Yavana kings Sanskrit name for Greek rulers, derived from the Greek name for the area of western Asia Minor called Ionia, a term that then extended to anyone who spoke Greek or came from the Mediterranean.

yellow press Newspapers that sought a mass circulation by featuring sensationalist reporting.

Yellow Turbans One of several local Chinese religious movements that emerged across the empire, especially under Wang Mang's officials, who considered him a usurper. The Yellow Turbans, so called because of the yellow scarves they wore around their heads, were Daoist millenarians.

Yin City that became the capital of the Shang in 1350 BCE, ushering in a golden age.

Young Egypt Antiliberal, fascist group that gained a large following in Egypt during the 1930s.

Young Italy Nationalist organization made up of young students and intellectuals, devoted to the unification and renewal of the Italian state.

Yuan dynasty Dynasty established by the Mongols after the defeat of the Song. The Yuan dynasty was strong from 1280 to 1368; its capital was at Dadu, or modern-day Beijing.

Yuan Mongols Mongol rulers of China who were overthrown by the Ming dynasty in 1368.

Yuezhi A Turkic nomadic people who roamed on pastoral lands to the west of the Xiongnu territory of central Mongolia. They had friendly relationships with the farming societies in China, but the Yuezhi detested the Xiongnu and had frequent armed clashes with them.

Zaibatsu Large-scale, family-owned corporations in Japan consisting of factories, import-export businesses, and banks that dominated the Japanese economy until 1945.

Zamindars Archaic tax system of the Mughal Empire where decentralized lords collected tribute for the emperor.

Zapatistas Group of indigenous rebels that rose up against the Mexican government in 1994 and drew inspiration from an earlier Mexican rebel, Emiliano Zapata.

Zheng King during the Qin era who defeated what was left of the Warring States between 230 and 221 BCE. He assumed the mandate of heaven from the Zhou and declared himself Shi Huangdi ("First August Emperor"), to distinguish himself from other kings.

Zheng He (1371–1433) Ming naval leader who established tributary relations with Southeast Asia, Indian Ocean ports, the Persian Gulf, and the east coast of Africa.

Zhong Shang Administrative central complex of the Shang.

Zhongguo Term originating in the ancient period and subsequently used to emphasize the central cultural and geographical location of China in the world; means "Middle Kingdom."

ziggurat By the end of the third millennium BCE, the elevated platform base of a Sumerian temple had transformed into a stepped platform called a *ziggurat*.

Zionism Political movement advocating the reestablishment of a Jewish homeland in Palestine.

Zoroaster Sometimes known as Zarathustra, thought to have been a teacher around 1000 BCE in eastern Iran and credited with having solidified the region's religious beliefs into a unified system that moved away from animistic nomadic beliefs. The main source for his teachings is a compilation called the Avesta.

Zoroastrianism Religion based on the teachings of Zoroaster that became the dominant religion of the Persian Empire.

Zulus African tribe that, under Shaka, created a ruthless warrior state in southern Africa in the early 1800s.

Credits

CHAPTER 1

Photo Credits Pages 2–3: Erich Lessing/Art Resource; p. 6 & 7: Volker Steger/Photo Researchers; p. 8: Robert Preston/Alamy; p. 11: John Reader/Photo Researchers; p. 12: Staffan Widstrand/Corbis; p. 13: Pascal Goetgheluck/Photo Researchers; p. 14: Lionel Bret/Photo Researchers; p. 21: Images of Africa Photobank/Alamy; p. 22: Erich Lessing/Art Resource; p. 27: © Christie's Images Ltd. All rights reserved/Corbis; p. 32: Boltin Picture Library/Bridgeman Art Library; p. 34 (top): Bruce Smith, The Emergence of Agriculture (New York: Diane Publishing Company, 1998), pg. 104; p. 34 (bottom): De Agostini Picture Library/M. Seemuller/Bridgeman Art Library; p. 42 (left): French Ministry of Culture and Communication, Regional Direction for Cultural Affairs, Rhône-Alpes Region–Regional Department of Archaeology; p. 42 (right): French Ministry of Culture and Communication, Regional Direction for Cultural Affairs, Rhône-Alpes Region–Regional Department of Archaeology; p. 43 (top left): Wikimedia Commons; p. 43 (bottom left): Wikimedia Commons; p. 43 (top right): Archivo Iconografico, S.A./Corbis.

Text Credits Primary Source 1.1 (p. 38): Ainslee T. Embree (ed.), from Sources of Indian Tradition, Vol. 1, From the Beginning to 1800, 2nd ed., pp. 18–19. Edited and revised by Ainslie T. Embree. Copyright © 1988 Columbia University Press. Reprinted with permission of the publisher. Primary Source 1.2 (pp. 38–39): Genesis 1:1–31. The Scripture quotations contained herein are from the New Revised Standard Version Bible, copyright © 1989, by the Division of Christian Education of the National Council of the Churches of Christ in the U.S.A., and are used by permission. All rights reserved. Primary Source 1.4 (pp. 39–40): Adrian Recinos, *Popol Vuh: The Sacred Book of the Ancient Quiche Maya*, English version by Delia Goetz & Sylvanus G. Morley, from the translation of Adrian Recinos. Copyright © 1950 The University of Oklahoma Press. Reproduced with permission. All rights reserved. Primary Source 1.5 (pp. 40–41): "Yoruba Creation Narrative" as translated by P.J. Criss. Reprinted by permission of the Estate of P.J. Criss.

CHAPTER 2

Photo Credits Pages 44–45: British Museum/Bridgeman Art Library; p. 46: Granger Collection; p. 52: Peter Bull Art Studio; p. 53: University of Pennsylvania Museum of Archaeology and Anthropology; p. 60 (left): Gianni Dagli Orti/Corbis; p. 60 (right): Christine Osborne/Corbis; p. 61 (left): Scala/Art Resource; p. 61 (right): Sandro Vannini/Corbis; p. 64 & 65: © Eric & David Hosking/Corbis; p. 67: Diego Lezama Orezzoli/Corbis; p. 68: Wikimedia Commons; p. 70: Asian Art & Archaeology, Inc./Corbis; p. 71: HIP/Art Resource; p. 74: Adam Woolfitt/Corbis; p. 79 (top): Wikimedia Commons; p. 79 (bottom): Borromeo/Art Resource; p. 80 (left): From Luo, Zhenyu ji, Yin xu shu qi jing hua. China: Shangyu Luo shi, Minguo 3: 1914; p. 80 (right): From Arthur Cotterell's "The Minoan World". Charles Scribner's Sons. New York: 1979; p. 81 (top left): Egyptian National Museum, Cairo, Egypt/Bridgeman Art Library; p. 81 (center): HIP/Art Resource; p. 81 (right): Réunion des Musées Nationaux/Art Resource; p. 81 (bottom left): Ashmolean Museum, University of Oxford.

Text Credits Primary Source 2.1 (p. 78): J. A. Black, G. Cunningham, E. Fluckiger-Hawker, E. Robson, and G. Zólyomi, from *The Electronic Text Corpus of Sumerian Literature* (University of Oxford, 1998–2006), www-etcsl.orient.ox.ac.uk/. Primary Source 2.2 (pp. 78–79): James P. Allen (trans.), "Egyptian Mouth-Opening Ritual" from *Writings of the Ancient World: The Ancient Pyramid Texts*, pp. 19–20. © 2005 The Society of Biblical Literature. Reprinted with the permission of the publisher.

CHAPTER 3

Photo Credits Pages 82–83: Scala/Art Resource; p. 85 (left): Art Resource; p. 85 (top right): Scala/Art Resource; p. 85 (bottom right): JTB Photo Communications/Alamy; p. 90: Roger Wood/Corbis; p. 93: Sandro Vannini/Corbis; p. 94: Eric Lessing/Art Resource; p. 95: Berlin Museum; p. 97: National Museum of India, New Delhi; p. 103: Yale University Art Gallery/Art Resource; p. 106: Albrecht G. Schaefer/Corbis; p. 108: Institute of Nautical Archaeology, Bodrum, Turkey; p. 110: Erich Lessing/Art Resource; p. 118 (left): Granger Collection; p. 118 (right): Granger Collection; p. 119: Wikimedia Commons.

Text Credits Primary Source 3.3 (pp. 115–116): "The Ten Commandments," from Exodus 20:1-17. The Scripture quotations contained herein are from the New Revised Standard Version Bible, copyright © 1989, by the Division of Christian Education of the National Council of the Churches of Christ in the U.S.A., and are used by permission. All rights reserved. Primary Source 3.5 (p. 116): Earnest Caldwell, "Social Change and Written law in Early Chinese Legal Thought," From *Law and History Review* 32(1), p. 15. Reprinted by permission of Cambridge University Press.

CHAPTER 4

Photo Credits Pages 120–121: Dagli Orti/Louvre/Bridgeman Art Library; p. 123 (left): © A. Paul Jenkin/ Animals Animals; p. 123 (right): S. Muller/Peter Arnold/Getty Images; pp. 126 & 127: Wikimedia Commons; p. 129: British Museum; p. 130: British Museum/Bridgeman Art Library; p. 133: EmmePi Iran/Alamy; p. 134: Erich Lessing/Art Resource, NY; p. 136: Scala/Art Resource, NY; p. 139 (left): Dagli Orti/Art Archive; p. 139 (right): © North Wind Picture Archives/The Image Works; p. 143: British Museum; p. 145: Giraudon/Art Resource; p. 147: Asia Society, New York: Mr. and Mrs. John D. Rockefeller 3rd Collection 1979. Photograph by Lynton Gardiner; p. 156 (left): British Museum; p. 156 (right): Bridgeman Art Library; p. 157: The Metropolitan Museum of Art.

Text Credits Primary Source 4.2 (p. 153): Roland G. Kent, from *Old Persian: Grammar, Texts, Lexicon*, 2nd Revised Ed. pp. 131–32. Copyright © 1953 American Oriental Society. Reprinted with permission. Primary Source 4.3 (pp. 153–154): Burton Watson (ed.), "Zhou Succession Story" from *Early Chinese Literature*, pp. 35–36. Edited by Burton Watson. Copyright © 1962 Columbia University Press. Reprinted with permission of the publisher.

CHAPTER 5

Photo Credits p. 158 (left): National Library of China; p. 158 (right): Scala/ Art Resource; p. 159: Erich Lessing/Art Resource; p. 165: Wikimedia Commons; p. 167: Erich Lessing/Art Resource; p. 169 (left): Paul Almasy/ Corbis; p. 169 (right): Corbis; p. 171: Borromeo/Art Resource; p. 172: National Library of China; p. 173: Scala/Art Resource, NY; p. 175: The Bridgeman Art Library; p. 176 (left): Erich Lessing/ Art Resource; p. 176 (right): HIP/Art Resource; p. 177: Scala/Art Resource; p. 181 (left): Gillett Griffin; p. 181 (right): Gillett Griffin; p. 186: Wikimedia Commons; p. 194 (left): Erich Lessing/Art Resource; p. 194 (right): Erich Lessing/ Art Resource; p. 195 (left): Princeton University Art Museum; p. 195 (right): Bridgeman Art Library.

Text Credits Primary Source 5.1 (p. 190): K.D. Irani (ed. & trans.), "Yasna 33" from *The Gathas: The Hymns of Zarathushtra* (Mumbai: K.R. Cama Oriental Institute, 1999), pp. 47–50. Used by permission of K.D. Irani. Primary Source 5.2 (p. 191): Confucius, from *The Analects of Confucius,* translated by Simon Leys. Copyright © 1997 by Pierre Ryckmans. Used by permission of W.W. Norton & Company, Inc. Primary Source 5.4 (p. 192): Plato, "Socrates' Defense," from *The Apology of Socrates.* Translated by Cathal Woods and Ryan Pack. Reprinted by permission of Cathal Woods.

CHAPTER 6

Photo Credits Pages 196–197: © The Cleveland Museum of Art; p. 199 (top): Erich Lessing/Art Resource; p. 199 (bottom): Lauros/Giraudon/Bridgeman Art Library; p. 203: Vanni/Art Resource; pp. 208 & 209: Wikimedia Commons; p. 210 (left): Brian A. Vikander/Corbis; p. 210 (right): Bridgeman Art Library; p. 211 (all): Courtesy of Bill Welch, "What I Like About Ancient

Coins", http://www.forumancientcoins .com/moonmoth/ancientcoins.html; p. 212: © The Cleveland Museum of Art; p. 214 (left): The Metropolitan Museum of Art. Gift of Muneichi Nitta, 2003 (2003.593.1) Image © The Metropolitan Museum of Art; p. 214 (right): © The Metropolitan Museum of Art/Art Resource; p. 219: The Art Archive/Palmyra Museum Syria/Dagli Orti; p. 220: NASA/JPL; p. 230 (top left): American Numismatic Society; p. 230 (top center left): American Numismatic Society; p. 230 (bottom left): Courtesy of Bill Welch, "What I Like About Ancient Coins", http://www.forumancientcoins. com/moonmoth/ancientcoins.html; p. 230 (top right center): American Numismatic Society; p. 230 (top right): American Numismatic Society; p. 230 (bottom right): American Numismatic Society; p. 231: HIP/Art Resource, NY.

Text Credits Primary Source 6.2 (pp. 228–229): Asoka, "The Kalinga Edict," from *Inscriptions of Asoka*, translated by D.C. Sircar. Reprinted from the Publications Division of the Ministry of Information and Broadcasting of India, 1967.

CHAPTER 7

Photo Credits Pages 232–233: Erich Lessing/Art Resource; p. 237: Snark/ Art Resource; p. 238 (top): Louis Mazzatenta/National Geographic Image Collection; p. 238 (bottom): Bridgeman Art Library; p. 239: British Museum/Art Resource, NY; p. 240: Model of House, Chinese. 1st century C.E., Eastern Han Dynasty (25-220 C.E.). Earthenware with unfired coloring, 52 x 33 1/2 x 27 inches (132.1 x 85.1 x 68.6 cm). The Nelson-Atkins Museum of Art, Kansas City, Missouri. Purchase: Nelson Trust, 33-521. Photograph by Jamison Miller; p. 241 (top left): Asian Art & Archaeology, Inc./Corbis; p. 241 (bottom left): Royal Ontario Museum/Corbis; p. 241 (right): Asian Art & Archaeology, Inc./ Corbis; p. 250: Vanni/Art Resource;

p. 251: Atlantide Phototravel/Corbis; p. 252 (bottom left): Roger Wood/Corbis; p. 252 (bottom right): Scala/Art Resource; p. 253: HIP/Art Resource; p. 257: Erich Lessing/Art Resource; pp. 258 & 259: The Metropolitan Museum of Art/Art Resource; p. 264 (left): Corbis; p. 264 (top right): Alamy; p. 264 (bottom right): Alamy; p. 265 (left): Wikimedia Commons; p. 265 (right): Getty Images.

Text Credits Primary Source 7.1 (p. 262): Dong Zhongshu, "Responsibilities of Han Rulership" from *Sources of Chinese Tradition, Volume 1*, Edited by Wm. Theodore de Bary and Irene Bloom, Copyright © 1999 Columbia University Press. Reprinted with permission of the publisher. Primary Source 7.3 (p. 263): Ban Zhao, from *Pan Chao: Foremost Woman Scholar of China*. Translated by Nancy Lee Swann (New York: Russell & Russell, 1932, 1968). Used by permission of the American Historical Association. Primary Source 7.4 (p. 263): Mary R. Lefkowitz & Maureen B. Fant, eds. *Women's Life in Greece and Rome: A Source Book in Translation. Third Edition*. pp. 50–51. © 1982, 1992, 2005 Mary F. Lefkowitz and Maureen B. Fant. Reprinted with permission of Johns Hopkins University Press.

CHAPTER 8

Photo Credits Pages 266–267: Charles & Josette Lenars/Corbis; p. 269: Granger Collection; p. 272: Scala/Art Resource; p. 277: Corbis Images; p. 280: Julian Chichester/Bridgeman Art Library; p. 281 (bottom left): Art Resource; p. 282 (bottom right): Dean Conger/Corbis; p. 284: akg-images/Werner Forman; p. 287: Réunion des Musées Nationaux/Art Resource; p. 288: National Palace Museum, Taipei, China; p. 292: Gianni Dagli Orti/Corbis; p. 293: Angelo Hornak/Corbis; p. 294: Werner Forman/Art Resource; p. 300 (left): Getty Images; p. 300 (right): Art

Resource; p. 301 (left): Art Resource; p. 301 (right): Art Resource.

Text Credits Primary Source 8.1 (p. 298): Excerpt from *Egeria: Diary of a Pilgrimage,* from the Ancient Christian Writers Series, translated and annotated by George E. Gingras, Ph. D. Copyright © 1970 by Rev. Johannes Quasten, Rev. Walter J. Burghardt, SJ and Thomas Comerford Lawler. The Newman Press-Paulist Press. Used with permission www.paulistpress.com. Primary Source 8.3 (p. 299): A.C. Bhaktivedanta Swami Prabhupāda (trans.), from *Srimad Bhagavatam: Third Canto* (Bhaktivedanta Book Trust, 1974), p. 16. Quoted text courtesy of The Bhaktivedanta Book Trust International, Inc. www.Krishna.com. Used with permission.

CHAPTER 9

Photo Credits Pages 302–303: Patrick Ward/Corbis; p. 304: Suhaib Salem/Reuters/Corbis; p. 311 (left): Vanni Archive/Corbis; p. 311 (right): Patrick Ward/Corbis; p. 313 (left): Gavin Hellier/JAI/Corbis; p. 313 (right): Christine Osborne/Corbis; p. 318 (left): Werner Forman/Art Resource; p. 318 (right): Kurt Scholz/SuperStock; p. 324: Julia Waterlow/Eye Ubiquitous/Corbis; p. 326 (left): CulturalEyes-AusGS/Alamy; p. 326 (right): Wikimedia Commons; p. 329: Giraudon/Bridgeman Art Library; p. 330 (left): Alamy; p. 330 (right): Alamy; p. 332: Werner Forman/Art Resource; p. 333: Alamy; p. 338 (left): British Library; p. 338 (right): British Library; p. 339 (top left): British Library; p. 339 (center left): University of Cambridge; p. 339 (bottom left): University of Cambridge; p. 339 (top right): Getty Images Editorial.

Text Credits Primary Source 9.1 (p. 336): Marmaduke Pickthall (trans.), "Sura 4" from *Qur'an: A Norton Critical Edition*, edited by Jane Dammen McAuliffe. Copyright © 2014 by

W.W. Norton & Company, Inc. Used by permission of W.W. Norton & Company, Inc. Primary Source 9.3 (p. 337): Heying Jenny Zhan and Robert Bradshaw (trans.), "The Book of Analects for Women: Consort Song," from *Journal of Historical Sociology* 9(3), pp. 261–269. Copyright © 1996 Blackwell Publishers Ltd. Reprinted by permission of John Wiley & Sons, Inc.

CHAPTER 10

Photo Credits Pages 340–341: HIP/Art Resource; p. 342: Granger Collection; p. 343: Nik Wheeler/Corbis; p. 345: Alamy; p. 351: Keren Su/Corbis; p. 355 (top): Granger Collection; p. 355 (bottom): Christophe Loviny/Corbis; p. 359: The Art Archive; pp. 360 & 361: Snark/Art Resource; p. 364: Werner Forman/Art Resource; p. 366 (top): Charles & Josette Lenars/Corbis; p. 366 (bottom): Otto Lang/Corbis; p. 369: akg-images; p. 380: Giraudon/Art Resource; p. 381 (top): Wikimedia Commons; p. 381 (bottom): Art Resource.

Text Credits Primary Source 10.1 (p. 376): *The Monks of Ḳûblâi Khân, Emperor of China, or, The history of the life and travels of Rabban Ṣâwmâ, envoy and plenipotentiary of the Mongol khans to the kings of Europe, and Markôs who as Mâr Yahbh-Allâhâ III became Patriarch of the Nestorian Church in Asia*. Edited and translated by E.A. Wallis Budge (London: Religious Tract Society, 1928). Reprinted by permission of the Lutterworth Press. Primary Source 10.3 (p. 377): *Ibn Battuta: Travels in Asia & Africa, 1325–1354* translated by H. A. R. Gibb, pp. 55–56. Copyright © 1929 George Routledge & Sons. Reprinted by permission of Taylor & Francis Books (UK).

CHAPTER 11

Photo Credits Pages 382–383: Snark/Art Resource; p. 385: Granger Collection;

Index

NORTH POLAR REGION

ARCTIC

NORTH AMERICA

ASIA

ARCTIC OCEAN

North Magnetic Pole

North Pole

GREENLAND

Iceland

ARCTIC CIRCLE

GREENLAND

NORTH AMERICA

NORTH PACIFIC OCEAN

NORTH ATLANTIC OCEAN

TROPIC OF CANCER

Hawaii

EQUATOR

GULF OF MEXICO

CENTRAL AMERICA

CARIBBEAN SEA

MID ATLANTIC RIDGE

Amazon Basin

SOUTH AMERICA

TROPIC OF CAPRICORN

SOUTH PACIFIC OCEAN

SOUTH ATLANTIC OCEAN

Easter Island

Falkland Islands

Cape Horn

ANTARCTIC CIRCLE

ANTARCTIC PENINSULA

WEDDELL SEA

Marie Byrd Land

ANTA

GLOBAL SATELLITE MOSAIC

The beauty and complexity of Earth's landscapes above and below the
oceans is revealed with the Global Satellite Mosaic. The mosaic was produced
for the National Geographic Society by NASA's Jet Propulsion Laboratory using
more than 500 satellite images from the National Oceanic and Atmospheric
Administration. The cloud-free images show Earth in its natural colors as it would be
seen from space. One can easily identify the world's major glaciers, deserts, mountain
ranges, and rain forests. For example, follow the green ribbon of lush vegetation along
the Nile into the stark, dry Sahara. The mountain ranges seem to rise off the map
in digital elevation databases from the Department of Defense. The deepest areas of the
ocean realm are colored dark blue in contrast to the light blue areas highlighting
continental shelves, submarine ridges, and underwater mountains.

BIOSPHERE

Thousands of satellite images are
combined to show a picture of biospheric
productivity. In the oceans, red, yellow, and
green indicate waters rich in phytoplankton. On land,
green areas show high-potential plant productivity; tan areas
suffer from productivity limitations due to aridity and temperature.

THE

SAT

Weddell Sea

Queen Maud Land

Drake Passage

ANTARCTIC CIRCLE

Antarctic Peninsula

Alexander I.

Bellingshausen Sea

ANTARCTICA

WEST ANTARCTICA

EAST ANTARCTICA

South Pole

Marie Byrd Land

Wilkes Land

Ross Ice Shelf

Ross Sea

South Magnetic Pole

ANTARCTIC CIRCLE

OCEAN

NORTH

PACIFIC

OCEAN

TROPIC OF CANCER

PHILIPPINE SEA

SOUTH CHINA SEA

MICRONESIA

MELANESIA

EQUATOR

INDONESIA

CORAL SEA

Fiji Islands

AUSTRALIA

TROPIC OF CAPRICORN

SOUTH PACIFIC OCEAN

TASMAN SEA

NEW ZEALAND

North Island

South Island

EUROPE

ASIA

SIBERIA

Ural Mountains

Lake Baikal

Kamchatka Peninsula

ARCTIC CIRCLE

Black Sea

Aral Sea

Plateau of Tibet

ARABIAN PENINSULA

ARABIAN SEA

INDIA

BAY OF BENGAL

AFRICA

Congo Basin

Lake Tanganyika

Madagascar

Kalahari Desert

Cape of Good Hope

INDIAN OCEAN

SOUTHWEST INDIAN RIDGE

SOUTHEAST INDIAN RIDGE

KERGUELEN PLATEAU

Wilkes Land

ARCTIC

Franz Josef Land

BARENTS SEA

THE NEED FOR SATELLITES

The Global Satellite Mosaic along with the biosphere image (lower left) and topographic image (lower right) provides an integrated view of our world. Extremely high elevations of the Himalaya and Tibet show up as a cold area (blue). Temperature imagized as a plant-poor area (tan, biosphere image). Temperature, topography, and landscape are interrelated. The need to understand the forces shaping environmental change has led to a space race among various countries. In 1997 alone some 85 rockets launched more than 140 satellites—mostly from China, Europe, Japan, Russia, and the United States. Some satellites provide vital communication links propelling economic development; other satellites supply data on patterns and trends associated with agricultural productivity, pollution monitoring, weather forecasting, and many other environmental concerns.

SURFACE TEMPERATURE

Reddish colors vividly show average high temperatures on the two largest continents, Africa and Asia, from the Sahara to Central Asia. Latitude, mountains, and oceans influence land temperatures.

WINKEL TRIPEL PROJECTION, CENTRAL MERIDIAN 0°

SCALE 1:38,931,000

1 CENTIMETER = 389 KILOMETERS; 1 INCH = 614 MILES AT THE EQUATOR

RLD

MAP

TICA

Political World

SOUTH POLAR REGION